T0215754

Lecture Notes in Computer Science 11958

More information about this series at http://www.springer.com/series/7407

Ivan Lirkov · Svetozar Margenov (Eds.)

Large-Scale Scientific Computing

12th International Conference, LSSC 2019
Sozopol, Bulgaria, June 10–14, 2019
Revised Selected Papers

 Springer

Editors
Ivan Lirkov 🆔
Bulgarian Academy of Sciences
Sofia, Bulgaria

Svetozar Margenov 🆔
Bulgarian Academy of Sciences
Sofia, Bulgaria

ISSN 0302-9743   ISSN 1611-3349 (electronic)
Lecture Notes in Computer Science
ISBN 978-3-030-41031-5   ISBN 978-3-030-41032-2 (eBook)
https://doi.org/10.1007/978-3-030-41032-2

LNCS Sublibrary: SL1 – Theoretical Computer Science and General Issues

This Springer imprint is published by the registered company Springer Nature Switzerland AG
The registered company address is: Gewerbestrasse 11, 6330 Cham, Switzerland

Preface

The 12th International Conference on Large-Scale Scientific Computations (LSSC 2019) was held in Sozopol, Bulgaria, June 10–14, 2019. The conference was organized by the Institute of Information and Communication Technologies at the Bulgarian Academy of Sciences in cooperation with Sozopol municipality.

The plenary invited speakers and lectures were:

- H. Bock, "Inverse Optimal Control Problems and Applications to Modeling Human Locomotion"
- R. Falgout, "Parallel Time Integration with Multigrid Reduction"
- S. MacLachlan, "Parameter-Robust Preconditioners for Singularly Perturbed PDEs"
- C. Rodrigo, "Robust Discretizations and Solvers for Poromechanics"
- Y. Shi, "Big Data Analytics: Theory and Applications"
- E. Tyrtyshnikov, "Tensor Decompositions Using Incomplete Data and Their Applications in Numerical Computations"

The success of the conference and the present volume are the outcome of the joint efforts of many partners from various institutions and organizations. First, we would like to thank all the members of the Scientific Committee for their valuable contribution forming the scientific face of the conference, as well as for their help in reviewing contributed papers. We especially thank the organizers of the special sessions. We are also grateful to the staff involved in the local organization.

Traditionally, the purpose of the conference is to bring together scientists working with large-scale computational models in natural sciences and environmental and industrial applications, as well as specialists in the field of numerical methods and algorithms for modern high-performance computers. The invited lectures reviewed some of the most advanced achievements in the field of numerical methods and their efficient applications. The conference talks were presented by researchers from academic institutions and practical industry engineers including applied mathematicians, numerical analysts, and computer experts. The general theme for LSSC 2019 was "Large-Scale Scientific Computing" with a particular focus on the organized special sessions.

The special sessions and organizers were:

- Control and Optimization of Dynamical Systems—M. Krastanov and V. Veliov
- Meshfree and Particle Methods—P. Bochev, N. Trask, and P. Kuberry
- Fractional Diffusion Problems: Numerical Methods, Algorithms and Applications—S. Harizanov, B. Jin, R. Lazarov, and P. Vabishchevich
- Recent Advances in Numerical Methods for Flow in Deformable Porous Media—J. Adler, X. Hu, J. Kraus, M. Lymbery, and C. Rodrigo
- Pore Scale Flow and Transport Simulation—S. Majid Hassanizadeh and O. Iliev
- Tensors Based Algorithms and Structures in Optimization and Applications—E. Tyrtyshnikov

- HPC and Big Data: Algorithms and Applications—A. Karaivanova, T. Gurov, and E. Atanassov
- Large-Scale Models: Numerical Methods, Parallel Computations and Applications —K. Georgiev and Z. Zlatev
- Monte Carlo Algorithms: Innovative Applications in Conjunctions with Other Methods—I. Dimov, C. Medina Bailon, and M. Nedjalkov
- Application of Metaheuristics to Large-Scale Problems—S. Fidanova and G. Luque
- Large Scale Machine Learning: Multiscale Algorithms and Performance Guarantees —J. Murphy, L. Zikatanov, and X. Hu

About 150 participants from all over the world attended the conference representing some of the strongest research groups in the field of advanced large-scale scientific computing. This volume contains 72 papers by authors from 23 countries.

The next international conference on LSSC will be organized in June 2021.

November 2019

Ivan Lirkov
Svetozar Margenov

Organization

Scientific Committee

James Adler	Tufts University, USA
Emanouil Atanassov	Institute of Information and Communication Technologies, BAS, Bulgaria
Pavel Bochev	Sandia National Laboratories, USA
Hans Georg Bock	University of Heidelberg, Germany
Ivan Dimov	Institute of Information and Communication Technologies, BAS, Bulgaria
Stefka Dimova	Sofia University, Bulgaria
Robert Falgout	Lawrence Livermore National Laboratory, USA
Stefka Fidanova	Institute of Information and Communication Technologies, BAS, Bulgaria
Ivan Georgiev	Institute of Information and Communication Technologies, BAS, Bulgaria
Krassimir Georgiev	Institute of Information and Communication Technologies, BAS, Bulgaria
Todor Gurov	Institute of Information and Communication Technologies, BAS, Bulgaria
Stanislav Harizanov	Institute of Information and Communication Technologies, BAS, Bulgaria
S. Majid Hassanizadeh	Utrecht University, The Netherlands
Xiaozhe Hu	Tufts University, USA
Bangti Jin	University College London, UK
Aneta Karaivanova	Institute of Information and Communication Technologies, BAS, Bulgaria
Mikhail Krastanov	Sofia University, Bulgaria
Johannes Kraus	University of Duisburg-Essen, Germany
Paul Kuberry	Sandia National Laboratories, USA
Ulrich Langer	Johannes Kepler University Linz, Austria
Raytcho Lazarov	Texas A&M University, USA
Ivan Lirkov	Institute of Information and Communication Technologies, BAS, Bulgaria
Gabriel Luque	University of Málaga, Spain
Maria Lymbery	University of Duisburg-Essen, Germany
Scott MacLachlan	Memorial University, Newfoundland and Labrador, Canada
Svetozar Margenov	Institute of Information and Communication Technologies, BAS, Bulgaria
Cristina Medina Bailon	University of Glasgow, UK

Contents

HPC and Big Data: Algorithms and Applications

**Large-Scale Models: Numerical Methods, Parallel Computations
and Applications**

Monte Carlo Algorithms: Innovative Applications in Conjunctions with Other Methods

Application of Metaheuristics to Large-Scale Problems

Large Scale Machine Learning: Multiscale Algorithms and Performance Guarantees

Additional Contributed Papers

Invited Papers

First-Order System Least Squares Finite-Elements for Singularly Perturbed Reaction-Diffusion Equations

James H. Adler[1]📵, Scott MacLachlan[2(✉)]📵, and Niall Madden[3]📵

[1] Department of Mathematics, Tufts University, Medford, USA
James.Adler@tufts.edu
[2] Department of Mathematics and Statistics,
Memorial University of Newfoundland, St. John's, Canada
smaclachlan@mun.ca
[3] School of Mathematics, Statistics, and Applied Mathematics,
National University of Ireland Galway, Galway, Ireland
Niall.Madden@NUIGalway.ie

Abstract. We propose a new first-order-system least squares (FOSLS) finite-element discretization for singularly perturbed reaction-diffusion equations. Solutions to such problems feature layer phenomena, and are ubiquitous in many areas of applied mathematics and modelling. There is a long history of the development of specialized numerical schemes for their accurate numerical approximation. We follow a well-established practice of employing *a priori* layer-adapted meshes, but with a novel finite-element method that yields a symmetric formulation while also inducing a so-called "balanced" norm. We prove continuity and coercivity of the FOSLS weak form, present a suitable piecewise uniform mesh, and report on the results of numerical experiments that demonstrate the accuracy and robustness of the method.

Keywords: First-order system least squares (FOSLS) finite elements · Singularly perturbed differential equations · Parameter-robust discretizations

1 Introduction

The numerical solution of singularly perturbed differential equations (SPDEs) is of great interest to numerical analysts, given the importance of these equations in computational modelling, and the challenges they present for classical numerical schemes and the mathematical methods used to analyse them; see [15] for a survey. In this work, we focus on linear second-order *reaction-diffusion problems* of the form

$$- \varepsilon \Delta u + bu = f \text{ on } \Omega := (0,1)^d \qquad u|_{\partial \Omega} = 0, \tag{1}$$

The work of S.M. was partially supported by NSERC discovery grants RGPIN-2014-06032 and RGPIN-2019-05692.

I. Lirkov and S. Margenov (Eds.): LSSC 2019, LNCS 11958, pp. 3–14, 2020.
https://doi.org/10.1007/978-3-030-41032-2_1

for $d = 1, 2, 3$, where we assume there exist constants $0 < b_0 < b(\boldsymbol{x}) < b_1$ for every $\boldsymbol{x} \in \Omega$. Like all SPDEs, (1) is characterised by a small positive parameter that multiplies the highest derivative. It is "singular" in the sense that the problem is ill-posed if one formally sets $\varepsilon = 0$. As ε approaches this limit, the solution typically exhibits layers: regions of rapid change, whose length is determined by ε. The over-arching goal is to devise methods that resolve these layers, and for which the error (measured in a suitable norm) is independent of ε. Many classical techniques make the tacit assumption that derivatives of u are bounded, which does not hold, uniformly in ε, for solutions to (1). Numerous specialised methods, usually based around layer-adapted meshes, have been developed with the goal of resolving these layers and the attendant mathematical conundrums. The celebrated piecewise uniform meshes of Shishkin have been particularly successful in this regard; and analyses of finite-difference methods for (1) and its many variants is largely complete [13].

Finite-element methods (FEMs) applied on layer-adapted meshes have also been successfully applied to (1), but their analysis is more problematic. This is highlighted to great effect by Lin and Stynes who demonstrated that the usual energy norm associated with (1) is too weak to adequately express the layers present in the solution [10]. They proposed a first-order FEM (see Sect. 2) for which the associated norm is sufficiently strong to capture layers; they coined the term "balanced norm" to describe this.

A flurry of activity on balanced norms was prompted by [10], including the first-order system Petrov-Galerkin (FOSPeG) approach proposed by the authors [1], and we refer to its introduction for a survey of the progress up to 2015. Since then, developments have continued apace. Broadly speaking, studies can be classified as one of two types.

1. Those that give analyses of standard FEMs, but in norms that are not induced by the associated bilinear forms; see, e.g., [16] on sparse grid FEMs, and [12] on hp-FEMs.
2. Those that propose new formulations for which the associated norm is naturally "balanced"; see, e.g., the discontinuous Petrov-Galerkin method of Heuer and Karulik [7].

The present study belongs to the second of these classes: we propose a new FEM for which the induced norm is balanced. This method is related to our earlier work [1], but instead uses a weighted least-squares FEM to obtain a symmetric discrete system. In this first-order system least-squares (FOSLS) approach [4,5], care is taken in choosing the weight, so that the resulting norms are indeed balanced.

The remainder of the paper is outlined as follows. Section 2 gives a brief discussion on balanced norms, where the Lin and Stynes and FOSPeG methods are summarized. In Sect. 3, we discuss the weighted least-squares approach and provide the necessary analysis, which applies in one, two and three dimensions. In Sect. 4, we focus on the particular case of $d = 2$; we present a suitable Shishkin mesh of the problem, and present numerical results that support our findings. Some concluding remarks are given in Sect. 5.

2 Balanced Norms

In [10], Lin and Stynes propose a first-order system reformulation of (1), writing the equivalent system as

$$L_{\text{div}}\, \mathcal{U} := \begin{pmatrix} \varepsilon^{1/4}(\boldsymbol{w} - \nabla u) \\ -\varepsilon \nabla \cdot \boldsymbol{w} + bu \end{pmatrix} = \begin{pmatrix} 0 \\ f \end{pmatrix} =: \mathcal{F}_{\text{div}}, \tag{2}$$

for $\mathcal{U} = (u, \boldsymbol{w})^T$. Rather than forming a least-squares finite-element discretization as in [4,5], they choose to close the system in a nonsymmetric manner, defining $\mathcal{V} = (v, \boldsymbol{z})^T$ and

$$M_{\text{div}}\, \mathcal{V} := \begin{pmatrix} \varepsilon^{1/4}(\boldsymbol{z} - \nabla v) \\ -\varepsilon^{1/2} b^{-1} \nabla \cdot \boldsymbol{z} + v \end{pmatrix},$$

then writing the solution of (1) as that of the weak form

$$a_{\text{div}}(\mathcal{U}, \mathcal{V}) := \langle L_{\text{div}}\, \mathcal{U}, M_{\text{div}}\, \mathcal{V} \rangle = \langle \mathcal{F}_{\text{div}}, M_{\text{div}}\, \mathcal{V} \rangle \quad \forall \mathcal{V} \in H^1(\Omega) \times H(\text{div}). \tag{3}$$

In [10], it is shown that a_{div} is coercive and continuous with respect to the norm,

$$|||\mathcal{U}|||_{\text{div}}^2 := b_0 \|u\|_0^2 + \frac{\varepsilon^{1/2}}{2} \|\nabla u\|_0^2 + \frac{\varepsilon^{1/2}}{2} \|\boldsymbol{w}\|_0^2 + \varepsilon^{3/2} \|\nabla \cdot \boldsymbol{w}\|_0^2, \tag{4}$$

which is shown to be a *balanced* norm for the problem, in the sense that all the components in (4) have the same order of magnitude with respect to the perturbation parameter, ε.

In [1], the authors augmented the first-order system approach proposed by Lin and Stynes to include a curl constraint, in the same style as [5], leading to the first-order system reformulation of (1) as

$$L\mathcal{U} := \begin{pmatrix} \varepsilon^{1/4}(\boldsymbol{w} - \nabla u) \\ -\varepsilon \nabla \cdot \boldsymbol{w} + bu \\ \varepsilon \nabla \times \boldsymbol{w} \end{pmatrix} = \begin{pmatrix} \boldsymbol{0} \\ f \\ \boldsymbol{0} \end{pmatrix} =: \hat{\mathcal{F}}. \tag{5}$$

Then, writing

$$M_k \mathcal{V} := \begin{pmatrix} \varepsilon^{1/4}(\boldsymbol{z} - \nabla v) \\ -\varepsilon^{1/2} b^{-1} \nabla \cdot \boldsymbol{z} + v \\ \varepsilon^{k/2} \nabla \times \boldsymbol{z} \end{pmatrix}, \tag{6}$$

leads to the weak form

$$a_k(\mathcal{U}, \mathcal{V}) := \langle L\mathcal{U}, M_k \mathcal{V} \rangle = \langle \hat{\mathcal{F}}, M_k \mathcal{V} \rangle \quad \forall \mathcal{V} \in \left(H^1(\Omega) \right)^{1+d}. \tag{7}$$

Building on the theory of [10], this form is shown to be coercive and continuous with respect to the balanced norm

$$|||\mathcal{U}|||_k^2 = b_0 \|u\|_0^2 + \frac{\varepsilon^{1/2}}{2} \|\nabla u\|_0^2 + \frac{\varepsilon^{1/2}}{2} \|\boldsymbol{w}\|_0^2 + \varepsilon^{3/2} \|\nabla \cdot \boldsymbol{w}\|_0^2 + \varepsilon^{1+k/2} \|\nabla \times \boldsymbol{w}\|_0^2. \tag{8}$$

Furthermore, in [1], the authors show that, when discretized using piecewise bilinear finite elements on a tensor-product Shishkin mesh, this weak form leads to a *parameter-robust* discretization, with an error estimate independent of the perturbation parameter ε.

3 First-Order System Least Squares Finite-Element Methods

While theoretical and numerical results in [1] show the effectiveness of the first-order system Petrov-Galerkin approach proposed therein, the non-symmetric nature of the weak form also has disadvantages. Primary among these is that the weak form no longer can be used as an accurate and reliable error indicator, contrary to the common practice for FOSLS finite-element approaches [2–6]. Standard techniques to symmetrize the weak form in (7) fail, however, either sacrificing the balanced nature of the norm (and, thus, any guarantee of parameter robustness of the resulting discretization) or coercivity or continuity of the weak form (destroying standard error estimates). Here, we propose a FOSLS approach for the problem in (1), made possible by considering a weighted norm with spatially varying weight function. Weighted least-squares formulations have been used for a wide variety of problems including those with singularities due to the domain [8,9].

To this end, we define the weighted inner product on both scalar and vector $H^1(\Omega)$ spaces, writing

$$\langle u, v \rangle_\beta = \int_\Omega \beta(\boldsymbol{x}) u(\boldsymbol{x}) v(\boldsymbol{x}) \, d\boldsymbol{x},$$

with the associated norm written as $\|u\|_\beta$. Slightly reweighting the first-order system from (5), we have

$$\mathcal{L}\mathcal{U} := \begin{pmatrix} \varepsilon^{1/2}(\boldsymbol{w} - \nabla u) \\ -\varepsilon b^{-1/2} \nabla \cdot \boldsymbol{w} + b^{1/2} u \\ \varepsilon^{k/2} \nabla \times \boldsymbol{w} \end{pmatrix} = \begin{pmatrix} \boldsymbol{0} \\ b^{-1/2} f \\ \boldsymbol{0} \end{pmatrix} =: \mathcal{F}. \tag{9}$$

and pose the weighted FOSLS weak form as

$$a(\mathcal{U}, \mathcal{V}) = \langle \mathcal{L}\mathcal{U}, \mathcal{L}\mathcal{V} \rangle_\beta = \langle \mathcal{F}, \mathcal{L}\mathcal{V} \rangle_\beta \quad \forall \mathcal{V} \in \left(H^1(\Omega) \right)^{1+d}.$$

This form leads to a natural weighted product norm given by

$$\|\|\mathcal{U}\|\|_{\beta,k}^2 = \|u\|_\beta^2 + \varepsilon \|\nabla u\|_\beta^2 + \varepsilon \|\boldsymbol{w}\|_\beta^2 + \varepsilon^2 \|\nabla \cdot \boldsymbol{w}\|_\beta^2 + \varepsilon^k \|\nabla \times \boldsymbol{w}\|_\beta^2.$$

As shown below, under a reasonable assumption on the weight function, β, the FOSLS weak form is coercive and continuous with respect to this norm.

Theorem 1. *Let $\beta(\boldsymbol{x})$ be given such that there exists $C > 0$ for which*

$$\nabla \beta \cdot \nabla \beta < \frac{b_0 \beta^2(\boldsymbol{x})}{\varepsilon(1+C)^2},$$

for every $\boldsymbol{x} \in \Omega$, and let $k \in \mathbb{R}$ be given. Then,

$$|a(\mathcal{U}, \mathcal{V})| \leq \left(3 + 2 \max(b_0^{-1}, b_1) \right) \|\|\mathcal{U}\|\|_{\beta,k} \|\|\mathcal{V}\|\|_{\beta,k}$$

$$\min\left(\frac{C \min(1, b_0)}{1+C}, b_1^{-1}, 1 \right) \|\|\mathcal{U}\|\|_{\beta,k}^2 \leq a(\mathcal{U}, \mathcal{U})$$

for all $\mathcal{U}, \mathcal{V} \in \left(H^1(\Omega) \right)^{1+d}$.

Proof. For the continuity bound, we note that

$$a(\mathcal{U}, \mathcal{V}) = \varepsilon\langle \boldsymbol{w} - \nabla u, \boldsymbol{z} - \nabla v\rangle_\beta$$
$$+ \langle -\varepsilon b^{-1/2}\nabla \cdot \boldsymbol{w} + b^{1/2}u, -\varepsilon b^{-1/2}\nabla \cdot \boldsymbol{z} + b^{1/2}v\rangle_\beta$$
$$+ \varepsilon^k\langle \nabla \times \boldsymbol{w}, \nabla \times \boldsymbol{z}\rangle_\beta.$$

Thus, by the Cauchy-Schwarz and triangle inequalities, we have

$$|a(\mathcal{U}, \mathcal{V})| \leq \varepsilon\left(\|\boldsymbol{w}\|_\beta + \|\nabla u\|_\beta\right)\left(\|\boldsymbol{z}\|_\beta + \|\nabla v\|_\beta\right)$$
$$+ \left(\varepsilon b_0^{-1/2}\|\nabla \cdot \boldsymbol{w}\|_\beta + b_1^{1/2}\|u\|_\beta\right)\left(\varepsilon b_0^{-1/2}\|\nabla \cdot \boldsymbol{z}\|_\beta + b_1^{1/2}\|v\|_\beta\right)$$
$$+ \varepsilon^k\|\nabla \times \boldsymbol{w}\|_\beta\|\nabla \times \boldsymbol{z}\|_\beta$$
$$\leq \left(3 + 2\max(b_0^{-1}, b_1)\right) |||\mathcal{U}|||_{\beta,k}|||\mathcal{V}|||_{\beta,k}.$$

For the coercivity bound, we note

$$a(\mathcal{U}, \mathcal{U}) = \varepsilon\|\boldsymbol{w} - \nabla u\|_\beta^2 + \varepsilon^2\|b^{-1/2}\nabla \cdot \boldsymbol{w}\|_\beta^2 + \|b^{1/2}u\|_\beta^2 + \varepsilon^k\|\nabla \times \boldsymbol{w}\|_\beta^2$$
$$- 2\varepsilon\langle \nabla \cdot \boldsymbol{w}, u\rangle_\beta$$
$$\geq \varepsilon\|\boldsymbol{w} - \nabla u\|_\beta^2 + \varepsilon^2 b_1^{-1}\|\nabla \cdot \boldsymbol{w}\|_\beta^2 + b_0\|u\|_\beta^2 + \varepsilon^k\|\nabla \times \boldsymbol{w}\|_\beta^2$$
$$- 2\varepsilon\langle \nabla \cdot \boldsymbol{w}, u\rangle_\beta.$$

Now consider

$$-2\varepsilon\langle \nabla \cdot \boldsymbol{w}, u\rangle_\beta = -2\varepsilon\int_\Omega (\nabla \cdot \boldsymbol{w})\, u\beta d\boldsymbol{x}$$
$$= 2\varepsilon\int_\Omega \boldsymbol{w} \cdot \nabla(u\beta)d\boldsymbol{x}$$
$$= 2\varepsilon\int_\Omega (\boldsymbol{w} \cdot \nabla u)\, \beta d\boldsymbol{x} + 2\varepsilon\int_\Omega (\nabla\beta \cdot \boldsymbol{w})\, u d\boldsymbol{x}$$
$$= 2\varepsilon\langle \boldsymbol{w}, \nabla u\rangle_\beta + 2\varepsilon\int_\Omega (\nabla\beta \cdot \boldsymbol{w})\, u d\boldsymbol{x},$$

where we use the fact that $u = 0$ on the boundary in the integration by parts step. Note that

$$\langle \boldsymbol{w}, \nabla u\rangle_\beta = \frac{1}{4}\|\boldsymbol{w} + \nabla u\|_\beta^2 - \frac{1}{4}\|\boldsymbol{w} - \nabla u\|_\beta^2,$$

and, consequently, that

$$\varepsilon\|\boldsymbol{w} - \nabla u\|_\beta^2 + 2\varepsilon\langle \boldsymbol{w}, \nabla u\rangle_\beta = \frac{\varepsilon}{2}\|\boldsymbol{w} + \nabla u\|_\beta^2 + \frac{\varepsilon}{2}\|\boldsymbol{w} - \nabla u\|_\beta^2 = \varepsilon\|\boldsymbol{w}\|_\beta^2 + \varepsilon\|\nabla u\|_\beta^2.$$

Thus,

$$a(\mathcal{U}, \mathcal{U}) \geq b_0\|u\|_\beta^2 + \varepsilon\|\boldsymbol{w}\|_\beta^2 + \varepsilon\|\nabla u\|_\beta^2 + \varepsilon^2 b_1^{-1}\|\nabla \cdot \boldsymbol{w}\|_\beta^2 + \varepsilon^k\|\nabla \times \boldsymbol{w}\|_\beta^2$$
$$+ 2\varepsilon\int_\Omega (\nabla\beta \cdot \boldsymbol{w})\, u d\boldsymbol{x}.$$

Finally, consider

$$2\varepsilon \left| \int_\Omega (\nabla\beta \cdot \boldsymbol{w})\, u d\boldsymbol{x} \right| = 2\varepsilon \left| \left\langle \boldsymbol{w}, \frac{u}{\beta}\nabla\beta \right\rangle_\beta \right| \leq 2\varepsilon \|\boldsymbol{w}\|_\beta \left\| \frac{u}{\beta}\nabla\beta \right\|_\beta .$$

By our assumption on β,

$$\left\| \frac{u}{\beta}\nabla\beta \right\|_\beta^2 \leq \frac{b_0}{\varepsilon(1+C)^2}\|u\|_\beta^2,$$

and, so,

$$2\varepsilon \left| \int_\Omega (\nabla\beta \cdot \boldsymbol{w})\, u d\boldsymbol{x} \right| \leq 2\frac{\varepsilon^{1/2}b_0^{1/2}}{1+C}\|\boldsymbol{w}\|_\beta \|u\|_\beta .$$

This gives

$$a(\mathcal{U},\mathcal{U}) \geq b_0\|u\|_\beta^2 + \varepsilon\|\boldsymbol{w}\|_\beta^2 + \varepsilon\|\nabla u\|_\beta^2 + \varepsilon^2 b_1^{-1}\|\nabla\cdot\boldsymbol{w}\|_\beta^2 + \varepsilon^k\|\nabla\times\boldsymbol{w}\|_\beta^2$$
$$- 2\frac{\varepsilon^{1/2}b_0^{1/2}}{1+C}\|\boldsymbol{w}\|_\beta\|u\|_\beta$$
$$\geq b_0\left(1 - \frac{1}{(1+C)}\right)\|u\|_\beta^2 + \varepsilon\left(1 - \frac{1}{(1+C)}\right)\|\boldsymbol{w}\|_\beta^2$$
$$+ \varepsilon\|\nabla u\|_\beta^2 + \varepsilon^2 b_1^{-1}\|\nabla\cdot\boldsymbol{w}\|_\beta^2 + \varepsilon^k\|\nabla\times\boldsymbol{w}\|_\beta^2$$
$$\geq \min\left(\frac{C\min(1,b_0)}{1+C}, b_1^{-1}, 1\right) \||\mathcal{U}\||_{\beta,k}^2.$$

A natural question, in light of this result, is whether a suitable choice of $\beta(\boldsymbol{x})$ exists. We now give a concrete construction of one such family of functions, $\beta(\boldsymbol{x})$, for which the assumption above is satisfied. This family is constructed for the case of $\Omega = [0,1]^d$ with boundary layers along each boundary adjacent to the origin (i.e., where $x_i = 0$ for some i). The extension to boundary layers along all $2d$ boundary faces is straightforward from the construction.

Theorem 2. *Let $C > 0$ be given, and define $\gamma = \frac{b_0^{1/2}}{(1+C)\sqrt{d}}$. Take*

$$\beta(\boldsymbol{x}) = \left(1 + \frac{1}{\sqrt{\varepsilon}}e^{-\gamma x_1/\sqrt{\varepsilon}}\right) \cdots \left(1 + \frac{1}{\sqrt{\varepsilon}}e^{-\gamma x_d/\sqrt{\varepsilon}}\right) \qquad (10)$$

Then,

$$\nabla\beta \cdot \nabla\beta < \frac{b_0\beta^2(\boldsymbol{x})}{\varepsilon(1+C)^2},$$

for every $\boldsymbol{x} \in \Omega$.

Proof. A direct calculation shows that

$$\frac{\partial\beta}{\partial x_i} = \frac{\frac{-\gamma}{\varepsilon}e^{-\gamma x_i/\sqrt{\varepsilon}}}{\left(1 + \frac{1}{\sqrt{\varepsilon}}e^{-\gamma x_i/\sqrt{\varepsilon}}\right)}\beta(\boldsymbol{x}).$$

Consequently,

$$\nabla\beta \cdot \nabla\beta = \sum_{i=1}^{d} \left(\frac{\frac{-\gamma}{\varepsilon} e^{-\gamma x_i/\sqrt{\varepsilon}}}{\left(1 + \frac{1}{\sqrt{\varepsilon}} e^{-\gamma x_i/\sqrt{\varepsilon}}\right)} \right)^2 \beta^2(\boldsymbol{x}).$$

Note, however, that

$$\left(\frac{\frac{-\gamma}{\varepsilon} e^{-\gamma x_i/\sqrt{\varepsilon}}}{\left(1 + \frac{1}{\sqrt{\varepsilon}} e^{-\gamma x_i/\sqrt{\varepsilon}}\right)} \right)^2 = \frac{\gamma^2}{\varepsilon} \left(\frac{\frac{1}{\sqrt{\varepsilon}} e^{-\gamma x_i/\sqrt{\varepsilon}}}{\left(1 + \frac{1}{\sqrt{\varepsilon}} e^{-\gamma x_i/\sqrt{\varepsilon}}\right)} \right)^2 \leq \frac{\gamma^2}{\varepsilon}.$$

This gives

$$\nabla\beta \cdot \nabla\beta \leq \frac{d\gamma^2}{\varepsilon} \beta^2(\boldsymbol{x}).$$

Substituting in the chosen value for γ gives the stated result.

The final question to be resolved is whether $\beta(\boldsymbol{x})$ as given in (10) is a "good" choice, in the sense of whether quasi-optimal approximation in the resulting norm is expected to give a good approximation to the layer structure in a typical solution. We consider the case of $d = 2$, the unit square. Following Lemmas 1.1 and 1.2 of [11], we require that the problem data satisfy the assumptions of [11, §2.1], specifically that $f, b \in C^{4,\alpha}(\bar{\Omega})$ and that f vanishes at the corners of the domain. Denoting the four edges of the domain by Γ_i, $1 \leq i \leq 4$, numbered clockwise with the edge $y = 0$ as Γ_1, and the four corners of the domain by c_i, $1 \leq i \leq 4$, numbered clockwise with the origin as c_1, we have the following result.

Lemma 1 ([11, Lemmas 1.1 and 1.2]). *The solution u of (1) can be decomposed as*

$$u = V + W + Z = V + \sum_{i=1}^{4} W_i + \sum_{i=1}^{4} Z_i, \tag{11a}$$

where each W_i is a layer associated with the edge Γ_i and each Z_i is a layer associated with the corner c_i. There exists a constant C such that

$$\left| \frac{\partial^{m+n} V}{\partial x^m \partial y^n}(x, y) \right| \leq C(1 + \varepsilon^{1-m/2-n/2}), \qquad 0 \leq m+n \leq 4, \tag{11b}$$

$$\left| \frac{\partial^{m+n} W_1}{\partial x^m \partial y^n}(x, y) \right| \leq C(1 + \varepsilon^{1-m/2})\varepsilon^{-n/2} e^{-y\sqrt{b_0/(2\varepsilon)}}, \quad 0 \leq m+n \leq 3, \tag{11c}$$

$$\left| \frac{\partial^{m+n} W_2}{\partial x^m \partial y^n}(x, y) \right| \leq C\varepsilon^{-m/2}(1 + \varepsilon^{1-n/2})e^{-x\sqrt{b_0/(2\varepsilon)}}, \quad 0 \leq m+n \leq 3, \tag{11d}$$

$$\left| \frac{\partial^{m+n} Z_1}{\partial x^m \partial y^n}(x, y) \right| \leq C\varepsilon^{-m/2-n/2} e^{-(x+y)\sqrt{b_0/(2\varepsilon)}}, \qquad 0 \leq m+n \leq 3, \tag{11e}$$

with analogous bounds for W_3, W_4, Z_2, Z_3 and Z_4.

Thus, as a "stereotypical" solution of (1) in the case where boundary layers only form along the edges $x = 0$ and $y = 0$ of $[0,1]^2$, we can consider

$$u(x) = u_0(x) + c_1 e^{-x\sqrt{b_0/(2\varepsilon)}} + c_2 e^{-y\sqrt{b_0/(2\varepsilon)}} + c_3 e^{-(x+y)\sqrt{b_0/(2\varepsilon)}}.$$

Next, we check if $|||\mathcal{U}|||_{\beta,k}$ is "balanced", not only in the sense of all terms having the same order, but in addition that each component in the stereotypical solution above is well-represented in the norm. This means the norm can be bounded from above and below by ε-independent values, so that it is not seen as being well-approximated by zero in the norm (unless truly vanishingly small), nor that the norm blows up as $\varepsilon \to 0$. For this case, (10) simplifies as

$$\beta(x,y) = \beta_1(x)\beta_1(y) \quad \text{where} \quad \beta_1(x) = 1 + \frac{1}{\sqrt{\varepsilon}} e^{-\gamma x_1/\sqrt{\varepsilon}},$$

and the checks rely on two direct calculations:

$$\int_0^1 \beta_1(x)dx = 1 + \frac{1}{\gamma}\left(1 - e^{-\gamma/\sqrt{\varepsilon}}\right) \approx 1 + \frac{1}{\gamma},$$

$$\int_0^1 \beta_1(x)\left(e^{-x\sqrt{b_0/(2\varepsilon)}}\right)^2 dx = \frac{1}{\gamma + \sqrt{2b_0}}\left(1 - e^{-\gamma/\sqrt{\varepsilon}-\sqrt{2b_0/\varepsilon}}\right)$$

$$+ \sqrt{\frac{\varepsilon}{2b_0}}\left(1 - e^{-2\sqrt{b_0/(2\varepsilon)}}\right)$$

$$\approx \frac{1}{\gamma + \sqrt{2b_0}},$$

With this, assuming that $u_0(x)$ is $\mathcal{O}(1)$ over a nontrivial fraction of the domain, we conclude that

$$|||(u_0, \nabla u_0)^T|||_{\beta,k} \approx 1 + \frac{1}{\gamma},$$

because of the separable nature of the calculation. Thus, the regular part of the solution is well-represented in the norm.

For the W_2 layer term, we write $w_2(x,y) = e^{-x\sqrt{b_0}/2\varepsilon}$ and calculate from the above that

$$\|w_2\|_\beta^2 \approx \left(1 + \frac{1}{\gamma}\right)\frac{1}{\gamma + \sqrt{2b_0}}.$$

Noting that all derivatives of this term with respect to y are zero and that $\partial_x^\ell w_2 = (-\sqrt{b_0/(2\varepsilon)})^\ell w_2$, we compute

$$|||(w_2, \nabla w_2)^T|||_{\beta,k}^2 = \|w_2\|_\beta^2 + \varepsilon\|\nabla w_2\|_\beta^2 + \varepsilon\|\nabla w_2\|_\beta^2 + \varepsilon^2\|\nabla \cdot \nabla w_2\|_\beta^2$$

$$+ \varepsilon^k\|\nabla \times \nabla w_2\|_\beta^2$$

$$= \|w_2\|_\beta^2 + \frac{b_0}{2}\|w_2\|_\beta^2 + \frac{b_0}{2}\|w_2\|_\beta^2 + \left(\frac{b_0}{2}\right)^2\|w_2\|_\beta^2 + 0$$

$$\approx \left(1 + b_0 + \left(\frac{b_0}{2}\right)^2\right)\left(1 + \frac{1}{\gamma}\right)\frac{1}{\gamma + \sqrt{2b_0}}.$$

Again, this shows that the W_2 layer term is well-represented in the norm. Similar calculations show the same to be true for the W_1 layer and Z_1 corner terms in the stereotypical solution.

4   Numerical Results

To test the above approach, we consider a two-dimensional problem with constant $b = 1$ posed on the unit square. We construct a problem whose solution mimics the stereotypical solution discussed above, with two edge layers and one corner layer. Specifically, we choose f so that the solution is

$$u(x,y) = \left(\cos\left(\frac{\pi x}{2}\right) - \frac{e^{-x/\sqrt{\varepsilon}} - e^{-1/\sqrt{\varepsilon}}}{1 - e^{-1/\sqrt{\varepsilon}}} \right) \left(1 - y - \frac{e^{-y/\sqrt{\varepsilon}} - e^{-1/\sqrt{\varepsilon}}}{1 - e^{-1/\sqrt{\varepsilon}}} \right).$$

We note that this has somewhat more complex layer behaviour than the stereotypical solution, but still obeys the bounds of Lemma 1. Also, the solution is constructed so as to obey the homogeneous Dirichlet boundary conditions. For numerical stability, we rescale the equations by defining $w = \sqrt{\varepsilon}\nabla u$ and making corresponding changes in weights to preserve the balanced nature of the norm. With this, we pick k to match the powers of ε in the weighting terms of both $\|\nabla \cdot w\|_\beta^2$ and $\|\nabla \times w\|_\beta^2$ in $\|\|\mathcal{U}\|\|_{\beta,k}$, equivalent to taking $k = 2$ above.

We discretize the test problem on a tensor-product Shishkin mesh (see, e.g., [1, §3] for more details). To do this, we select a transition point, $\tau > 0$, and construct a one-dimensional mesh with $N/2$ equal-sized elements on each of the intervals $[0, \tau]$ and $[\tau, 1]$. The two-dimensional mesh is created as a tensor-product of this mesh with itself, with rectangular (quadrilateral) elements. For the choice of τ, we slightly modify the standard choice from the literature (see, for example, [1,10,11]) to account for both the layer functions present in the solution decomposition and in the definition of $\beta(x)$ in (10). As such, we take

$$\tau = \min\left\{ \frac{1}{2}, (p+1)\sqrt{\frac{2\varepsilon}{b_0}}\gamma^{-1}\ln N \right\}$$

where p is the degree of the polynomial space ($p = 1$ for bilinear elements, $p = 2$ for biquadratic, and $p = 3$ for bicubic), so that this factor matches the expected L^2 rate of convergence of the approximation, while the terms $\sqrt{2\varepsilon/b_0}\gamma^{-1}$ decrease appropriately as ε does, but increase (corresponding to increasing layer width) with decreases in b_0 or γ. In the results that follow, we take $\gamma = 0.5$, implying $C = \sqrt{2} - 1$. All numerical results were computed using the software for automating the finite-element method, Firedrake [14], for the discretization and a direct solver for the resulting linear systems.

Table 1 shows the expected reduction rates in errors with respect to the mesh parameter, N, if we were to have standard estimates of approximation error in the β-norm on the Shishkin meshes considered here. Tables 2, 3 and 4 show the measured errors (relative to the manufactured solution) for the bilinear, biquadratic, and bicubic discretizations, respectively. Expected behaviour for

Table 1. Expected error reduction rates on a Shishkin mesh.

	$N = 64$	$N = 128$	$N = 256$	$N = 512$
$N^{-1} \ln N$	0.60	0.58	0.57	0.56
$(N^{-1} \ln N)^2$	0.36	0.34	0.33	0.32
$(N^{-1} \ln N)^3$	0.22	0.20	0.19	0.18
$(N^{-1} \ln N)^4$	0.13	0.12	0.11	0.10

Table 2. β-weighted norm and discrete max norm errors for model problem with bilinear discretization.

$||| \mathcal{U}^* - \mathcal{U}^N |||_{\beta,2}$ (Reduction Rate w.r.t. N)

ε/N	32	64	128	256	512
10^{-6}	3.086e−01	1.921e−01 (0.62)	1.137e−01 (0.59)	6.531e−02 (0.57)	3.680e−02 (0.56)
10^{-8}	3.086e−01	1.921e−01 (0.62)	1.137e−01 (0.59)	6.532e−02 (0.57)	3.681e−02 (0.56)
10^{-10}	3.086e−01	1.921e−01 (0.62)	1.137e−01 (0.59)	6.533e−02 (0.57)	3.681e−02 (0.56)
10^{-12}	3.086e−01	1.921e−01 (0.62)	1.137e−01 (0.59)	6.533e−02 (0.57)	3.681e−02 (0.56)

$|| u^* - u^N ||_{\ell_\infty}$ (Reduction Rate w.r.t. N)

ε/N	32	64	128	256	512
10^{-6}	6.935e−02	1.981e−02 (0.29)	6.436e−03 (0.32)	2.051e−03 (0.32)	6.448e−04 (0.31)
10^{-8}	6.945e−02	1.983e−02 (0.29)	6.444e−03 (0.32)	2.053e−03 (0.32)	6.455e−04 (0.31)
10^{-10}	6.946e−02	1.984e−02 (0.29)	6.445e−03 (0.32)	2.054e−03 (0.32)	6.456e−04 (0.31)
10^{-12}	6.946e−02	1.984e−02 (0.29)	6.445e−03 (0.32)	2.054e−03 (0.32)	6.456e−04 (0.31)

Table 3. β-weighted norm and discrete max norm errors for model problem with biquadratic discretization.

$||| \mathcal{U}^* - \mathcal{U}^N |||_{\beta,2}$ (Reduction Rate w.r.t. N)

ε/N	32	64	128	256	512
10^{-6}	9.307e−02	3.854e−02 (0.41)	1.394e−02 (0.36)	4.655e−03 (0.33)	1.484e−03 (0.32)
10^{-8}	9.306e−02	3.854e−02 (0.41)	1.394e−02 (0.36)	4.656e−03 (0.33)	1.485e−03 (0.32)
10^{-10}	9.306e−02	3.854e−02 (0.41)	1.394e−02 (0.36)	4.656e−03 (0.33)	1.485e−03 (0.32)
10^{-12}	9.306e−02	3.854e−02 (0.41)	1.394e−02 (0.36)	4.656e−03 (0.33)	1.485e−03 (0.32)

$|| u^* - u^N ||_{\ell_\infty}$ (Reduction Rate w.r.t. N)

ε/N	32	64	128	256	512
10^{-6}	1.512e−02	1.817e−03 (0.12)	2.715e−04 (0.15)	3.609e−05 (0.13)	4.133e−06 (0.11)
10^{-8}	1.518e−02	1.823e−03 (0.12)	2.730e−04 (0.15)	3.622e−05 (0.13)	4.145e−06 (0.11)
10^{-10}	1.519e−02	1.823e−03 (0.12)	2.733e−04 (0.15)	3.624e−05 (0.13)	4.147e−06 (0.11)
10^{-12}	1.519e−02	1.823e−03 (0.12)	2.734e−04 (0.15)	3.625e−05 (0.13)	4.147e−06 (0.11)

the bilinear case is a reduction like $N^{-1} \ln N$ for $||| \mathcal{U}^* - \mathcal{U}^N |||_{\beta,2}$ (where $\mathcal{U}^*$ represents the manufactured solution, u^* and its gradient) and like $(N^{-1} \ln N)^2$ for the discrete maximum norm of the error, $|| u^* - u^N ||_{\ell_\infty}$, which is measured

Table 4. β-weighted norm and discrete max norm errors for model problem with bicubic discretization.

$|||\mathcal{U}^* - \mathcal{U}^N|||_{\beta,2}$ (Reduction Rate w.r.t. N)				
ε/N	32	64	128	256	512
10^{-6}	2.786e−02	7.800e−03 (0.28)	1.748e−03 (0.22)	3.419e−04 (0.20)	6.185e−05 (0.18)
10^{-8}	2.785e−02	7.800e−03 (0.28)	1.749e−03 (0.22)	3.420e−04 (0.20)	6.187e−05 (0.18)
10^{-10}	2.785e−02	7.800e−03 (0.28)	1.749e−03 (0.22)	3.420e−04 (0.20)	6.187e−05 (0.18)
10^{-12}	2.785e−02	7.800e−03 (0.28)	1.749e−03 (0.22)	3.420e−04 (0.20)	6.187e−05 (0.18)

$\|u^* - u^N\|_{\ell_\infty}$ (Reduction Rate w.r.t. N)				
ε/N	32	64	128	256	512
10^{-6}	4.364e−03	6.989e−04 (0.16)	9.807e−05 (0.14)	1.148e−05 (0.12)	1.198e−06 (0.10)
10^{-8}	4.370e−03	6.993e−04 (0.16)	9.812e−05 (0.14)	1.149e−05 (0.12)	1.199e−06 (0.10)
10^{-10}	4.371e−03	6.994e−04 (0.16)	9.813e−05 (0.14)	1.149e−05 (0.12)	1.199e−06 (0.10)
10^{-12}	4.371e−03	6.994e−04 (0.16)	9.813e−05 (0.14)	1.149e−05 (0.12)	1.199e−06 (0.10)

at the nodes of the mesh corresponding to the finite-element degrees of freedom. These are both expected to be raised by one power in the biquadratic case, and a further one power for bicubics. In Tables 2, 3, and 4, we see convergence behaviour comparable to these rates, with the exception of the results for the discrete maximum norm in Table 3. These seem to show a superconvergence-type phenomenon, although we have no explanation for this observation at present.

5   Conclusions

In the paper, we propose and analyse a new weighted-norm first-order system least squares methodology tuned for singularly perturbed reaction-diffusion equations that lead to boundary layers. The analysis includes a standard ellipticity result for the FOSLS formulation in a weighted norm, and shows that this norm is suitably weighted to be considered a "balanced norm" for the problem. Numerical results confirm the effectiveness of the method. Future work includes completing the error analysis by proving the necessary interpolation error estimates, with respect to $||| \cdot |||_{\beta,2}$, investigating the observed superconvergence properties, generalizing the theory to convection-diffusion equations, and investigating efficient linear solvers for the resulting discretizations.

References

1. Adler, J.H., MacLachlan, S., Madden, N.: A first-order system Petrov-Galerkin discretisation for a reaction-diffusion problem on a fitted mesh. IMA J. Numer. Anal. **36**(3), 1281–1309 (2016)
2. Berndt, M., Manteuffel, T.A., McCormick, S.F.: Local error estimates and adaptive refinement for first-order system least squares (FOSLS). Electron. Trans. Numer. Anal. **6**, 35–43 (1997)

3. Brezina, M., Garcia, J., Manteuffel, T., McCormick, S., Ruge, J., Tang, L.: Parallel adaptive mesh refinement for first-order system least squares. Numer. Linear Algebra Appl. **19**, 343–366 (2012)
4. Cai, Z., Lazarov, R., Manteuffel, T., McCormick, S.: First-order system least squares for second-order partial differential equations: part I. SIAM J. Numer. Anal. **31**, 1785–1799 (1994)
5. Cai, Z., Manteuffel, T., McCormick, S.: First-order system least squares for second-order partial differential equations: part II. SIAM J. Numer. Anal. **34**(2), 425–454 (1997). https://doi.org/10.1137/S0036142994266066
6. De Sterck, H., Manteuffel, T., McCormick, S., Nolting, J., Ruge, J., Tang, L.: Efficiency-based *h*- and *hp*-refinement strategies for finite element methods. Numer. Linear Algebra Appl. **15**(2–3), 89–114 (2008). https://doi.org/10.1002/nla.567
7. Heuer, N., Karkulik, M.: A robust DPG method for singularly perturbed reaction-diffusion problems. SIAM J. Numer. Anal. **55**(3), 1218–1242 (2017). https://doi.org/10.1137/15M1041304
8. Lee, E., Manteuffel, T.A., Westphal, C.R.: Weighted-norm first-order system least squares (FOSLS) for problems with corner singularities. SIAM J. Numer. Anal. **44**(5), 1974–1996 (2006)
9. Lee, E., Manteuffel, T.A., Westphal, C.R.: Weighted-norm first-order system least-squares (FOSLS) for div/curl systems with three dimensional edge singularities. SIAM J. Numer. Anal. **46**(3), 1619–1639 (2008)
10. Lin, R., Stynes, M.: A balanced finite element method for singularly perturbed reaction-diffusion problems. SIAM J. Numer. Anal. **50**(5), 2729–2743 (2012). https://doi.org/10.1137/110837784
11. Liu, F., Madden, N., Stynes, M., Zhou, A.: A two-scale sparse grid method for a singularly perturbed reaction-diffusion problem in two dimensions. IMA J. Numer. Anal. **29**(4), 986–1007 (2009). https://doi.org/10.1093/imanum/drn048
12. Melenk, J.M., Xenophontos, C.: Robust exponential convergence of *hp*-FEM in balanced norms for singularly perturbed reaction-diffusion equations. Calcolo **53**(1), 105–132 (2016). https://doi.org/10.1007/s10092-015-0139-y
13. Miller, J.J.H., O'Riordan, E., Shishkin, G.I.: Fitted Numerical Methods for Singular Perturbation Problems, revised edn. World Scientific Publishing Co., Pte. Ltd., Hackensack (2012). https://doi.org/10.1142/9789814390743
14. Rathgeber, F., et al.: Firedrake: automating the finite element method by composing abstractions. ACM Trans. Math. Softw. (TOMS) **43**(3), 24 (2017)
15. Roos, H.G., Stynes, M., Tobiska, L.: Robust Numerical Methods for Singularly Perturbed Differential Equations. Springer Series in Computational Mathematics, vol. 24, 2nd edn. Springer, Berlin (2008). https://doi.org/10.1007/978-3-540-34467-4
16. Russell, S., Stynes, M.: Balanced-norm error estimates for sparse grid finite element methods applied to singularly perturbed reaction-diffusion problems. J. Numer. Math. **27**(1), 37–55 (2019). https://doi.org/10.1515/jnma-2017-0079

Big Data Analysis: Theory and Applications

Yong Shi[1,2,3,4(✉)] and Pei Quan[5]

[1] School of Economics and Management, University of Chinese Academy of Sciences,
Beijing 100190, China
yshi@ucas.ac.cn
[2] Key Lab of Big Data Mining and Knowledge Management,
Chinese Academy of Sciences, Beijing 100190, China
[3] Research Center on Fictitious Economy and Data Science,
Chinese Academy of Sciences, Beijing 100190, China
[4] College of Information Science and Technology, University of Nebraska at Omaha,
Omaha, NE 68182, USA
[5] School of Computer and Control, University of Chinese Academy of Sciences,
Beijing 100190, China

Abstract. With the continuous improvement of data processing capabilities and storage capabilities, Big Data Era has entered the public sight. Under such a circumstance, the generation of massive data has greatly facilitated the development of data mining algorithms. This paper describes the status of data mining and presents three of our works: optimization-based data mining, intelligent knowledge and the intelligence quotient of Artificial Intelligence respectively. Besides that, we also introduced some applications that have emerged in the context of big data. Furthermore, this paper indicates three potential directions for future research of big data analysis.

Keywords: Big data · Data mining · Optimization-based data mining · Intelligent knowledge

1 Introduction

Since the beginning of the 21st century, computer technology and computer network technology have begun to develop rapidly, and the extension of data and information has been further expanded. The traditional digital data have been expanded into video, audio, graphics, images and other types, which not only make the expression of information more diversified, but also generate a qualitative leap in the speed of information generation. Take the Internet as an example, the, global Internet traffic reached more than 45,000 GB/second in 2017. Scientists expect that the global information volume will exceed 40ZB by 2020 [23]. The emergence of Internet technology has made people's information interaction and cooperation more comfortable, and the amount of information has grown exponentially.

© Springer Nature Switzerland AG 2020
I. Lirkov and S. Margenov (Eds.): LSSC 2019, LNCS 11958, pp. 15–27, 2020.
https://doi.org/10.1007/978-3-030-41032-2_2

As we all know, the data can contain a lot of useful information. Especially when the accumulation of data reaches a certain level, the knowledge contained therein will be a precious treasure. If this information can be extracted and utilized in a proper way, it will be of great benefit to the development of the enterprise and the development of society. The traditional method of relying on manual analysis is not only very dependent on the level of personal expertise, but also very time consuming and labor intensive. In this context, many data mining methods have emerged.

Data mining is a process of discovering the hidden patterns from massive quantities of data that businesses generate [19]. Concretely speaking, it contains four periods of selecting, transforming, mining and interpreting. The data sources include databases, data warehouses, webs, other information repositories, or the data that flows dynamically into the system. The current data mining algorithms can be roughly classified into association, clustering, classification, prediction, sequence pattern analysis and time series analysis. Benefiting from the extraordinary analysis ability of these methods, data mining has achieved great success in a large number of domains, ranging from medical [1], finance [6], education [15] and et al.

In this paper, we shall present our three different works in optimization-based data mining, intelligent knowledge and the intelligence quotient (IQ) of Artificial Intelligence (AI) respectively, which can be regard as form three different perspective of big data theory: data analysis method, application and evaluation. The contributions of this paper are list as follow:

- We present three important topics in big data theory: optimization-based data mining, intelligent knowledge and the IQ of AI respectively.
- We briefly introduce some significant applications of big data analysis methods in our daily life.
- Through the analysis of existing methods, we propose several open challenges in big data domain.

2   Optimization-Based Data Mining

Over the past few decades, data mining algorithms have been significantly developed and deeply rooted in our everyday life. Linear programming, which is formulated with a single criterion and a single resource availability level [16], has always been a fundamental part of the data mining field. Owing to the simplicity and stability of linear programming, it has achieved superior performances in a huge number of tasks. However, linear programming is not a perfect method to deal with data mining problems with conflict objectives. Such problems, therefore, should be handled by multi-criteria linear programming.

In this section, we review multi-criteria data mining [5] to cope with the challenge mentioned above. In linear discriminate analysis, data separation can be achieved by two opposite objectives. The first objective separates the observations by minimizing the sum of the deviations (MSD) among the observations.

The second maximizes the minimum distances (MMD) of observations from the critical value [2]. However, it is difficult for traditional linear programming to optimize MMD and MSD simultaneously. According to the concept of Pareto optimality, we can seek the best tradeoff of two measurements [5, 20, 22]. A Multiple Criteria Linear Programming (MCLP) can be formulated as follows:

$$\text{Min } \sum_{i=1}^{n} \alpha_i$$

$$\text{Max } \sum_{i=1}^{n} \beta_i$$

$$\text{S.T. } (\mathbf{x}_i, \mathbf{w}) = b + y_i (\alpha_i - \beta_i), \quad i = 1, \ldots, n$$
$$\boldsymbol{a}, \boldsymbol{\beta} \geq 0$$

(1)

Here, α_i, β_i denote overlapping and the distance from the training sample to the discriminator $(\mathbf{x}_i, \mathbf{w})$ respectively. $y_i \in 1, -1$ denotes the label of $\mathbf{x_i}$ and n is the number of samples, a training set can be interpreted as pair $\mathbf{x}_i, y_i$, where $\mathbf{x}_i$ is the vector value of the variables and $y_i \in -1, 1$ is the label in the classification case. The weights vector $\mathbf{w}$ and the bias b are the unknown variables to be optimized for the two objectives. Note that alternatively, the constraint of MCLP can also be written as $((\mathbf{x}_i, \mathbf{w}) - b) = \alpha_i - \beta_i$. The geometric meaning of the model is shown in Fig. 1 (Fig. 2).

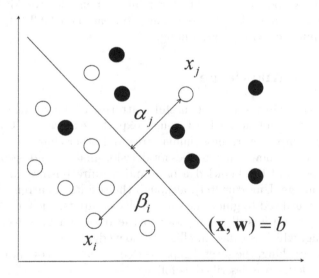

Fig. 1. The two criteria of classification.

As the multi-criteria problem become more and more complex, several variants of MCLP, shown in Fig. 1, have been designed to deal with different problems.

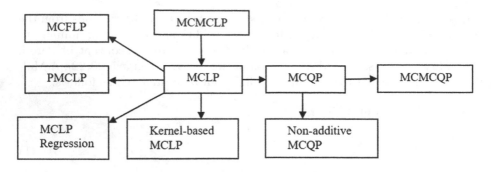

Fig. 2. Evolution of multi-criteria models in data mining.

[7] proposed a penalized MCLP (PMCLP) method to cope with the problem of the unbalanced training set. To obtain a better classifier, [3] introduced Multiple Criteria Fuzzy Linear Programming (MCFLP). [4, 13] proposed several MCQP methods by using different norms to measure the overlapping degree and distance. [5] introduced Multi-Class Multiple Criteria Programming to solve the multi-Class classification task, namely MCMCLP and MCMCQP, respectively. Considering data distributed with non-linear patterns, [26] introduced a Kernel-based Multiple Criteria Linear Program (Kernel-based MCLP). Also, [24] applied the Choquet integral to formulate a non-additive MCQP model, while [25] designed an MCLP Regression method based on MCLP to extend the framework of multi-criteria programming.

3   Intelligent Knowledge

Data mining can always extract useful patterns of knowledge from large databases, which is not accessible through experts' experience. Owing to the high efficiency, comprehensiveness, human-free and other characteristics of data mining, it has bought new opportunities for decision-making and become a meaningful way to expand the knowledge base and acquire business intelligence in this information age. Unfortunately, although the results of current data mining methods can be utilized to guide the same tasks as inputs, such as classification and regression, there is still a long way to the data can be directly used for decision-making, which is called intelligent knowledge.

Concretely speaking, the several gaps between the results of data mining and intelligent knowledge are described as follow:

First, the primary purpose of traditional data mining is to extract hidden patterns underlying massive data rather than summarize the corresponding knowledge obtained from given data. Most researchers halt immediately after obtaining rules through data mining from data and rarely go further to evaluate or formalize the result of mining to support business decisions [11]. For example, there is a data mining project which aims to divide users into "current users, freezing users and lost users" by using their personal information and transaction records.

In this project, they utilize the decision tree classification algorithm producing 245 rules [18]. However, surprisingly, business personnel cannot acquire right knowledge from these rules [18]. Therefore, the knowledge should not be just limited in the form of symbols or numbers. Some more humanistic expressions, such as natural languages, flow charts and other visualization techniques are encouraged to design for the representation of intelligent knowledge and facility the process of decision-making. To this end, the current data mining method needs to be further investigated.

Second, the current data mining methods ignore domain knowledge, expertise, users' intentions and situational factors [14]. Therefore, the result of data mining methods cannot be directly converted to general intelligent knowledge. Here we indicate that although knowledge and information are related to meaning, knowledge is a concept about operations and it always exists for a "certain purpose". Namely that, knowledge is in accordance with the specific situation and acquires associated attributes [12,28]. To obtain better knowledge from data, patterns, or rules generated from data mining must be combined with a specific context. Here, the context contains relevant physics, business and other externally environmental and contextual factors, which also covers cognition, experience, psychology and other internal factors of the subject. Therefore, context is crucial for the process that generalizing results obtained by data mining method to meaningful knowledge, which should be regarded as a focal point in studies of generating intelligent knowledge automatically.

Third, the data mining process stops at the beginning of knowledge acquisition. It is well known that knowledge can be viewed as a higher-order representation of statistical results. However, common data mining algorithms are just designed to obtain statistical results from the given data. There are seldom works involve how to conduct a second-order analysis to apply the knowledge to practical business. In the ontology of data mining process, the discovered patterns are always viewed as the end of the work. It is very necessary to explain the process of knowledge creation at the organizational level from the aspects of knowledge realization, knowledge certification, knowledge internal process, organizational knowledge assets, and knowledge recreation. A deep study of the process of data - information - knowledge - wisdom is urgently needed.

In order to better represent intelligent knowledge, we have rigorously defined some concepts related to intelligent knowledge [27], such as Data, Information, Rough Knowledge and so on. Some specific definitions are shown as follow:

- **Data** is a certain form of the representation of facts.
- **Information** is any data that has been pre-processed to all aspects of human's interests.
- **Rough Knowledge** is the hidden pattern or "knowledge" discovered from information that has been analyzed by the known data mining algorithms or tools.

Figure 3 illustrates the process of transformations from data to rough knowledge, to intelligent knowledge and to actionable knowledge in a flow way.

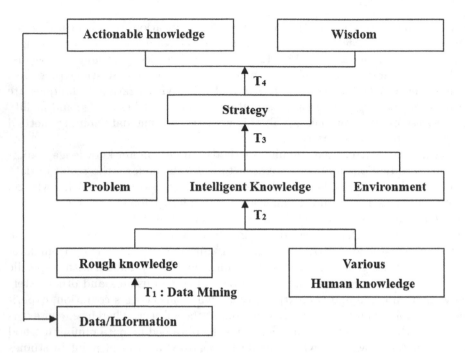

Fig. 3. Data $\Rightarrow$ Rough Knowledge $\Rightarrow$ Intelligent Knowledge $\Rightarrow$ Actionable Knowledge

T_1 represents the necessary processing and analyzing of raw data/information to obtain the rough knowledge (hidden pattern, rules, etc.). In the process of T_2, based on the rough knowledge extracted previous, user preferences, scenarios, domain knowledge and others, the process carries out a "second-order" mining for knowledge used to support intelligent decision-making and intelligent action. The process carries out deep processing of the original knowledge, which is the core step in intelligent knowledge management. T_3 represents the process of transforming intelligent knowledge to intelligent strategy through consideration of problem statement and solving environment. Finally, T_4 denotes the process from intelligent strategy to actionable knowledge. And the actionable knowledge as the final output of intelligent knowledge, can be regard as data source for decision support.

4   The Intelligence Quotient of Artificial Intelligence

In today's big data era, the improvement of computing power and storage capacity has promoted the development of artificial intelligent (AI) algorithms. Some new AI products appear in our daily life, including smart speakers, intelligent refrigerators, intelligent air conditioning, and facility our daily life significantly. However, it still cannot change the point that artificial intelligence is a potential threat to human resource, which has been insisted since the birth of artificial intelligence. An opening question is that if we could compare the developmental levels of AI and systems with measured human intelligence quotients (IQs), scilicet, can we design a quantitative analysis method to measure the degree of artificial intelligence threat?

There are two main challenges before the realization of quantitative evaluation of artificial intelligence [9,10]: there is no unified model of an artificially intelligent system, and there is no unified model for comparing artificially intelligent systems with human beings. These challenges can be coped with in the same way that conducts a unified model to describe all living behavior, especially human behavior, and all artificial intelligence systems.

Inspired by David Wechsler's theory, and the von Neumann architecture, we conclude the following criteria for defining a standard intelligence system [9]:

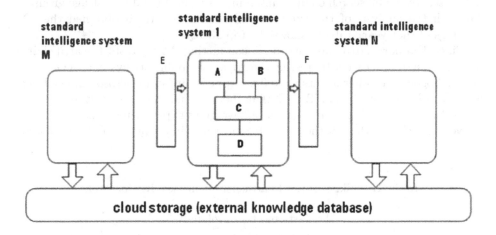

A. arithmetic logic unit

B. control unit

C. internal memory unit

D. innovation generator

E. input device

F. output device

Fig. 4. Expanded von Neumann architecture

- The system should have the ability to obtain data, information or knowledge from the outside environment via aural, image, and/or textual input.
- The system should have the ability to transform external data, information, and knowledge into internal knowledge that can be utilized by system.
- The system should have the ability to use its own knowledge in an innovative manner to deal with the demand generated by external data, information and knowledge. And this innovative ability is expected to include associate, create, imagine, discover, etc.

– The system should have the ability to feedback data, information, and knowledge generated by itself to the outside environment through the aural, image, or textual according to different situation.

To express human, machine and artificial intelligence systems in a more explicit way, we extend two additional components based on five components of von Neumann architecture (an arithmetic logic unit, a control unit, a memory unit, an input unit, and an output unit). The extended von Neumann architecture is shown in Fig. 4.

Based on this unified model of intelligent systems mentioned above, we established an artificial intelligence IQ evaluation system in 2014 [8]. Considering the four major ability types, 15 sub-tests were established, and an artificial intelligence scale was formed. We applied this scale to set up relevant question databases, tested 50 search engines and humans from three different age groups. Through the analysis of the experimental results, our team obtained the IQ rankings of that year. Table 1 shows the top 13 IQs.

Since February 2016, we have been conducting AI IQ tests for artificially intelligent systems circa 2016, testing the artificial intelligence systems of Google, Baidu, Sogou, and other agents as well as Apple's Siri and Microsoft's Xiaobing [9]. It can be observed from Table 2 that the artificial intelligence systems produced by Google, Baidu, and others still have giant gaps when compared with a six-year-old child although they have dramatically improved over the past two years.

Table 1. Ranking of top 13 artificial intelligence IQs for 2014.

ID	Test object	Absolute IQ
1	18 years old	97
2	12 years old	84.5
3	6 years old	55.5
4	Google	26.5
5	Baidu	23.5
6	so	23.5
7	Sogou	22
8	yell	20.5
9	Yandex	19
10	ramber	18
11	His	18
12	seznam	18
13	clix	16.5

Table 2. IQ scores of artificial intelligence systems in 2016

ID	Test object	Absolute IQ
1	18 years old	97
2	12 years old	84.5
3	6 years old	55.5
4	Google	47.28
5	duer	37.2
6	Baidu	32.92
7	Sogou	32.25
8	Bing	31.98
9	Microsoft's Xiaobing	24.48
10	SIRI	23.94

5   Application of Big Data Analysis

With the continuous development of data science, big data analysis technology plays an increasingly important role in our daily life. In this section, we briefly summarize two real-world application cases to illustrate how big data analytics technology is widely used in finance and healthcare.

5.1   China's National Credit Scoring System

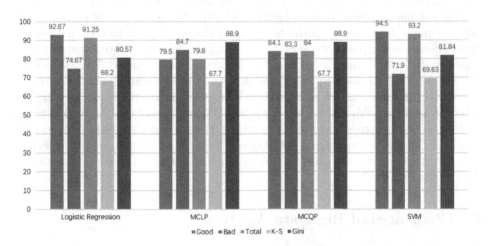

Fig. 5. Models comparison in China's national credit scoring system (China score)

The first author leads his research and technical group at the People's Bank of China from 2006 to 2009 to develop China's National Credit Scoring System called "China Score" based on the National Personal Credit Database, which is the world largest database of credit and contains all Chinese banking records. The following figure shows the computation results of the "China score" that has been implemented by the methods of optimization-based data mining and intelligent knowledge [21].

Figure 5 shows the comparison of four data mining results: Logistic Regression (LR), Multiple Criteria Linear Programming (MCLP), Multiple Criteria Quadratic Programming (MCQP) and Support Vector Machine (SVM) over a big credit data. Among them, MCLP and MCQP are our proposed optimization-based data mining methods. In addition, the implementation of the intelligent knowledge has provided the highest accuracy in bad accounts classification over most known credit scoring models in the field.

5.2   ChunYu Doctors App

ChunYu Doctors is an internet company in China, which focus on the internet medical treatment. The main product of ChunYu is an application named ChunYu Doctors App, which is an online platform for doctors and patients to communicate efficiently. After continuous development and improvement, this app currently has two core subsystems, the Accurate Inquiry & Triage System (AITS) and Doctor Recommendation System (DRS). By analyzing the symptoms, medication history, individual health situation and other information supplied by patients, which are always in unstructured forms, AITS can assign appropriate subjects based on each patient's condition. After the classification, the DRS can recommend a suitable online doctor for the patient by matching their expertise, major and comments from patients with the feature of patients.

By utilizing Support Vector Machine (SVM), MCLP, Linear Regression and other popular data mining methods, ChunYu Doctors App have been witnessed great success in the past few years. Specifically, the accuracy of automatic triage remains above 90%, the overall users' satisfaction is more than 95%. Moreover, the average time of doctor-patient matching and online communication is conducted within 3 min. Also, the ChunYu Doctors has become the leader in Chinese Internet Medical field, which cooperate with 17 first-class hospitals and attract millions of users, expert doctors. At present, the big data analytic platform of ChunYu Doctors is supporting 600,000 registered medical doctors and serving over 200 million patients, which is the largest internet based medical consultant App in the world.

6   Challenges of Big Data Analysis

Even though big data analysis has achieved a great success in manifolds and rooted in our daily life, they are still not good enough to offer satisfying results for all cases. In this section, we share several open problems about big data analysis with the readers [17].

- **Structuralize the Unstructured Data.** Big data environments mean large volumes, fast speeds, diverse types, and low-value density. In the data mining of the era of big data, it is necessary to consider all-round and multi-angle of big data, not only including structured data, but also typical semi-structured data such as HTML files, SGML documents and WEB data in the Internet, and text, images, videos, etc. cannot directly describe the unstructured data of the content. Due to these unstructured data are the carriers of most of the information in our lives, data analysis for unstructured data is very important.
- **The Complexity and Uncertainty of Big Data.** Due to the emergence of big data, people have acquired unprecedented large-scale samples when dealing with computational problems, but they also have to face more complex data objects. The inherent complexity of big data makes the data perception, expression, understanding and calculation face many challenges, which leads to the proliferation of time complexity and space complexity. Many traditional data analysis and mining tasks, such as retrieval, topic discovery, semantics, and sentiment analysis, become extremely difficult. In addition, as data continues to accumulate, internal data patterns may change over time. This phenomenon is called data drift, how to perform dynamic data analysis to ensure the long-term effectiveness of results is of outstanding interest.
- **The Relation between Data and Decision.** Big data means that the amount of data is enormous and contains multiple data types. The use of big data analysis technology to obtain information from data and then combine it with the knowledge of decision-makers is an essential part of intelligent knowledge acquisition. How to dig out knowledge from big data for management decision-making is the core value of big data research. With the continuous development of big data, the amount of data has exploded, and the complexity of decision-making has increased, but the response time required for decisionmaking has been gradually shortened. This makes research on the relationship between data structures and decision structures important. How to design a big data analysis system for decision-making has attracted the attention of many researchers.

7 Conclusion

The era of big data brings new opportunities and challenges to the field of data science. In this paper, we have first introduced the current environment status of big data. Then, we have elaborated our works on optimization-based data mining, intelligent knowledge and the intelligence quotient of Artificial Intelligence respectively from three aspects: data mining method, mining result application, and model evaluation. We have also shown some practical big data analytics projects in our daily life. Finally, we have shared our view about the challenges of big data analysis. Nevertheless, the big data analysis is still an ongoing research and there will be more and more findings in the near future.

Acknowledgement. This work was partially supported by the National Natural Science Foundation of China [Grant No. 7193000078, No. 91546201, No. 71331005, No. 71110107026, No. 11671379, No. 11331012] and UCAS Grant [No. Y55202LY00].

References

1. Cios, K.J., Moore, G.W.: Uniqueness of medical data mining. Artif. Intell. Med. **26**(1–2), 1–24 (2002)
2. Freed, N., Glover, F.: Simple but powerful goal programming models for discriminant problems. Eur. J. Oper. Res. **7**(1), 44–60 (1981)
3. He, J., Liu, X., Shi, Y., Xu, W., Yan, N.: Classifications of credit cardholder behavior by using fuzzy linear programming. Int. J. Inf. Technol. Decis. Making **3**(04), 633–650 (2004)
4. Kou, G.: Multi-class multi-criteria mathematical programming and its applications in large scale data mining problems. Ph.D. thesis, University of Nebraska at Omaha (2006)
5. Kou, G., Liu, X., Peng, Y., Shi, Y., Wise, M., Xu, W.: Multiple criteria linear programming approach to data mining: models, algorithm designs and software development. Optim. Methods Softw. **18**(4), 453–473 (2003)
6. Kovalerchuk, B., Vityaev, E.: Data Mining in Finance: Advances in Relational and Hybrid Methods, vol. 547. Springer, Heidelberg (2006)
7. Li, A., Shi, Y., He, J.: MCLP-based methods for improving bad catching rate in credit cardholder behavior analysis. Appl. Soft Comput. **8**(3), 1259–1265 (2008)
8. Liu, F., Shi, Y.: The search engine IQ test based on the internet IQ evaluation algorithm. Proc. Comput. Sci. **31**, 1066–1073 (2014)
9. Liu, F., Shi, Y., Liu, Y.: Intelligence quotient and intelligence grade of artificial intelligence. Ann. Data Sci. **4**(2), 179–191 (2017)
10. Liu, F., Shi, Y., Wang, B.: World search engine IQ test based on the internet IQ evaluation algorithms. Int. J. Inf. Technol. Decis. Making **14**(02), 221–237 (2015)
11. McGarry, K.: A survey of interestingness measures for knowledge discovery. Knowl. Eng. Rev. **20**(1), 39–61 (2005)
12. Nonaka, I., Toyama, R., Konno, N.: SECI, Ba and leadership: a unified model of dynamic knowledge creation. Long Range Plan. **33**(1), 5–34 (2000)
13. Peng, T., Zuo, W., He, F.: SVM based adaptive learning method for text classification from positive and unlabeled documents. Knowl. Inf. Syst. **16**(3), 281–301 (2008)
14. Peng, Y., Kou, G., Shi, Y., Chen, Z.: A descriptive framework for the field of data mining and knowledge discovery. Int. J. Inf. Technol. Decis. Making **7**(04), 639–682 (2008)
15. Romero, C., Ventura, S.: Data mining in education. Wiley Interdisc. Rev.: Data Min. Knowl. Discov. **3**(1), 12–27 (2013)
16. Shi, Y.: Multiple Criteria and Multiple Constraint Levels Linear Programming: Concepts, Techniques and Applications. World Scientific Publishing Company, Singapore (2001)
17. Shi, Y.: Big data: History, current status, and challenges going forward. Bridge **44**(4), 6–11 (2014)
18. Shi, Y., Li, X.: Knowledge management platforms and intelligent knowledge beyond data mining. In: Shi, Y., Olsen, D.L., Stam, A. (eds.) Advances in Multiple Criteria Decision Making and Human Systems Management: Knowledge and Wisdom, pp. 272–288. IOS Press, Amsterdam (2007)

19. Shi, Y.: Introduction to Business Data Mining. New York, New York (2007)
20. Shi, Y., Peng, Y., Xu, W., Tang, X.: Data mining via multiple criteria linear pro-
    gramming: applications in credit card portfolio management. Int. J. Inf. Technol.
    Decis. Making **1**(01), 131–151 (2002)
21. Shi, Y., Tian, Y., Kou, G., Peng, Y., Li, J.: Optimization Based Data Mining:
    Theory and Applications. Springer, Heidelberg (2011). https://doi.org/10.1007/
    978-0-85729-504-0
22. Shi, Y., Wise, M., Luo, M., Lin, Y.: Data mining in credit card portfolio man-
    agement: a multiple criteria decision making approach. In: Köksalan, M., Zionts,
    S. (eds.) Multiple Criteria Decision Making in the New Millennium. LNE, vol.
    507, pp. 427–436. Springer, Heidelberg (2001). https://doi.org/10.1007/978-3-642-
    56680-6_39
23. Turner, V., Gantz, J.F., Reinsel, D., Minton, S.: The digital universe of opportuni-
    ties: rich data and the increasing value of the internet of things. IDC Anal. Future
    16 (2014)
24. Yan, N., Shi, Y., Chen, Z.: Multiple criteria nonlinear programming classification
    with the non-additive measure. In: Ehrgott, M., Naujoks, B., Stewart, T., Walle-
    nius, J., et al. (eds.) Multiple Criteria Decision Making for Sustainable Energy and
    Transportation Systems. LNE, vol. 634, pp. 289–297. Springer, Heidelberg (2010).
    https://doi.org/10.1007/978-3-642-04045-0_25
25. Zhang, D., Tian, Y., Shi, Y.: A regression method by multiple criteria linear pro-
    gramming. In: 19th International Conference on Multiple Criteria Decision Making
    (2008)
26. Zhang, J., Shi, Y., Zhang, P.: Several multi-criteria programming methods for
    classification. Comput. Oper. Res. **36**(3), 823–836 (2009)
27. Zhang, L., Li, J., Shi, Y., Liu, X.: Foundations of intelligent knowledge manage-
    ment. Hum. Syst. Manag. **28**(4), 145–161 (2009)
28. Zhang, L., Li, J., Zheng, X., Li, X., Shi, Y.: Study on a process-oriented knowledge
    management model. JAIST PRESS Publications (2007). http://hdl.handle.net/
    10119/4140

Control and Optimization of Dynamical Systems

Solutions to the Hamilton-Jacobi Equation for Bolza Problems with State Constraints and Discontinuous Time Dependent Data

Julien Bernis and Piernicola Bettiol[(⊠)]

Univ Brest, UMR CNRS 6205, Laboratoire de Mathématiques de Bretagne
Atlantique, 29200 Brest, France
{julien.bernis,piernicola.bettiol}@univ-brest.fr

Abstract. This paper concerns the characterization of the value function associated with a state constrained Bolza problem in which the data are allowed to be discontinuous w.r.t. the time variable on a set of zero measure and have everywhere left and right limits. Using techniques coming from viability theory and nonsmooth analysis, we provide a characterization of the value function as the unique solution to the Hamilton-Jacobi equation, in a generalized sense which employs the lower Dini derivative and the proximal normal vectors.

Keywords: Hamilton-Jacobi equation · Value function · State constraints

1 Introduction

We consider the following family of minimization problems indexed by initial data $(t, x) \in [S, T] \times \mathbb{R}^n$:

$$
(SC_{t,x}) \begin{cases}
\text{Minimize } g(x(T)) + \int_t^T L(s, x(s), \dot{x}(s)) \mathrm{d}s \\
\text{over arcs } x(\cdot) \in W^{1,1}([t, T], \mathbb{R}^n) \text{ satisfying} \\
\dot{x}(s) \in F(s, x(s)) \text{ for a.e. } s \in [S, T], \\
x(s) \in A \text{ for all } s \in [S, T], \\
x(t) = x,
\end{cases}
$$

in which $g : \mathbb{R}^n \to \mathbb{R} \cup \{+\infty\}$ and $L : [S, T] \times \mathbb{R}^n \times \mathbb{R}^n \to \mathbb{R}$ are given functions, $F : [S, T] \times \mathbb{R}^n \rightsquigarrow \mathbb{R}^n$ is a given multivalued function, and A is a given nonempty closed set in $\mathbb{R}^n$. An F-trajectory on the interval $[s, t] \subset [S, T]$ is an absolutely continuous arc $x(\cdot) : [s, t] \to \mathbb{R}^n$ which satisfies the reference differential inclusion $\dot{x}(\sigma) \in F(\sigma, x(\sigma))$ for a.e. $\sigma \in [s, t]$. We say that $x(\cdot) \in W^{1,1}([s, t], \mathbb{R}^n)$ is *feasible* on $[s, t]$ if $x(\sigma) \in A$ for all $\sigma \in [s, t]$.

The value function $V : [S, T] \times \mathbb{R}^n \to \mathbb{R} \cup \{+\infty\}$ is defined by the infimum cost of $(SC_{t,x})$:

$$V(t, x) = \inf(SC_{t,x}),$$

© Springer Nature Switzerland AG 2020
I. Lirkov and S. Margenov (Eds.): LSSC 2019, LNCS 11958, pp. 31–39, 2020.
https://doi.org/10.1007/978-3-030-41032-2_3

taking into account the convention that $V(t,x) = +\infty$ whenever $x \notin A$ (in particular we are interpreting '$+\infty$' the cost of an F-trajectory $x(\cdot)$ which is not feasible). The aim of this paper is to characterize the value $V(\cdot,\cdot)$ as the unique solution in the class of lower semicontinuous (lsc) functions, in a suitable generalized sense, which involves the notion of lower Dini derivative and the proximal normal vectors to the epigraph of V, to the Hamilton-Jacobi equation associated with $(SC_{t,x})$. This is a long-standing research topic and a lot of work has been done in this context (we refer the reader to [3,5–9] also for further references and a comparison with viscosity solutions techniques).

We shall consider the case when we may have a discontinuous behaviour of F and L w.r.t. the time variable t in the following sense: F and L have everywhere one-sided limits in t and are continuous on the complement of a zero-measure subset of $[S,T]$. This class of time discontinuity has been introduced in [3] to provide an 'everywhere in t' characterization of the value function for optimal control Mayer problems ($L = 0$). In our case, the Lagrangian L is merely continuous w.r.t. the state variable x. Moreover, we do not impose any *a priori* regularity condition on the epigraph of the candidate solutions. As a consequence, the class of problems that we are considering is not covered by previous work; in particular a state augmentation technique would not allow to employ, for instance, the results obtained in [3] and would not reduce the difficulties, either.

Our results (see Theorems 1 and 2 below) provide an extension of [3, Theorems 4.1 and 4.2] to the context of Bolza problems when we have a single 'smooth' state constraint (see condition (H1) below): the first theorem considers a lsc (on A) final cost function g assuming an 'outward pointing' constraint qualification; the second concerns the case of a continuous function g coupled with an 'inward pointing' constraint qualification. We also give an illustrative example showing that the right coupling between 'regularity of g' and 'constraint qualification' plays a crucial role in these results: if g is just lsc a bad constraint qualification ('inward pointing' in this case) would not yield the desired characterization.

A further important feature is that, in our context, it is necessary to have at hand a $W^{1,1}$ 'distance estimate' (we recall that for [3, Theorems 4.1 and 4.2] only an $\mathbb{L}^\infty$ distance estimate result was necessary): this is an analytical tool which allows to construct, from an arbitrary F-trajectory, a feasible F-trajectory having, in our case, a suitable $W^{1,1}$-distance from the reference F-trajectory. In this paper we provide the structure of the proofs of Theorems 1 and 2 developing in detail a crucial part of the proof of Theorem 2 to highlight the role of the $W^{1,1}$-distance estimate result.

2   Notation and Standing Assumptions

Notation. In this paper we write $\mathbb{B}$ for the closed unit ball in $\mathbb{R}^n$. We denote the Lebesgue subsets of $[S,T]$ and the Borel subsets of $\mathbb{R}^n$ by $\mathcal{L}$ and $\mathcal{B}^n$ respectively. The (associated) product σ-algebra of sets in $[S,T] \times \mathbb{R}^n$ is written $\mathcal{L} \times \mathcal{B}^n$. Let $D \subset \mathbb{R}^m$, we denote by $\mathrm{co}D$ and $\overline{\mathrm{co}}D$ respectively the convex hull and the closed convex hull of D. The distance of x from the set D is written $d_D(x) :=$ $\inf_{y \in D}\{|x - y|\}$. Consider a point $x \in \overline{D}$ and a multifunction $G(\cdot) : D \rightsquigarrow \mathbb{R}^m$. The limit inferior and the limit superior of $G(\cdot)$ at x along D (in the Kuratowski sense) are the sets

$$\liminf_{y \xrightarrow{D} x} G(y) := \left\{ v \in \mathbb{R}^m \ : \ \limsup_{y \xrightarrow{D} x} d_{G(y)}(v) = 0 \right\},$$

$$\limsup_{y \xrightarrow{D} x} G(y) := \left\{ v \in \mathbb{R}^m \ : \ \liminf_{y \xrightarrow{D} x} d_{G(y)}(v) = 0 \right\},$$

where $y \xrightarrow{D} x$ means that we take convergent sequences $(y_i)_i$ such that $y_i \to x$ and $y_i \in D$ for all i. We recall that $v \in \liminf_{y \xrightarrow{D} x} G(y)$ if and only if for every $\varepsilon > 0$ we can find $\delta > 0$ such that $(v + \varepsilon \mathbb{B}) \cap G(y) \neq \emptyset$ for all $y \in (x + \delta \mathbb{B}) \cap D$, and $v \in \limsup_{y \xrightarrow{D} x} G(y)$ if and only if there exist a sequence $y_i \xrightarrow{D} x$ and a sequence $v_i \to v$ such that $v_i \in G(y_i)$ for all i. For arbitrary nonempty closed sets in $\mathbb{R}^n$, C' and C, we denote by $d_H(C, C')$ the 'Hausdorff distance' between C and C':

$$d_H(C, C') := \max \left\{ \inf\{\beta > 0 \,|\, C' \subset C + \beta \mathbb{B}\}, \ \inf\{\beta > 0 \,|\, C \subset C' + \beta \mathbb{B}\} \right\}.$$

The *proximal normal cone* to C at $x \in C$, denoted $N_C^P(x)$ is defined by:

$$N_C^P(x) := \{\eta \in \mathbb{R}^m \,|\, \exists M \geq 0 \quad \text{s.t.} \quad \eta \cdot (y - x) \leq M|y - x|^2, \ \forall y \in C\}.$$

Consider an extended valued function $\varphi : \mathbb{R}^m \to \mathbb{R} \cup \{\pm \infty\}$. We write $\mathrm{dom}\,(\varphi) := \{x \in \mathbb{R}^m \,|\, \varphi(x) \neq \pm \infty\}$, $\mathrm{epi}\,\varphi := \{(x, r) \in \mathbb{R}^{m+1} \,|\, r \geq \varphi(x)\}$. Take $x \in \mathrm{dom}\,(\varphi)$ and $d \in \mathbb{R}^m$. The *lower Dini derivative* (also called *the contingent epiderivative*) of φ at x in the direction $d \in \mathbb{R}^m$, denoted $D_\uparrow \varphi(x, d)$, is defined by:

$$D_\uparrow \varphi(x, d) := \liminf_{\substack{h \downarrow 0 \\ e \to d}} h^{-1}(\varphi(x + he) - \varphi(x)).$$

Let $[s, t] \subset [S, T]$ an interval. We write $W^{1,1}([s, t], \mathbb{R}^n)$, the space of absolutely continuous function for the Lebesgue measure endowed with the norm:

$$\|f\|_{W^{1,1}} := |f(s)| + \int_s^t |\dot{f}(\tau)| d\tau, \text{ for all } f \in W^{1,1}([s, t], \mathbb{R}^n).$$

Hypotheses. We assume that for every $R_0 > 0$ there exist functions $c_F(\cdot) \in \mathbb{L}^1([S, T], \mathbb{R})$ and $k_F(\cdot) \in \mathbb{L}^1([S, T], \mathbb{R}_+)$, a modulus of continuity $\omega(\cdot) : \mathbb{R}_+ \to \mathbb{R}_+$, and constants $c_0 > 0$, $M_0 > 0$, $\gamma_0 > 0$, such that

(H1): (i) The multivalued function $F : [S, T] \times \mathbb{R}^n \rightsquigarrow \mathbb{R}^n$ takes convex, closed, nonempty values. For every $x \in \mathbb{R}^n$, $F(\cdot, x)$ is Lebesgue mesurable.
(ii) The function $g : \mathbb{R}^n \to \mathbb{R} \cup \{+\infty\}$ is lsc, with nonempty domain.

(iii) The subset $A \subset \mathbb{R}^n$ is closed with nonempty interior. Moreover it admits a functional inequality representation: $A := \{x \in \mathbb{R}^n \mid h(x) \leq 0\}$, where $h : \mathbb{R}^n \to \mathbb{R}$ is a differentiable function such that ∇h is locally Lipschitz continuous.

(H2): (i) For almost every $t \in [S, T]$ and $x \in \mathbb{R}^n$: $F(t, x) \subset c_F(t)(1 + |x|)\mathbb{B}$.

(ii) For any $(t, x) \in [S, T] \times R_0\mathbb{B}$: $F(t, x) \subset c_0\mathbb{B}$.

(H3): (i) $d_H(F(t, x'), F(t, x)) \leq \omega(|x - x'|)$, for all $x, x' \in R_0\mathbb{B}$ and $t \in [S, T]$;

(ii) $F(t, x') \subset F(t, x) + k_F(t)|x - x'|\mathbb{B}$, for all $x, x' \in R_0\mathbb{B}$ for a.e. $t \in [S, T]$.

(H4): (i) For each $x \in \mathbb{R}^n$, $s \in [S, T[$, and $t \in]S, T]$ the following limits (in the sense of Kuratowski) exist and are nonempty:

$$F(s^+, x) := \lim_{s' \downarrow s} F(s', x) \text{ and } F(t^-, x) := \lim_{t' \uparrow t} F(t', x).$$

(ii) For almost every $s \in [S, T[$ and $t \in]S, T]$, and every $x \in \mathbb{R}^n$ we have:

$$F(s^+, x) = F(s, x) \text{ and } F(t^-, x) = F(t, x).$$

(H5): (i) The Lagrangian $L : [S, T] \times \mathbb{R}^n \times \mathbb{R}^n \longrightarrow \mathbb{R}$ is $\mathcal{L} \times \mathcal{B}^{n+n}$-measurable. For every $t \in [S, T]$ and $x \in \mathbb{R}^n$, $L(t, x, \cdot)$ is convex.

(ii) L is locally bounded in the following sense:

$$|L(t, x, v)| \leq M_0, \quad \text{for all} \quad (t, x, v) \in [S, T] \times R_0\mathbb{B} \times 2c_0\mathbb{B} .$$

(H6): (i) $|L(t, x', v) - L(t, x, v)| \leq \omega(|x - x'|)$, for all $x, x' \in R_0\mathbb{B}$, $t \in [S, T]$ and $v \in c_0\mathbb{B}$.

(ii) $L(t^-, x, v) := \lim_{t' \uparrow t} L(t', x, v)$ exists for every $(t, x, v) \in]S, T] \times R_0\mathbb{B} \times c_0\mathbb{B}$, and $L(t^-, x, v) = L(t, x, v)$ for a.e. $t \in]S, T]$.

(iii) $L(s^+, x, v) := \lim_{s' \downarrow s} L(s', x, v)$ exists for every $(s, x, v) \in [S, T[\times R_0\mathbb{B} \times c_0\mathbb{B}$, and $L(s^+, x, v) = L(s, x, v)$ for a.e. $s \in [S, T[$.

(H7): $\min_{v \in F(t, x)} \nabla h(x) \cdot (-v) \leq -\gamma_0$, for all $(t, x) \in [S, T] \times (R_0\mathbb{B} \cap \partial A)$.

(H8): $\min_{v \in F(t, x)} \nabla h(x) \cdot v \leq -\gamma_0$, for all $(t, x) \in [S, T] \times (R_0\mathbb{B} \cap \partial A)$.

3   Two Characterizations of the Value Function

Theorem 1 (Characterization of lsc extended valued Value Functions). *Assume (H1)–(H6) and (H7). Let $U : [S, T] \times \mathbb{R}^n \to \mathbb{R} \cup \{+\infty\}$ be an extended valued function. Then (a), (b), and (c) below are equivalent:*

(a) The function U is the value function for $(SC_{t,x})$: $U = V$.

(b) The function U is lsc, satisfies $U(t, x) = +\infty$ whenever $x \notin A$ and:

(i) for every $(t, x) \in ([S, T[\times A) \cap \text{dom}(U)$,

$$\inf_{v \in F(t^+, x)} \left[D_\uparrow U((t, x), (1, v)) + L(t^+, x, v) \right] \leq 0;$$

(ii) for every $(t, x) \in (]S, T] \times \text{int } A) \cap \text{dom}(U)$,

$$\sup_{v \in F(t^-, x)} \left[D_\uparrow U((t, x), (-1, -v)) - L(t^-, x, v) \right] \leq 0;$$

(iii) for every $x \in A$, $\liminf_{\{(t',x') \to (T,x) \,|\, t' < T, x' \in \text{int } A\}} U(t',x') = U(T,x) = g(x)$.

(c) The function U *is lsc, satisfies* $U(t,x) = +\infty$ *whenever* $x \notin A$ *and:*

(i) for every $(t,x) \in (]S,T[\times A) \cap \text{dom}(U)$:

$$\xi^0 + \inf_{v \in F(t^+,x)} \left[\xi^1 \cdot v + \lambda L(t^+,x,v)\right] \leq 0, \quad \forall(\xi^0,\xi^1,-\lambda) \in N^P_{\text{epi}\,U}((t,x),U(t,x));$$

(ii) for every $(t,x) \in (]S,T[\times\text{int } A) \cap \text{dom}(U)$:

$$\xi^0 + \inf_{v \in F(t^-,x)} \left[\xi^1 \cdot v + \lambda L(t^-,x,v)\right] \geq 0, \quad \forall(\xi^0,\xi^1,-\lambda) \in N^P_{\text{epi}\,U}((t,x),U(t,x));$$

(iii) for every $x \in A$, $\liminf_{\{(t',x') \to (S,x) \,|\, t' > S\}} U(t',x') = U(S,x)$,

$$\liminf_{\{(t',x') \to (T,x) \,|\, t' < T, x' \in \text{int } A\}} U(t',x') = U(T,x) = g(x). \tag{1}$$

Theorem 2 (Characterization of lsc extended valued Value Functions when the final cost is continuous). *Assume that (H1)–(H6), (H8) are satisfied and that* g *is continuous on* A. *Let* $U : [S,T] \times \mathbb{R}^n \to \mathbb{R} \cup \{+\infty\}$ *be an extended valued function. Then (a), (b), and (c) below are equivalent:*

(a) The function U *is the value function for* $(SC_{t,x})$: $U = V$.

(b) The function U *is lsc, satisfies* $U(t,x) = +\infty$ *whenever* $x \notin A$ *and:*

(i) for every $(t,x) \in (]S,T[\times A) \cap \text{dom}(U)$,

$$\inf_{v \in F(t^+,x)} \left[D_\uparrow U((t,x),(1,v)) + L(t^+,x,v)\right] \leq 0;$$

(ii) for every $(t,x) \in (]S,T] \times \text{int } A) \cap \text{dom}(U)$,

$$\sup_{v \in F(t^-,x)} \left[D_\uparrow U((t,x),(-1,-v)) - L(t^-,x,v)\right] \leq 0;$$

(iii) for every $x \in A$, $U(T,x) = g(x)$.

(c) The function U *is lsc, satisfies* $U(t,x) = +\infty$ *whenever* $x \notin A$ *and:*

(i) for every $(t,x) \in ([S,T[\times A) \cap \text{dom}(U)$:

$$\xi^0 + \inf_{v \in F(t^+,x)} \left[\xi^1 \cdot v + \lambda L(t^+,x,v)\right] \leq 0, \quad \forall(\xi^0,\xi^1,-\lambda) \in N^P_{\text{epi}\,U}((t,x),U(t,x));$$

(ii) for every $(t,x) \in (]S,T] \times \text{int } A) \cap \text{dom}(U)$:

$$\xi^0 + \inf_{v \in F(t^-,x)} \left[\xi^1 \cdot v + \lambda L(t^-,x,v)\right] \geq 0, \quad \forall(\xi^0,\xi^1,-\lambda) \in N^P_{\text{epi}\,U}((t,x),U(t,x));$$

(iii) $\liminf_{\{(t',x') \to (S,x) \,|\, t' > S\}} U(t',x') = U(S,x)$ *and* $U(T,x) = g(x)$, *for all* $x \in A$.

Remarks. – If we assume in addition that $L(\cdot,x,v)$ is a lsc function for all $(x,v) \in R_0\mathbb{B} \times c_0\mathbb{B}$, then the assertions of Theorems 1 and 2 remain valid when we replace $L(t^+,x,v)$ by $L(t,x,v)$ in conditions (b) (i) and (c) (i).

– It is not difficult to see that, under hypotheses considered in Theorem 2, the value function is continuous on $[S,T] \times A$. However, its characterization is provided in the class of lsc functions. As a consequence, the theorem not only identifies V as the unique generalized solution to reference Hamilton-Jacobi equation, but gives the important information that there are no 'hidden' generalized solutions in the larger class of lsc functions.

The following example illustrates two crucial facts. First, condition (H7) cannot be replaced by (H8) in Theorem 1. Second, the continuity of g cannot be dropped in Theorem 2.

Example 1. Take $n = 1$, $[S,T] = [0,1]$, $h(x) := -x$, $F(t) := [0,1]$, $L = 0$, and $g(x) := -x - 2$, if $x \leq 0$ and $g(x) = -x$ if $x > 0$. Observe that all the assumptions in Theorem 1 are satisfied except (H7), and that (H8) is valid. Then for all $(t,x) \in [0,1] \times \mathbb{R}$, we have:

$$V(t,x) = \begin{cases} t - x - 1, & \text{if } x > 0, \\ -2, & \text{if } x = 0, \\ +\infty, & \text{if } x < 0, \end{cases}$$

and we obtain $\liminf_{\{(t',x') \to (1,0) \,|\, x' > 0\}} V(t',x') = 0 \neq V(1,0) = -2$. Therefore, the value function does not satisfy condition (iii) of (b) and (c). On the other hand, all the hypotheses of Theorem 2 are satisfied, except the continuity of g. As a consequence, (b) and (c) do not characterize the value function as shown by the following function W which satisfies (b) (i)–(iii) of Theorem 2:

$$W(t,x) := \begin{cases} t - x - 1, & \text{if } x > 0, \\ -3/2, & \text{if } x = 0 \text{ and } t \neq 1, \\ -2, & \text{if } (t,x) = (1,0), \\ +\infty, & \text{if } x < 0. \end{cases}$$

4   Proofs of Theorems 1 and 2

The Role of (H7) and (H8). Using [4, Theorem 2.1], (H7) has the following consequence: any 'backward' F-trajectory starting from A can be approximated (for the $W^{1,1}$ topology) by a feasible 'backward' F-trajectory that starts from the same initial point and then evolves in int A. Assuming (H8) gives the analogous property for 'forward' F-trajectories emanating from A.

Proofs Structure. To prove Theorems 1 and 2, a convenient approach is to establish the following sequence of implications $(a) \Rightarrow (b) \Rightarrow (c) \Rightarrow (a)$.

The first and second steps $(a) \Rightarrow (b) \Rightarrow (c)$ of the proof of Theorem 1 are based on standard arguments (see for instance [3,9], and we refer the reader to [2] for the facts that V satisfies (b) (i) and (ii)). Condition (1) can be proved using estimations of backward F-trajectories, the principle of optimality and (H5) (ii). The difficult part in the step $(c) \Rightarrow (a)$ is establishing that $U \leq V$ whenever

U satisfies (c) (ii) and (iii). This part of the proof is somewhat involved: a crucial role is played by hypothesis (H7) which combined with condition (1) allows to construct suitable approximating 'backward' F-trajectories; subsequently, to derive the desired inequality, one can apply Carathéodory's parametrization theorems [1, Theorems 9.6.2 and 9.7.2] to the multivalued function F and a local Weak Invariance Theorem to an appropriate constrained differential inclusion (cf. [2,3]). The proof of Theorem 2 follows almost entirely along the lines of the proof of Theorem 1, and is simpler. Here we explain more in detail why $U \leq V$ whenever U satisfies (c) (ii) and (iii) to give the reader some insight of the crucial part of the proof in which a $W^{1,1}$ distance estimate result intervenes.

A step of the proof of Theorem 2: $U \leq V$. Let $(\bar{t}, \bar{x}) \in ([S,T] \times A) \cap \mathrm{dom}(U)$, and $x(\cdot) \in W^{1,1}([\bar{t}, T], \mathbb{R}^n)$ a feasible F-trajectory s.t. $x(\bar{t}) = \bar{x}$. We can assume that $g(x(T)) < +\infty$. Using hypothesis (H8) and the $W^{1,1}$ distance estimate theorem in [4], there exists $(x_j)_{j \geq 1}$ in $W^{1,1}([\bar{t}, T], \mathbb{R}^n)$ such that for every $j \geq 1$, $x_j(\bar{t}) = \bar{x}$, $x_j(s) \in \mathrm{int}\, A$ for all $s \in]\bar{t}, T]$, and:

$$\|x - x_j\|_{W^{1,1}([\bar{t},T],\mathbb{R}^n)} \leq \frac{1}{j}. \tag{2}$$

Take a strictly decreasing sequence $(t_j)_{j \geq 1}$ in $]\bar{t}, T[$ that converges to $\bar{t}$. For every $j \geq 1$, there exists $\delta_j \in]0, +\infty[$ s.t. for every $t \in [t_j, T]$: $x_j(t) + \delta_j \mathbb{B} \subset \mathrm{int}\, A$.

Let $f : [S,T] \times \mathbb{R}^n \times \mathbb{B} \to \mathbb{R}^n$ be a measurable/Lipschitz Carathéodory parameterization of F (cf. [1, Theorem 9.7.2]). Applying Filippov's selection theorem for a.e. $t \in [t_j, T]$, $\dot{x}_j(t) = f(t, x_j(t), u_j(t))$, for some mesurable control $u_j : [t_j, T] \to \mathbb{B}$.

Fix any $j \geq 1$ and $i \in \mathbb{N}$ such that $i \geq 2\delta_j^{-1}$. Lusin's theorem allows us to find a pair of functions $(x_j^i, u_j^i) \in W^{1,1}([t_j, T], \mathbb{R}^n) \times \mathcal{C}([t_j, T], \mathbb{B})$ such that:

$$\begin{cases} \dot{x}_j^i(t) = f(t, x_j^i(t), u_j^i(t)), \text{ for almost every } t \in [t_j, T]; \\ \|x_j - x_j^i\|_{\mathrm{L}^\infty([t_j,T],\mathbb{R}^n)} \leq \frac{1}{i} \text{ and } x_j^i(t_j) = x_j(t_j); \\ \mathrm{meas}\left(\{t \in [t_j, T] \,|\, u_j(t) - u_j^i(t) \neq 0\}\right) \leq \frac{1}{i}. \end{cases}$$

We notice that $x_j^i(\cdot)$ is strictly feasible on $[t_j, T]$ for every integer $i \geq 2\delta_j^{-1}$. We now define the arc $(\tilde{\sigma}, \tilde{z}, \tilde{\ell})$ on $[t_j, T]$ by $\tilde{\sigma}(t) := t$, $\tilde{z}(t) := x_j^i(T - t)$ and $\tilde{\ell}(t) := U(T, x_j^i(T)) + \int_0^t L(T - s, x_j^i(T - s), \dot{x}_j^i(T - s)) \mathrm{d}s$, for every $t \in [t_j, T]$. We also define $\tilde{U}(s, y) := U(T - s, y)$, for every $s \in [0, T - S]$ and $y \in \mathbb{R}^n$.

For every $(t, x) \in [t_j, T] \times \mathbb{R}^n$, we write $v^+(t, x) := f(t^+, x, u_j^i(t))$, $v^-(t, x) := f(t^-, x, u_j^i(t))$ (For a proof of the existence of the limits $f(t^+, x, u_j^i(t))$ and $f(t^-, x, u_j^i(t))$) we refer the reader to [3]; a similar analysis can be employed to show that the limits $L(t^-, x, v^-(t, x))$ and $L(t^+, x, v^+(t, x))$ used below also exist.). We consider the multivalued functions $F_{j,i} : [t_j, T] \times \mathbb{R}^n \rightsquigarrow \mathbb{R}^n$, $\Lambda_{j,i} : [t_j, T] \times \mathbb{R}^n \rightsquigarrow \mathbb{R}$ and $\Gamma_{j,i} : [0, T - t_j] \times \mathbb{R}^n \times \mathbb{R} \rightsquigarrow \mathbb{R} \times \mathbb{R}^n \times \mathbb{R}$ defined by:

$$F_{j,i}(t, x) := \mathrm{co}\,\{v^-(t, x), v^+(t, x)\},$$

$$\Lambda_{j,i}(t,x) := \mathrm{co}\left\{L(t^-, x, v^-(t,x)), L(t^+, x, v^+(t,x))\right\},$$

$$\Gamma_{j,i}(t,x,\ell) := \{1\} \times -F_{j,i}(T-t,x) \times \Lambda_{j,i}(T-t,x), \text{ for all } t \in [0, T-t_j].$$

Owing to our hypotheses and (c) (ii), we can apply the local Weak Invariance Theorem (see [3]) and find out that $(\tilde{\sigma}, \tilde{z}, \tilde{\ell})$ is a solution to the constrained differential inclusion

$$\begin{cases} (\dot{\tau}(t), \dot{y}(t), \dot{\ell}(t)) \in \Gamma_{j,i}(\tau(t), y(t), \ell(t)), \text{ for a.e. } t \in [0, T-t_j], \\ \tau(0) = 0, y(0) = x_j^i(T), \ell(0) = \tilde{U}(0, x_j(T)) = g(x_j(T)), \\ (\sigma(t), y(t), \ell(t)) \in \mathrm{epi}\,\tilde{U}, \text{ for all } t \in [0, T-t_j]. \end{cases}$$

This shows that for any $j \geq 1$ and any integer $i \geq \frac{2}{\delta_j}$, we have:

$$U(t_j, x_j^i(t_j)) \leq g(x_j(T)) + \int_{t_j}^T L(s, x_j^i(s), \dot{x}_j^i(s))\mathrm{d}s.$$

Since U is lower semicontinuous and $x_j^i(t_j) \xrightarrow[i \to +\infty]{} x_j(t_j)$, we have:

$$U(t_j, x_j(t_j)) \leq g(x_j(T)) + \liminf_{i \to +\infty} \int_{t_j}^T L(s, x_j^i(s), \dot{x}_j^i(s))\mathrm{d}s, \text{ for any } j \geq 1.$$

It can be established that $\dot{x}_j^i(\cdot)$ converges to $\dot{x}_j(\cdot)$ in $\mathbb{L}^1([t_j, T], \mathbb{R}^n)$. Therefore the Lebesgue's dominated convergence theorem gives (possibly extracting a subsequence we do not relabel):

$$U(t_j, x_j(t_j)) \leq g(x_j(T)) + \int_{t_j}^T L(s, x_j(s), \dot{x}_j(s))\mathrm{d}s, \text{ for any } j \geq 1.$$

Since $x_j(T) \xrightarrow[j \to +\infty]{A} x(T)$ and $g(\cdot)$ is continuous on A, we obtain:

$$U(\bar{t}, \bar{x}) \leq \liminf_{j \to +\infty} U(t_j, x_j(t_j)) \leq g(x(T)) + \liminf_{j \to +\infty} \int_{t_j}^T L(s, x_j(s), \dot{x}_j(s))\mathrm{d}s,$$

From (2), $x_j(\cdot)$ converges to $x(\cdot)$ in $W^{1,1}$, so the Lebesgue's dominated convergence theorem yields (possibly for a subsequence):

$$U(\bar{t}, \bar{x}) \leq g(x(T)) + \int_{\bar{t}}^T L(s, x(s), \dot{x}(s))\mathrm{d}s,$$

which shows that $U(\bar{t}, \bar{x}) \leq V(\bar{t}, \bar{x})$.

References

1. Aubin, J.P., Frankowska, H.: Set-Valued Analysis. Springer, Heidelberg (2009). https://doi.org/10.1007/978-0-8176-4848-0

2. Bernis, J., Bettiol, P.: Solutions to the Hamilton-Jacobi equation for Bolza problems with discontinuous time dependent data. ESAIM Control Optim. Calc. Var. https://doi.org/10.1051/cocv/2019041

3. Bettiol, P., Vinter, R.B.: The Hamilton Jacobi equation for optimal control problems with discontinuous time dependence. SIAM J. Control Optim. **55**(2), 1199–1225 (2017)

4. Bettiol, P., Bressan, A., Vinter, R.B.: On trajectories satisfying a state constraint: $W^{1,1}$ estimates and counterexamples. SIAM J. Control Optim. **48**(7), 4664–4679 (2010)

5. Clarke, F.H., Ledyaev, Y.S., Stern, R.J., Wolenski, P.R.: Nonsmooth Analysis and Control Theory, Graduate Texts in Mathematics, vol. 178. Springer, Heidelberg (1998). https://doi.org/10.1007/b97650

6. Frankowska, H., Mazzola, M.: Discontinuous solutions of Hamilton-Jacobi-Bellman equation under state constraints. Calc. Var. Partial Differ. Equ. **46**, 725–747 (2013)

7. Frankowska, H., Vinter, R.B.: Existence of neighbouring feasible trajectories: applications to dynamic programming for state constrained optimal control problems. J. Optim. Theory Appl. **104**(1), 21–40 (2000)

8. Frankowska, H.: Lower semicontinuous solutions of Hamilton-Jacobi-Bellman equations. SIAM J. Control Optim. **31**, 257–272 (1993)

9. Vinter, R.B.: Optimal Control. Springer, Heidelberg (2010). https://doi.org/10.1007/978-0-8176-8086-2

Optimal Control Problem
of a Metronomic Chemotherapy

Dieter Grass[1] and Valeriya Lykina[2]([✉])

[1] Research Unit Operations Research and Control of Systems (ORCOS),
Vienna University of Technology,
Wiedner Hauptstrasse 8, E-105/4, 1040 Vienna, Austria
dieter.grass@tuwien.ac.at
[2] Institute for Mathematics, Department of Optimization,
Brandenburg University of Technology at Cottbus-Senftenberg,
Platz der Deutschen Einheit 1, 03046 Cottbus, Germany
Valeriya.Lykina@b-tu.de

Abstract. In this paper we consider a metronomic chemotherapy model which is optimally controlled over the expected future lifetime of the particular patient. Under certain assumptions concerning the distribution of the future lifetime of the patient, it can be easily transformed to a purely deterministic optimal control problem with infinite horizon. To solve the latter the open source software package OCMat was used. Solutions to optimal control problems with L_2- and regularized L_1-objective functionals have been compared.

Keywords: Infinite horizon optimal control · Metronomic chemotherapy · Numerical analysis

1 Introduction

In recent years the question of modeling a low-dosed cancer treatment by means of chemotherapy agents has been paid a broad attention. It has become evident through numerous experiments that "more is not necessarily better" for certain type of cancers, cf. [5]. The papers [1] and [6] gave birth to a new research field in medicine called metronomic chemotherapy. The two mostly spread definitions of what metronomic chemotherapy means say: "The frequent administration of chemotherapy drugs at relatively low, non-toxic doses, without prolonged drug-free breaks" and the recent one "the minimum biologically effective dose of a chemotherapeutic agent, which, when given at a regular dosing regiment with no prolonged drug-free breaks, leads to antitumor activity", cf. [13]. The main assumption while trying to model a metronomic chemotherapy with only one drug is that besides of a cytotoxic effect on tumor cells, small doses of a chemotherapeutic agent have both antiangiogenic and immune stimulatory effect, while toxicity level on healthy tissues stays low or even neglectful. This fact is illustrated by a generic dynamic model of cancer treatment by means of

© Springer Nature Switzerland AG 2020
I. Lirkov and S. Margenov (Eds.): LSSC 2019, LNCS 11958, pp. 40–47, 2020.
https://doi.org/10.1007/978-3-030-41032-2_4

chemotherapy, cf. the book [10], where the model has been analyzed with respect to equilibria, their stability and bifurcations as well as an optimal control problem with a free finite terminal time T. In dependence on involved parameters, the above dynamic system may have scenarios varying from a unique, asymptotically stable benign (tumour-free) equilibrium point (situation of immune surveillance) to a situation with both benign and malignant equilibria (co-existent equilibria) to the situation when only unique, asymptotically stable malignant (death) equilibrium point exists, cf. [10], p. 358.

Since it is very important not only how much of drug to give, but also how to give, the finding of the drug administration regiment (protocol) becomes one of the most important tasks on the way to a successful therapy.

Our task in the present paper is to consider the problem of metronomic chemotherapy as an optimal control problem, where the tumor size and the side effects of the therapy are being minimized over the treatment horizon, which gives rise to an integral objective in Lagrange form. Through finding the optimal solution to this optimal control problem we obtain the best possible drug administration protocol automatically, including the doses and rest periods if there should be some. In case of continuous optimal solutions which are less practicable, the latter may be replaced by piecewise constant suboptimal controls which are still good enough to satisfy the treatment goal.

One of our key ideas is to assume that we have enough time to treat the patient and the goal is not to fight the cancer as fast as possible. Moreover, we consider the cancer as a chronic disease, which will be treated over the whole remaining future lifetime of the particular patient. The aim is to figure out whether such "chronic" formulation of control problem leads to considerably lower doses, and, consequently, less toxic treatments, or structurally different solutions in comparison to the short fixed finite treatment horizons. We would like to mention that through minimizing the expectation value of the cost functional the optimal control problem becomes stochastic. Nevertheless, in some cases it can easily be transformed to a purely deterministic control problem with infinite horizon. The solutions of the latter provide long-term therapies for cancer treatment.

To handle the obtained infinite horizon optimal control problem, we use on the one hand its rigorous formulation in weighted functional spaces. The advantage of such a functional analytical approach was addressed in details in [9]. According to this approach, a weighted Sobolev and a weighted Lebesgue spaces are chosen as the state space and the control space respectively. Although we don't give a detailed theoretical analysis here, we still retain a rigorous analytic formulation of the optimal control problem. On the other hand, to obtain numerical solutions to the considered problem, the open source software package OCMat was applied, which is available at http://orcos.tuwien.ac.at/research/ocmat_software/and has been described in [4].

Our paper is structured as follows. Section 2 contains the necessary definitions from functional analysis. Section 3 presents the metronomic chemotherapy model as an optimal control problem. Sections 4 and 5 present the numerical analysis of optimal control problems arising with L_2- and regularized L_1-objective functionals respectively. Discussion, comparison of obtained results and an outlook of future work in Sect. 6 complete our paper.

2 Main Definitions

Let us write $[0, \infty) = \mathbb{R}^+$. We denote by $\mathcal{M}(\mathbb{R}^+)$, $L_p(\mathbb{R}^+)$ and $C^0(\mathbb{R}^+)$ the spaces of all functions $x : \mathbb{R}^+ \to \mathbb{R}$ which are Lebesgue measurable, in the pth power Lebesgue integrable or continuous, respectively, see [2], p. 146 and p. 285; [3], p. 228. The Sobolev space $W_p^1(\mathbb{R}^+)$ is then defined as the space of all functions $x : \mathbb{R}^+ \to \mathbb{R}$ which belong to $L_p(\mathbb{R}^+)$ and admit distributional derivative $\dot{x}$ ([12], p. 49) belonging to $L_p(\mathbb{R}^+)$ as well.

Definition 1. (a) *A continuous function $\nu : \mathbb{R}^+ \to \mathbb{R}$ with positive values is called a weight function.*

(b) *A weight function ν will be called a density function iff it is Lebesgue integrable over $\mathbb{R}^+$, i.e. $\int\limits_0^\infty \nu(t)dt < \infty$, (cf. [7], p. 18).*

(c) *By means of a weight function $\nu \in C^0(\mathbb{R}^+)$ we define for any $1 \le p < \infty$ the weighted Lebesgue space*

$$L_p(\mathbb{R}^+, \nu) = \left\{ x \in \mathcal{M}(\mathbb{R}^+) \mid \|x\|_{L_p(\mathbb{R}^+, \nu)} = \left(\int\limits_0^\infty |x(t)|^p \, \nu(t) dt \right)^{1/p} < \infty \right\}.$$

(d) *For $x \in L_p(\mathbb{R}^+, \nu)$ let the distributional derivative $\dot{x}$ be defined according to [12], p. 46. We introduce the weighted Sobolev space of all $L_p(\mathbb{R}^+, \nu)$ functions having its distributional derivative in $L_p(\mathbb{R}^+, \nu)$:*

$$W_p^1(\mathbb{R}^+, \nu) = \left\{ x \in \mathcal{M}(\mathbb{R}^+) \mid x \in L_p(\mathbb{R}^+, \nu), \ \dot{x} \in L_p(\mathbb{R}^+, \nu) \right\}$$

(see [7], p. 11).

Equipped with the norm $\|x\|_{W_p^1(\mathbb{R}^+, \nu)} = \|x\|_{L_p(\mathbb{R}^+, \nu)} + \|\dot{x}\|_{L_p(\mathbb{R}^+, \nu)}$, the space $W_p^1(\mathbb{R}^+, \nu)$ becomes a Banach space (this can be confirmed analogously to [7], p. 19).

3 Metronomic Chemotherapy Model as an Optimal Control Problem

Let a be the current age of the particular patient to be treated against cancer and T_a be the random variable denoting the future lifetime of the patient. Then our purpose is to minimize either L_2- or L_1-objective functional

$$J_\infty^i(x, u) = \mathbb{E}_{T_a} \left\{ \int\limits_0^{T_a} \frac{1}{2} \left(p(t) + q(t) - r(t) + u^i(t) \right) dt \right\} \to \min! \quad i = 1, 2$$

with respect to all $(x, u) := (p, q, r, u) \in W_2^{1,3}(\mathbb{R}^+, e^{-\rho t}) \times L_2^1(\mathbb{R}^+, e^{-\rho t})$ satisfying the differential equations:

$$\dot{p}(t) = -\xi p(t) \ln\left(p(t)/q(t)\right) - \theta p(t) r(t) - \phi_1 p(t) u(t), \tag{1}$$

$$\dot{q}(t) = bp(t) - (\mu + dp^{2/3}(t))q(t) - \phi_2 q(t) u(t), \tag{2}$$

$$\dot{r}(t) = \alpha(p(t) - \beta p^2(t))r(t) + \gamma - \delta r(t) + \phi_3 r(t) u(t), \tag{3}$$

as well as the pointwise and isoperimetrical control constraints

$$\forall\, t \in \mathbb{R}^+ : u(t) \in [0, u_{max}] \quad \text{and} \quad \int_0^\infty u(t) e^{-\rho t} dt < \infty, \tag{4}$$

where $p(t)$, $q(t)$ and $r(t)$ denote the tumor volume, the carrying capacity of vasculature and the immunocompetent cell density respectively. The control $u(t)$ stands for the dose of a chemotherapeutic agent and ξ, μ, d, β, γ, δ, ϕ_i ($i = 1, 2, 3$) are parameters of the model.

It is well known, cf. [11], that under the assumption of the mortality force μ_a given by $\mu_a = k a^n$, $k > 0, n \geq 0$ the random variable T_a is distributed with the density $k(a + T_a)^n e^{-\frac{k}{n+1}((a+T_a)^{n+1} - a^{n+1})}$. Therefore, calculating the expectation value in the objective (1) and changing the order of integration we obtain

$$\mathbb{E}_{T_a}\left\{\int_0^{T_a} \frac{1}{2}\left(p(t) + q(t) - r(t) + u^i(t)\right) dt\right\}$$

$$= \int_0^\infty \left(\int_0^{T_a} \frac{1}{2}\left(p(t) + q(t) - r(t) + u^i(t)\right) dt\right) k(a + T_a)^n e^{-\frac{k}{n+1}((a+T_a)^{n+1} - a^{n+1})} dT_a$$

$$= \int_0^\infty \int_t^\infty \frac{1}{2}\left(p(t) + q(t) - r(t) + u^i(t)\right) k(a + T_a)^n e^{-\frac{k}{n+1}((a+T_a)^{n+1} - a^{n+1})} dT_a dt.$$

Calculating the inner integral in the above expression we arrive at

$$J_\infty^i(x, u) = e^{\frac{k}{n+1} a^{n+1}} \int_0^\infty \frac{1}{2}\left(p(t) + q(t) - r(t) + u^i(t)\right) e^{-\frac{k}{n+1}(a+t)^{n+1}} dt \tag{5}$$

Thus, we have arrived at a purely deterministic optimal control problem with infinite horizon, namely (1)–(4), (5). In the subsequent sections we consider this optimal control problem and denote it by (P_∞). Our goal is to choose such a parameter set that the dynamic system possesses at least one stable benign equilibrium. Therefore, we set the parameters as it is stated in Table 1, cf. also [10], p. 371. In this paper we only consider the case of constant mortality force, i.e. $n = 0$.

Table 1. Values of parameters used in numerical computations

Parameter	Interpretation	Numerical value	Dimension
p	Tumor volume		10^6 cells
q	Carrying capacity		10^6 cells
r	Immuno-competent cells density		Non-dimensional
u	Concentration of the cytotoxic agent		mg of dose/10^6 cells
α	Tumor stimulated proliferation rate of immune system	0.0529	Non-dimensional
β	Inverse threshold of tumor suppression	0.00291	Non-dimensional
γ	Constant influx into immune system	0.05	10^6 Cells/day
δ	Death rate	0.3743	Non-dimensional
θ	Tumor immune system interaction rate	1	
ξ	Tumor growth parameter	0.0347	
b	Tumor induced stimulation parameter of vasculature	5	Cells/day
d	Tumor induced inhibition parameter of vasculature	0.0667	Non-dimensional
μ	Loss of vascular support through natural causes	0	Cells/day
ϕ_1	Cytotoxic killing parameter	0.005	10^6 cells/mg of dose
ϕ_2	Antiangiogenic elimination parameter	0.06	10^6 cells/mg of dose
ϕ_3	Immune stimulatory parameter	0.02	10^6 cells/mg of dose
ρ	Weighting parameter of the space	0.03	Non-dimensional

4   Numerical Analysis of a Model with an L_2-objective

The assumption of a constant mortality force $\mu_a \equiv k > 0$ leads to the exponentially distributed random variable T_a, which has the density function ke^{-kt}. Consequently, for $n = 0$, $i = 2$ the optimal control problem to solve is that of minimizing the functional

$$J^2_\infty(x, u) = \int_0^\infty \frac{1}{2}\left(p(t) + q(t) - r(t) + u^2(t)\right) e^{-kt} dt. \tag{6}$$

over all pairs $(x, u) := (p, q, r, u) \in W_2^{1,3}(\mathbb{R}^+, e^{-\rho t}) \times L_2^1(\mathbb{R}^+, e^{-\rho t})$ under the constraints (1)–(4). The numerical solutions for different values of the maximal allowed pointwise doses can be seen in Fig. 1. Red parts of the graphs correspond to the treatment with the maximal allowed dose, while the blue parts correspond to a lower dose of the cytotoxic drug. It can be easily observed that the optimal control depends on the value of u_{max} and for the values of u_{max} large enough the control constraint does not become active. In all considered cases the tumor volume p tends to zero, while the immune-competent cells variable r tends toward

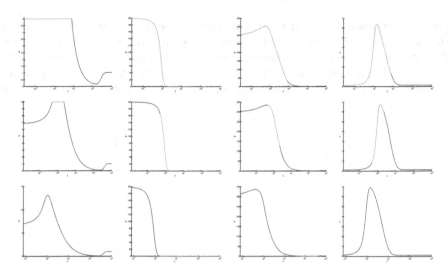

Fig. 1. Optimal solution for $u_{max} = 5$ (first row), $u_{max} = 10$ (second row) and $u_{max} = 15$ (third row). From the left to the right: control, tumor volume, carrying capacity, immune cells. (Color figure online)

some positive level after having some boost. Other remarkable fact is that the lower pointswise control constraint does not become active at all. Moreover, the height of the dose tends to some low constant level.

5 Numerical Analysis of a Model with a Regularized L_1-objective

Setting $n = 0$, $i = 1$ in (5) and introducing a regularization term $\epsilon u^2(t)$ in the integrand, we arrive at a nearly linear in control optimal control problem with the functional

$$J_\infty^1(x, u) = \int_0^\infty \frac{1}{2} \left(p(t) + q(t) - r(t) + u(t) + \epsilon u^2(t) \right) e^{-kt} dt \qquad (7)$$

which has to be minimized under the same restrictions as in the previous section. The purpose of considering the regularized objective functional lies on the one hand in obtaining a nonlinear in control problem which can be analyzed and solved numerically by means of the OCMat package designed for solving nonlinear in control optimal control problems. On the other hand, optimal solution of the regularized optimal control problem has a more convenient structure as for applications in practice. The corresponding optimal solutions for $\epsilon = 10^{-4}$ computed by means of OCMat package can be found in Fig. 2. In addition to the previously explained red and blue parts of the solution graphs, here the green parts of the graphs correspond to the rest periods (no treatment). As one could expect in a problem linear in control variable, we obtain also for the problem with the regularized L_1-functional a bang-bang-singular structure of the optimal control u with a maximal allowed dose at the beginning, a rest period with $u(t) = 0$ and some singular control at the end tending to some low positive constant level. The period with the maximal dose treatment becomes shorter if u_{max} value grows.

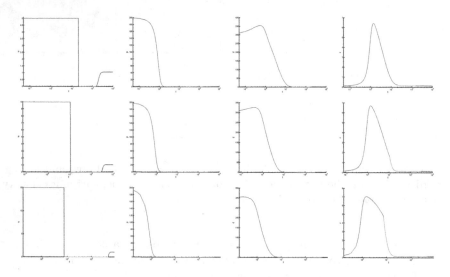

Fig. 2. Optimal solution for $u_{max} = 5$ (1.row), $u_{max} = 10$ (2.row) and $u_{max} = 15$ (3.row). From the left to the right: control, tumor volume, carrying capacity, immune cells. (Color figure online)

6   Conclusions

We have considered an optimal control problem of metronomic chemotherapy in the so called "chronic" setting, i.e. where the patient is treated over the whole remained lifetime. This lead us under the assumption of a constant mortality force to an exponentially distributed random variable T_a and correspondingly to an objective functional with an exponential density function e^{-kt} inside. The obtained numerical solutions for the problem with an L_2-functional show that after treatment with a relatively high dose replaced by nearly rest period, the optimal control tends to some low positive constant level, whereas the tumor volume tends to zero. Considering the regularized L_1-functional with a nearly zero regularization parameter ϵ shows that instead of a continuous control one could apply a more practical bang-bang-singular control consisting of the most tolerated dose u_{max} followed by a rest period and then apply a control which is close to some positive low level for the whole remaining lifetime. The analysis of the corresponding model under more realistic assumption of the growing mortality force represents the issue of the subsequent paper.

References

1. Browder, T., et al.: Antiangiogenic scheduling of chemotherapy improves efficacy against experimental drug-resistant cancer. Cancer Res. **60**, 1878–1886 (2000)
2. Dunford, N., Schwartz, J.T.: Linear Operators. Part I: General Theory. Wiley-Interscience, New York (1988)
3. Elstrodt, J.: Maß und Integrationstheorie. Springer, Berlin (1996). https://doi.org/10.1007/978-3-662-08528-8
4. Graß, D.: Numerical computation of the optimal vector field in a fishery model. J. Econ. Dyn. Control **36**(10), 1626–1658 (2012)
5. Hanahan, D., Bergers, G., Bergsland, E.: Less is more, regularly: metronomic dosing of cytotoxic drugs can target tumor angiogenesis in mice. J. Clin. Invest. **105**(8), 145–147 (2000)
6. Klement, G., et al.: Continuous low-dose therapy with vinblastine and VEGF receptor-2 antibody induces sustained tumor regression without over toxicity. J. Clin. Invest. **105**(8), R15–R24 (2000)
7. Kufner, A.: Weighted Sobolev Spaces. Wiley, Chichester (1985)
8. Ledzewicz, U., Schättler, H.: A review of optimal chemotherapy protocols: from MTD towards metronomic therapy. J. Math. Model. Nat. Phenom. **9**(4), 131–152 (2014)
9. Lykina, V., Pickenhain, S.: Weighted functional spaces approach in infinite horizon optimal control problems: a systematic analysis of hidden advantages and opportunities. J. Math. Anal. Appl. **454**(1), 195–218 (2017)
10. Schättler, H., Ledzewicz, U.: Optimal Control for Mathematical Models of Cancer Therapies. An Application of Geometric Methods, Interdisciplinary Applied Mathematics, vol. 42. Springer, New York (2015). https://doi.org/10.1007/978-1-4939-2972-6
11. Valdez, E.A.: Survival models (2014). https://studylib.net/doc/8854157/survival-models
12. Yosida, K.: Functional Analysis. Springer, New York (1974)
13. Pasquier, E., Ledzewicz, U.: More is not necessarily better: metronomic chemotherapy. Newslett. Soc. Math. Biol. **26**(2) (2013)

Asymptotic Behaviour of Controllability Gramians and Convexity of Small-Time Reachable Sets

Mikhail Gusev[✉] [ID]

N.N. Krasovskii Institute of Mathematics and Mechanics,
S.Kovalevskaya str., 16, 620108 Ekaterinburg, Russia
gmi@imm.uran.ru

Abstract. We study the convexity of reachable sets for a nonlinear control-affine system on a small time interval under integral constraints on control variables. The convexity of a reachable set for a nonlinear control system under integral constraints was proved by B. Polyak under assumption that linearization of the system is controllable and L_2 norms of controls are bounded from above by a sufficiently small number. Using this result we propose sufficient conditions for the convexity of reachable sets of a control-affine system on a small time interval. These conditions are based on the estimates for the asymptotics of the minimal eigenvalue of controllability Gramian of the system linearization, which depends on a small parameter (a length of the interval). A procedure for calculating estimates using the expansion of the Gramian into a series with respect to the small parameter degrees is described and some illustrative examples are presented.

Keywords: Control system · Small-time reachable set · Integral constraints · Convexity

1 Introduction

The reachable sets for nonlinear systems may have a complex structure, in particular be non convex [1,4,11,12,15]. In the paper [13] however it has been proven that the reachable sets are convex assuming that the system linearization is controllable and control inputs are restricted from above in $\mathbb{L}_2$ norm by a sufficiently small number. The proof uses the convexity of a nonlinear image of a small ball in a Hilbert space [14]. In the present paper this result is adapted to provide sufficient conditions for the convexity of reachable sets for a nonlinear control-affine system on a small time interval. These sufficient conditions require knowledge of lower bounds of the minimal eigenvalue of the controllability Gramian of the system linearization. In this regard, we are studying the asymptotics of controllability Gramians for a linear time-invariant system containing a small parameter. The resulting asymptotics allows us to prove the convexity of small-time reachable sets of two-dimensional nonlinear time-invariant systems with a single

© Springer Nature Switzerland AG 2020
I. Lirkov and S. Margenov (Eds.): LSSC 2019, LNCS 11958, pp. 48–55, 2020.
https://doi.org/10.1007/978-3-030-41032-2_5

control input. Reachability problems for control systems under integrally constrained controls and algorithms for constructing reachable sets were considered in the papers [2,6–9]. Asymptotics of small-time reachable sets of linear systems with integral control constraints was studied in [5].

2   Convexity of Small Time Reachable Sets

Let X, Y be real Hilbert spaces and $B(x, \mu_0) \subset X$ be a closed ball of radius μ_0 centered at x. Consider a nonlinear map $f : B(a, \mu_0) \to Y$ with Lipschitz continuous derivative on $B(a, \mu_0)$: $\|f'(x) - f'(y)\| \leq L\|x - y\|$, $x, y \in B(a, \mu_0)$. Assume that the linear operator $f'(a)$ maps X onto Y: $f'(a)X = Y$. This implies that for some $\gamma > 0$ $\|f'(a)^*y\| \geq \gamma\|y\|$, $\forall y \in Y$ ($f'(a)^*$ is an adjoint linear operator). The last inequality is equivalent to $(f'(a)f'(a)^*y, y) \geq \gamma^2\|y\|^2$, hence we can take $\gamma^2 = \nu$, where ν is the minimal eigenvalue of $f'(a)f'(a)^*$. In [14] the convexity of the image of $B(a, \mu)$ for sufficiently small μ was proved.

Theorem 1. *Let the inequality $\mu \leq \min\{\mu_0, \frac{\gamma}{2L}\}$ holds. Then the set $G = \{f(x) : x \in B(a, \mu)\}$ is convex.*

Let $\mu_0 > 0$ be given. Further we consider a control system

$$\dot{x}(t) = f_1(t, x(t)) + f_2(t, x(t))u(t), \ x(t_0) = x^0, \tag{1}$$

where $t_0 \leq t \leq t_1$, $x \in \mathbb{R}^n$, $u \in \mathbb{R}^r$, the functions $f_1 : [t_0, t_1] \times \mathbb{R}^n \to \mathbb{R}^n$, $f_2 : [t_0, t_1] \times \mathbb{R}^n \to \mathbb{R}^{n \times r}$ are assumed to be continuous and continuously differentiable in x. Consider a space of square integrable vector-functions with an inner product defined as

$$(u(\cdot), v(\cdot)) = \int_{t_0}^{t_1} u^\top(t)v(t)dt,$$

for this space we use the notation $\mathbb{L}_2$. The constraints on $u(\cdot)$ are given as a ball $B(0, \mu) = \{u(\cdot) \in \mathbb{L}_2 : (u(\cdot), u(\cdot)) \leq \mu^2\}$ of radius $\mu > 0$.

Suppose that for any $u(\cdot) \in B(0, \mu_0)$ there exists a unique absolutely continuous solution $x(t)$ of system (1) which is defined on the interval $[t_0, t_1]$ and all trajectories of system (1) corresponding to controls from $B(0, \mu_0)$ are lying in some compact set $D \subset \mathbb{R}^n$. In what follows we assume that $0 < \mu \leq \mu_0$.

Denote $G(t_1) = \{x \in \mathbb{R}^n : \exists u(\cdot) \in \mathbb{L}_2 : (u(\cdot), u(\cdot)) \leq \mu^2, \ x = x(t_1, u(\cdot))\}$, $G(t_1)$ is the reachable set of system (1) at a given time instant t_1.

Assumption 1. *The functions $f_1(t, x)$, $f_2(t, x)$ have continuous derivatives in x which satisfy the Lipschitz conditions: for all $t \in [t_0, t_1]$, $x_1, x_2 \in D$*

$$\left\|\frac{\partial f_1}{\partial x}(t, x_1) - \frac{\partial f_1}{\partial x}(t, x_2)\right\| \leq L_3\|x_1 - x_2\|, \ \left\|\frac{\partial f_2}{\partial x}(t, x_1) - \frac{\partial f_2}{\partial x}(t, x_2)\right\| \leq L_4\|x_1 - x_2\|,$$

where $L_i \geq 0$ for $i = 3, 4$.

As L_1, L_2 denote Lipschitz constants in the variable x on $[t_0, t_1] \times D$ for f_1, f_2 respectively.

Let $A(t) = A(t, u(\cdot))$, $B(t) = B(t, u(\cdot))$ be the matrices of the linearizations of system (1) along the pair $(u(\cdot), x(\cdot))$:

$$A(t) = \frac{\partial f_1}{\partial x}(t, x(t)) + \frac{\partial}{\partial x}[f_2(t, x(t))u(t)], \ B(t) = f_2(t, x(t)).$$

For $u_i(\cdot) \in B(0, \mu)$, $i = 1, 2$ denote corresponding matrices as $A_i(t)$, $B_i(t)$. Let $X(t, s) = X(t, s, u(\cdot))$, $X_i(t, s) = X(t, s, u_i(\cdot))$, $i = 1, 2$ be the fundamental matrices of the systems $\dot{x}(t) = A(t)x(t)$, $\dot{x}(t) = A_i(t)x(t)$, $i = 1, 2$. Supposing Assumption 1 to be fulfilled and applying Theorem 3 in [3] one can get the following inequalities (see, for example, [8])

$$\|x_1(\cdot) - x_2(\cdot)\|_C \le K\|u_1(\cdot) - u_2(\cdot)\|_{\mathbb{L}_2}, \tag{2}$$

$$\int_{t_0}^{t_1} \| A_1(t) - A_2(t) \| \, dt \le C_1\|u_1(\cdot) - u_2(\cdot)\|_{\mathbb{L}_2}, \tag{3}$$

$$\| B_1(\cdot) - B_2(\cdot) \|_C \le C_2\|u_1(\cdot) - u_2(\cdot)\|_{\mathbb{L}_2}, \tag{4}$$

$$\|X_1(t, s) - X_2(t, s)\| \le C_3\|u_1(\cdot) - u_2(\cdot)\|_{\mathbb{L}_2}, \ t, s \in [t_9, t_1], \tag{5}$$

$x_i(t) = x(t, u_i(\cdot))$ are trajectories corresponding to the controls $u_i(\cdot)$, $i = 1, 2$,

$$K = k_1 \exp\left(L_1(t_1 - t_0) + L_2\mu(t_1 - t_0)^{1/2}\right),$$

$$k_1 = ((t_1 - t_0) \max_{[t_0, t_1] \times D} \|f_2(t, x)\|)^{1/2},$$

and $C_1 > 0$, $C_2 > 0$, $C_3 > 0$ are constants that depend on L_i, $i = 1, ..., 4$ and do not depend on $u_1(\cdot), u_2(\cdot)$.

Define the map $F : B(0, \mu_0) \to \mathbb{R}^n$ by the equality $F(u(\cdot)) = x(t_1)$, here $x(t)$ is a trajectory of system (1), corresponding to the control $u(\cdot)$. The map has a continuous Fréchet derivative $F' : \mathbb{L}_2 \to \mathbb{R}^n$ $F'(u(\cdot))\Delta u(\cdot) = \Delta x(t_1)$. where $\Delta x(t)$ is a solution of the linearization along $(u(t), x(t))$ of system (1) with zero initial vector and the control $\Delta u(t)$.

From (2) we get that $F'(u(\cdot)) = X(t_1, s, u(\cdot))B(s, u(\cdot))$, $s \in [t_0, t_1]$. Using inequalities (4), (5) one may prove that $F'(u(\cdot))$ is Lipschitz continuous with a constant $L > 0$.

In [13] Theorem 1 is applied to the mapping $F(u(\cdot))$ to prove the convexity of $G(t_1)$. Equality $F'(0)X = Y$ means here that the linearization of (1) is controllable and hence its controllability Gramian

$$W = W(t_1) = F'(0)F'(0)^* = \int_{t_0}^{t_1} X(t_1, s, 0)B(s, 0)B^\top(s, 0)X^\top(t_1, s, 0)ds$$

is positive definite. Here 0 is a null element of the space $\mathbb{L}_2$. The estimate

$$\mu \le \min\{\mu_0, \frac{\gamma}{2L}\}, \tag{6}$$

where $\nu = \gamma^2$ is a minimal eigenvalue of W, implies the convexity of $G(t_1) = F(B(0, \mu))$ [13].

Further we propose sufficient conditions for the reachable set $G(t_1)$ to be convex in the case when a value of μ is fixed but the time interval $[t_0, t_1]$ is sufficiently small.

In what follows we assume that system (1) is defined on the interval $[t_0, \bar{t}_1]$, all the trajectories of system (1) corresponding to $u(\cdot) \in B(0, \mu)$, $t_1 \in (t_0, \bar{t}_1]$ belong to a compact set D, and Assumption 1 is satisfied on $[t_0, \bar{t}_1]$. Consider $t_0 < t_1 \leq \bar{t}_1$ and denote $t_1 - t_0 = \varepsilon$. Applying a change of variables $t = \varepsilon\tau + t_0$ and taking $y(\tau) = x(\varepsilon\tau + t_0)$, $v(\tau) = \varepsilon u(\varepsilon\tau + t_0)$ we get

$$\dot{y}(\tau) = \tilde{f}_1(\tau, y(\tau)) + \tilde{f}_2(\tau, y)v(\tau), \ 0 \leq \tau \leq 1, y(0) = x^0, \tag{7}$$

where $\tilde{f}_1(\tau, y) = \varepsilon f_1(\varepsilon\tau + t_0, y)$, $\tilde{f}_2(\tau, y) = f_2(\varepsilon\tau + t_0, y)$, with constraints on the control $v(\cdot)$ given by the inequality

$$\int_0^1 v^\top(t)v(t)dt \leq (\mu\sqrt{\varepsilon})^2. \tag{8}$$

Note that trajectories of (7), (8) are also lying in D for $\varepsilon \leq \bar{t}_1 - t_0$, and that $y(\tau, 0) = x(\varepsilon\tau + t_0, 0)$. The Lipschitz constants for $\tilde{f}_1$, $\tilde{f}_2$, $\partial\tilde{f}_1/\partial y$, $\partial\tilde{f}_2/\partial y$ on the set D equal respectively to εL_1, L_2, εL_3, L_4. The inequality (2) being applied to system (7) gives

$$\|y_1(\cdot) - y_2(\cdot)\|_C \leq \tilde{K}\|v_1(\cdot) - v_2(\cdot)\|_{L_2}, \tag{9}$$

for some $\tilde{K}$, which does not depend on ε (here we use the same notations C, L_2 for spaces of functions defined on a segment $[0, 1]$). Similarly, from (3), (4) we get

$$\int_{t_0}^{t_1} \| \tilde{A}_1(t) - \tilde{A}_2(t) \| \ dt \leq (\tilde{C}_1\varepsilon + \tilde{C}_0)\|v_1(\cdot) - v_2(\cdot)\|_{L_2}, \tag{10}$$

$$\| \tilde{B}_1(\cdot) - \tilde{B}_2(\cdot) \|_C \leq \tilde{C}_2\|v_1(\cdot) - v_2(\cdot)\|_{L_2}, \tag{11}$$

for some $\tilde{C}_i \geq 0$. The matrices $\tilde{A}_i(t)$, $\tilde{B}_i(t)$ denote here the matrices of the linearization of system (7) along the pairs $(y_i(\cdot), v_i(\cdot))$.

Note that in the case when $f_2(t, x)$ does not depend on x, the constant $\tilde{C}_0$ equals to zero.

Denote by $\tilde{F}$ an analog of the map F for the system (7). The mapping $\tilde{F}'$ is Lipschitz continuous with a constant $L(\varepsilon) = \tilde{L}_1\varepsilon + \tilde{L}_0$ for some $\tilde{L}_i \geq 0$. As above $\tilde{L}_0 = 0$ if $f_2(t, x) = f_2(t)$. The inequality (6) takes here the form $4\mu^2\varepsilon L^2(\varepsilon) \leq \nu$, this inequality gives the sufficient conditions for the reachable set $\tilde{G}(1)$ of the system (7) under constraints (8) to be convex. Taking into account that $G(t_1) = \tilde{G}(1)$ we come to the following

Proposition 1. *Suppose $\nu(\varepsilon)$ to be a minimal eigenvalue of the controllability Gramian of the linearization of system (7) along the trajectory $y(t, 0)$ corresponding to control $v(t) \equiv 0$, $0 \leq t \leq 1$. Let there exist $C > 0, \alpha > 0, \bar{\varepsilon} > 0$ such that for all $\varepsilon \leq \bar{\varepsilon}$ $\nu(\varepsilon) \geq C\varepsilon^{1-\alpha}$, or $\nu(\varepsilon) \geq C\varepsilon^{3-\alpha}$ in the case $f_2(t, x) = f_2(t)$. Then $G(t_1)$ is convex for all sufficiently small t_1.*

3 Estimates for Minimal Eigenvalues of Controllability Gramian

Consider the autonomous control system

$$\dot{x}(t) = f(x(t)) + Bu(t), \ x(0) = x^0, \ 0 \leq t \leq t_1, \tag{12}$$

where $f : \mathbb{R}^n \to \mathbb{R}^n$ is a continuously differential mapping, B is an $n \times r$ matrix. Suppose that $f(x^0) = 0$, in this case the solution corresponding to zero control $x(t, 0) \equiv x^0$, hence, $A(t) = \frac{\partial f}{\partial x}(x(t, 0)) = \frac{\partial f}{\partial x}(x^0) = A$ is a constant matrix. The linearization of system (12) along the pair $(x^0, 0)$ may be written as follows

$$\dot{y}(t) = \varepsilon A y(t) + Bv(t), \ t \in [0, 1], \tag{13}$$

where $\varepsilon > 0$ is a small parameter. If the pair (A, B) is completely controllable then $(\varepsilon A, B)$ is also controllable for any $\varepsilon \neq 0$. In this case the minimal eigenvalue $\nu(W_\varepsilon)$ of the controllability Gramian W_ε of (13) is positive for every value $\varepsilon > 0$. The controllability Gramian is defined by the equality

$$W_\varepsilon(t) = \int_0^t X_\varepsilon(t, \tau) B B^\top X_\varepsilon^\top(t, \tau) d\tau, \tag{14}$$

where $X_\varepsilon(t, \tau)$ is a Cauchy matrix of system (13) $(\dot{X}_\varepsilon(t, \tau) = \varepsilon A X_\varepsilon(t, \tau), X(\tau, \tau) = I)$. From (14) we get

$$\dot{W}_\varepsilon = \varepsilon A W_\varepsilon + \varepsilon W_\varepsilon A^\top + B B^\top, \ W_\varepsilon(0) = 0. \tag{15}$$

We may look for $W_\varepsilon(t)$ as a sum of a series in powers of ε

$$W_\varepsilon(t) = V_0(t) + \varepsilon V_1(t) + \varepsilon^2 V_2(t) + ..., \ V_k(0) = 0, \ k = 0, 1, ... \tag{16}$$

Differentiating (16) and equating multipliers at equal degrees of ε we have

$$\dot{V}_0(t) = B B^\top, \ \dot{V}_k(t) = A V_{k-1}(t) + V_{k-1}(t) A^\top, \ k = 1, 2, ... \tag{17}$$

Integrating Eq. (17) yields

$$V_0(t) = t U_0, \ V_i(t) = \frac{t^{i+1}}{(i+1)!} U_i, \ i = 1, 2, ...,$$

where $U_0 = B B^\top$, $U_i = A U_{i-1} + U_{i-1} A^\top$, $k = 1, 2, ...$ Thus, the matrix $W_\varepsilon = W_\varepsilon(1)$ is represented by the sum of series, uniformly convergent on every bounded subset of $\mathbb{R}$

$$W_\varepsilon = \sum_{k=0}^{\infty} \frac{\varepsilon^k}{(k+1)!} U_k. \tag{18}$$

We need to investigate the asymptotics of the minimal eigenvalue $\nu(W_\varepsilon)$ under $\varepsilon \to 0$. Note that all the matrices U_k in (18) are symmetric but not necessarily positive semi-definite. For U_0 we obviously have $\nu(U_0) \geq 0$. If $\nu(U_0) > 0$ then there exists $\alpha > 0$ such that $\nu(W_\varepsilon) \geq \alpha$ for sufficiently small ε. Further we assume that $\nu(U_0) = 0$, hence $\nu(W_\varepsilon) \to 0$ as $\varepsilon \to 0$.

Definition 1. *The pair (A, B) is linearly equivalent to the pair (A_1, B_1) if there exists a nonsingular matrix S such that $A_1 = SAS^{-1}$, $B_1 = SB$.*

Note that the pair (A, B) is controllable iff (A_1, B_1) is controllable.

Lemma 1. *Let (A, B), (A_1, B_1) be linearly equivalent pairs and let W_ε, W_ε^1 be the corresponding controllability Gramians. There exist $\alpha > 0$, $\beta > 0$ such that $\alpha \nu(W_\varepsilon) \le \nu(W_\varepsilon^1) \le \beta \nu(W_\varepsilon)$ for all ε.*

Proof. Denote by U_k^1, $k = 0, 1, 2, \ldots$ matrices in the expansion (18) for W_ε^1. Then by induction we get

$$U_0^1 = B_1 B_1^\top = SBB^\top S^\top = SU_0 S^\top, \ U_k^1 = A_1 U_{k-1}^1 + U_{k-1}^1 A_1^\top =$$

$$SAS^{-1}SU_{k-1}S^\top + SU_{k-1}S^\top(S^{-1})^\top A^\top S^\top = S(AU_{k-1} + U_{k-1}A^\top)S^\top = SU_k S^\top.$$

The last implies the equality $W_\varepsilon^1 = SW_\varepsilon S^\top$ that means that W_ε^1 and W_ε are congruent matrices. For symmetric congruent matrices the following is true (see, for example, [10, Theorem 4.5.9]): for any symmetric matrix D there exist the numbers θ_i, $\lambda_1(SS^\top) \le \theta_i \le \lambda_n(SS^\top)$, $i = 1, \ldots, n$ such that $\lambda_i(SDS^\top) = \theta_i \lambda_i(D)$. Here λ_i denote eigenvalues of the matrices, ordered by ascending. The last implies the assertion of the lemma.

Consider a linear system with a single control input. In this case A is an $n \times n$ matrix and B is a column n-vector.

Theorem 2. *Assume that the pair A, B is controllable. If $n = 2$ then there exist $\alpha > 0, \beta > 0$ such that for all sufficiently small $\varepsilon > 0$ the following inequality holds $\alpha \varepsilon^2 \le \nu(W_\varepsilon) \le \beta \varepsilon^2$. If $n \ge 3$ then there exists $\beta > 0$ such that for all sufficiently small $\varepsilon > 0$ we have $0 < \nu(W_\varepsilon) \le \beta \varepsilon^{2n-2}$.*

Proof. Since the pair (A, B) is controllable, there exists a nonsingular matrix S such

$$A_1 = SAS^{-1} = \begin{pmatrix} 0 & 1 & 0 & \ldots & 0 \\ 0 & 0 & 1 & \ldots & 0 \\ \ldots & \ldots & \ldots & \ldots & \ldots \\ 0 & 0 & 0 & \ldots & 1 \\ a_1 & a_2 & a_3 & \ldots & a_n \end{pmatrix}, \ B_1 = SB = \begin{pmatrix} 0 \\ 0 \\ \ldots \\ 0 \\ 1 \end{pmatrix}. \tag{19}$$

Here $a_1, a_2, \ldots, a_n$ are the coefficients of the characteristic polynomial of matrix A. Taking into account Lemma 1 one can assume without loss of generality that the pair (A, B) itself has the form (19).

For $m \ge 1$ represent W_ε in the form $W_\varepsilon = S^m(\varepsilon) + \varepsilon^{m+1} R^{m+1}(\varepsilon)$, where $S^m(\varepsilon)$ is a partial series sum. Consider $n = 2$, in this case

$$A = \begin{pmatrix} 0 & 1 \\ a_1 & a_2 \end{pmatrix}, \ B = \begin{pmatrix} 0 \\ 1 \end{pmatrix}, \ U_0 = \begin{pmatrix} 0 & 0 \\ 0 & 1 \end{pmatrix}, \ U_1 = \begin{pmatrix} 0 & 1 \\ 1 & 2a_2 \end{pmatrix},$$

$$U_2 = \begin{pmatrix} 2 & 3a_2 \\ 3a_2 & 2a_1 + 4a_2^2 \end{pmatrix}, \ S^2(\varepsilon) = \begin{pmatrix} \varphi_1(\varepsilon) & \varphi_2(\varepsilon) \\ \varphi_2(\varepsilon) & \varphi_3(\varepsilon) \end{pmatrix}$$

where $\varphi_1(\varepsilon) = 1/3\varepsilon^2$, $\varphi_2(\varepsilon) = a_2/2\varepsilon^2 + 1/2\varepsilon$, $\varphi_3(\varepsilon) = (a_1 + 2a_2^2)/3\varepsilon^2 + a_2\varepsilon + 1$. Calculating a minimal eigenvalue of $S^2(\varepsilon)$ we get $\nu(S^2(\varepsilon)) = \frac{\varepsilon^2}{12} + o(\varepsilon^2)$. From theorems on the perturbation of eigenvalues of a symmetric matrix [10, Sect. 6.3, page 406] it follows that $\nu(W_\varepsilon) \geq \nu(S^2(\varepsilon)) - \varepsilon^3 \|R^3(0)\|/2 \geq \frac{\varepsilon^2}{12} + o(\varepsilon^2)$, for sufficiently small positive ε, this proves the fist part of the theorem.

In the case $n \geq 3$ by induction we prove that the elements in the left top corners of the matrices U_i are equal to zero for all $i = 1, ..., 2n - 3$. Hence, these matrices $S^i(\varepsilon)$ are singular, that implies inequalities $\nu(S^i(\varepsilon)) \leq 0$ for all $i = 1, ..., 2n - 3$. From the equality $W_\varepsilon = S^{2n-3}(\varepsilon) + \varepsilon^{2n-2}R^{2n-2}(\varepsilon)$ we get the estimate $\nu(W_\varepsilon) \leq \beta\varepsilon^{2n-2}$.

From Proposition 1 and Theorem 2 we get the following:

Corollary 1. *Consider system (12) with a single control input ($r = 1$). Suppose that $f(x^0) = 0$ and the linearization of the system (12) at the point x^0 is controllable. If $n = 2$ then the reachable set $G(t_1)$ is convex for all sufficiently small t_1. For $n \geq 3$ the sufficient conditions of convexity of $G(t_1)$ are not satisfied.*

As an illustrative example consider the Duffing equation

$$\dot{x}_1 = x_2, \quad \dot{x}_2 = -x_1 - 10x_1^3 + u, \quad 0 \leq t \leq t_1 \tag{20}$$

which describes the motion of nonlinear stiff spring on impact of an external force u, satisfying quadratic integral constraints. Estimating the derivative of a Lyapunov-type function $V(x) = 5/2x_1^4 + 1/2x_1^2 + 1/2x_2^2$ along the trajectory one can prove that trajectories of system (20) belong to the compact set $D = \{x \in \mathbb{R}^2 : V(x) \leq \mu^2 t_1\}$. The linearization of (20) along $x(t) \equiv 0$ after time variable change $\dot{y}_1 = t_1 y_2$, $\dot{y}_2 = -y_1 + v$, $x(0) = (0,0)$, $0 \leq t \leq 1$ is controllable. From Corollary 1 it follows that in this example the reachable sets $G(t_1)$ are convex for small t_1.

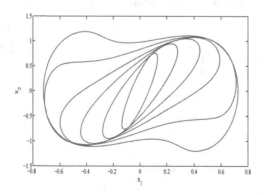

Fig. 1. The reachable sets for the Duffing system.

The Fig. 1 presents the plot of the reachable sets, obtained by algorithms from [8,9], for $\mu^2 = 2$ at times $t_1 = 0.3, 0.5, 0.7, 0.9, 1.2, 1.5$ respectively. Note that $G(t_1) \subset G(\hat{t}_1)$ if $t_1 < \hat{t}_1$. The plot shows that reachable sets remain convex till the value $t_1 \approx 0.9$ and lose their convexity as t_1 increase.

References

1. Baier, R., Gerdts, M., Xausa, I.: Approximation of reachable sets using optimal control algorithms. Numer. Algebra Control Optim. **3**(3), 519–548 (2013)
2. Dar'in, A.N., Kurzhanskii, A.B.: Control under indeterminacy and double constraints. Differ. Equ. **39**(11), 1554–1567 (2003)
3. Filippov, A.F.: Differential Equations with Discontinuous Righthand Sides. Kluwer Academic Press, Boston (1988)
4. Filippova, T.F.: Estimation of star-shaped reachable sets of nonlinear control systems. In: Lirkov, I., Margenov, S. (eds.) LSSC 2017. LNCS, vol. 10665, pp. 210–218. Springer, Cham (2018). https://doi.org/10.1007/978-3-319-73441-5_22
5. Goncharova, E., Ovseevich, A.: Small-time reachable sets of linear systems with integral control constraints: birth of the shape of a reachable set. J. Optim. Theory Appl. **168**(2), 615–624 (2016)
6. Guseinov, K.G., Ozer, O., Akyar, E., Ushakov, V.N.: The approximation of reachable sets of control systems with integral constraint on controls. Nonlinear Differ. Equ. Appl. **14**(1–2), 57–73 (2007)
7. Guseinov, K.G., Nazlipinar, A.S.: Attainable sets of the control system with limited resources. Trudy Inst. Mat. i Mekh. Uro RAN **16**(5), 261–268 (2010)
8. Gusev, M.: On reachability analysis of nonlinear systems with joint integral constraints. In: Lirkov, I., Margenov, S. (eds.) LSSC 2017. LNCS, vol. 10665, pp. 219–227. Springer, Cham (2018). https://doi.org/10.1007/978-3-319-73441-5_23
9. Gusev, M.I., Zykov, I.V.: On extremal properties of the boundary points of reachable sets for control systems with integral constraints. Proc. Stekl. Inst. Math. **300**(suppl.1), 114–125 (2018)
10. Horn, R.A., Jonson, C.R.: Matrix Analysis, 2nd edn. Cambridge University Press, New York (2013)
11. Krastanov, M.I., Veliov, V.M.: High-order approximations to nonholonomic affine control systems. In: Lirkov, I., Margenov, S., Waśniewski, J. (eds.) LSSC 2009. LNCS, vol. 5910, pp. 294–301. Springer, Heidelberg (2010). https://doi.org/10.1007/978-3-642-12535-5_34
12. Patsko, V.S., Pyatko, S.G., Fedotov, A.A.: Three-dimensional reachability set for a nonlinear control system. J. Comput. Syst. Sci. Int. **42**(3), 320–328 (2003)
13. Polyak, B.T.: Convexity of the reachable set of nonlinear systems under L2 bounded controls. Dyn. Continuous Discrete Impulsive Syst. Ser. A: Math. Anal. **11**, 255–267 (2004)
14. Polyak, B.T.: Local programming. Comput. Math. Math. Phys. **41**(9), 1259–1266 (2001)
15. Sinyakov, V.V.: Method for computing exterior and interior approximations to the reachability sets of bilinear differential systems. Differ. Equ. **51**(8), 1097–1111 (2015)

On the Regularity of Mayer-Type Affine Optimal Control Problems

Nikolai P. Osmolovskii[1,2,3] and Vladimir M. Veliov[4(✉)]

[1] Department of Informatics and Mathematics,
University of Technology and Humanities in Radom, Radom, Poland
osmolovski@uph.edu.pl
[2] Systems Research Institute, Polish Academy of Sciences, Warszawa, Poland
[3] Department of Applied Mathematics,
Moscow State University of Civil Engineering, Moscow, Russia
[4] Institute of Statistics and Mathematical Methods in Economics,
Vienna University of Technology, Vienna, Austria
veliov@tuwien.ac.at

Abstract. The paper presents a sufficient condition for strong metric sub-regularity (SMsR) of the system of first order optimality conditions (optimality system) for a Mayer-type optimal control problem with a dynamics affine with respect to the control. The SMsR property at a reference solution means that any solution of the optimality system, subjected to "small" disturbances, which is close enough to the reference one is at a distance to it, at most proportional to the size of the disturbance. The property is well understood for problems satisfying certain coercivity conditions, which however, are not fulfilled for affine problems.

1 Introduction

In the paper, we analyze the question of strong metric sub-regularity (SMsR) of the system of optimality conditions at a reference point $\hat{u}$ for the following affine optimal control problem, presented in the Mayer form:

$$\min g(x(T)) \tag{1}$$

subject to

$$\dot{x}(t) = a(t, x(t)) + B(t, x(t))u(t), \quad x(0) = x^0, \tag{2}$$

$$u(t) \in U, \quad t \in [0, T], \tag{3}$$

where the state x is a vector in $\mathbb{R}^n$, the control u has values $u(t)$ that belong to a given set U in $\mathbb{R}^m$ for almost every (a.e.) $t \in [0, T]$. The initial state x^0 and the final time $T > 0$ are fixed. The set of feasible control functions u, denoted

This research is supported by the Austrian Science Foundation (FWF) under grant No P31400-N32.

I. Lirkov and S. Margenov (Eds.): LSSC 2019, LNCS 11958, pp. 56–63, 2020.
https://doi.org/10.1007/978-3-030-41032-2_6

in the sequel by $\mathcal{U}$, consists of all Lebesgue measurable and bounded functions $u : [0, T] \to U$. Accordingly, the state trajectories x, that are solutions of (2) for feasible controls, are Lipschitz continuous functions of time $t \in [0, T]$. For brevity we denote $f(t, x, u) := a(t, x) + B(t, x)u$.

Assumption (A1). The set U is convex and compact, the components of the functions a, B, g (of dimensions $n \times 1$, $n \times m$ and 1, correspondingly) are two times differentiable with respect to x, the second derivatives are continuous in x locally uniformly in t,[1] a and B and their first and second derivatives in x are measurable and bounded in t.

Here, and in the squeal, we use the following standard notations. The euclidean norm and the scalar product in $\mathbb{R}^n$ (the elements of which are regarded as column-vectors) are denoted by $|\cdot|$ and $\langle \cdot, \cdot \rangle$, respectively. The transpose of a matrix (or vector) E is denoted by $E^\top$. For a function $\psi : \mathbb{R}^p \to \mathbb{R}^r$ of the variable z we denote by $\psi_z(z)$ its derivative (Jacobian), represented by an $(r \times p)$-matrix. If $r = 1$, $\nabla_z \psi(z) = \psi_z(z)^\top$ denotes its gradient (a vector-column of dimension p). Also for $r = 1$, $\psi_{zz}(z)$ denotes the second derivative (Hessian), represented by a $(p \times p)$-matrix. For a function $\psi : \mathbb{R}^{p \times q} \to \mathbb{R}$ of the variables (z, v), $\psi_{zv}(z, v)$ denotes its mixed second derivative, represented by a $(p \times q)$-matrix. The space $L^k = L^k([0, T], \mathbb{R}^r)$, with $k = 1, 2$ or $k = \infty$, consists of all (classes of equivalent) Lebesgue measurable r-dimensional vector-functions defined on the interval $[0, T]$, for which the standard norm $\| \cdot \|_k$ is finite. As usual, $W^{1,k} = W^{1,k}([0, T], \mathbb{R}^r)$ denotes the space of absolutely continuous r-dimensional vector-functions on $[0, T]$ for which the first derivative belongs to L^k, with the usual norm, $\| \cdot \|_{1,k}$. Often the specification $([0, T], \mathbb{R}^r)$ will be omitted in the notations. In any metric space we denote by $\mathbf{B}_a(x)$ the closed ball of radius a centered at x.

Define the Hamiltonian associated with problem (1)–(3) as usual:

$$H(t, x, u, p) := \langle p, f(t, x, u) \rangle, \quad p \in \mathbb{R}^n.$$

Although the feasible controls $u \in \mathcal{U}$ are bounded, we consider the control-trajectory pairs (x, u) as elements of the space $W^{1,1}([0, 1], \mathbb{R}^n) \times L^1([0, 1], \mathbb{R}^m)$.

The local form of the Pontryagin maximum (here minimum) principle for problem (1)–(3) can be represented by the following optimality system for (x, u) and an absolutely continuous (here Lipschitz) function $p : [0, T] \to \mathbb{R}^n$: for a.e. $t \in [0, T]$

$$0 = -\dot{x}(t) + f(t, x(t), u(t)), \quad x(0) - x^0 = 0, \tag{4}$$

$$0 = \dot{p}(t) + \nabla_x H(t, x(t), u(t), p(t)), \tag{5}$$

$$0 = p(T) - \nabla_x g(x(T)), \tag{6}$$

$$0 \in \nabla_u H(t, x(t), u(t), p(t)) + N_U(u(t)), \tag{7}$$

---

[1] Applied to a, for example, this means that for every bounded set $S \subset \mathbb{R}^n$ there exists a function (called *modulus of continuity*) $\omega : (0, +\infty) \to [0, +\infty)$ with $\lim_{s \to 0} \omega(s) = 0$, such that $|a(t, x') - a(t, x)| \le \omega(|x' - x|)$ for every $t \in [0, T]$ and $x, x' \in S$.

where the normal cone $N_U(u)$ to the set U at $u \in \mathbb{R}^m$ is defined as

$$N_U(u) = \begin{cases} \{y \in \mathbb{R}^n \mid \langle y, v - u \rangle \le 0 \text{ for all } v \in U\} & \text{if } u \in U, \\ \emptyset & \text{otherwise.} \end{cases}$$

Introduce the spaces

$$\mathcal{Y} := W_0^{1,1} \times \mathcal{U} \times W^{1,1}, \qquad \mathcal{Z} := L^1 \times L^1 \times \mathbb{R}^n \times L^\infty,$$

where $W_0^{1,1}$ is the affine space consisting of those $x \in W^{1,1}$ for which $x(0) = x^0$ and $\mathcal{U}$ is endowed with the L^1-metric. Norms in this spaces are also defined as usual: for $y = (x, u, p) \in \mathcal{Y}$ and $z = (\xi, \pi, \nu, \rho) \in \mathcal{Z}$

$$\|y\| = \|x\|_{1,1} + \|u\|_1 + \|p\|_{1,1}, \qquad \|z\| = \|\xi\|_1 + \|\pi\|_1 + |\nu| + \|\rho\|_\infty.$$

Then the optimality system (4)–(7) can be recast as the generalized equation

$$0 \in \psi(y) + \Psi(y), \tag{8}$$

where $y = (x, u, p)$ and

$$\mathcal{Y} \ni y \mapsto \psi(y) := \begin{pmatrix} -\dot{x} + f(\cdot, x, u) \\ \dot{p} + \nabla_x H(\cdot, y) \\ p(T) - \nabla_x g(x(T)) \\ \nabla_u H(\cdot, y) \end{pmatrix} \in \mathcal{Z}, \ \mathcal{Y} \ni y \Rightarrow \Psi(y) := \begin{pmatrix} 0 \\ 0 \\ 0 \\ N_{\mathcal{U}}(u) \end{pmatrix} \subset \mathcal{Z}.$$

Here $N_{\mathcal{U}}(u) := \{v \in L^\infty : v(t) \in N_U(u(t)) \text{ for a.e. } t \in [0, T]\}$ is the normal cone to the set $\mathcal{U}$ (considered as a subset of L^1) at $u \in \mathcal{U}$. For $u \notin \mathcal{U}$ the normal cone is empty.

Below we remind one of the several equivalent definitions of the notion of strong metric sub-regularity, adapted to our notations, see e.g. [2, p. 202].

Definition 1. *The set-valued mapping $\psi + \Psi : \mathcal{Y} \rightrightarrows \mathcal{Z}$ is Strongly Metrically sub-Regular (SMsR) at the point $\hat{y}$ for $\hat{z}$ if $\hat{z} \in \psi(\hat{y}) + \Psi(\hat{y})$ and there exist numbers $\alpha_0 > 0$, $\beta_0 > 0$ and c_0 such that for any $z \in \mathcal{Z}$ with $\|z - \hat{z}\| \le \alpha_0$ and for any solution $y \in \mathcal{Y}$ of the inclusion $z \in \psi(y) + \Psi(y)$ with $\|y - \hat{y}\| \le \beta_0$, it holds that $\|y - \hat{y}\| \le c_0 \|z - \hat{z}\|$.*

We will prove the SMsR property of the mapping $\psi + \Psi$ in the optimality system (8) under an additional assumption, given in the next section. At the end of the next section we will also compare our result with the few existing ones. Here we only mention that in contrast to the case of the so-called "coercive" problems, where a Legendre-type condition is satisfied, the investigation of regularity properties for affine control problems started just a few years ago and is still in progress.

2   Main Result

Let a solution $\hat{y} = (\hat{x}, \hat{u}, \hat{p}) \in W^{1,1} \times \mathcal{U} \times W^{1,1}$ of the optimality system (4)–(7) be fixed. To shorten the notations we skip arguments with "hat" in functions, shifting the "hat" on the top of the notation of the function, so that $\hat{f}(t) := f(t, \hat{x}(t), \hat{u}(t))$, $\hat{B}(t) := B(t, \hat{x}(t))$, $\hat{H}(t) := H(t, \hat{x}(t), \hat{u}(t), \hat{p}(t))$, $\hat{H}(t, u) := H(t, \hat{x}(t), u, \hat{p}(t))$, etc. Moreover, denote

$$\hat{A}(t) := \hat{f}_x(t) = f_x(t, \hat{x}(t), \hat{u}(t)), \quad \hat{\sigma}(t) := \nabla_u \hat{H}(t, \hat{x}(t), \hat{u}(t), \hat{p}(t)) = \hat{B}(t)^\top \hat{p}(t).$$

Remark 1. Due to Assumption (A1), and since the solution $\hat{x}$ of (2) with $u = \hat{u}$, exists on $[0, T]$, there exist a number $r > 0$ and a convex compact set $\bar{S} \subset I\!\!R^n$ such that for every $u \in \mathcal{U}$ with $\|u - \hat{u}\|_1 \leq r$ the solution x of (2) exists on $[0, T]$ and $\mathbf{B}_1(x(t)) \subset \bar{S}$ for all $t \in [0, T]$. By taking $\bar{S}$ sufficiently large we may also ensure that $\mathbf{B}_1(\hat{p}(t)) \subset \bar{S}$ for all $t \in [0, T]$. Using Assumption (A1), we denote by L a Lipschitz constant with respect to $x \in \bar{S}$ (uniformly with respect to $t \in [0, T]$, $u \in U$, $p \in \bar{S}$) of the functions a, B, g, f, and H and their first derivatives in x. Further, we denote by M a bound of all these functions, their first and second derivatives in x, for $(t, x, u, p) \in [0, T] \times \bar{S} \times U \times \bar{S}$. Finally, we denote by $\bar{\omega}$ a modulus of continuity of the second derivative in x of the functions a, B, g, f, and H, uniformly with respect to $(t, u, p) \in [0, T] \times U \times \bar{S}$ (see Footnote 1). Due to the Grönwal inequality, the following estimation holds for every $u \in \mathcal{U}$ with $\|u - \hat{u}\|_1 \leq r$: $\|x - \hat{x}\|_C \leq c_f \|u - \hat{u}\|_1$ where $c_f = Me^{LT}$.

According to this remark, for any $u \in \mathcal{U}$ with $\|u - \hat{u}\|_1 \leq r$ the value of the objective functional $J(u) := g(x(T))$ is well defined. For any function $\delta u \in \mathcal{U} - \hat{u}$ we introduce the linearized version of Eq. (2) for the function $\delta x : [0, T] \to I\!\!R^n$ (with $\delta \dot{x}$ denoting its derivative):

$$\delta \dot{x}(t) = \hat{A}(t)\delta x + \hat{B}(t)\delta u(t), \quad \delta x(0) = 0, \quad t \in [0, T]. \tag{9}$$

Denote by Γ the set of all pairs $(\delta x, \delta u) \in W^{1,1} \times L^1$ such that $\delta u \in \mathcal{U} - \hat{u}$ and δx is the solution of the linearized Eq. (9). Let us introduce the following quadratic functional of $(\delta x, \delta u) \in W^{1,1} \times L^1$:

$$\Omega(\delta x, \delta u) := \frac{1}{2} \langle g_{xx}(\hat{x}(T)) \, \delta x(T), \delta x(T) \rangle$$

$$+ \int_0^T \left[\frac{1}{2} \langle \hat{H}_{xx}(t)\delta x(t), \delta x(t) \rangle + \langle \hat{H}_{ux}(t)\delta x(t), \delta u(t) \rangle \right] \mathrm{d}t. \tag{10}$$

Assumption (A2). There exists a constant $c_0 > 0$ such that

$$\int_0^T \langle \hat{\sigma}(t), \delta u(t) \rangle \, \mathrm{d}t + 2\,\Omega(\delta x, \delta u) \geq c_0 \|\delta u\|_1^2 \quad \text{for all } (\delta x, \delta u) \in \Gamma. \tag{11}$$

Consider the following "perturbed" version of (8):

$$z \in \psi(y) + \Psi(y), \qquad (12)$$

where $z = (\xi, \pi, \nu, \rho) \in \mathcal{Z}$.

Theorem 1. *Let assumptions (A1) and (A2) be fulfilled. Then there exist constants $\alpha_0 > 0$, $\beta_0 > 0$ and c_0 such that for any $z \in \mathcal{Z}$ with $\|z\| \leq \alpha_0$ and for any solution $y = (x, u, p) \in \mathcal{Y}$ of the disturbed optimality system (12), with $\|u - \hat{u}\|_1 \leq \beta_0$, it holds that*

$$\|x - \hat{x}\|_{1,1} + \|u - \hat{u}\|_1 + \|p - \hat{p}\|_{1,1} \leq c_0 \|z\|. \qquad (13)$$

Thus, the mapping $\psi + \Psi$, associated with problem (1)–(3), is strongly metrically sub-regular at $\hat{y} = (\hat{x}, \hat{u}, \hat{p})$ for zero.   ∎

It is interesting to note that Assumption (A2) guarantees not only strong metric sub-regularity of the mapping $\psi + \Psi$ at the point $(\hat{x}, \hat{u}, \hat{p})$, but also that $\hat{u}$ is a strict L^1-local minimizer. Moreover, it can be proved that even a weaker condition than (A2) guarantees such a minimum at $\hat{u}$ (see [3, Corollary 2.1]). This weakened condition differs from (A2) only by changing 2Ω with Ω in the inequality (11) (and then it follows from (A2) since $\langle \hat{\sigma}(t), \delta u(t) \rangle \geq 0$ a.e. in $[0, T]$ for all $\delta u \in \mathcal{U} - \hat{u}$).

The following more demanding condition than (A2) appears in [1, Sect. 5] and is used for error analysis of the Euler discretization scheme:

$$\int_0^T \langle \hat{\sigma}(t), \delta u(t) \rangle \, dt \geq c_1 \|\delta u\|_1^2 \qquad \text{for all } (\delta x, \delta u) \in \Gamma, \qquad (14)$$

$$2\,\Omega(\delta x, \delta u) \geq c_2 \|\delta u\|_1^2 \qquad \text{for all } (\delta x, \delta u) \in \Gamma$$

with $c_1 + c_2 > 0$. Sufficient conditions for (14) are known in the case of a box-like set U; see [4] and the forthcoming paper [3] for the relevant bibliography, and also for the case of a general compact convex polyhedral set U.

3   Proof of Theorem 1

We give the proof omitting some details. The positive numbers α_0 and β_0 will be fixed later as depending only on L, M and $\bar{\omega}$ (see Remark 1). Now take an arbitrary $z = (\xi, \pi, \nu, \rho) \in \mathcal{Z}$ with $\|z\| \leq \alpha_0$ and a solution $y = (x, u, p) \in \mathcal{Y}$ of (12) satisfying $\|u - \hat{u}\|_1 \leq \beta_0$. In detail, inclusion (12) reads as

$$\dot{x}(t) = f(t, x(t), u(t)) - \xi(t), \quad x(0) = x^0, \qquad (15)$$

$$\dot{p}(t) = -\nabla_x H(t, x(t), u(t), p(t)) + \pi(t), \qquad (16)$$

$$p(T) = \nabla_x g(x(T)) + \nu, \qquad (17)$$

$$-N_U(u(t)) \ni \nabla_u H(t, x(t), u(t), p(t)) - \rho(t), \qquad (18)$$

where differential Eqs. (15), (16) and inclusion (18) have to be fulfilled for a.e. $t \in [0, T]$. Denote $\Delta x(t) = x(t) - \hat{x}(t)$, $\Delta \dot{x}(t) = \dot{x}(t) - \dot{\hat{x}}(t)$, $\Delta u(t) = u(t) - \hat{u}(t) = \delta u(t)$, $\Delta f(t) = f(t, x(t), u(t)) - \hat{f}(t)$, etc. Then

$$\Delta \dot{x}(t) = \Delta f(t) - \xi(t), \quad \Delta x(0) = 0, \tag{19}$$

$$\Delta \dot{p}(t) = -\Delta(\nabla_x H)(t) + \pi(t), \quad \Delta p(T) = \Delta(\nabla_x g)(T) + \nu, \tag{20}$$

$$\Delta \sigma(t) = \Delta(\nabla_u H)(t) - \rho(t). \tag{21}$$

Applying the Grönwall inequality to Eq. (19) we obtain

$$\|\Delta x\|_C \le e^{LT}(M\|\delta u\|_1 + \|\xi\|_1) \le c_f(\|\delta u\|_1 + \|\xi\|_1) \le c_f(\|\delta u\|_1 + \|z\|), \tag{22}$$

where $c_f = e^{LT} \max\{M, 1\}$. Similarly applying the Grönwall inequality to Eq. (20) and using (22) we get

$$\|\Delta p\|_C \le c_H(\|\delta u\|_1 + \|z\|), \tag{23}$$

where $c_H = e^{MT} \max\{L(T+1)c_f + M, 1\}$. The following obvious equality serves as a source for further key estimations:

$$\int_0^T \langle \Delta \dot{p}(t), \Delta x(t) \rangle \, dt + \int_0^T \langle \Delta p(t), \Delta \dot{x}(t) \rangle \, dt = \langle \Delta p(T), \Delta x(T) \rangle,$$

whence in view of (19) and (20), we get

$$\langle \Delta(\nabla_x g)(T), \Delta x(T) \rangle + \int_0^T \Big(\langle \Delta(\nabla_x H)(t), \Delta x(t) \rangle - \langle \Delta p(t), \Delta f(t) \rangle \Big) \, dt$$

$$= -\langle \nu, \Delta x(T) \rangle + \int_0^T \Big(\langle \pi(t), \Delta x(t) \rangle - \langle \Delta p(t), \xi(t) \rangle \Big) \, dt. \tag{24}$$

Further, simple expansions and transformations show that

$$\langle \Delta(\nabla_x H)(t), \Delta x(t) \rangle = \langle \hat{H}_{xu}(t)\delta u(t), \Delta x(t) \rangle + \langle \hat{H}_{xx}(t)\Delta x(t), \Delta x(t) \rangle$$
$$+ \langle \hat{H}_{xp}(t)\Delta p(t), \Delta x(t) \rangle + r_{H_x},$$
$$\langle \Delta p(t), \Delta f(t) \rangle = \langle \hat{H}_{pu}(t)\delta u(t), \Delta p(t) \rangle + \langle \hat{H}_{px}(t)\Delta x(t), \Delta p(t) \rangle + r_{H_p}(t),$$
$$\langle \hat{H}_{pu}(t)\delta u(t), \Delta p(t) \rangle = \langle \Delta(\nabla_u H)(t), \delta u(t) \rangle - \langle \hat{H}_{ux}(t)\Delta x(t), \delta u(t) \rangle + r_\sigma(t),$$

where

$$\|r_{H_x}\|_1 \le \big(T\bar{\omega}(\|\Delta x\|_C) + MT\|\Delta p\|_C + M\|\delta u\|_1\big)\|\Delta x\|_C^2 + M\|\Delta x\|_C\|\Delta p\|_C\|\delta u\|_1,$$
$$\|r_{H_p}\|_1 \le \big(T\bar{\omega}(\|\Delta x\|_C) + M\|\delta u\|_1\big)\|\Delta x\|_C\|\Delta p\|_C,$$
$$\|r_\sigma\|_1 \le \bar{\omega}(\|\Delta x\|_C)\|\Delta x\|_C\|\delta u\|_1 + M\|\Delta x\|_C\|\delta u\|_1\|\Delta p\|_C.$$

Using these formulas together with (22) and (23), we obtain

$$\langle \Delta(\nabla_x g)(T), \Delta x(T) \rangle + \int_0^T \Big(\langle \Delta(\nabla_x H)(t), \Delta x(t) \rangle - \langle \Delta p(t), \Delta f(t) \rangle \Big) \, dt$$

$$= 2\Omega(\Delta x, \delta u) - \int_0^T \langle \Delta(\nabla_u H)(t), \delta u(t) \rangle \, dt + r_\Omega, \tag{25}$$

where

$$|r_\Omega| \leq c_{r_\Omega}[\bar{\omega}(c_f(\|z\| + \|\delta u\|_1)) + \|z\| + \|\delta u\|_1](\|z\| + \|\delta u\|_1)^2, \qquad (26)$$

and $c_{r_\Omega} > 0$ depends only on L, M, T (therefore also on $\hat{x}, \hat{u}$).

The next step involves replacing $(\Delta x, \delta u)$ with $(\delta x, \delta u) \in \Gamma$ in the quadratic form Ω. Let $\delta x(t)$ be the solution of linear Eq. (9). Then it follows from (19) and (9) that

$$\frac{\mathrm{d}}{\mathrm{d}t}(\Delta x(t) - \delta x(t)) = \hat{A}(t)(\Delta x(t) - \delta x(t)) + r_f(t) - \xi(t),$$

where $|r_f(t)| \leq M|\Delta u(t)||\Delta x(t)| + \frac{1}{2}L|\Delta x(t)|^2$. Using the Grönwall inequality and estimate (22) we obtain that

$$\|\Delta x - \delta x\|_C \leq e^{MT}(\|r_f\|_1 + \|\xi\|_1) \leq c_f e^{MT}(M + \frac{1}{2}LTc_f)(\|\xi\|_1 + \|\delta u\|_1)^2 + e^{MT}\|\xi\|_1.$$

Since $\|\xi\|_1 \leq \alpha_0$ and hence $(\|\xi\|_1 + \|\delta u\|_1)^2 \leq 2\alpha_0\|\xi\|_1 + 2\|\delta u\|_1^2$, we get

$$\|\Delta x - \delta x\|_C \leq \tilde{d}\|\delta u\|_1^2 + \hat{d}\|\xi\|_1 \leq \tilde{d}\|\delta u\|_1^2 + \hat{d}\|z\|_1, \qquad (27)$$

where $\tilde{d}$ and $\hat{d}$ depend only on L, M, and T. Now we can estimate the difference $r_{\Delta\Omega}(\delta u) := \Omega(\Delta x, \delta u) - \Omega(\delta x, \delta u)$ as follows:

$$|r_{\Delta\Omega}(\delta u)| \leq M\left[\frac{1}{2}(1 + T)(\|\Delta x\|_C + \|\delta x\|_C) + \|\delta u\|_1\right]\|\Delta x - \delta x\|_C.$$

In view of (9) we have $\|\delta x\|_C \leq e^{MT}M\|\delta u\|_1 =: c_M\|\delta u\|_1$. Using this estimate together with (22) and (27), we obtain

$$|r_{\Delta\Omega}(\delta u)| \leq c_{\Delta\Omega}(\|\delta u\|_1 + \|z\|)(\|\delta u\|_1^2 + \|z\|), \qquad (28)$$

where $c_{\Delta\Omega} := M(\frac{1}{2}(1+T)c_f + c_M)(\tilde{d} + \hat{d})$. It follows from (25) and the definition of $r_{\Delta\Omega}$ that

$$\langle\Delta(\nabla_x g), \Delta x(T)\rangle + \int_0^T \left(\langle\Delta(\nabla_x H)(t), \delta x(t)\rangle - \langle\Delta p(t), \Delta f(t)\rangle\right) \mathrm{d}t$$

$$= 2\Omega(\delta x, \delta u) - \int_0^T \langle\Delta(\nabla_u H)(t), \delta u(t)\rangle \,\mathrm{d}t + r_\Omega + 2r_{\Delta\Omega}. \qquad (29)$$

According to (21) $\sigma(t) - \hat{\sigma}(t) = \Delta(\nabla_u H)(t) - \rho(t)$. This and the inequality $\langle\sigma(t), \delta u(t)\rangle \leq 0$ a.e. in $(0, T)$, following from (18), imply

$$\int_0^T \langle\Delta(\nabla_u H)(t), \delta u(t)\rangle \,\mathrm{d}t \leq -\int_0^T \langle\hat{\sigma}(t), \delta u(t)\rangle \,\mathrm{d}t + \int_0^T \langle\rho(t), \delta u(t)\rangle \,\mathrm{d}t,$$

and then in view of Assumption (A2) we get from (29) that

$$\langle \Delta(\nabla_x g), \Delta x(T) \rangle + \int_0^T \Big(\langle \Delta(\nabla_x H)(t), \delta x(t) \rangle - \langle \Delta p(t), \Delta f(t) \rangle \Big)\, dt$$

$$\geq 2\Omega(\delta x, \delta u) + \int_0^T \langle \hat{\sigma}(t), \delta u(t) \rangle\, dt - \int_0^T \langle \rho(t), \delta u(t) \rangle\, dt + r_\Omega + 2 r_{\Delta\Omega}$$

$$\geq c_0 \|\delta u\|_1^2 - \int_0^T \langle \rho(t), \delta u(t) \rangle\, dt + r_\Omega + 2 r_{\Delta\Omega}. \tag{30}$$

Combining this with (24) we get

$$c_0 \|\delta u\|_1^2 + r_\Omega + 2 r_{\Delta\Omega} \leq \int_0^T \Big(\langle \pi(t), \Delta x(t) \rangle\rangle - \langle \Delta p(t), \xi(t) \rangle + \langle \rho(t), \delta u(t) \rangle \Big)\, dt$$

$$- \langle \nu, \Delta x(T) \rangle \leq (|\Delta x(T)| + \|\Delta x\|_C + \|\Delta p\|_C + \|\delta u\|_1)\|z\|.$$

Using also (22) and (23) we obtain

$$c_0 \|\delta u\|_1^2 + r_\Omega + 2 r_{\Delta\Omega} \leq \hat{c}(\|\delta u\|_1 + \|z\|)\|z\|, \tag{31}$$

where $\hat{c} = (2c_f + c_H + 1)$. Take α_0 and β_0 such that $\bar{\omega}(c_f(\|z\| + \|\delta u\|_1)) + \|z\| + \|\delta u\|_1 \leq \varepsilon$ for all $\|z\| \leq \alpha_0$, $\|\delta u\|_1 \leq \beta_0$, where $\varepsilon \in (0,1)$ will be defined later. Then in view of (26) and (28), $|r_\Omega| \leq 2c_{r_\Omega}\varepsilon\|z\|^2 + 2c_{r_\Omega}\varepsilon\|\delta u\|_1^2$ and $|r_{\Delta\Omega}| \leq c_{\Delta\Omega}\varepsilon\|\delta u\|_1^2 + c_{\Delta\Omega}\|z\|(\|\delta u\|_1 + \|z\|)$. Using these estimates and inequality (31) we get

$$(c_0 - 2c_{r_\Omega}\varepsilon - 2c_{\Delta\Omega}\varepsilon)\|\delta u\|_1^2 \leq (\hat{c} + 2c_{r_\Omega}\varepsilon + 2c_{\Delta\Omega})(\|\delta u\|_1 + \|z\|)\|z\|.$$

Take $\varepsilon \in (0,1)$ such that $c_0 - 2c_{r_\Omega}\varepsilon - 2c_{\Delta\Omega}\varepsilon \geq \frac{1}{2}c_0$, and set $a = (\hat{c} + 2c_{r_\Omega} + 2c_{\Delta\Omega})/c_0$. Then $\|\delta u\|_1^2 \leq 2a(\|\delta u\|_1 + \|z\|)\|z\|$, whence $(\|\delta u\|_1 - a\|z\|)^2 \leq (a + 1)^2\|z\|^2$, which implies $\|\delta u\|_1 \leq (2a + 1)\|z\|$. Combined with (22) and (23) this inequality completes the proof. $\qquad \square$

References

1. Alt, W., Felgenhauer, U., Seydenschwanz, M.: Euler discretization for a class of nonlinear optimal control problems with control appearing linearly. Comput. Optim. Appl. **69**, 825–856 (2018)
2. Dontchev, A.L., Rockafellar, R.T.: Implicit Functions and Solution Mappings: A View from Variational Analysis, 2nd edn. Springer, New York (2014)
3. Osmolovskii, N.P., Veliov, V.M.: Metric sub-regularity in optimal control of affine problems with free end state. Submitted; available as Research Report 2019–04, ORCOS, TU Wien (2019). https://orcos.tuwien.ac.at/research/research_reports
4. Preininger, J., Scarinci, T., Veliov, V.M.: Metric regularity properties inbang-bang type linear-quadratic optimal control problems. Set-Valued Var. Anal. **27**, 381–404 (2019). https://doi.org/10.1007/s11228-018-0488-1.

Meshfree and Particle Methods

Mesh-Hardened Finite Element Analysis Through a Generalized Moving Least-Squares Approximation of Variational Problems

P. Bochev[(⊠)], N. Trask, P. Kuberry, and M. Perego

Center for Computing Research, Sandia National Laboratories,
Albuquerque, NM 87125, USA
{pbboche,natrask,pakuber,mperego}@sandia.gov

Abstract. In most finite element methods the mesh is used to both represent the domain and to define the finite element basis. As a result the quality of such methods is tied to the quality of the mesh and may suffer when the latter deteriorates. This paper formulates an alternative approach, which separates the discretization of the domain, i.e., the meshing, from the discretization of the PDE. The latter is accomplished by extending the Generalized Moving Least-Squares (GMLS) regression technique to approximation of bilinear forms and using the mesh only for the integration of the GMLS polynomial basis. Our approach yields a non-conforming discretization of the weak equations that can be handled by standard discontinuous Galerkin or interior penalty terms.

Keywords: Galerkin methods · Generalized Moving Least Squares · Nonconforming finite elements

1 Introduction

The vast majority of finite element methods uses the mesh to both approximate the computational domain and to define the shape functions necessary to discretize the weak forms of the governing PDEs. These dual roles of the mesh are often in conflict. On the one hand, the properties of the discrete equations depend strongly on the quality of the underlying mesh and may deteriorate to the point of insolvability on poor quality grids. For example, high-aspect or "sliver" elements lead to nearly singular shape functions, which result in ill-conditioned or even singular discrete equations [4,13]. On the other hand, automatic generation of high-quality grids remains a challenge. Currently, hexahedral grids can deliver

Sandia National Laboratories is a multimission laboratory managed and operated by National Technology and Engineering Solutions of Sandia, LLC., a wholly owned subsidiary of Honeywell International, Inc., for the U.S. Department of Energy's National Nuclear Security Administration under contract DE-NA-0003525.

I. Lirkov and S. Margenov (Eds.): LSSC 2019, LNCS 11958, pp. 67–75, 2020.
https://doi.org/10.1007/978-3-030-41032-2_7

robust results but require prohibitive manual efforts. Conversely, tetrahedral grids can be constructed more efficiently but their quality may be insufficient for traditional Finite Element Analysis (FEA) due to poor aspect ratios. Summarily, meshing can consume significant resources, creating a computational bottleneck in the finite element workflow [9]. Moreover, in some circumstances such as Lagrangian simulations of large-deformation mechanics [12], distorted grids are unavoidable. As a result, hardening finite element methods against substandard grids can have significant impacts towards enabling automated CAD-to-solution capabilities by reducing or even removing the performance barriers created by the mesh-quality requirements of conventional FEA.

Attaining these goals requires either reducing or altogether eliminating the dependency of the finite element shape functions on the underlying mesh. In this paper we aim for the latter by extending Generalized Moving Least Squares (GMLS) [15] regression techniques to approximate the weak variational forms of the PDE problems that are at the core of FEA. In so doing our approach limits the role of the underlying mesh to performing numerical integration and enables generation of well-conditioned discrete problems that are independent of its quality. These problems are obtained by (i) solving a small local quadratic program on each element; (ii) substituting the test and trial functions by the polynomial basis of the GMLS reproduction space, and (iii) integrating the resulting products of polynomials, which can be accomplished with relatively few quadrature points. The approximate weak forms generated by this process fall into the category of non-conforming FEM, which are supported by a mature and rigorous stability theory and error analysis. This allows us to borrow classical "off-the-shelf" stabilization techniques from, e.g., Discontinuous Galerkin [2,8] or Interior Penalty [1,16] methods.

These traits, i.e., formulations that require only integration of polynomials and can be stabilized by standard non-conforming FEM terms, set our approach apart from other techniques, such as meshfree Galerkin methods [3,5,10,11] that also aim to alleviate mesh quality issues. These methods use GMLS, or similar regression techniques, to define *meshfree shape functions* which replace the standard mesh-based finite element bases in the weak forms. However, the meshfree shape functions are not known in closed form and are non-polynomial. As a result, their integration requires a relatively large number of quadrature points, which increases the computational cost of such schemes, as every shape function evaluation involves a solution of a small linear algebra problem. This has prompted consideration of reduced order integration [6,7]; however, such integration leads to numerical instabilities due to underintegration and requires application-specific stabilizations. For the convenience of the reader we provide a brief overview of the GMLS technique in Sect. 2. The core of the paper is Sect. 3 where we extend GMLS to the approximation of weak variational forms and apply the new technique to a model PDE. Section 4 contains preliminary numerical results demonstrating the new approach.

2   Generalized Moving Least Squares (GMLS) Regression

GMLS is a non-parametric regression technique for the approximation of bounded linear functionals from scattered data [15, Section 4.3]. A typical GMLS setting includes (i) a function space U with a dual U^*; (ii) a finite dimensional space $\Phi \subset U$ with basis $\phi = \{\phi_1, \ldots, \phi_q\}$; (iii) a Φ-unisolvent[1] set of sampling functionals $S = \{\lambda_1, \ldots, \lambda_n\} \subset U^*$; and (iv) a locally supported kernel $w : U^* \times U^* \mapsto \mathbb{R}^+ \cup \{0\}$.

GMLS seeks an approximation $\widetilde{\tau}(u)$ of the *target* $\tau(u) \in U^*$ in terms of the sample vector $\boldsymbol{u} := (\lambda_1(u), \ldots, \lambda_n(u)) \in \mathbb{R}^n$, such that $\widetilde{\tau}(\phi) = \tau(\phi)$ for all $\phi \in \Phi$, i.e., the approximation is Φ-reproducing. To define $\widetilde{\tau}(u)$ we need the vector $\boldsymbol{\tau}(\phi) \in \mathbb{R}^q$ with elements $(\boldsymbol{\tau}(\phi))_i = \tau(\phi_i)$, $i = 1, \ldots, q$, the diagonal weight matrix $W(\tau) \in \mathbb{R}^{n \times n}$ with element $W_{ii}(\tau) = w(\tau; \lambda_i)$, and the basis sample matrix $B \in \mathbb{R}^{n \times q}$ with element $B_{ij} = \lambda_i(\phi_j)$; $i = 1, \ldots, n$; $j = 1, \ldots, q$. Let $|\cdot|_{W(\tau)}$ denote the Euclidean norm on $\mathbb{R}^n$ weighted by $W(\tau)$, i.e.,

$$|\boldsymbol{b}|^2_{W(\tau)} = \boldsymbol{b}^\mathsf{T} W(\tau) \boldsymbol{b} \qquad \forall \boldsymbol{b} \in \mathbb{R}^n \, .$$

The GMLS approximant of the target is then given by

$$\widetilde{\tau}(u) := \boldsymbol{c}(\boldsymbol{u}; \tau) \cdot \boldsymbol{\tau}(\phi), \tag{1}$$

where the GMLS coefficients $\boldsymbol{c}(\boldsymbol{u}; \tau) \in \mathbb{R}^q$ solve

$$\boldsymbol{c}(\boldsymbol{u}; \tau) = \underset{\boldsymbol{b} \in \mathbb{R}^q}{\operatorname{argmin}} \frac{1}{2} |B\boldsymbol{b} - \boldsymbol{u}|^2_{W(\tau)} \, . \tag{2}$$

It is straightforward to check that $\boldsymbol{c}(\boldsymbol{u}; \tau) = (B^\mathsf{T} W(\tau) B)^{-1} (B^\mathsf{T} W(\tau)) \boldsymbol{u}$. We refer to [14] for information about the efficient and stable solution of (2). Lastly, let $\mathbf{e}_i \in \mathbb{R}^n$ be the ith Cartesian unit vector and let $u_i^\tau := \boldsymbol{c}(\mathbf{e}_i; \tau) \cdot \phi \in \Phi$. We call the set $S^\tau = \{u_1^\tau, \ldots, u_n^\tau\} \subset \Phi$ a *GMLS reciprocal* of S *relative to* τ.

3   GMLS Approximation of Variational Equations

Let U and V denote Hilbert spaces with duals U^* and V^*, respectively. We consider the following abstract variational equation: *given $f \in V^*$ find $u \in U$ such that*

$$a(u, v) = f(v) \qquad \forall v \in V \, , \tag{3}$$

where $a(\cdot, \cdot) : U \times V \to \mathbb{R}$ is a given bilinear form. We refer to U and V as the trial and test space, respectively. To approximate (3) we will use two separate instances of the GMLS regression for the test and trial spaces, respectively. To differentiate between these instances we tag their entities with a sub/superscript indicating the underlying space, e.g., S_U and $\boldsymbol{c}^U(u)$ denote a sampling set and

---

[1] We recall that Φ-unisolvency implies $\{\phi \in \Phi \mid \lambda_i(\phi) = 0, i = 1, \ldots, n\} = \{0\}$.

a coefficient vector, respectively, for the *trial space*. One exception to this rule will be the reciprocal GMLS functions u_i^τ and v_i^τ.

We obtain the GMLS approximation of (3) in two steps. For any fixed $u \in U$ the form $a(u, \cdot)$ defines a bounded linear functional on V, i.e., $a(u, \cdot) \in V^*$. We shall assume that the kernel w is such that $W(a(u, \cdot)) = W(f)$. For this reason we retain the generic label τ to indicate dependence of various GMLS entities on their respective target functionals. Then, the GMLS approximants of $a(u, \cdot)$ and f can be written in terms of the same GMLS coefficient vector as

$$\widetilde{a}(u, v) := c^V(v; \tau) \cdot a(u, \phi^V) \quad \text{and} \quad \widetilde{f}(v) = c^V(v; \tau) \cdot f(\phi^V) \quad \forall v \in V,$$

respectively. Combining these representations yields the following approximation of (3): *find $u \in U$ such that $\widetilde{a}(u, v) = \widetilde{f}(v)$ for all $v \in V$*, or equivalently,

$$c^V(v; \tau) \cdot a(u, \phi^V) = c^V(v; \tau) \cdot f(\phi^V) \quad \forall v \in V. \tag{4}$$

The weak problem (4) has infinitely many "equations" and "variables". To reduce the number of equations we restrict the test space in (4) to the GMLS reciprocal set S_V^τ to obtain the following problem: *find $u \in U$ such that $\widetilde{a}(u, v_i^\tau) = \widetilde{f}(v_i^\tau)$ for all $v_i^\tau \in S_V^\tau$* or, which is the same,

$$c^V(\mathbf{e}_i; \tau) \cdot a(u, \phi^V) = c^V(\mathbf{e}_i; \tau) \cdot f(\phi^V) \quad i = 1, \ldots, n^V. \tag{5}$$

This completes the first step. The second step discretizes the trial space by restricting the search for a solution to the reciprocal GMLS space S_U^τ, i.e., we consider the problem: *find $u^\tau \in S_U^\tau$ such that*

$$\widetilde{a}(u^\tau, v_i^\tau) = \widetilde{f}(v_i^\tau) \quad \forall v_i^\tau \in S_V^\tau. \tag{6}$$

where $u^\tau := \sum_{j=1}^{n^U} a_j u_j^\tau$. Using (5) and $u_j^\tau := c(\mathbf{e}_j; \tau) \cdot \phi$ one can write (6) as

$$\sum_{j=1}^{n^U} \left(c^V(\mathbf{e}_i; \tau) \cdot a(\phi^U, \phi^V) \cdot c^U(\mathbf{e}_j; \tau) \right) a_j = c^V(\mathbf{e}_i; \tau) \cdot f(\phi^V) \quad i = 1, \ldots, n^V. \tag{7}$$

It is easy to see that this problem is equivalent to the following $n^V \times n^U$ system of linear algebraic equations

$$K a = F \tag{8}$$

where $a = \{a_1, \ldots, a_{n^U}\} \in \mathbb{R}^{n^U}$ are the GMLS degrees-of-freedom (DoF), while $K \in \mathbb{R}^{n^V \times n^U}$ and $F \in \mathbb{R}^{n^V}$ have elements

$$K_{ij} = c^V(\mathbf{e}_i; \tau) \cdot a(\phi^U, \phi^V) \cdot c^U(\mathbf{e}_j; \tau) \quad \text{and} \quad F_i = c^V(\mathbf{e}_i; \tau) \cdot f(\phi^V),$$

respectively. Problems (6) and (8) can be viewed as GMLS analogues of a conforming Petrov-Galerkin discretization of (3) and its equivalent linear algebraic form. In this context, the reciprocal fields u_j^τ and v_i^τ are analogues of modal bases for the trial and test spaces. As a result, in what follows we shall generate the necessary approximants by simply restricting bilinear forms and right hand side functionals to the reciprocal spaces. Just as in the finite element case "assembling" (8) amounts to computing the action of the bilinear form $a(\cdot, \cdot)$ and the right hand side functional f on the polynomial basis functions ϕ^U and ϕ^V.

However, application of (8) for the numerical solution of PDEs is subject to additional considerations, if one wishes to obtain a computationally effective scheme. This has to do with the fact that in the PDE context $a(\cdot, \cdot)$ and f usually involve integration over a domain Ω. In such a case one would have to consider a GMLS regression with a kernel w whose support contains the entire problem domain. Unfortunately, this renders (8) dense, making the discretization impractical for all but small academic problems.

The key to obtaining computationally efficient discretizations from (6), resp. (8) is to apply the GMLS formulation *locally*. In the following section we specialize the approach to generate a non-conforming scheme for a model PDE.

3.1   Application to a Model PDE

Consider the advection-diffusion equation with homogeneous Dirichlet boundary conditions

$$-\varepsilon \Delta u + \mathbf{b} \cdot \nabla u = f \text{ in } \Omega \quad \text{and} \quad u = 0 \text{ on } \Gamma, \tag{9}$$

where $\Omega \subset \mathbb{R}^d$, $d = 1, 2, 3$ is a bounded region with Lipschitz continuous boundary Γ, $\mathbf{b}$ is a solenoidal vector field, and f is a given function. The weak form of (9) is given by the abstract problem (3) with $U = V = H_0^1(\Omega)$,

$$a(u, v) = \int_\Omega \varepsilon \nabla u \cdot \nabla v + (\mathbf{b} \cdot \nabla u)v dx \quad \text{and} \quad f(v) = \int_\Omega f v dx.$$

Let Ω^h and $X^\eta \subset \Omega$ denote a conforming partition of the computational domain into finite elements $\{\mathcal{K}_k\}_{k=1}^{N_e}$ and a point cloud comprising points $\{\boldsymbol{x}_i\}_{i=1}^{N_p}$, respectively. We seek an approximation of u on the point cloud, i.e., the DoFs are associated with X^η rather than the underlying mesh. Furthermore, no relationship is assumed between Ω^h and X^η, in practice though one may define X^η using mesh entities such as element vertices, element centroids, etc.

Using the additive property of the integral $a(u, v) = \sum_{k=1}^{N_e} a_k(u, v)$ and $f(v) = \sum_{k=1}^{N_e} f_k(v)$, where $a_k(\cdot, \cdot)$ and $f_k(\cdot)$ are restrictions of $a(\cdot, \cdot)$ and $f(\cdot)$ to element $\mathcal{K}_k$. To discretize (9) we will apply GMLS *locally* to approximate $a_k(\cdot, \cdot)$ and $f_k(\cdot)$. Since $U = V$ we can use the same regression process for the trial and test spaces and drop the sub/superscripts used earlier to distinguish between them. We define the local GMLS kernel as $w(\mathcal{K}_k, \boldsymbol{x}_j) := \rho(|\boldsymbol{b}_k - \boldsymbol{x}_j|)$, where $\boldsymbol{b}_k$ is the centroid of $\mathcal{K}_k$ and $\rho(\cdot)$ is a radially symmetric function with $\operatorname{supp} \rho = O(h)$. This kernel satisfies the assumption $W(a_k(u, \cdot)) = W(f_k)$. The GMLS approximants of $a_k(\cdot, \cdot)$ and $f_k(\cdot)$ will be constructed from point samples close to $\boldsymbol{b}_k$ using the local sampling set $S_k = \{\delta_{\boldsymbol{x}_j} \mid w(\mathcal{K}_k, \boldsymbol{x}_j) > 0\}$ with cardinality n_k. We assume that the support of ρ is large enough to ensure that S_k is

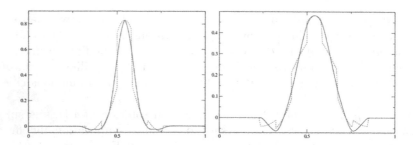

Fig. 1. Comparison of a Moving Least Squares basis function (black) and a composite reciprocal basis function $[u]_i$ (red) in one-dimensions for $\Phi = P^2$ and two different kernels. (Color figure online)

P^m-unisolvent. We also have the GMLS reciprocal set $S^k = \{u_1^k, \ldots, u_{n_k}^k\}$ with $u_i^k := \boldsymbol{c}(\boldsymbol{e}_i^k; \boldsymbol{b}_k) \cdot \boldsymbol{\phi}$ and $\boldsymbol{e}_i^k \in \mathbb{R}^{n_k}$. We obtain the local GMLS approximants of the elemental forms by restricting each $a_k(\cdot, \cdot)$ to $S^k \times S^k$, i.e.,

$$\widetilde{a}_k(u_j^k, u_i^k) := \boldsymbol{c}(\boldsymbol{e}_i^k; \boldsymbol{b}_k) \cdot a_k(\boldsymbol{\phi}, \boldsymbol{\phi}) \cdot \boldsymbol{c}(\boldsymbol{e}_j^k; \boldsymbol{b}_k)$$

The matrix $a_k(\boldsymbol{\phi}, \boldsymbol{\phi}) \in \mathbb{R}^{n_q \times n_q}$ has element

$$(a_k(\boldsymbol{\phi}, \boldsymbol{\phi}))_{st} = \int_{\mathcal{K}_k} \nabla \phi_s \cdot \nabla \phi_t dx$$

Likewise, we have that $\widetilde{f}_k(u_i^k) = \boldsymbol{c}(\boldsymbol{e}_i^k; \boldsymbol{b}_k) \cdot f_k(\boldsymbol{\phi})$ where $f_k(\boldsymbol{\phi}) \in \mathbb{R}^{n_q}$ with

$$(f_k(\boldsymbol{\phi}))_s = \int_{\mathcal{K}_k} f \, \phi_s dx \,.$$

The local approximants $\widetilde{a}_k(\cdot, \cdot)$ and $\widetilde{f}_k(\cdot)$ give rise to a local matrix $K_{ij}^k = \boldsymbol{c}(\boldsymbol{e}_i^k; \boldsymbol{b}_k) \cdot a_k(\boldsymbol{\phi}, \boldsymbol{\phi}) \cdot \boldsymbol{c}(\boldsymbol{e}_j^k; \boldsymbol{b}_k)$ and a local vector $F_i^k = \boldsymbol{c}^V(\boldsymbol{e}_i; \tau) \cdot f(\boldsymbol{\phi})$, respectively, which are analogues of the element stiffness matrix and load vector in FEA.

To define the global approximants of $a(\cdot, \cdot)$ and $f(\cdot)$ from the local ones we first need to define a global discrete space to supply the global test and trial functions. We construct this space as $[S] = \cup_{\mathcal{K}_k \in \Omega^h} S^k$ and denote its elements by $[u]$. Stacking all local DoF in a single vector $[\boldsymbol{a}] := \{\boldsymbol{a}^1, \ldots, \boldsymbol{a}^{N_e}\}$ produces the global DoF set for $[u]$. We now define the global approximants by summing over all elements, i.e.,

$$\widetilde{a}([u], [v]) := \sum_{\mathcal{K}_k \in \Omega^h} \widetilde{a}_k(u^k, v^k) \quad \text{and} \quad \widetilde{f}([v]) := \sum_{\mathcal{K}_k \in \Omega^h} \widetilde{f}_k(v^k),$$

where $u^k, v^k \in S^k$. In general, a sampling functional $\delta_{\boldsymbol{x}_j}$ can belong to multiple local sampling sets S_k, which means that $[u]$ will be multivalued at $\boldsymbol{x}_j$. In fact, one can show that the global approximants $\widetilde{a}(\cdot, \cdot)$ and $\widetilde{f}(\cdot)$ can be generated by using a composite "basis" of the global space $[S]$ assembled from the local reciprocal bases as

$$[u]_i := \sum_{\mathcal{K}_k \in \Omega^h} \chi_k u_i^k ,$$

where χ_k is the characteristic function of element $\mathcal{K}_k$. Figure 1 shows an example of a composite global basis function in one dimension and compares it to a Moving Least Squares basis function used in many meshfree Galerkin methods; see, e.g., [5,11].

The multivalued character of the global approximation space $[S]$ means that $\tilde{a}(\cdot, \cdot)$ and $\tilde{f}(\cdot)$ are *non-conforming* approximations of $a(\cdot, \cdot)$ and $f(\cdot)$, resembling the type of "broken" forms one sees in Discontinuous Galerkin (DG) and interior penalty methods. The similarity between $\tilde{a}(\cdot, \cdot)$ and a broken DG form indicates that the former may not be stable without any additional modifications. At the same time, this similarity also suggests that standard DG terms could be used to stabilize $\tilde{a}(\cdot, \cdot)$. Below we describe one possible scheme that results from this approach, focusing on the handling of the local bilinear forms and skipping for brevity the modifications to $f_k(\cdot)$

Following [8] we integrate the advective term in the element forms $a_k(\cdot, \cdot)$ and use the upwind trace $\vec{u}$ on each boundary facet to obtain the upwind element form

$$\vec{a}_k(u, v) = \sum_{\mathcal{K}_k \in \Omega^h} \int_{\mathcal{K}_k} \nabla u \cdot \nabla v dx - \int_{\mathcal{K}_k} u\mathbf{b} \cdot \nabla v dx + \int_{\partial \mathcal{K}_k} \vec{u}\, v\mathbf{b} \cdot \mathbf{n}_k dS$$

To stabilize the diffusive term we use the interior penalty method [1]. These steps transform the element forms into the following stabilized, "DG" versions

$$a_k^{DG}(u, v) = \vec{a}_k(u, v) - \sum_{\mathcal{F}} \int_{\mathcal{F}} \{\!\{\nabla u\}\!\} \cdot [\![v]\!] dS + \int_{\mathcal{F}} v \cdot [\![u]\!] dS - \frac{\delta}{h} \int_{\mathcal{F}} [\![u]\!] \cdot [\![v]\!]_{\mathcal{F}} dS,$$

where the sum is over all element facets in the mesh, $\{\!\{\cdot\}\!\}$ is the average operator, $[\![\cdot]\!]$ is the jump operator, and δ is stabilization parameter; see [8, p.1261].

We then restrict the elemental DG forms $a_k^{DG}(u, v)$ to the composite reciprocal space, i.e., $[S] \times [S]$ to obtain their local GMLS approximants $\tilde{a}_k^{DG}(\cdot, \cdot)$. Summation of the latter over all elements then yields the global DG form $\tilde{a}^{DG}(\cdot, \cdot)$.

4   Numerical Examples

To demonstrate the approach we have implemented the "DG" scheme from Sect. 3.1 in one-dimension using the element centroids to define the point cloud X^η. The left plot in Fig. 2 highlights the optimal convergence of the scheme for several different polynomial reproduction spaces. We see that in each case the numerical solution attains the best approximation-theoretic rate for the respective polynomial order.

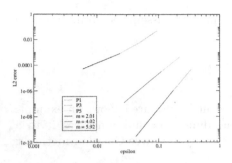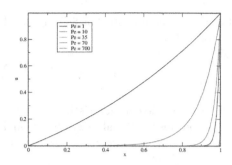

Fig. 2. Left: convergence of the nonconforming "DG" scheme for different polynomial orders. Right: nonconforming "DG" solution of one-dimensional advection-diffusion problem for increasing Péclet numbers.

The right plot in Fig. 2 demonstrates the scheme for increasing Péclet numbers. Solution plots in this figure reveal that the simple upwind strategy adopted in our implementation is adequate for low to moderate Péclet numbers. Future work will consider improved upwinding for strong advection-dominated problems, alternatives to the interior penalty stabilization, and extension to higher dimensions.

Acknowledgments. This material is based upon work supported by the U.S. Department of Energy, Office of Science, Office of Advanced Scientific Computing Research under Award Number DE-SC-0000230927, and the Laboratory Directed Research and Development program at Sandia National Laboratories.

References

1. Arnold, D.: An interior penalty finite element method with discontinuous elements. SIAM J. Numer. Anal. **19**(4), 742–760 (1982)
2. Arnold, D.N., Brezzi, F., Cockburn, B., Marini, L.D.: Unified analysis of discontinuous Galerkin methods for elliptic problems. SIAM J. Numer. Anal. **39**, 1749–1779 (2002)
3. Atluri, S.N., Zhu, T.: A new meshless local Petrov-Galerkin (MLPG) approach in computational mechanics. Comput. Mech. **22**(2), 117–127 (1998)
4. Babuška, I., Aziz, A.: On the angle condition in the finite element method. SIAM J. Numer. Anal. **13**(2), 214–226 (1976)
5. Belytschko, T., Lu, Y.Y., Gu, L.: Element-free Galerkin methods. Int. J. Numer. Methods Eng. **37**(2), 229–256 (1994)
6. Chen, J.S., Hillman, M., Rüter, M.: An arbitrary order variationally consistent integration for Galerkin meshfree methods. Int. J. Numer. Methods Eng. **95**(5), 387–418 (2013)
7. Chen, J.S., Wu, C.T., Yoon, S., You, Y.: A stabilized conforming nodal integration for Galerkin mesh-free methods. Int. J. Numer. Methods Eng. **50**(2), 435–466 (2001)

8. Cockburn, B., Dong, B., Guzmán, J.: Optimal convergence of the original DG method for the transport-reaction equation on special meshes. SIAM J. Numer. Anal. **46**(3), 1250–1265 (2008)
9. Harwick, M., Clay, R., Boggs, P., Walsh, E., Larzelere, A., Altshuler, A.: Dart system analysis. Technical report SAND2005-4647, Sandia National Laboratories (2005)
10. Mirzaei, D., Schaback, R., Dehghan, M.: On generalized moving least squares and diffuse derivatives. IMA J. Numer. Anal. **32**(3), 983–1000 (2012)
11. Nayroles, B., Touzot, G., Villon, P.: Generalizing the finite element method: diffuse approximation and diffuse elements. Comput. Mech. **10**(5), 307–318 (1992)
12. Puso, M.A., Chen, J.S., Zywicz, E., Elmer, W.: Meshfree and finite element nodal integration methods. Int. J. Numer. Methods Eng. **74**(3), 416–446 (2008)
13. Shewchuk, J.R.: What is a good linear element? Interpolation, conditioning, and quality measures. In: 11th International Meshing Roundtable, pp. 115–126 (2002)
14. Trask, N., Perego, M., Bochev, P.: A high-order staggered meshless method for elliptic problems. SIAM J. Sci. Comput. **39**(2), A479–A502 (2017)
15. Wendland, H.: Scattered Data Approximation, vol. 17. Cambridge University Press, Cambridge (2004)
16. Wheeler, M.F.: An elliptic collocation-finite element method with interior penalties. SIAM J. Numer. Anal. **15**(1), 152–161 (1978)

An Adaptive LOOCV-Based Algorithm for Solving Elliptic PDEs via RBF Collocation

R. Cavoretto[(✉)] [ID] and A. De Rossi [ID]

Department of Mathematics "Giuseppe Peano", University of Torino,
Via Carlo Alberto 10, 10123 Torino, Italy
{roberto.cavoretto,alessandra.derossi}@unito.it

Abstract. We present a new adaptive scheme for solving elliptic partial differential equations (PDEs) through a radial basis function (RBF) collocation method. Our adaptive algorithm is meshless and it is characterized by the use of an error indicator, which depends on a leave-one-out cross validation (LOOCV) technique. This approach allows us to locate the areas that need to be refined, also including the chance to add or remove adaptively any points. The algorithm turns out to be flexible and effective by means of a good interaction between error indicator and refinement procedure. Numerical experiments point out the performance of our scheme.

Keywords: Meshfree methods · Adaptive algorithms · Refinement techniques · Poisson problems

1 Introduction

In this paper we present a new adaptive refinement algorithm for solving 2D elliptic partial differential equations (PDEs) such as Poisson type problems. Our adaptive scheme is applied to Kansa's method, which is known as a nonsymmetric radial basis function (RBF) collocation scheme [6]. This approach has spawned several works, which engaged practitioners and scientists coming from many areas of science and engineering. Several adaptive techniques are used for modeling PDE problems through different RBF methods (see e.g. [2,9]). Basically, our adaptive algorithm is characterized by the use of a *leave-one-out cross validation* (LOOCV) technique, which was originally proposed by Rippa [10]. While the LOOCV was introduced to find an optimal value of the RBF

The authors acknowledge support from the Department of Mathematics "Giuseppe Peano" of the University of Torino via Project 2019 "Mathematics for applications". Moreover, this work was partially supported by INdAM – GNCS Project 2019 "Kernel-based approximation, multiresolution and subdivision methods and related applications". This research has been accomplished within RITA (Research ITalian network on Approximation).

I. Lirkov and S. Margenov (Eds.): LSSC 2019, LNCS 11958, pp. 76–83, 2020.
https://doi.org/10.1007/978-3-030-41032-2_8

shape parameter (see [4]), in this work it is used as an error indicator within the refinement procedure. This strategy enables us to identify which areas need to be refined by adding new points. After that phase, we further refine the discretization points based on information arising from another error estimate. This stage of adaptive refinement extends the residual subsampling method proposed in [3], thus allowing us to get an improvements in terms of accuracy. In our numerical experiments we show the performance of our algorithm, which is tested by solving a few Poisson problems. For solving large scale problems one could also think of applying our LOOCV-based scheme to local collocation methods [12].

The paper is organized as follows. In Sect. 2 we briefly describe Kansa's RBF collocation method. In Sect. 3 we present the adaptive refinement scheme proposed for solving elliptic PDE problems. Section 4 illustrates numerical experiments carried out to show the performance of our algorithm.

2   Kansa's Collocation Method

Given a domain $\Omega \subset \mathbb{R}^d$ and a linear elliptic partial differential operator $\mathcal{L}$, we define a PDE of the form

$$\mathcal{L}u(\boldsymbol{x}) = f(\boldsymbol{x}), \qquad \boldsymbol{x} \in \Omega, \tag{1}$$

with Dirichlet boundary conditions

$$u(\boldsymbol{x}) = g(\boldsymbol{x}), \qquad \boldsymbol{x} \in \partial\Omega. \tag{2}$$

For Kansa's approach we express the approximate solution $\hat{u}$ as a linear combination of basis functions as commonly happens for RBF interpolation (see e.g. [4]), i.e.

$$\hat{u}(\boldsymbol{x}) = \sum_{j=1}^{N} c_j \phi_\varepsilon(||\boldsymbol{x} - \boldsymbol{z}_j||_2), \tag{3}$$

where c_j denote unknown real coefficients, $|| \cdot ||_2$ is the Euclidean norm, and $\phi_\varepsilon : [0, \infty) \to \mathbb{R}$ is some RBF depending on a positive *shape parameter* ε such that

$$\phi_\varepsilon(||\boldsymbol{x} - \boldsymbol{z}||_2) = \phi(\varepsilon||\boldsymbol{x} - \boldsymbol{z}||_2), \qquad \forall \boldsymbol{x}, \boldsymbol{z} \in \Omega.$$

As an example, globally supported RBFs that are commonly used for solving PDEs are listed below along with their smoothness degrees (see [11]):

$$\phi_\varepsilon(r) = (1 + \varepsilon^2 r^2)^{-1/2}, \qquad \text{Inverse MultiQuadric } C^\infty,$$
$$\phi_\varepsilon(r) = \exp(-\varepsilon r)(\varepsilon^3 r^3 + 6\varepsilon^2 r^2 + 15\varepsilon r + 15), \quad \text{Matérn } C^6.$$

Note that the value of ε significantly affects stability and accuracy of a RBF method. In particular, in (3) the accuracy is typically high (low) when ε is small (large), but the ill-conditioning is severe (acceptable). For further details, see [4].

In (3) we distinguish between *centers* $Z_N = \{z_1, \ldots, z_N\}$ and *collocation points* $X_N = \{x_1, \ldots, x_N\} \subset \Omega$. Even though such sets of points can formally be distinct, for the following discussion we assume that $Z_N = X_N$ (see [4]). Then, for our purposes we split the set X_N in the two subsets X_{N_I} of interior points and X_{N_B} of boundary points, with $X_N = X_{N_I} \cup X_{N_B}$, N_I and N_B indicating the number of interior and boundary points, respectively.

When matching the differential equation (1) and the boundary conditions (2) at the collocation points X_N, we get the collocation system of linear equations

$$Ac = u,$$

where A is the collocation matrix

$$A = \begin{bmatrix} \hat{A}_{\mathcal{L}} \\ \hat{A} \end{bmatrix}, \tag{4}$$

whose two blocks in (4) are given by

$$(\hat{A}_{\mathcal{L}})_{ij} = \mathcal{L}\phi(\|x_i - z_j\|_2), \ x_i \in X_{N_I}, \ z_j \in Z_N,$$
$$\hat{A}_{ij} = \phi(\|x_i - z_j\|_2), \quad x_i \in X_{N_B}, \ z_j \in Z_N,$$

while u is the vector of entries

$$u_i = \begin{cases} f(x_i), & x_i \in X_{N_I}, \\ g(x_i), & x_i \in X_{N_B}. \end{cases}$$

Kansa's approach is known to be a nonsymmetric collocation method. Theoretical analysis and further considerations on this popular RBF method can be found, for instance, in [5,8].

3 Adaptive LOOCV-Based Scheme

3.1 Basics on LOOCV

The idea of LOOCV for Kansa's method can be depicted in the following way. At first, the data are split into two distinct sets: a *training set* $\{u(x_1), \ldots, u(x_{k-1}), u(x_{k+1}), \ldots, u(x_N)\}$, and a *validation set* that is merely made of the single value $u(x_k)$, i.e. the one left out when generating the training set [4].

Given an index $k \in \{1, \ldots, N\}$ and a fixed value of ε, the partial RBF approximant is given by

$$\hat{u}^{[k]}(x) = \sum_{j=1, \ j \neq k}^{N} c_j^{[k]} \phi_\varepsilon(\|x - z_j\|_2),$$

whose coefficients $c_j^{[k]}$ are found by collocating the training data, that is

$$\mathcal{L}\hat{u}^{[k]}(x_i) = f(x_i), \qquad x_i \in X_{N_I},$$
$$\hat{u}^{[k]}(x_i) = g(x_i), \qquad x_i \in X_{N_B}, \qquad \text{for } i = 1, \ldots, k-1, k+1, \ldots, N.$$

In order to give a measure of the quality of this attempt, we define the absolute error

$$e_k = |u(\boldsymbol{x}_k) - \hat{u}^{[k]}(\boldsymbol{x}_k)|, \tag{5}$$

at that validation point $\boldsymbol{x}_k$, which is not used to determine the approximant. Now, if we compute the error in (5), for all $k = 1, \ldots, N$, we get a vector $e = (e_1, \ldots, e_N)^T$, which can be viewed as an error indicator to identify the regions which require to be refined by adding any points in the neighborhood of the selected point. However, instead of using (5), the computation of the error components can be done in a more efficient way without solving N collocation problems, each of size $(N-1) \times (N-1)$. In fact, in [10] Rippa shows that the computation of the error terms can be simplified to a single formula. The rule (5) can thus be rewritten as

$$e_k = \left| \frac{c_k}{A_{kk}^{-1}} \right|, \qquad k = 1, \ldots, N, \tag{6}$$

where c_k is the k-th coefficient of the full approximate solution (3) and A_{kk}^{-1} is the k-th diagonal element of the inverse of the corresponding $N \times N$ collocation matrix A in (4).

3.2   Error Indicator and Refinement via LOOCV

At the beginning of our adaptive scheme, we define an initial set $X_{N^{(1)}}^1 \equiv X_N = \{\boldsymbol{x}_1^{(1)}, \ldots, \boldsymbol{x}_{N^{(1)}}^{(1)}\}$ of grid collocation points. It is then split into two subsets, i.e. the set $X_{N_I^{(j)}}^1 = \{\boldsymbol{x}_1^{(j)}, \ldots, \boldsymbol{x}_{N_I^{(j)}}^{(j)}\}$ of interior points, and the set $X_{N_B^{(j)}}^1 = \{\boldsymbol{x}_1^{(j)}, \ldots, \boldsymbol{x}_{N_B^{(j)}}^{(j)}\}$ of boundary points, where $j = 1, 2, \ldots$ identifies the iteration of the adaptive algorithm. Observe that the superscript [1] above denotes the first phase of our scheme, while the subscript $N^{(j)}$ defines the number of collocation points in the j-th iteration of that same phase.

Then, for a fixed tolerance $\tau > 0$ in our adaptive process, from (6) we can iteratively define an error indicator via LOOCV given by

$$e_k^{(j)} = \left| \frac{c_k}{A_{kk}^{-1}} \right|, \qquad k = 1, \ldots, N^{(j)}, \qquad j = 1, 2, \ldots, \tag{7}$$

where in the absolute value argument any reference to the iteration is omitted to avoid confusion in the notation. If the error indicator (7) is such that $e_k^{(j)} > \tau$, then a refinement is applied in the neighborhood of $\boldsymbol{x}_k$. However, in order to do that, first we have to compute the so-called *separation distance*

$$q_{X_{N^{(j)}}^1} = \frac{1}{2} \min_{u \neq v} \|\boldsymbol{x}_u^{(j)} - \boldsymbol{x}_v^{(j)}\|_2, \qquad \boldsymbol{x}_u^{(j)}, \boldsymbol{x}_v^{(j)} \in X_{N^{(j)}}^1, \qquad j = 1, 2, \ldots, \tag{8}$$

and then we sum up or subtract the quantity in (8) to one (both) coordinate(s) of the point $\boldsymbol{x}_k$. In particular, defining explicitly the coordinates of $\boldsymbol{x}_k$, i.e. setting

$\boldsymbol{x}_k = (\boldsymbol{x}_{k,1}, \boldsymbol{x}_{k,2})$, the refinement strategy consists in the addition of four points around $\boldsymbol{x}_k$. More precisely, the coordinates of these four points are $(\boldsymbol{x}_{k,1}, \boldsymbol{x}_{k,2} + q_{X^1_{N^{(j)}}})$, $(\boldsymbol{x}_{k,1} - q_{X^1_{N^{(j)}}}, \boldsymbol{x}_{k,2})$, $(\boldsymbol{x}_{k,1}, \boldsymbol{x}_{k,2} - q_{X^1_{N^{(j)}}})$ and $(\boldsymbol{x}_{k,1} + q_{X^1_{N^{(j)}}}, \boldsymbol{x}_{k,2})$. The refinement procedure stops when all components of error terms in (7) are less than or equal to the tolerance τ.

3.3 Further Adaptive Refinement

At the second phase of the algorithm we further refine the collocation points based on other information coming from a new error estimate. Here, this adaptive refinement is a sort of extension of the residual subsampling method given in [3], and later modified for RBF partition of unity collocation [1]. Basically, our procedure is obtained by means of an efficient combination between an error indicator and a refinement technique, which consists in solving, estimating and finally adding or removing adaptively any points in the areas selected by the process.

Therefore, we start from the output of the previous phase described in Subsect. 3.2 and re-name that final set as $X^2_{N^{(1)}}$, where the superscript ^{2} denotes the second stage of our adaptive process. Then, for $k = 1, 2, \ldots$, we compute iteratively two solutions of the form (3), called $\hat{u}$ and $\hat{u}^a$, respectively. In particular, $\hat{u}$ is found by considering the set $X^2_{N^{(k)}}$ of collocation points, while $\hat{u}^a$ is obtained by taking the same set $X^2_{N^{(k)}}$ with additional boundary points outside the domain. The resulting set is denoted as $X^{2,a}_{N^{(k)}}$. Further details on this strategy of adding points, which is here used to get two approximate RBF solutions, can be found in [4, Chapter 39].

After defining a set $Y^{(k)} = \{\boldsymbol{y}^{(k)}_1, \ldots, \boldsymbol{y}^{(k)}_{N^{(k)}}\}$ of check points, we validate the results via the error indicator defined by

$$E^{(k)}_i = |\hat{u}(\boldsymbol{y}^{(k)}_i) - \hat{u}^a(\boldsymbol{y}^{(k)}_i)|, \qquad \boldsymbol{y}^{(k)}_i \in Y^{(k)}. \tag{9}$$

At the moment we fix two thresholds τ_{low} and τ_{upp}, such that $0 < \tau_{low} < \tau_{upp}$, which allow us to refine the set of discretization points when the estimate indicator (9) does not give precise enough result, or coarsen the set of discretization points if the level of accuracy achieved is under the tolerance τ_{low}. This process thus leads to an addition or removal of points, thus making this scheme adaptive. The iterative procedure stops once the refinement process is completed.

4   Numerical Results

In this section we show some results derived from application of our adaptive algorithm, which is implemented in MATLAB. All results are carried out on a laptop with an Intel(R) Core(TM) i7-6500U CPU 2.50 GHz processor and 4 GB RAM.

In the following we restrict our attention on solution of some 2D elliptic PDE problems with Kansa's collocation method. More precisely, we consider some

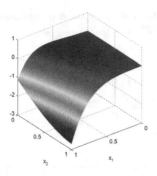 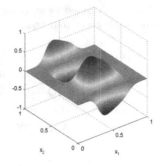

Fig. 1. Exact solutions of Poisson problems u_1 (left) and u_2 (right).

Poisson problems, taking the Laplace operator $\mathcal{L} = -\Delta$ in (1). To analyze the performance of our adaptive scheme, we take two test problems defined on the domain $\Omega = [0,1]^2$ (see [1,7]). The analytic solutions of such Poisson problems are given by

$$u_1(x_1, x_2) = \frac{1}{20} \exp(4x_1) \cos(2x_1 + x_2),$$

$$u_2(x_1, x_2) = \sinh(0.3(4x_1 - 4) \sin(8x_2 - 4) \exp(-(4x_1 - 2.1)^4)),$$

while their graphical representation is shown in Fig. 1.

Moreover, we remark that in the second stage of the algorithm we used Halton points [4] as check points. It is however obvious that the choice of these validation points is absolutely arbitrary and other possible distributions can be used.

In our tests we illustrate the performance of the adaptive algorithm applied to Kansa's approach by using RBFs of different smoothness as Inverse Multi-Quadric C^∞ (IMQ) and Matérn C^6 (M6) functions (see Sect. 2). In these experiments we begin the iterative process by considering $N = 225$ grid collocation points, consisting of $N_I = 169$ interior points and $N_B = 56$ boundary points. In order to investigate the accuracy of the adaptive scheme, we compute the Root Mean Square Error (RMSE), i.e.

$$\text{RMSE} = \sqrt{\frac{1}{N_{eval}} \sum_{i=1}^{N_{eval}} |u(\boldsymbol{\xi}_i) - \hat{u}(\boldsymbol{\xi}_i)|^2},$$

where the $\boldsymbol{\xi}_i$, $i = 1, \ldots, N_{eval}$, constitute a set of grid evaluation points and $N_{eval} = 40 \times 40$. Further, to analyze the stability of the numerical method, we evaluate the Condition Number (CN) of the collocation matrix A in (4) by making use of the MATLAB command cond.

After carrying out a preliminary analysis of the algorithm behavior with different values of ε in the interval $[1, 6]$, in Table 1 we show a summary of all results obtained by using IMQ and M6 with $\varepsilon = 4$, also indicating the total

Table 1. Results obtained by starting from $N = 225$ grid collocation points and using various RBFs with $\varepsilon = 4$ and $(\tau_{low}, \tau_{upp}) = (10^{-8}, 10^{-4})$.

Problem	RBF	N_{fin}	RMSE	CN	no. iter	τ
u_1	M6	547	9.22e−6	7.57e+11	6	0.05
u_1	IMQ	810	4.54e−5	5.88e+15	9	0.05
u_2	M6	1086	2.97e−5	3.91e+11	6	0.1
u_2	IMQ	695	2.23e−5	3.50e+14	4	0.1

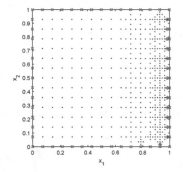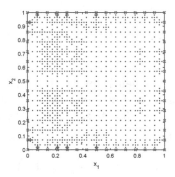

Fig. 2. Final discretization points for u_1 (left) and u_2 (right) using M6 with $\varepsilon = 4$.

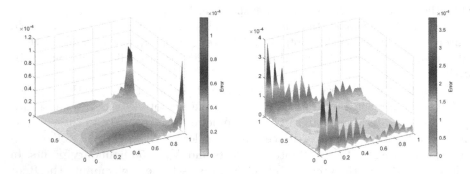

Fig. 3. Absolute error for u_1 (left) and u_2 (right) using M6 with $\varepsilon = 4$.

number N_{fin} of collocation points obtained to achieve the final result. While the value of τ associated with the LOOCV is related to the PDE problem, the values of $(\tau_{low}, \tau_{upp}) = (10^{-8}, 10^{-4})$ are kept fixed. In Fig. 2 we show some graphs with the final configurations of discretization points, while Fig. 3 shows some plots of the absolute error for RBF solution, i.e. $|u(\boldsymbol{\xi}_i) - \hat{u}(\boldsymbol{\xi}_i)|$, $i = 1, \ldots, N_{eval}$, computed on the grid of $N_{eval} = 40 \times 40$ evaluation points.

From an analysis of the numerical results, we can note that our adaptive refinement scheme works well for both differential problems. The algorithm identifies the areas of Ω with significant variations, increasing the number of collocation points only in those domain parts in which the accuracy is not enough.

As regards the stability, we remark that the CN assumes values around 10^{+11}–10^{+15}. Even though RBF-based methods can suffer from severe ill-conditioning (see e.g. [4]), we observe as a good refinement strategy allows us to control it, thus avoiding the number of discretization points increasing by too much. Finally, in Table 1 we indicate the number of iteration required, observing that our iterative algorithm completes its refinement process in only a few seconds.

References

1. Cavoretto, R., De Rossi, A.: Adaptive meshless refinement schemes for RBF-PUM collocation. Appl. Math. Lett. **90**, 131–138 (2019)
2. Chen, W., Fu, Z.-J., Chen, C.S.: Recent Advances on Radial Basis Function Collocation Methods. Springer Briefs in Applied Science and Technology. Springer, Heidelberg (2014). https://doi.org/10.1007/978-3-642-39572-7
3. Driscoll, T.A., Heryudono, A.R.H.: Adaptive residual subsampling methods for radial basis function interpolation and collocation problems. Comput. Math. Appl. **53**, 927–939 (2007)
4. Fasshauer, G.E.: Meshfree Approximation Methods with MATLAB. Interdisciplinary Mathematical Sciences, vol. 6. World Scientific Publishing Co., Singapore (2007)
5. Hon, Y.C., Schaback, R.: On unsymmetric collocation by radial basis functions. Appl. Math. Comput. **119**, 177–186 (2001)
6. Kansa, E.J.: Multiquadrics-a scattered data approximation scheme with applications to computational fluid-dynamics-II solutions to parabolic, hyperbolic and elliptic partial differential equations. Comput. Math. Appl. **19**, 147–161 (1990)
7. Larsson, E., Shcherbakov, V., Heryudono, A.: A least squares radial basis function partition of unity method for solving PDEs. SIAM J. Sci. Comput. **39**, A2538–A2563 (2017)
8. Lee, C.-F., Ling, L., Schaback, R.: On convergent numerical algorithms for unsymmetric collocation. Adv. Comput. Math. **30**, 339–354 (2009)
9. Oanh, D.T., Davydov, O., Phu, H.X.: Adaptive RBF-FD method for elliptic problems with point singularities in 2D. Appl. Math. Comput. **313**, 474–497 (2017)
10. Rippa, S.: An algorithm for selecting a good value for the parameter c in radial basis function interpolation. Adv. Comput. Math. **11**, 193–210 (1999)
11. Wendland, H.: Scattered Data Approximation. Cambridge Monographs on Applied and Computational Mathematics, vol. 17. Cambridge University Press, Cambridge (2005)
12. Yang, J., Liu, X., Wen, P.H.: The local Kansa's method for solving Berger equation. Eng. Anal. Bound. Elem. **57**, 16–22 (2015)

Adaptive Refinement Techniques
for RBF-PU Collocation

R. Cavoretto and A. De Rossi$^{(\boxtimes)}$

Department of Mathematics "Giuseppe Peano", University of Torino,
Via Carlo Alberto 10, 10123 Torino, Italy
{roberto.cavoretto,alessandra.derossi}@unito.it

Abstract. We propose new adaptive refinement techniques for solving
Poisson problems via a collocation radial basis function partition of unity
(RBF-PU) method. As the construction of an adaptive RBF-PU method
is still an open problem, we present two algorithms based on different
error indicators and refinement strategies that turn out to be particularly suited for a RBF-PU scheme. More precisely, the first algorithm
is characterized by an error estimator based on the comparison of two
collocation solutions evaluated on a coarser set and a finer one, while the
second one depends on an error estimate that is obtained by a comparison between the global collocation solution and the associated local RBF
interpolant. Numerical results support our study and show the effectiveness of our algorithms.

Keywords: Adaptive algorithms · Refinement strategies · RBF
methods · Meshless methods · Elliptic PDEs

1 Introduction

In this work we face the problem of designing new adaptive refinement algorithms
for solving 2D Poisson problems via radial basis functions (RBFs) methods.
Here, we focus on the construction of adaptive techniques based on the use of the
partition of unity (RBF-PU) method, which is known in literature in the context
of meshless methods for solution of interpolation and collocation problems (see
[5,6]). More precisely, we present two algorithms within a RBF-PU framework,
which in this paper we will call Algorithm 1 and Algorithm 2. The former is
characterized by an error estimator based on the comparison of two collocation
solutions evaluated on a coarser set and a finer one, the latter instead depends on
an error estimate that is obtained by a comparison between the global collocation

The authors acknowledge support from the Department of Mathematics "Giuseppe
Peano" of the University of Torino via Project 2019 "Mathematics for applications".
Moreover, this work was partially supported by INdAM – GNCS Project 2019 "Kernel-
based approximation, multiresolution and subdivision methods and related applications". This research has been accomplished within RITA (Research ITalian network
on Approximation).

I. Lirkov and S. Margenov (Eds.): LSSC 2019, LNCS 11958, pp. 84–91, 2020.
https://doi.org/10.1007/978-3-030-41032-2_9

solution and the associated local RBF interpolant. Numerical experiments show performance of both adaptive procedures.

The paper is organized as follows. Section 2 contains a description of the RBF-PU method for solving Poisson PDE problems. In Sect. 3 we present two adaptive algorithms that involve different refinement strategies. In Sect. 4 we show some numerical results obtained to illustrate the performance of the refinement techniques.

2   RBF-PU Method for 2D Poisson PDEs

2.1   The RBF-PU Method

Given an open and bounded domain $\Omega \subseteq \mathbb{R}^2$ and a function $u : \Omega \to \mathbb{R}$, we consider a set $X_N = \{x_i\}_{i=1}^N \subseteq \Omega$ of collocation points. The domain Ω is then covered by d subdomains Ω_j such that $\bigcup_{j=1}^d \Omega_j \supseteq \Omega$ with some mild overlaps among them [6]. In addition, we assume that the subdomains are circles of fixed radius so that the covering of Ω is given by $\{\Omega_j\}_{j=1}^d$. Associated with each subdomain Ω_j we introduce a family of compactly supported, nonnegative and continuous weights w_j, with $\mathrm{supp}(w_j) \subseteq \Omega_j$. The weight functions w_j form a partition of unity, i.e.

$$\sum_{j=1}^d w_j(x) = 1, \qquad \forall x \in \Omega.$$

As functions w_j we choose to use Shepard's weights, which involve compactly supported functions such as Wendland C^2 functions defined on Ω_j (see [5]). The RBF-PU method can thus be expressed as follows

$$\tilde{u}(x) = \sum_{j=1}^d w_j(x)\tilde{u}_j(x), \qquad x \in \Omega, \tag{1}$$

where $\tilde{u}_j$ defines the local RBF approximant

$$\tilde{u}_j(x) = \sum_{i=1}^{N_j} c_i^j \phi_\varepsilon(||x - x_i^j||_2). \tag{2}$$

In (2) N_j indicates the number of points $x_i^j \in X_{N_j} = X_N \cap \Omega_j$, c_i^j represents an unknown real coefficient, $||\cdot||_2$ is the Euclidean norm, and $\phi : \mathbb{R}_{\geq 0} \to \mathbb{R}$ denotes a RBF depending on a positive *shape parameter* ε such that

$$\phi_\varepsilon(||x - z||_2) = \phi(\varepsilon||x - z||_2), \qquad \forall x, z \in \Omega.$$

Some examples of popular RBFs [3,6] are given by

$$\phi_\varepsilon(r) = \sqrt{1 + \varepsilon^2 r^2}, \qquad\qquad \text{MultiQuadric (MQ)},$$
$$\phi_\varepsilon(r) = \exp(-\varepsilon r)(\varepsilon^3 r^3 + 6\varepsilon^2 r^2 + 15\varepsilon r + 15), \quad \text{Matérn } C^6 \text{ (M6)}.$$

2.2   Solution of Poisson Problems

In order to show some applications of the RBF-PU collocation method to elliptic PDEs, we define a Poisson problem with Dirichlet boundary conditions

$$
\begin{aligned}
-\Delta u(\boldsymbol{x}) &= f(\boldsymbol{x}), && \boldsymbol{x} \in \Omega, \\
u(\boldsymbol{x}) &= g(\boldsymbol{x}), && \boldsymbol{x} \in \partial\Omega,
\end{aligned}
\tag{3}
$$

where Δ is the Laplace operator [4]. Moreover, for convenience, we split the set X_N of discretization points into a set X_{N_I} of interior points and a set X_{N_B} of boundary points such that $X_N = X_{N_I} \cup X_{N_B}$, where N_I and N_B represent the number of interior and boundary collocation points, respectively.

Now, to find an approximate solution of the form (1), the problem (3) is discretized as follows

$$
\begin{aligned}
-\Delta \tilde{u}(\boldsymbol{x}_i) &= -\sum_{j=1}^{d} \Delta\left(w_j(\boldsymbol{x}_i)\tilde{u}_j(\boldsymbol{x}_i)\right) = f(\boldsymbol{x}_i), && \boldsymbol{x}_i \in X_{N_I}, \\
\tilde{u}(\boldsymbol{x}_i) &= \sum_{j=1}^{d} w_j(\boldsymbol{x}_i)\tilde{u}_j(\boldsymbol{x}_i) = g(\boldsymbol{x}_i), && \boldsymbol{x}_i \in X_{N_B}.
\end{aligned}
\tag{4}
$$

The differential operator can be expanded to get

$$
\begin{aligned}
-\Delta\left(w_j(\boldsymbol{x}_i)\tilde{u}_j(\boldsymbol{x}_i)\right) = {}&-\Delta w_j(\boldsymbol{x}_i)\tilde{u}_j(\boldsymbol{x}_i) - 2\nabla w_j(\boldsymbol{x}_i) \cdot \nabla\tilde{u}_j(\boldsymbol{x}_i) \\
&-w_j(\boldsymbol{x}_i)\Delta\tilde{u}_j(\boldsymbol{x}_i), && \boldsymbol{x}_i \in X_{N_I}.
\end{aligned}
\tag{5}
$$

We then define the vector $\tilde{\boldsymbol{u}}_j = (\tilde{u}_j(\boldsymbol{x}_1^j), \ldots, \tilde{u}_j(\boldsymbol{x}_{N_j}^j))^T$ of local nodal values and the local coefficient vector $\boldsymbol{c}_j = (c_1^j, \ldots, c_{N_j}^j)^T$. Further, if we denote by $A_j \in \mathbb{R}^{N_j \times N_j}$ the matrix of entries $A_{ki} = \phi_\varepsilon(\|\boldsymbol{x}_k^j - \boldsymbol{x}_i^j\|_2)$, $k,i = 1, \ldots, N_j$, from (2) we know that $\boldsymbol{c}_j = A_j^{-1}\tilde{\boldsymbol{u}}_j$, and so we obtain

$$
\Delta\tilde{\boldsymbol{u}}_j = A_j^{\Delta} A_j^{-1}\tilde{\boldsymbol{u}}_j, \qquad \nabla\tilde{\boldsymbol{u}}_j = A_j^{\nabla} A_j^{-1}\tilde{\boldsymbol{u}}_j,
\tag{6}
$$

where A_j^{Δ} and A_j^{∇}, $j = 1, \ldots, N_j$, are the matrices whose entries are

$$
(A_j^{\Delta})_{ki} = \Delta\phi(\|\boldsymbol{x}_k^j - \boldsymbol{x}_i^j\|_2), \qquad (A_j^{\nabla})_{ki} = \nabla\phi(\|\boldsymbol{x}_k^j - \boldsymbol{x}_i^j\|_2).
$$

Associated with each subdomain Ω_j, we consider the following diagonal matrix

$$
W_j^{\Delta} = \operatorname{diag}\left(\Delta w_j(\boldsymbol{x}_1^j), \ldots, \Delta w_j(\boldsymbol{x}_{N_j}^j)\right),
$$

with W_j^{∇} and W_j defined in similar way. To derive the discrete operator P_j, we differentiate (4) by using a product derivative rule and then apply the relations given in (6). By means of (5) and incorporating the Dirichlet boundary conditions, the discrete local Laplacian is given by

$$
(P_j)_{ki} = \begin{cases} (\bar{P}_j)_{ki}, & \boldsymbol{x}_i^j \in X_{N_I}, \\ \delta_{ki}, & \boldsymbol{x}_i^j \in X_{N_B}, \end{cases}
$$

where δ_{ki} is the Kronecker delta and

$$\bar{P}_j = \left(W_j^\Delta A_j + 2W_j^\nabla \cdot A_j^\nabla + W_j A_j^\Delta \right) A_j^{-1}.$$

By assembling the local matrices P_j into the global matrix P, i.e.

$$(P_j)_{ki} = \sum_{j=1}^{d} (P_j)_{\eta_{kj}, \eta_{ij}}, \qquad k, i = 1, \ldots, N,$$

we can obtain the global discrete operator and solve the sparse linear system

$$Py = u, \tag{7}$$

where $u = (u_1, \ldots, u_N)^T$ is defined by

$$u_i = \begin{cases} f(x_i), & x_i \in X_{N_I}, \\ g(x_i), & x_i \in X_{N_B}, \end{cases}$$

and the numerical solution $y = (\tilde{u}(x_1), \ldots, \tilde{u}(x_N))^T$ is obtained by inverting the collocation matrix P in (7) (see [1]).

3 Adaptive Refinement Techniques

In this section we present two refinement algorithms that can be used to solve a Poisson problem via the RBF-PU method. They are based on different error indicators and refinement strategies, which are applied in the adaptive process.

3.1 Algorithm 1

At first, we define two sets of grid collocation points of size $N_1^{(0)}$ and $N_2^{(0)}$, such that $N_1^{(0)} < N_2^{(0)}$, where the symbol $^{(0)}$ identifies the iteration number. For the sake of clarity, we denote these sets as $X_{N_1^{(0)}}$ and $X_{N_2^{(0)}}$, respectively. Then, the iterative procedure starts and, for $k = 0, 1, \ldots$, the collocation solutions $\tilde{u}_{N_1^{(k)}}$ and $\tilde{u}_{N_2^{(k)}}$ of the form (1) are computed on $N_1^{(k)}$ and $N_2^{(k)}$ collocation points. In order to know where we need to refine, we compare the two approximate solutions evaluated at the (coarser) set $X_{N_1^{(k)}}$, supposing that the solution computed on the set $X_{N_2^{(k)}}$ is more accurate than the previous one. So the error indicator is given by

$$E_i^{(k)} = |\tilde{u}_{N_2^{(k)}}(x_i^{(k)}) - \tilde{u}_{N_1^{(k)}}(x_i^{(k)})|, \qquad x_i^{(k)} \in X_{N_1^{(k)}}.$$

After fixing a tolerance τ, we detect all points $x_i^{(k)} \in X_{N_1^{(k)}}$ such that

$$E_i^{(k)} > \tau. \tag{8}$$

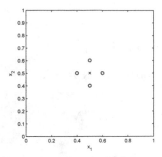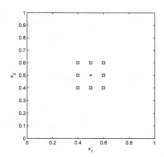

Fig. 1. Example of refinement around the point $\boldsymbol{x}_i^{(k)}$, marked by a black cross, to generate the new sets $X_{N_1^{(k+1)}}$ (left) and $X_{N_2^{(k+1)}}$ (right).

To refine the distribution of discretization points, we compute the *separation distance*

$$q_{X_{N_1}^{(k)}} = \frac{1}{2} \min_{i \neq j} \| \boldsymbol{x}_i^{(k)} - \boldsymbol{x}_j^{(k)} \|_2, \qquad \boldsymbol{x}_i^{(k)}, \boldsymbol{x}_j^{(k)} \in X_{N_1^{(k)}}, \tag{9}$$

and, afterward, for $k = 0, 1, \ldots$, we update the sets $X_{N_1^{(k+1)}}$ and $X_{N_2^{(k+1)}}$ of collocation points. In particular, if the condition (8) is satisfied, we add to $\boldsymbol{x}_i^{(k)}$ four and eight points to generate the sets $X_{N_1^{(k+1)}}$ and $X_{N_2^{(k+1)}}$, respectively (see Fig. 1, left to right). In both cases the new sets are obtained by either adding or subtracting the value of (9) to the components of $\boldsymbol{x}_i^{(k)}$. Notice that these new sets are such that $X_{N_1^{(k)}} \subset X_{N_2^{(k)}}$, for $k = 1, 2, \ldots$. Finally, the adaptive algorithm stops when there are no points anymore that satisfy the condition (8), returning the set $X_{N_2^{(k^*)}}$, with k^* denoting the last iteration.

3.2 Algorithm 2

At the beginning, we define a set $X_{N^{(0)}}$ of grid collocation points, i.e. $X_{N^{(0)}} = X_N$, with the symbol $^{(0)}$ identifying – as in Algorithm 1 – the iteration of our adaptive procedure. So for $k = 1, 2, \ldots$ we compute the collocation solution $\tilde{u}_{N^{(k)}}$ of the form (1), and then for each subdomain Ω_j, $j = 1, \ldots, d$, we construct a local RBF interpolant $I\tilde{u}_{\Omega_j}^{(k)}$. It is obtained by using the (local) approximate values, which are obtained by solving the global collocation system (7). Acting in this way, we can give an error estimate evaluating $\tilde{u}_{N^{(k)}}$ and $I\tilde{u}_{\Omega_j}^{(k)}$ on a set $\Xi^{(k)} = \{\boldsymbol{\xi}_i\}_{i=1}^{n_k}$ of check points, being n_k the number of check points at the k-th iteration. Thus, the error indicator is given by

$$E_i^{(k)} = |\tilde{u}_{N^{(k)}}(\boldsymbol{\xi}_i^{(k)}) - I\tilde{u}_{\Omega_j}^{(k)}(\boldsymbol{\xi}_i^{(k)})|, \qquad \boldsymbol{\xi}_i^{(k)} \in \Xi^{(k)}. \tag{10}$$

Now, fixed two positive tolerances $\tau_{\min} < \tau_{\max}$ and the k-th iteration, if $E_i^{(k)}$ in (10) is larger than $\tau_{\max}$, we add the point $\boldsymbol{\xi}_i^{(k)}$ among the collocation points.

Instead, if $E_i^{(k)}$ is smaller than $\tau_{\min}$, the check point is removed along with its nearest point. We can thus define the sets

$$Z_{T_{\max}^{(k)}} = \{\boldsymbol{\xi}_i^{(k)} \in \Xi^{(k)} : E_i^{(k)} > \tau_{\max}, i = 1, \dots, T_{\max}^{(k)}\}$$

and

$$Z_{T_{\min}^{(k)}} = \{\bar{\boldsymbol{x}}_i^{(k)} \in X_{N^{(k)}} : E_i^{(k)} < \tau_{\min}, i = 1, \dots, T_{\min}^{(k)}\},$$

where $\bar{\boldsymbol{x}}_i^{(k)}$ is the point closest to $\boldsymbol{\xi}_i^{(k)}$. Iteratively, for $k = 2, 3, \dots$, we can therefore obtain a new set of discretization points

$$X_{N^{(k)}} = X_{N_I^{(k)}} \cup X_{N_B^{(k)}}, \quad \text{where} \quad X_{N_I^{(k)}} = (X_{N_I^{(k-1)}} \cup Z_{T_{\max}^{(k-1)}}) \backslash Z_{T_{\min}^{(k-1)}}.$$

The process stops when the set $Z_{T_{\min}^{(k)}}$ is empty. Note that this adaptive refinement technique, which obeys the common paradigm of solve-estimate-refine/coarsen till a stopping criterion is satisfied, is based on the adaptive scheme given in [2].

4   Numerical Experiments

In this section we summarize the results obtained by the use of the refinement algorithms, described in Sect. 3 and implemented in MATLAB. All tests are carried out on a laptop with an Intel(R) Core(TM) i7-6500U CPU 2.50 GHz processor and 8 GB RAM.

In this study we focus on two Poisson problems of the form (3) defined on the unit square, i.e. the domain $\Omega = [0, 1]^2$. The exact solutions of our elliptic problems are

$$T1 : u_1(x_1, x_2) = \sin(x_1 + 2x_2^2) - \sin(2x_1^2 + (x_2 - 0.5)^2),$$
$$T2 : u_2(x_1, x_2) = \exp(-8((x_1 - 0.5)^2 + (x_2 - 0.05)^2)).$$

In Fig. 2 we give a graphical representation of these analytic solutions.

In the tests we illustrate the performance of the adaptive RBF-PU scheme obtained by using the M6-RBF with $\varepsilon = 3$ and applying each of the two refinement algorithms. On the one hand, for Algorithm 1 the two starting sets defined in Subsect. 3.1 consist of $N_1^{(0)} = 289$ and $N_2^{(0)} = 1089$ grid collocation points, while the tolerance is $\tau = 10^{-5}$. On the other hand, for Algorithm 2 described in Subsect. 3.2 we start with $N^{(0)} = 121$ grid collocation points, whose stepsize is h_0 and tolerances are given by $(\tau_{\min}, \tau_{\max}) = (10^{-8}, 10^{-5})$; then, we refine such points by generating iteratively grid points, which have a stepsize $h_k = h_{k-1}/2$, $k = 1, 2, \dots$, and are used as check points in (10). To measure the quality of our results, we compute the Root Mean Square Error (RMSE), that is,

$$\text{RMSE} = \left(\frac{1}{N_{eval}} \sum_{i=1}^{N_{eval}} |u(\boldsymbol{z}_i) - \tilde{u}(\boldsymbol{z}_i)|^2\right)^{1/2}.$$

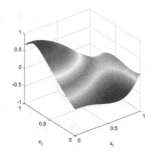 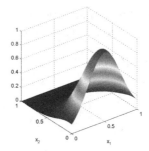

Fig. 2. Graphs of exact solutions of Poisson problems T1 (left) and T2 (right).

Table 1. Results obtained by using Algorithm 1 with M6, $\varepsilon = 3$ and $\tau = 10^{-5}$.

Test Problem	N_{fin}	RMSE	CN	Time
T1	1058	5.54e−6	1.35e+07	4.1
T2	1445	3.88e−6	1.03e+07	4.7

Table 2. Results obtained by using Algorithm 2 with M6, $\varepsilon = 3$ and $(\tau_{\min}, \tau_{\max}) = (10^{-8}, 10^{-5})$.

Test Problem	N_{fin}	RMSE	CN	Time
T1	920	1.64e−5	4.76e+06	3.2
T2	1079	1.19e−5	9.16e+06	4.4

which is evaluated on a grid of $N_{eval} = 40 \times 40$ evaluation points. Then, to analyze the stability of the method, we evaluate the Condition Number (CN) of the sparse collocation matrix P in (7) by using the MATLAB command condest. As to efficiency we report the CPU times computed in seconds.

Therefore, in Tables 1 and 2 we present the results obtained, also reporting the final number N_{fin} of discretization points. In addition, in Fig. 3 we show the "final grids" obtained by applying the adaptive refinement techniques.

From these results, we observe as Algorithm 1 increases the number of points only in some more specific areas where the solution behavior varies, while Algorithm 2 distributes the points in a more uniform way. This results in greater accuracy of Algorithm 1, even if it is paid with a larger final number of points returned by the iterative procedure. These differences are also evident in terms of efficiency, because Algorithm 2 turns out to converge slightly more quickly than Algorithm 1. However, we note that both algorithms complete their work in few seconds. Similar conclusions can be done as regards the CN.

Finally, to assess the advantage of our adaptive schemes, as a comparison in case of the problem T1 we report the results obtained by applying the RBF-PU method on a uniform point set. In particular, in order to achieve a similar level of accuracy as found in Tables 1 and 2, we need 6400 collocation points to get

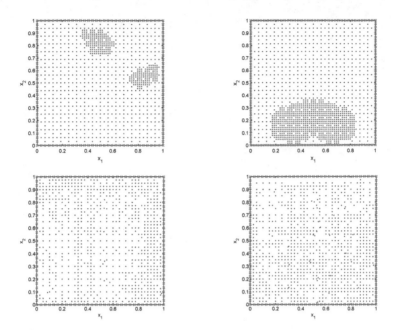

Fig. 3. Final distribution of discretization points obtained by applying the adaptive algorithms with M6, $\varepsilon = 3$, for problems T1 (left) and T2 (right). Top: Algorithm 1, bottom: Algorithm 2.

a RMSE $=$ 5.57e$-$6 in 6.5 s (cf. Table 1), and 2500 collocation points to reach a RMSE $=$ 1.74e$-$5 in 3.3 s (cf. Table 2). As evident from these experiments, the adaptive algorithms are useful to reduce discretization error and CPU time, mainly when a higher level of accuracy is required.

References

1. Cavoretto, R., De Rossi, A.: Adaptive meshless refinement schemes for RBF-PUM collocation. Appl. Math. Lett. **90**, 131–138 (2019)
2. Driscoll, T.A., Heryudono, A.R.H.: Adaptive residual subsampling methods for radial basis function interpolation and collocation problems. Comput. Math. Appl. **53**, 927–939 (2007)
3. Fasshauer, G.E., McCourt, M.J.: Kernel-Based Approximation Methods Using MATLAB. Interdisciplinary Mathematical Sciences, vol. 19. World Scientific Publishing Co., Singapore (2015)
4. Heryudono, A., Larsson, E., Ramage, A., Sydow, L.V.: Preconditioning for radial basis function partition of unity methods. J. Sci. Comput. **67**, 1089–1109 (2016)
5. Safdari-Vaighani, A., Heryudono, A., Larsson, E.: A radial basis function partition of unity collocation method for convection-diffusion equations. J. Sci. Comput. **64**, 341–367 (2015)
6. Wendland, H.: Scattered Data Approximation. Cambridge Monographs on Applied and Computational Mathematics, vol. 17. Cambridge University Press, Cambridge (2005)

Fractional Diffusion Problems: Numerical Methods, Algorithms and Applications

A Second Order Time Accurate Finite Volume Scheme for the Time-Fractional Diffusion Wave Equation on General Nonconforming Meshes

Fayssal Benkhaldoun[1,2] and Abdallah Bradji[3(✉)]

[1] LAGA, University of Paris 13, Paris, France
fayssal@math.univ-paris13.fr
[2] UM6P, Benguerir, Morocco
Fayssal.BENKHALDOUN@um6p.ma
[3] LMA (Laboratoire de Mathématiques Appliquées) Faculty of Sciences,
University of Annaba, Annaba, Algeria
abdallah.bradji@gmail.com, abdallah.bradji@etu.univ-amu.fr,
bradji@math.univ-paris13.fr
https://www.math.univ-paris13.fr/~fayssal/
https://www.i2m.univ-amu.fr/~bradji/

Abstract. SUSHI (Scheme Using Stabilization and Hybrid Interfaces) is a finite volume method has been developed at the first time to approximate heterogeneous and anisotropic diffusion problems. It has been applied later to approximate several types of partial differential equations. The main feature of SUSHI is that the control volumes can only be assumed to be polyhedral. Further, a consistent and stable Discrete Gradient is developed.

In this note, we establish a second order time accurate implicit scheme for the TFDWE (Time Fractional Diffusion-Wave Equation). The space discretization is based on the use of SUSHI whereas the time discretization is performed using a uniform mesh. The scheme is based on the use of an equivalent system of two low order equations. We sketch the proof of the convergence of the stated scheme. The convergence is unconditional. This work is an improvement of [3] in which a first order scheme, whose convergence is conditional, is established.

Keywords: Finite volume · Time Fractional Diffusion Wave Equation · System · Unconditional convergence · Second order time accurate

1 Problem to Be Solved and Aim of This Paper

Let us consider the following time-fractional equation:

$$\partial_t^\alpha u(\boldsymbol{x},t) - \Delta u(\boldsymbol{x},t) = f(\boldsymbol{x},t), \ (\boldsymbol{x},t) \in \Omega \times (0,T), \tag{1}$$

© Springer Nature Switzerland AG 2020
I. Lirkov and S. Margenov (Eds.): LSSC 2019, LNCS 11958, pp. 95–104, 2020.
https://doi.org/10.1007/978-3-030-41032-2_10

where Ω is an open bounded connected subset of $\mathbb{R}^d$ ($d \in \mathbb{N}^\star$), $T > 0$, and f is a given function. The operator ∂_t^α denotes the Caputo derivative of order α whose general formula is given by, for $m - 1 < \rho < m$ with $m \in \mathbb{N}^\star$

$$\partial_t^\rho u(t) = \frac{1}{\Gamma(m - \rho)} \int_0^t (t - s)^{m-1-\rho} u^{(m)}(s) ds. \tag{2}$$

We are concerned with the case of TFDWE in which α, which appears in the first term on the left hand side of (1), is satisfying

$$1 < \alpha < 2.$$

In this case the operator ∂_t^α is given by

$$\partial_t^\alpha u(t) = \frac{1}{\Gamma(2 - \alpha)} \int_0^t (t - s)^{1-\alpha} u''(s) ds. \tag{3}$$

Initial conditions are given by, for all $\boldsymbol{x} \in \Omega$:

$$u(\boldsymbol{x}, 0) = u^0(\boldsymbol{x}) \quad \text{and} \quad u_t(\boldsymbol{x}, 0) = u^1(\boldsymbol{x}), \tag{4}$$

where u^0 and u^1 are given functions defined on Ω.

Homogeneous Dirichlet boundary conditions are given by

$$u(\boldsymbol{x}, t) = 0, \ (\boldsymbol{x}, t) \in \partial\Omega \times (0, T). \tag{5}$$

The TFDWE arises in several applications and several numerical methods have been devoted to approximate such equation, see [7,8] and references therein. In this note, we establish a second order time accurate implicit finite volume scheme using SUSHI [5] for TFDWE in any space dimension along with a brief study for its convergence analysis in several discrete norms. The scheme is based on an equivalent system of low order equations for (1). This work improves [3] which deal with a first order scheme with a conditional convergence.

2   Definition of a Consistent and Stable Discrete Gradient

We consider as discretization in space the mesh of [5]. In brief, such mesh is defined as the triplet $\mathcal{D} = (\mathcal{M}, \mathcal{E}, \mathcal{P})$ where $\mathcal{M}$ is the set of cells, $\mathcal{E}$ is the set of edges, and $\mathcal{P}$ is a set of points $\boldsymbol{x}_K$ in each cell K. We assume that, for all $K \in \mathcal{M}$, there exists a subset $\mathcal{E}_K$ of $\mathcal{E}$ such that $\partial K = \cup_{\sigma \in \mathcal{E}_K} \overline{\sigma}$. For any $\sigma \in \mathcal{E}$, we denote by $\mathcal{M}_\sigma = \{K, \sigma \in \mathcal{E}_K\}$. We then assume that, for any $\sigma \in \mathcal{E}$, either $\mathcal{M}_\sigma$ has exactly one element and then $\sigma \subset \partial\Omega$ (the set of these interfaces, called boundary interfaces, denoted by $\mathcal{E}_{\text{ext}}$) or $\mathcal{M}_\sigma$ has exactly two elements (the set of these interfaces, called interior interfaces, denoted by $\mathcal{E}_{\text{int}}$). For all $\sigma \in \mathcal{E}$, we denote by $\boldsymbol{x}_\sigma$ the barycentre of σ. For all $K \in \mathcal{M}$ and $\sigma \in \mathcal{E}$, we denote by $\mathbf{n}_{K,\sigma}$ the unit vector normal to σ outward to K. Denoting by $d_{K,\sigma}$ the Euclidean distance between $\boldsymbol{x}_K$ and the hyperplane including σ, one assumes that $d_{K,\sigma} > 0$. We then denote by $\mathcal{D}_{K,\sigma}$ the cone with vertex $\boldsymbol{x}_K$ and basis σ. Also, h_K is used to denote the diameter of K. For more details on the mesh, we refer to [5, Definition 2.1, Page 1012].

We define the discrete space $\mathcal{X}_{\mathcal{D},0}$ as the set of all $v = \left((v_K)_{K \in \mathcal{M}}, (v_\sigma)_{\sigma \in \mathcal{E}} \right)$, where $v_K, v_\sigma \in \mathbb{R}$ and $v_\sigma = 0$ for all $\sigma \in \mathcal{E}_{\text{ext}}$. Let $H_\mathcal{M}(\Omega) \subset L^2(\Omega)$ be the space of functions which are constant on each control volume K of the mesh $\mathcal{M}$. For all $v \in \mathcal{X}_\mathcal{D}$, we denote by $\Pi_\mathcal{M} v \in H_\mathcal{M}(\Omega)$ the function defined by $\Pi_\mathcal{M} v(\boldsymbol{x}) = v_K$, for a.e. $\boldsymbol{x} \in K$, for all $K \in \mathcal{M}$. In order to analyze the convergence, we need to consider the size of the discretization $\mathcal{D}$ defined by $h_\mathcal{D} = \sup \{ \text{diam}(K), K \in \mathcal{M} \}$ and the regularity of the mesh given by

$$\theta_\mathcal{D} = \max \left(\max_{\sigma \in \mathcal{E}_{\text{int}}, K, L \in \mathcal{M}} \frac{d_{K,\sigma}}{d_{L,\sigma}}, \max_{K \in \mathcal{M}, \sigma \in \mathcal{E}_K} \frac{h_K}{d_{K,\sigma}} \right).$$

The formulation of the scheme we want to consider involves the discrete gradient, denoted by $\nabla_\mathcal{D}$, developed in [5]. The value of $\nabla_\mathcal{D} u$, where $u \in \mathcal{X}_{\mathcal{D},0}$, is defined by, for all $K \in \mathcal{M}$, for a.e. $\boldsymbol{x} \in \mathcal{D}_{K,\sigma}$

$$\nabla_\mathcal{D} u(\boldsymbol{x}) = \frac{1}{\text{m}(K)} \sum_{\sigma \in \mathcal{E}_K} \text{m}(\sigma) \left(u_\sigma - u_K \right) \mathbf{n}_{K,\sigma}$$

$$+ \left(\frac{\sqrt{d}}{d_{K,\sigma}} \left(u_\sigma - u_K - \nabla_K u \cdot (\boldsymbol{x}_\sigma - \boldsymbol{x}_K) \right) \right) \mathbf{n}_{K,\sigma}. \tag{6}$$

We define now the inner product defined on $\mathcal{X}_{\mathcal{D},0} \times \mathcal{X}_{\mathcal{D},0}$ and given by

$$\langle u, v \rangle_F = \int_\Omega \nabla_\mathcal{D} u(\boldsymbol{x}) \cdot \nabla_\mathcal{D} v(\boldsymbol{x}) d\boldsymbol{x}. \tag{7}$$

The time discretization is performed with a constant time step $k = \dfrac{T}{N+1}$, where $N \in \mathbb{N}^\star$, and we shall denote $t_n = nk$, for $n \in [\![0, N+1]\!]$. We denote by ∂^1 the discrete first time derivative given by $\partial^1 v^{j+1} = \dfrac{v^{j+1} - v^j}{k}$.

Throughout this paper, the letter C stands for a positive constant independent of the parameters of the space and time discretizations.

3 A High Order Approximation for the Caputo Derivative and Its Properties

For the sake of completeness, we recall in this section some results concerning a second order approximation for the time fractional derivative $\partial_t^\beta \Phi$ with $0 < \beta < 1$ and Φ is smooth, i.e. $\Phi \in \mathcal{C}^3[0, T]$, and its properties. This approximation is given by the so-called $L2-1_\sigma$ formula developed in [1,6]. Such approximation will help to derive a second order time accurate scheme for the considered problem (1)–(5). To construct this high order approximation for the Caputo derivative, we consider the "fractional mesh points" $t_{n+\sigma} = (n + \sigma)k$, for $n \in [\![0, N]\!]$, where

$$\sigma = 1 - \frac{\beta}{2}. \tag{8}$$

Using (2) when $\rho = \beta \in (0,1)$ and consequently $m = 1$, the value $\partial_t^\beta \Phi(t_{n+\sigma})$ is given by

$$\frac{1}{\Gamma(1-\beta)} \left(\sum_{j=1}^{n} \int_{t_{j-1}}^{t_j} (t_{n+\sigma} - s)^{-\beta} \Phi_s(s) ds + \int_{t_n}^{t_{n+\sigma}} (t_{n+\sigma} - s)^{-\beta} \Phi_s(s) \right) ds. \quad (9)$$

For each $j \in [\![1, N]\!]$, let $\Pi_{2,j}\Phi$ be the quadratic interpolation defined on (t_{j-1}, t_j) on the points t_{j-1}, t_j, t_{j+1} of Φ. An explicit expansion for $\Pi_{2,j}\Phi$ yields:

$$(\Pi_{2,j}\Phi(s))' = \partial^1\Phi(t_{j+1}) + \partial^2\Phi(t_{j+1})\left(s - t_{j+\frac{1}{2}}\right)$$
$$= \partial^1\Phi(t_j) + \partial^2\Phi(t_{j+1})\left(s - t_{j-\frac{1}{2}}\right).$$

When approximating the terms of the sum (resp. the last term) using quadratic interpolations (resp. a linear interpolation) in (9) of $\partial_t^\beta \Phi(t_{n+\sigma})$, we have to compute the following integrals:

1. **First set of integrals:**

$$\int_{t_{j-1}}^{t_j} \left(s - t_{j-\frac{1}{2}}\right)(t_{n+\sigma} - s)^{-\beta} ds = \frac{k^{2-\beta}}{1-\alpha} b_{n-j}^\sigma,$$

where
$$b_l^\sigma = \frac{1}{2-\beta}\left((l+\sigma+1)^{2-\beta} - (l+\sigma)^{2-\beta}\right) - \frac{1}{2}\left((l+\sigma+1)^{1-\beta} + (l+\sigma)^{1-\beta}\right).$$

2. **Second set of integrals:**

$$\int_{t_{j-1}}^{t_j} (t_{n+\sigma} - s)^{-\beta} ds = \frac{k^{1-\beta}}{1-\beta} d_{n+\sigma-j,\beta}, \quad (10)$$

with, for all $s > 0$, $d_{s,\beta}$ is given by $d_{s,\beta} = (s+1)^{1-\beta} - s^{1-\beta}$.

3. **Third set of integrals:**

$$\int_{t_n}^{t_{n+\sigma}} (t_{n+\sigma} - s)^{-\beta} ds = \frac{k^{1-\beta}}{1-\beta} \sigma^{1-\beta}. \quad (11)$$

We then obtained approximation for the fractional derivative $\partial_t^\beta \Phi(t_{n+\sigma})$ using (9)–(11)

$$\frac{1}{\Gamma(1-\beta)} \left(\sum_{j=1}^{n} \int_{t_{j-1}}^{t_j} (t_{n+\sigma} - s)^{-\beta} (\Pi_{2,j}\Phi(s))' ds + \frac{k^{1-\beta}}{1-\beta} \sigma^{1-\beta} \partial^1 \Phi(t_{n+1}) \right)$$

$$= \frac{k^{1-\beta}}{\Gamma(2-\beta)} \left(\sum_{j=1}^{n} \partial^1\Phi(t_j) d_{n+\sigma-j,\beta} + \partial^2\Phi(t_{j+1}) k b_{n-j}^\sigma + \sigma^{1-\beta} \partial^1\Phi(t_{n+1}) \right).$$

This gives, after re-ordering the sum (see [1, (27)-(28), Page 429])

$$\partial_t^\beta \Phi(t_{n+\sigma}) \approx \frac{k^{1-\beta}}{\Gamma(2-\beta)} \sum_{j=0}^{n} c_{n-j}^{\sigma,n} \partial^1 \Phi(t_{j+1}), \qquad (12)$$

where $c_0^{\sigma,0} = \sigma^{1-\beta}$ and for all $n \geq 1$

$$c_0^{\sigma,n} = \sigma^{1-\beta} + b_0^\sigma, \quad c_j^{\sigma,n} = d_{j+\sigma-1,\beta} + b_j^\sigma - b_{j-1}^\sigma, \quad \forall j \in [\![1, n-1]\!], \quad (13)$$
$$c_n^{\sigma,n} = d_{n+\sigma-1,\beta} - b_{n-1}^\sigma.$$

Let us denote

$$\lambda_j^{n+1} = \frac{c_{n-j}^{\sigma,n}}{k^\beta \Gamma(2-\beta)}. \qquad (14)$$

The following lemma summarizes some properties of the approximation given by (12). Some of these results are proved in [1] whereas the other ones can be justified using the explicit form (14).

Lemma 1 (Some results concerning the time discretization, cf. [1,6]).
  Let $\beta \in (0,1)$ be given and λ_j^{n+1} be defined by (14). Then the following results hold:
1. Properties of the coefficients λ_j^{n+1}, cf. [1, Lemma 4, Page 431].

$$\lambda_n^{n+1} > \lambda_{n-1}^{n+1} > \ldots > \lambda_0^{n+1} > \lambda_0 = \frac{1}{2T^\alpha \Gamma(1-\beta)}, \qquad (15)$$

$$\sum_{j=0}^{n} k\lambda_j^{n+1} \leq \frac{T^{1-\beta}}{\Gamma(2-\beta)}, \qquad k\sum_{n=1}^{N} \lambda_1^{n+1} \leq \frac{(4-\beta)T^{1-\beta}}{\Gamma(3-\beta)}, \qquad (16)$$

and for all $j \in [\![0,n]\!]$ and $i \in [\![0,m]\!]$ such that $n - j = m - i$, $i \neq 0$, and $j \neq 0$, we have $\lambda_j^{n+1} = \lambda_i^{m+1}$.
2. Stability result, cf. [1, Corollary 1, Page 427]. *For all $\left(\beta^j\right)_{j=0}^{N+1} \in \mathbb{R}^{N+2}$, for any $n \in [\![0, N+1]\!]$:*

$$\left(\sigma\beta^{n+1} + (1-\sigma)\beta^n\right) \sum_{j=0}^{n} \lambda_j^{n+1}(\beta^{j+1} - \beta^j) \geq \frac{1}{2} \sum_{j=0}^{n} \lambda_j^{n+1} \left((\beta^{j+1})^2 - (\beta^j)^2\right).$$

$$(17)$$

3. Consistency result, cf. [1, Lemma 2, Page 429]. *For any $\Phi \in \mathcal{C}^3([0,T])$:*

$$\left| \partial^\beta \Phi(t_{n+\sigma}) - \sum_{j=0}^{n} k\lambda_j^{n+1} \partial^1 \Phi(t_{j+1}) \right| \leq Ck^{3-\beta} \left| \Phi^{(3)} \right|_{\mathcal{C}([0,T])}. \qquad (18)$$

4   Principles of the Scheme

The principles of the scheme we want to present are:

1. First step. Taking the "fractional mesh point" $t = t_{n+\sigma}$, with σ is given by (8) and $\beta = \alpha - 1$, in (1) and using the general formula (2) implies that (which gives $\partial_t^\alpha u(t) = \partial_t^{\alpha-1}(u_t)$)

$$\partial_t^{\alpha-1}\overline{u}(t_{n+\sigma}) - \Delta u(t_{n+\sigma}) = f(t_{n+\sigma}) \quad \text{and} \quad \overline{u} = u_t. \tag{19}$$

2. Second step. Approximation of $\partial_t^{\alpha-1}\overline{u}(t_{n+\sigma})$, which is the first term in (19), can be deduced from (18) by choosing $\beta = \alpha - 1$ and $\Phi(t) = \overline{u}(t) = u_t$:

$$\partial_t^{\alpha-1}\overline{u}(t_{n+\sigma}) = \sum_{j=0}^n k\lambda_j^{n+1}\partial^1\overline{u}(t_{j+1}) + \mathbb{T}_1^{n+1}(\overline{u}), \tag{20}$$

where $|\mathbb{T}_1^{n+1}(\overline{u})| \leq Ck^{4-\alpha}\left|u^{(4)}\right|_{\mathcal{C}([0,T])}$.

3. Third step. Approximation of the first equation of (19). We have, thanks to a convenient Taylor expansion

$$u^{n+\sigma} = \sigma u(t_{n+1}) + (1-\sigma)u(t_n) = u(t_{n+\sigma}) + \mathbb{T}_2^{n+1}, \tag{21}$$

where $|\mathbb{T}_2^{n+1}| \leq \dfrac{k^2}{2}\|u\|_{\mathcal{C}^2([0,T])}$. From (19)–(21), we deduce that

$$\sum_{j=0}^n k\lambda_j^{n+1}\partial^1\overline{u}(t_{j+1}) - \Delta u^{n+\sigma} = f(t_{n+\sigma}) + \mathbb{T}_3^{n+1}, \tag{22}$$

where $|\mathbb{T}_3^{n+1}| \leq Ck^2\|u\|_{\mathcal{C}^4([0,T])}$.

4. Fourth step. Approximation of the second equation of (19) when $n \geq 1$. The derivative $u_t(t_{n+\sigma})$ is approximated (to get the stability property) by $\dfrac{(2\sigma + 1)u(t_{n+1}) - 4\sigma u(t_n) + (2\sigma - 1)u(t_{n-1})}{2k}$. Using a suitable Taylor expansion yields

$$\frac{(2\sigma + 1)u(t_{n+1}) - 4\sigma u(t_n) + (2\sigma - 1)u(t_{n-1})}{2k} = \overline{u}(t_{n+\sigma}) + \mathbb{T}_4^{n+1}, \tag{23}$$

where $|\mathbb{T}_4^{n+1}| \leq Ck^2\|u\|_{\mathcal{C}^3([0,T])}$.

The system (19) is used for instance in [8] to establish a finite difference scheme in one space dimension. Such scheme is based on a Crank-Nicolson method.

5   Formulation of a Second Order Time Accurate Finite Volume Scheme and Statement of Its Convergence

After having explained the principles of the finite volume scheme for problem (1)–(5), we are able now to set its definition. We will denote by $(\cdot, \cdot)_{L^2(\Omega)}$ the $L^2(\Omega)$-inner product and by $v^{n+\sigma}$ the barycentric element given by $v^{n+\sigma} = \sigma v^{n+1} + (1-\sigma)v^n$.

Definition 1 (Definition of a finite volume scheme for (1)–(5)). *Let* $\langle \cdot, \cdot \rangle$ *be the inner product given by (7):*
1. *Discretization of initial conditions (4): Find* $u_{\mathcal{D}}^0, \overline{u}_{\mathcal{D}}^0 \in \mathcal{X}_{\mathcal{D},0}$ *such that, for all* $v \in \mathcal{X}_{\mathcal{D},0}$

$$\langle u_{\mathcal{D}}^0, v \rangle_F = -\left(\Delta u^0, \Pi_{\mathcal{M}} v\right)_{L^2(\Omega)} \quad \text{and} \quad \langle \overline{u}_{\mathcal{D}}^0, v \rangle_F = -\left(\Delta u^1, \Pi_{\mathcal{M}} v\right)_{L^2(\Omega)}.$$
(24)

2. *Discretization of Eq. (22): For any* $n \in [\![0, N]\!]$*, find* $u_{\mathcal{D}}^{n+1}, \overline{u}_{\mathcal{D}}^{n+1} \in \mathcal{X}_{\mathcal{D},0}$ *such that*

$$\sum_{j=0}^{n} \lambda_j^{n+1} \left(\Pi_{\mathcal{M}}(\overline{u}_{\mathcal{D}}^{j+1} - \overline{u}_{\mathcal{D}}^j), \Pi_{\mathcal{M}} v\right)_{L^2(\Omega)} + \langle u_{\mathcal{D}}^{n+\sigma}, v \rangle_F$$

$$= (f(t_{n+\sigma}), \Pi_{\mathcal{M}} v)_{L^2(\Omega)}, \quad \forall v \in \mathcal{X}_{\mathcal{D},0}.$$
(25)

3. *Discretization of the second equation of (19):*

$$\overline{u}_{\mathcal{D}}^{\frac{1}{2}} = \partial^1 u_{\mathcal{D}}^1 \quad \text{and}$$
(26)

$$\overline{u}_{\mathcal{D}}^{n+\sigma} = \frac{1}{2k}\left((2\sigma + 1)u_{\mathcal{D}}^{n+1} - 4\sigma u_{\mathcal{D}}^n + (2\sigma - 1)u_{\mathcal{D}}^{n-1}\right), \quad \forall n \in [\![1, N]\!].$$

We now state one of the main results of this note, that is the convergence of scheme (24)–(26).

Theorem 1 (Error estimates for scheme (24)–(26)). *Let* Ω *be a polyhedral open bounded subset of* $\mathbb{R}^d$*, where* $d \in \mathbb{N} \setminus \{0\}$*. Assume that the solution of (1)–(5) satisfies* $u \in \mathcal{C}^4([0, T]; \mathcal{C}^2(\overline{\Omega}))$ *and* $\theta_{\mathcal{D}}$ *satisfies* $\theta \geq \theta_{\mathcal{D}}$*. Let* $\nabla_{\mathcal{D}}$ *be the discrete gradient defined as in (6) and* $\langle \cdot, \cdot \rangle$ *be the inner product given by (7). Let* $k = \frac{T}{N+1}$*, with* $N \in \mathbb{N}^*$*, and denote by* $t_n = nk$*, for* $n \in [\![0, N+1]\!]$*. Let* σ *be defined by (8) with* $\beta = \alpha - 1$*. For any* $n \in [\![0, N]\!]$*, for any* $j \in [\![0, n]\!]$*, we define the coefficients* λ_j^{n+1} *as in (14).*

Then there exists a unique solution $(\overline{u}_{\mathcal{D}}^n)_{n=0}^{N+1}$*,* $(u_{\mathcal{D}}^n)_{n=0}^{N+1} \in \mathcal{X}_{\mathcal{D},0}^{N+2}$ *for scheme (24)–(26) and the following error estimates in* $L^\infty(H^1)$ *and* $H^1(L^2)$ *discrete semi-norms hold:*

$$\max_{n=0}^{N+1} \|\nabla_{\mathcal{D}} u_{\mathcal{D}}^n - \nabla u(t_n)\|_{L^2(\Omega)^d} + \left(\sum_{n=0}^{N+1} k\|\Pi_{\mathcal{M}} \overline{u}_{\mathcal{D}}^n - u_t(t_n)\|_{L^2(\Omega)}^2\right)^{\frac{1}{2}}$$

$$\leq C(h_{\mathcal{D}} + k^2)\|u\|_{\mathcal{C}^4(0,T;\mathcal{C}^2(\overline{\Omega}))}.$$
(27)

The proof of Theorem 1 is based on the following new a priori estimate result:

Theorem 2 (A priori estimate for the discrete problem) *Under the same hypotheses of Theorem 1, assume that there exists* $(\overline{\eta}^n)_{n=0}^{N+1}$*,* $(\eta^n)_{n=0}^{N+1} \in (\mathcal{X}_{\mathcal{D},0})^{N+2}$ *such that* $\eta_{\mathcal{D}}^0 = \overline{\eta}^0 = 0$ *and for all* $n \in [\![0, N]\!]$

$$\sum_{j=0}^{n} \lambda_j^{n+1} \left(\Pi_{\mathcal{M}}(\overline{\eta}_{\mathcal{D}}^{j+1} - \overline{\eta}_{\mathcal{D}}^j), \Pi_{\mathcal{M}} v\right)_{L^2(\Omega)} + \langle \eta_{\mathcal{D}}^{n+\sigma}, v \rangle_F = \left(\mathcal{S}^{n+1}, \Pi_{\mathcal{M}} v\right)_{L^2(\Omega)},$$

(28)

where $\mathcal{S}^{n+1} \in L^2(\Omega)$, for all $n \in [\![0, N]\!]$. Then, the following estimate holds:

$$\max_{n=0}^{N+1} \|\nabla_\mathcal{D} \eta_\mathcal{D}^n\|_{L^2(\Omega)^d} + \left(\sum_{n=0}^{N+1} k \|\Pi_\mathcal{M} \overline{\eta}_\mathcal{D}^n\|_{L^2(\Omega)}^2 \right)^{\frac{1}{2}} \leq C\overline{\mathcal{S}}, \qquad (29)$$

where

$$\overline{\mathcal{S}} = \max_{n=1}^{N} \left\| \nabla_\mathcal{D} \left(\overline{\eta}_\mathcal{D}^{n+\sigma} - \frac{(2\sigma+1)\eta_\mathcal{D}^{n+1} - 4\sigma\eta^n + (2\sigma-1)\eta_\mathcal{D}^{n-1}}{2k} \right) \right\|_{L^2(\Omega)^d}$$
$$+ \max_{n=0}^{N} \|\mathcal{S}^{n+1}\|_{L^2(\Omega)} + \|\nabla_\mathcal{D}(\partial^1 \eta_\mathcal{D}^1 - \overline{\eta}_\mathcal{D}^{\frac{1}{2}})\|_{L^2(\Omega)^d} \qquad (30)$$

An Overview on the Proof of Theorem 2: In addition to Lemma 1, the proof of Theorem 2 is based on the following inequality:

$$\langle \sigma\eta_\mathcal{D}^{n+1} + (1-\sigma)\eta_\mathcal{D}^n, (2\sigma+1)\eta_\mathcal{D}^{n+1} - 4\sigma\eta_\mathcal{D}^n + (2\sigma-1)\eta_\mathcal{D}^{n-1} \rangle_F \geq \mathbb{E}^{n+1} - \mathbb{E}^n, \quad (31)$$

where

$$\mathbb{E}^{n+1} = \frac{2\sigma^2 + \sigma - 1}{2} \|\nabla_\mathcal{D}(\eta_\mathcal{D}^{n+1} - \eta_\mathcal{D}^n)\|_{L^2(\Omega)^d}^2 + \frac{2\sigma+1}{2} \|\nabla_\mathcal{D}\eta_\mathcal{D}^{n+1}\|_{L^2(\Omega)^d}^2$$
$$- \frac{2\sigma - 1}{2} \|\nabla_\mathcal{D}\eta_\mathcal{D}^n\|_{L^2(\Omega)^d}^2.$$

In addition to this $\mathbb{E}^{n+1} \geq \dfrac{1}{2\sigma} \|\nabla_\mathcal{D}\eta_\mathcal{D}^{n+1}\|_{L^2(\Omega)^d}^2$. However, Theorem 2 demands a rather longer proof. We will detail this in a future paper. $\qquad \square$

Sketch of the proof of Theorem 1

The uniqueness for schemes (24) stems from the fact that $\|\nabla_\mathcal{D} \cdot \|_{L^2(\Omega)^d}$ is a norm on $X_{\mathcal{D},0}$. This uniqueness implies the existence since the matrix involved is square. The uniqueness for scheme (25) with (26) can be justified using a priori estimate (29). This uniqueness implies the existence since the matrix involved in (25) is square. To prove estimate (27), we compare (24)–(26) with the following auxiliary schemes: For any $n \in [\![0, N+1]\!]$, find $\Xi_\mathcal{D}^n, \Upsilon_\mathcal{D}^n \in X_{\mathcal{D},0}$ such that

$$\langle \Xi_\mathcal{D}^n, v \rangle_F = -(\Delta u(t_n), \Pi_\mathcal{D}v)_{L^2(\Omega)} \quad \text{and} \qquad (32)$$
$$\langle \Upsilon_\mathcal{D}^n, v \rangle_F = -(\Delta u_t(t_n), \Pi_\mathcal{D}v)_{L^2(\Omega)}, \quad \forall v \in X_{\mathcal{D},0}.$$

Taking $n = 0$ in (32), using the fact that $u(0) = u^0$ and $u_t(0) = u^1$ (subject of (4)), and comparing with scheme (24), we get $\overline{\eta}_\mathcal{D}^0 = \eta_\mathcal{D}^0 = 0$, where, for all $n \in [\![0, N+1]\!]$, $\overline{\eta}_\mathcal{D}^n, \eta_\mathcal{D}^n \in X_{\mathcal{D},0}$ are given by $\eta_\mathcal{D}^n = u_\mathcal{D}^n - \Xi_\mathcal{D}^n$ and $\overline{\eta}_\mathcal{D}^n = \overline{u}_\mathcal{D}^n - \Upsilon_\mathcal{D}^n$.

First step: Comparison between (u, u_t) and $(\Xi_\mathcal{D}^n, \Upsilon_\mathcal{D}^n)$. We have (see [4,5])

$$\|\partial^1 u(t_n) - \Pi_\mathcal{M}\partial^1 \Xi_\mathcal{D}^n\|_{L^2(\Omega)} + \|\nabla u(t_n) - \nabla_\mathcal{D}\Xi_\mathcal{D}^n\|_{L^2(\Omega)^d} \leq Ch_\mathcal{D}\|u\|_{\mathcal{C}^1(0,T;\mathcal{C}^2(\overline{\Omega}))}. \qquad (33)$$

and

$$\|u_t(t_n) - \Pi_{\mathcal{M}}\Upsilon_{\mathcal{D}}^n\|_{L^2(\Omega)} + \|\partial^1 (u_t(t_n) - \Pi_{\mathcal{M}}\Upsilon_{\mathcal{D}}^n)\|_{L^2(\Omega)} \leq Ch_{\mathcal{D}}\|u\|_{C^2(0,T;C^2(\overline{\Omega}))}.$$
(34)

Second step: Comparison between $(\Xi_{\mathcal{D}}^n, \Upsilon_{\mathcal{D}}^n)$ **and** $(u_{\mathcal{D}}^n, \overline{u}_{\mathcal{D}}^n)$. From (25), (22), and (32), we deduce that

$$\sum_{j=0}^{n} \lambda_j^{n+1} \left(\Pi_{\mathcal{M}}(\overline{\eta}_{\mathcal{D}}^{j+1} - \overline{\eta}_{\mathcal{D}}^j), \Pi_{\mathcal{M}}v\right)_{L^2(\Omega)} + (\nabla_{\mathcal{D}}\eta_{\mathcal{D}}^{n+\sigma}, \nabla_{\mathcal{D}}v)_{L^2(\Omega)^d}$$

$$= (\mathcal{S}^{n+1}, \Pi_{\mathcal{M}}v)_{L^2(\Omega)}, \tag{35}$$

where $\mathcal{S}^{n+1} = \sum_{j=0}^{n} k\lambda_j^{n+1}\partial^1 \left(u_t(t_{j+1}) - \Pi_{\mathcal{M}}\Upsilon_{\mathcal{D}}^{j+1}\right) - \mathbb{T}_3^{n+1}$. Using the a priori estimate (29) yields

$$\max_{n=0}^{N+1} \|\nabla_{\mathcal{D}}\eta_{\mathcal{D}}^n\|_{L^2(\Omega)^d} + \left(\sum_{n=0}^{N+1} k\|\Pi_{\mathcal{M}}\overline{\eta}_{\mathcal{D}}^n\|_{L^2(\Omega)}^2\right)^{\frac{1}{2}} \leq C\overline{\mathcal{S}}, \tag{36}$$

where

$$\overline{\mathcal{S}} = \max_{n=1}^{N} \left\|\nabla_{\mathcal{D}} \left(\overline{\eta}_{\mathcal{D}}^{n+\sigma} - \frac{(2\sigma+1)\eta_{\mathcal{D}}^{n+1} - 4\sigma\eta^n + (2\sigma-1)\eta_{\mathcal{D}}^{n-1}}{2k}\right)\right\|_{L^2(\Omega)^d}$$

$$+ \max_{n=0}^{N} \|\mathcal{S}^{n+1}\|_{L^2(\Omega)} + \|\nabla_{\mathcal{D}}(\partial^1\eta_{\mathcal{D}}^1 - \overline{\eta}_{\mathcal{D}}^{\frac{1}{2}})\|_{L^2(\Omega)^d}. \tag{37}$$

Using the triangle inequality, (16), and (34) yields (recall that $\mathbb{T}_3^{n+1}$ is of order two, see (22)) $\mathcal{S} \leq C(h_{\mathcal{D}} + k^2)\|u\|_{C^4(0,T;C^2(\overline{\Omega}))}$. Using (26) implies that $\overline{\eta}_{\mathcal{D}}^{\frac{1}{2}} - \partial^1\eta_{\mathcal{D}}^1 = -\Upsilon_{\mathcal{D}}^{\frac{1}{2}} + \partial^1\Xi_{\mathcal{D}}^1$. On the other hand, using (32) implies that $\left(\nabla_{\mathcal{D}} \left(\partial^1\Xi_{\mathcal{D}}^1 - \Upsilon_{\mathcal{D}}^{\frac{1}{2}}\right), \nabla_{\mathcal{D}}v\right)_{L^2(\Omega)^d} = -\left(\Delta\left(\partial^1 u(t_1) - u_t^{\frac{1}{2}}\right), \Pi_{\mathcal{M}}v\right)_{L^2(\Omega)}$. By taking $v = \partial^1\Xi_{\mathcal{D}}^1 - \Upsilon_{\mathcal{D}}^{\frac{1}{2}}$ in this equation and using the Cauchy Schwarz inequality and the Poincaré inequality [5, Lemma 5.4] imply that $\left\|\nabla_{\mathcal{D}} \left(\overline{\eta}_{\mathcal{D}}^{\frac{1}{2}} - \partial^1\eta_{\mathcal{D}}^1\right)\right\|_{L^2(\Omega)^d} \leq Ck^2\|u\|_{C^3(0,T;C^2(\overline{\Omega}))}$. In the same manner, we justify that the first term in (37) is bounded above by $Ck^2\|u\|_{C^3(0,T;C^2(\overline{\Omega}))}$. These estimates for the terms of (37) and estimate (36) imply that $\max_{n=0}^{N+1} \|\nabla_{\mathcal{D}}\eta_{\mathcal{D}}^n\|_{L^2(\Omega)^d}$ and $\left(\sum_{n=0}^{N+1} k\|\Pi_{\mathcal{M}}\overline{\eta}_{\mathcal{D}}^n\|_{L^2(\Omega)}^2\right)^{\frac{1}{2}}$ are bounded above by $C(h_{\mathcal{D}}+k^2)\|u\|_{C^4(0,T;C^2(\overline{\Omega}))}$. This with the triangle inequality and estimates (33)–(34) imply the required estimate (27). This completes the proof of Theorem 1. $\qquad\square$

6   Some Concluding Remarks and Perspectives

Using an equivalent system of low order equations for TFDWE, we established a second order time accurate finite volume scheme using the discrete gradient of [5]. The time discretization uses the approximation of Caputo derivative of order $0 < \beta < 1$ developed in [1,6]. We *sketched* a proof for the convergence under the *strong regularity assumption* $\mathcal{C}^4(\mathcal{C}^2)$. This regularity can be weakened to $\mathcal{C}^3(H^2)$ in the particular cases when $d = 2$ or $d = 3$, see [5, Remark 4.9, Pages 1033–1034]. Strong regularity assumptions are usually needed when we would like to improve the convergence, see for instance the regularity $\mathcal{C}^3(\mathcal{C}^4)$ in [1, Lemma 5]. The convergence stated in this note includes a convergence in $L^\infty(H^1)$ and $H^1(L^2)$ discrete semi-norms. As mentioned in Abstract and Introduction, the present notes improve [3]. We plan in the near future to detail these notes and to address for instance the technique of graded meshes to get high order approximations.

References

1. Alikhanov, A.A.: A new difference scheme for the fractional diffusion equation. J. Comput. Phys. **280**, 424–438 (2015)
2. Bradji, A.: Convergence order of gradient schemes for time-fractional partial differential equations. C. R. Math. Acad. Sci. Paris **356**(4), 439–448 (2018)
3. Bradji, A.: Some convergence results of a multi-dimensional finite volume scheme for a time-fractional diffusion-wave equation. In: Cancès, C., Omnes, P. (eds.) FVCA 2017. Springer Proceedings in Mathematics & Statistics, vol. 199, pp. 391–399. Springer, Cham (2017). https://doi.org/10.1007/978-3-319-57397-7_32
4. Bradji, A.: An analysis of a second-order time accurate scheme for a finite volume method for parabolic equations on general nonconforming multidimensional spatial meshes. Appl. Math. Comput. **219**(11), 6354–6371 (2013)
5. Eymard, R., Gallouët, T., Herbin, R.: Discretization of heterogeneous and anisotropic diffusion problems on general nonconforming meshes. IMA J. Numer. Anal. **30**(4), 1009–1043 (2010)
6. Gao, G.-H., Sun, Z.-Z., Zhang, H.-W.: A new fractional numerical differentiation formula to approximate the Caputo fractional derivative and its applications. J. Comput. Phys. **259**, 33–50 (2014)
7. Jin, B., Lazarov, R., Zhou, Z.: Two fully discrete schemes for fractional diffusion and diffusion-wave equations with nonsmooth data. SIAM J. Sci. Comput. **38**, A146–A170 (2016)
8. Sun, Z.-Z., Wu, X.: A fully discrete difference scheme for a diffusion-wave system. Appl. Numer. Math. **56**, 193–209 (2006)

Identification of a Time-Dependent Right-Hand Side of an Unsteady Equation with a Fractional Power of an Elliptic Operator

Petr N. Vabishchevich[1,2](✉)(iD)

[1] Nuclear Safety Institute, Russian Academy of Sciences, Moscow, Russia
vabishchevich@gmail.com
[2] Akhmet Yasawi International Kazakh-Turkish University, Turkistan, Kazakhstan

Abstract. An inverse problem of identifying the right-hand side is considered for an unsteady equation with a fractional power of the elliptic operator. We consider the case when the time-dependent right-hand side is unknown. The redefinition (additional information) is associated with the known solution at an internal point (points) of the computational domain. The computational algorithm is based on a special decomposition of the solution of the unsteady problem during a transition from the previous time level to the next one. The related auxiliary problems are direct boundary value problems for stationary equations with fractional powers of elliptic operators. Some features of the proposed computational algorithm are demonstrated by the results of numerical experiments for a model 2D inverse problem.

Keywords: Inverse problem · Fractional power of an elliptic operator · Parabolic equation · Identifying the right-hand side

1 Introduction

Many new non-local mathematical models are associated with fractional powers of elliptic operators [15]. An example is the problem of super-diffusion (fractional in space). At present, for numerical solving of such non-classical problems, there are actively developed approaches based on some rational approximation of the fractional power of the elliptic operator [1,3]. Another class of methods is associated with considering some auxiliary problem for a PDE of higher dimension. In [8], a boundary value problem is considered for an elliptic equation. We (see [16]) suggested the Cauchy problem method that is based on a transition to a pseudo-parabolic equation.

This research was supported by the Russian Foundation for Basic Research (project 20-01-00207) and the Ministry of Education and Science of the Republic of Kazakhstan (project AP05133873).

© Springer Nature Switzerland AG 2020
I. Lirkov and S. Margenov (Eds.): LSSC 2019, LNCS 11958, pp. 105–112, 2020.
https://doi.org/10.1007/978-3-030-41032-2_11

In the theory and practice of inverse problems for PDEs, much attention is paid to the problem of identification of coefficients from some additional information [2]. An important class of inverse problems for partial differential equations is connected with evaluation of the unknown right-hand side of the equation. An additional condition is most often formulated as a specification of the solution at an interior point or as the average value that results from integration over the whole domain. The existence and uniqueness of the solution to such an inverse problem and well-posedness of this problem in various functional classes are examined, for example, in the works [5, 10].

Currently, inverse problems for equations with fractional derivatives are actively studied (see, e.g., [6]). Separately, we can distinguish investigations on time-fractional and space-fractional parabolic problems. As for problems of identification of the right-hand side, the emphasis is on problems of identifying the dependence of the right-hand side on the spatial variables, where the known solution at the final time moment is considered (the final redefinition). Such time-fractional problems were considered, for example, in works [4, 7], whereas space-fractional parabolic problems where studied in [14, 20]. Inverse problems of determining the dependence of the right-hand side on time were investigated for time-fractional boundary value problems, e.g., in [11].

In the present paper, we study the problem of identifying a right-hand side with an unknown dependence on time for an evolutionary equation with a fractional power of an elliptic operator in a rectangular domain with an additional information about the solution of the boundary value problem at an interior point of the computational domain. Difference approximations of the Laplace operator with a homogeneous Dirichlet boundary condition are used on a uniform rectangular grid. The approximation in time is based on the backward Euler scheme. An iteration-free computational algorithm is employed to solve the inverse problem. We use a special decomposition of the solution of the equation, where a transition to a new time level is based on solving two standard grid elliptic problems. We have successfully applied this approach [17–19] for solving problems of identification of a right-hand side and coefficients that depend on time for parabolic equations.

2   Problem Formulation

For simplicity, we restrict ourselves to a 2D problem in a rectangle. Let $x = (x_1, x_2)$ and

$$\Omega = \{x \mid x = (x_1, x_2), \quad 0 < x_\alpha < l_\alpha, \quad \alpha = 1, 2\}.$$

Let $(\cdot, \cdot), \| \cdot \|$ be the scalar product and norm in $H = L_2(\Omega)$, respectively:

$$(u, v) = \int_\Omega u(x)v(x)dx, \quad \|u\| = (u, u)^{1/2}.$$

Define an elliptic operator $\mathcal{A}$ such that

$$\mathcal{A}u = -\triangle u, \quad x \in \Omega. \tag{1}$$

We use calligraphic letters for denoting operators in infinite dimensional spaces and standard capital letters for their finite dimensional approximations. The operator $\mathcal{A}$ is defined on the set of functions $u(\boldsymbol{x})$ that satisfy on the boundary $\partial\Omega$ the following conditions:

$$u(\boldsymbol{x}) = 0, \quad \boldsymbol{x} \in \partial\Omega. \tag{2}$$

For the spectral problem

$$\mathcal{A}\varphi_k = \lambda_k\varphi_k, \quad \boldsymbol{x} \in \Omega, \quad \varphi_k(\boldsymbol{x}) = 0, \quad \boldsymbol{x} \in \partial\Omega,$$

we have $0 < \lambda_1 \leq \lambda_2 \leq ...$, and the eigenfunctions φ_k, $\|\varphi_k\| = 1$, $k = 1, 2, ...$ form a basis in $L_2(\Omega)$. Therefore

$$u = \sum_{k=1}^{\infty}(u, \varphi_k)\varphi_k.$$

Let the operator $\mathcal{A}$ satisfy the following restrictions:

$$D(\mathcal{A}) = \{u \mid u(\boldsymbol{x}) \in L_2(\Omega), \ \sum_{k=0}^{\infty}|(u, \varphi_k)|^2\lambda_k < \infty\}.$$

The operator $\mathcal{A}$ is self-adjoint and positive definite:

$$\mathcal{A} = \mathcal{A}^* \geq \delta\mathcal{I}, \tag{3}$$

where $\mathcal{I}$ is the identity operator in H. For δ, we have $\delta = \lambda_1$. In applications, the value of λ_1 is unknown (the spectral problem must be solved). Therefore, we assume that $\delta \leq \lambda_1$ in (3). Let us assume for the fractional power of the operator $\mathcal{A}$:

$$\mathcal{A}^{\alpha}u = \sum_{k=0}^{\infty}(u, \varphi_k)\lambda_k^{\alpha}\varphi_k, \quad 0 < \alpha < 1.$$

The direct problem is formulated as follows. We search $u(t) = u(\boldsymbol{x}, t)$, $0 \leq t \leq T$, $T > 0$ such that it is the solution of the following first-order evolutionary equation:

$$\frac{du}{dt} + \mathcal{A}^{\alpha}u = p(t)f, \quad 0 < t \leq T. \tag{4}$$

The initial condition is specified as

$$u(0) = u_0. \tag{5}$$

The formulation (4), (5) presents the direct problem, where the right-hand side (functions $p(t)$, $f(\boldsymbol{x})$) are given as the boundary and initial conditions.

Let us consider the inverse problem, where in Eq. (4), the coefficient $p(t)$ is unknown. An additional condition is often formulated as

$$u(\boldsymbol{x}^*, t) = \varphi(t), \quad 0 < t \leq T. \tag{6}$$

We assume that the above inverse problem of finding a pair of $u(\boldsymbol{x}, t)$, $p(t)$ from Eqs. (4), (5) and additional conditions (6) is well-posed. The corresponding conditions for existence and uniqueness of the solution for parabolic problems (for $\alpha = 1$) are available in paper [9]. These results are presented in detail in the book [10] (section 1.5, the bibliographic commentary on pages 647, 648). The key requirement for well-posedness of the inverse problem is $|f(\boldsymbol{x}^*)| > 0$.

3   Semi-discrete Problem

To solve numerically the time-dependent problem (4), (5), we introduce the uniform grid in the domain Ω:

$$\bar{\omega} = \omega \cup \partial\omega = \{\boldsymbol{x} \mid \boldsymbol{x} = (x_1, x_2), \; x_\beta = i_\beta h_\beta,$$
$$i_\beta = 0, 1, ..., N_\beta, \; N_\beta h_\beta = l_\beta, \; \beta = 1, 2\},$$

where ω is the set of interior points, whereas $\partial\omega$ is the set of boundary points. For the grid functions $y(\boldsymbol{x}) = 0$, $\boldsymbol{x} \in \partial\omega$, we define the Hilbert space $H = L_2(\omega)$, where the scalar product and norm are given as follows:

$$(y, w) \equiv \sum_{\boldsymbol{x} \in \omega} y(\boldsymbol{x}) w(\boldsymbol{x}) h_1 h_2, \quad \|y\| \equiv (y, y)^{1/2}.$$

The grid operator A can be written as

$$Ay(\boldsymbol{x}) = -\frac{1}{h_1^2}(y(x_1 + h_1, x_2) - 2y(\boldsymbol{x}) + y(x_1 - h_1, x_2))$$
$$-\frac{1}{h_2^2}(y(x_1, x_2 + h_2) - 2y(\boldsymbol{x}) + y(x_1, x_2 - h_2)), \quad \boldsymbol{x} \in \omega. \tag{7}$$

Consider the spectral problem

$$A\psi_k = \mu_k \psi_k, \quad \boldsymbol{x} \in \omega, \quad k = (k_1, k_2), \quad k_\beta = 1, 2, ..., N_\beta - 1, \quad \beta = 1, 2.$$

For the eigenfunctions and eigenvalues, we have (see, e.g., [13]):

$$\psi_k(\boldsymbol{x}) = \prod_{\beta=1}^{2} \sqrt{\frac{2}{l_\beta}} \sin(k_\beta \pi x_\beta), \quad \boldsymbol{x} \in \omega,$$

$$\mu_k = \sum_{\beta=1}^{2} \frac{4}{h_\beta^2} \sin^2 \frac{k_\beta \pi}{2N_\beta}, \quad k_\alpha = 1, 2, ..., N_\alpha - 1, \quad \alpha = 1, 2.$$

Certain direct calculations yield (see (3))

$$A = A^* \geq \delta I. \tag{8}$$

where $\delta = \mu_1$ and

$$\mu_1 = \sum_{\beta=1}^{2} \frac{4}{h_\beta^2} \sin^2 \frac{\pi}{2N_\beta} \geq 8\left(\frac{1}{l_1^2} + \frac{1}{l_2^2}\right).$$

For the fractional power of the operator A, we obtain

$$A^\alpha y = \sum_{k=1}^{K} (y, \psi_k) \mu_k^\alpha \psi_k, \quad K = (N_1 - 1)(N_2 - 1), \quad 0 < \alpha < 1.$$

The problem (4), (5) is associated with the Cauchy problem

$$\frac{dy}{dt} + A^\alpha y = p(t)f, \quad 0 < t \le T, \tag{9}$$

$$y(0) = u_0, \quad x \in \omega. \tag{10}$$

4   Algorithm for Solving the Inverse Problem

Let us define a uniform grid in time $t^n = n\tau$, $n = 0, 1, ..., N$, $\tau N = T$ and denote $y^n = y(t^n)$, $t^n = n\tau$. We start with discretization in time for approximate solving the direct problem (9), (10). Let us apply the unconditionally stable [12] implicit scheme

$$\frac{y^{n+1} - y^n}{\tau} + A^\alpha y^{n+1} = \rho^{n+1} f, \quad n = 0, 1, ..., N - 1, \tag{11}$$

$$y^0 = u_0. \tag{12}$$

After discretization of the direct problem (4), (5) both in space and in time, according to (11), (12), we arrive at the problem of identifying the coefficient $p(t) \approx \rho(t)$ in the right-hand side. We restrict ourselves to the case when an additional information about the solution is defined as the solution value at the point of observation x^* (see (6)), which is some interior point of the grid. Assume that

$$y^{n+1}(x^*) = \varphi^{n+1}, \quad x^* \in \omega, \quad n = 0, 1, ..., N - 1. \tag{13}$$

For the approximate solution of the problem (11)–(13) at the new time level y^{n+1}, we use (see [17–19]) the decomposition

$$y^{n+1}(x) = v^{n+1}(x) + \rho^{n+1} w(x), \quad x \in \omega. \tag{14}$$

To evaluate $v^{n+1}(x)$, we solve the grid equation

$$\frac{v^{n+1} - y^n}{\tau} + A^\alpha v^{n+1} = 0, \quad n = 0, 1, ..., N - 1. \tag{15}$$

The grid function $w(x)$, $x \in \omega$ is evaluated from the equation

$$\frac{1}{\tau} w + A^\alpha w = f. \tag{16}$$

Using the decomposition (14)–(16), Eq. (11) holds for any ρ^{n+1}.

The condition (13) is used to evaluate ρ^{n+1}. Substituting (14) into (13), we get

$$\rho^{n+1} = \frac{1}{w(x^*)} (\varphi^{n+1} - v^{n+1}(x^*)). \tag{17}$$

The key issue of applicability of this algorithm is associated with the condition $w(\boldsymbol{x}^*) \neq 0$. The grid function $w(\boldsymbol{x}^*)$ is defined as the solution of the grid Eq. (16). The assumption that $w(\boldsymbol{x}^*) \neq 0$ is closely related to the constraint on the well-posedness of the inverse problem $|f(\boldsymbol{x}^*)| > 0$. It becomes obvious when considering problem (16) with $\tau \to 0$. Such restrictions can be provided via the corresponding measurement scheme, i.e., the observation point $\boldsymbol{x}^*$.

To validate the computational algorithm, we obtain the corresponding estimates of stability for the difference solution using the maximum principle for grid equations. For parabolic equations ($\alpha = 1$), such a consideration was done in [19].

The computational implementation is based on the method of variable separation with the decomposition of the solution via known eigenfunctions of the operator A. For the solution of the problem (16), we have

$$w(\boldsymbol{x}) = \sum_{k=1}^{K} \frac{\tau}{\tau + \mu_k^\alpha} (f, \psi_k)\psi_k(\boldsymbol{x}), \quad \boldsymbol{x}^* \in \omega.$$

In a similar way, for $v^{n+1}(\boldsymbol{x})$ in (15), we get

$$v^{n+1}(\boldsymbol{x}) = \sum_{k=1}^{K} \frac{\tau}{\tau + \mu_k^\alpha} (y^n, \psi_k)\psi_k(\boldsymbol{x}), \quad \boldsymbol{x}^* \in \omega, \quad n = 0, 1, ..., N - 1.$$

Thus, approximate solving the problem with the fractional power of the elliptic operator is implemented in the simplest way.

5   Numerical Examples

To demonstrate the possibilities of the above numerical algorithm for solving the RHS identification problem for the parabolic equation, we study the following model problem. In the examples below, we consider the problem in the unit square ($l_1 = l_2 = 1$). Suppose

$$f(\boldsymbol{x}) = x_1 x_2, \quad u_0(\boldsymbol{x}) = 0, \quad \boldsymbol{x} \in \Omega.$$

The problem is considered on the grid with $N_1 = N_2 = 256$. Note that for the studied inverse problems, the influence of spatial computational grid is practically not observed when we consider a sequence of grids. The observation point is located at the square center ($\boldsymbol{x}^* = (0.5, 0.5)$). The coefficient $p(t)$ is taken in the form

$$p(t) = 20\sin(10\pi t), \tag{18}$$

with $T = 0.1$. For the right-hand side (18), integrating in time the Fourier coefficients, we can obtain the exact solution of the semi-discrete problem. It is treated as a reference solution.

The approximate solution of the direct problem (1)–(5) at the final time moment $t = T$ is shown in Fig. 1. We highlight the principle dependence of the

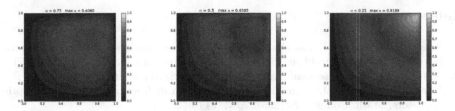

Fig. 1. Solution $y(x,t)$ of the direct problem at the final time moment $t = T$ for various α

solution on the power α. As α tends to zero, we observe the singularity of the solution. The solution of the direct problem at the observation point (see (6)) is depicted in Fig. 2. When solving the inverse problem of finding the coefficient $p(t)$, this data is treated as an input.

In the approximate solving problem (11)–(13), the emphasis is on a reconstruction of the dependence of the right-hand side on time for various time steps. The accuracy is evaluated via the solution error $\varepsilon = \rho(t) - p(t)$. The dependence of the solution error on the parameter α is presented in Figs. 3, 4 and 5. We observe the first-order convergence in time.

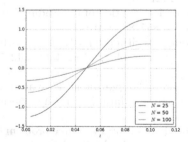

Fig. 2. Solution $\varphi(t)$ of the direct problem

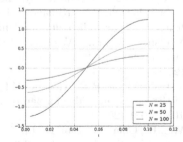

Fig. 3. Solution error $\varepsilon(t)$ of the inverse problem for $\alpha = 0.75$

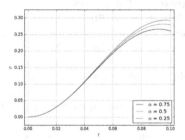

Fig. 4. Solution error $\varepsilon(t)$ of the inverse problem for $\alpha = 0.5$

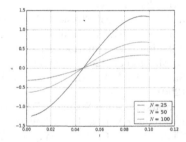

Fig. 5. Solution error $\varepsilon(t)$ of the inverse problem for $\alpha = 0.25$

References

1. Aceto, L., Novati, P.: Rational approximation to the fractional Laplacian operator in reaction-diffusion problems. SIAM J. Sci. Comput. **39**(1), A214–A228 (2017)
2. Alifanov, O.M.: Inverse Heat Transfer Problems. Springer, Heidelberg (2011)
3. Bonito, A., Pasciak, J.: Numerical approximation of fractional powers of elliptic operators. Math. Comput. **84**(295), 2083–2110 (2015)
4. Furati, K.M., Iyiola, O.S., Kirane, M.: An inverse problem for a generalized fractional diffusion. Appl. Math. Comput. **249**, 24–31 (2014)
5. Isakov, V.: Inverse Problems for Partial Differential Equations, 3rd edn. Springer, Cham (2017). https://doi.org/10.1007/978-3-319-51658-5
6. Jin, B., Rundell, W.: A tutorial on inverse problems for anomalous diffusion processes. Inverse Prob. **31**(3), 035003 (2015)
7. Kirane, M., Malik, S.A., Al-Gwaiz, M.A.: An inverse source problem for a two dimensional time fractional diffusion equation with nonlocal boundary conditions. Math. Methods Appl. Sci. **36**(9), 1056–1069 (2013)
8. Nochetto, R.H., Otárola, E., Salgado, A.J.: A PDE approach to fractional diffusion in general domains: a priori error analysis. Found. Comput. Math. **15**(3), 733–791 (2015)
9. Prilepko, A., Soloviev, V.: The solvability theorems and Rothe's method in inverse problems for a parabolic equation. Part I. Differ. Equ. **23**(10), 1791–1799 (1987). in Russian
10. Prilepko, A.I., Orlovsky, D.G., Vasin, I.A.: Methods for Solving Inverse Problems in Mathematical Physics. Marcel Dekker, Inc., New York (2000)
11. Sakamoto, K., Yamamoto, M.: Initial value/boundary value problems for fractional diffusion-wave equations and applications to some inverse problems. J. Math. Anal. Appl. **382**(1), 426–447 (2011)
12. Samarskii, A.A.: The Theory of Difference Schemes. Marcel Dekker, New York (2001)
13. Samarskii, A.A., Nikolaev, E.S.: Numerical Methods for Grid Equations, vol. I, II. Birkhauser Verlag, Basel (1989)
14. Tian, W., Li, C., Deng, W., Wu, Y.: Regularization methods for unknown source in space fractional diffusion equation. Math. Comput. Simul. **85**, 45–56 (2012)
15. Uchaikin, V.V.: Fractional Derivatives for Physicists and Engineers. Higher Education Press, Beijing (2013)
16. Vabishchevich, P.N.: Numerically solving an equation for fractional powers of elliptic operators. J. Comput. Phys. **282**(1), 289–302 (2015)
17. Vabishchevich, P.N., Klibanov, M.V.: Numerical identification of the leading coefficient of a parabolic equation. Differ. Equ. **52**(7), 855–862 (2016)
18. Vabishchevich, P.N., Vasil'ev, V.I.: Computational algorithms for solving the coefficient inverse problem for parabolic equations. Inverse Probl. Sci. Eng. **24**(1), 42–59 (2016)
19. Vabishchevich, P.N., Vasil'ev, V.I., Vasil'eva, M.V.: Computational identification of the right-hand side of a parabolic equation. Comput. Math. Math. Phys. **55**(6), 1015–1021 (2015)
20. Wei, H., Chen, W., Sun, H., Li, X.: A coupled method for inverse source problem of spatial fractional anomalous diffusion equations. Inverse Probl. Sci. Eng.; Former. Inverse Probl. Eng. **18**(7), 945–956 (2010)

Pore Scale Flow and Transport Simulation

Computational Identification of Adsorption and Desorption Parameters for Pore Scale Transport in Random Porous Media

Vasiliy V. Grigoriev[1], Oleg Iliev[2,4]([✉]), and Petr N. Vabishchevich[3]

[1] North-Eastern Federal University, 58 Belinskogo Street, 677000 Yakutsk, Russia
[2] Fraunhofer Institute for Industrial Mathematics ITWM,
Fraunhofer-Platz 1, 67663 Kaiserslautern, Germany
iliev@itwm.fraunhofer.de
[3] Nuclear Safety Institute, Russian Academy of Sciences,
52, B. Tulskaya, Moscow, Russia
[4] Institute of Mathematics and Informatics, Bulgarian Academy of Science,
Sofia, Bulgaria

Abstract. Reactive flow at pore scale in random porous media is considered at low Pecklet and Damkoler numbers, and computational identification of unknown adsorption and desorption rates is discussed. The reactive transport is governed by steady state Stokes equations, coupled with convection-diffusion equation for species transport. The surface reactions, namely adsorption and desorption, are accounted via Robin boundary condition. Finite element approximation in space and implicit time discretization are exploited. Measured concentration of the specie at the outlet of the domain is provided to carry out the identification procedure. The impact of the noise in the measurement on the parameter identification procedure is studied. Stochastic parameter identification approach is adopted. Computational results demonstrating the potential of the considered parameter identification approaches are presented.

1 Introduction

In the case of surface reactions, at pore scale the species transport is coupled to surface reaction via boundary conditions. When the reaction rates are not known, their identification falls into the class of boundary value inverse problems, [1]. The so called breakthrough curves, i.e. the average concentration of the specie at the outlet as a function of time, are usually used as extra information which is needed to identify the unknown adsorption and desorption parameters. In the literature, inverse problems for porous media flow are discussed mainly in connection with parameter identification for macroscopic, Darcy scale problems (see, e.g., [7]). Identification of parameters for pore scale models is discussed in this paper.

© Springer Nature Switzerland AG 2020
I. Lirkov and S. Margenov (Eds.): LSSC 2019, LNCS 11958, pp. 115–122, 2020.
https://doi.org/10.1007/978-3-030-41032-2_12

Gradient methods for minimizing the functional of the difference between measured and computed quantities, are broadly used for solving inverse problems. Opposite to this approach, our target is not to find exactly the minimum of the functional, but to identify an admissible set of parameters for which the functional is smaller then a prescribed threshold. We show that in the considered here case this ensures also certain accuracy for the identified parameters. We adopt here a stochastic approach for global optimization in its simplest form, consisting only of a random search, known as Pure Random Search [9]. In this case the residual functional is evaluated at randomly chosen points from the feasible set. Sobol sequences [6] can be used for sampling. An advantage of this approach is that unlike the gradient methods, its parallelization is straightforward. The solution of the inverse problems we are interested in, is composed of two ingredients: (multiple) solution of the direct (called also forward) problem, and the parameter identification algorithm.

This paper is continuation of [3] where parameter identification for small Pecklet and Damkoler numbers was studied in conjunction with periodic porous media. The goal here is to study the parameter identification in random porous media under the same Pe and Da assumptions. Due to the page limitation, results on parameter identification from noisy data for only one realization of the random porous media are presented here. The results from the systematic study for many realizations and for different porosities will be presented elsewhere.

2   Mathematical Model

2D pore scale transport of a dissolved substance in the presence of adsorption and desorption is considered. Random porous media geometry used here is shown on Fig. 1. A part of the domain (covered by a grid on the figure), namely Ω_f is occupied by a fluid, while the other part is occupied be the obstacles Ω_s. The obstacle surfaces (where the reaction occurs) are denoted by Γ_s, while periodicity lines are denoted by Γ_{per}. It is supposed that dissolved substance is introduced via the inlet boundary Γ_{in}, and the part of the substance which did not react flows out via the outlet Γ_{out}. The computational domain consists from Ω_f. *Flow problem.* The flow is described by the incompressible steady state Stokes equations:

$$\nu\nabla^2\boldsymbol{u} = \nabla p, \quad \boldsymbol{x} \in \Omega_f, \quad t > 0, \tag{1}$$

where ν, $\boldsymbol{u}(\boldsymbol{x})$ and $p(\boldsymbol{x})$ are the viscosity, fluid velocity and pressure, respectively. Boundary conditions which are typical for such problems are considered. No-slip and no-penetration conditions are prescribed on the solid walls. Periodic conditions are prescribed on the periodic boundary of the computational domain. Uniform flow is prescribed at the inlet. Zero normal component of the stress tensor is prescribed at the outlet. *Species Transport.* The unsteady solute transport in absence of homogeneous reactions is governed by the following dimensionless convection diffusion equation

$$\frac{\partial c}{\partial t} + \nabla(\boldsymbol{u}c) - \frac{1}{\text{Pe}}\nabla^2 c = 0, \quad \boldsymbol{x} \in \Omega_f, \quad t > 0, \tag{2}$$

where $c(\boldsymbol{x}, t)$ stands for the dimensionless concentration and $\mathrm{Pe} = \frac{l\bar{u}}{D}$ is the Peclet number.

The concentration of the solute at the inlet has been used to scale the concentration, thus $c = 1, \boldsymbol{x} \in \Gamma_{in}$. Zero diffusive flux of the solute at the outlet and on the external boundaries of the domain is prescribed. Note that nonzero convective flux via the outlet is implicitly allowed by the above boundary conditions. The surface reactions that occur at the obstacles' surface Γ_s satisfy the mass conservation law, in this particular case meaning that the change in the adsorbed surface concentration is equal to the flux from the fluid to the surface. This in dimensionless form is described as

$$\frac{\partial m}{\partial t} = -\nabla c \cdot \boldsymbol{n}, \quad \boldsymbol{x} \in \Gamma_s, \tag{3}$$

where m is scaled as $\bar{m} = l\bar{c}$. In dimensionless form the adsorption relations, in the case of Henry isotherm, are written as follows

$$\frac{\partial m}{\partial t} = \mathrm{Da}_a c - \mathrm{Da}_d m, \quad \boldsymbol{x} \in \Gamma_s, \tag{4}$$

where the adsorption and desorption Damkoler numbers are given by

$$\mathrm{Da}_a = \frac{k_a}{\bar{u}}, \quad \mathrm{Da}_d = \frac{k_d l}{\bar{u}}.$$

3   Numerical Solution of the Direct Problem

Finite Element Method, FEM, is used for space discretization of the above problem, together with implicit discretization in time. The algorithm used here for solving the direct problem is practically identical of the algorithm used to study oxidation in [2]. Therefore the details, e.g., functional spaces, grid convergence studies, etc., will be omitted here due to space limitation.

Geometry and Grid. The computational domain for one realization of the random geometry, together with a generated grid with 13746 nodes, are shown on Fig. 1. Note, that as it is usual for pore scale simulations, some pure fluid regions are added in front of the inflow and behind the outflow.

Computation of Steady State Flow. One way coupling is considered here. The fluid flow influences the species transport, but there is no back influence of the species concentration on the fluid flow. Based on this, the flow is computed in advance. The FEM approximation of the steady state flow problem is based on variational formulation of the considered boundary value problem (1), together with the respective boundary conditions.

For the FEM approximation of the velocity and the pressure, Taylor-Hood $P_2 - P_1$ elements [8] are used here. The computations are carried out using the computing platform for partial differential equations FEniCS (website fenicsproject.org) [5].

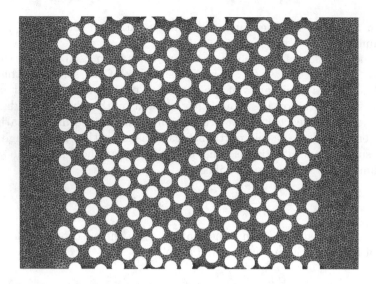

Fig. 1. The computational domain and the grid for one realization of the random geometry with porosity $\phi = 0.56$.

Simulation of Reactive Transport. The unsteady species transport problem (2), (3), (4) is solved numerically using standard Lagrangian P_1 finite elements. For details on the FE discretization see [2,3]. In the considered here case, zero initial conditions for the concentration are posed, the used time step is 0.1.

The basic set of parameters used in the forward simulations in this articles reads as follows: $\text{Pe} = 10, \text{Da}_a = 0.005, \text{Da}_d = 0.05$. The unsteady problem (2) is solved on dimensionless time interval $(0, T)$, $T = 40$, using time step $\tau = 0.1$.

The concentration field at two time moments is shown on Fig. 2.

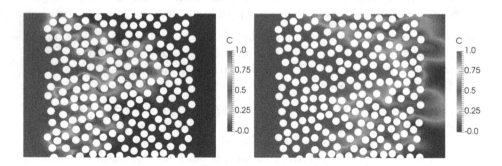

Fig. 2. Concentration at $t = 5$ (left), and $t = 10$ (right).

The breakthrough curves for these three different realizations of the porous media are relatively close to each other. Note, that the identified admissible set for those three realizations are also very close to each other for the considered

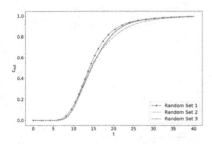 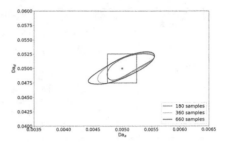

Fig. 3. Left: Breakthrough curves without noise for three different realizations of the porous media; Right: Exact and identified parameters in the case of no noise

here low Pe and Da case, but these results are not shown here due to space limitation. Below we show results for only one realization of the random porous media.

4   Numerical Solution of the Inverse Problem

Breakthrough Curves and Residual Functional. Consider an inverse problem for determining unknown adsorption and desorption rates (so called parameter identification problem). Breakthrough curve (presenting the dynamics of the average outlet concentration) defined as:

$$c_{out}(t) = \frac{\int_{\Gamma_{out}} c(\boldsymbol{x}, t) d\boldsymbol{x}}{\int_{\Gamma_{out}} d\boldsymbol{x}}, \tag{5}$$

is used as input for the parameter identification procedure. The breakthrough curves for three realizations of random porous media with the same porosity and same size of inclusions are shown on Fig. 3, left.

In fact, the breakthrough curves are a quantity which relatively easy can be measured in the Lab. Denote by $\widetilde{c}_{out}(t)$ the measured breakthrough curve (which is often noisy). The starting point in parameter identification procedure is the monitoring of the difference (residual) between the measured $\widetilde{c}_{out}(t)$ and the computed $c_{out}(t)$ average outflow concentration for different value of the parameters Da_a and Da_d in Henry isotherm Eq. (4). Let us consider the problem for identifying the adsorption and desorption rates, Da_a, Da_d, respectively, using given measurement results $\widetilde{c}_{out}(t)$. The functional of the residual is given by

$$J(\mathrm{Da}_a, \mathrm{Da}_d) = \int_0^T (c_{out}(t) - \widetilde{c}(t))^2 dt, \tag{6}$$

where $c_{out}(t)$ is given by (5) after solving (1), and (2), (3), (4).

Note that in this paper we work with synthetic data. Namely, using the basing set of parameters, a breakthrough curve is generated, and later on this breakthrough curve is used in the identification procedure.

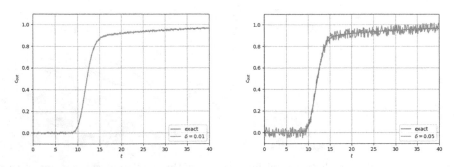

Fig. 4. Breakthrough curves with noise: a—$\delta = 0.01$, b—$\delta = 0.05$

Pure Random Search Based Parameter Identification. The problem for identifying adsorption parameters in this case is formulated as follows. Find Da_a, Da_d from a set of admissible parameters G, satisfying (7). A stochastic approach for global optimization in its simplest form consists only of a random search and it is called Pure Random Search [9]. In this case the residual functional is evaluated at randomly chosen points belonging to the admissible set. Such an stochastic approach is very easy to parallelize.

Consider the case when the admissible set G is defined in a simple way:

$$0 \leq Da_a \leq \overline{Da_a}, \quad 0 \leq Da_d \leq \overline{Da_d}.$$

To generate uniformly distributed points D from G, Sobol sequences [6] are used. The software implementation is based on the sensitivity analysis library SALib [4].

The result of the statistical identification in the case of no noise for $\overline{Da_a} = 0.005, \overline{Da_d} = 0.05$ is shown on Fig. 3, right for different number of sample points. The star $\star$ on the picture shows the exact values of the parameters, while the cross $\times$ shows the identified parameters. In this case (no noise, small Pe and Da) the identified parameters coincide with the exact ones.

The Influence of the Noise in the Measured Data. In the reality the measurement data are often noisy, therefore it is important to understand how the noise influences the parameter identification. Suppose that the measurement are carried out at each time step. Instead of (5), let us define

$$\widetilde{c}_{out}(t^n) = c_{out}(t^n; \widetilde{Da}_a, \widetilde{Da}_d) + \delta\sigma(t^n), \quad n = 1, 2, ..., N, \quad N\tau = T.$$

Here the parameter δ quantifies the amplitude of the noise, while $\sigma(t^n)$ is a random variable, uniformly distributed on the interval $[-1, 1]$.

Noisy data for a breakthrough curve are shown on Fig. 4, left for the case $\delta = 0.01$, and Fig. 4, right for the case $\delta = 0.05$.

Square root of the residual functional for the noisy data is shown on Fig. 5. On the left side of Fig. 5 the results for the case of $\delta = 0.01$ are shown. Similar to the case of no noise, the star $\star$ on the picture points to the exact value of the parameters, while the cross × points to the set of parameters in which the minimum of the functional is achieved. The red square on the picture, centered around the star, is a drawing of $(0.99 \times 1.01)\mathrm{Da}_a, (0.99 \times 1.01)\mathrm{Da}_d$ isolines of the residual. This means that all the values of the parameters within the red square approximate the exact parameters with less than one percent error (recall that in this case the amplitude of the noise is also one percent). On the right side of Fig. 5 the results for the case of $\delta = 0.05$ are shown. In this case the star ⋆ and the cross × do not coincide, what means that the minimum of the residual functional in the case of noise does not coincide with the minimum in the case of no noise. The red square on the picture, centered around the star, in this case is a drawing of $(0.95 \times 1.05)\mathrm{Da}_a, (0.95 \times 1.05)\mathrm{Da}_d$ lines of the residual. This means that all the values of the parameters within the red square approximate the exact parameters with less than five percent error (recall that in this case the amplitude of the noise is also five percent). As it can be expected, the large amplitudes of the noise lead to reduced accuracy of identification. However, in the case of large amplitude of the noise, also the requirements to the accuracy of the identified parameters are often relaxed in the practice. It is a common case to target identification accuracy which is at the same order as the level of the noise in the measurements.

For cases when instead of trying to identify an unique set of single values for the parameters of interest, one should identify an admissible set of parameters for which the value of the residual functional is below (prescribed) critical tolerance, one has to prescribe properly such a tolerance. Having in mind the dispersion of the uniformly distributed random variable σ, we define the set of the admissible parameters by the inequality

$$J(\mathrm{Da}_a, \mathrm{Da}_d) \leq \gamma \delta^2 \frac{T}{3}, \tag{7}$$

where $\gamma > 1$ is a numerical parameter (in our calculations it is set to 1.1). For the calculated admissible sets of parameters with different noise levels shown on Fig. 5, obviously, larger amplitude of the noise leads to larger set of admissible parameters. It is seen that the red squares are not completely within the identified admissible set of parameters, on the other hand keeping the residual functional below a prescribed tolerance is more important and more informative.

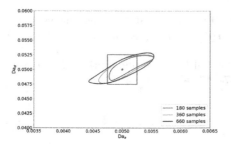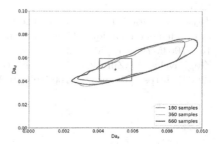

Fig. 5. Results with noise: left—$\delta = 0.01$, right—$\delta = 0.05$

5   Summary

Stochastic algorithm for identification of unknown adsorption and desorption rates is presented in conjunction with pore scale simulation of reactive flow in 2D random porous media. Breakthrough curves are the extra data needed for the solution of the parameter identification problem. Exact and noisy data are considered. In the latter case the impact of the noise on the identification procedure is discussed. It should be pointed that in the real problem, especially in the case of noisy data, the target should be not identifying a single set of the seeked parameters, in which the minimum of the residual functional is achieved. Instead, it is more reasonable to seek admissible sets of parameters for which the residual functional is less than a prescribed threshold. The threshold should be consistent with the amplitude in the noise in the data.

Acknowledgements. The work was supported by Mega-grant of the Russian Federation Government (N 14.Y26.31.0013), and by grant from the Russian Foundation for Basic Research (project 19-31-90108).

References

1. Alifanov, O.M.: Inverse Heat Transfer Problems. Springer, Berlin (2011)
2. Churbanov, A.G., Iliev, O., Strizhov, V.F., Vabishchevich, P.N.: Numerical simulation of oxidation processes in a cross-flow around tube bundles. Appl. Math. Model. **59**, 251–271 (2018)
3. Grigoriev, V.V., Iliev, O., Vabishchevich, P.N.: Computational identification of adsorption and desorption parameters for pore scale transport in periodic porous media. J. Comput. Appl. Math. **370**, 112661 (2020). https://doi.org/10.1016/j.cam.2019.112661
4. Herman, J., Usher, W.: SALib: an open-source python library for sensitivity analysis. J. Open Source Softw. **2**(9) (2017). https://doi.org/10.21105/joss.00097
5. Logg, A., Mardal, K.A., Wells, G.N., et al.: Automated Solution of Differential Equations by the Finite Element Method. Springer, Heidelberg (2012). https://doi.org/10.1007/978-3-642-23099-8
6. Sobol', I.M.: On the systematic search in a hypercube. SIAM J. Numer. Anal. **16**(5), 790–793 (1979)
7. Sun, N.Z.: Inverse Problems in Groundwater Modeling, vol. 6. Springer, Dordrecht (2013)
8. Taylor, C., Hood, P.: A numerical solution of the Navier-Stokes equations using the finite element technique. Comput. Fluids **1**(1), 73–100 (1973). https://doi.org/10.1016/0045-7930(73)90027-3
9. Zhigljavsky, A., Žilinskas, A.: Stochastic Global Optimization. Springer, New York (2008). https://doi.org/10.1007/978-0-387-74740-8

Weighted Time-Semidiscretization Quasilinearization Method for Solving Rihards' Equation

Miglena N. Koleva and Lubin G. Vulkov[✉]

University of Ruse, 8 Studentska Street, 7017 Ruse, Bulgaria
{mkoleva,lvalkov}@uni-ruse.bg

Abstract. This paper concerns efficient σ - weighted ($0 < \sigma < 1$) time-semidiscretization quasilinearization technique for numerical solution of Richards' equation. We solve the classical and a new α - time-fractional ($0 < \alpha < 1$) equation, that models anomalous diffusion in porous media. High-order approximation of the $\alpha = 2(1 - \sigma)$ fractional derivative is applied. Numerical comparison results are discussed.

1 Introduction

The Richards' equation is one of the most used model for simulations of water transport in soil and has many applications in hydrology, meteorology, agronomy and agriculture. It has been derived by L. Richards (1931) on the base of Darcy's law for saturated flow in porous media. When an anomalous diffusion is considered in porous media, fractional derivative appears in the new model due to the scaling between time and space variables. A generalization of the Richards' equation, which indicates presence of memory effects in soil water transport phenomena, by introducing fractional time derivative is suggested in [8,9,15]. So, without loss of generality, we consider a slightly modification of the classical Richards' equation using fractional derivative of water content on time:

$$\frac{\partial^\alpha u}{\partial t^\alpha} = Lu, \ \ 0 < \alpha \le 1, \ \ Lu = L(x,t)[u] = \frac{\partial}{\partial x}\left(k(x)a(u)\left(\frac{\partial u}{\partial x} + g\right)\right), \quad (1)$$

where $g \ge 0$ is a constant, $u = u(t,x)$, $x \in \Omega = (0,L)$, $L > 0$, $t \in (0,T_f)$, $k(x) \ge 0$ for $x \in [0,1]$. The coefficient $k(x)$ can degenerate, i.e. $k(0) = 0$, in the fully saturated zone. In this work, we consider Eq. (1) for *constant* $k > 0$ with the following initial and boundary conditions

$$u(x,0) = u^0(x), \ \ x \in \Omega, \ \ u(0,t) = u_l(t), \ \ u(L,t) = u_r(t), \ \ t \in [0,T_f]. \quad (2)$$

The problem (1), (2), for $0 < \alpha < 1$, $g = 0$, $k = 1$, so called fractional generalization of Richards' equation, is derived in [8,9,15]. In this formulation, u is the volumetric soil water content ($L^3 L^{-3}$), $a(u)$ is the fractional diffusivity ($L^2 T^{-\alpha}$), depending on the water content, x is the distance from one of the ends of the

I. Lirkov and S. Margenov (Eds.): LSSC 2019, LNCS 11958, pp. 123–130, 2020.
https://doi.org/10.1007/978-3-030-41032-2_13

column (L), t is time (T). Soil bulk density changes and soil water hysteresis are ignored. The water flux w_f is governed by the Darcy law $w_f = -a(u)\frac{\partial u}{\partial x}$.

The model, suggested by Richards [17], has been extensively studied from many researchers [13,16]. Existence and uniqueness of a weak solution is discussed in [13]. Numerous numerical methods for solving the classical Richards' equation ($\alpha = 1$) in its different forms (h (or pressure)-based, θ (or moisture)-based and mixed form) are available in the literature. For example, Picard's and Newton's linearizations based schemes are proposed in [4,5,14,18] etc.

For time-fractional problem (1), (2), $g = 0$, $k = 1$ a finite difference schemes are developed, using $O(\tau)$ approximation of the fractional time derivative and solved by Gauss elimination [15] and Adams-Bashforth-Moulton algorithm, realized by iterative Newton-Raphson method [8,9].

In the present work we focus on the construction of fast numerical algorithms for solving (1), (2), $0 < \alpha \leq 1$ and at this stage for constant $k > 0$. We develop and examine weighted quasilinearization scheme, combined with $O(\tau^{3-\alpha})$ approximation [1] of the fractional time derivative (for $0 < \alpha < 1$).

The quasilinearization method (QLM) has been introduced by [3] and has developed for solving non-linear differential equations. Two-grid extension of the QLM is proposed in [11].

The remaining part of the paper is organized as follows. In the next two sections, we introduce the time-discretization quasilinearization for the classical and fractional (generalized) Richards' equations, respectively. The full approximation of the Dirichlet problem is discussed in Sect. 4. In Sect. 5 we present numerical results. We end the paper with some conclusions.

2   Quasilinearization of the Problem (1)–(2) for $\alpha = 1$

For clarity, first we look at the case $\alpha = 1$. Consider an uniform partition of the interval $J = [0, T_f]$ with points $t_n = n\tau$, $n = 0, 1, \ldots, N$ and uniform step size $\tau = T_f/N$, where N is the number of subintervals. Denote by $f^n(x)$ the function $f(t_n, x)$ from $\Omega \times J$. The σ - weight time semidiscretization of the Eq. (1) leads to the following approximation:

$$\frac{u^{n+1}(x) - u^n(x)}{\tau} = \sigma L(x, t_{n+1})[u^{n+1}] + (1 - \sigma)L(x, t_n)[u^n]. \tag{3}$$

Let us denote

$$v^{n+1} = \frac{\partial u^{n+1}}{\partial x}, \qquad w^{n+1} = \frac{\partial^2 u^{n+1}}{\partial x^2} \tag{4}$$

and suppose that u_0^{n+1}, v_0^{n+1} and w_0^{n+1} are the initial approximations of the corresponding exact values of u^{n+1}, v^{n+1} and w^{n+1} at the $(n+1)$-th time layers. Then

$$u^{n+1} = u_0^{n+1} + (u^{n+1} - u_0^{n+1}) = u_0^{n+1} + \delta u^{n+1}, \quad v^{n+1} = v_0^{n+1} + \delta v^{n+1},$$
$$w^{n+1} = w_0^{n+1} + \delta w^{n+1}. \tag{5}$$

Following the quasilinearization technique of Bellman and Kalaba [3], we consider u^{n+1}, v^{n+1} and w^{n+1} as independent variables. Suppose that $\delta u^{n+1}, \delta v^{n+1}$ and δw^{n+1} are small values, denote $a'(u) = da/du$ and rewrite $L(x, t_{n+1})[u^{n+1}]$ in the form

$$L(x, t_{n+1})[u^{n+1}] = ka'(u^{n+1})(v^{n+1})^2 + ka(u^{n+1})w^{n+1} + kga'(u^{n+1})v^{n+1}. \quad (6)$$

Then, using (5), we perform the quasilinearization for the first term, to find:

$$a'(u_0^{n+1} + \delta u^{n+1})(v_0^{n+1} + \delta v^{n+1})^2 = 2v_0^{n+1}a'(u_0^{n+1})v^{n+1}$$
$$+ (v_0^{n+1})^2 a''(u_0^{n+1})u^{n+1} - (v_0^{n+1})^2 a'(u_0^{n+1}) - u_0^{n+1}(v_0^{n+1})^2 a''(u_0^{n+1}). \quad (7)$$

In a similar way, for the second term of (6), we get:

$$a(u^{n+1})w^{n+1} = a(u_0^{n+1})w^{n+1} + w_0^{n+1}a'(u_0^{n+1})u^{n+1} - u_0^{n+1}.w_0^{n+1}a'(u_0^{n+1}). \quad (8)$$

Further, the convection term of (6), we rewrite as

$$a'(u^{n+1})v^{n+1} = a'(u_0^{n+1})v^{n+1} + a''(u_0^{n+1})v_0^{n+1}u^{n+1} - a''(u_0^{n+1})v_0^{n+1}u_0^{n+1}. \quad (9)$$

Collecting all the results (6)–(9), substituting in (3), rearranging the terms and in view of (4), we obtain

$$\left(\frac{1}{\tau} + B^{n+1}(x)\right) u^{n+1} + C^{n+1}(x)\frac{\partial u^{n+1}}{\partial x} + D^{n+1}(x)\frac{\partial^2 u^{n+1}}{\partial x^2} = F_1^n(x) + F_2^{n+1}(x), \quad (10)$$

$$B^{n+1}(x) = -\sigma\left(kw_0^{n+1}a'(u_0^{n+1}) + k(v_0^{n+1})^2 a''(u_0^{n+1}) + kgv_0^{n+1}a''(u_0^{n+1})\right),$$
$$C^{n+1}(x) = -\sigma k(2v_0^{n+1} + g)a'(u_0^{n+1}), \quad D^{n+1}(x) = -\sigma ka(u_0^{n+1}),$$
$$F_2^{n+1}(x) = -k\sigma\Big((v_0^{n+1})^2 a'(u_0^{n+1}) + (v_0^{n+1})^2 u_0^{n+1}a''(u_0^{n+1}) + u_0^{n+1}w_0^{n+1}a'(u_0^{n+1})$$
$$+ gv_0^{n+1}u_0^{n+1}a''(u_0^{n+1})\Big), \quad F_1^n(x) = \frac{u^n}{\tau} + (1-\sigma)L(x, t_n)[u^n].$$

The Eq. (10) is subjected to the initial and boundary conditions (2).

3 Time Discretization and Quasilinearization of the Problem (1)–(2) for $0 < \alpha < 1$

Following [8,9,15], in (1) we consider Caputo fractional derivative of order α, defined by

$$\frac{\partial^\alpha u}{\partial t^\alpha} = D_c^\alpha u_t := \frac{1}{\Gamma(1-\alpha)} \int_0^t (t-\eta)^{-\alpha}\frac{\partial u(x,\eta)}{\partial \eta}d\eta, \quad 0 < \alpha < 1.$$

There are many approximations of the subdiffusion fractional derivatives in the literature, see e.g. [1,6,12] and references therein.

For the fractional derivative $D_c^\alpha u_t$ we apply $O(\tau^{3-\alpha})$ approximation at $t_{n+\sigma} = (n+\sigma)\tau$, $\sigma = 1 - \alpha/2$, $n = 0, 1, \ldots, N-1$, derived in [1].

$$D_c^\alpha u_t \approx D_c^\alpha U_t := \frac{\tau^{-\alpha}}{\Gamma(2-\alpha)} \sum_{j=0}^{n} c_j^{(n,\alpha,\sigma)} \left(u(t_{n-j+1}, x) - u(t_{n-j}, x)\right), \qquad (11)$$

where, $c_0^{(0,\alpha,\sigma)} = a_0^{(\alpha,\sigma)}$ for $n = 0$ and for $n \geq 1$

$$c_j^{(n,\alpha,\sigma)} = \begin{cases} a_0^{(\alpha,\sigma)} + b_1^{(\alpha,\sigma)}, & j = 0, \\ a_j^{(\alpha,\sigma)} + b_{j+1}^{(\alpha,\sigma)} - b_j^{(\alpha,\sigma)}, & 1 \leq j \leq n-1, \\ a_n^{(\alpha,\sigma)} - b_n^{(\alpha,\sigma)}, & j = n, \end{cases}$$

$$a_l^{(\alpha,\sigma)} = \begin{cases} \sigma^{1-\alpha}, & l = 0, \\ (l+\sigma)^{1-\alpha} - (l-1+\sigma)^{1-\alpha}, & l \geq 1, \end{cases}$$

$$b_l^{(\alpha,\sigma)} = \frac{1}{2-\alpha}[(l+\sigma)^{2-\alpha} - (l-1+\sigma)^{2-\alpha}] - \frac{1}{2}[(l+\sigma)^{1-\alpha} + (l-1+\sigma)^{1-\alpha}], \; l \geq 1.$$

Now, incorporating (11), the σ - weighted finite difference semidiscretization of the Eq. (1), $0 < \alpha < 1$, leads to the following approximation:

$$D_c^\alpha U_t = \sigma L(x, t_{n+1})[u^{n+1}] + (1-\sigma)L(x, t_n)[u^n]. \qquad (12)$$

The quasilinearization of the convection-diffusion part at new time level is similar as for the case $\alpha = 1$. Consequently, from (4)–(9), (11), for (12) we have

$$\left(\frac{\sigma^{1-\alpha}}{\Gamma(1-\alpha)\tau^\alpha} + B^{n+1}(x)\right)u^{n+1} + C^{n+1}(x)\frac{\partial u^{n+1}}{\partial x} + D^{n+1}(x)\frac{\partial^2 u^{n+1}}{\partial x^2} = F_1^n(x)$$

$$+ F_2^{n+1}(x) - \frac{1}{\Gamma(1-\alpha)\tau^\alpha} \sum_{j=1}^{n} c_j^{(n,\alpha,\sigma)} \left(u(t_{n-j+1}, x) - u(t_{n-j}, x)\right),$$

$$F_1^n(x) = (1-\sigma)L(x, t_n)[u^n] + \frac{\sigma^{1-\alpha}}{\Gamma(1-\alpha)\tau^\alpha} u^n,$$

$$(13)$$

where $B^{n+1}(x)$, $C^{n+1}(x)$, $D^{n+1}(x)$, $F_2^{n+1}(x)$ are defined as in (10).

The problem is completed by the initial and boundary conditions (2).

4   Full Discretization

Observing that for $\alpha = 1$, the Eq. (13) coincides with (10), further we discuss the full discretization of (13) for $0 < \alpha \leq 1$ and $\sigma = 1 - \alpha/2$.

Consider uniform mesh $\overline{\omega}_h$ in Ω: $\overline{\omega}_h = \{x_i = ih, \; i = 0, 1, \ldots, M, \; h = L/M\}$ and denote by U_i^n and $(U_0)_i^n$ the numerical solution of u and u_0 at point (t_n, x_i).

Next, we approximate all derivatives in (13) by second-order central finite differences, using the representation (6) for $L(x, t_n)[U_i^n]$, involve the notation

B_i^n for the resulting approximation of $B^n(x)$ and similarly for C_i^n, D_i^n, $(F_1)_i^n$, $(F_2)_i^n$, we obtain the full discretization of the problem (1), (2), $0 < \alpha \leq 1$:

$$\left(\frac{\sigma^{1-\alpha}}{\Gamma(1-\alpha)\tau^\alpha} + B_i^{n+1} - \frac{2D_i^{n+1}}{h^2}\right) U_i^{n+1} + \left(\frac{D_i^{n+1}}{h^2} + \frac{C_i^{n+1}}{2h}\right) U_{i+1}^{n+1}$$

$$+ \left(\frac{D_i^{n+1}}{h^2} - \frac{C_i^{n+1}}{2h}\right) U_{i-1}^{n+1} = (F_2)_i^{n+1} + \mathcal{F}_i, \quad i = 1, 2, \ldots, M-1,$$

$$\mathcal{F}_i = (F_1)_i^n - \frac{1}{\Gamma(1-\alpha)\tau^\alpha} \sum_{j=1}^{n} c_j^{(n,\alpha,\sigma)} (U_i^{n-j+1} - U_i^{n-j}),$$

$$U(x_i, 0) = u^0(x_i), \quad i = 1, 2, \ldots, M-1,$$

$$U(0, t_{n+1}) = u_l(t_{n+1}), \quad U(L, t_{n+1}) = u_r(t_{n+1}), \quad \text{where} \quad n = 0, 1, \ldots, N-1.$$

$$\tag{14}$$

To solve the non-linear system of algebraic equations (14), at each time layer we initiate iteration procedure, computing B^{n+1}, C^{n+1} and D^{n+1} at old iteration up to reaching the desired accuracy ε, measured as a difference of the solutions (in max norm) on two consecutive iterations. As initial guess we take the solution of the previous time level. Further, for shortness, we refer to this method as QLS.

5   Numerical Results

In this section we compare the efficiency and convergence order in maximum norm of QLS with other linearization methods.

First, we consider a test example with exact solution [7]: $a(u) = 1.01 + \tanh((u-0.5)/0.1)$, $k = 1$, $g = 2$, adding residual function in the right-hand side of (1), such that $u = 2e^{-t/2} \sin \pi x$ to be the exact solution. Initial and boundary conditions are chosen according to the exact solution. The error in maximum discrete norm and convergence order are computed at final time T_f by

$$E_M = \max_{0 \leq i \leq M} |u(x_i, T_f) - U_i^N|, \quad CR = \log_2(E_{2M}/E_M).$$

As the expected order of convergence for $0 < \alpha \leq 1$ is $O(\tau^2 + h^2)$ [1], we perform computations for fixed $\tau = h$. The other parameters are $\varepsilon = 10^{-6}$, $L = 1$ and $T_f = 1$.

Picard's and Newton's linerarizations and their modifications are often used for solving classical Richards' equation [4,5,14,18]. That is why, as a benchmark test we consider the σ-weighed discritization of (1), (2)

$$D_c^\alpha U_t = \frac{\sigma}{h} \left(A_{i+1/2}^{n+1}(U_i) - A_{i-1/2}^{n+1}(U_{i-1})\right) + \frac{(1-\sigma)}{h} \left(A_{i+1/2}^n(U_i) - A_{i-1/2}^n(U_{i-1})\right),$$

where $A_{i+1/2}^n(U_i) = 0.5k \left(a(U_{i+1}^n) + a(U_i^n)\right) \left((U_{i+1}^n - U_i^n)/h + g\right)$, realized by the classical Newton's method (NMS) and Picard's method (PMS), computing $a(U^{n+1})$ on the old iteration.

In Table 1 we compare the results from computations with all schemes: PMS, NMS, QLS for $\alpha = 1$. With 'iter' we denote the average number of iterations

Table 1. $\alpha = 1$

M	PMS			NMS			QLS		
	E_M	CR	iter	E_M	CR	iter	E_M	CR	iter
161	3.66139e−3		65.487	3.66211e−3		3.006	2.49534e−3		3.000
321	9.28298e−4	1.9844	27.209	9.24778e−4	1.9855	3.000	7.85718e−4	1.6672	3.000
641	2.31991e−4	1.9958	14.583	2.31795e−4	1.9963	2.005	2.10479e−4	1.9003	2.000
1281	5.80825e−5	1.9979	8.994	5.79868e−5	1.9991	2.000	5.36132e−5	1.9730	2.000
2561	1.42573e−5	2.0264	5.864	1.44994e−5	1.9997	2.000	1.34651e−5	1.9934	2.000
5121	3.58647e−6	1.9911	4.153	3.62502e−6	1.9999	2.000	3.37017e−6	1.9983	2.000

Table 2. $0 < \alpha < 1$, NMS

	$\alpha = 0.25$			$\alpha = 0.5$			$\alpha = 0.75$		
	E_M	CR	iter	E_M	CR	iter	E_M	CR	iter
161	3.07373e−3		3.006	3.22127e−3		3.006	3.40080e−3		3.000
321	7.80594e−4	1.9773	2.991	8.18600e−4	1.9764	2.990	8.57956e−4	1.9869	2.990
641	1.95254e−4	1.9992	2.995	2.04724e−4	1.9995	2.995	2.13067e−4	2.0096	2.000
1281	4.87550e−5	2.0017	2.000	1.10874e−5	2.0026	2.000	5.24587e−5	2.0221	2.000
2561	1.21963e−5	1.9991	2.000	1.27559e−5	2.0018	2.000	1.27995e−5	2.0351	2.000
5121	3.08308e−6	1.9840	2.002	3.17704e−6	2.0054	2.000	3.07176e−6	2.0590	2.000

at each time level. We observe that for all considered methods, the accuracy is $O(\tau^2 + h^2)$ and PMS executes more iterations. With QLM we attain better precision of the numerical solution than NMS, for the same number of iterations.

Consider the case $0 < \alpha < 1$. Numerical tests showed that for $0 < \alpha < 1$, PMS requires very fine mesh and large number of iterations, especially at the first time layers. For example, if $\alpha = 0.75$ and $N < 1281$, we observe oscillations of the numerical solution around the point $x = 0.05$. For $N = 1281$, the solution is computed successfully and the average number of iterations at each time level is 58. As smaller is α, we need the finer mesh and more iterations.

In Tables 2 and 3 we give the results from the computations with NMS and QLS for $0 < \alpha < 1$. The order of convergence $O(\tau^2 + h^2)$ for both schemes is confirmed. Comparing NMS and QLS, we may conclude that for $\alpha \geq 0.5$, QLS approximates the exact solution more precisely. For $\alpha < 0.5$ QLS provides better accuracy on the coarser meshes, while NMS is more accurate on the finer meshes.

Now, we consider van Genutchen-Mualem model (1)–(2) with pore size distribution indices $n = 2$ and $m = 1/n$ [10,13]:

$$a(u) = \begin{cases} (1 + u^2)^{-5/4}(\sqrt{1 + u^2} + u)^{-2}, & u > 0, \\ 1, & u \leq 0. \end{cases}$$

The other model parameters are:, $g = 2$, $u_l = 0$, $u_r = 1$, $u^0 = 1$, the depth $L = 100\,\text{cm}$, $T_f = 200\,\text{min}$, $\tau = 6\,\text{s}$, $h = 1.5625\,\text{mm}$. On Fig. 1 we depict the solution, computed by QLS at final time for different values of α and k. Advancing

Table 3. $0 < \alpha < 1$, QLS

M	$\alpha = 0.25$			$\alpha = 0.5$			$\alpha = 0.75$		
	E_M	CR	iter	E_M	CR	iter	E_M	CR	iter
161	2.41278e−3		3.000	2.42218e−3		3.000	2.43814e−3		3.000
321	7.38222e−4	1.7086	2.990	7.46388e−4	1.6983	2.991	7.53483e−4	1.6939	2.991
641	1.96031e−4	1.9130	2.995	1.98536e−4	1.9105	2.995	1.99105e−4	1.9202	1.998
1281	4.97533e−5	1.9782	2.000	5.03800e−5	1.9785	2.000	4.97894e−5	1.996	2.000
2561	1.25264e−5	1.9898	2.000	1.26271e−5	1.9963	2.000	1.21519e−5	2.0347	2.000
5121	3.10703e−6	2.0114	2.000	3.14623e−6	2.0048	2.000	2.89800e−6	2.0681	2.000

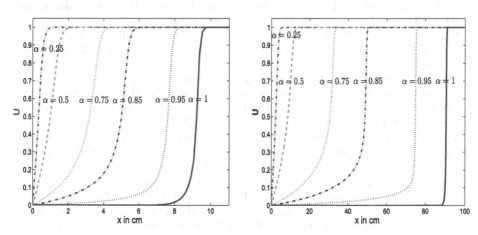

Fig. 1. QLS for Genutchen-Mualem model; $k = 0.1$, x-cutted plot (*left*); $k = 1$ (*right*)

in time, solution profiles move to the right boundary. The speed of this evolution depends significantly on the values of k and α. The larger k and α, the faster the solution approaches the right boundary.

6   Conclusions

A time-discretization quasilinearization method is proposed for numerical solving classical and time-fractional Richards' equation. For fixed time level, at each quasilinearization iteration we solve a linear ODE boundary value problem by finite difference method. Numerical results show the efficiency of QLS in comparison with NMS and PMS. By virtue of the simulations with PMS, we conclude that not each numerical method, developed for classical differential equation is efficient for solving the corresponding time-fractional order differential equation.

In the future investigations we plan to focus on the following two issues: (i) Construction and analysis of fitted finite volume method for the degenerate porosity soil case, $k(0) = 0$, see e.g. [2]; (ii) Extension of the present investigations for 2D Richards' equation.

Acknowledgements. This research is supported by the Bulgarian National Science Fund under Bilateral Project DNTS/Russia 02/12 from 2018.

References

1. Alikhanov, A.A.: A new difference scheme for the time fractional diffusion equation. J. Comput. Phys. **280**, 424–438 (2015)
2. Arbogast, T., Taicher, A.L.: A cell-centered finite difference method for a denerate elliptic equation arising from two-phase mixtures. Comput. Geosci. **21**(4), 700–712 (2017)
3. Bellman, R., Kalaba, R.: Quasilinearization and Nonlinear Boundary-Value Problems. Elsevier Publishing Company, New York (1965)
4. Casulli, V., Zanolli, P.: A nested Newton-type algorithm for finite volume methods solving Richards' equation in mixed form. SIAM J. Sci. Comput. **32**, 2255–2273 (2010)
5. Celia, M., Boulout, F., Zarba, R.L.: A general mass-conservativ numerical solution for the unsaturated flow equation. Water Resour. Res. **26**(7), 1483–1496 (1990)
6. Dimitrov, Y.: Three-point approximation for the Caputo fractional derivative. Commun. Appl. Math. Comput. **31**(4), 413–442 (2017)
7. Evans, C., Pollock, S., Rebholz, L.G., Xiao, M.: A proof that Anderson acceleration increases the convergence rate in linearly converging fixed point methods (but not in quadratically converging ones). arXiv:1810.08455v1 [math.NA], 19 October 2018
8. Gerolymatou, E., Vardoulakis, I., Hilfer, R.: Modelling infiltration by means of a nonlinear fractional diffusion model. J. Phys. D Appl. Phys. **39**, 4104–4110 (2006)
9. Gerolymatou, E., Vardoulakis, I., Hilfer, R.: Simulating the saturation front using a fractional diffusion model. In: 5th GRACM International Congress on Computational Mechanics Limassol, 29 June–1 July 2005 (2005). https://www.icp.uni-stuttgart.de/~hilfer/publikationen/pdfo/ZZ-2005-GRACM-653.pdf
10. van Genuchten, M.: A closed-form equation for predicting the hydraulic conductivity of unsaturated soils. Soil Sci. Soc. Am. J. **44**, 892–898 (1980)
11. Koleva, M., Vulkov, L.: Two-grid quasilinearization approach to ODEs with applications to model problems in physics and mechanics. Comput. Phys. Commun. **181**, 663–670 (2010)
12. Koleva, M., Vulkov, L.: Numerical solution of time-fractional Black-Scholes equation. Comput. Appl. Math. **36**(4), 1699–1715 (2017)
13. Misiats, O., Lipnikov, K.: Second-order accurate finite volume scheme for Richards' equation. J. Comput. Phys. **239**, 125–137 (2013)
14. Mitra, K., Pop I.S.: A modified L-scheme to solve nonlinear diffusion problems. Comput. Math. Appl. (in press). https://doi.org/10.1016/j.camwa.2018.09.042
15. Pachepsky, Y., Timlin, D., Rawls, W.: Generalized Richards' equation to simulate water transport in saturated soils. J. Hydrol. **272**, 3–13 (2003)
16. Popova, Z., Crevoisier, D., Mailhol, J., Ruelle, P.: Assessment and simulation of water and nitrogen transfer under furrow irrigation: application of hydrus2D model to simulate nitrogen transfer. In: ICID 22nd European Regional Conference 2007, Pavia, Italy, 2–7 September 2007 (2007). https://doi.org/10.13140/2.1.1268.2242
17. Richards, L.A.: Capillary conduction of liquids through porous mediums. Physics **1**(5), 318–333 (1931)
18. Zadeh, K.S.: A mass-conservative switching algorithm for modeling fluid flow in variably saturated porous media. J. Comput. Phys. **230**, 664–679 (2011)

Tensors Based Algorithms and Structures in Optimization and Applications

On the Problem of Decoupling Multivariate Polynomials

Stanislav Morozov[1], Dmitry A. Zheltkov[2(✉)], and Nikolai Zamarashkin[2]

[1] Lomonosov Moscow State University,
GSP-1, Leninskie Gory, Moscow 119991, Russian Federation
stanis-morozov@yandex.ru
[2] Marchuk Institute of Numerical Mathematics, Russian Academy of Sciences,
Gubkin Street, 8, Moscow 119333, Russian Federation
dmitry.zheltkov@gmail.com

Abstract. In this paper we address the application properties of the decoupling multivariate polynomials problem algorithm proposed in [2]. By numerous examples we demonstrate that this algorithm, unfortunately, fails to provide a solution in some cases. Therefore we empirically determine the application scope of this algorithm and show that it is connected with the uniqueness conditions of the CP-decomposition (Canonical Polyadic Decomposition). We also investigate the approximation properties of this algorithm and show that it is capable of construction the best low-rank polynomial approximation provided that the CP-decomposition is unique.

Keywords: Low-parametric representation · Polynomial · Tensor decomposition

1 Introduction

The problem addressed in this paper is a low-rank function representation of the form

$$f(u) = WG(V^T u), \tag{1}$$

where $W \in \mathbb{R}^{m \times r}$, $V \in \mathbb{R}^{n \times r}$ and G is a polynomial map, that is $G : \mathbb{R}^r \to \mathbb{R}^r$ defined as:

$$G(x_1, \ldots, x_r) = \begin{bmatrix} g_1(x_1) \ldots g_r(x_r) \end{bmatrix}^T \tag{2}$$

with g_k being a polynomial of degree d. Here and further m denotes the number of inputs, n denotes the number of outputs and r denotes the rank of representation. Such a representation often provides an efficient low-parametric form of a given function. This can be utilized, for example, for nonlinear block-oriented system identification [3], nonlinear state-space identification [1,4] and more generally in signal processing [5,6]. To the best of our knowledge for the first time the way of constructing low-rank function approximation (1) was proposed in [2]. However,

I. Lirkov and S. Margenov (Eds.): LSSC 2019, LNCS 11958, pp. 133–139, 2020.
https://doi.org/10.1007/978-3-030-41032-2_14

the existing approach has a number of disadvantages which is the concern of this paper.

The rest of the paper is organized as follows: in Sect. 2 we briefly remind the algorithm from [2]. In Sect. 3 we empirically investigate its application scope and in Sect. 4 we demonstrate the problems of the existing algorithms by several examples. We study the approximation properties in Sect. 5 and in Sect. 6 we conclude the paper.

2 Decoupling Algorithm

In this section we briefly review the algorithm of decoupling multivariate polynomials which is proposed in [2]. Besides the given function f, the method also requires the possibility to calculate the Jacobi matrix

$$J(u) = \begin{bmatrix} \dfrac{\partial f_1}{\partial u_1}(u) & \cdots & \dfrac{\partial f_1}{\partial u_m}(u) \\ \vdots & \ddots & \vdots \\ \dfrac{\partial f_n}{\partial u_1}(u) & \cdots & \dfrac{\partial f_n}{\partial u_m}(u) \end{bmatrix} \tag{3}$$

at a given point u. In [2] the following lemma has been proved:

Lemma 1. *The first-order derivatives of the parameterization (1) are given by*

$$J(u) = W \operatorname{diag}(g_i'(v_i^T u)) V^T, \tag{4}$$

where $W \in \mathbb{R}^{m \times r}$, $V \in \mathbb{R}^{n \times r}$ and v_i is the i-th column of matrix V.

Provided a sample of values $u^{(k)}$, $k = 1, \ldots, N$ the lemma implies that the first-order derivatives of the parameterization (1), evaluated at points $u^{(k)}$ give the simultaneous diagonalization of a set of matrices $J(u^{(k)})$ which is equivalent to CP-decomposition of tensor

$$\mathcal{J}_{ijk} = \frac{\partial f_i}{\partial u_j}(u^{(k)}). \tag{5}$$

Then the algorithm can be summarized as follows [2].

1. Evaluate the Jacobian matrix $J(u)$ in N sampling points $u^{(k)}$;
2. Stack the Jacobian matrices into a three-way tensor $\mathcal{J}$ of dimensions $n \times m \times N$;
3. Compute the CP decomposition:

$$\mathcal{J} = \sum_{t=1}^{r} w_t \otimes v_t \otimes h_t. \tag{6}$$

Note that in this decomposition we have

$$h_i = \begin{bmatrix} g_i'(v_i^T u^{(1)}) & \ldots & g_i'(v_i^T u^{(N)}) \end{bmatrix}^T. \tag{7}$$

4. For given matrices W and V solve the linear least squares problem to find the coefficients of polynomials g_i.

3 Uniqueness Conditions

The key problem of the described algorithm is that it substantially relies on the uniqueness of CP-decomposition. Of course, the CP-decomposition is not unique up to columnwise scaling and permutation of columns. The term essential uniqueness is used to denote the uniqueness of the CP-decomposition up to the columnwise scaling and permutation of the columns.

Two the most known results about CP-decomposition uniqueness are Kruskal [7,8] and De Lathauwer [9] conditions. The Kruskal condition relies on the notion of the Kruskal rank k_X of matrix X which is defined as the largest number k for which any set of k columns of X is linearly independent.

Theorem 1 *(Kruskal). The CP decomposition of rank-r tensor $\mathcal{J}$ (6) is unique provided that*

$$k_W + k_V + k_H \geq 2r + 2. \tag{8}$$

In our case we can state that $k_W = \min\{n, r\}$, $k_V = \min\{m, r\}$ and $k_H = r$ with probability 1. Then sufficient uniqueness condition is:

$$\min\{n, r\} + \min\{m, r\} \geq r + 2, \tag{9}$$

where m denotes the number of inputs and n denotes the number of outputs. Another uniqueness condition is given below.

Theorem 2 *(De Lathauwer). The CP decomposition of $\mathcal{J}$ (6) is unique with probability 1 for $r \leq N$ if*

$$n(n - 1)m(m - 1) \geq 2r(r - 1). \tag{10}$$

The last theorem provides stronger conditions hence we compare with it. We varied m, n and r generated random matrices W, V and polynomial G of degree 3 and tried to restore the representation by given Jacoby matrix and function values. For every n and m we report the maximal value r for which the algorithm succeeded in Table 1. It can be seen that the results are consistent with the De Lathauwer uniqueness conditions. However, the De Lathauwer uniqueness conditions are only sufficient and for $n = 3$, $m = 4$ they state that $r = 6$ while $r = 7$ is also valid.

4 Uniqueness Problem

It was shown in [2] that if tensor $\mathcal{J}$ provides an essential CP-decomposition uniqueness then the decoupling algorithm gives the solution. However, if it is not the case, then representation (1) cannot be constructed. The reason is that in (7) the vectors h_i are assumed to have values corresponding to the values of function g_i'. Consider a simple example:

$$f(u_1, u_2) = u_1 u_2. \tag{11}$$

Table 1. The maximal rank for which the algorithm can successfully restore the low-rank representation. $d = 3$, $N = 1,000$. A "7+" sign means that the rank is possibly higher, however we managed to find exact CP-decomposition only for rank 7. A "*" sign means that we didn't manage to find precise decomposition.

n, m	1	2	3	4
1	$+\infty$	1	1	1
2	$+\infty$	2	3	4
3	$+\infty$	3	4	7+
4	$+\infty$	4	7+	*

In this case

$$\mathcal{J}_{ijk} = \mathcal{J}_{jk} = \begin{bmatrix} u_2^{(1)} & u_1^{(1)} \\ \vdots & \vdots \\ u_2^{(N)} & u_1^{(N)} \end{bmatrix} \qquad (12)$$

and tensor $\mathcal{J}$ has rank $r = 2$. However it is actually a matrix and its skeleton decomposition

$$\mathcal{J}^T = VH^T \qquad (13)$$

is not unique. We assume that

$$W = \begin{bmatrix} 1 & 1 \end{bmatrix}. \qquad (14)$$

Due to formula (7) we have $h_{ij} = g_i'(v_i^T u^{(j)})$. Hence the following set of points $(v_i^T u^{(j)}, h_{ij})$, $j = 1, \ldots, N$ should lie on the curve of the polynomial $g_i'(x)$. Figure 1 shows the described set of points as well as the best fitting polynomial with the same degree as $g_i'(x)$. It can be seen that the set of points resembles a cloud and cannot be well approximated by a curve. Hence there are no such polynomials g_i for matrices W and V which satisfy (1). Nevertheless for this choice of matrices W and V we can construct the perfect CP-decomposition of tensor $\mathcal{J}$ given in (12).

Consider another example:

$$f(u_1, u_2) = u_1 u_2^2. \qquad (15)$$

In this case

$$\mathcal{J}_{ijk} = \mathcal{J}_{jk} = \begin{bmatrix} (u_2^{(1)})^2 & 2u_1^{(1)} u_2^{(1)} \\ \vdots & \vdots \\ (u_2^{(N)})^2 & 2u_1^{(N)} u_2^{(N)} \end{bmatrix} \qquad (16)$$

and tensor $\mathcal{J}$ has rank $r = 2$. We write out the formula (4) again

$$[u_2^2 \ 2u_1 u_2] = [w_1 \ w_2] \begin{bmatrix} \alpha_0 + \alpha_1(v_{11}u_1 + v_{21}u_2) + \alpha_2(v_{11}u_1 + v_{21}u_2)^2 \\ \beta_0 + \beta_1(v_{12}u_1 + v_{22}u_2) + \beta_2(v_{12}u_1 + v_{22}u_2)^2 \end{bmatrix} \begin{bmatrix} v_{11} & v_{21} \\ v_{12} & v_{22} \end{bmatrix}$$
$$(17)$$

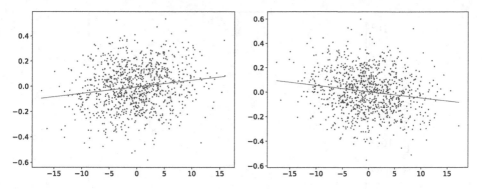

Fig. 1. The set of points $(v_i^T u^{(j)}, h_{ij})$, $j = 1, \ldots, N$ for $i = 1, 2$ and the best fitting curve of degree 1.

which gives:

$$\begin{cases} \alpha_2 v_{11}^3 + \beta_2 v_{12}^3 = 0 \\ \alpha_2 v_{12} v_{21}^2 + \beta_2 v_{12} v_{22}^2 = 1 \\ \alpha_2 v_{11}^2 v_{21} + \beta_2 v_{12}^2 v_{22} = 0 \\ \alpha_2 v_{21} v_{11}^2 + \beta_2 v_{22} v_{12}^2 = 0 \\ \alpha_2 v_{21}^3 + \beta_2 v_{22}^3 = 0 \\ \alpha_2 v_{21}^2 v_{11} + \beta_2 v_{22}^2 v_{12} = 1/2 \end{cases} \tag{18}$$

where we put $w_1 = w_2 = 1$ without loss of generality. It can be easily seen that $\alpha_2, \beta_2, v_{ij} \neq 0$. Then from the first and fifth equations we obtain:

$$\begin{cases} \dfrac{\alpha_2}{\beta_2} = -\left(\dfrac{v_{12}}{v_{11}}\right)^3 \\ \dfrac{\alpha_2}{\beta_2} = -\left(\dfrac{v_{22}}{v_{21}}\right)^3 \end{cases}. \tag{19}$$

Hence $v_{12}v_{21} - v_{11}v_{22} = 0$ which implies $\det V = 0$. But then tensor $\mathcal{J}$ (which is actually a matrix) has rank less then 2 which is the contradiction. This means that despite tensor $\mathcal{J}$ has rank 2, the representation (1) has rank at least 3. But it is clear that rank-3 decomposition of tensor $\mathcal{J}$ is not unique since this tensor has rank 2.

5   Stability Study

We also study the approximation properties of the algorithm. That is, in previous sections we outlined the conditions which allows to determine the exact representation (1). But now we want to investigate the problem

$$\mathbb{E}_u \min_{W,G,V} \|f(u) - WG(V^T u)\|. \tag{20}$$

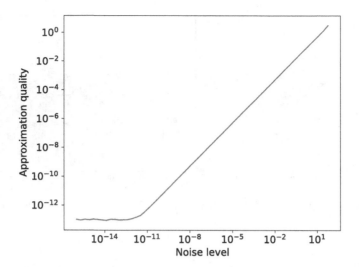

Fig. 2. The dependence of the approximation quality on the noise level.

We generated a random model of the form

$$f(u) = WG(V^T u) \tag{21}$$

with $n = 4$, $m = 6$ and $r = 5$ of degree 3. Then we added a noise in the following way:

$$\widetilde{f}(u) = WG(V^T u) + \varepsilon \begin{bmatrix} \sin u_1 + \sin u_2 \\ \cos u_2 + \sin u_6 \\ \cos u_4 + \cos u_5 \\ \sin u_3 + \cos u_6 \end{bmatrix}. \tag{22}$$

It is clear that $\widetilde{f}(u)$ is not of rank 5 and degree 3, but we try to restore $f(u)$ using its perturbed version $\widetilde{f}(u)$. We use the values and Jacobi matrix only for function $\widetilde{f}(u)$ during the identification and measured approximation quality (20) with respect to the function $f(u)$. The dependence of the approximation quality on the noise level ε is shown on Fig. 2. The results show that the algorithm is stable and capable of function approximation, but under the condition that CP-decomposition approximation reaches its global optimum.

6   Conclusion

In this paper we studied the application properties of the decoupling multivariate polynomials problem algorithm proposed in [2]. It was shown that the algorithm has limitations connected with the uniqueness problem of CP-decomposition which lead to the restrcitions on the model rank. We also proposed an example which demonstrates that decoupling rank should not coincide with the CP-rank. Hence the algorithm is also inappropriate if this is the case. We also investigated the stability properties of the algorithm and concluded that it is capable of approximating functions with higher rank and degree.

Acknowledgements. The work was supported by the Russian Science Foundation, grant 19-11-00338.

References

1. Relan, R., Tiels, K., Marconato, A., Dreesen, P., Schoukens, J.: Data driven discrete-time parsimonious identification of a nonlinear state-space model for a weakly nonlinear system with short data record. Mech. Syst. Signal Process. **104**, 929–943 (2018)
2. Dreesen, P., Ishteva, M., Schoukens, J.: Decoupling multivariate polynomials using first-order information and tensor decompositions. SIAM J. Matrix Anal. Appl. **36**(2), 864–879 (2015)
3. Giri, F., Bai, E.W.: Block-oriented Nonlinear System Identification. Lecture Notes in Control and Information Sciences. Springer, New York (2010). https://doi.org/10.1007/978-1-84996-513-2
4. Paduart, J., Lauwers, L., Swevers, J., Smolders, K., Schoukens, J., Pintelon, R.: Identification of nonlinear systems using polynomial nonlinear state space models. Automatica **46**, 647–656 (2010)
5. Cichocki, A., et al.: Tensor decompositions for signal processing applications: from two-way to multiway component analysis. IEEE Signal Process. Mag. **32**, 145–163 (2015)
6. Comon, P.: Tensors: a brief introduction. IEEE Signal Process. Mag. **31**, 44–53 (2014)
7. Kruskal, J.B.: Three-way arrays: rank and uniqueness of trilinear decompositions, with application to arithmetic complexity and statistics. Linear Algebra Appl. **18**, 95–138 (1977)
8. Kruskal, J.B.: Rank decomposition, and uniqueness for 3-way and N-way arrays. In: Coppi, R., Bolasco, S. (eds.) Multiway Data Analysis, pp. 8–18. North-Holland, Amsterdam (1988)
9. De Lathauwer, L.: A link between the canonical decomposition in multilinear algebra and simultaneous matrix diagonalization. SIAM J. Matrix Anal. Appl. **28**, 642–666 (2006)

Model Order Reduction Algorithms in the Design of Electric Machines

Sergey Petrov[✉]

Marchuk Institute of Numerical Mathematics, Moscow, Russia
spetrov.msk@gmail.com

Abstract. Although model order reduction techniques based on searching for a solution in a low-rank subspace are researched well for the case of linear differential equations, it is still questionable if such model order reduction techniques would work well for nonlinear PDEs. In this work, model order reduction via POD-DEIM (Proper Orthogonal Decomposition via Discrete Empirical Interpolation) method is applied to a particular nonlinear parametric PDE that is used for the modeling of electric machines. The idea of the POD-DEIM algorithm is to use statistical data about 'typical solutions' that correspond to 'typical' parameter values, to approximate solutions for other parameter values. Practical POD-DEIM application to the particular PDE has met a number of difficulties, and several improvements to the selection of initial approximation, selection of interpolation nodes, selection of interpolation basis and handling moving physical entities were made to make the method to work. These improvements, along with some numerical experiments, are presented.

1 Introduction

Design optimization for electrical machines may require solving a 2D nonlinear magnetostatic PDE over magnetic potential a large number of times for different values of problem parameters, such as mechanical angle between the rotor and the stator, phase angle between currents, stator current modulus, and others [4–6]. The considered 2D magnetostatic problem has the following notable properties:

- The problem is described with a nonlinear parametric PDE, where the nonlinearity comes from the possibly nonlinear properties of machine materials. The exact formulation of the problem will be given later in the experiments section.
- Certain part of the problem region ('rotor' part) can move with respect to another part, the 'stator' part.

In this work, the application of model order reduction (MOR) using POD-DEIM to the 2D magnetostatic equation is considered. In Sect. 2, the original POD-DEIM method [2,8] will be described. In Sect. 3, several improvements to POD-DEIM will be proposed. In Sect. 4, numerical results of application of POD-DEIM with the proposed modifications to the considered magnetostatic PDE will be described.

© Springer Nature Switzerland AG 2020
I. Lirkov and S. Margenov (Eds.): LSSC 2019, LNCS 11958, pp. 140–147, 2020.
https://doi.org/10.1007/978-3-030-41032-2_15

2 POD-DEIM Description

It is assumed that the nonlinear numerical scheme used to solve the considered parametric PDE is organised in the following form

$$Ay_\mu + F_\mu(y_\mu) = 0, \tag{1}$$

where $A \in \mathbb{R}^M \to \mathbb{R}^M$ is a linear operator, $F_\mu \in \mathbb{R}^M \to \mathbb{R}^M$ is a nonlinear operator, that depends on parameter μ, and the problem size M is very large. The POD (Proper Orthogonal Decomposition, [2,8]) method is based on searching for the solution in a low-rank linear subspace; that subspace is selected using statistical data. Denoting by y_μ a solution of (1) corresponding to parameter μ, POD method requires the following assumption:

$$numrank_\epsilon([y_{\mu_1} y_{\mu_2} \cdots y_{\mu_k}]) \approx const, \forall k \tag{2}$$

Here, $numrank_\epsilon(B)$ denotes the 'numerical rank' of a matrix B, which equals to $\max\{i : \sigma_i(B) > \epsilon\sigma_1(B)\}$, where $\sigma_j(B)$ denotes the j-th singular value of the matrix B. Then, a low-rank linear subspace V of rank r_a is selected as linear span over top singular vectors V of matrix of a large number k (yet $k \ll M$) 'typical' solutions ('snapshots') corresponding to 'typical' parameters, organized columnwise, which means that the optimal rank-r_a approximation for the snapshot matrix is defined by

$$[y_{\mu_1} \, y_{\mu_2} \, \cdots \, y_{\mu_k}] \approx V\Sigma Q_V^T \tag{3}$$

The original discrete system is then projected onto V:

$$V^T AV x_\mu + V^T F_\mu(V x_\mu) = 0.$$

To reduce the computational complexity of computing $F(V x_\mu)$, which still depends on original problem size M, DEIM (Discrete Empirical Interpolation, [2]) method implies that F_μ is approximated by it's projection PF_μ with a certain projector P:

$$V^T AV x_\mu + V^T PF_\mu(V x_\mu) = 0.$$

Intuitively, the projector P is defined in such a way that it only uses a small fraction of elements of a given vector x to compute Px. Formally, $P : \mathbb{R}^M \to \mathbb{R}^M$ is a linear projector with a special structure

$$P = U(S^T U)^{-1} S^T, \tag{4}$$

where U is a matrix of size $M \times r_i$ (r_i is 'interpolation' rank, r_a is 'approximation' rank, $r_i > r_a$), and S is a matrix with only one nonzero element in each column:

$$S = [e_{i_1} \, e_{i_2} \cdots e_{i_k}].$$

Such a projector P is uniquely defined by it's image U and a set of indices $I_{int} = \{i_1, i_2, \ldots, i_k\}$. The structure of P implies that vector y elements $y_{i_1} \cdots y_{i_k}$, 'selected' by columns of S, are enough to compute Py, and only a small fraction of elements of $F(Vx)$ are used to compute $V^T PF(Vx)$. Projector P is also sometimes called 'interpolative' projector as it preserves the values of vector corresponding to 'selected' indeces.

Now consider the case where the PDE numerical scheme equations are 'local': for each j, the value of $F(y)_j$ depends only on a small number of elements of y. Let $C(j)$ define the set of indeces of y, which define the value of $F(y)_j$. Let $C(I_{int}) = \cup_k C(i_k)$. Then let $D_{C(I_{int})}$ be a diagonal matrix, such that

$$\begin{cases} (D_{C(I_{int})})_{jj} = 1, j \in C(I_{int}) \\ (D_{C(I_{int})})_{jj} = 0, j \notin C(I_{int}) \end{cases}$$

Then, we have $V^T PF(Vx) = V^T PF(D_{C(I_{int})}Vx)$, thus a small fraction of elements of Vx is enough to compute $V^T PF(Vx)$.

The original DEIM papers [2,3] suggest selecting U in the same statistical way as V, using SVD of the matrix containing $F(x_\mu)$ organized columnwise, where x_μ are the MOR snapshots. From the final structure of the POD-DEIM system of reduced equations

$$V^T AV x_\mu + V^T U(S^T U)^{-1} S^T F_\mu (D_{C(I_{int})}Vx_\mu) = 0,$$

it can be seen that two matrices $V^T AV$ and $V^T U(S^T U)^{-1}$ can be computed in advance (during the so called 'offline' stage, when the snapshot bases are computed), and then the dimensionality of the resulting reduced problem is independent on the original problem dimensionality M.

3   POD-DEIM Improvements

3.1   Interpolation Points Selection

One of the offline stages of POD-DEIM algorithm is the selection of interpolation indeces I_{int}. The interpolative projector P qualities could be assessed with

$$\begin{aligned} \|(I - P))f\| &= \|(I - U(S^T U)^{-1}S^T)f\| \\ &= \|(I - U(S^T U)^{-1}S^T)(I - UU^T)f\| \le \|(S^T U)^{-1}\|\epsilon_U(f) \end{aligned}$$

where $\epsilon_U(f) = \|(I - UU^T)f\|$ is the best possible approximation of f using orthonormal columns of U. Thus, I_{int} should be selected in such a way that $\|(S^T U)^{-1}\|$ is small, or a square submatrix of U with smallest possible inverse norm should be selected. Original DEIM papers suggest that Gaussian pivoting is used for index selection, which results in exponential bounds for $\|(S^T U)^{-1}\|$ [3]. However, if $S^T U$ is chosen as the maximum volume submatrix of U, $\|(S^T U)^{-1}\| \le \sqrt{r_i(M - r_i + 1)}$. The proof of this bound, as well as detailed descriptions of algorithms for searching for a submatrix with a 'large' volume are presented in [7].

3.2   Initial Approximation

If for solving the small reduced nonlinear system of equations, Newton iterations are used, their convergence depend on the initial point selection. As for the basis V generation, SVD of the 'snapshot' matrix is used, additional information is available: consider the short SVD

$$\begin{bmatrix} y_{\mu_1} \, y_{\mu_2} \, \cdots \, y_{\mu_k} \end{bmatrix} = \begin{bmatrix} V \, V_2 \end{bmatrix} \begin{bmatrix} \Sigma & 0 \\ 0 & \Sigma_2 \end{bmatrix} \begin{bmatrix} W^T \\ W_2^T \end{bmatrix} = \begin{bmatrix} V \, V_2 \end{bmatrix} \begin{bmatrix} \Sigma W^T \\ \Sigma_2 W_2^T \end{bmatrix}$$

where $V \in \mathbb{R}^{M \times r_a}, V_2 \in \mathbb{R}^{M \times k-r_a}, \Sigma \in \mathbb{R}^{r_a \times r_a}, \Sigma_2 \in \mathbb{R}^{k-r_a \times k-r_a}, W^T \in \mathbb{R}^{r_a \times k}, W_2^T \in \mathbb{R}^{k-r_a \times k}$. According to the SVD properties, matrix ΣW^T contains optimal coefficients for the basis V approximations of the snapshots $y_{\mu_1} \ldots y_{\mu_k}$. In other words,

$$\Sigma W^T = \begin{bmatrix} x_{\mu_1} \, x_{\mu_2} \, \cdots \, x_{\mu_k} \end{bmatrix}$$

where $V x_{\mu_j}$ is the optimal basis V approximation of $y_{\mu_j}, \forall j \in 1 \ldots k$. As $\Sigma W^T \in \mathbb{R}^{r_a \times k}$, that matrix dimensionalities are low enough to make it available to store that matrix as well as the values of parameters $\mu_1 \ldots \mu_k$ as additional data for MOR.

Then, it is proposed to use that data for selection of initial point for Newton iterations. If a solution is to be found for a set of parameter values μ, it is suggested to find the closest parameter set μ_j from $\mu_1 \ldots \mu_k$ (in some metric in the parameter space. In our further experiments, we used scaled sum of modules of parameter values), and use corresponding x_{μ_j} as initial Newton point.

3.3   Shift Parameter and Moving Objects

Moving physical entities can disprove the solution low-rank assumption (2). Consider two solutions graphs that correspond to two different values of the rotor-stator cyclic shift:

 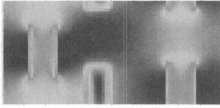

The solutions are 'concentrated' in different areas of the solution vector, thus the low-rank assumption is likely false. But the rotor-stator shift parameter has important physical sense and cannot be discarded. A special procedure is proposed to handle that parameter. This parameter is assumed to be discrete: only shifts of values $h, 2h, 3h \ldots$, where h is the grid square size, are allowed. In order to find a solution for a fixed shift parameter, we propose to apply the same shift to the bases V, U. Mathematically that means multiplying the basis matrices by a permutation matrix Z

$$V \to ZV, \; U \to ZU, \; S \to ZS \tag{5}$$

that would lead to the following system transformation:

$$V^T A V x_\mu + V^T U (S^T U)^{-1} S^T F_\mu (D_{C(I_{int})} V x_\mu) = 0 \rightarrow$$
$$\rightarrow V^T Z^T A Z V x_\mu + V^T U (S^T U)^{-1} S^T Z^T F_\mu (Z D_{C(I_{int})} V x_\mu) = 0$$

From these transformations we can see:

- Auxiliary matrix $V^T U (S^T U)^{-1}$ is still present in the same form (does not depend on basis permutation), thus no additional actions corresponding to this matrix are to be done in the offline stage of the algorithm.
- $S^T F_\mu (D_{C(I_{int})} y)$ is transformed into $S^T Z^T F_\mu (Z D_{C(I_{int})} y), y = V x$. That transformation is a renumbering of nodes that are used in the nonlinear vector-function F interpolation. The vector elements of y that are required to find $(F_\mu(y))_j$ and $(Z^T F_\mu(Zy))_j$ are different for nodes j located along the cyclic shift edge (because edge nodes' neighbors change when the shift is applied); this is handled by adding $O(N)$ indeces to the $C(I_{int})$, and saving $O(N)$ additional rows of V as auxiliary data, where N is the vertical grid size ($N = O(\sqrt{M})$).
- The auxiliary matrix $V^T A V$ is changed to $V^T Z^T A Z V$. In order to keep the online phase complexity low, a fast algorithm of finding $V^T Z^T A Z V$ using $V^T A V$ should be provided. Such an algorithm can be established using the structure of particular A; for the used numerical scheme, A is a block matrix with diagonal blocks and circulant blocks, thus cyclic renumeration does not change A except for the positions close to the edge of the cyclic shift.

3.4   Nonlinear Function Interpolation

The original DEIM (Discrete Empirical Interpolation) method suggests that the basis U is selected using statistical data, just like the basis V:

$$\left[F_{\mu_1}(V x_{\mu_1}), F_{\mu_2}(V x_{\mu_2}) \dots F_{\mu_k}(V x_{\mu_k}) \right] \approx U \Sigma Q_U^T$$

However, contrary to the approximation basis, it may be not enough for U to interpolate well the nonlinear functions of solutions y_μ. If the reduced small nonlinear system of equations is solved iteratively (using Newton iterations), $F(Vx)$ should be also well approximated with $PF(Vx)$ for the vectors x that arise in the iterative process. Another assumption should be required:

$$numrank_\epsilon([F_{\mu_1}(V x_1), F_{\mu_2}(V x_2) \dots F_{\mu_k}(V x_k)]) = const \ll k, \forall k$$

Our practical experiments have shown that this rank grows much faster with $\epsilon \to 0$ than the rank of V for the considered magnetostatic PDE. To deal with that problem and obtain reasonable interpolation ranks r_i, we used random numbers to generate $x_1 \dots x_k$. For vectors $x_1 \dots x_k$, each component j was selected using Gaussian distribution with mean 0 and norm expectation of σ_j, where σ_j are the singular values of the snapshot matrix that is used to compute V. That distribution was selected to limit the possible values of vectors x to a smaller class that could still describe well the vectors that arise in the iterative process.

4 Numerical Results

Electric synchronous machine is typically modelled with a rectangle in polar coordinates (sector) for symmetry reasons. In this work, in order to focus on model order reduction (MOR) and omit engineering details, a simplified model problem will be considered, with the problem region being a rectangle in Cartesian coordinates.

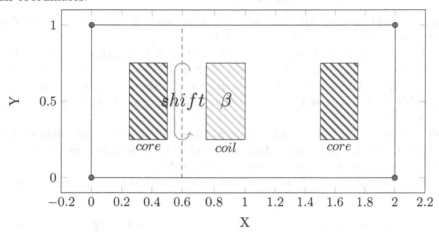

The picture above is a scheme of the considered problem. The considered electric machine model has one 'coil' (region where the right hand side is nonzero) and two cores (machine areas made of materials with nonlinear properties). The model is split into a model 'rotor' and 'stator' regions (see dashed line on the picture above); the rotor movement is modelled with a vertical cyclic shift of the part of the problem region to the right of the dashed line. The model problem is described by the following equations over magnetic potential ϕ:

$$\begin{cases} \nabla(\nu(\|\nabla\phi(x,y)\|; x, y)\nabla\phi(x,y)) = \hat{f}(x,y), (x,y) \in [0,2] \times [0,1] \\ \phi(0,y) = 0, y \in [0,1], \\ \phi(2,y) = 0, y \in [0,1], \\ \phi(x,0) = \phi(x,1), x \in [0,2], \\ \phi_y(x,0) = \phi_y(x,1), x \in [0,2], \end{cases} \quad (6)$$

where

$$\begin{cases} f(x,y) = \beta, (x,y) \in coil \\ f(x,y) = 0, (x,y) \notin coil \end{cases}$$

$$\begin{cases} \nu(s; x, y) = 4\pi 10^{-7}, (x,y) \notin core \\ \nu(s; x, y) = \frac{s^3}{s^4 + 6.25 \times 10^{10}} + 4\pi 10^{-7}, (x,y) \in core \end{cases}$$

The model problem has two parameters: right side value of coil β and a vertical cyclic shift of the model rotor. For this model problem, control volume mixed FE scheme on a uniform quadrilateral grid was developed, and trust region based modification of Newton iterations [1] was used to solve the nonlinear discretized system of equations.

The first experiments that we have carried out with the original POD-DEIM applied to the model problem, did not show good results. Reduced system Newton iterations converged only for very small ranks of the subspace V up to 7–10; for larger ranks, Newton iterations got stuck at a local minimum with the residual values around 0.01–0.1 of the initial residual.

With all the proposed above improvements implemented, testing was carried out using the following problem setup:

– Regular grids of sizes 40×80 or 80×160 were used: $N = 40, M = 6N^2 + N = 9640$ or $N = 80, M = 6N^2 + N = 38480$.
– Two parameters were considered, right side constant value β and vertical cyclic shift. Each parameter had a set of 20 possible values: β possible values ranged from $3.0e + 4$ to $3.0e + 6$ uniformly in the logarithmic scale; shift possible values ranged in $[0, 1)$ uniformly (with a step of two grid square sizes h).
– 80 (out of possible 400) random combinations of these two parameters were selected, and the full model solver was used to build solutions for these combinations. These solutions were used as 'snapshots'.
– 2000 random nonlinear function samples were used to form the interpolation basis.

Then, random parameter combinations that were not present in the 'snapshot' parameter list were chosen to make POD-DEIM experiments. We obtained the following average error values (over 50 experiments for each grid size, r_a is the rank of V, r_i is the rank of U):

	L_2 relative error	C-norm relative error
Values, 40×80, $r_a = 40, r_i = 300$	0.001793	0.003583
Fluxes, 40×80, $r_a = 40, r_i = 300$	0.001581	0.001942
Values, 80×160, $r_a = 40, r_i = 600$	0.000624	0.002642
Fluxes, 80×160, $r_a = 40, r_i = 600$	0.000328	0.002374

With our implementations of full and reduced solvers, reduced solver produced its approximate solution 100−1000 times faster than the full solver:

	$40 \times 80, r_a = 40, r_i = 300$	$80 \times 160, r_a = 40, r_i = 600$
Full model solver	3.384 s	41.13 s
Reading auxiliary data from a file	0.0254 s	0.0533 s
Transforming $V^T AV$	0.000131 s	0.000286 s
Reduced solver iterations	0.007770 s	0.0154 s

5   Conclusion

With certain modifications, a stable performance of POD-DEIM for 2D magnetostatic parametric PDE was established: practical computational complexity of finding a POD-DEIM approximate solution turned out to be hundreds-thousands times smaller than that of a full solver, for the simplified model problem.

Acknowledgments. The work was supported by the Russian Science Foundation, grant 19-11-00338.

References

1. Dennis Jr., J.E., Schnabel, R.B.: Numerical Methods for Unconstrained Optimization and Nonlinear Equations, vol. 16. SIAM, Philadelphia (1996)
2. Chaturantabut, S., Sorensen, D.C.: Nonlinear model reduction via discrete empirical interpolation. SIAM J. Sci. Comput. **32**(5), 2737–2764 (2010)
3. Sorensen, D.C., Embree, M.: A DEIM induced cur factorization. SIAM J. Sci. Comput. **38**(3), A1454–A1482 (2016)
4. Montier, L., Henneron, T., Clénet, S., Goursaud, B.: Transient simulation of an electrical rotating machine achieved through model order reduction. Adv. Model. Simul. Eng. Sci. **3**(1), 10 (2016)
5. Henneron, T., Clenet, S.: Model order reduction of non-linear magnetostatic problems based on POD and DEI methods. IEEE Trans. Magn. **50**(2), 33–36 (2014)
6. Henneron, T., Clenet, S.: Model order reduction applied to the numerical study of electrical motor based on POD method taking into account rotation movement. Int. J. Numer. Model. Electron. Netw. Devices Fields **27**(3), 485–494 (2014)
7. Osinsky, A. Rectangular maximum volume and projective volume search algorithms. arXiv preprint arXiv:1809.02334 (2018)
8. Berkooz, G., Holmes, P., Lumley, J.L.: The proper orthogonal decomposition in the analysis of turbulent flows. Annu. Rev. Fluid Mech. **25**(1), 539–575 (1993)

Discrete Vortices and Their Generalizations for Scattering Problems

Alexey Setukha[1,2](✉)

[1] Marchuk Institute of Numerical Mathematics Russian Academy of Sciences,
Gubkin str. 8, Moscow, Russia
setuhaav@rambler.ru
[2] Lomonosov Moscow State University, GSP-1, Leninskie Gory,
Moscow, Russia

Abstract. In the numerical solving of boundary integral equations of electrodynamics, the problem is reduced to a system of linear algebraic equations with dense matrix. A significant increase in the number of cells of the partition used for the solution can be achieved by applying special methods for compressing dense matrices and fast matrix algorithms. At the same time, the extension of the classes of solved wave scattering problems requires the progress in the of the boundary integral equations method. The problem of electromagnetic diffraction in a piecewise homogeneous medium that can consist of domains with different dielectric properties and can contain ideally conducting inclusions in the form of solid objects and screens is considered in the present work. The proposed numerical method for solving of boundary hypersingular integral equations is based on ideas borrowed from the vortex frame method, widely used in computational aerodynamics.

Keywords: Integral equations · Numerical methods · Electromagnetic scattering

1 Introduction

The method of boundary integral equations are widely used in wave scattering problems (refer, for example, [1,2]). Recently, methods based on the reduction to integral equations with singular and hypersingular integrals have been widely used for the numerical soluton of three-dimensional applied problems of electrodynamics. This approach is specified by the possibility to apply it both to diffraction problems on bodies and to diffraction problems on thin screens as well as when modeling the boundary between different dielectric media.

The known approach to the theoretical study and numerical solution of hypersingular integral equations is related to the interpretation of such equations as pseudodifferential equations in Sobolev spaces [3]. In this case, numerical schemes are usually based on the finite-element version of the Galerkin method [4].

The work was supported by the Russian Science Foundation, grant 19-11-00338.

I. Lirkov and S. Margenov (Eds.): LSSC 2019, LNCS 11958, pp. 148–155, 2020.
https://doi.org/10.1007/978-3-030-41032-2_16

In the present article a different approach based on the collocation method is applied to the arising boundary equations. In this case the strongly singular integrals are understood in the sense of a finite value according to Hadamard. For discretization such equations a piecewise-constant approximation of unknown functions is used. This approach underlies the vortex frame method used in computational aerodynamics [5,6]. As shown in book [5], the method of vortex frames for problems of potential flow around a body is a method for solving a boundary hypersingular integral equation on its surface.

For boundary value problems of electrodynamics a method of this type with piecewise constant approximation of the surface currents was proposed in [7]. Further development of such approach to the problems of waves scattering by perfectly conducting body is given in articles [8,9], where the numerical scheme of the piecewise constant approximations and collocations method is implemented, similar to the vortex frame method. The Numerical schemes of similar type for problems of scattering by some combinations of dielectric and perfectly conducting bodies were constructed in papers [10,11].

This article describes the idea of expanding the method for the scattering problems by an arbitrary system of dielectric medias and perfect conducting bodies. Examples of calculations are given.

2   Statement of the Problem

The problem of monochromatic electromagnetic wave scattering by the system of dielectric medias and perfectly conducting bodies and screens is considered. It is assumed that the all dielectric medias and external environment is homogeneous, isotropic and free of electric charges (see Fig. 1, at left).

Let Ω_1 be a domain occupied by the external environment, $\Omega_2, ..., \Omega_K$ – are domains occupied by the dielectrics medias. Each of the domains $\Omega_1, ..., \Omega_K$ can include ideally perfectly conducting bodies or screens.

The intensities of electric and magnetic fields are sought in the following form respectively: $\mathbf{E}^*(x,t) = \mathbf{E}_{tot}(x)e^{-i\omega t}$, $\mathbf{H}^*(x,t) = \mathbf{H}_{tot}(x)e^{-i\omega t}$, where ω is the angular frequency of electromagnetic field, t—time, $x = (x_1, x_2, x_3) \in R^3$—points of space, $\mathbf{E}_{tot}(x)$, $\mathbf{H}_{tot}(x)$—spatial components of the total electric and magnetic fields. It is assumed that the full field is induced by the defined incident field, in which the intensities of electric and magnetic fields have the following form: $\mathbf{E}_{inc}(x)e^{-i\omega t}$, $\mathbf{H}_{inc}(x)e^{-i\omega t}$, respectively. At that, the spatial components of intensities of the total electric and magnetic fields in the external domain Ω_1 are sought in the form [12]:

$$\mathbf{E}_{tot}(x) = \mathbf{E}_{inc}(x) + \mathbf{E}(x), \quad \mathbf{H}_{tot}(x) = \mathbf{H}_{inc}(x) + \mathbf{H}(x), \qquad (1)$$

$\mathbf{E}, \mathbf{H}$—unknown intensities of the scattered electric and magnetic fields. We also denote $\mathbf{E}, \mathbf{H}$—unknown intensities of the scattered electric and magnetic fields in the domains $\Omega_2, ..., \Omega_K$, and we assume that the formula (1) is fulfilled in these domains with $\mathbf{E}_{inc}(x) = \mathbf{H}_{inc}(x) = 0$.

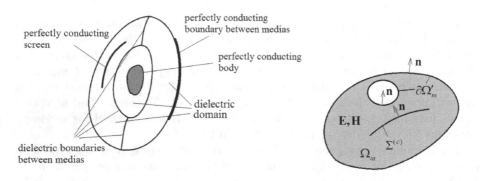

Fig. 1. To the statement of the problem

The electric and magnetic fields should satisfy the Maxwell equations:

$$rot\,\mathbf{E} = i\mu_m\mu_0\omega\mathbf{H}, \quad rot\,\mathbf{H} = -i\varepsilon_m\varepsilon_0\omega\mathbf{E} \quad in \quad \Omega_m, \quad m = 1, ..., K,$$

here μ_0 end ε_0 – the electric constant and magnetic constant, ε_m and μ_m – the relative permittivity end the relative permeability of the medium in domain Ω_m, respectively. The following boundary conditions must be satisfied:

$\mathbf{E}_{tot} \times \mathbf{n} = 0$ on the surfaces of perfectly conducting bodies of screens, as well as on ideally-conducting boundaries between medias;

$\left[\mathbf{E}_{tot}^+ - \mathbf{E}_{tot}^-\right] \times \mathbf{n} = 0,\quad \left[\mathbf{H}_{tot}^+ - \mathbf{H}_{tot}^-\right] \times \mathbf{n} = 0$ on the dielectric boundaries between medias. Here we single out the case of direct contact of various dielectrics—dielectric boundaries between medias, and the case when between different dielectrics there is an ideally conductive infinitely thin layer—ideally-conducting boundaries between medias. By an ideally conducting screen, we mean an infinitely thin ideally conducting layer that lies inside a single dielectric medium, not a boundary between different dielectrics.

We pose the conditions of radiation at infinity (in the Sommerfeld form):

$$\mathbf{E}(x) \to 0, \mathbf{H}(x) \to 0, \quad \frac{\partial \mathbf{E}}{\partial \tau} - ik\mathbf{E} = o\left(\frac{1}{|x|}\right), \quad \frac{\partial \mathbf{H}}{\partial \tau} - ik\mathbf{H} = o\left(\frac{1}{|x|}\right)$$

as $|x| \to \infty$, where $\partial/\partial\tau$ – derivative in the direction of vector $\tau = x/|x|$, $o(r)$ – infinitesimally small function of a higher order of smallness than r, and the condition: $\int_D \mathbf{E}^2 dv < \infty$, $\int_D \mathbf{H}^2 dv < \infty$ for any bounded domain $D \subset \Omega$, dv – element of the spatial volume.

3 Method of Integral Equations

Let Ω_m be one of the domains occupied by the dielectric, $\partial\Omega_m$—the boundary of Ω_m. The boundary $\partial\Omega_m$ is some total surface, which may contain surface $\Sigma^{(c)}$ – the total surface of perfectly conducting screens lying in this domain. Let $\partial\Omega_m'$ be the part of the surface $\partial\Omega_m$ without the surface $\Sigma^{(c)}$ (see Fig. 1 at right).

Then for the electric and magnetic fields in the region, the following integral representation is valid (the Stretton - Chu formulas [12]):

$$\mathbf{E}(\mathbf{x}) = \frac{i}{\omega\varepsilon_m}\mathbf{K}_m[\partial\Omega'_m,\mathbf{j}_E] - \mathbf{R}_m[\partial\Omega'_m,\mathbf{j}_M] + \frac{i}{\omega\varepsilon_m}\mathbf{K}_m[\Sigma^{(c)},\mathbf{j}_E],$$

$$\mathbf{H}(\mathbf{x}) = \frac{i}{\omega\mu_m}\mathbf{K}_m[\partial\Omega'_m,\mathbf{j}_M] + \mathbf{R}_m[\partial\Omega'_m,\mathbf{j}_E] + \frac{i}{\omega\mu_m}\mathbf{R}_m[\Sigma^{(c)},\mathbf{j}_E]$$

where $\mathbf{j}_E$ and $\mathbf{j}_M$ are complex tangent vector fields on the surfaces Ω'_m and $\Sigma^{(c)}$, defined by the formulas

$$\mathbf{j}_E = -\mathbf{n}\times\mathbf{H},\ \mathbf{j}_M = \mathbf{n}\times\mathbf{E} \text{ on surface } \partial\Omega'\ \mathbf{j}_E = \mathbf{j}_E^+ - \mathbf{j}_E^- \text{ on surface } \Sigma^{(c)}, \quad (2)$$

$\mathbf{n}$ is the surface normal vector that is external to the domain Ω_m in these formulas, $\mathbf{K}_m$ and $\mathbf{R}_m$—are the follow integral operators:

$$\mathbf{K}_m[\Sigma,\mathbf{j}] = grad\,div\int_\Sigma \mathbf{j}(y)F_m(x-y)d\sigma_y + k^2\int_\Sigma \mathbf{j}(y)F_m(x-y)d\sigma_y, \quad (3)$$

$$\mathbf{R}_m[\Sigma,\mathbf{j}](x) = \int_\Sigma rot_x[\mathbf{j}(y)F_m(x-y)]d\sigma_y,\ x\in\Omega_m, \quad (4)$$

$$F_m(x-y) = \frac{e^{ikR}}{R},\ R = |x-y|,\ k = \frac{\omega}{c_m},\ c_m = \frac{1}{\sqrt{\varepsilon_m\mu_m}}.$$

To write the system of integral equations, we use the following properties of the boundary values of this operators. Let's denote $\mathbf{E}_1 = \mathbf{K}[\Sigma_0,\mathbf{j}]$, where $\mathbf{j}$—twice continuously differentiable complex tangent vector field on a some surface Σ_0. It has been proved in [8] that in each point $x\in\Sigma^{in}$, where $\Sigma^{in} = \Sigma_0\backslash\partial\Sigma_0$, there are boundary values $\mathbf{E}_1^+$ and $\mathbf{E}_1^-$ of field $\mathbf{E}_1$, for which the following formula is true:

$$\mathbf{E}_1^\pm(x) = \mathbf{E}_1(x) \mp \frac{1}{2}\mathbf{n}(x)\,Div\,\mathbf{j}(x),\ x\in\Sigma_0^{in}, \quad (5)$$

where $Div\,\mathbf{j}(x)$—surface divergence of vector field $\mathbf{j}(x)$, $\mathbf{E}_1(x)$—direct value of the vector field under consideration at point $x\in\Sigma_0^{in}$, obtained directly from expression (3), wherein arising integral should be understood in the sense of Hadamard finite value:

$$\mathbf{E}_1(x) = \lim_{\varepsilon\to 0+}\left(\int_{\Sigma_0\backslash B(x,\varepsilon)}\mathbf{K}(\mathbf{j}(y),x,y)d\sigma_y - \frac{\mathbf{j}(x)}{4\varepsilon}\right),$$

$B(x,\varepsilon)$ is the neighborhood of x of radius ε.

Further, let $\mathbf{E}_2 = \mathbf{R}[\Sigma_0,\mathbf{j}]$, where $\mathbf{j}(x)$—Hölder continuous tangent vector field on surface Σ_0. It is easy to show (refer, for example, [10]), that the field $\mathbf{E}_2$ has boundary values at each point $x\in\Sigma_0^{in}$, for which the following formula is true:

$$\mathbf{E}_2^\pm(x) = \mathbf{E}_2(x) \pm \frac{1}{2}\mathbf{j}(x)\times\mathbf{n}(x),\ x\in\Sigma_0^{in}, \quad (6)$$

where $\mathbf{E}_2(x)$ – direct value obtained for this point from the expression (4), where the integral is understood in the sense of principal value.

For each domain Ω_m, we place on its boundary unknown tangent vector fields (surface currents) defined by formulas (2). From formulas (5) and (6) we have equations:

$$\frac{1}{2}\mathbf{j}_M + \mathbf{n} \times \left\{ \frac{i}{\omega\varepsilon_m}\mathbf{K}_m[\partial\Omega'_m, \mathbf{j}_E] - \mathbf{R}_m[\partial\Omega'_m, \mathbf{j}_M] + \frac{i}{\omega\varepsilon_m}\mathbf{K}_m[\Sigma^{(c)}, \mathbf{j}_E] \right\} \tag{7}$$
$$= -\delta_1^m \mathbf{n} \times \mathbf{E}_{inc} \; on \; \partial\Omega'_m,$$

$$\mathbf{n} \times \left\{ \frac{i}{\omega\varepsilon_m}\mathbf{K}_m[\partial\Omega'_m, \mathbf{j}_E] - \mathbf{R}_m[\partial\Omega'_m, \mathbf{j}_M] + \frac{i}{\omega\varepsilon_m}\mathbf{K}_m[\Sigma^{(c)}, \mathbf{j}_E] \right\} \tag{8}$$
$$= -\delta_1^m \mathbf{n} \times \mathbf{E}_{inc} \; on \; \Sigma^{(c)} \subset \bar{\Omega}_m,$$

where $\delta_i^j = 1$ for $i = j$, $\delta_i^j = 0$ for $i \neq j$.

Note that on the surface, which is the boundary between two different areas, we have unknown currents on both its sides. Let Σ be one of such surfaces, which is supposed to be oriented. Let $\mathbf{j}_E^+$, $\mathbf{j}_M^+$ be the unknown currents on the positive side of this surface and $\mathbf{j}_E^-$, $\mathbf{j}_M^-$ on the negative side. Then we have the following relations between the currents on this surface:

$$\mathbf{j}_E^- = -\mathbf{j}_E^+ - \delta_i^1 \mathbf{j}_{E\_ent}, \; \mathbf{j}_M^- = -\mathbf{j}_M^+ - \delta_i^1 \mathbf{j}_{M\_ent} \; \text{on the dielectric boundary}, \tag{9}$$

$$\mathbf{j}_M^+ = -\delta_i^1 \mathbf{j}_{M\_ent}, \; \mathbf{j}_M^- = 0 \; \text{on the perfectly conducting boundary}, \tag{10}$$

where $\mathbf{j}_{E\_ent} = -\mathbf{n} \times \mathbf{E}_{(inc)}$, $\mathbf{j}_{H\_ent} = -\mathbf{n} \times \mathbf{H}_{(inc)}$ on the boundary $\partial\Omega_1$.

Thus, we can solve the system (7)–(8) with respect to the vectors $\mathbf{j}_1 = \mathbf{j}_E^+$, $\mathbf{j}_2 = \mathbf{j}_M^+$ on the dielectric boundary, $\mathbf{j}_1 = \mathbf{j}_E^+$, $\mathbf{j}_2 = \mathbf{j}_E^-$ on the perfectly conducting boundary between difference medias, $\mathbf{j}_1 = \mathbf{j}_E$, $\mathbf{j}_2 = 0$ on the surface of the perfectly conducting objects.

We approximate all the surfaces between dielectric media and all the surfaces of ideally conducting bodies and screens with a system of four coal cells σ_k, $k = 1, ..., N$. We select a collocation point $x^k \in \sigma_k$ on each cell of the partition and construct the vector $\mathbf{n}_k = \mathbf{n}(x^k)$. Let's also construct for each cell σ_k, the vectors $\mathbf{e}_k^1$ as arbitrary unit vectors, that are orthogonal to vectors $\mathbf{n}_k$ and the vectors $\mathbf{e}_k^2 = \mathbf{n}_k \times \mathbf{e}_k^1$. On each cell σ_k we place the following unknown vectors:

$$\mathbf{j}_{1\,i} = j_1^1{}_i \mathbf{e}_i^1 + j_1^2{}_i \mathbf{e}_i^2, \; \mathbf{j}_{2\,i} = j_2^1{}_i \mathbf{e}_i^1 + j_2^2{}_i \mathbf{e}_i^2$$

We approximate the operators $\mathbf{K}[\Sigma_0, \mathbf{j}]$ and $\mathbf{K}[\Sigma_0, \mathbf{j}]$ as:

$$\mathbf{K}[\Sigma_0, \mathbf{j}] \approx \sum_{k=1}^{N} \tilde{\mathbf{K}}[\sigma_k, \mathbf{j}_k], \; \mathbf{R}[\Sigma_0, \mathbf{j}] \approx \sum_{k=1}^{n} \tilde{\mathbf{R}}[\sigma_k, \mathbf{j}_k], \tag{11}$$

where $\tilde{\mathbf{K}}[\sigma_k, \mathbf{j}_k]$ and $\tilde{\mathbf{R}}[\sigma_k, \mathbf{j}_k]$ – approximations of the respective integrals for the area of surface Σ_0, approximated by cell σ_k.

By approximating the system of equations (7)–(8) at the collocation points and using equations (9)–(10), we obtained a system of linear equations for the coordinates of the current j_{1i}^m and j_{2i}^m of the following type:

$$\sum_{J=1,...,\tilde{N},\ l=1,2} a_{IJ}^{ml} J_J^l = F_I^m, \quad I = 1, ..., \tilde{N}, \quad m = 1, 2, \tag{12}$$

$$a_{IJ}^{ml} = (\mathbf{A}_{IJ}\mathbf{e}_j^l, \mathbf{e}_i^m), \quad F_I^m = (\mathbf{F}_I, \mathbf{e}_i^m),$$

where $\mathbf{A}_{IJ}$ and $\mathbf{F}_I$– operators of the following form:

$$\mathbf{A}_{IJ}\mathbf{J} = \alpha\, \mathbf{n}_i \times \mathbf{G}\left[\sigma_j, \mathbf{J}\right](x^i) + \beta_i^j \mathbf{J}, \quad \mathbf{F}_I = -\sum_{J=1,....N} \mathbf{A}_{IJ}^{ent} \mathbf{J}_J^{inc} - \gamma \delta_m^1 \mathbf{n} \times \mathbf{E}_{inc},$$

$$\mathbf{A}_{IJ}^{inc}\mathbf{J}_J^{inc} = \alpha^{inc}\, \mathbf{n}_i \times \mathbf{G}^{inc}\left[\sigma_j, \mathbf{J}_J^{inc}\right](x^i) + \beta_i^j \mathbf{J}_J^{inc},$$

$J_J^l = j_{1i}^l$ or $J_J^l = j_{2i}^l$, $i = i(I), j = j(J)$ – the partitioning cell numbers that correspond to indices I and J in the system, $\mathbf{G} = \tilde{\mathbf{K}}$ or $\mathbf{G} = \tilde{\mathbf{R}}$, $\mathbf{G}^{inc} = \tilde{\mathbf{K}}$ or $\mathbf{G}^{inc} = \tilde{\mathbf{R}}$, the type of operators $\mathbf{G}$, $\mathbf{G}^{inc}$ and the values of the coefficients in this formulas are selected depending on the types of surfaces on which the cells σ_i and σ_j lie.

4 Numerical Result and Discussion

The computational costs for the constructed algorithm are determined not only by the complexity of the geometry of the irradiated object, but also by its electrodynamic size: the ratio of the object size to the wavelength. As an example calculation results and calculation costs are shown for the problem of plane wave scattering by a circular cylinder of finite length. Figure 2 shows the backscatter diagrams for a cylinder. The values of the radar cross section σ in dB(m*m) are presented. The incident field had the form of a plane wave: $\mathbf{E}_{inc}(x) = \mathbf{E}_0 exp(i(\mathbf{k}, r)$, r – thr radius-vector of the point x, $\mathbf{k}$ – wave vector, $|\mathbf{k}| = k$, $\mathbf{E}_0$ – polarization vector. We considered the polarization in which the vector $\mathbf{E}_0$ lies in the same plane in which the scatter diagram is constructed (horizontal polarization).

Calculations were made for frequencies 4 GHz (wave length $\lambda = 7.5$ cm $=$ H/3.3), 8 GHz ($\lambda = 3.75$ cm $=$ H/6.6) and 16 GHz ($\lambda = 1.875$ cm $=$ H/13.2), where H—cylinder height. Calculation results (gray line) are compared to experimental data (black line) received from ITAE RAS. The captions to the figure show data on the number of partition cells, at which agreement between the calculated and experimental data was achieved. The calculations for frequencies 4 and 8 GHz were carried out on a personal computer. The calculation for the frequency of 8 GHz (45784 cells) was carried out using the method of low-rank approximations of the matrix of the system of linear equations [13,14]. The calculation for the frequency of 16 GHz (273600 cells) was carried out using the low-rank approximation method on the supercomputer "Chebychev" at HPC Lomonosov Moscow State University (about 100 cores were involved).

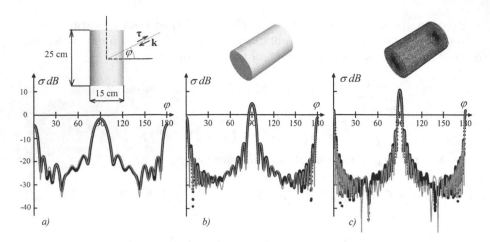

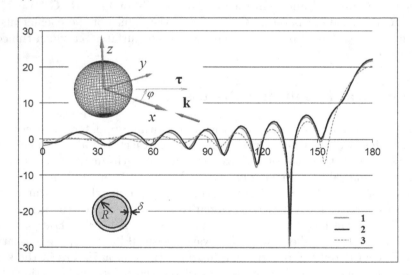

Fig. 2. Backscatter on the cylinder. 4 GHz (a) 13482 cells; 8 GHz (b) 45784 cells; 16 GHz (c) 273600 cells

Fig. 3. Bistatic scattering by coated sphere. 1 – coated sphere (theory), 2 – coated sphere (calculation), 3 – uncoated sphere (theory). $R = 1\,\mathrm{m}$, $\delta = 0.02\,\mathrm{m}$, $k = 10\,\mathrm{m}^{-1}$

Figure 3 shows a bistatic scattering pattern by an ideally conducting sphere with a dielectric coating for the case of horizontal polarization. The curve obtained in the calculation is compared with the theoretical curve. Also, for comparison, the theoretical curve for an uncoated sphere is shown.

Thus, a mathematical model has been created for solving monochromatic wave scattering problems by complex combinations of dielectric and ideally conducting objects. The problem is reduced to a system of linear equations in which the number of equations strongly depends on the electrodynamic size of the objects. Further development of this model should be based on the application of efficient fast matrix algorithms.

References

1. Volakis, J.L., Sertel, K.: Integral Equation Methods for Electromagnetics. SciTech Publishing (2012)
2. Gibson W.: The Method of Moments in Electromagnetics. Chapman & Hall/CRC, Boca Raton (2008)
3. Smirnov, Y.G.: Convergence of the Galerkin methods for equations with elliptic operators on subspaces and solving the electric field equation. Comput. Math. Math. Phys. **47**(1), 126–135 (2007)
4. Rao, S.M., Wilton, D.R., Glisson, A.W.: Electromagnetic scattering by surfaces of arbitrary shape. IEEE Trans. Antennas Propag. **AP-30**(3), 409–418 (1982)
5. Lifanov, I.K.: Singular Integral Equations and Discrete Vortices. VSP, The Netherlands (1996)
6. Belotserkovsky, S.M., Lifanov, I.K.: Method of Discrete Vortices. SRC Press, Boca Raton (1993)
7. Davydov, A.G., Zakharov, E.V., Pimenov, Y.V.: A method for the numerical solution of problems of diffraction of electromagnetic waves by nonclosed surfaces of arbitrary shape. Dokl. Akad. Nauk **276**(1), 96–100 (1984). (in Russian)
8. Zakharov, E.V., Ryzhakov, G.V., Setukha, A.V.: Numerical solution of 3D problems of electromagnetic wave diffraction on a system of ideally conducting surfaces by the method of hypersingular integral equations. Differ. Equ. **50**(9), 1240–1251 (2014)
9. Setukha, A., Fetisov, S.: The method of relocation of boundary condition for the problem of electromagnetic wave scattering by perfectly conducting thin objects. J. Comput. Phys. **373**, 631–647 (2018)
10. Zakharov, E.V., Setukha, A.V., Bezobrazova, E.N.: Method of hypersingular integral equations in a three-dimensional problem of diffraction of electromagnetic waves on a piecewise homogeneous dielectric body. Differ. Equ. **51**(9), 1197–1210 (2015)
11. Setukha, A.V., Bezobrazova, E.N.: The method of hypersingular integral equations in the problem of electromagnetic wave diffraction by a dielectric body with a partial perfectly conducting coating. Russ. J. Numer. Anal. Math. Model. **32**(6), 371–380 (2017)
12. Colton, D., Kress, R.: Integral Equation Methods in Scattering Theory. SIAM (2013)
13. Aparinov, A.A., Setukha, A.V., Stavtsev, S.L.: Parallel implementation for some applications of integral equations method. Lobachevskii J. Math. **39**(4), 477–485 (2018)
14. Aparinov, A., Setukha, A., Stavtsev, S.: Supercomputer modelling of electromagnetic wave scattering with boundary integral equation method. Commun. Comput. Inf. Sci. **793**, 325–336 (2017)

Nonnegative Tensor Train Factorizations and Some Applications

Elena Shcherbakova[1(✉)] and Eugene Tyrtyshnikov[2]

[1] Lomonosov Moscow State University, Moscow, Russia
lena1959@mail.ru
[2] Marchuk Institute of Numerical Mathematics of Russian Academy
of Sciences, Moscow, Russia
eugene.tyrtyshnikov@gmail.com

Abstract. Nowadays as the amount of available data grows, the problem of managing information becomes more difficult. In many applications data can be represented as a multidimensional array. However, in the big data case and as well as when we aim at discovering some structure in the data, we are often interested to construct some low-rank tensor approximations, for instance, using tensor train (TT) decomposition. If the original data is nonnegative, we may be interested to guarantee that an approximant keeps this property. Nonnegative tensor train factorization is an utterly nontrivial task when we cannot afford to see each data element because it may be too expensive in the case of big data.

A natural solution is to build tensor trains with all carriages (cores) to be nonnegative. This means that skeleton decompositions (approximations) have to be constructed nonnegative. Nonnegative factorizations can be used as models for recovering suitable structures in data, e.g., in machine learning and image processing tasks. In this work we suggest a new method for nonnegative tensor train factorizations, estimate its accuracy and give numerical results for different problems.

Keywords: Nonnegative tensor factorization · Tensor train · Low rank approximation · Cross method

1 Introduction

In many applications data can be represented as a multidimensional array but even when the number of dimensions is not tremendously high (say, several tens) it is next to impossible to handle the data picking up each of its elements due to the so called "curse of dimensionality". We certainly need some low-parametric models one of which is a tensor train or TT-decomposition.

The TT-SVD algorithm to build a tensor train consists of successive use of SVD, which yields optimal Frobenius norm approximation, and the resulting matrix factors may not have nonnegative values. However, there are often

---

The work was supported by the Russian Science Foundation, grant 19-11-00338.

I. Lirkov and S. Margenov (Eds.): LSSC 2019, LNCS 11958, pp. 156–164, 2020.
https://doi.org/10.1007/978-3-030-41032-2_17

nonnegative constraints for tensor elements, and we may wish to maintain this property in the approximations. This requirement appears in machine learning and image processing tasks or in physical models where it allows one to interpret the results. Thus, it is important to develop techniques called nonnegative tensor factorization (NTF).

NTF algorithms for canonical or PARAFAC decomposition, Tucker decomposition, Tucker and TT hybrid (the NTT-Tucker model proposed in [1]) are considered in the literature. To the best of our knowledge there is only one algorithm for building a nonnegative tensor train to approximate original tensor described in [1]. The method is called NTT-HALS, the authors use it for estimating the nonnegative TT (NTT) model and a hybrid model called the NTT-Tucker. The ranks of decomposition are to be given on the input, then the tensor train is initialized via an alternating linear scheme and the approximation is improved by an iterative process using a hierarchical alternating least squares approach. At this moment there are no accuracy estimations of the result.

In this article we propose a new algorithm for nonnegative tensor train factorization (NTTF) along with error estimates and demonstrate and discuss some numerical experiments.

2   Nonnegative Tensor Train

Tensor train (TT) decomposition is used for compact representation and approximation of high-dimensional tensors. The nonnegative TT decomposition is written as a tensor train of the form:

$$a(i_1,\ldots,i_d) = \sum_{\alpha_1,\ldots,\alpha_{d-1}} G_1(i_1,\alpha_1)G_2(\alpha_1,i_2,\alpha_2)\ldots G_{d-1}(\alpha_{d-2},i_{d-1},\alpha_{d-1})G_d(\alpha_{d-1},i_d),$$

with tensor carriages $G_1,\ldots,G_d$, where any two neighbors have a common summation index. The summation indices α_k run from 1 to r_k and are called auxiliary indices. The quantities r_k are referred to as tensor train (TT) ranks. The tensor carriages $G_2,\ldots,G_{d-1} \in \mathbb{R}_+^{r_{k-1}\times n_k \times r_k}$. It is sometimes easier to assume that G_1, G_d are not two-dimensional but three-dimensional with additional auxiliary indices $\alpha_0 = \alpha_d = 1$ and tensor train ranks $r_0 = r_d = 1$. This assumption helps to simplify some algorithms.

3   NTTF

In order to achieve the nonnegativity of TT-decomposition elements we suggest to use in TT-SVD algorithm one of the nonnegative matrix factorization (NMF) methods instead of the SVD method. In literature the first articles about NMF appeared in 1994 [2], but the problem became really popular in 1999 after Lee and Seung's publication [3]. Let us formulate the NMF problem: we have an $m \times n$ matrix V with $V_{ij} \geq 0$, $i = \overline{1,m}$, $j = \overline{1,n}$ (further nonnegativity of matrix elements will be denoted as $V \geq 0$) and natural number $r < \min(m,n)$, and we should find matrices $W \in \mathbb{R}^{m \times r}$ and $H \in \mathbb{R}^{r \times n}$ with nonnegative elements such as $V \approx WH$. The minimum r such that $V = WH$ is called nonnegative rank of V.

In general NMF is considered to be NP-hard even when the nonnegative matrix rank is known [4]. The same can be said about complexity of searching for the nonnegative matrix rank. In general NMF is not unique. If W, H is a solution then $W_1 = WD, H_1 = D^{-1}H$ also is a solution if D is nonsingular and preserves nonnegativity of factors.

For nonnegative factorization rank the following theorem holds:

Theorem 1 ([5]). *Let all the elements of an $m \times n$ matrix V be nonnegative: $\mathbb{R}^{m \times n} \ni V \geq 0$. Then nonnegative rank of V (rank$_+(V)$) satisfies this inequality:*

$$\text{rank}(V) \leq \text{rank}_+(V) \leq \min(m, n).$$

The proof is simple. If $\text{rank}_+(V) < \text{rank}(V)$, then from nonnegative factorization rank definition follows that $\text{rank}_+(V) = \text{rank}(V)$. Thus we have a contradiction with our assumption so $\text{rank}_+(V) \geq \text{rank}(V)$. The upper bound is correct because as factors for decomposition we can always consider matrix V and identity matrix.

The usual approach to find W and H is by minimizing the difference between V and WH: $\min\limits_{W \geq 0, H \geq 0} ||V - WH||_F^2$, where $|| \cdot ||_F$ is the Frobenius norm. The problem is non-convex and may have several local minima.

For NTTF it is possible to choose any nonnegative matrix factorization technique, and we suggest to use lraNMF – low-rank approximation based NMF proposed in [6]. There the authors analyzed two well known NMF algorithms (multiplicative update rules and HALS) and noticed that each iteration has more than $O(mn)$ complexity. The most time consuming operation is matrix multiplication with the original large matrix V. So the authors suggested to replace it by a low-rank factorization to increase the method efficiency. They considered the following optimization problem:

$$\min\limits_{\widetilde{W}, \widetilde{H}, W, H} ||V - \widetilde{W}\widetilde{H}||_F^2 + ||\widetilde{W}\widetilde{H} - WH||_F^2$$

such that $\widetilde{W} \in \mathbb{R}^{m \times s}$, $\widetilde{H} \in \mathbb{R}^{s \times n}$, $W \in \mathbb{R}^{m \times r} \geq 0$, $H \in \mathbb{R}^{r \times n} \geq 0$.

The authors of [6] used a two-step method to solve it. First, a low-rank decomposition of V with small rank s is constructed. Then NMF problem $\min_{W,H} ||\widetilde{W}\widetilde{H} - WH||_F^2$ has to be solved. One of the algorithms proposed for it in [6] is called lraNMF_HALS. It has $O((m + n)r^2)$ complexity per iteration, where r is the rank for the nonnegative factorization. The authors claim that lraNMF_HALS always converges to a stationary point. Also in [6] some analysis is given on how the the low-rank approximation error affects the final fitting error of lraNMF.

Here, we suggest to use the cross low-rank approximation methods [7–10] which have $O((m+n)s^2)$ complexity and use for its construction only $O((m+n)s)$

elements of the original matrix V. Thus, using the cross method with the lraNMF_HALS algorithm allows us to significantly reduce the number of operations.

Below a pseudocode for the new method NTTF (nonnegative tensor train factorization) is presented. The functions employed there are the standard Matlab functions. Function reshape($A, [n_1, n_2, \ldots, n_t]$) returns array of size $n_1 \times n_2 \times \ldots \times n_t$ whose elements are taken column-wise from A. Command eye(m) returns $m \times m$ matrix and rank(C) returns rank of C.

Data: Tensor $A(i_1, \ldots, i_d)$, accuracy ε, maximum number of iterations $maxIter$.
Result: Nonnegative TT $B(i_1, \ldots, i_d)$ with cores $G_1, \ldots, G_d$.
1 $C = A$;
2 $r_0 = 1$;
3 **for** $i = 1:(d\text{-}1)$ **do**
4      $C = $ reshape($C, [r_{i-1}n_i, \frac{numel(C)}{r_{i-1}n_i}]$);
5   First estimate for the nonnegative rank: $k = $ rank(C);
6   **while** $k < $ min(size(C)) **do**
7         $iter = 1$;
8   Find factorization of rank k: $C = WH + E$, $W \geq 0$, $H \geq 0$.
9   **while** $||E|| > \frac{\varepsilon}{d-1} \wedge iter \leq maxIter$ **do**
10   Find factorization of rank k: $C = WH + E$, $W \geq 0$, $H \geq 0$.
11           $iter = iter + 1$;
12   **end**
13   **if** $||E|| < \frac{\varepsilon}{d-1}$ **then**
14   break;
15   **end**
16        $k = k + 1$;
17   **end**
18   **if** $||E|| > \frac{\varepsilon}{d-1}$ **then**
19   **if** (size($C, 1$) > size($C, 2$)) **then**
20           $W = C$; $H = $ eye(k);
21   **else**
22           $W = $ eye(k); $H = C$;
23   **end**
24   **end**
25     $r_{i+1} = k$;
26     $H = ||W||_F H$;
27     $W = \frac{W}{||W||_F}$;
28   New core: $G_i = $ reshape($W, [r_{i-1}, n_i, r_i]$);
29     $C = H$;
30 **end**
31 $G_d = C$;

Algorithm 1. Pseudocode for NTTF.

In Algorithm 1 we iteratively use some NMF method to factorize an unfolding matrix and that guarantees elementwise nonnegativity of the tensor train cores. But NMF methods require the nonnegative factorization rank as an input. Because the only known bounds for it are from the Theorem 1, at first we initialize variable k as the rank of an unfolding matrix. Then we try to find the nonnegative factorization of rank k with accuracy $\frac{\varepsilon}{d-1}$. If it is possible then we have found new nonnegative tensor train rank. Otherwise k is incremented by one and the process is repeated. Thus, we check values for the nonnegative rank one by one. Another way is to use a binary search as we have done for numerical experiments. Here Algorithm 1 is formulated for any NMF method, in case we use lraNMF with the cross approximation we can set the start value for k equal low-rank approximation rank.

In theory NMF algorithm converges to local minima. It means that results may considerably differ given different initialization. In order to avoid the possible problem with "bad" initialization the NMF method can be repeated several times (in Algorithm 1 the maximum number of iterations depends on variable *maxIter*).

Theorem 2. *Algorithm 1 finds a tensor train B such that*

$$\|A - B\|_F \leq \varepsilon$$

Proof. For $d = 2$ we have to deal with simple NMF, and the statement correctness immediately follows from the algorithm for constructing B.

Let $d > 2$. Then the fist unfolding matrix A_1 will be represented as $A_1 = W_1 H_1 + E_1$, where $\|E_1\| \leq \frac{\varepsilon}{d-1}$, $W_1 \in \mathbb{R}^{n_1 \times r_1}$, $\|W_1\|_F = 1$. The matrix H_1 can be considered as tensor with elements $H_1(\alpha_1 i_2, i_3, \ldots, i_d)$ for which the algorithm will be used. Then H_1 will be approximated by multiplication of some $W_2 H_2$, and $\|H_1 - W_2 H_2\|_F \leq \frac{\varepsilon}{d-1}$, $\|W_2\|_F = 1$. Then for the second iteration of the method the following is correct:

$$\|A_1 - W_1 W_2 H_2\|_F = \|A_1 - W_1(W_2 H_2 - H_1 + H_1)\|_F \leq$$
$$\leq \|A_1 - W_1 H_1\|_F + \|W_1(H_1 - W_2 H_2)\|_F \leq \frac{\varepsilon}{d-1} + \|W_1\|_F \|W_2 H_2 - H_1\|_F \leq 2\frac{\varepsilon}{d-1}.$$

We can proceed by induction. Assume for the n-th iteration ($n < d - 1$) holds:

$$\|A_1 - W_1 \ldots W_n H_n\|_F \leq n\frac{\varepsilon}{d-1}.$$

Then for the (n+1)-th step for H_n we will get this approximation: $\|H_n - W_{n+1} H_{n+1}\|_F \leq \frac{\varepsilon}{d-1}$, $\|W_{n+1}\|_F = 1$. It means that

$$\|A_1 - W_1 \ldots W_{n+1} H_{n+1}\|_F = \|A_1 - W_1 \ldots W_n(W_{n+1} H_{n+1} - H_n + H_n)\|_F$$

$$\leq \|A_1 - W_1 \ldots W_n H_n\|_F + \|W_1 \ldots W_n(W_{n+1} H_{n+1} - H_n)\|_F \leq n\frac{\varepsilon}{d-1}$$

$$+ \|W_1\|_F \ldots \|W_n\|_F \|H_n - W_{n+1} H_{n+1}\|_F \leq (n+1)\frac{\varepsilon}{d-1}.$$

Thus for $(d-1)$-th (the last step of the method) we will construct nonnegative TT $B(i_1, \ldots, i_d)$ for which $\|A - B\|_F \leq \varepsilon$. □

4 Numerical Experiments

The method NTTF was implemented in Matlab. As the NMF algorithm lraNMF was chosen where the cross method implemented in TT-Toolbox [11] was combined with lraNMF_HALS from TDALAB [12]. For all experiments presented here the relative accuracy is computed as $\frac{\|A-B\|_F}{\|A\|_F} \times 100\%$, where B is a constructed nonnegative TT approximation of the original nonnegative tensor A. Experiments were performed on a desktop computer with an Intel CPU at 2.20 GHz using 8.0 GB of RAM running Windows 8 Professional and Matlab R2016a.

Table 1. NTTF (Algorithm 1) to positive tensors with nonnegative TT ranks $r_1 = r_2 = r_3 = 5$.

Size	Relative error (%)	Time (s, $\pm$ std)	Average ranks	Min ranks	Max ranks
$10 \times 10 \times 10 \times 10$	1.14	0.12 ± 0.01	5, 5, 6	4, 5, 5	5, 8, 8
$100 \times 100 \times 10 \times 10$	1.2	0.6 ± 0.05	5, 5, 8	4, 5, 4	5, 5, 10
$100 \times 100 \times 100 \times 100$	1.66	75.6 ± 3	5, 5, 8	5, 5, 5	5, 5, 8

4.1 An Artificial Dataset

For this experiment random tensor trains with positive elements were generated with a function from the TT-toolbox [11]. Algorithm 1 was applied to their full forms to compare the original and resulting nonnegative tensor train ranks. We considered $10 \times 10 \times 10 \times 10$, $100 \times 100 \times 10 \times 10$ and $100 \times 100 \times 100 \times 100$ tensors. For each experiment 100 tensors were generated, and the results are summarized in Table 1. For maximum and minimum ranks the largest and the smallest values respectively along each r_k, $k = \overline{1,3}$ were chosen. The found nonnegative tensor train ranks do not always coincide with the real ones, but the difference between maximum and minimum ranks is acceptable because we still achieve a serious gain in memory.

4.2 ERP Data

It is easy to change Algorithm 1 so that it will construct tensor train with fixed ranks. Then it becomes possible to compare the performance of our method with the results from [1]. For this purpose we considered a power spectrum obtained from the event-related potential (ERP) data as it was done in [1]. Thus, we have fourth-order tensor of size $71 \times 60 \times 42 \times 9$ [13,14]. Each dimension corresponds to the spectral, temporal, subject and spatial modes.

   In [1] the authors present the results for constructing the NTT-Tucker decomposition of the ERP tensor. They perform the two-step procedure by applying the NTT-HALS algorithm. Firstly, the nonnegative tensor train (NTT) is built. Next, each third-order core tensor is further factored into a third-order core tensor and a factor matrix to get Tucker decomposition for further analysis of the data. Unfortunately, the authors do not present separate measurements for each step. We plan to run more cross-performance tests with NTT-HALS in the future.

We can get estimates for nonnegative tensor train ranks from [1]. They are 4, 10, 6. The computations for Algorithm 1 with fixed ranks were repeated 100 times. The average relative error for the resulting nonnegative tensor train approximation is 13.6% which is close to 13.8% for NTT-Tucker from [1]. The time to construct nonnegative TT with such accuracy is in average 2.5 s of CPU time whereas algorithm for construction of NTT-Tucker needs 4.4 s [1].

4.3   Coagulation Kernel for Smoluchowski Equation

In the introduction we mentioned that nonnegative factorization methods can be used for physical problems. The Smoluchowski equation is a conventional mathematical model of coagulation processes involving huge numbers of inelastically colliding particles. Such collisions play an important role in various physical processes, for example, in aerosol dynamics, polymerization, blood clotting and even in formation of stars. In the case when the particles are uniformly distributed in space and can have only pairwise collisions we get the Smoluchowski coagulation equation:

$$\frac{\partial n(v,t)}{\partial t} = \frac{1}{2} \int_0^v K(v-u,u)n(v-u,t)n(u,t)du - n(v,t) \int_0^\infty K(v,u)n(u,t)du.$$

This equation describes the time-evolution of the concentration function $n(v,t)$ of the particles of size v per the unit volume of the system at the moment t. When the particles consist of l different components, their sizes form a vector $\overline{v} = (v_1, \ldots, v_l)$. Then the coagulation process can be described by a multicomponent version of the Smoluchowski equation. Usually coagulation kernel $K(\overline{v}, \overline{u})$ depends on the features of the considered physical system. In [15] nonnegative functions were used as kernels for which the tensor train approximations were constructed. However, the nonnegativity condition is not guaranteed, but NTTF can help to solve this problem. We have considered coagulation kernel $K(\overline{u}, \overline{v}) = (u_1 + u_2)^\mu (v_1 + v_2)^\nu + (u_1 + u_2)^\nu (v_1 + v_2)^\mu$, $u_i \geq 0$, $i = \overline{1,2}$, $v_i \geq 0$, $i = \overline{1,2}$, where we chose different parameters μ, ν such that $\mu + \nu \leq 1$, $|\mu - \nu| \leq 2$. Variables u_i, v_i, $i = \overline{1,2}$ take values from 0.1 to 10 with step 0.1. Hence, we get a fourth-order tensor with 10^8 elements. For each set of μ, ν we repeated our experiments 10 times. The results for this test are presented in Table 2.

As we can see, even in the worst case for the nonnegative tensor train we have to store less than one percent of the original amount of values. At the same time, the achieved accuracy is good and the CPU time is acceptable for the tensors of this size.

Table 2. NTTF (Algorithm 1) to $K(\overline{u},\overline{v})$, size: $(100\times 100\times 100 \times 100)$

μ	ν	Relative error (%)	Time (s, $\pm$ std)	Average ranks	Min ranks	Max ranks
0.1	−0.05	0.14	55.8 ± 4.5	2, 21, 22	2, 2, 2	2, 96, 100
0.2	0.1	0.12	63.2 ± 2.8	3, 25, 41	3, 1, 3	3, 85, 100

5 Conclusion

In this article we propose a new nonnegative tensor factorization method called NTTF (Nonnegative Tensor Train Factorization). We also estimate the accuracy of our algorithm. Similar to TT-SVD, our NTTF method uses successive decompositions of unfolding matrices, but instead of SVD different NMF methods can be used to ensure the elementwise nonnegativity. For fast nonnegative factorization we recommend to use the low-rank approximation based NMF proposed in [6]. As a way to further reduce the number of operations we propose to employ the cross low-rank approximation method.

The question about the ranks of nonnegative tensor trains remains open. In general it is impossible to obtain an upper bound of the matrix nonnegative rank smaller than minimum of the matrix dimensions so in the worst case we will not get any gain in memory. In order to avoid this problem the chosen NMF method is executed several times iteratively to decrease the probability of the "bad" initialization.

In the future we plan to analyze the classes of tensors for which the nonnegative ranks can be estimated. Also the elaboration of NTTF strongly depends on improvement of used NMF methods in regard to the speed of convergence and complexity.

References

1. Lee, N., Phan, A.-H., Cong, F., Cichocki, A.: Nonnegative tensor train decompositions for multi-domain feature extraction and clustering. In: Hirose, A., Ozawa, S., Doya, K., Ikeda, K., Lee, M., Liu, D. (eds.) ICONIP 2016. LNCS, vol. 9949, pp. 87–95. Springer, Cham (2016). https://doi.org/10.1007/978-3-319-46675-0_10
2. Paatero, P., Tapper, U.: Positive matrix factorization: a non-negative factor model with optimal utilization of error estimates of data values. Environmetrics **5**, 111–126 (1994)
3. Lee, D., Seung, H.: Learning the parts of objects by nonnegative matrix factorization. Nature **401**, 788–791 (1999)
4. Vavasis, S.: On the complexity of nonnegative matrix factorization. SIAM J. Optim. **20**(3), 1364–1377 (2007)
5. Cohen, J., Rothblum, U.: Nonnegative ranks, decompositions and factorizations of nonnegative matrices. Linear Algebra Appl. **190**, 149–168 (1993)
6. Zhou, G., Cichocki, A., Xie, S.: Fast nonnegative matrix/tensor factorization based on low-rank approximation. IEEE Trans. Signal Process. **60**(6), 2928–2940 (2012)
7. Goreinov, S., Tyrtyshnikov, E., Zamarashkin, N.: A theory of pseudo-skeleton approximations. Linear Algebra Appl. **261**, 1–21 (1997)

8. Tyrtyshnikov, E.: Incomplete cross approximation in the mosaic-skeleton method. Computing **64**(4), 367–380 (2000)
9. Goreinov, S., Tyrtyshnikov, E.: The maximal-volume concept in approximation by low-rank matrices. Contemp. Math. **208**, 47–51 (2001)
10. Goreinov, S., Oseledets, I., Savostyanov, D., Tyrtyshnikov, E., Zamarashkin, N.: How to find a good submatrix. In: Olshevsky, V., Tyrtyshnikov, E. (eds.) Matrix Methods: Theory, Algorithms and Applications, pp. 247–256. World Scientific Publishers, New York (2010)
11. TT-Toolbox (TT=Tensor Train) by Oseledets, I. et al.: Version 2.2.2, Institute of Numerical Mathematics, Moscow, Russia. 2009–2013. https://github.com/oseledets/TT-Toolbox
12. TDALAB - MATLAB Toolbox for High-order Tensor Data Decompositions and Analysis. https://github.com/andrewssobral/TDALAB. Current version 1.1, released 1st May 2013
13. Cong, F., Lin, Q.-H., Kuang, L.-D., Gong, X.-F., Astikainen, P., Ristaniemi, T.: Tensor decomposition of EEG signals: a brief review. J. Neurosci. Methods **248**, 59–69 (2015)
14. Cong, F., et al.: Benefits of multi-domain feature of mismatch negativity extracted by nonnegative tensor factorization from low-density array EEG. Int. J. Neural Syst. **22**(6), 1250025 (2012)
15. Matveev, S., Zheltkov, D., Tyrtyshnikov, E., Smirnov, A.: Tensor train versus Monte Carlo for the multicomponent Smoluchowski coagulation equation. J. Comput. Phys. **316**, 164–179 (2016)

Low Rank Structures in Solving Electromagnetic Problems

Stanislav Stavtsev(✉) ⓘD

Marchuk Institute of Numerical Mathematics Russian Academy of Sciences,
Gubkin Street 8, Moscow, Russia
sstass2000@mail.ru

Abstract. Hypersingular integral equations are applied in various areas of applied mathematics and engineering. The paper presents a method for solving the problem of diffraction of an electromagnetic wave on a perfectly conducting object of complex form. In order to solve the problem of diffraction with large wave numbers using the method of integral equations, it is necessary to calculate a large dense matrix.

In order to solve the integral equation, the author used low-rank approximations of large dense matrices. The low-rank approximation method allows multiplying a matrix of size $N \times N$ by a vector of size N in $\mathcal{O}(N \log(N))$ operations instead of $\mathcal{O}(N^2)$. An iterative method (GMRES) is used to solve a system with a large dense matrix represented in a low-rank format, using fast matrix-vector multiplication.

In the case of a large wave number, the matrix becomes ill-conditioned; therefore, it is necessary to use a preconditioner to solve the system with such a matrix. A preconditioner is constructed using the uncompressed matrix blocks of a low-rank matrix representation in order to reduce the number of iterations in the GMRES method. The preconditioner is a sparse matrix. The MUMPS package is used in order to solve system with this sparse matrix on high-performance computing systems.

Keywords: Parallel algorithm · Fast matrix method ·
Preconditioner · Electromagnetic scattering

1 Introduction

Solving large problems on a computer often involves the use of huge computational resources; therefore, for solving large problems, computing systems with distributed memory are used, as well as special numerical approximation methods for dense matrices. In this paper, using the example of solving the problem of diffraction of electromagnetic waves, the features of the application of low-rank approximation methods for supercomputers are presented.

In our work we used "Zhores" supercomputer installed at Skolkovo Institute of Science and Technology [1]. The work was supported by the Russian Science Foundation, grant 19-11-00338.

I. Lirkov and S. Margenov (Eds.): LSSC 2019, LNCS 11958, pp. 165–172, 2020.
https://doi.org/10.1007/978-3-030-41032-2_18

Solving problem of diffraction of electromagnetic waves is equivalent to solving a hypersingular integral equation (as in [2–4]). A low-rank approximation method has been developed for supercomputers in order to solve a system with a large dense matrix. The system with the compressed matrix is solved by the GMRES method. In order to reduce the number of iterations in an iterative algorithm in this paper is proposed a preconditioner using a mosaic structure of the original matrix.

2   Electrodynamics Problem

Let us consider the diffraction problem on a perfectly conducting surface Σ, which can be either closed or open.

A monochrome wave with a frequency ω satisfies the Maxwell equations,

$$\nabla \times \boldsymbol{E} = i\mu\mu_0\omega\boldsymbol{H}; \nabla \times \boldsymbol{H} = -i\varepsilon\varepsilon_0\omega\boldsymbol{E}.$$

On a perfectly conducting surface the following boundary condition holds,

$$\boldsymbol{n} \times (\boldsymbol{E}_0 + \boldsymbol{E}) = 0,$$

where $\boldsymbol{E}_0$ is a given function, defined by the incident wave (we assume that the incident wave is planar), and $\boldsymbol{n}$ is a normal vector to the surface.

To find a unique solution it is necessary to pose additional conditions

$$\boldsymbol{E} \in L_2^{\mathrm{loc}}(\Omega)$$

and

$$\frac{d}{d\tau}\begin{pmatrix} \boldsymbol{E} \\ \boldsymbol{H} \end{pmatrix} - ik\begin{pmatrix} \boldsymbol{E} \\ \boldsymbol{H} \end{pmatrix} = o\left(\frac{1}{|\boldsymbol{x}|}\right), \ \tau = |\boldsymbol{x}|, \ \tau \to \infty.$$

In accordance with [2], the problem can be reduced to the electric field integral equation on the unknown $\boldsymbol{j}(y)$:

$$\boldsymbol{n} \times \iint\limits_{\Sigma} \boldsymbol{j}(y)\Big(\mathrm{grad\ div\ } F(x-y) + k^2 F(x-y)\Big)d\sigma_y = -\boldsymbol{n} \times \boldsymbol{E}_0(x), \ x \in \Sigma, \ (1)$$

where $k = \omega\sqrt{\varepsilon\varepsilon_0\mu\mu_0}$ is the wave number, and

$$F(R) = \frac{\exp(ikR)}{R}, \ R = |x - y|.$$

In Eq. (1) the integral can be understood in the sense of the Hadamard finite part.

For the numerical solution of the Eq. (1) we use a numerical scheme presented in [5]. In this scheme the surface is uniformly divided into cells σ_i, $i = 1, n$, and for each cell an orthonormal basis $\boldsymbol{e}_{i1}$, $\boldsymbol{e}_{i2}$ is introduced. For each cell σ_i it is assumed that $\boldsymbol{j}_i = \boldsymbol{j}(x_i)$, where x_i is the center of mass of the cell. Each cell is considered to be planar. Discretization of the integral operator produces a matrix that consists of 2×2 blocks:

$$A_{ij} = \begin{pmatrix} E_{1j}(x_i) \cdot e_{1i} & E_{2j}(x_i) \cdot e_{1i} \\ E_{1j}(x_i) \cdot e_{2i} & E_{2j}(x_i) \cdot e_{2i} \end{pmatrix},$$

$$E_{1j}(x_i) = \int_{\partial \sigma_j} Q(x_i) de_2 + k^2 e_{1j} \int_{\sigma_j} \frac{\exp(ikR)}{R} d\sigma; \tag{2}$$

$$E_{2j}(x_i) = - \int_{\partial \sigma_j} Q(x_i) de_1 + k^2 e_{2j} \int_{\sigma_j} \frac{\exp(ikR)}{R} d\sigma, Q(x) = \nabla_y \frac{\exp(ik|x-y|)}{|x-y|}.$$

In (2) the contour and surface integrals are calculated numerically.

3 Mosaic Skeleton Approximations

The problem reduces to the solution of the linear system of algebraic equations

$$A z = b \tag{3}$$

with a dense matrix A. To approximate the matrix we use the mosaic-skeleton method [6–8]. It partitions the matrix hierarchically into blocks, and the low-rank matrix blocks can be calculated independently using the incomplete cross approximation algorithm.

Let us investigate the approximation algorithm. In all examples below the surface Σ in Eq. (1) is a round cylinder with a diameter 15 cm and height 25 cm.

In Fig. 1 we present the inverse Radar Cross Section (RCS) for the frequency 16 GHz. The σ value for different directions τ of the wave vectors of the incident wave is calculated as

$$\sigma(\tau) = \frac{4\pi}{|E_0|^2} \left| \sum_{i=1}^{n} (j_i - \tau \cdot (\tau \cdot j_i)) k^2 \exp(-ik\tau \cdot x_i)\sigma_i \right|^2. \tag{4}$$

The black points show the results of the experiment, the grey line shows the results of the numerical simulation.

In all calculations the number of cells is 192 156, the number of right-hand sides is 2048, the accuracy of approximation of the matrix is 10^{-3}, the accuracy of solving system is $5 \cdot 10^{-3}$.

The accuracy of the matrix approximation and the accuracy of the solution of the system is determined by comparing the RSC obtained from experiments and from approximate calculations for a large number of problems.

In Table 1 one can see the number of necessary iterations for solving the system with 2048 right-hand sides up to the accuracy $5 \cdot 10^{-3}$ for different frequencies and numbers of cells n.

It can be seen from Table 1 that the number of iterations increases significantly with respect to the frequency, and it requires a lot of memory and computational time.

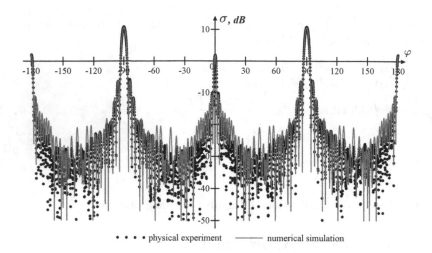

Fig. 1. RCS, 16 GHz, vertical polarization, $n = 192\,156$

Table 1. Number of iterations for various parameters of the electrodynamics problem.

n	2 GHz	4 GHz	8 GHz	16 GHz
7872	1862	2355	4390	9410
21760	2821	4261	6025	11237
30400	3651	4791	7285	12990
45784	4262	5689	8269	21103

4   Preconditioner

Let us reduce the number of iterations in the GMRES method using the preconditioner for solving the system (3). The technology for building and using the preconditioner is described in the monograph [9].

The matrix is divided into blocks according to the mosaic-skeleton approximations method. The blocks corresponding to the interaction of distant domains are assumed to have low rank. All elements of the remaining blocks are calculated. Non-low-rank blocks will be called dense. For low-rank blocks, an approximation is constructed with a given accuracy [6,10]. Suppose that for a block of size $m \times n$, an approximation of rank r is constructed. If the $m \cdot n < r(m + n)$ condition is satisfied for a block with m, n, r parameters, then such block is also assumed to be dense. Dense blocks are shown in red in Fig. 2.

A matrix from the mosaic-skeleton representation is selected as the M preconditioner of the system (3), in which the only dense blocks are left and the low-rank blocks are assumed to be zero (see Fig. 3). The M matrix is sparse; therefore, the LU decomposition is quickly built for this matrix. The LU decomposition factors are also sparse, so small amount of RAM is needed to store the L and U matrices, and the system with a preconditioner is quickly solved:

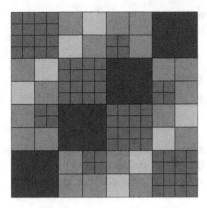

Fig. 2. Mosaic matrix structure (Color figure online)

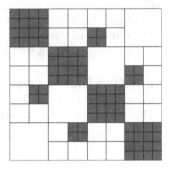

Fig. 3. Nonzero blocks of the preconditioner (Color figure online)

$$M\,y = c. \tag{5}$$

The construction of LU decomposition for sparse systems on multiprocessor computing systems is implemented in many packages. In this paper, the author used the MUMPS package [11].

Let us apply MUMPS to solve the system (3):

1. the original A matrix is represented in a low-rank format, and the structure of the matrix and the location of dense blocks in it are determined;
2. information about the found dense blocks is collected on a single processor by the MUMPS package, the distribution of the calculated elements of the M matrix by processors is determined;
3. the M preconditioner is calculated;
4. the LU decomposition of a sparse matrix is calculated in parallel using the MUMPS package;
5. in order to solve the (3) system by the GMRES method using the MUMPS package and the LU decomposition of the M matrix, the system (5) is solved at each iteration.

Table 2. Number of iterations for solving of system without using a preconditioner and with using a preconditioner.

N	34 122	94 872	167 676	376 800
p_1	4 684	7 563	9 777	14 514
p_2	949	1 051	1 116	1 488

The MUMPS package provides for the use of different methods for constructing LU decomposition of sparse systems. In this paper, the authors used the method that leads to the least full L and U matrices [11].

5   Numerical Results

Table 2 shows the effectiveness of the preconditioner for solving systems of different sizes N. In the table p_1 is the number of iterations without a preconditioner, p_2 is the number of iterations with a preconditioner. The frequency in the example is 8 GHz.

It is possible to construct RCS for cylinder on supercomputers without using a preconditioner only for frequency equal to the 16 GHz (see Fig. 1). Preconditioner allows to obtain a solution of the integral equation and $\sigma(\tau)$ (4) for 32 GHz and 64 GHz.

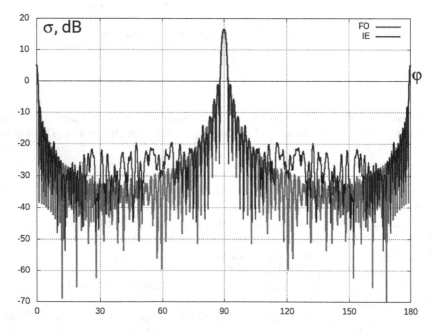

Fig. 4. RCS, 32 GHz, horizontal polarization, $N = 1\,507\,200$ (Color figure online)

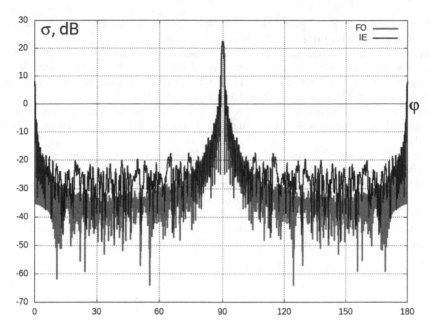

Fig. 5. RCS, 64 GHz, horizontal polarization, $N = 2\,006\,928$ (Color figure online)

In Figs. 4, 5, the RCS obtained from the solution of the integral equation (IE) is shown in black, the RCS obtained by the physical optics method (FO) [12] is shown in red.

In this section we used "Zhores" supercomputer installed at Skolkovo Institute of Science and Technology [1]. The work was supported by the Russian Science Foundation, grant 19-11-00338.

References

1. Zacharov, I., et al.: Zhores - Petaflops supercomputer for data-driven modeling, machine learning and artificial intelligence installed in Skolkovo Institute of Science and Technology. arxiv:1902.07490
2. Colton, D., Kress, R.: Integral Methods in Scattering Theory. Willey, New York (1983)
3. Fetisov, S., Setukha, A.: The method of relocation of boundary condition for the problem of electromagnetic wave scattering by perfectly conducting thin objects. J. Comput. Phys. **373**, 631–647 (2018)
4. Lifanov, I.K., Stavtsev, S.L.: Integral equations and sound propagation in a shallow sea. Differ. Equ. **40**(9), 1330–1344 (2004)
5. Stavtsev, S.L.: $\mathcal{H}^2$ matrix and integral equation for electromagnetic scattering by a perfectly conducting object. In: Constanda, C., Dalla Riva, M., Lamberti, P.D., Musolino, P. (eds.) Integral Methods in Science and Engineering, vol. 2, pp. 255–264. Springer, Cham (2017). https://doi.org/10.1007/978-3-319-59387-6_25

6. Tyrtyshnikov, E.E.: Incomplete cross approximation in the mosaic skeleton method. Computing **64**(4), 367–380 (2000)
7. Aparinov, A., Setukha, A., Stavtsev, S.: Supercomputer modelling of electromagnetic wave scattering with boundary integral equation method. In: Voevodin, V., Sobolev, S. (eds.) RuSCDays 2017. CCIS, vol. 793, pp. 325–336. Springer, Heidelberg (2017). https://doi.org/10.1007/978-3-319-71255-0_26
8. Aparinov, A.A., Setukha, A.V., Stavtsev, S.L.: Parallel implementation for some applications of integral equations method. Lobachevskii J. Math. **39**(4), 477–485 (2018)
9. Chen, K.: Matrix Preconditioner Techniques and Applications. Cambridge University Press, Cambridge (2005)
10. Osinsky, A.I., Zamarashkin, N.L.: Pseudo-skeleton approximations with better accuracy estimates. Linear Algebra Appl. **537**, 221–249 (2018)
11. MUMPS. http://mumps.enseeiht.fr/
12. Saez de Adana, F., Gutierrez, O., Gonzalez, I., Catedra, M.F., Lozano, L.: Practical Applications of Asymptotic Techniques in Electromagnetics. Artech House, Boston (2011)

Tensors in Modelling Multi-particle Interactions

Daniil A. Stefonishin[1], Sergey A. Matveev[1,2(✉)], and Dmitry A. Zheltkov[2,3]

[1] Skolkovo Institute of Science and Technology, Moscow, Russia
{d.stefonishin,s.matveev}@skoltech.ru
[2] Marchuk Institute of Numerical Mathematics RAS, Moscow, Russia
dmitry.zheltkov@gmail.com
[3] Moscow Institute of Physics and Technology, Moscow, Russia
https://www.skoltech.ru/
https://www.inm.ras.ru/

Abstract. In this work we present recent results on application of low-rank tensor decompositions to modelling of aggregation kinetics taking into account multi-particle collisions (for three and more particles). Such kinetics can be described by system of nonlinear differential equations with right-hand side requiring N^D operations for its straight-forward evaluation, where N is number of particles' size classes and D is number of particles colliding simultaneously. Such a complexity can be significantly reduced by application low rank tensor decompositions (either Tensor Train or Canonical Polyadic) to acceleration of evaluation of sums and convolutions from right-hand side. Basing on this drastic reduction of complexity for evaluation of right-hand side we further utilize standard second order Runge-Kutta time integration scheme and demonstrate that our approach allows to obtain numerical solutions of studied equations with very high accuracy in modest times. We also show preliminary results on parallel scalability of novel approach and conclude that it can be efficiently utilized with use of supercomputers.

Keywords: Tensor train · Aggregation kinetics · Parallel algorithms

1 Introduction

Aggregation of inelastically colliding particles plays important role in many technological and natural phenomena. In case of spatially homogeneous systems aggregation process can be described by famous Smoluchowski kinetic equations [1]. These equations describe time-evolution of mean concentrations n_k of particles of size k per unit volume of media:

$$\frac{dn_k}{dt} = \frac{1}{2} \sum_{i+j=k} C_{i,j} n_i n_j - n_k \sum_{i=1}^{\infty} C_{k,i} n_i.$$

The work was supported by the Russian Science Foundation, grant 19-11-00338.

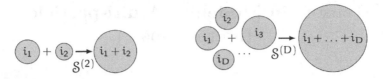

Fig. 1. On the left panel binary aggregation of particles is presented, and multi-particle collision on the right panel

Such a model is well-studied by lots of analytical and numerical methods but allows to take into account only pairwise particles' collisions. In this work we consider a generalization of aggregation equations for case of multi-particle interactions

$$\frac{d\mathbf{n}}{dt} = \sum_{d=2}^{D} \mathcal{S}^{(D)}[\mathbf{n}] = \sum_{d=2}^{D} \left[\mathcal{P}^{(D)}[\mathbf{n}] + \mathcal{Q}^{(D)}[\mathbf{n}] \right],$$

where operators $\mathcal{P}^{(d)} = \left[p_1^{(d)}, p_2^{(d)}, \ldots \right]^T$ and $\mathcal{Q}^{(d)} = \left[q_1^{(d)}, d_2^{(d)}, \ldots \right]^T$ are defined as

$$p_k^{(d)}[\mathbf{n}] = \frac{1}{d!} \sum_{|\mathbf{i}_d|=k} C_{\mathbf{i}_d}^{(d)} n_{i_1} n_{i_2} \ldots n_{i_d}, \quad k \in \mathbb{N},$$

$$q_k^{(d)}[\mathbf{n}] = -\frac{n_k}{(d-1)!} \sum_{\mathbf{i}_{d-1} \in \mathbb{N}^{d-1}} C_{\mathbf{i}_{d-1},k}^{(d)} n_{i_1} n_{i_2} \ldots n_{i_{d-1}}, \quad k \in \mathbb{N},$$

$$\mathbf{i}_d = (i_1, i_2, \ldots, i_d), \quad |\mathbf{i}_d| = i_1 + i_2 + \ldots + i_d, \quad 2 \le d \le D.$$

Those operators $p^{(d)}$ and $q^{(d)}$ correspond to description of simultaneous collisional aggregation of d particles. We represent such a model informally in Fig. 1.

In case of defined initial conditions $n_k(t=0)$ we obtain a Cauchy problem which is known to be well-posed under assumption of bounded non-negative symmetric coefficients [2]. There also exist a very few examples of known analytical solutions for the Cauchy problem for multi-particle aggregation kinetic equations [3]. Unfortunately, such class of mathematical models is much less studied numerically than class of aggregation equations accounting only binary collisions. The reason lies in higher order of non-linearity and exponential growth of complexity of evaluation of the right-hand side with respect to number D of simultaneously colliding particles. It makes the numerical treatment of such systems extremely time-consuming.

In our recent work we proposed a novel approach based on application of low-rank tensor train (TT) decomposition [5,6] to acceleration of computations and presented its high accuracy [7,8]. This allowed us to reduce the complexity of evaluation of sums from the right-hand side from $O(N^D)$ operations to $O(NDR^2 \log N)$ operations, where $R \ll N$ is the maximal TT-rank of kinetic coefficients. In case of pre-defined low-rank Canonical Polyadic (CP) decomposition of kernel coefficients the complexity can be reduced even to $O(NDR \log N)$ but we do not know a robust way finding CP-decomposition even for 3-dimensional tensors. Nevertheless, assumption that $R \ll N$ is crucial for efficiency of proposed approach.

In the current work we prove that TT-ranks of a wide class of generalized Brownian kernels are low and do not depend on the number N of accounted kinetic equations for arbitrary dimension D. We also present an efficient parallel implementation of our TT-based approach and present preliminary tests of scalability our method.

2   Estimates of TT-ranks for Generalized Brownian Kernels

In this section we present estimates of tensor ranks for generalized Brownian kernel $\mathscr{C}^{(D)} = \left[C_{i_D}^{(D)} \right]$ (see example of exact Brownian coefficients e.g. at [4]) with the elements of the following form:

$$C_{i_D}^{(D)} \equiv C_{i_D}^{(D)}[\mu_1, \mu_2, \ldots, \mu_D] = \sum_{\sigma} i_{\sigma(1)}^{\mu_1} \cdot i_{\sigma(2)}^{\mu_2} \cdot \ldots \cdot i_{\sigma(D)}^{\mu_D} \tag{1}$$

Here we assume the sum to be over all permutations σ of the set $\{1, 2, \ldots, D\}$.

Recall the definition of a TT-decomposition for a kernel $\mathscr{C}^{(D)}$ which is of the form

$$C_{i_D}^{(D)} = \sum_{r_0, r_1, \ldots, r_D} H_{r_0, i_1, r_1}^{(1)} \cdot H_{r_1, i_2, r_2}^{(2)} \cdot \ldots \cdot H_{r_{D-1}, i_D, r_D}^{(D)}, \tag{2}$$

$$1 \le r_\lambda \le R_\lambda, \quad 0 \le \lambda \le D; \quad R_0 = R_D = 1.$$

For the kernel $\mathscr{C}^{(D)}$ of dimension D with the elements (1) there holds an estimate on the TT-ranks R_λ:

$$\max\{R_\lambda : 0 \le \lambda \le D\} = \binom{D}{\lceil D/2 \rceil} \equiv O\left(2^D/\sqrt{D}\right).$$

Such estimate can be verified by the means of the following theorem.

Theorem 1. *Let the parameters $\mu_1, \mu_2, \ldots, \mu_D$ be fixed. For a given tensor $\mathscr{C}^{(D)}$ in D dimensions of sizes $N \times N \times \ldots \times N$ with the elements (1) one can prove the following estimates on its TT-ranks R_λ:*

$$R_\lambda \le \binom{D}{\lambda} \equiv \frac{D!}{\lambda! \cdot (D-\lambda)!}, \quad 0 \le \lambda \le D.$$

Proof. Let us put $R_\lambda := \binom{D}{\lambda}$ for $0 \le \lambda \le D$. To prove the theorem we simply need to construct a tensor train decomposition of the tensor $\mathscr{C}^{(D)}$ with these predefined ranks R_λ.

Further we assume that for each number $1 \leq \lambda \leq D$ it is chosen a bijection $r_\lambda \rightarrow (r_{1,\lambda}, r_{2,\lambda}, \ldots, r_{\lambda,\lambda})$ between the sets

$$\{r_\lambda \in \mathbb{N} \colon 1 \leq r_\lambda \leq R_\lambda\},$$
$$\mathcal{R}_\lambda := \{(r_{1,\lambda}, r_{2,\lambda}, \ldots, r_{\lambda,\lambda}) \in \mathbb{N}^\lambda \colon 1 \leq r_{1,\lambda} < r_{2,\lambda} < \ldots < r_{\lambda,\lambda} \leq D\}.$$

One can specify such mappings for sure due to the coincidence of the cardinalities of the considered sets.

Note, that for all numbers $1 \leq \lambda \leq D-1$ one can check the correctness of the identity

$$C_{i_{\lambda+1}}^{(\lambda+1)}[\mu_1, \mu_2, \ldots, \mu_{\lambda+1}] \equiv \sum_{\xi=1}^{\lambda+1} C_{i_\lambda}^{(\lambda)}[\mu_1, \ldots, \mu_{\xi-1}, \mu_{\xi+1}, \ldots, \mu_{\lambda+1}] \cdot i_{\lambda+1}^{\mu_\xi}. \quad (3)$$

With the given identity we show by induction on $1 \leq \lambda \leq D$, that it is always possible to choose the values $H_{r_{\tau-1}, i_\tau, r_\tau}^{(\tau)}$ in order to satisfy the constraints

$$\sum_{r_0, r_1, \ldots, r_{\lambda-1}} H_{r_0, i_1, r_1}^{(1)} \cdot H_{r_1, i_2, r_2}^{(2)} \cdot \ldots \cdot H_{r_{\lambda-1}, i_\lambda, r_\lambda}^{(\lambda)} = C_{i_\lambda}^{(\lambda)}[\mu_{r_{1,\lambda}}, \mu_{r_{2,\lambda}}, \ldots, \mu_{r_{\lambda,\lambda}}], \quad (4)$$

$$r_0 = 1, \quad 1 \leq i_\tau \leq N, \quad 1 \leq r_\tau \leq R_\tau, \quad 1 \leq \tau \leq \lambda.$$

Thus, the equality (4) with $\lambda = D$ gives us the required TT-decomposition for the tensor with the elements of the form (1).

The base of induction is trivial, if choose

$$H_{r_0, i_1, r_1}^{(1)} := C_{i_1}^{(1)}[\mu_{r_1}] \equiv i_1^{\mu_{r_1}}, \quad 1 \leq i_1 \leq N, \quad 1 \leq r_1 \leq R_1.$$

Next we rewrite the Eq. (1) for $D = 2, 3$:

$$C_{i_1, i_2}^{(2)}[\mu_1, \mu_2] \equiv \begin{bmatrix} i_1^{\mu_1} & i_1^{\mu_2} \end{bmatrix} \cdot \begin{bmatrix} i_2^{\mu_2} \\ i_2^{\mu_1} \end{bmatrix};$$

$$C_{i_1, i_2, i_3}^{(3)}[\mu_1, \mu_2, \mu_3] \equiv \begin{bmatrix} i_1^{\mu_1} & i_1^{\mu_2} & i_1^{\mu_3} \end{bmatrix} \cdot \begin{bmatrix} 0 & i_2^{\mu_3} & i_2^{\mu_2} \\ i_2^{\mu_3} & 0 & i_2^{\mu_1} \\ i_2^{\mu_2} & i_2^{\mu_1} & 0 \end{bmatrix} \cdot \begin{bmatrix} i_3^{\mu_1} \\ i_3^{\mu_2} \\ i_3^{\mu_3} \end{bmatrix}.$$

This representation allows us to describe the structure of factors $\mathscr{H}^{(\tau)}$ for each τ. If the equality (4) is already proven for a given λ, then it is sufficient to choose

$$H_{r_\lambda, i_{\lambda+1}, r_{\lambda+1}}^{(\lambda+1)} := \begin{cases} i_{\lambda+1}^{\mu_{r_{\xi,\lambda+1}}}, & \{r_{\xi,\lambda+1}\} \cup \mathcal{R}_\lambda = \mathcal{R}_{\lambda+1}, \\ 0, & \text{otherwise}; \end{cases}$$

$$1 \leq r_\lambda \leq R_\lambda, \quad 1 \leq i_{\lambda+1} \leq N, \quad 1 \leq r_{\lambda+1} \leq R_{\lambda+1}.$$

Now it is not hard to prove, that by the virtue of the proposed choice for all numbers $1 \leq i_1, i_2, \ldots, i_{\lambda+1} \leq N$ and $1 \leq r_{\lambda+1} \leq R_{\lambda+1}$ we have the identity

$$\sum_{r_\lambda=1}^{R_\lambda} C_{i_\lambda}^{(\lambda)} \left[\mu_{r_{1,\lambda}}, \mu_{r_{2,\lambda}}, \ldots, \mu_{r_{\lambda,\lambda}} \right] \cdot H_{r_\lambda, i_{\lambda+1}, r_{\lambda+1}}^{(\lambda+1)} =$$

$$= \sum_{\xi=1}^{\lambda+1} C_{i_\lambda}^{(\lambda)} \left[\mu_{r_{1,\lambda+1}}, \ldots, \mu_{r_{\xi-1,\lambda+1}}, \mu_{r_{\xi+1,\lambda+1}}, \ldots, \mu_{r_{\lambda+1,\lambda+1}} \right] \cdot i_{\lambda+1}^{\mu_{r_{\xi,\lambda+1}}}.$$

Therefore, to verify an induction step we just need to use the identity (3), where it is necessary to use parameters $\mu_{r_{1,\lambda+1}}, \mu_{r_{2,\lambda+1}}, \ldots, \mu_{r_{\lambda+1,\lambda+1}}$ instead of parameters $\mu_1, \mu_2, \ldots, \mu_{\lambda+1}$ respectively. The last statement proves the theorem.

3 Parallel Algorithm and Numerical Experiments

In our work we exploit organization of parallel computations along particle size coordinate with dimension N. It is worth to note that alternative way of parallelization of our approach along TT-ranks leads to dramatic overheads in terms of data exchanges and collective operations and does not lead to speedup of computations.

Let us assume that we have P processors and number N of studied kinetic equations is divisible by P. Thus, we introduce the following notation for getting p-th block of taken vector $\mathbf{a}_N = [sa_1, a_2, \ldots, a_N]^T$:

$$\{\mathbf{a}_N\}_p := \left[a_{(p-1)N/P+1}, a_{(p-1)N/P+2}, \ldots, a_{pN/P} \right]^T, \qquad 1 \leqslant p \leqslant P.$$

With use of those notations we can denote the blocks $\mathcal{H}^{(\lambda,p)}$ of cores $\mathcal{H}^{(\lambda)}$ of TT-decomposition of kernel kinetic coefficients $\mathscr{C}^{(D)}$ which will be used at processor with number p ($1 \leq p \leq P$) :

$$\mathbf{h}_{r_{\lambda-1},r_\lambda}^{(\lambda)} := \left[H_{r_{\lambda-1},1,r_\lambda}^{(\lambda)}, H_{r_{\lambda-1},2,r_\lambda}^{(\lambda)}, \ldots, H_{r_{\lambda-1},N,r_\lambda}^{(\lambda)} \right]^T \in \mathbb{R}^N,$$

$$\mathbf{H}_{r_\lambda}^{(\lambda,p)} := \left[\left\{ \mathbf{h}_{1,r_\lambda}^{(\lambda)} \right\}_p, \left\{ \mathbf{h}_{2,r_\lambda}^{(\lambda)} \right\}_p, \ldots, \left\{ \mathbf{h}_{R_{\lambda-1},r_\lambda}^{(\lambda)} \right\}_p \right]^T \in \mathbb{R}^{R_{\lambda-1} \times N/P},$$

$$\mathscr{H}^{(\lambda,p)} := \left[\left\{ \mathbf{h}_{r_{\lambda-1},r_\lambda}^{(\lambda)} \right\}_p \right] \equiv \left[\mathbf{H}_{r_\lambda}^{(\lambda,p)} \right] \in \mathbb{R}^{R_{\lambda-1} \times N/P \times R_\lambda}.$$

The algorithm for operator $\mathcal{P}^{(d)}$ is presented in Fig. 2 and for $\mathcal{Q}^{(d)}$ in Fig. 3. On the input algorithms require to have blocks $\mathscr{H}^{(1,i)}$ of TT-decomposition for kinetic coefficients and vector of concentrations. For time-integration of the

```
 1: function PARALLEL TT-CONVOLUTION(𝓗^(1,p), 𝓗^(2,p),..., 𝓗^(D,p), {n_N}_p)
 2:     for r_{D-1} ← 1, 2, ..., R_{D-1} do
 3:         {x_{r_{D-1}}^{(D-1)}}_p ← {h_{r_{D-1},1}^{(D)}}_p ∘ {n_N}_p              ▷ Elementwise product
 4:     end for
 5:     for λ ← D - 1, D - 2, ..., 1 do
 6:         for r_{λ-1} ← 1, 2, ..., R_{λ-1} do
 7:             {x_{r_{λ-1}}^{(λ-1)}}_p ← 0
 8:             for r_λ ← 1, 2, ..., R_λ do
 9:                 {y}_p ← {h_{r_{λ-1},r_λ}^{(λ)}}_p ∘ {n_N}_p                   ▷ Elementwise product
10:                 {y}_p ← {x_{r_λ}^{(λ)} * y}_p                                ▷ Parallel discrete convolution
                                                                                ▷ Collective communications of all processes
11:                 {x_{r_{λ-1}}^{(λ-1)}}_p ← {x_{r_{λ-1}}^{(λ-1)}}_p + {y}_p
12:             end for
13:         end for
14:     end for
15:     {x_1^{(0)}}_p ← (1/D!) · {x_1^{(0)}}_p
16:     Logical shift of vector x_1^{(0)} on D - 1 position to the right
                                                                                ▷ Transfers of D - 1 components between processes with adjusent identifiers p
17:     return {x_1^{(0)}}_p
18: end function
```

Fig. 2. Parallel algorithm for $\mathcal{P}^{(D)}$.

```
 1: function PARALLEL TT-PRODUCT(𝓗^(1,p), 𝓗^(2,p), ..., 𝓗^(D,p), {n_N}_p)
 2:     y_D ← 1
 3:     for λ ← D, D - 1, ..., 2 do
 4:         for r_λ ← 1, 2, ..., R_λ do
 5:             z_{r_λ}^{(λ,p)} ← H_{r_λ}^{(λ,p)} {n_N}_p                        ▷ Matrix-vector product
 6:             z_{r_λ}^{(λ,p)} ← Σ_{q=1}^{P} z_{r_λ}^{(λ,q)}                   ▷ Parallel sum reduction
                                                                                ▷ Collective communications of all processes
 7:         end for
 8:         y_{λ-1} ← [z_1^{(λ,p)}, z_2^{(λ,p)}, ..., z_{R_λ}^{(λ,p)}] y_λ       ▷ Matrix-vector product
 9:     end for
10:     x ← -(1/(D-1)!) 𝔥^{(1,p)} y_1                                           ▷ Matrix-vector product
11:     x ← x ∘ {n_N}_p                                                         ▷ Elementwise product
12:     return x
13: end function
```

Fig. 3. Parallel algorithm for $\mathcal{Q}^{(D)}$.

Table 1. Speedup of computations with use of ClusterFFT operation for pure ternary aggregation in case of 3-dimensional generalized Brownian kernel with $N = 2^{19}$ equations. Benchmark for 100 time-integration steps with use of second order Runge-Kutta method. "Zhores" supercomputer of Skolkovo Institute of Science and Technology tables.

Number of CPU-cores	Time, Sec	Speedup
1	257.80	1.00
2	147.62	1.75
4	80.21	3.21
8	43.65	5.91
16	22.63	11.39
32	14.83	17.38
64	13.15	19.60
128	12.22	21.09

Cauchy problem we utilize standard explicit second order Runge-Kutta method, hence, each time-step requires two evaluations of $\mathcal{P}^{(d)}$ and $\mathcal{Q}^{(d)}$.

We present results of benchmarks of the presented algorithm for the generalized Brownian coefficients in Table 1. In our experiments we used ClusterFFT library included into Intel MKL^{TM}. As soon as FFT is a dominating operation in our algorithm in terms of complexity, we obtain similar performance of our code to performance of ClusterFFT library. From these experiments we obtain speedup of calculations for modelling of ternary aggregation with use of 128 cores by order of magnitude in comparison with sequential computations. This allows us to consider a broader class of problems of potential interest which can be studied in modest computational time.

4   Conclusions

In this paper we present recent developments of tensor based methods for modelling of multi-particle aggregation. We prove estimates of TT-ranks for generalized Brownian kinetic coefficients depending only on the dimensionality D but not on the mode-sizes N of used arrays. We also propose an efficient way of parallel implementation of TT-based approach and demonstrate preliminary results of its parallel scalability.

Acknowledgments. In our work we used "Zhores" supercomputer installed at Skolkovo Institute of Science and Technology [9]. We also would like to acknowledge Talgat Daulbaev for an idea of representation of generalized Brownian coefficients in TT-format in case of $D = 3$. The work was supported by the Russian Science Foundation, grant 19-11-00338.

References

1. Galkin, V. A. : Smoluchowski equation.: Fizmatlit, Moscow (2001)
2. Galkin, V.A.: Kinetic method for solving systems of differential equations. Doklady Mathematics **288**, 508–509 (2013)
3. Krapivsky, P.L.: Aggregation processes with n-particle elementary reactions. Journal of Physics A: Mathematical and General **24**(19), 4697–4703 (1991)
4. Matveev, S.A., Krapivsky, P.L., Smirnov, A.P., Tyrtyshnikov, E.E., Brilliantov, N.V.: Oscillations in aggregation-shattering processes. Physical review letters **119**(26), 260601 (2017)
5. Oseledets, I.V.: Tensor-train decomposition. SIAM Journal on Scientific Computing **33**(5), 2295–2317 (2011)
6. Oseledets, I.V., Tyrtyshnikov, E.E.: TT-cross approximation for multidimensional arrays. Linear Algebra and its Applications **432**(1), 70–88 (2010)
7. Stefonishin, D.A., Matveev, S.A., Smirnov, A.P., Tyrtyshnikov, E.E.: Tensor decompositions for solving the equations of mathematical models of aggregation with multiple collisions of particles (In Russian). Vychislitel'nye Metody i Programmirovanie **19**(4), 390–404 (2018)
8. Stefonishin, D.A., Matveev, S.A., Smirnov, A.P., Tyrtyshnikov, E.E.: An efficient finite-difference method for solving Smoluchowski-type kinetic equations of aggregation with three-body collisions (In Russian). Vychislitel'nye Metody i Programmirovanie **19**(3), 261–269 (2018)
9. Zacharov, I., et al.: Zhores - Petaflops supercomputer for data-driven modeling, machine learning and artificial intelligence installed in Skolkovo Institute of Science and Technology. arxiv:1902.07490

Tensorisation in the Solution of Smoluchowski Type Equations

Ivan Timokhin[1,2(✉)]

[1] Department of Computational Mathematics and Cybernetics,
Lomonosov Moscow State University, Moscow, Russia
timokhin.iv@gmail.com
[2] Marchuk Institute of Numerical Mathematics, Russian Academy of Sciences,
Moscow, Russia

Abstract. We investigate the structure of the non-linear operator featured in the Smoluchowski-type system of ordinary differential equations, and find a way to express it algebraically in terms of the parameters of the problem and a few auxiliary tensors, describing, in a sense, the "shape" of the system. We find compact representations of these auxiliary tensors in terms of a Tensor Train decomposition. Provided the parameters admit a compact representation in this format as well, this allows us to rather straightforwardly reuse standard numerical algorithms for a wide range of associated problems, obtaining $O(\log N)$ asymptotic complexity.

1   Introduction

Smoluchowski-type equations describe a spatially-uniform system of coagulating particles; specifically, they describe time evolution of concentrations of particles of various sizes, denoted traditionally as n_k for particles of size k. The main effect modelled is coagulation, i.e. constructive collision of particles of sizes i and j, resulting in a single particle of size $i + j$. Over time, the original equations were extended to include a number of other effects, such as spontaneous fragmentation, influx of new particles over time, or destructive collision. Assuming that aggregates, whether spontaneously or as a result of a collision, always shatter completely into monomers, we arrive at the following system of equations (see, e.g. [4]):

$$\frac{dn_1}{dt} = J_1 - n_1 \sum_{j \geq 1} C_{1j} n_j + n_1 \sum_{j \geq 2} j A_{1j} n_j \tag{1}$$

$$+ \frac{1}{2} \sum_{i,j \geq 2} A_{ij}(i+j) n_i n_j + k B_k n_k \,,$$

$$\frac{dn_k}{dt} = J_k + \frac{1}{2} \sum_{i+j=k} C_{ij} n_i n_j - \sum_{i \geq 1} (C_{ik} + A_{ik}) \, n_i n_k - B_k n_k \,. \tag{2}$$

© Springer Nature Switzerland AG 2020
I. Lirkov and S. Margenov (Eds.): LSSC 2019, LNCS 11958, pp. 181–188, 2020.
https://doi.org/10.1007/978-3-030-41032-2_20

Here C_{ij} gives the rates at which aggregates of sizes i and j merge to produce a cluster of size $i+j$, while A_{ij} fulfils the same role for destructive collisions; these are typically proportional, $A_{ij} = \lambda C_{ij}$. B_k characterises the rates of spontaneous fragmentation. Finally, J_k denotes the intensity of a source of particles of size k; typically, only a few values of J_k are non-zero.

Rather naturally, we put additional constraints both on parameters and the solution:

$$n_k(t) \geq 0 \qquad C_{ij} = C_{ji} \geq 0$$
$$B_k \geq 0 \qquad A_{ij} = A_{ji} \geq 0$$

To solve system (1–2) or its derivatives (e.g. stationary problems) numerically, it is usually necessary to transition to a finite system; for better approximation of the original problem, it is desirable to make the system as large as possible. In doing so, one runs into problems with both the representation of matrices C and A, and the complexity of the operations used.

One approach, investigated recently by various authors, including that of the present paper, is to use low-rank decompositions of kernels C and A, leading to algorithms with typical complexity of $O(N \log N)$; see e. g. [5,6]. Another approach, used e.g. in [7], is to group neighbouring concentrations in progressively larger "windows", and write equations for total concentrations in these; the disadvantage being the inability to detect rapid changes within windows. In this paper, we investigate an alternative approach, based on a Tensor Train decomposition [1], which promises algorithms with complexity of $O(\log N)$, possibly at the expense of a larger constant factor.

2   Structure of the Operator

While Eqs. (1–2) are fairly terse, we find it more illuminating to disentangle different effects into their own operators:

$$\frac{dn}{dt} = \mathcal{S}(n, n) + \mathcal{F}(n, n) + Bn + J, \tag{3}$$

where

$$(\mathcal{S}(x,y))_k := \frac{1}{2} \sum_{i+j=k} C_{ij} x_i y_j - \frac{1}{2} x_k \sum_{i \geq 1} C_{ik} y_i - \frac{1}{2} y_k \sum_{i \geq 1} C_{ik} x_i, \tag{4}$$

$$(\mathcal{F}(x,y))_k := \frac{\delta_{k1}}{2} \sum_{i,j \geq 1} (i+j) A_{ij} x_i y_j - \frac{1}{2} x_k \sum_{i \geq 1} A_{ik} y_i - \frac{1}{2} y_k \sum_{i \geq 1} A_{ik} x_y, \tag{5}$$

are two symmetric bilinear operators, corresponding to constructive and destructive collisions correspondingly, and $(Bn)_k = B_k n_k$.

For convenience, we can name the operator on the right-hand-side of the system $\mathcal{G}$ and rewrite Eq. (3) as

$$\frac{dn}{dt} = \mathcal{G}(n)$$
$$\mathcal{G}(n) = \mathcal{S}(n, n) + \mathcal{F}(n, n) + Bn + J.$$

One important advantage of such representation is that it allows us to manipulate the operator much more conveniently than by transforming equations directly. For example, we can derive a formula for a directional derivative (equivalently, a product of a Jacobi matrix by a vector):

$$\frac{d}{dn}\mathcal{G}(n) \times \nu = 2\mathcal{S}(n, \nu) + 2\mathcal{F}(n, \nu) + B\nu. \tag{6}$$

This means that further investigation into the structure of the operators $\mathcal{S}$ and $\mathcal{F}$, specifically concerning their fast evaluation, will improve not only the performance of evaluating $\mathcal{G}$ by itself, but also of its directional derivatives; access to later allows us to solve non-linear systems involving $\mathcal{G}$, which arise both in stationary problems and in implicit integration.

Similar to how we associate matrices with linear operators (which we did almost implicitly with B above), we may associate three-dimensional tensors with bilinear operators. Specifically, we define

$$S_{ijk} = \frac{1}{2}C_{ij}\left([i + j = k] - [i = k] - [j = k]\right) \tag{7}$$

$$F_{ijk} = \frac{1}{2}A_{ij}\left((i + j)[k = 1] - [i = k] - [j = k]\right), \tag{8}$$

where $[P]$ is an Iverson bracket: $[P] = 1$ if P, and 0 otherwise.

With these tensors we can rewrite (4–5) more succinctly as

$$(\mathcal{S}(x, y))_k = \sum_{i,j \geq 1} S_{ijk}x_i y_j =: S \times_1 x \times_2 y,$$

$$(\mathcal{F}(x, y))_k = \sum_{i,j \geq 1} F_{ijk}x_i y_j =: F \times_1 x \times_2 y,$$

so Eq. (3) can now be rewritten as

$$\frac{dn}{dt} = S \times_1 n \times_2 n + F \times_1 n \times_2 n + Bn + J. \tag{9}$$

3   Tensorisation

We now task ourselves with finding a compact representation for the tensors S and F. To do so, we utilise the Tensor Train decomposition [1], specifically, its tensorised version. It is especially attractive to us because it supports all basic operations required in our formulas—linear combination of tensors and a product of tensorised matrices—allowing us to evaluate the operator precisely in the TT-format, assuming the tensors involved are already given in it. Furthermore, it admits an efficient algorithm for solving linear systems with matrices in the format [3]. This, together with the Eq. (6), allows us to implement a Newton's method, effectiveness of which for stationary and quasi-stationary problems for Smoluchowski equations was recently demonstrated in [6].

Very briefly, the main idea of the tensorisation for a low-dimensional tensor—say, of size $2^d \times 2^d \times 2^d$—is to recast it as a high dimensional one, by splitting each index into d independent ones, and then regroup them together, like so:

$$T(\overline{i_1 \ldots i_d}, \overline{j_1 \ldots j_d}, \overline{k_1 \ldots k_d}) = \tilde{T}(\overline{i_1 j_1 k_1}, \ldots, \overline{i_d j_d k_d}),$$

and then apply the Tensor Train decomposition to the resulting tensor. For details, please refer to [2]. Crucially, all operations in the format have the complexity of $O(dr^\alpha)$ for different values of α, where r is the maximum of the ranks of the decomposition; for $r = O(1)$, this gives us the desired $O(\log N)$.

We seek, then, a representation of tensors S, F, B and J in a TTT (Tensorised Tensor Train) format; or rather, estimates of their ranks. For B and J the task is rather straightforward—ranks B depend entirely on the ranks of the original vector. In many important applications, B is simply zero, in which case all ranks are zero as well. J, having typically only a few non-zero elements, has its ranks bounded by their number. S and F are more interesting.

Unfortunately, these depend substantially on the parameters of the problem—namely, kernels C_{ij} and A_{ij}. Luckily, we can easily recast our definitions of S and F in terms of a small number of basic tensors and operations on them:

$$S = \frac{1}{2}\hat{C} \odot (\mathbf{T}^{(1)} - \mathbf{T}^{(2)} - \mathbf{T}^{(3)}), \tag{10}$$

$$F = \frac{1}{2}\hat{A} \odot (\mathbf{T}^{(4)} - \mathbf{T}^{(2)} - \mathbf{T}^{(3)}). \tag{11}$$

Here, $\odot$ is a Hadamard product, and $\hat{\ }$ denotes extension of a tensor with additional index:

$$\hat{X}_{ijk} := X_{ij}.$$

The "basic" tensors $\mathbf{T}^{(i)}$ themselves are defined as follows:

$$\mathbf{T}^{(1)}_{ijk} = [i + j = k], \qquad \mathbf{T}^{(2)}_{ijk} = [i = k],$$
$$\mathbf{T}^{(3)}_{ijk} = [j = k], \qquad \mathbf{T}^{(4)}_{ijk} = (i + j)[k = 1]$$

Fortunately, operations used in our representation (10–11) are readily expressible in TT format. Using estimates given in [1], we have the following estimates:

$$\text{ttrank}_s\, S \leq \text{ttrank}_s\, C \times (\text{ttrank}_s\, \mathbf{T}^{(1)} + \text{ttrank}_s\, \mathbf{T}^{(2)} + \text{ttrank}_s\, \mathbf{T}^{(3)})$$
$$\text{ttrank}_s\, F \leq \text{ttrank}_s\, A \times (\text{ttrank}_s\, \mathbf{T}^{(4)} + \text{ttrank}_s\, \mathbf{T}^{(2)} + \text{ttrank}_s\, \mathbf{T}^{(3)})$$

Estimating $\text{ttrank}_s \mathbf{T}^{(i)}$ for $i = 2, 3$ is trivial; for them we have $\text{ttrank}_s \mathbf{T}^{(1)} = \text{ttrank}_s \mathbf{T}^{(2)} = 1$.

For $\mathbf{T}^{(4)}$, we need to consider unfolding matrices:

$$
\begin{aligned}
\mathbf{T}_l^{(3)} & (\overline{i_1 j_1 k_1}, \overline{i_2 j_2 k_2}) \\
&= \mathbf{T}^{(3)}(i_1 + (i_2 - 1)N_l, j_1 + (j_2 - 1)N_l, k_1 + (k_2 - 1)N_l) \\
&= ((i_1 + j_1) + N_l(i_2 + j_2 - 2))\,[k_1 = 1]\,[k_2 = 1] \\
&= (i_1 + j_1)\,[k_1 = 1]\,[k_2 = 1] + N_l\,[k_1 = 1]\,(i_2 + j_2 - 2)\,[k_2 = 1].
\end{aligned}
$$

The rank of each unfolding matrix is, therefore, 2, and so is $\text{ttrank}_s \mathbf{T}^{(3)}$. Finally, consider $\mathbf{T}^{(1)}$. Once again, we consider the unfolding matrices

$$
\mathbf{T}_l^{(1)}(\overline{i_1 j_1 k_1}, \overline{i_2 j_2 k_2}) = [(i_1 + j_1 - k_1) + N_l(i_2 + j_2 - k_2 - 1) = 0]. \tag{12}
$$

Here, we have rewritten the expression for the element of the tensor to better highlight the separation between indices.

Since $1 \le i_1, j_1, k_1 \le N_l$, $2 - N_l \le i_1 + j_1 - k_1 \le 2N_l - 1$. In order for the entire expression inside the Iverson bracket to evaluate to zero, this number has to be divisible by N_l; fortunately, there are only two such numbers in the specified range, namely 0 and N_l. With this in mind, we can rewrite Eq. (12) as

$$
\begin{aligned}
\mathbf{T}_l^{(1)} & (\overline{i_1 j_1 k_1}, \overline{i_2 j_2 k_2}) \\
&= [i_1 + j_1 = k_1]\,[i_2 + j_2 = k_2 + 1] + [i_1 + j_1 = k_1 + N_l]\,[i_2 + j_2 = k_2 + 2], \tag{13}
\end{aligned}
$$

and now it is obvious that $\text{ttrank}_s \mathbf{T}^{(1)}$ is 2 as well.

Summarising these results, we arrive at the following lemma:

Lemma 1. *TT-ranks of S and F are bounded by multiples of ranks of C and A respectively; specifically*

$$
\text{ttrank}_s\, S \le 4\,\text{ttrank}_s\, C,
$$

$$
\text{ttrank}_s\, F \le 4\,\text{ttrank}_s\, A.
$$

In case $A = \lambda C$, furthermore:

$$
\text{ttrank}_s(S + F) \le 6\,\text{ttrank}_s\, C.
$$

4 Numerical Experiments

One crucial variable left unexplored in the discussion above is the kernel C_{ij} itself; its ranks feature prominently in the estimates of the ranks of resulting tensors. We consider a simple kernel

$$
C_{ij} = i^a j^{-a} + i^{-a} j^a, \tag{14}
$$

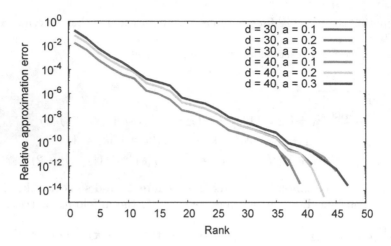

Fig. 1. Total relative approximation error of the C kernel depending on the rank cutoff, for various values of kernel parameter a and problem size $N = 2^d$.

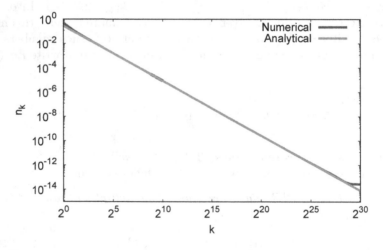

Fig. 2. Comparison of numerical and analytical stationary solution for the investigated kernel in the simplest case $a = 0$, for $N = 2^{30}$.

and evaluate the error of its approximations with bounded TT-ranks for different values of a and N. The case of $a = 0$ is degenerate; here, $C_{ij} = 2$, so $ttrank_s\, C \equiv 1$. The results are represented in Fig. 1.

While the ranks required to obtain high precision are unacceptably high (complexity is heavily grows dramatically with even small increases in ranks), it is possible to obtain decent precision even for modest ranks, such as $ttrank_s\, C \leq 15$. More importantly, the errors essentially do not depend on the size of the problem, so the promise of logarithmic complexity is realised.

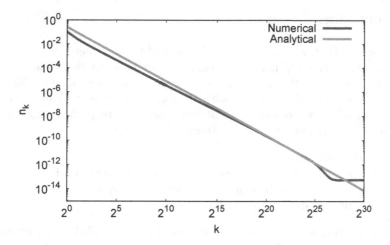

Fig. 3. Comparison of numerical and analytical stationary solution for the investigated kernel for $a = 0.2$, rounded to ttrank$_s$ $C \leq 5$. See the text for the discussion

Unfortunately, as the Figs. 2 and 3 demonstrate, this is not necessarily enough. These demonstrate the numerical solution for the stationary problem $\mathcal{G}(n) = 0$ in the simple case of $A = 0$, $B = 0$, $J_k = \delta_{k1}$, obtained via Newton's method with the stopping criteria $\|\mathcal{G}(n)\|_2 \leq 10^{-13}$ for $a = 0$ and 10^{-10} for $a = 0.2$. While for the trivial kernel we get excellent agreement, for the more complicated kernel, where we had to resort to a crude approximation, we observe significant divergence for small k, likely owning to larger relative errors in elements of the kernel for those indices. Increasing the rank could alleviate these issues, but at the cost of dramatic increase in the solution time.

Finally, in Table 1 we present the time required to solve the same stationary system with a constant kernel (i.e. $a = 0$). The timings clearly demonstrate complexity much lower than $O(N)$, although the behaviour is somewhat erratic. The dependence on the rank is much more pronounced; the same system with $a = 0.1$, rounded to rank 5 takes 20 min to solve for $N = 2^{20}$ and 25 min for $N = 2^{22}$.

Table 1. Time to solve the system with constant kernel, depending on its size.

$\log_2 N$	Time, s
20	10.8
22	12.7
24	19.2
26	19.4
28	20.1
30	20.7

5   Conclusion

We have proven that, assuming the TTT-ranks of the parameter tensors C, A, B and J, are low, corresponding ranks of the tensors participating in our principal $\mathcal{G}$ operator, describing the right-hand-side of the Smoluchowski-type differential equation, are low as well. Together with the explicit representations (3) and (6), as well as algorithms provided in [1,3], this allows us to perform the following operations efficiently, entirely in the Tensor Train format:

- evaluate the right hand side;
- evaluate the directional derivative of the corresponding non-linear operator, or, equivalently, the product of the Jacobi matrix by a vector;
- solve the linear system with the Jacobi matrix.

These, in turn, are sufficient to implement either explicit time integration schemes for the original ODE system, or, via Newton's method, solve stationary problems or implement implicit time integration methods, all with $O(\log N)$ complexity. A remaining open problem, and a direction of future work, is to search for adequate low-rank approximations for common kernels, which would allow us to lower the constant factors in these algorithms.

Acknowledgements. The work was supported by the Russian Science Foundation, grant 19-11-00338.

References

1. Oseledets, I.V.: Tensor-train decomposition. SIAM J. Sci. Comput. **33**(5), 2295–2317 (2011). https://doi.org/10.1137/090752286
2. Oseledets, I.V.: Approximation of $2^d \times 2^d$ matrices using tensor decomposition. SIAM J. Matrix Anal. Appl. **31**(4), 2130–2145 (2010). https://doi.org/10.1137/090757861
3. Dolgov, S.V., Savostyanov, D.V.: Alternating minimal energy methods for linear systems in higher dimensions. SIAM J. Sci. Comput. **36**(5), A2248–A2271 (2014). https://doi.org/10.1137/140953289
4. Brilliantov, N.V., et al.: Size distribution of particles in Saturn's rings from aggregation and fragmentation. Proc. Nat. Acad. Sci. U.S.A. **112**(31), 9536–9541 (2015)
5. Matveev, S.A., Smirnov, A.P., Tyrtyshnikov, E.E.: A fast numerical method for the Cauchy problem for the Smoluchowski equation. J. Comput. Phys. **282**, 23–32 (2015). https://doi.org/10.1016/j.jcp.2014.11.003
6. Timokhin, I.V., Matveev, S.A., Siddharth, N., Tyrtyshnikov, E.E., Smirnov, A.P., Brilliantov, N.V.: Newton method for stationary and quasi-stationary problems for Smoluchowski-type equations. J. Comput. Phys. **382**, 124–137 (2019). https://doi.org/10.1016/j.jcp.2019.01.013
7. Lee, M.H.: On the validity of the coagulation equation and the nature of runaway growth. Icarus **143**(1), 74–86 (2000)

On Tensor-Train Ranks of Tensorized Polynomials

Lev Vysotsky[1,2](✉) (iD)

[1] Moscow State University, Moscow, Russia
vysotskylev@yandex.ru
[2] Marchuk Institute of Numerical Mathematics of Russian Academy of Sciences,
Moscow, Russia

Abstract. Discretization followed by tensorization (mapping from low-dimensional to high-dimensional data) can be used to construct low-parametric approximations of functions. For example, a function f defined on $[0, 1]$ may be mapped to a d-dimensional tensor $A \in \mathbb{R}^{b \times \cdots \times b}$ with elements $A(i_1, \ldots, i_d) = f(i_1 b^{-1} + \cdots + i_d b^{-d})$, $i_k \in \{0, \ldots, b-1\}$. The tensor A can now be compressed using one of the tensor formats, e.g. tensor train format. It has been noticed in practice that approximate TT-ranks of tensorizations of degree-n polynomials grow very slowly with respect to n, while the only known bound for them is $n+1$. In this paper we try to explain the observed effect. New bounds of the described TT-ranks are proved and shown experimentally to quite successfully capture the observed distribution of ranks.

Keywords: Tensor train format · TT-ranks · TT-decomposition · Discretization · Tensorization

1 Introduction

Relatively recent advances in overcoming the "curse of dimensionality" have allowed for working with functions on very fine grids and thus achieving very low approximation errors. One example workflow is as follows (similar to [5]): let us assume we are given a function f defined on $[0, 1]$ (any other segment can be easily mapped to $[0, 1]$) and discretize it on a uniform grid with step b^{-d} where $b, d \in \mathbb{N}$. We thus obtain a vector

$$a \in \mathbb{R}^{b^d}, \ a(i) = f(ib^{-d}), \ i \in \{0, \ldots, b^d - 1\}.$$

It can, however, be viewed (in spirit of [1]) as an d-dimensional array, or tensor $A \in \mathbb{R}^{b \times \cdots \times b}$ with elements

$$A(i_1, \ldots, i_d) = f(i_1 b^{-1} + \cdots + i_d b^{-d}), \ i_k \in \{0, \ldots, b-1\}.$$

The work was supported by the Russian Science Foundation, grant 19-11-00338.

I. Lirkov and S. Margenov (Eds.): LSSC 2019, LNCS 11958, pp. 189–196, 2020.
https://doi.org/10.1007/978-3-030-41032-2_21

This tensor sometimes can be approximated by another one (let us denote it $\widetilde{A}$) that admits low-parametric representation. For example, tensor train (TT-) format [2,3] may be used:

$$\widetilde{A}(i_1,\ldots,i_d) = \sum_{\alpha_1,\ldots,\alpha_{d-1}} G_1(i_1,\alpha_1)G_2(\alpha_1,i_2,\alpha_2)\ldots G_d(\alpha_{d-1},i_d),$$

where α_k takes values from $\{1,\ldots,r_k\}$. The numbers r_k are called "TT-ranks" of $\widetilde{A}$, and 2- and 3-dimensional tensors $G_1,\ldots,G_d$ are called "carriages". When the TT-ranks are not very large (as is often the case in practice) the described format can break the "curse of dimensionality", as the time and memory needed for storing and performing common operations with a tensor in tensor-train format depend only linearly on d.

Thus the main question to answer when considering applicability of TT-approximations is "are the TT-ranks small?". It is certainly not an easy question in the general case of a function tensorization, but for certain particular cases some results are known. For example, one interesting and important class of functions are polynomials. It has been known [4,6] that all the TT-ranks for tensorized degree-n polynomial does not exceed $n+1$.

However, in practice it has been noticed that actual TT-ranks of tensor train approximations are much lower that $n+1$. In this paper we present new bounds for approximate TT-ranks of tensorized polynomials, which appear to capture more closely the observed behavior of these values. Moreover, the largest rank is shown to grow as $O(n^{\frac{1}{3}+\gamma})$ as $n \to \infty$, where $\gamma > 0$ can usually be taken arbitrarily small.

Formally, we consider a polynomial $p(x) = p_0 + p_1 x + \cdots + p_n x^n$ with real coefficients and its tensorization on the segment $[0,1]$, i.e. tensor $P(i_1,\ldots,i_d)$:

$$P(i_1,\ldots,i_d) = p(i_1 b^{-1} + \cdots + i_d b^{-d}), \quad \text{where } i_k \in \{0,\ldots,b-1\}.$$

By approximate TT-rank $r_k(\varepsilon)$, $\varepsilon > 0$, we will denote the smallest k-th TT-rank of a tensor $\widetilde{P}$ such that $||P - \widetilde{P}||_F \le \varepsilon$ (here $||\cdot||_F$ denotes Frobenius norm of a tensor, i.e. square root of the sum of squares of its elements).

To study the values $r_k(\varepsilon)$ it is sufficient to consider the unfolding matrices $P_k(i_1\ldots i_k; i_{k+1}\ldots i_d)$ and estimate their approximate ranks. The reason is that the k-th TT-rank of a tensor coincides with the rank of the corresponding unfolding matrix (see [2]) and, moreover, Frobenius norm is invariant to reshaping of a tensor. Let us denote $i := (i_1,\ldots,i_k)$ and $j := (i_{k+1},\ldots,i_d)$. We will also identify multiindices with a single base-b number:

$$i = i_1 b^{k-1} + \cdots + i_k, \quad j = i_{k+1} b^{d-k-1} + \cdots + i_d.$$

2   Taylor Expansion-Based Approach

In this section we fix k and denote $A(i,j) := P_k(i;j)$. Using the Taylor expansion for $p(x)$ at $x_0 = ib^{-k}$ we get:

$$p(ib^{-k} + jb^{-d}) = p(ib^{-k}) + \frac{1}{1!}p'(ib^{-k})jb^{-d} + \cdots + \frac{1}{n!}p^{(n)}(ib^{-k})(jb^{-d})^n.$$

Denote $A_s(i, j)$ the s-th summand:

$$A_s(i, j) := \frac{1}{s!} p^{(s)}(ib^{-k})(jb^{-d})^s$$

and notice that the matrix A_s has rank at most 1. The proposed rank-r approximation of A is obtained by taking the first r summands:

$$B_r := A_0 + \cdots + A_{r-1}.$$

To get the estimate for the Frobenius norm of the approximation error $E_r := A - B_r$ let us first bound $|A_s(i, j)|$.

Lemma 1. *For any $i \in I$ and $j \in J$*

$$|A_s(i, j)| \leq M \sum_{t=0}^{n-s} \binom{s+t}{s} (ib^{-k})^t (jb^{-d})^s,$$

where M denotes the largest absolute value of coefficients of polynomial $p(x)$.

Proof. It follows directly from the following inequality holding for $x \in [0, 1]$:

$$|p^{(s)}(x)| = \left| p_s s! + p_{s+1} \frac{(s+1)!}{1!} x + \cdots + p_n \frac{n!}{(n-s)!} x^{n-s} \right| \leq M \sum_{t=0}^{n-s} \frac{(s+t)!}{t!} x^t.$$

Now it is possible to prove the estimate of $\|E_r\|_F$.

Lemma 2.

$$\|E_r\|_F \leq M b^{\frac{d}{2}} \sum_{s=r}^{n} \sum_{t=0}^{n-s} \binom{s+t}{s} \frac{b^{-ks}}{\sqrt{s+1}\sqrt{t+1}}.$$

Proof. From Lemma 1 it follows that

$$|E_r(i, j)| \leq M \sum_{s=r}^{n} \sum_{t=0}^{n-s} \binom{s+t}{s} (ib^{-k})^t (jb^{-d})^s,$$

thus

$$E_r^2(i, j) \leq M^2 \sum_{s'=r}^{n} \sum_{t'=0}^{n-s'} \sum_{s''=r}^{n} \sum_{t''=0}^{n-s''} \binom{s'+t'}{s'} \binom{s''+t''}{s''} (ib^{-k})^{t'+t''} (jb^{-d})^{s'+s''}.$$

Next, notice that

$$\sum_{i \in I} i^{t'+t''} \leq \int_0^{b^k} x^{t'+t''} \, dx = \frac{b^{k(t'+t''+1)}}{t'+t''+1}. \tag{1}$$

Note also the following simple inequality holding for any $s', s'' \geq 0$:

$$\frac{1}{s' + s'' + 1} \leq \frac{1}{\sqrt{s'+1}\sqrt{s''+1}}. \tag{2}$$

Thus the square of Frobenius norm of E_r is

$$\|E_r\|_F^2 = \sum_{i \in I}\sum_{j \in J} E_r^2(i,j) \leq \qquad\qquad \text{(reorder the summands)}$$

$$\leq M^2 \sum_{s',t'}\sum_{s'',t''} \binom{s'+t'}{s'}\binom{s''+t''}{s''} \sum_{i \in I}(ib^{-k})^{t'+t''} \sum_{j \in J}(jb^{-d})^{s'+s''} \leq \quad \text{(use (1) twice)}$$

$$\leq M^2 b^d \sum_{s',t'}\sum_{s'',t''} \binom{s'+t'}{s'}\binom{s''+t''}{s''} \frac{b^{-k(s'+s'')}}{(s'+s''+1)(t'+t''+1)} \leq \quad \text{(use (2) twice)}$$

$$\leq M^2 b^d \sum_{s',t'}\sum_{s'',t''} \binom{s'+t'}{s'}\binom{s''+t''}{s''} \frac{b^{-ks'}b^{-ks''}}{\sqrt{s'+1}\sqrt{s''+1}\sqrt{t'+1}\sqrt{t''+1}} \leq$$

$$\leq M^2 b^d \left(\sum_{s=r}^{n}\sum_{t=0}^{n-s} \binom{s+t}{s} \frac{b^{-ks}}{\sqrt{s+1}\sqrt{t+1}} \right)^2.$$

Using the previous lemma the following result can be easily seen.

Theorem 1. *The ε-rank $r_k(\varepsilon)$ of the k-th unfolding matrix of the tensor $P(i_1,\ldots,i_d)$ satisfies the following inequality:*

$$r_k(\varepsilon) \leq \min\left\{ r : M b^{\frac{d}{2}} \sum_{s=r}^{n}\sum_{t=0}^{n-s} \binom{s+t}{s} \frac{b^{-ks}}{\sqrt{s+1}\sqrt{t+1}} \leq \varepsilon \right\}.$$

To make the meaning of the above theorem clearer, let us bound from above the double sum in the inequality. Using the well-known inequality (e.g. see [7])

$$\binom{n}{k} \leq \left(\frac{en}{k}\right)^k$$

that holds for $n, k > 0$, we can write

$$M b^{\frac{d}{2}} \sum_{s=r}^{n}\sum_{t=0}^{n-s} \binom{s+t}{s} \frac{b^{-ks}}{\sqrt{s+1}\sqrt{t+1}} \leq M b^{\frac{d}{2}} \sum_{s=r}^{n}\sum_{t=0}^{n-s} \left(\frac{e(s+t)}{s}b^{-k}\right)^s \leq$$

$$\leq M b^{\frac{d}{2}} n \sum_{s=r}^{n} \left(\frac{en}{r}b^{-k}\right)^s = M b^{\frac{d}{2}} n \left(\frac{en}{r}b^{-k}\right)^r \frac{\left(\frac{en}{r}b^{-k}\right)^{n-r+1} - 1}{\left(\frac{en}{r}b^{-k}\right) - 1}$$

Thus if $b^k > en$ then for $r \geq 2$ the above sum can be bound by

$$M b^{\frac{d}{2}} n \left(\frac{en}{b^k r}\right)^r \frac{1}{1 - r^{-1}} \leq 2 M b^{\frac{d}{2}} n \left(\frac{en}{b^k r}\right)^r.$$

To estimate $r_k(\varepsilon)$ let us elaborate on the inequality

$$2 M b^{\frac{d}{2}} n \left(\frac{en}{b^k r}\right)^r \leq \varepsilon \Leftrightarrow r(k + \log_b r - \log_b(en)) \geq \log_b \frac{M}{\varepsilon} + \frac{d}{2} + \log_b(2n).$$

Thus we have come to

Corollary 1.

$$r_k(\varepsilon) \leq \min\left\{ r : r(k + \log_b r - \log_b(en)) \geq \log_b \frac{M}{\varepsilon} + \frac{d}{2} + \log_b(2n) \right\}.$$

From this we can obtain the following two corollaries to be used in constructing a more tight estimate later in Sect. 4.

Corollary 2. *For $k > \log_b(en)$*

$$r_k(\varepsilon) \leq \left\lceil \frac{1}{k - \log_b(en)} \left(\log_b \frac{M}{\varepsilon} + \frac{d}{2} + \log_b(2n) \right) \right\rceil.$$

Corollary 3. *For $1 \leq k \leq \lceil \log_b(en) \rceil$*

$$r_k(\varepsilon) \leq b^{\lceil \log_b(en) \rceil + 1 - k} \left\lceil \log_b \frac{M}{\varepsilon} + \frac{d}{2} + \log_b(2n) \right\rceil. \tag{3}$$

Proof. From Corollary 1 we can see that $r_{k-1}(\varepsilon) \leq b r_k(\varepsilon)$, as

$$br(k - 1 + \log_b(br) - \log_b(en)) \geq r(k + \log_b r - \log_b(en)).$$

3 Low-Degree Approximation Approach

The estimates of $r_k(\varepsilon)$ derived in the previous section are quite low for large enough k. For $k < \log_b(en)$ we must demand $r > enb^{-k}$ and thus r grows quite fast as k decreases. A bit better result for lower values of k can be obtained using another approach.

Theorem 2.

$$r_k(\varepsilon) \leq \min\left\{ r < 2b^k : -r\log_b\left(1 - \frac{r}{2}b^{-k}\right) \geq 2\log_b \frac{M}{\varepsilon} + d + 2k \right\}. \tag{4}$$

Proof. Fix some $m \in \mathbb{N}$ (to be chosen later) and split the set of row indices of the matrix P_k into two disjoint subsets, namely, $I_1 = \{0, \ldots, b^k - m - 1\}$ and $I_2 = \{b^k - m, \ldots, b^k - 1\}$. The rows with indices from I_1 will be approximated with the rows of matrix

$$C \in \mathbb{R}^{(b^k - m) \times b^{d-k}}, \quad C(i,j) = q(x_{ij}),$$

where $q(x)$ is a polynomial of degree $\ell - 1$, $q_s = p_s$ for $s = 0, \ldots, \ell - 1$. According to [6], $\operatorname{rank} C \leq \ell$. Let us denote

$$x_{ij} := ib^{-k} + jb^{-d},$$

Then the approximation error for any given matrix entry doesn't exceed

$$|P_k(i,j) - C(i,j)| = |p(x_{ij}) - q(x_{ij})| \leq M|x_{ij}^\ell + \cdots + x_{ij}^n| \leq Mx_{ij}^\ell \frac{1}{1 - x_{ij}}.$$

Note also that $x_{ij} < (b^k - m)b^{-k}$ for $i \in I_1$. Thus, we conclude:

$$\|P_k(I_1, :) - C\|_F \leq b^{\frac{d}{2}} M(1 - mb^{-k})^\ell \frac{1}{mb^{-k}}.$$

The rows with indices from I_2 are just copied as-is. So we arrive at the approximation

$$\widetilde{P}_k \approx \begin{bmatrix} C \\ P_k(I_2, :) \end{bmatrix}$$

of rank $\ell + m$. To bound $r_k(\varepsilon)$ we require that

$$b^{\frac{d}{2}} M(1 - mb^{-k})^\ell \frac{1}{mb^{-k}} \leq \varepsilon \iff -\ell \log_b(1 - mb^{-k}) + \log_b(m) \geq \log_b \frac{M}{\varepsilon} + \frac{d}{2} + k.$$

We additionally require that $\ell = m = \frac{r}{2}$ and obtain the simpler inequality:

$$-r \log_b \left(1 - \frac{r}{2}b^{-k}\right) \geq 2 \log_b \frac{M}{\varepsilon} + d + 2k,$$

from which follows the estimate (4).

4   Asymptotic Estimates

Let us try to establish some intuition behind proved theorems. For this purpose we fix b and let both $\log_b \frac{M}{\varepsilon}$ and d grow slower than some power of n:

$$d(n) = o(n^\gamma) \text{ and } \log_b \frac{M(n)}{\varepsilon(n)} = o(n^\gamma) \text{ for some } 0 < \gamma < \frac{1}{3}.$$

In such setting the above estimates can be used alternately to get the tightest bound. Indeed, let us first elaborate on (4). Denote u the right-hand side of the inequality ($u = o(n^\gamma)$). To bound the left-hand side we note that

$$\log_b(1 - x) \leq \left(-x + \frac{x^2}{2} - \ldots\right) \log_b e \leq \left(-x + \frac{x^2}{2}\right) \log_b e.$$

Thus we arrive at a simpler inequality:

$$r^2 b^{-k} - \frac{1}{2} r^3 b^{-2k} \geq \frac{2u}{\log_b e}.$$

It's not hard to see that for $k > 2\gamma \log_b n$ we get

$$r_k(\varepsilon) = O(n^\gamma b^{\frac{k}{2}}). \tag{5}$$

Denote $\widehat{k} = \lceil \frac{2}{3} \log_b(en) \rceil$. For $2\gamma \log_b n \leq k \leq \widehat{k}$ we will use (5), thus obtaining

$$r_k(\varepsilon) = O(n^{\frac{1}{3}+\gamma}),$$

and for $\widehat{k} < k \leq \lceil \log_b(en) \rceil$ we will use Corollary 3 arriving at the same bound. Corollary 2 is used for $k > \log_b(en)$ giving

$$r_k(\varepsilon) = O\left(\frac{n^\gamma}{k - \log_b(en)}\right).$$

For $1 \leq k \leq \lceil 2\gamma \log_b n \rceil$ we can use the trivial bound $r_k(\varepsilon) \leq b^k$. For a brief summary of all the used bounds see Fig. 1.

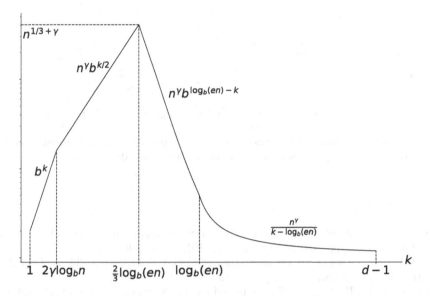

Fig. 1. Sketch of bounds for $r_k(\varepsilon)$ from Sect. 4. The vertical axis has logarithmic scale. $O(\cdot)$ symbol is omitted for brevity from all labels except the ones under the k-axis

5   Numerical Examples

We can also compare estimates from the above theorems with actual ε-ranks of the unfolding matrices P_k. We generate polynomials of degree n with coefficients distributed uniformly in $[-1, 1]$. The tensor P is constructed and ε-ranks of the unfolding matrices are computed using SVD. One result (for a degree-300 polynomial) is visualized in Fig. 2.

What we noticed during the experiments is that while largest rank in our estimate grows roughly proportional to $n^{1/3}$ as $n \to \infty$, the largest rank of a random degree-n polynomial tensorization doesn't demonstrate such behavior: it stagnates for quite low values of n. Our hypothesis is that the probability of generating a "bad" polynomial decreases as $n \to \infty$. Of course, another explanation could be that our upper bound is too high. Anyway, there is something left to explore in this problem.

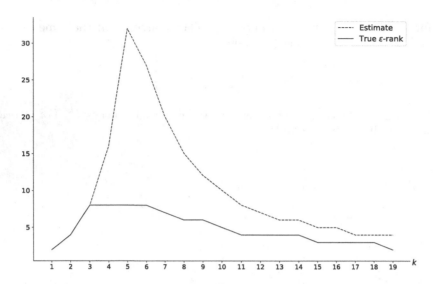

Fig. 2. Actual approximate TT-ranks of a random degree-300 polynomial tensorization compared with estimates developed in this work. Here $\varepsilon = 10^{-8}$, $b = 2$

References

1. Oseledets, I.V.: Approximation of $2^d \times 2^d$ matrices using tensor decomposition. SIAM J. Matrix Anal. Appl. **31**(4), 2130–2145 (2010). https://doi.org/10.1137/090757861
2. Oseledets, I.: Tensor-Train Decomposition. SIAM J. Sci. Comput. **33**(5), 2295–2317 (2011). https://doi.org/10.1137/090752286
3. Grasedyck, L., Hackbusch, W.: An introduction to hierarchical (H-) rank and TT-rank of tensors with examples. Comput. Methods Appl. Math. Comput. Methods Appl. Math. **11**(3), 291–304 (2011). https://doi.org/10.2478/cmam-2011-0016
4. Oseledets, I.: Constructive representation of functions in low-rank tensor formats. Constr. Approx. **37**(1), 1–18 (2013). https://doi.org/10.1007/s00365-012-9175-x
5. Tyrtyshnikov, E.E.: Tensor approximations of matrices generated by asymptotically smooth functions. Sb. Math. **194**(6), 941–954 (2003). https://doi.org/10.4213/sm747
6. Khoromskij, B.N.: $O(d \log N)$-quantics approximation of N-d tensors in high-dimensional numerical modeling. Constr. Approx. **34**(2), 257–280 (2011). https://doi.org/10.1007/s00365-011-9131-1
7. Cormen, T., Leiserson, C., Rivest, R., Stein, C.: Introduction to Algorithms, 3rd edn. The MIT Press, Cambridge (2009)

Global Optimization Algorithms Using Tensor Trains

Dmitry A. Zheltkov$^{(\boxtimes)}$ and Alexander Osinsky

Marchuk Institute of Numerical Mathematics, Moscow, Russia
dmitry.zheltkov@gmail.com, sasha_o@list.ru

Abstract. Global optimization problem arises in a huge amount of applications including parameter estimation of different models, molecular biology, drug design and many others. There are several types of methods for this problem: deterministic, stochastic, heuristic and metaheuristic. Deterministic methods guarantee that found solution is the global optima, but complexity of such methods allows to use them only for problems of relatively small dimensionality, simple functional and area of optimization.

Non-deterministic methods are based on some simple models of stochastic, physical, biological and other processes. On practice such methods are often much faster then direct methods. But for the most of them there is no proof of such fast convergence even for some simple cases.

In this paper we consider global optimization method based on tensor train decomposition. The method is non-deterministic and exploits tensor structure of functional. Theoretical results proving its fast convergence in some simple cases to global optimum are provided.

1 Introduction

Tensor train (TT) decomposition [5,6] allows to represent multidimensional array (tensor) $A \in \mathbb{R}^{n_1 \times \cdots \times n_d}$ using only $O(dnr^2)$ parameters, where $n = \max\limits_{i=\overline{1,\ldots,d}} n_i$, $r = \max\limits_{i=\overline{1,\ldots,d-1}} r_i$ – is so called TT-rank of tensor:

$$A(i_1, \ldots, i_d) = \sum_{\alpha_1=1,\ldots,\alpha_{d-1}=1}^{r_1,\ldots,r_{d-1}} G_1(i_1,\alpha_1)G_2(\alpha_1,i_2,\alpha_2)\ldots G_d(\alpha_{d-1},i_d) \qquad (1)$$

If r is small enough then tensor is represented by logarithmic number of parameters. Moreover:

- Evaluation of tensor element is fast—$O(dr^2)$ arithmetic operations.
- Tensor arithmetic is fast—most of them have complexity $O(dnr^3)$ or even less.
- There is fast and robust round (recompression) procedure.
- TT approximation of tensor can be robustly obtained using TT-SVD procedure.

© Springer Nature Switzerland AG 2020
I. Lirkov and S. Margenov (Eds.): LSSC 2019, LNCS 11958, pp. 197–202, 2020.
https://doi.org/10.1007/978-3-030-41032-2_22

However, many tensors in practice are given as functions of integer arguments and so huge that all of the elements can not be evaluated in a reasonable time or stored in computer memory. To work with such tensors TT-Cross method [7] was developed. This method allows to obtain TT-approximation of the tensor using only $O(dnr^2)$ evaluations of tensor element.

To obtain approximation TT-Cross method performs "smart" search of tensor elements of large magnitude and use them as interpolation nodes. It was noted, that the method with high probability finds element with the largest magnitude even if approximation quality is not very high. This fact allowed to develop global optimization algorithm.

2   TT-Global Optimization

The crucial part of TT-Cross method and TT global optimization method is matrix cross interpolation method [1–4].

2.1   Matrix Cross Interpolation Method

The method allows to obtain approximation of matrix $A \in \mathbb{R}^{m \times n}$ using only $O((m+n)r)$ matrix element evaluations and $O((m+n)r^2)$ arithmetic operations.

The idea of the method is based on such fact: if rank $A = r$, matrix $\hat{A} \in \mathbb{R}^{r \times r}$—nonsingular submatrix of A, $C \in \mathbb{R}^{m \times r}$ columns of A containing $\hat{A}$, $R \in \mathbb{R}^{r \times n}$ rows of A containing $\hat{A}$, then:

$$A = C \hat{A}^{-1} R \tag{2}$$

Moreover if rank $A \approx r$ (that means $\mathrm{rank}(A + E) = r$, $\|E\| \leqslant \varepsilon$ for sufficiently small ε), and $\hat{A}$ is submatrix of order r with maximal volume (magnitude of determinant), then:

$$A \approx C \hat{A}^{-1} R \tag{3}$$

And such approximation is quasioptimal [1–4]:

$$\|A - C \hat{A}^{-1} R\|_C \leqslant (r + 1)\sigma_{r+1}(A) \tag{4}$$

$$\|A - C \hat{A}^{-1} R\|_2 \leqslant (r + 1)^2 \sigma_{r+1}(A) \tag{5}$$

If volume of $\hat{A}$ is not maximal but large enough, such approximation still would be quasioptimal [2].

Matrix cross interpolation with heuristic rank estimation is, in fact, incomplete LU-decomposition with special pivoting.

After k steps of the method approximation $A_k = U_k V_k$, interpolation rows $i_1, \ldots, i_k$ and columns $j_1, \ldots, j_k$ (these rows and columns are zero in the matrix $E_k = A - A_k$) are obtained. At the next step:

1. A random row with index $\tilde{i}$ is selected from the rows that was not interpolated yet ($\tilde{i} \neq i_1, \ldots, i_k$).

2. Row $\tilde{i}$ of the matrix E_k is computed.
3. Position containing maximal magnitude element of this row is denoted as j_{k+1}.
4. Column j_{k+1} of the matrix E_k is computed and denoted as c_{k+1}.
5. Maximal magnitude element of c_{k+1} is denoted as a_{k+1}, its position as i_{k+1}.
6. Row i_{k+1} of the matrix E_k is computed and denoted as r_{k+1}.
7. Algorithm stops if $a_{k+1}, c_{k+1}, r_{k+1}$ are small enough. Otherwise an update (similar to the LU-decomposition step using a_{k+1} as pivot) is performed:

$$u_{k+1} = \frac{c_{k+1}}{\sqrt{|a_{k+1}|}} \tag{6}$$

$$v_{k+1} = \frac{r_{k+1}\sqrt{|a_{k+1}|}}{a_{k+1}} \tag{7}$$

$$U_{k+1} = \begin{bmatrix} U_k u_{k+1} \end{bmatrix} \tag{8}$$

$$V_{k+1} = \begin{bmatrix} V_k \\ v_{k+1} \end{bmatrix} \tag{9}$$

The algorithm is often modified to perform more searches of maximal magnitude elements in rows and columns (steps 3–6). For example, until element that have maximal magnitude in both row and column it containing is found.

2.2   TT-Cross Interpolation Method

To describe TT-cross approximation method it is helpful to introduce special matrices associated with tensor—TT-unfolding matrices: $A_k \in \mathbb{R}^{n_1 \ldots n_k \times n_{k+1} \ldots n_d}$ is called k-th TT-unfolding of tensor $A \in \mathbb{R}^{n_1 \times \cdots \times n_d}$, if its elements are such reorder of tensor elements that:

$$A(i_1 \ldots i_k, i_{k+1} \ldots i_d) = A(i_1, \ldots, i_d) \tag{10}$$

Let P_k be set of tensor elements that correspond to "good" interpolation interpolation points of k-th TT-unfolding matrix (at the start of the method all these sets could be empty).

Left to right sweep of TT-Cross method works consecutively with TT-unfolding matrices from A_1 to A_{d-1}:

1. Set of k-th TT-unfolding row indices I_k is generated by addition for each $i = (i_1, \ldots, i_d) \in P_{k-1}$ such n_k row indices: $(i_1, \ldots, i_{k-1}, 1), \ldots, (i_1, \ldots, i_{k-1}, n_k)$.
2. If $2|I_k|$ is greater than number of columns of A_k set J_k consist of all possible column indices. Else J_k constructed by such rules:
   (a) For each $i = (i_1, \ldots, i_d) \in P_{k-1} \cup P_k$ column $(i_{k+1}, \ldots, i_d)$ is added to J_k.
   (b) Random columns are being added to J_k until $|J_k|$ is less than $2|I_k|$.
3. Matrix cross interpolation of the matrix $A_k(I_k, J_k)$ is performed with tolerance $\frac{\varepsilon}{\sqrt{d-1}}$, where ε—target tensor approximation tolerance.
Set P_k is replaced by set of interpolation points, $r_k = |P_k|$.
Indices of A_k rows and columns that contain interpolation points are denoted as $\tilde{I}_k$ and $\tilde{J}_k$ correspondingly.

4. Matrix $A_k(I_k, \tilde{J}_k)A_k(\tilde{I}_k, \tilde{J}_k)^{-1}$ is reshaped to tensor of sizes $r_{k-1} \times n_k \times r_k$ and assigned to TT carriage G_k.

Matrix $A_{d-1}(\tilde{I}_{d-1}, :)$ is assigned to TT carriage G_d.

Right to left sweep is left to right sweep for tensor B such that:

$$B(i_1, \ldots, i_d) = A(i_d, \ldots, i_1) \tag{11}$$

The algorithm stops when relative difference between consecutive tensor approximations is small enough.

Complexity of TT-Cross interpolation method is $O(dnr^2)$ tensor element evaluations and $O(dnr^3)$ arithmetic operations.

2.3   Global Optimization Using on Tensor Train Decomposition

Consider a problem of global optimization of the functional $f(x)$ on d-dimensional parallelepiped. A grid among every dimension could easily be introduced, values of the functional $f(x)$ on the grid form a tensor $A \in \mathbb{R}^{n_1 \times \cdots \times n_d}$. If the grid is fine enough and $f(x)$ is continuous in the vicinity of its optima then the value and the position of an optimal tensor element would be close to the functional global optimum.

Tensor part of the global optimization method performs a search for an element with the maximal magnitude, therefore the problem should be transformed to a problem of the largest magnitude search. It is quite important to find a good mapping from the original problem to an equivalent problem of magnitude maximization. Such mapping should be:

- Strictly monotonic.
- Continuous and smooth (otherwise TT-rank may grow).
- Not leading to large amount of machine zeros.
- Leaving close (by value) optima as distinct as possible.

For example, for a global minimization problem of the functional with unknown field of value $\text{arccot}(f - f_*)$ is often a good choice, where f_* – current approximation to the global minimum.

Denote as P a set of indices corresponding to the best found values of tensor A, as P_k – a set of indices of tensor A for k-th TT unfolding. The method iteration consists of such steps:

1. Tensor $B(i_1, \ldots, i_d) = g(A(i_1, \ldots, i_d))$ is constructed (but not computed), where g – selected mapping to the magnitude maximization problem.
2. For each of TT unfolding B_k independently:
   (a) A set of random tensor indices R_k is generated. $|R_k| = |P \cup P_{k-1} \cup P_k \cup P_{k+1}|$.
   (b) Sets of TT unfolding row indices I_k and column indices J_k are produced: for each $i = (i_1, \ldots, i_d) \in P \cup P_{k-1} \cup P_k \cup P_{k+1} \cup R_k$ such indices are added:

- To I_k: row indices $(i_1, \ldots, i_{k-1}, 1) \ldots (i_1, \ldots, i_{k-1}, n_k)$.
- To J_k: column indices $(1, i_{k+2}, \ldots, i_d) \ldots (n_{k+1}, i_{k+2}, \ldots, i_d)$.

(c) Matrix cross interpolation of $B_k(I_k, J_k)$ with the rank bound r_{max} is performed.

(d) P_k is overwritten by interpolation points. Optionally, a projection to the grid of the points obtained from interpolation points by "rough" local optimization are added to P_k

3. Set P is overwritten by the best r_{max} points of all P_k and P.

Complexity of the method is $O(dnr^2)$ functional evaluations, $O(dnr^3)$ arithmetic operations and $O(dr)$ local optimizations.

2.4 Theoretical Results for Matrix Case

Consider a matrix $A \in \mathbb{R}^{m \times n}$ such that $A = \sigma uv^T + E, \|u\|_2 = \|v\|_2 = 1$. Denote $\|E\|_C$ as δ, $\frac{\|E\|_C}{\sigma \|uv^T\|_C}$ as ε. Let $\varepsilon < \frac{1}{8}$.

Theorem 1 (Matrix cross magnitude maximization starting from a set of columns). *Let v be uniformly distributed on the unit sphere.*

Let the starting row of cross interpolation method be a row containing maximal magnitude element of first $k = \beta \ln n$ columns.

Then with probability not less than $1 - O(n^{-\beta \ln 2})$:

1. *After three search steps (two in rows and one in column) of the matrix cross method such element a_{ij} is found that $|u_i v_j| \geqslant (1 - 4\varepsilon)^2 \|uv^T\|_C$.*
2. *If an element a_{ij} has the maximal magnitude in both i-th row and j-th column, then $|u_i v_j| \geqslant \left(\frac{1 + \sqrt{1 - 8\varepsilon}}{2}\right)^2 \|uv^T\|_C$.*

Theorem 2 (Matrix cross magnitude maximization starting from random column). *Let $m = n$, vectors u, v be uniformly distributed on the unit sphere, matrix E to consist of independently uniformly distributed elements on the interval $[-\delta, \delta]$.*

The with probability not less then

$$1 - O\left(\left(\frac{n}{\ln n}\right)^{-k}\right)$$

1. *If after k steps of matrix cross method element a_{ij} has maximal magnitude in both i-th row and j-th column, then $|u_i v_j| \geqslant \left(\frac{1 + \sqrt{1 - 8\varepsilon}}{2}\right)^2 \|uv^T\|_C$.*
2. *After $k + 3$ steps of matrix cross method element a_{ij} is such that $|u_i v_j| \geqslant (1 - 4\varepsilon)^2 \|uv^T\|_C$.*

Proofs of the theorems are based on the ideas for the probabilistic estimation of the rank-1 approximation accuracy of matrix cross method [8]:

1. To show that if matrix cross approximation method starts from row i (or column j) and ratio $\frac{|u_i|}{\max\limits_{k=1,..,m} |u_k|}$ $\left(\frac{|v_i|}{\max\limits_{k=1,..,n} |v_k|}\right)$ is not very small, then:

(a) After three steps pivot element suggested by the method will be close enough to the element with the largest magnitude.

(b) If pivot element suggested by the method has the largest magnitude in both its row and column, than it is even closer to the element with the largest magnitude.

2. To estimate a probability that starting row (or column) is good enough.

3   Conclusion

Global optimization method based on tensor train allows to solve high-dimensional global optimization problems. It is relatively fast and has high parallel effectiveness. This allowed to use it for different global optimization problems such as protein-ligand docking [10], ODE model parameter estimation [9] and others.

In this work theoretical statements explaining why the method works in simple cases is provided.

Acknowledgments. The work was supported by the RAS presidium program 1 "Fundamental mathematics and its applications" and by program 26 "Fundamental foundations of design of algorithms and software for prospective and high-performance computing systems".

References

1. Goreinov, S.A., Tyrtyshnikov, E.E., Zamarashkin, N.L.: A theory of pseudo-skeleton approximations. Linear Algebra Appl. **261**(1–3), 1–21 (1997)
2. Tyrtyshnikov, E.E.: Incomplete cross approximation in the mosaic-skeleton method. Computing **64**(4), 367–380 (2000)
3. Goreinov, S.A., Tyrtyshnikov, E.E.: The maximal-volume concept in approximation by low-rank matrices. Contemp. Math. **208**, 47–51 (2001)
4. Goreinov, S.A., Oseledets, I.V., Savostyanov, D.V., Tyrtyshnikov, E.E., Zamarashkin, N.L.: How to find a good submatrix. In: Olshevsky, V., Tyrtyshnikov, E. (eds.) Matrix Methods: Theory, Algorithms, Applications, pp. 247–256. World Scientific, Hackensack (2010)
5. Oseledets, I.V., Tyrtyshnikov, E.E.: Breaking the curse of dimensionality, or how to use SVD in many dimensions. SIAM J. Sci. Comput. **31**(5), 3744–3759 (2009)
6. Oseledets, I.V.: Tensor-train decomposition. SIAM J. Sci. Comput. **33**(5), 2295–2317 (2011)
7. Oseledets, I.V., Tyrtyshnikov, E.E.: TT-cross approximation for multidimensional arrays. Linear Algebra Appl. **432**(1), 70–88 (2010)
8. Osinsky A.I.: Probabilistic estimation of the rank-1 cross approximation accuracy. arXiv preprint arXiv:1706.10285 (2017)
9. Zheltkova, V.V., Zheltkov, D.A., Grossman, Z., Bocharov, G.A., Tyrtyshnikov, E.E.: Tensor based approach to the numerical treatment of the parameter estimation problems in mathematical immunology. J. Inverse Ill-posed Prob. **26**(1), 51–66 (2008)
10. Sulimov, A.V., et al.: Evaluation of the novel algorithm of flexible ligand docking with moveable target-protein atoms. Comput. Struct. Biotechnol. J. **15**, 275–285 (2017)

Application of the Global Optimization Methods for Solving the Parameter Estimation Problem in Mathematical Immunology

V. V. Zheltkova[1,2] , Dmitry A. Zheltkov[1(✉)], G. A. Bocharov[1] ,
and Eugene Tyrtyshnikov[1]

[1] Marchuk Institute of Numerical Mathematics of the Russian Academy of Sciences,
Moscow, Russia
`valeryaaziattseva@yandex.ru`, `dmitry.zheltkov@gmail.com`,
`gbocharov@gmail.com`, `eugene.tyrtyshnikov@gmail.com`
[2] Lomonosov Moscow State University, Moscow, Russia

Abstract. Mathematical modeling is widely used in modern immunology. The availability of biologically meaningful and detailed mathematical models permits studying the complex interactions between the components of a biological system and predicting the outcome of the therapeutic interventions. However, the incomplete theoretical understanding of the immune mechanism leads to the uncertainty of model structure and the need of model identification. This process is iterative and each step requires data-based model calibration. When the model is highly detailed, the considerable part of model parameters can not be measured experimentally or found in literature, so one has to solve the parameter estimation problem. Using the maximum likelihood framework, the parameter estimation leads to minimization problem for least square functional, when the observational errors are normally distributed. In this work we presented different computational approaches to the treatment of global optimization problem, arising in parameter estimation. We consider two high-dimensional mathematical models of HIV (human immunodeficiency virus)-infection dynamics as examples. The ODE (ordinary differential equations) and DDE (delay differential equations) versions of models were studied. For these models we solved the parameter estimation problem using a number of numerical global optimization techniques, including the optimization method, based on the tensor-train decomposition (TT). The comparative analysis of obtained results showed that the TT-based optimization technique is in the leading group of the methods ranked according to their performance in the parameter estimation for ODE and DDE versions of both models.

Keywords: Mathematical immunology · Parameter estimation · Global optimization · Model identification

Supported by Russian Foundation for Basic Research (RFBR), research projects 18-31-00356 and research project 17-01-00636.

I. Lirkov and S. Margenov (Eds.): LSSC 2019, LNCS 11958, pp. 203–209, 2020.
https://doi.org/10.1007/978-3-030-41032-2_23

1   Introduction

Mathematical modeling is widely used in modern biological sciences [1]. The development of meaningful models, describing immunological processes with enough level of detail is in great demand, because these models can be used for numerical experiments and predictions. However, the process of model development involves a number of difficulties: complexity and large number of components and interactions in studied processes, uncertainty and incompleteness of theoretical knowledge, the impossibility or difficulty of obtaining experimental or clinical data. Thus, there is a need to solve the model identification and selection problems, and the data-based model parameter estimation is an essential part of these tasks. Parameter estimation problem can be computationally-intensive, especially for multiscale and highly-detailed models, so the development of efficient numerical tools for this task is relevant.

In this work we considered a parameter estimation problem for two high-dimensional models of HIV-infection. For each model we examined both the ODE and DDE versions. The problem was formulated using a maximum likelihood framework and solved with a number of numerical global optimization techniques, including the TT-based optimization method, proposed in [2].

2   Parameter Estimation

2.1   Maximum Likelihood Framework

The detailed description of maximum likelihood estimation (MLE) is given [3]. The mathematical model based on ODE or DDE system can be written in general form of the initial value problem:

$$\mathbf{y}'(t;\mathbf{p}) = \mathbf{f}(t, \mathbf{y}(t;\mathbf{p}), \mathbf{y}(t - \tau;\mathbf{p});\mathbf{p}) \text{ for } t \in [t_0, T];$$
$$\mathbf{y}(t;\mathbf{p}) = \phi(t;\mathbf{p}), \text{ for } t \in [t_0 - \tau, t_0].$$

Here $\mathbf{y}(t) = \mathbf{y}(t;\mathbf{p}) \in \mathbf{R}^M$ - model solution, $\mathbf{p} = [p_1, p_2, ..., p_L]^T \in \mathbf{R}^L$ - vector of parameters. Experimental data is presented by $\{\mathbf{y_j}\}$ with components $y_j^i, i = 1, ... M, j = 1, ..., N$, corresponding times $t_j, j = 1, ..., N, t_j \in [t_0, T]$. We search for a parameter vector $\mathbf{p}*$ from $\Omega = \{\mathbf{p} : p_i \in [\alpha_i, \beta_i]\}$, where α_i, β_i – biologically meaningful boundaries for corresponding paramer, obtained from literature, which gives the best approximation of the experimental data according to a suitable objective function $\Phi(\mathbf{p})$:

$$\mathbf{p}* = \arg\min_{\mathbf{p} \in \Omega \subseteq \mathbf{R}^L} \Phi(\mathbf{p}) \tag{1}$$

The specific form of objective function $\Phi(\mathbf{p})$ depends on the statistical framework used for parameter estimation. When we don't have any information about the parameters, we can use the uniform distribution as a prior. In this case the more general Bayesian framework can be reformulated as a maximum likelihood estimation. In this study we assume the observational errors to be log-normally distributed, time- and component-independent and to have the same variance of observation errors for all the state variables and observation times. In this case the MLE can be formulated as minimization problem for the log-least-squares function:

$$\Phi(\mathbf{p}) = \sum_{j=1}^{N} \sum_{i=1}^{M} \left(\log(y_j^i) - \log(y_i(t_j))\right)^2 \qquad (2)$$

2.2   Optimization Methods

The minimization problem (1) can be solved using different optimization techniques, including local, global and hybrid methods [4,5]. Local optimization methods are fast and have proved convergence to the local minima, but in general they can escape global minima. The global optimization techniques can be slow and do not have theoretically proved convergence, but they can be used for exploring large regions of parameter space. Hybrid methods use global optimization algorithms for searching suitable start points for further local optimization. In this work we analyzed a number of hybrid and global optimization methods, including the TT-based optimization approach [2,6]. This method is based on the useful features of Tensor-Train decomposition [7] and TT-cross approximation method [8]. A parallel implementation of the method is available. The application of TT-based global optimization method to the solution of the parameter estimation problem was described in [6], and for solution of a docking problem in [2].

3   Mathematical Modeling of HIV Dynamics

HIV infection is a disease, which is characterized by long-term course and gradual decrease of CD4 T-cell number and involves many aspects of the immune system. At the moment, there is no clear answer to the question of what exactly is the cause of this decline and the onset AIDS [9,10]. Researchers have developed many mathematical models of varying degrees of detail, describing different aspects of the disease [11,12]. In this work we focused on two deterministic models of immune response dynamics in the acute phase of HIV infection. The first model is a modification of Marchuk-Petrov model of infectious disease [13]. The second model describes the dynamics of regulatory T-lymphocytes during HIV infection [14]. In [15] it was shown, that delay differential equation models are more consistent with the nature of biological underlying processes, so we examined both ODE and DDE versions of models.

3.1   Marchuk-Petrov Model of HIV Infection

In [6] we presented the ODE system based modification of the Marchuk-Petrov model [13], which describes some features of the HIV infection. This model considers the antigen-presenting cells, both cytotoxic and humoral immune reactions. Denote this model as M1-ODE. The model scheme, equations and parameters are given in [6]. In [16] we also described the DDE version of this model, where the equations for the corresponding state variables are written in the following way:

$$\frac{dP}{dt} = b_P^p \xi \rho_P (D_V(t - \tau_P) + D_V^*(t - \tau_P))(H_{Bsp}(t - \tau_P)$$
$$+ H_{Bsp}^*(t - \tau_P))B_{sp}(t - \tau_P) + \alpha_P(\theta P_0 - P);$$

$$\frac{dH_{Bsp}}{dt} = \alpha_{H_B}(\xi \theta H_B^0 - H_{Bsp}) - \sigma_{H_B} H_{Bsp} V - \sigma_{H_B}^D H_{Bsp} D_V^*$$
$$+ b_{H_B}(2(D_V(t - \tau_{HB}) + D_V^*(t - \tau_{HB}))H_{Bsp}(t - \tau_{HB}) - (D_V + D_V^*)H_{Bsp})$$
$$- b_{H_B}^P(D_V + D_V^*)H_{Bsp}B_{sp};$$

$$\frac{dH_{Esp}}{dt} = \alpha_{H_E}(\xi \theta H_E^0 - H_{Esp}) - \sigma_{H_E} H_{Esp} V - \sigma_{H_E}^D H_{Esp} D_V^*$$
$$+ b_{H_E}(2(D_V(t - \tau_{HE}) + D_V^*(t - \tau_{HE}))H_{Esp}(t - \tau_{HE}) - (D_V + D_V^*)H_{Esp})$$
$$- b_{H_E}^P(D_V + D_V^*)H_{Esp}E_{sp};$$

$$\frac{dB_{sp}}{dt} = \alpha_B(\theta B^0 - B_{sp}) + b_B^P$$
$$(2(D_V(t - \tau_B) + D_V^*(t - \tau_B))(H_{Bsp}(t - \tau_B) + H_{Bsp}^*(t - \tau_B))B_{sp}(t - \tau_B));$$

$$\frac{dE_{sp}}{dt} = \alpha_E(\theta E^0 - E_{sp}) + 2b_E^P(D_V(t - \tau_E) + D_V^*(t - \tau_E))(H_{Esp}(t - \tau_E)$$
$$+ H_{Esp}^*(t - \tau_E))E_{sp}(t - \tau_E) - b_{ED_V} D_V^* E_{sp} - b_{EH_E} H_E^* E_{sp} - b_{EH_B} H_B^* E_{sp};$$

We denote the DDE version of the model as M1-DDE. Both the ODE and DDE models have 19 variables. For the ODE version we estimated 32 parameters, for the DDE – 37 parameters.

3.2   Model with Regulatory T-Cell Dynamics

The regulatory T-cells (Tregs) are a subset of CD4 T-cells, and their activity during HIV infection has both beneficial and deleterious effects on patient recovery [14]. However, vast majority of HIV mathematical models do not describe their dynamics. In [14] a mathematical model, describing Treg dynamics during HIV infection, is presented. In this model the following populations are considered: T - CD4 T-lymphocytes, T^* - infected CD4 T-lymphocytes, E_i - immature effectors, E_m - mature effectors, V - virions, R - normal Tregs, R_α - adaptive Tregs. The parameters are given in Table 1. We considered the ODE version of this model with slightly modified equations (we amended them to satisfy the condition of positive invariance):

$$\frac{dT}{dt} = \lambda - d_T T - kVT - \alpha_1 RT; \quad \frac{dT^*}{dt} = kVT - \delta T^* - mE_m T^*;$$
$$\frac{dE_i}{dt} = p_{E_i} - d_{E_i} E_i - k_E V E_i - \alpha_2 RE_i; \quad \frac{dE_m}{dt} = k_E V E_i - \delta_E E_m - \alpha_3 R_\alpha E_m;$$
$$\frac{dV}{dt} = N\delta T^* - cV; \quad \frac{dR}{dt} = p_R - d_r R - \gamma RV; \quad \frac{dR_\alpha}{dt} = \gamma RV - \delta_R R_\alpha.$$

Denote the model as M2-ODE. In the respective DDE version (M2-DDE) the equation for the mature effectors is written as follows:

$$\frac{dE_m}{dt} = k_E V(t - \tau)E_i(t - \tau) - \delta_E E_m - \alpha_3 R_\alpha E_m$$

Table 1. Parameters for model M2

Parameter	Biological meaning	Meas. unit
λ	T-cells production rate	cell/(ml $\cdot$ day)
d_T	T-cells death rate	1/day
k	Infection rate of T cells by V	ml/(part. $\cdot$ day)
δ	Infected cell death rate	1/day
N	Viral production rate	part./cell
c	Viral death rate	1/day
m	Infected cell elimination rate	ml/(cell $\cdot$ day)
δ_E	Mature effectors death rate	1/day
α_1	Downregulation rate of nTregs on T-cells	ml/(cell $\cdot$ day)
p_{E_i}	Immature effectors production rate	cell/(ml $\cdot$ day)
d_{E_i}	Immature effectors death rate	1/day
k_E	Transition rate $E_i->E_m$	ml/(part. $\cdot$ day)
α_2	Downregulation rate of nTregs on immature effectors	ml/(cell $\cdot$ day)
α_3	Downregulation rate of aTregs on mature effectors	ml/(cell $\cdot$ day)
p_R	nTreg production rate	cell/(ml $\cdot$ day)
d_R	nTreg death rate	1/day
γ_R	Transition rate $R->R_\alpha$	ml/(part. $\cdot$ day)
δ_R	aTregs death rate	1/day

4   Numerical Experiments

In numerical experiments the optimization of the log-least squares functional using the TT global optimization and different global optimization methods of NLopt library [17] was performed. The considered methods are listed below:

TT – TT global optimization method.
CRS2 – Controlled Random Search with local mutation [18].
rMLSL – Multi-Level Single-Linkage [19] with pseudo-random start points.
qrMLSL – Multi-Level Single-Linkage with quasi-random start points.
rMLSL+SBPLX – Multi-Level Single-Linkage with pseudo-random start points, Sublex [20] method used for local optimizations.
qrMLSL+SBPLX – Multi-Level Single-Linkage with quasi-random start points, Sublex method used for local optimizations.
ISRES – Improved Stochastic Ranking Evolution Strategy [21].
ESCH – Evolutionary Algorithm [22].

For both models we used a set of clinical data, describing the standard course of infectious process [23]. It contained 17 time points for each of the three infection characteristics related model variables: viral load, CD4+ T cell and CD8+ T lymphocyte counts. All methods were set to perform 10^6 functional evaluations. For numerical solution of the initial value problems for ODE systems we used the BDF method, implemented in Sundials [24], and for the DDE model

Table 2. Minima values, obtained after local optimization, ϵ - system integration tolerance.

Method ϵ	M1-ODE 10^{-6}	M1-DDE 10^{-4}	M2-ODE 10^{-6}	M2-DDE 10^{-6}
TT	2.28	2.56	1.75	1.86
CRS2	2.47	5.06	19.76	18.47
rMLSL	2.50	3.20	3.69	4.44
qrMLSL	2.51	2.89	2.14	4.49
rMLSL+SBPLX	2.13	2.82	1.88	2.06
qrMLSL+SBPLX	2.22	3.00	1.91	1.93
ISRES	2.34	2.72	14.93	1.59
ESCH	3.49	4.38	3.41	2.05

system - the BDF (backward differential formulas) method, implemented in DIFSUBDEL [25]. Also local optimization was performed for the final points, obtained by each of the global optimization methods. The corresponding results are presented in Table 2.

5   Results and Discussion

In this work we presented two mathematical models of HIV infection dynamics, focused on different key aspects of infectious process (antigen presentation, the antigen-specific humoral and cytotoxic immune reactions, the effects of regulatory T-cells). Both models were formulated in two versions: as ODE and DDE systems. We formulated parameter estimation problem for each of the models using the maximum likelihood framework and solved them by various global and hybrid optimization methods, including the TT-based global optimization technique. The obtained parameter values are biologically meaningful as the area of their search was limited by the values given in the literature [6,9,14]. Based on the results we can conclude, that TT, rMLSL+SBPLX, qrMLSL+SBPLX show the best performance for ODE versions of the models, and TT, ISRES demonstrate the best execution results for DDE versions of the models.

References

1. Germain, R., Meier-Schellersheim, M.: Systems biology in immunology: a computational modeling perspective. Annu. Rev. Immunol. **29**, 527–85 (2011)
2. Zheltkov, D., Oferkin, I., Katkova, E., Sulimov, A., Sulimov, V., Tyrtyshnikov, E.: TTDock: a docking method based on tensor train decompositions. Vychislitel'nye Metody i Programmirovanie **4**(3), 279–291 (2013)
3. Bocharov, G., et al.: Mathematical Immunology of Virus Infections. Springer, Cham (2018). https://doi.org/10.1007/978-3-319-72317-4

4. Ashyraliyev, M., Fomekong-Nanfack, Y., Kaandorp, J., Blom, J.: Systems biology: parameter estimation for biochemical models. FEBS J. **276**, 886–902 (2009)
5. Lillacci, G., Khammash, M.: Parameter estimation and model selection in computational biology. PLOS Comput. Biol. **6**(3), e1000696 (2010)
6. Zheltkova, V., Zheltkov, D., Grossman, Z., Bocharov, G., Tyrtyshnikov, E.: Tensor based approach to the numerical treatment of the parameter estimation problems in mathematical immunology. J. Inverse Ill-posed Probl. **26**(1), 51–66 (2018)
7. Oseledets, I., Tyrtyshnikov, E.: TT-cross approximation for multidimensional arrays. Linear Algebra Appl. **432**(1), 70–88 (2010)
8. Oseledets, I.: Tensor-train decomposition. SIAM J. Sci. Comput. **33**(5), 2295–2317 (2011)
9. Bocharov, G., Chereshnev, V., et al.: Human immunodeficiency virus infection: from biological observations to mechanistic mathematical modelling. Math. Model. Nat. Phenom. **7**(5), 78–104 (2012)
10. Grossman, Z., et al.: CD4+ T-cell depletion in HIV infection: are we closer to understanding the cause? Nat. Med. **8**(4), 319 (2002)
11. Perelson, A.: Modelling viral and immune system dynamics. Nat. Rev. Immunol. **2**(1), 28 (2002)
12. Adams, B., et al.: HIV dynamics: modeling, data analysis, and optimal treatment protocols. J. Comput. Appl. Math. **184**(1), 10–49 (2005)
13. Marchuk, G.: Mathematical Modelling of Immune Response in Infectious Diseases, vol. 395. Springer, Heidelberg (2013). https://doi.org/10.1007/978-94-015-8798-3
14. Simonov, M.: Modeling adaptive regulatory T-cell dynamics during early HIV infection. PLoS ONE **7**(4), e33924 (2012)
15. Baker, C., Bocharov, G., Rihan, F.: A report on the use of delay differential equations in numerical modelling in the biosciences. Manchester Centre for Computational Mathematics, Manchester, UK (1999)
16. Zheltkova, V., Zheltkov, D., Bocharov, G. : Modelling HIV infection: model identification and global sensitivity analysis. Math. Biol. Bioinform. **14**(1), 19–33 (2019). (in Russian)
17. The NLopt nonlinear-optimization package. http://ab-initio.mit.edu/wiki/index.php/NLopt. Accessed 27 Feb 2019
18. Kaelo, P., Ali, M.: Some variants of the controlled random search algorithm for global optimization. J. Optim. Theory Appl. **130**(2), 253–264 (2006)
19. Kan, R.: Stochastic global optimization methods. Math. Program. **39**(1) (1987)
20. Rowan, T.: Functional stability analysis of numerical algorithms (1990)
21. Runarsson, T., Yao X.: Search biases in constrained evolutionary optimization. IEEE Trans. Syst. Man Cybern. Part C (Appl. Rev.) **35**(2), 233–243 (2005)
22. Santos, C., Goncalves, M., Hernandez-Figueroa, H.: Designing novel photonic devices by bio-inspired computing. IEEE Photonics Technol. Lett. **22**(15), 1177–1179 (2010)
23. Munier, M., Kelleher, A.: Acutely dysregulated, chronically disabled by the enemy within: T-cell responses to HIV-1 infection. Immunol. Cell Biol. **85**(1), 6–15 (2007)
24. Hindmarsh, A., et al.: SUNDIALS: suite of nonlinear and differential/algebraic equation solvers. ACM Trans. Math. Softw. (TOMS) **31**(3), 363–396 (2005)
25. Bocharov, G., Romanyukha, A.: Numerical solution of delay-differential equations by linear multistep methods: algorithm and programme. Preprint No. 117. Institute of Numerical Mathematics, Russian Academy of Sciences, Moscow (1986). (in Russian)

HPC and Big Data: Algorithms and Applications

Statistical Moments of the Vertical Distribution of Air Pollution over Bulgaria

Georgi Gadzhev[✉], Kostadin Ganev, and Plamen Mukhtarov

National Institute of Geophysics, Geodesy and Geography,
Bulgarian Academy of Sciences, Acad. G. Bonchev Street, bl. 3, 1113 Sofia, Bulgaria
ggadzhev@geophys.bas.bg

Abstract. The air quality has a key impact on the quality of life and human health. The atmospheric composition fields are formed as a result of complex interaction of processes with different temporal and spatial scales from global to regional to a chain of local scales. The earth surface heterogeneities, including the complex terrain, have a very significant impact on the atmospheric dynamics, hence on the formation of air pollution pattern. The incredible diversity of dynamic processes, the complex chemical transformations of the compounds and complex emission configuration together lead to the formation of a complex vertical structure of the atmospheric composition. The detailed analysis of this vertical structure with its temporal/spatial variability jointly with the atmospheric dynamics characteristics can enrich significantly the knowledge about the processes and mechanisms, which form air pollution, including near earth surface. The present paper presents some results of a study, which aims at performing reliable, comprehensive and detailed analysis of the atmospheric composition fields 3D structure and its connection with the processes, which lead to their formation.

The numerical simulations of the vertical structure of atmospheric composition fields over Bulgaria have been performed using the US EPA Model–3 system as a modelling tool for 3D simulations and the system nesting capabilities were applied for downscaling the simulations from 81 km to 9 km grid resolution over Bulgaria. The national emission inventory was used as an emission input for Bulgaria, while outside the country the emissions are from the TNO high resolution inventory.

Keywords: Vertical structure · Air pollution · Atmospheric composition · Numerical simulation · High performance computing

1 Introduction

The parameters of the atmosphere have key impact on quality of life and human health. Because of this, quite naturally, the surface air quality is mostly studied. From the other hand the atmospheric composition fields are formed as a result

© Springer Nature Switzerland AG 2020
I. Lirkov and S. Margenov (Eds.): LSSC 2019, LNCS 11958, pp. 213–219, 2020.
https://doi.org/10.1007/978-3-030-41032-2_24

of complex interaction of processes with different temporal and spatial scales—from global to synoptic to a chain of local scales. A very significant role in the formation of air pollution pattern play also the atmospheric turbulence and the atmospheric boundary layer processes. The impact of terrain heterogenity is also important. The picture becomes even more complex in urban environment, where human activities leads to the formation of specific urban climate, urban heat island and urban boundary layer with complex structure [1].

The incredible diversity of dynamic processes, the complex chemical transformations of the compounds and complex emission configuration together lead to the formation of a complex vertical structure of the atmospheric composition. The detailed analysis of this vertical structure with its temporal/spatial variability jointly with the atmospheric dynamics characteristics can enrich significantly the knowledge about the processes and mechanisms, which form air pollution, including near earth surface.

In this paper we are presenting some results of a study, which aims at performing analysis of the atmospheric composition fields 3D structure and its connection with the processes, which lead to their formation.

2   Methodology

The study is based on performed day by day for 7 years (2008–2014) ensemble of computer simulations of the atmospheric composition fields in Bulgaria, which is comprehensive enough as to provide statistically reliable assessment of the atmospheric composition climate. By averaging over the ensemble the "typical" seasonal and annual pollution concentration fields were constructed with their spatial variability and diurnal course. Some characteristics of the concentration fields vertical distribution—center of masses, vertical dispersion, skewness and kurtosis, vertical mean and maximal concentration, the maximal concentration level ans cross correlations [2] have been calculated for the so constructed "typical" seasonal and annual pollution concentration fields.

The simulations have been performed using US EPA Model-3 system as modeling tools for 3D simulations: Meteorological model WRF [3], Atmosphere Composition Model CMAQ [4] and Emission model SMOKE [5]. The NCEP Global Analysis Data meteorological background with $1° × 1°$ resolution was used. The models nesting capabilities were applied to downscale the simulations to 9 km for Bulgaria. The TNO high resolution emission inventory [6,7] and National emission inventory as emission input for Bulgaria have been used. More detailed description of the experiments can be seen in [8,9].

The computer resource requirements of the modeling system are very big [10,11] and so the numerical experiments were organized in effective HPC environment [12]. The calculations were implemented on the Supercomputer System "Avitohol" at IICT-BAS.

3   Results

2D maps, of the diurnal course of the annual vertical center of masses Z and surface concentrations C_0 for Sulfur dioxide (SO_2) are shown in Fig. 1 as a demonstration of the complexity of the vertical pollution field structure. As it can be seen the center of masses has well displayed horizontal and diurnal variability, which reflects both the complexity of the atmospheric dynamics and the emission sources configuration. It should be noted that Z and C_0 always change in anti–phase, which is a good illustration of the role of the vertical pollution transport. As stated in [13] the diurnal behaviour of Z in the case of complex, horizontally heterogeneous meteorological fields and complex emission sources configuration is dramatically different from the classic case of pollution from a point source in a 1D boundary layer.

A good impression of the complexity of the pollution fields vertical structure give the cross correlations of the concentrations at earth surface and aloft (Fig. 2).

The main features of the cross correlations of Coarse Particulate Mater (CPRM), calculated for the averaged over the domain concentrations are: *Annually*—there is a well displayed diurnal course and at the height at about 1 km a reverse change in the phase of the diurnal course can be seen. The time lag in cross correlations at above the ground is due to the time needed for transport of surface concentration in height. *Summer*—they are quite similar to the annuals. *Winter*—the layer of good cross correlation narrows and the diurnal course almost disappears. The lag of reactions to the surface concentrations is bigger and can be negative as well as positive. These tree effects are evidence of the slower (less intensive) vertical transport, which is most probably not the only dominant one near surface in Winter.

Considering the Fine Particulate Mater (FPRM) one can see that there is almost no diurnal course in annual and seasonal cross correlations near ground. During the *Summer* only above 1 km delay in the cross correlations can be seen, which is connected with upward movements, as under 1 km the correlations are symmetric. The fact that the diurnal course (result of the diurnal course of atmospheric stability) of the cross correlations is not well manifested probably tells that FPRM concentration pattern is formed as result of interaction also of many other processes, which makes the vertical transport impact not so visible.

For SO_2 one can see that *Annually* at heights up to 1 km positive and negative time lag (overtaking and delay) appears in the same range in cross correlations which tells that upward and downward transport are of similar importance. This is due to the fact that some major SO_2 sources are high (power plants), so the surface concentrations are formed also by downward transport. At higher levels only a delay can be seen which is again connected with upward transport from high sources. In *Summer* the cross correlation behaviour is quite similar to the annual one as near ground the delay is bigger than the annual and reaches up to 48 h. This means that there is a not so intensive and slow rising of surface SO_2. Again this is most probably a joint effect of different processes, including local circulations. In *Winter* the situation is exactly opposite to the summer one. The prominent overtake again reflects the SO_2 source height.

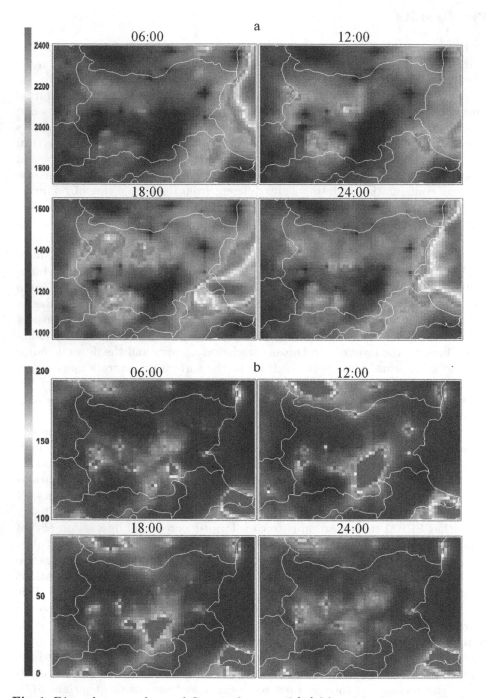

Fig. 1. Diurnal course of annual Centre of masses **Z** [m] (a) and Surface concentration C_0 [μg/m^3] (b) horizontal distribution over Bulgaria for SO_2

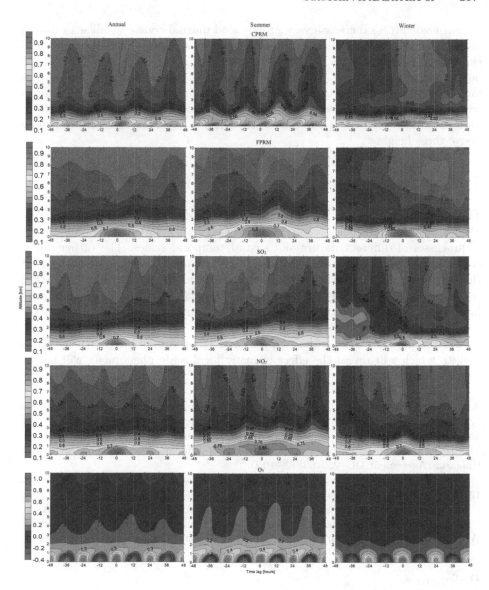

Fig. 2. Annual, Summer and winter cross correlations between averaged over the domain surface and height concentrations of CPRM, FPRM, SO_2, NO_2 and O_3.

For Nitrogen dioxide (NO_2) *Annually* the diurnal course is well manifested, but due to the symmetry of cross correlations at all heights, it is difficult to draw conclusions based only on these characteristics. For *Summer* for height up to 1 km the positive lag predominates, which is an evidence of upward transport. In *Winter* there is a slight top-down transport in the lower layers. In general, cross correlations across all seasons are balanced, as can be seen in the annuals.

For Ozone (O_3) there is a very pronounced diurnal course at all seasons and annually. The very well displayed diurnal course is a very good illustration of the O_3 photochemical cycle. *Annually* at height above 1 km there is a slight delay (effect of downward vertical transport), and in the *Summer* this delay is more pronounced. During the *Winter*, the layer with significant cross correlations reaches 2–3 km, and above this height the cross correlation disappears, which indicates a lack of connection between the surface O_3 concentrations and those above these heights.

4   Conclusion

The results shown in the present paper are a good demonstration of the complexity of the atmospheric composition 3D structure and of the joint impact of processes of different nature and spatial/temporal scales. The rather different behaviour of the cross correlations of the different compounds shows that the vertical profiles are compound specific. They do not reflect only the vertical transport (governed largely by atmospheric stability), but also the emission configurations, local circulation systems, chemical transformations, possibly aerosol processes, and etc.

Performing simulations and analysis with finer resolution (down to urban scales), which will reveal the effect of many local scale phenomena will be the task for future work.

Acknowledgments. This work has been carried out in the framework of the National Science Program "Environmental Protection and Reduction of Risks of Adverse Events and Natural Disasters", approved by the Resolution of the Council of Ministers 577/17.08.2018 and supported by the Ministry of Education and Science (MES) of Bulgaria (Agreement DO–230/06–12–2018).

The studies are funded by the Bulgarian National Science Fund (DN–04/2 13.12.2016) Program for career development of young scientists, BAS.

Deep gratitude to the organizations and institutes (TNO, NCEP–NCAR, ECA&D, Unidata, MPI–M and all others), which provide free of charge software and data. Without their innovative data services and tools this study would not be possible.

References

1. Kanakidou, M., et al.: Megacities as hot spots of air pollution in the East Mediterranean. Atmos. Environ. **45**, 1223–1235 (2010)
2. Korn, G.A., Korn, T.M.: Mathematical Handbook for Scientists and Engineers, 2nd edn. McGraw-Hill, NewYork (1968)
3. Shamarock, W., et al.: A description of the Advanced Research WRF Version 2 (2007). http://www.mmm.ucar.edu/wrf/users/docs/arw_v2.pdf
4. CMAQ user guide (2006). https://www.cmascenter.org/help/documentation.cfm?model=cmaq&version=4.6
5. CEP: Sparse Matrix Operator Kernel Emission (SMOKE) Modeling System, University of Carolina, Research Triangle Park, North Carolina (2003)

6. Visschedijk, A., Zandveld, P., van der Gon, H.: A high resolution gridded European emission database for the EU integrated project GEMS, TNO report 2007-A-R0233/B, The Netherlands (2007)
7. Brunekreef, B., Holgate, S.: Air pollution and health. Lancet **360**, 1233–1242 (2002)
8. Gadzhev, G., Ganev, K., Miloshev, N., Syrakov, D., Prodanova, M.: Numerical study of the atmospheric composition in Bulgaria. Comput. Math. Appl. **65**, 402–422 (2013)
9. Gadzhev, G., Ganev, K., Prodanova, M., Syrakov, D., Atanasov, E., Miloshev, N.: Multi-scale atmospheric composition modelling for Bulgaria. In: Steyn, D., Builtjes, P., Timmermans, R. (eds.) Air Pollution Modeling and its Application XXII. NAPSC, pp. 381–385. Springer, Dordrecht (2013). https://doi.org/10.1007/978-94-007-5577-2_64
10. Todorova, A., et al.: Grid computing for atmospheric composition studies in Bulgaria. Earth Sc. Inf. **3**(4), 259–282 (2010)
11. Marécal, V., et al.: A regional air quality forecasting system over Europe: the MACC-II daily ensemble production. Geosci. Model Dev. **8**, 2777–2813 (2015)
12. Atanassov, E., Gurov, T., Karaivanova, A., Ivanovska, S., Durchova, M., Dimitrov, D.: On the parallelization approaches for Intel MIC architecture. In: AIP Conference Proceedings, vol. 1773, p. 070001 (2016). https://doi.org/10.1063/1.4964983
13. Gadzhev, G., Ganev, K.: Vertical structure of some pollutant over Bulgaria - Ozone and Nitrogen Dioxide. In: SGEM 2018, vol. 18, issue 4.3, pp. 449–454 (2018). https://doi.org/10.5593/sgem2018/4.3. ISBN 978-619-7408-70-6. ISSN 1314-2704

Distributed Deep Learning
on Heterogeneous Computing Resources
Using Gossip Communication

Dobromir Georgiev[✉] and Todor Gurov

Institute of Information and Communication Technologies,
Bulgarian Academy of Sciences, Acad. G. Bonchev St., Block 25A,
1113 Sofia, Bulgaria
{dobromir,gurov}@parallel.bas.bg

Abstract. With the increased usage of deep neural networks, their structures have naturally evolved, increasing in size and complexity. With currently used networks often containing millions of parameters, and hundreds of layers, there have been many attempts to leverage the capabilities of various high-performance computing architectures. Most approaches are focused on either using parameter servers or a fixed communication network, or exploiting particular capabilities of specific computational resources. However, few experiments have been made under relaxed communication consistency requirements and using a dynamic adaptive way of exchanging information.

Gossip communication is a peer-to-peer communication approach, that can minimize the overall data traffic between computational agents, by providing a weaker guarantee on data consistency - eventual consistency. In this paper, we present a framework for gossip-based communication, suitable for heterogeneous computing resources, and apply it to the problem of parallel deep learning, using artificial neural networks. We present different approaches to gossip-based communication in a heterogeneous computing environment, consisting of CPUs and MIC-based co-processors, and implement gossiping via both shared and distributed memory. We also provide a simplistic approach to load balancing in a heterogeneous computing environment, that proves efficient for the case of parallel deep neural network training.

Further, we explore several approaches to communication exchange and resource allocation, when considering parallel deep learning using heterogeneous computing resources, and evaluate their effect on the convergence of the distributed neural network.

Keywords: Deep learning · Gossip communication · Heterogeneous high-performance computing

© Springer Nature Switzerland AG 2020
I. Lirkov and S. Margenov (Eds.): LSSC 2019, LNCS 11958, pp. 220–227, 2020.
https://doi.org/10.1007/978-3-030-41032-2_25

1   Introduction

1.1   Deep Neural Networks

Deep Learning (DL) algorithms are Machine Learning methods, focused on learning data representations. Deep neural networks (DNN), artificial neural networks, which contain multiple layers of interconnected neurons. They are one of the most common ways to store the model of the DL algorithm. DNNs are able to represent highly non-linear models and are successfully applied in an ever-growing number of problems, in domains like image recognition, climate modeling, finance, and engineering. Their increased usage, especially on large and complex datasets, has naturally caused their structures to evolve and increase in size and complexity, with currently used DNNs containing hundreds of layers and millions of parameters [7,8]. This has resulted in numerous attempts to leverage the capabilities of modern high-performance computing resources, to tackle the computational demands of such large networks. While using shared memory parallelization or co-processor devices, like GPUs, is widely researched, efficient use of distributed memory and heterogeneous computational resources is still a topic of high interest.

Typically, DL algorithms use some form of the Gradient Descent method to iteratively update neurons in different layers based on the predictions of the DNN and the expected output. The most widely used form of Gradient Descent is the Mini-Batch Gradient Descent, where at each iteration a random subset of inputs is executed against the neural network, and subsequently, weights are updated based on the output of the network. These steps are known as feed-forward and back-propagation.

Most approaches to distributed memory DL algorithms are centered around the usage of a central parameter server [2], whose only purpose is to store the most up-to-date version of the model, while other computational agents, perform the network training. Periodically, each process that performs the training, sends either gradient updates, or the entire network to the parameter server while requesting the most up-to-date version of the model. Information exchange with the parameter server can be synchronous or asynchronous and symmetrical or not. Naturally, with the increased number of processes, using a single parameter server becomes a bottleneck, and using multiple parameter servers results in wasted resources and increased complexity in maintaining the model.

1.2   Gossip Communication

Gossip communication is a communication paradigm, which aims to reduce the overall communication traffic in systems that work under relaxed constraints on data consistency - eventual consistency. It is inspired by the real-life way of decentralized information exchange of the same name. Gossip communication substitutes message broadcasts and all-to-all communication with peer-to-peer information exchange. Additionally, with an adequate approach to peer selection, it can provide guarantees that data will take no more than $log(N)$ communication exchanges to reach all participating computational agents. Gossip communication can be applied in a wide variety of algorithms in machine learning, evolutionary computations, financial mathematics [6], control theory, etc.

1.3 Heterogeneous Computing Environments

While any computing environment, which consists of non-identical computing resources, can be considered to be heterogeneous, the term is usually either applied to environments consisting of resources that are provisioned differently, i.e. hybrid usage of traditional HPC resources, and elastic Cloud resources, or to environments consisting of traditional CPU computational resources and co-processors - be it GPUs or Many Integrated Core (MIC) devices. In our experiments, we consider the latter and predominantly use a CPU and MIC based computing environment.

2 Implementation

In our implementation, we consider the scenario where multiple DNN workers are running in parallel. All workers store a DNN with identical layout initialized with the same random values. Each worker iteratively performs a Mini-Batch Gradient Descent and asynchronous and asymmetrical Gossip communication exchange.

2.1 Processing Overview

Each worker hosts a single network and performs iterations, consisting of a learning step - Gradient Descent Step, and a Gossip Exchange Step. The latter consists of sending gossip, dependent on a random variable, and consuming inbound gossip messages.

Gradient Descent Step: During this step, the worker performs a stochastic gradient descent, based on a random Mini-Batch, and updates the weights of its network.

Send Gossip Step: After each Gradient Descent step, the worker may send its current state to another peer. The state of the worker consists:

- Weights and biases;
- Number of iterations;
- Number of outbound gossip messages;
- Number of inbound gossip messages.

These can be utilized in the inbound message consuming of the receiving worker.

Whether a message will be sent and peer selection approaches are considered in further detail in subsequent sections.

Recv Gossip Step: While within the Send Gossip Step, it is possible to send only a single message, when receiving Gossip messages, due to the asynchronous and asymmetrical way of communication, it is possible to receive more than one message. In that case, messages are simply sequentially processed. A standard approach to consuming other model weights in consensus Gossip protocols is to do a weighted average of the current model and the inbound. For n participants, usually the coefficients are *(n-1)/n* and *1/n*, respectively. As dealing with heterogeneous computing resources, will most likely result in workers with different iteration speeds, a more adequate approach is to also weigh in the number of iterations of both sender and receiver as described in 2.

Algorithm 1. Gossip exchange step	**Algorithm 2.** Gossip message consume
1: **function** GOSSIPEXCHANGE	1: **Input:** e_j: epochs of receiver, e_i: epochs of sender, n: workers, W_j: weights of receiver, W_i: weights of sender
2: **if** RAND **then**	
3: $r \leftarrow$ SELECTRECEIVER	
4: SENDGOSSIP(message, r)	
5: **end if**	2: **function** CONSUMEGOSSIP
6: **while** !INQUEUE.EMPTY **do**	3: $m \leftarrow \frac{1}{n}\frac{e_j}{e_i}$
7: CONSUMEGOSSIP()	4: $W_j \leftarrow (1-m)W_j + mW_i$
8: **end while**	5: **end function**
9: **end function**	

2.2   Implementation Details

Deep Neural Network: For our experiments, we developed our own small DNN framework, focused on exposing an idiomatic C++ interface, while enabling fine control of memory allocations. Apart from a C++ compliant allocator based on Intel MKL allocation procedures, our framework provides the facilities to store the entire model in a single piece of memory, with each layer properly padded for optimal memory access. This enables copying the entire model with a single allocation.

MPI Gossip Communication: Communication exchange between processes is implemented in terms of non-blocking MPI procedures. This naturally requires buffering of the whole network, the cost of which is negligible as it constitutes a single, though large copy operation. The outbound messages and their associated **MPI_Request** objects are stored in a list, whose oldest entry is repeatedly polled for completion with **MPI_Test**. Polling for inbound Gossip is based on **MPI_Iprobe** with **MPI_ANY_SOURCE** and subsequent **MPI_Recv**.

Sending Gossip: Generating outbound gossip messages is currently determined in one of two ways. Either a worker sends messages at a fixed number of iterations, or with a specific probability.

Peer Selection: Peer selection can be done in one of two ways - uniform selection, or through a predefined virtual topology (Fig. 1).

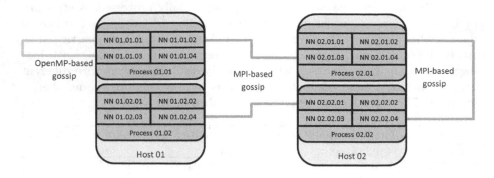

Fig. 1. Gossip communication channels between worker instances

Hybrid MPI-OpenMP Gossip Communication: A similar approach for Gossip communication, can be utilized in a shared memory environment. In such an environment, we consider multiple DNN algorithms sharing a single process. This facilitates lowering the overall memory usage and training dataset loading times. To enable the execution of multiprocess multi-threaded training of a distributed gossiping DLL, however, the purely MPI-based approach must be modified. In our experiments, we chose to enable direct communication between threads residing in different processes. For that purpose, at the start of the execution, using the **MPI_Alltoall** procedure, a virtual thread topology is created, mapping threads to MPI ranks. Subsequently, each thread can send to and receive gossip from each other thread.

3   Numerical Experiments

The system that we've used for our numerical experiments is the Avitohol High-performance computing system at IICT-BAS. It consists of 150 HP Cluster Platform SL250S GEN8 servers, each equipped with 2 Intel Xeon E5-2650 v2 CPUs and 2 Intel Xeon Phi 7120P co-processors. Thus, each server provides 16 physical/32 logical CPU cores and 122 physical/488 logical MIC cores. The server interconnect is FDR InfiniBand. To fully utilize the MIC capabilities, Intel MKL is extensively used.

We've based our experiments mostly on CIFAR-10 [3]. The network we've used for CIFAR-10 is described in [1] - (3, 28) C(64, 24) P(64, 12) C(128, 8) P(128, 4) C(64, 2) D(256, 1) S(10, 1).

Before running experiments in a heterogeneous environment, naturally, we explored the capabilities of the devices with regard to epoch velocity - epochs per second. Table 1 shows the achieved epochs per second with different execution configurations on the CPUs and the MIC co-processors.

Table 1. Epoch velocity per devices Processes/Threads per process.

CPU	CPU velocity	MIC	MIC velocity
1/1	5.97	1/1	0.52
1/4	24.04	1/2	1.09
4/1	23.83	1/4	2.22
1/8	48.08	1/8	4.40
8/1	48.04	1/16	8.90
1/16	94.76	1/32	17.75
4/4	95.16	1/60	32.34
16/1	95.39	1/64	34.30
1/32	108.29	1/128	45.02

Table 2. Epoch velocity per nodes used.

Nodes	Epoch velocity
1	157.79
2	157.95
3	154.24
4	154.44
6	150.62
8	150.78
12	153.17
16	150.51
20	151.23

With that in mind, we consider the following execution setup for a compute node - a single process with 16 threads on the CPU, and a single process with 60 threads on each MIC device. Considering Table 1, this results in an expected average of 160.07 iterations per second. The actually achieved on a node are 157.79.

Table 2 shows the average velocity in terms of an epoch, achieved with different execution configurations, showing a good level of scalability, considering that each node executes 136 DNNs.

Figure 2 shows the achieved classification accuracy at a given epoch, comparing a serial execution with a parallel one on 10 nodes, demonstrating an

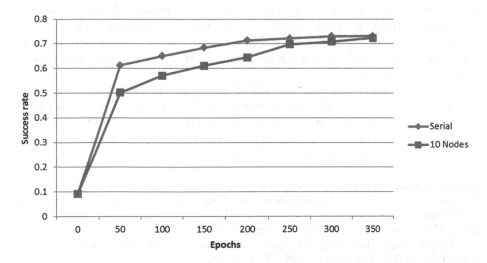

Fig. 2. The accuracy of a serial execution vs. a parallel execution on 10 nodes on the CIFAR-10 set

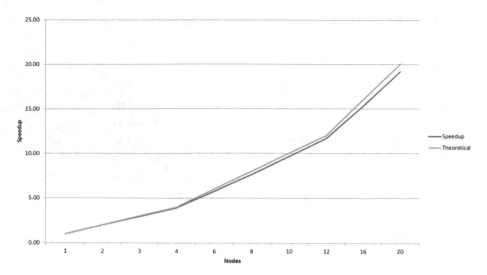

Fig. 3. The speedup achieved in terms of epochs per second

overall minor difference, considering the substantial speedup. Figure 3 compares the achieved speedup, in terms of epochs per second, to the theoretical speedup when different numbers of nodes are used, demonstrating the excellent parallel efficiency and the low communication overhead of our approach.

4   Conclusions and Future Work

In this paper, we have presented our experiments with distributed deep learning in a heterogeneous computing environment. The numerical experiments on a well-known training set and a well-studied network architecture, have proven the validity of our approach, achieving excellent results in terms of training. Additionally, the scalability testing has demonstrated the efficiency of our communication approach.

While sufficiently efficient, the gossip selection approach can be further expanded with the notion of a communicational hierarchy, based on thread coresidence and co-processor location. Additionally, experiments with different architectures and different datasets can further demonstrate the effectiveness of the approach, or provide further opportunities for perfecting it.

Acknowledgments. This work was supported by the Bulgarian Ministry of Education and Science under the National Research Programme "Environmental Protection and Reduction of Risks of Adverse Events and Natural Disasters", approved by the RCM #577/17.08.2018 and signed Agreement DO-#230/06.12.2018, as well as by the "Program for Support of Young Scientists and PhD Students at the Bulgarian Academy of Sciences - 2017" under the project DFNP-17-91.

References

1. Wan, L., Zeiler, M., Zhang, S., Le Cun, Y., Fergus, R.: Regularization of neural networks using DropConnect. In: Proceedings of the 30th International Conference on Machine Learning, vol. 28, no. 3, pp. 1058–1066. PMLR (2013)
2. Zhang, S., Choromanska, A., LeCun, Y.: Deep learning with elastic averaging SGD. In: Cortes, C., Lawrence, N.D., Lee, D.D., Sugiyama, M., Garnett, R. (eds.) Advances in Neural Information Processing Systems 28 (NIPS), pp. 685–693 (2013)
3. Krizhevsky, A.: Learning Multiple Layers of Features from Tiny Images (2009). http://www.cs.toronto.edu/~kriz/learning-features-2009-TR.pdf
4. Blot, M., Picard, D., Cord, M., Thome, N.: Gossip training for deep learning. arXiv preprint arXiv:1611.09726 (2016)
5. Daily, J., Vishnu, A., Siegel, C., Warfel, T., Amatya, V.: GossipGraD: scalable deep learning using gossip communication based asynchronous gradient descent. arXiv preprint arXiv:1803.05880 (2018)
6. Atanassov, E., Ivanovska, S., Dimitrov, D.: Parallel implementation of option pricing methods on multiple GPUs, MIPRO. In: Proceedings of the 35th International Convention, pp. 368–373. IEEE (2012)
7. Szegedy, C., Vanhoucke, V., Ioffe, S., Shlens, J., Wojna, Z.: Rethinking the inception architecture for computer vision. In: Proceedings of the IEEE Conference on Computer Vision and Pattern Recognition, pp. 2818–2826 (2015)
8. He, K., Zhang, X., Ren, S., Sun, J.: Deep residual learning for image recognition. In: Proceedings of the IEEE Conference on Computer Vision and Pattern Recognition, pp. 770–778 (2016)

Process Analysis of Atmospheric Composition Fields in Urban Area (Sofia City)

Ivelina Georgieva[✉], Georgi Gadzhev, Kostadin Ganev, and Nikolay Miloshev

National Institute of Geophysics, Geodesy and Geography,
Bulgarian Academy of Sciences, Acad. G. Bonchev Street, bl. 3, 1113 Sofia, Bulgaria
iivanova@geophys.bas.bg

Abstract. The air pollution pattern is formed as a result of interaction of different processes, so knowing the contribution of each one of the processes for different meteorological conditions and given emission spatial configuration and temporal profiles could be helpful for understanding the atmospheric composition and air pollutants behavior. Analysis of the contribution of these different processes (chemical and dynamical) which form the atmospheric composition in chosen region will be demonstrated in the present paper. To analyze the contribution of different dynamic and chemical processes for the air pollution formation over Sofia the CMAQ Integrated Process Rate Analysis option was applied. The procedure allows the concentration change for each compound to be presented as a sum of the contribution of each one of the processes, which determine the air pollution concentration. A statistically robust ensemble of the atmospheric composition over Sofia, taking into account the two-way interactions of local to urban scale and tracking the main pathways and processes, which lead to different scale atmospheric composition formation should be constructed in order to understand the atmospheric composition climate and air pollutants behavior.

On the basis of 3D modeling tools an extensive data base was created and this data was used for different studies of the atmospheric composition, carried out with good resolution using up-to-date modeling tools and detailed and reliable input data. All the simulations were based on the US EPA (Environmental Protection Agency) Model–3 system for the 7 years period (2008 to 2014). The modeling system consists of 3 models, meteorological pre–processor, the emission pre–processor SMOKE and Chemical Transport Model (CTM) CMAQ.

Keywords: Air pollution modeling · Dynamical and chemical processes · Ensemble of numerical simulation · Atmospheric composition · Process analysis

1 Introduction

An ensemble of the atmospheric composition over Sofia, taking to account the two-way interactions of different processes and track the main pathways and

© Springer Nature Switzerland AG 2020
I. Lirkov and S. Margenov (Eds.): LSSC 2019, LNCS 11958, pp. 228–236, 2020.
https://doi.org/10.1007/978-3-030-41032-2_26

processes, which lead to different scale atmospheric composition formation is constructed. This ensemble is statistically robust enough in order to understand the atmospheric composition climate and air pollutants behavior. Results about the atmospheric composition climate modelling over Bulgaria are published in a number of papers [1–11], but a detailed examination of the processes determining the atmospheric composition in urban areas have not yet been made and will be presented in the current paper. On the basis of 3D modeling tools the extensive data base was created and this data was used for different studies of the atmospheric composition, carried out with good resolution using up-to-date modeling tools and detailed and reliable input data. The air pollution pattern is formed as a result of interaction of different processes, so knowing the contribution of each one of these processes for different meteorological conditions and given emission spatial configuration and temporal profiles is useful for understanding the atmospheric composition and air pollutants origin and behavior. To analyze the contribution of different dynamic and chemical processes for the air pollution formation over Sofia city special option of the model CMAQ "Integrated Process Rate Analysis" option was applied. Process analysis allows determining the change of the concentration of the individual pollutant depending on the variation of the contribution of the individual processes that determine it.

2   Methods

On the basis of 3D modeling tools the extensive data base was created and these data were used for different studies of the atmospheric composition. All the simulations were based on the USEPA Model-3 system consists of 3 models, meteorological model WRF (Weather Research and Forecasting model) [12], the emission pre-processor SMOKE (Sparse Matrix Operator Kernel Emissions Modeling System) [13] and Chemical Transport Model (CTM) CMAQ (Community Multiscale Air Quality System) [14,15]. The data used as meteorological background is a large scale data from the NCEP Global Analysis Data with $1° \times 1°$ horizontal grid resolution. The nesting capabilities of the models are used for downscaling the simulations to a 1 km horizontal resolution for the city of Sofia. For emission input outside Bulgaria, the TNO high resolution inventory is exploited with resolution $0.25° \times 0.125°$ longitude-latitude. The inventory is produced by proper disaggregation of the EMEP 50 km inventory data base [16,17]. For the territory of Bulgaria the national emission inventory was used. Special pre-processing procedures are created for introducing temporal profiles and speciation of the emissions [7]. All the simulations are performed for 7 years period from 2008 to 2014. The Models-3 "Integrated Process Rate Analysis" option was applied to discriminate the role of different dynamic and chemical processes for the air pollution pattern formation: The procedure allows the concentration change for each compound for an hour Δc to be presented as a sum of the contribution of the processes, which determine the concentration. The involved processes here are horizontal diffusion (HDIF); horizontal advection (HADV); vertical diffusion (VDIF); vertical advection (VADV); dry deposition (DDEP); emission (EMIS); chemical transformations (CHEM); aerosol processes (AERO); cloud processes (CLDS), and in that way the Δc—sum of the contribution of the processes, that presents the concentration change is: $\sum_{i=1}^{N} \Delta c_i$, where $\Delta c_i^1 = \frac{1}{h_1} \int_0^{h_1} (c_i(t+\Delta t) - c_i(t))dz$ is the mean concentration change for the time from t to $t + \Delta t$. The equation for transport and transformation of pollutants can be written in the form:

$$\Delta c_i^1 = (\Delta c_i^1)_{hdif} + (\Delta c_i^1)_{vdif} + (\Delta c_i^1)_{hadv} + (\Delta c_i^1)_{vadv} + (\Delta c_i^1)_{drydep} + (\Delta c_i^1)_{emis} +$$
$$(\Delta c_i^1)_{chem} + (\Delta c_i^1)_{cloud} + (\Delta c_i^1)_{aero}$$

Where each right-hand term of this equation shows the change of the mean concentration due to the contribution of the respective proces for the time period from t to $t + \Delta t$.

3   Results

To analyze the contribution of different dynamic and chemical processes for the air pollution formation over Sofia the CMAQ Integrated Process Rate Analysis option was applied. The procedure allows the concentration change for each compound to be presented as a sum of the contribution of each one of the processes, which determine the air pollution concentration. The Integrated Process Rate Analysis option, allows determining not only the contributions of individual processes to a particular pollutant but also a group of pollutants. One group of gas pollutants GNOY $= NO + NO_2 + NO_3 + 2*N_2O_5 + (HONO + HNO_3 + PNA) -$ nitrogen oxides, which will be present here and also for the ozone (O_3). The outputs were averaged over the whole 7–year ensemble and so the "typical" seasonal and annual evaluations were obtained. The simulations aimed at constructing of ensemble of daily simulations for a large period (from 2008 to 2014). The "ensemble" in the present paper means a set of daily simulations for a large number of days. The annual behavior of the processes contribution to concentrations of ozone (O_3), nitrogen oxides (GNOY) for Sofia are presented.

In all the maps the contribution of the advections HADV and VADV reflect very clearly the topography of the region. They are effected also by a local circulation systems. The mountain regions in the domain are very well displayed on the map. The HADV and VADV contributions have always opposite signs, which is a manifestation of the atmosphere continuity equation. For the O_3 Fig. 1, the HADV has maximal and positive contribution in the mountain foot, while over the mountains the contribution is negative, while in that region (over Vitosha) the VADV has contribution opposite to HADV. The contribution of HDIF to the formation of O_3 is negative over the highest part of the mountain and positive in the mountain foot. The contribution of HDIF is small compared to advections and VDIF contributions, but the HDIF acts for compensating the O_3 deficiency and is in opposite phase with the CHEM, which have strictly negative impact. The road networks in the domain are powerful GNOY sources, so can be followed as O_3 sinks. The contribution of VDIF is positive and has maximum over Vitosha Mountain, because of the intensive turbulent transport of O_3 from the upper layers. This effect is very well manifested in the urban areas, where the very large GNOY surface sources cause big O_3 deficiency.

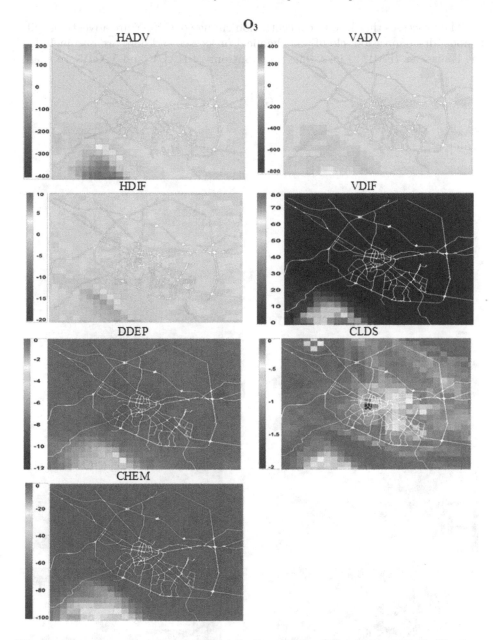

Fig. 1. Annually averaged surface contributions of the different processes to the formation of O_3 $[(\mu g/m^3)/h]$ over territory of Sofia at 06:00 GMT.

The contributions of DDEP and CLDS are negative and have maximal values over the big sources in the city—TPP Sofia in the centre and TPP Iztok.

The processes that lead to concentration change of GNOY are advections, diffusions, dry deposition, cloud and chemical processes and here are also included the Emissions (EMIS) Fig. 2. The contributions of HADV and VADV are again

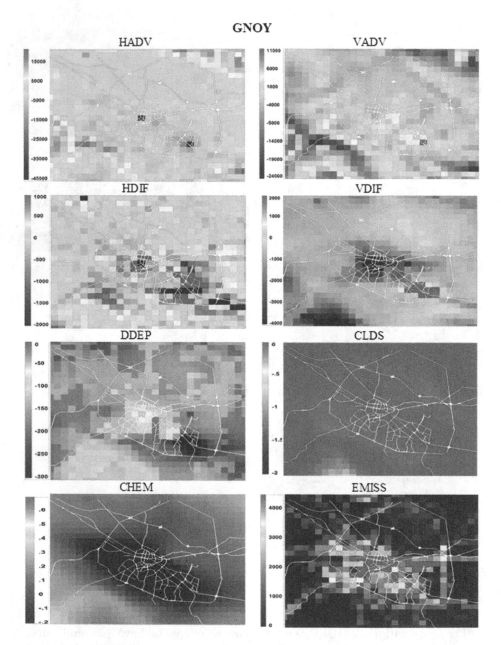

Fig. 2. Annually averaged surface contributions of the different processes to the formation of GNOY $[(\mu g/m^3)/h]$ over territory of Sofia at 06:00 GMT.

with opposite sign, but in the same order of magnitude. The diffusion impacts, are strictly opposite of these of O_3, especially where the very large nitrogen oxide surface sources cause big O_3 gaps and big negative vertical GNOY gradients. The maximal positive HDIF contribution is over the mountains foot and near the sources, while maximal negative impact is over the sources. The DDEP and CLDS contributions are negative with maximal values over the sources and mountains. The CHEM has really small impact to the formation of GNOY. The EMIS has very big impact to the formation of GNOY and the contribution is strictly positive and has maximal values over the whole city. It is easy to follow where are the big sources (TPPs Iztok and Sofia) and also the busiest road networks and autobahns. Maximal values of positive EMIS contribution are over TPPs. Figure 3 shows annual and seasonal surface contribution of the processes to the formation of GNOY and ozone. The total concentration change (Δc) in black line, which is sum of the contributions of all processes is also shown in the graphs. The Δc could be with positive or with negative sign and this depending on the type of emissions, emission sources, also weather conditions and topography of the region. The total concentration change (Δc) is a result of superposition of the contributions of all the processes, which may have large, compared to Δc values and different changing signs. To the formation of GNOY the lead contribution is of the advection (HADV and VADV) and VDIF. HADV has positive contribution in morning and afternoon hours, while it is negative around noon. The contribution of VADV is with totally oposite phase. The VDIF has strictly negative contribution with maximal values around noon. During the

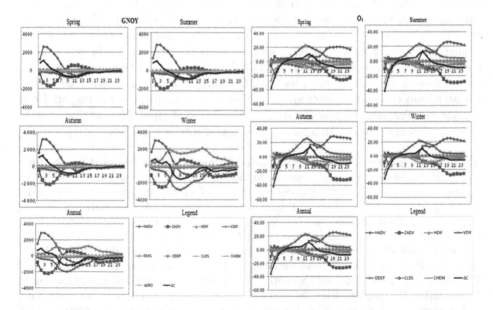

Fig. 3. Annual, seasonal and diurnal course of the contribution of the processes to the formation of (a) GNOY and (b) O_3, $[(\mu g/m^3)/h]$ averaged for the territory of Sofia.

all the seasons the contribution of EMIS is positive with small values, but it should be noticed that, during the winter this impact of EMIS is one of the dominant contribution with values bigger than those of VADV. All other processes have minimal impact. The leading contribution to the formation of O_3 has the VDIF, with total positive impact during the all the seasons, with maximum around noon. The second dominant processes that lead to concentration change of ozone is HADV in the afternoon hours, where the VADV is in anti phase according to atmosphere continuity equation. The contribution of DDEP and CHEM is negative with maximum at noon, and also they are in anti phase with VDIF. All other processes have minimal contributions.

4   Discussion and Conclusion

The results produced by the CMAQ "Integrated Process Rate Analysis" demonstrate the very complex behavior and interaction of the different processes. Further analysis of these processes, their spatial, diurnal and seasonal variability and interaction could be helpful for explanation of the overall picture and origin of the pollution in the considered region. For the whole domain Sofia, and for each of the selected items, the total concentration change (Δc) is determined mainly by a small number of dominating processes which have large values, and could be with opposite sign and phases. The total concentration change (Δc) is a result of all the processes which may have large values with opposite sign and phases and that is why the Δc could be positive, as well as negative and is different for each pollutant, the sign of the Δc depending on the type of emissions, emission sources, as well as weather conditions and topography. For the whole domain the contribution of EMIS during the winter is dominant to the formation of surface concentration of GNOY, which means that the city is largely polluting itself with nitrogen oxides. The VDIF has a major positive contribution to the surface ozone, which indicates that the surface ozone is mostly due to the transfer from the higher levels and is probably a consequence of transport from outside the domain. In general, it can be concluded that the contributions of different processes have a different behavior and interact in a very complex way.

Acknowledgments. This work is supported by projects: The National Science Program "Environmental Protection and Reduction of Risks of Adverse Events and Natural Disasters", approved by the Resolution of the Council of Ministers №577/17.08.2018 and supported by the Ministry of Education and Science (MES) of Bulgaria (Agreement №DO-230/06-12-2018; Program for career development of young scientists, BAS and Bulgarian National Science Fund (grant DN-04/2/13.12.2016).

Deep gratitude to the next organizations and institutes National Center for Environmental Prediction (NCEP) and National Center for Atmospheric Research (NCAR), The European Monitoring and Evaluation Programme (EMEP) and The Netherlands Organization for Applied Scientific Research (TNO) for providing free-of-charge data and software, the high-resolution European anthropogenic emission inventory and all others.

References

1. Georgieva, I.: Study of the air quality index climate for Bulgaria. In: Proceedings of the International Conference on Numerical Methods for Scientific Computations and Advanced Applications, Bansko, 19–22 May 2014, pp. 39–42 (2014)
2. Georgieva, I., Gadzhev, G., Ganev, K., Prodanova, M., Syrakov, D., Miloshev, N.: Numerical study of the air quality in the city of Sofia–some preliminary results. Int. J. Environ. Pollut. **57**(3/4), 162–174 (2015). https://doi.org/10.1136/jech.2009.087999
3. Georgieva, I., Gadzhev, G., Ganev, K., Melas, D., Wang, T.: High performance computing simulations of the atmospheric composition in Bulgaria and the City of Sofia. Cybern. Inf. Technol. **17**(5), 37–48 (2017)
4. Georgieva, I., Gadzhev, G., Ganev, K., Miloshev, N.: Analysis of dynamical and chemical processes which form atmospheric composition over Bulgaria. In: Proceedings of the SGEM Vienna Green 2018, vol. 18, issue 4.3, pp. 167–179 (2018). https://doi.org/10.5593/sgem2018/4.3
5. Syrakov, D., et al.: Downscaling of Bulgarian chemical weather forecast from Bulgaria region to Sofia city. In: AIP Conference Proceedings, vol. 1561, pp. 120–132. American Institute of Physics (2013)
6. Gadzhev, G., Jordanov, G., Ganev, K., Prodanova, M., Syrakov, D., Miloshev, N.: Atmospheric composition studies for the Balkan region. In: Dimov, I., Dimova, S., Kolkovska, N. (eds.) NMA 2010. LNCS, vol. 6046, pp. 150–157. Springer, Heidelberg (2011). https://doi.org/10.1007/978-3-642-18466-6_17
7. Gadzhev, G., Ganev, K., Miloshev, N., Syrakov, D., Prodanova, M.: Numerical study of the atmospheric composition in Bulgaria. Comput. Math. Appl. **65**, 402–422 (2013)
8. Gadzhev, G., Ganev, K., Prodanova, M., Syrakov, D., Miloshev, N.: Some statistical evaluations of numerically obtained atmospheric composition fields in Bulgaria. In: Proceedings of the 15th International Conference on Harmonisation within Atmospheric Dispersion Modeling for Regulatory Purposes (2013)
9. Gadzhev, G., Ganev, K., Miloshev, N., Syrakov, D., Prodanova, M.: Analysis of the processes which form the air pollution pattern over Bulgaria. In: Lirkov, I., Margenov, S., Waśniewski, J. (eds.) LSSC 2013. LNCS, vol. 8353, pp. 390–396. Springer, Heidelberg (2014). https://doi.org/10.1007/978-3-662-43880-0_44
10. Gadzhev, G., Ganev, K., Miloshev, N.: Numerical study of the atmospheric composition climate of Bulgaria-Validation of the computer simulation results. Int. J. Environ. Pollut. **57**(3–4), 189–201 (2015)
11. Gadzhev, G., Ganev, K., Miloshev, N., Syrakov, D., Prodanova, M.: HPC simulations of the fine particulate matter climate of Bulgaria. In: Dimov, I., Fidanova, S., Lirkov, I. (eds.) NMA 2014. LNCS, vol. 8962, pp. 178–186. Springer, Cham (2015). https://doi.org/10.1007/978-3-319-15585-2_20
12. Skamarock, W.C., et al.: A Description of the Advanced Research WRF Version 2 (2007). http://www.dtic.mil/dtic/tr/fulltext/u2/a487419.pdf
13. CEP: Sparse Matrix Operator Kernel Emission (SMOKE) Modeling System, University of Carolina, Carolina Environmental Programs, Research Triangle Park, North Carolina (2003)
14. Byun, D.: Dynamically consistent formulations in meteorological and air quality models for multiscale atmospheric studies Part I: governing equations in a generalized coordinate system. J. Atmos. Sci. **56**, 3789–3807 (1999)

15. Byun, D., Ching, J.: Science Algorithms of the EPA Models-3 Community Multi-scale Air Quality (CMAQ) Modeling System. EPA Report 600/R-99/030, Washington, D.C., EPA/600/R-99/030 (NTIS PB2000-100561) (1999). https://cfpub. epa.gov/si/si_public_record_report.cfm?Lab=NERL&dirEntryId=63400
16. Vestreng, V.: Emission data reported to UNECE/EMEP: evaluation of the spatial distribution of emissions. Meteorological Synthesizing Centre - West, The Norwegian Meteorological Institute, Oslo, Norway, Research Note 56, EMEP/MSC-W Note 1 (2001)
17. Vestreng, V., et al.: Inventory Review 2005 (Emission Data reported to LRTAP Convention and NEC Directive), Technical Report MSC-W 1/2005, EMEP (2005)

Modeling of PM10 Air Pollution in Urban Environment Using MARS

Snezhana G. Gocheva-Ilieva[✉], Atanas V. Ivanov, Desislava S. Voynikova, and Maya P. Stoimenova

University of Plovdiv Paisii Hilendarski, 24 Tsar Asen Street, 4000 Plovdiv, Bulgaria
{snow,aivanov,desi_voynikova,mstoimenova}@uni-plovdiv.bg

Abstract. In the modern world, attention is increasingly drawn to the pressing problem of atmospheric air pollution, which is a serious threat to human health. Worldwide, China, India, Indonesia and some of the countries in Europe, including Bulgaria, are the most polluted countries. To help solve these issues, a very large number of scientific studies have been devoted, including the study, analysis and forecasting of atmospheric air pollution with particulate matter PM10. In this study the PM10 concentrations in the town of Smolyan, Bulgaria are examined and mathematical models with high performance for prediction and forecasting depending on weather conditions are developed. For this purpose, the powerful method of multivariate adaptive regression splines (MARS) is implemented. The examined data cover a period of 9 years - from 2010 to 2018, on a daily basis. As independent variables, 7 meteorological factors are used - minimum and maximum daily temperatures, wind speed and direction, atmospheric pressure, etc. Additional predictors also used are lagged PM10 and meteorological variables with a delay of 1 day. Three time variables are included to account for time. Multiple models are created with interactions between predictors up to the 4th order. The obtained best MARS models fit to over 80% of measured data. The models are used to forecast PM10 concentrations for 7 days ahead of time. This approach could be applied for real predictions and development of computer and mobile applications.

Keywords: Air pollution · Particulate matter PM10 · Multivariate adaptive regression splines (MARS) · Forecasting

1 Introduction

Worldwide, attention is increasingly drawn to the quality of atmospheric air and the negative impact of air pollutants on the human health. In the field of ecology, there are numerous scientific studies, which indicate the worrying statistics related to bad air quality and the growing number of people who suffer

This work has been accomplished with the financial support of the MES by the Grant No. D01-221/03.12.2018 for NCDSC, part of the Bulgarian National Roadmap on RIs.

from disease and die as the result of air pollution [1,2]. Recent data show that Bulgaria ranks among the European countries with the most polluted air and the highest levels of particulate matter $10\,\mu m$ in diameter or smaller (PM10) [3,4]. The main reasons, which facilitate the generation of PM10 are the emissions of various fuel-based commercial and domestic processes, busy traffic and other, predominantly during the winter periods. In Bulgaria, 36 automated measuring stations constantly monitor the levels of 12 main pollutants, including PM10, and are controlled by the national Executive Environment Agency (EExA) [5].

In the literature, various methods for investigation and forecasting of air pollutant concentrations are used in order to ensure air quality and to prevent pollution. Multivariate linear and non-linear regression, principal component analysis, factor analysis, cluster analysis, and other have a wide range of applications [6,7]. In a large number of publications, stochastic methods for modeling time series of air pollutants are applied (see [8,9] and the literature cited therein). The most frequently used methods of this type are ARIMA, transfer function methods and others, based on the methodology of Box-Jenkins [10].

In recent years, alongside these methods, the scientific community is increasingly more interested in new computer-oriented machine-learning data-driven methods. These methods extract direct dependencies and generate mathematical models from the data. The most widely-used methods are: Artificial neural networks (ANN), Support vector machine (SVM) regression, Random Forest (RF), Multivariate adaptive regression splines (MARS), etc. In [11] forecasts are made for the concentrations of SO2 by applying three different methods - least square SVR, MARS, and M5 Model Tree. It was found that the MARS method is the second best for predicting SO2 concentrations. Authors of [12] present predicted results for PM10 concentrations for the city of Sarajevo, obtained using the ANN method and input data for meteorological variables (wind speed, humidity, temperature and pressure) over the period from 2010 to 2013. Predictive RF models are built and analyzed in [13] for data from 31 air quality monitoring sites in Switzerland using surface meteorological, synoptic scale, boundary layer height, and time variables to explain daily PM10 concentrations. A recent summary paper [14] presents the current state of air pollution forecasting methods and published results.

This study applies the non-parametric data-driven regression technique MARS to analyze and model the concentrations of PM10 in the town of Smolyan, Bulgaria. The objective of the developed empirical case study is to construct the most suitable models, which describe the measured data with the highest degree of predictive power and to forecast the future pollution for up to 7 days ahead.

Statistical procedures are carried out using the software package Salford Predictive Modeler (SPM) [15] and IBM SPSS [16].

2   Description of the Study Area and Data

The town of Smolyan is located in South Bulgaria and is the administrative center of Smolyan municipality and Smolyan province. The town has a population of 28,000 people and is the smallest main provincial town in Bulgaria. The climate of Smolyan is transitional-continental with predominant Aegean influence. The terrain is mountainous with an abundance of coniferous forests. The average altitude is around 1000 m. Winters are mild and snowy with a stable snow-cover between 80 and 120 days, and summers are cool and humid. The average temperature in January is between -1 and $-5\,°C$, and in July—between 13 and $20°$. The town of Smolyan was chosen for this study as representative of mountain settlements, regional centers in Bulgaria, with systemic pollution of PM10. Similar examples are the cities of Blagoevgrad, Kardzhali and others.

The investigation is conducted using average daily measurements of the pollutant PM10 ($\mu g/m^3$) in the town of Smolyan over a period of 9 years from 1 January 2010 to 30 November 2018 or the total number of observations is $N = 3254$. The missing data for the observed time interval of the PM10 variable are 167, which is about 5%. In the modeling procedures, the missing data are replaced using linear interpolation. The analysis also includes 13 initial predictors: CLOUD - cloud cover, HUMID - relative air humidity, MAXT - maximum daily temperature, MINT - minimum daily temperature, PRESS - atmospheric pressure, WINDSP - winds speed, PRECIP - precipitation, as well as the lagged variables: PM10_1, MINT_1, and others with the values from the previous day. In order to maintain correspondence with the weather, the models also use 3 time variables: YEAR_MONTH, MONTH, and MONTH_DAY.

Table 1 shows descriptive statistics of the initial data for the town of Smolyan. The table indicates that the average value of the pollutant PM10 is $44.14\,\mu g/m^3$, which is close to the maximum permissible average daily threshold of $50\,\mu g/m^3$ as per European and national standards [17,18]. The maximum recorded value is $260.5\,\mu g/m^3$, which exceeds the threshold by a factor of five. The initial analysis clearly shows that the PM10 air pollutant is problematic for the town.

Figure 1 shows the sequence plot of the time series for the PM10 pollutant over the considered 9-year period. The horizontal line in the plot represents the regulatory requirements of $50\,\mu g/m^3$. It clearly outlines multiple instances where this threshold value is exceeded. The exceedances for the pollutant are observed

Table 1. Descriptive statistics of the initial data.

Variable	Mean	Median	Std. dev.	Skewness	Kurtosis	Minimum	Maximum
PM10, $\mu g/m^3$	44.14	33.48	29.59	1.858	4.334	1.64	260.5
MINT, °C	8.78	9.00	9.745	-0.260	-0.592	-23	29
MAXT, °C	14.19	15.00	8.984	-0.263	-0.784	-15	33
PRESS, mbar	1016	1016	6.864	0.211	0.315	990	1039
HUMID, %	0.767	0.77	0.131	-0.260	-0.694	0.28	1
CLOUD, %	0.345	0.27	0.270	0.727	-0.478	0	1
PRECIP, cm	4.781	0.80	9.00	3.874	24.833	0	126.1
WINDSP, m/s	6.808	6.00	3.179	1.459	3.639	1	28

Note. Std. Err. of Skewness for all variables is 0.044 and Std. Err. of Kurtosis is 0.088.

mainly during the cold months of the year. This is explained by the fact that households use mainly solid fuel and coal for heating.

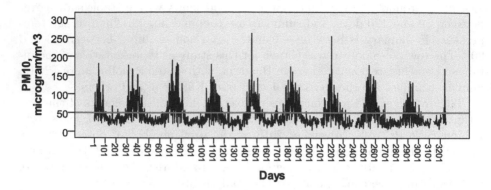

Fig. 1. Sequence plot of the measured daily concentrations of PM10 for the town of Smolyan.

3   MARS Method

The MARS method was developed by the American statistician and physicist Friedman in 1990–1991 [19]. The advantage of the MARS method lies in its ability to process both small- and large-scale datasets. If the dependent variable (here PM10) is $y = y(X)$ and the predictors $X = (X_1, X_2, \ldots, X_p)$ are vectors with dimension N, the MARS model $\widehat{y} = \widehat{y}_{[M]}$ has the following form:

$$\widehat{y}_{[M]} = b_0 + \sum_{j=1}^{M} b_j BF_j(X), \tag{1}$$

where $b_0, b_j, j = 1, 2, \ldots, M$ are the coefficients in the model, $BF_j(X)$ are its basis functions (BFs), M is their number, p is the number of predictors in the model. The form of one-dimensional BFs is one of the follows

$$BF_j(X) = \max_{X_k}(0, X_k - c_{k,j}), \quad BF_j(X) = \max_{X_k}(c_{k,j} - X_k, 0), \tag{2}$$

where $c_{k,j} \in X_k$ are nodes selected and fixed by the MARS algorithm, X_k is a variable (predictor), $k = 1, 2, \ldots, p$. For the non-linear interactions BFs are built as products of other BFs.

When constructing the model, some control parameters need to be set by the researcher. The maximum number of basis functions (L_0) and the maximum r of multipliers (i.e. degree of interactions) in BFs are set, where $L_0 \geq 3p$. The algorithm consists of two steps. During the first step, initial value for b_0 is taken (for example $b_0 = \min_i y_i$) and consequently the model is complemented by

BFs of type (2). For the current model with L number of BFs, the selection of variables and nodes is determined by the condition for minimizing the sum

$$SSL_{[L]} = \sum_{i=1}^{N} \left[y_i - \widehat{y}_{[L],i}(X) \right]^2. \tag{3}$$

The second step of the method includes an assessment of the accuracy of the constructed MARS model and reduction of the number of BFs using the general cross-validation (GCV) criterion, which takes into account not only the residuals error but also the overall error of the model [19]. BFs which do not contribute significantly to the accuracy of the model are removed. The form of the criterion is:

$$GCV_{[m]} = \frac{\sum_{i=1}^{N} \left[y_i - \widehat{y}_{[m],i}(X) \right]^2}{N(1 - C(n)/N)^2}, \quad m = 1, 2, \ldots, L_1, \quad L_1 \leq L_0. \tag{4}$$

Here $C(m) = m + \delta(m-1)/2 \in [2,3]$. The second step of the algorithm prevents the overfitting of the model. The best MARS models were selected with the highest coefficient of determination R^2, the highest GCV R^2, obtained after step 2, and the minimum values of the root mean square error (RMSE), given by the expressions

$$R^2 = \frac{\sum_{i=1}^{N}(\widehat{y}_i - \overline{y})^2}{\sum_{i=1}^{N}(y_i - \overline{y})^2}, \quad RMSE = \sqrt{\frac{1}{N} \sum_{i=1}^{N}(y_i - \widehat{y}_i)^2} \tag{5}$$

where y_i are the observed values of the dependent variable $y = PM10$, $\overline{y}$ is its mean, $\widehat{y}_i$ are the predicted values by the MARS model.

4   Results and Discussion

4.1   Construction of MARS Models

An important part in constructing MARS models is the choice of control parameters. With a relatively large volume N of the sample, a maximum number of BFs of 100, 200 and 300, and a maximum degree of interactions between the predictors r = 2, 3 and 4 were selected. Furthermore, a more detailed analysis of the PM10 observations showed only two very high measured values - 260.5 $\mu g/m^3$ and 253 $\mu g/m^3$, respectively. In order not to unnecessarily complicate the models, these two outliers were replaced by linear interpolation.

The conducted model procedures showed that the best predictive results could be obtained with the use of all 7 meteorological variables from Table 1 and their lagged variables and lagged variable PM10_1, taking into account the PM10 pollution from the previous day. As predictors, the following time variables were also used: MONTH, YEAR_MONTH and MONTH_DAY respectively, given by the expressions:

$$YEAR\_MONTH = YEAR + (MONTH - 0.5)/12, \tag{6}$$

$$MONTH\_DAY = MONTH + (DAY - 0.5)/31 \qquad (7)$$

Interactions between these time variables was ruled out. In order to assess the future forecasting model capabilities, the data for the last 7 days of the sample (24–30 November 2018) were not included in the modeling process and were used as holdout data. The total maximum number of predictors is 18. Table 2 shows the main statistics of selected best MARS models.

Table 2. Summary statistics of the selected best MARS models of PM10.

MARS model (L_0 r)	Number of BFs	$R^2, \%$	$GCV R^2$	RMSE
M1 (200; 2)	112	81.34	78.21	12.460
M2 (200; 3)	138	84.23	80.00	11.497
M3 (200; 4)	152	86.66	82.86	10.699
M4 (300; 2)	161	83.64	78.13	11.711
M5 (300; 3)	179	86.32	81.35	10.707

The obtained best MARS models describe the observed PM10 data with R2 = 86% and GCV R^2 = 83%. Models M3 (200; 4) and M5 (300; 3) have the highest performance, followed by M2 (200; 3). Since their respective RMSEs are not significantly different, we choose models M2 and M5 as the simplest models with interaction between predictors up to 3th degree. Figure 2 shows the correspondence between M5 and PM10 with a 5% confidence interval.

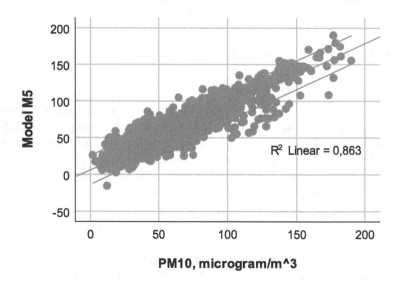

Fig. 2. Comparison of the predicted PM10 values using model M5 and the measured PM10 values.

4.2   Application of Models for Forecasting Future Pollution

The MARS method has the advantage over many other methods that it generates flexible models which allow to obtain very easy the predictions and forecasts through formulas (1)–(2) at given predictor values. Figure 3 illustrates the calculated estimates of M2 and M5 models compared to PM10 data for 7 days ahead. Very good correspondence is observed.

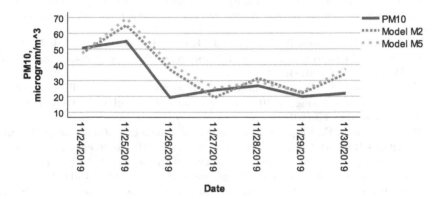

Fig. 3. Forecasting results obtained using MARS models M2 and M5 against the measured PM10 values for 7 days ahead.

5   Conclusion

With the help of the powerful data-driven method MARS statistical models for analyzing and forecasting of PM10 atmospheric air pollution data, depending on changes in weather conditions are built. Models with very good statistical characteristics were obtained. The agreement of models with measured data and their high performance for predicting future pollution concentrations has been demonstrated.

The performed analyzes and obtained results suggest that MARS can successfully be used to model other air pollutants as well as similar time series of ecology data.

References

1. Maji, J.K., Dikshit, A.K., Deshpande, A.: Disability - adjusted life years and economic cost assessment of the health effects related to PM2.5 and PM10 pollution in Mumbai and Delhi, in India from 1991 to 2015. Environ. Sci. Poll. Res. **24**(5), 4709–4730 (2017)

2. Wang, C., Zhou, X., Chen, R., Duan, X., Kuang, X., Kan, H.: Estimation of the effects of ambient air pollution on life expectancy of urban residents in China. Atmos. Environ. **80**, 347–351 (2013)
3. Piepoli, M., et al.: 2016 European Guidelines on cardiovascular disease prevention in clinical practice: the Sixth Joint Task Force of the European Society of Cardiology and Societies on cardiovascular disease prevention in clinical practice. Eur. Heart J. **37**(29), 2315–2381 (2016)
4. European Environment Agency, Air quality in Europe - 2018 report. https://www.eea.europa.eu//publications/air-quality-in-europe-2018. Accessed 22 Feb 2019
5. Executive Environment Agency. http://eea.government.bg/en/. Accessed 22 Feb 2019
6. Stadlober, E., Hubnerova, Z., Michalek, J., Kolar, M.: Forecasting of daily PM10 concentrations in Brno and Graz by different regression approaches. Austrian J. Stat. **41**(4), 287–310 (2012)
7. Ng, K.Y., Awang, N.: Multiple linear regression and regression with time series error models in forecasting PM10 concentrations in Peninsular Malaysia. Environ. Monit. Assess. **190**, 63 (2018)
8. Zheleva, I., Veleva, E., Filipova, M.: Analysis and modeling of daily air pollutants in the city of Ruse, Bulgaria. In: Todorov, M. (ed.) AIP Conference Proceedings, vol. 1895, no. 1, p. 030007. American Institute of Physics, Melville (2017)
9. Gocheva-Ilieva, S.G., Ivanov, A.V., Voynikova, D.S., Boyadzhiev, D.T.: Time series analysis and forecasting for air pollution in small urban area: an SARIMA and factor analysis approach. Stoch. Environ. Res. Risk Asses. **28**(4), 1045–1060 (2014)
10. Box, G.E.P., Jenkins, G.M., Reinsel, G.S.: Time Series Analysis, Forecasting and Control, 3rd edn. Prentice-Hall Inc., New Jersey (1994)
11. Kisi, O., Parmar, K.S., Soni, K., Demir, V.: Modeling of air pollutants using least square support vector regression, multivariate adaptive regression spline, and M5 model tree models. Air Qual. Atmos. Health **10**(7), 873–883 (2017)
12. Dedovic, M.M., Avdakovic, S., Turkovic, I., Dautbasic, N., Konjic, T.: Forecasting PM10 concentrations using neural networks and system for improving air quality. In: Proceedings of the 11th International Symposium Telecommunications (BIHTEL), Article no. 7775721. IEEE (2016)
13. Grange, S.K., Carslaw, D.C., Lewis, A.C., Boleti, E., Hueglin, C.: Random forest meteorological normalisation models for Swiss PM10 trend analysis. Atmos. Chem. Phys. **18**(9), 6223–6239 (2018)
14. Bai, L., Wang, J., Ma, X., Lu, H.: Air pollution forecasts: an overview. Int. J. Environ. Res. Public Health **15**(4), 780 (2018)
15. Salford Predictive Modeler 8. https://www.salford-systems.com. Accessed 22 Feb 2019
16. SPSS IBM 25. https://www.ibm.com/products/. Accessed 22 Feb 2019
17. Directive 2008/50/EC of the European Parliament and of the council of 21 May 2008 on ambient air quality and cleaner air for Europe. Official Journal of the European Union, L 152/1 (2008)
18. European Commission, Environment, Air, Air Quality Standards (2018). http://ec.europa.eu/environment/air/quality/standards.htm. Accessed 22 Feb 2019
19. Friedman, J.H.: Multivariate adaptive regression splines (with discussion). Ann. Stat. **19**(1), 1–141 (1991)

Application of Orthogonal Polynomials
and Special Matrices
to Orthogonal Arrays

Nikolai L. Manev[✉]

Institute of Mathematics and Informatics, BAS, Sofia, Bulgaria
nlmanev@math.bas.bg

Abstract. Special matrices are explored in many areas of science and technology. Krawtchouk matrix is such a matrix that plays important role in coding theory and theory of orthogonal arrays also called fractional factorial designs in planning of experiments and statistics. In this paper we give explicitly Smith normal forms of Krawtchouk matrix and its extended matrix. Also we propose a computationally effective method for determining the Hamming distance distributions of an orthogonal array with given parameters. The obtained results facilitate the solving of many existence and classification problems in theory of codes and orthogonal arrays.

Keywords: Orthogonal polynomials · Smith normal form · Distance distribution · Orthogonal arrays · Linear programming bound

1 Introduction

Definition 1. *Let $\mathcal{A}$ be an alphabet of q symbols. An **Orthogonal Array** $OA(M, n, q, t)$ of strength t with M rows, n columns ($n \geq t$), and q levels is an $M \times n$ matrix (array) with entries from $\mathcal{A}$ so that every $M \times t$ submatrix contains each of the q^t possible t-tuples equally often as a row (say λ times).*

Other often used notations for $OA(M, n, q, t)$ are also $OA(M, q^n, t)$ and $t - (q, n, \lambda)$, where $\lambda = M/q^t$ is called ***index***.

Orthogonal arrays are introduced by Rao in 1946 and they have been a subject of intensive investigations by many researchers coming from different scientific areas. A comprehensive study of the subject is the book [7]. Herein we give only those basic properties of orthogonal array that are necessary for presenting the goal and the place of our work.

Similar to the other combinatorial structures the problems of main interest for orthogonal arrays are ones of existence and classification up to isomorphism of orthogonal arrays with given parameters. In partial such a problem is to **find the minimal index λ for which $OA(\lambda q^t, n, q, t)$ exists.** Let $n \geq t \geq 2, q \geq 2$, $M = \lambda q^t$. An equivalent form of this problem is to determine

$$F(n, q, t) \stackrel{def}{=} \min M : there\ exists\ OA(M, n, q, t),\ i.e.,\ t - (q, n, M/q^t).$$

© Springer Nature Switzerland AG 2020
I. Lirkov and S. Margenov (Eds.): LSSC 2019, LNCS 11958, pp. 245–253, 2020.
https://doi.org/10.1007/978-3-030-41032-2_28

A table of known minimal indexes for various q can be found in [7]. One can find improvements of that table in the web sites [12] and [13].

The alphabet $\mathcal{A}$ can be a commutative ring with unity, but for our combinatorial problems it is sufficiently to assume that $\mathcal{A} = \mathbb{Z}_q$, the ring of integers modulo q.

Hamming distance $d(\mathbf{x}, \mathbf{y})$ between two vectors x and y of $\mathcal{A}^n$ is the number of places in which they differ: $d(\mathbf{x}, \mathbf{y}) \overset{\text{def}}{=} |\{i | x_i \neq y_i\}|$.

Let C be a subset (in general multi subset) of $\mathcal{A}^n$ and $\mathbf{x} \in \mathcal{A}^n$ be a fixed vector. The $n + 1$-tuple of nonnegative integers $\mathbf{p}(\mathbf{x}) = (p_0, p_1, \ldots, p_n)$ defined by

$$p_i = |\{\mathbf{u} \in C \mid d(\mathbf{x}, \mathbf{u}) = i\}|$$

is called the **distance distribution of C with respect to x**.

The knowledge of distance distributions of C with respect to vectors of $\mathcal{A}^n$ is important for studying codes and orthogonal arrays. In [1–3] authors use knowledge of possible values of $\mathbf{p}(\mathbf{x})$ to prove nonexistence of orthogonal arrays with given parameters in order to determine the minimal index.

Unfortunately to obtain distance distributions $\mathbf{p}$ all nonnegative integer solutions of systems of linear Diophantine equations have to be found. It is a computationally hard problem even for small parameters. In Sect. 4 we show how to facilitate this task.

2   Preliminaries

2.1   Krawtchouk Polynomials

Let $\mathcal{R}_n$ be the linear space of polynomials of degree up to n over real numbers $\mathbb{R}$. Let $q \geq 2$ be an integer. It is easy to check that the bilinear map defined by

$$\langle f, g \rangle \overset{def}{=} \frac{1}{q^n} \sum_{i=0}^{n} \binom{n}{i} (q-1)^i f(i) g(i). \tag{1}$$

satisfies the axioms for scalar product.

The following polynomials introduced by Krawtchouk [8] form a family of orthogonal polynomials with respect to (1).

Definition 2. Krawtchouk polynomial *is a polynomial defined by*

$$K_k(x; n, q) = \sum_{j=0}^{k} (-1)^j \binom{x}{j} \binom{n-x}{k-j} (q-1)^{k-j}, \quad k = 0, 1 \ldots n.$$

Usually q and n have already been fixed or their values are known from context. Hence for simplicity we often omit n and q and write only $K_k(x)$.

$K_k(x; n, q)$ is a polynomial of degree k in x with leading coefficient $(-q)^k/k!$. The generating function of Krawtchouk polynomials is

$$\sum_{k=0}^{n} K_k(x; n, q) z^k = (1 + (q-1)z)^{n-x}(1-z)^x. \qquad (2)$$

For fixed q and n the Krawtchouk polynomials $K_0(x), K_1(x), \ldots, K_n(x)$ satisfy

$$\langle K_k, K_l \rangle = \frac{1}{q^n} \sum_{i=0}^{n} \binom{n}{i}(q-1)^i K_k(i) K_l(i) = \binom{n}{k}(q-1)^k \delta_{kl} \qquad (3)$$

for $k, l = 0, 1, \ldots, n$, where δ_{kl} is Kronecker delta. Therefore they form an **orthogonal basis** of $\mathcal{R}_n$.

Using the properties of Krawtchouk polynomials we can derive from (3) the so called *second orthogonality relation*.

$$\sum_{i=0}^{n} K_k(i) K_i(l) = q^n \delta_{kl} \qquad (4)$$

Theorem 1. *For any polynomial $f(x) \in \mathbb{R}[x]$ of degree $\leq n$ there is a unique expansion $f(x) = \sum_{k=0}^{n} f_k K_k(x)$, where*

$$f_k = \frac{1}{q^n \binom{n}{k}(q-1)^k} \sum_{i=0}^{n} \binom{n}{i}(q-1)^i f(i) K_k(i) = \frac{1}{q^n} \sum_{i=0}^{n} f(i) K_i(k).$$

Krawtchouk matrix is referred to be the $n \times n$ matrix $\mathbf{K} = (K_i(j)), i, j = 1, 2, \ldots, n$. The $(n+1) \times (n+1)$ matrix $\widehat{\mathbf{K}}$ obtained from $\mathbf{K}$ by adding all-ones vector as a first row and $\mathbf{b} = (K_0(0), K_1(0), K_2(0), \ldots, K_n(0))^\tau$ as a first column is called the **extended Krawtchouk matrix**. The second orthogonal relation (4) gives $\widehat{\mathbf{K}}^2 = q^n \mathbf{I}_{n+1}$, where $\mathbf{I}_{n+1}$ is identity matrix of order $n+1$.

Krawtchouk polynomials play important role in coding theory. Besides the general properties of orthogonal polynomials (e.g. [14]) they posses many other interesting properties. For more detail we refer to [9,10], where the reader can find the proofs of the aforesaid properties as well as many others useful facts.

2.2   Basic Properties of Orthogonal Arrays

The next results are due to Delsarte [4–6].

Lemma 1. *Let C be $OA(M, n, q, t)$ and $\mathbf{x} \in \mathbb{F}_q^n$. If $\mathbf{p}(\mathbf{x}) = (p_0, p_1, \ldots, p_n)$ is the distance distribution of C with respect to $\mathbf{x}$ then*

$$\sum_{i=0}^{n} p_i K_k(i) = 0 \qquad \text{for } k = 1, \ldots, t. \qquad (5)$$

Let C be a (multi-)subset of $\mathcal{A}^n$. The sequence of rational numbers $\{A_i\}$, $i = 0, 1, \ldots, n$, defined by

$$A_i \stackrel{def}{=} \frac{1}{|C|} \left| \{(\mathbf{x}, \mathbf{y}) \in C^2 \mid d(\mathbf{x}, \mathbf{y}) = i\} \right|$$

is called **distance distribution** of C. Obviously $(A_0, \ldots, A_i, \ldots, A_n)$ is the mean of $\mathbf{p}(\mathbf{x})$ on $\mathbf{x} \in C$.

The next theorem demonstrates the significance of Krawtchouk matrix for the theory of orthogonal arrays.

Theorem 2 (Linear programming bound for orthogonal arrays). *Let* $n, q \geq 2, t \in \mathbb{N}$. *Then*

$$F(n, q, t) \geq \min \sum_{i=0}^{n} A_i,$$

where A_i, $i = 0, 1, \ldots, n$ *satisfy the constrains* $A_i \geq 0, A_0 \geq 1$ *and*

$$\sum_{i=0}^{n} A_i K_k(i) = 0, 1 \leq k \leq t, \qquad and \qquad \sum_{i=0}^{n} A_i K_k(i) \geq 0, \quad k = t+1, \ldots, n$$

3   Smith Normal Forms of Krawtchouk Matrix

The content of the previous section shows that the studying orthogonal arrays requires computing nonnegative integer solutions of systems of linear equations and inequalities whose matrices are Krawtchouk matrix or part of Krawtchouk matrix. Herein we prove properties of $\mathbf{K}$ and $\widehat{\mathbf{K}}$ that facilitates the solving of this task.

Lemma 2. *Let* $\mathbf{R} = (r_{ij}) = \left(\binom{j}{i} \right)$ *where* $i, j = 0, 1, 2, \ldots, n$. *Its inverse matrix is*

$$\mathbf{R}^{-1} = \mathbf{RE} = \left((-1)^{i+j} \binom{j}{i} \right), \quad \mathbf{E} = diag(1, -1, 1, \ldots, (-1)^n)$$

Proof. The proof is based on the following combinatorial identity [11, §1.2]:

$$\sum_{j=k}^{m} (-1)^j \binom{m}{j} \binom{j}{k} = (-1)^k \delta_{mk}. \text{ Using it we have}$$

$$\sum_{j=0}^{n} r_{kj}((-1)^{j+m} r_{jm}) = (-1)^m \sum_{j=0}^{n} (-1)^j \binom{j}{k} \binom{m}{j} = (-1)^m (-1)^k \delta_{mk} = \delta_{mk}.$$

$\square$

Theorem 3. *Matrix* **K** *is a product of two triangle and one diagonal* $n \times n$ *matrices, namely* **K** = **PDQ**, *where*

$$\mathbf{P} = (p_{ki}) = \left((-1)^k \binom{i}{k} \right); \quad \mathbf{Q} = (q_{ij}) = \left((-1)^{i-j} \binom{n-j}{i-j} (q-1)^{i-j} \right). \quad (6)$$

and $\mathbf{D} = \boldsymbol{diag}(q^{n-1}, \ldots, q, 1)$, $k, i, j = 0, 1, \ldots, n$. *Also* **P** *is an idempotent matrix, while* $\mathbf{Q}^{-1}$ *is absolute value of* **Q**, *that is*

$$\mathbf{P}^{-1} = \mathbf{P}, \quad \mathbf{Q}^{-1} = (|q_{ij}|) = \left(\binom{n-j}{n-i} (q-1)^{i-j} \right). \quad (7)$$

Proof. Differentiating k times (see (2))

$$\sum_{i=0}^{n} K_i(j) z^i = (1 + (q-1)z)^{n-j} (1-z)^j, \quad j = 1, 2, \ldots, n$$

for $k = 1, 2, \ldots, n$ we get

$$k! \sum_{i=0}^{n} \binom{i}{k} K_i(j) z^{i-k} = \sum_{i=0}^{n} \binom{k}{i} \frac{\mathbf{d}(1 + (q-1)z)^{n-j}}{\mathbf{d}z^{k-i}} \frac{\mathbf{d}(1-z)^j}{\mathbf{d}z^i}$$

$$\sum_{i=0}^{n} \binom{i}{k} K_i(j) z^{i-k} = \sum_{i=0}^{n} \frac{1}{(k-i)!} \frac{\mathbf{d}(1+(q-1)z)^{n-j}}{\mathbf{d}z^{k-i}} \cdot \frac{1}{i!} \frac{\mathbf{d}(1-z)^j}{\mathbf{d}z^i}.$$

$$\frac{1}{(k-i)!} \frac{\mathbf{d}(1+(q-1)z)^{n-j}}{\mathbf{d}z^{k-i}} = \binom{n-j}{k-i} (q-1)(1+(q-1)z)^{n-j-k+i}.$$

$$\frac{1}{i!} \frac{\mathbf{d}(1-z)^j}{\mathbf{d}z^i} = (-1)^i \binom{j}{i} (1-z)^{j-i}, \quad i = 0, 1, \ldots, j.$$

Obviously for $z = 1$ the right side of the second equality is nonzero only for $i = j$. Therefore

$$\sum_{i=0}^{n} \binom{i}{k} K_i(j) z^{i-k} =$$

$$\sum_{i=0}^{n} \binom{k}{i} \binom{n-j}{k-i} (q-1)(1+(q-1)z)^{n-j-k+i} (-1)^i \binom{j}{i} (1-z)^{j-i}.$$

Now setting $z = 1$ and multiplying both sides by $(-1)^k$ we have

$$\sum_{i=0}^{n} (-1)^k \binom{i}{k} K_i(j) = (-1)^{k-j} (q-1)^{k-j} q^{n-k} \binom{k}{j} \binom{n-j}{k-j}, \quad (8)$$

which in matrix form for $k, j = 1, 2, \ldots, n$ is $\mathbf{PK} = \mathbf{DQ}$. Now multiplying by $\mathbf{P}^{-1} = \mathbf{P}$ we get $\mathbf{K} = \mathbf{PDQ}$.

The proof of (7) is similar to the proof of Lemma 2.   □

Corollary 4. $\widehat{\mathbf{K}} = \widehat{\mathbf{P}}\widehat{\mathbf{D}}\widehat{\mathbf{Q}}$, *where* $\widehat{\mathbf{Q}}$ *is* $\mathbf{Q}$ *for* $n := n + 1$, $\widehat{\mathbf{D}} = diag(q^n, q^{n-1}, \ldots, 1)$, *and*

$$\widehat{\mathbf{P}} = \begin{pmatrix} 1\,1\ldots1 \\ 0 \\ \vdots \quad \mathbf{P} \\ 0 \end{pmatrix}.$$

Proof. It is easy to check that $\widehat{\mathbf{P}}^{-1} = \widehat{\mathbf{P}}$. The equality $\widehat{\mathbf{P}}\widehat{\mathbf{K}} = \widehat{\mathbf{D}}\widehat{\mathbf{Q}}$ is also the matrix form of (8) but with k and j starting from zero, not from 1. Hence $\widehat{\mathbf{K}} = \widehat{\mathbf{P}}\widehat{\mathbf{D}}\widehat{\mathbf{Q}}$.

Theorem 5. *Let for* $i, j = 0, 1, 2, \ldots, n$

$$\mathbf{R} = (r_{ij}) = \left(\binom{j}{i} \right), \qquad \mathbf{L} = (l_{ij}) = \left((-1)^j \binom{n-j}{n-i} (q-1)^{i-j} \right) \tag{9}$$

and $\mathbf{B} = diag(1, q, \ldots, q^n)$ *then* $\qquad \widehat{\mathbf{K}} = \mathbf{LBR}.$

$(\mathbf{K} = \mathbf{L}_1\mathbf{BR}_1$, where $\mathbf{L}_1$ and $\mathbf{R}_1$ are $\mathbf{L}$ and $\mathbf{R}$ with deleted first row and respectively first column.)

Proof. Multiplying $\widehat{\mathbf{P}}\widehat{\mathbf{K}} = \widehat{\mathbf{D}}\widehat{\mathbf{Q}}$ from the right by $\widehat{\mathbf{K}}$ gives

$$q^n\widehat{\mathbf{P}} = \widehat{\mathbf{D}}\widehat{\mathbf{Q}}\widehat{\mathbf{K}} \qquad \Longrightarrow \qquad \widehat{\mathbf{K}} = \widehat{\mathbf{Q}}^{-1}(q^n\widehat{\mathbf{D}}^{-1})\widehat{\mathbf{P}}$$

But $\mathbf{R} = \mathbf{E}\widehat{\mathbf{P}}$ and $\mathbf{L} = \widehat{\mathbf{Q}}^{-1}\mathbf{E}$, where $\mathbf{E} = diag(1, -1, 1, \ldots, (-1)^n)$. Since $\mathbf{E}^2 = \mathbf{I}_{n+1}$ and $\widehat{\mathbf{D}}^{-1}\mathbf{E} = \mathbf{E}\widehat{\mathbf{D}}^{-1}$ we obtain the assertion of the theorem. $\qquad \square$

Theorem 6. $\mathbf{U}_n\widehat{\mathbf{K}} = \widehat{\mathbf{D}}\mathbf{V}_n$, *where for* $k, i, j = 0, 1, \ldots, n$

$$\mathbf{U}_n = (u_{ki}) = \left(\binom{n-i}{k} \right); \widehat{\mathbf{D}} = diag(q^n, \ldots, q, 1); \mathbf{V}_n = (v_{ij}) = \left(\binom{n-j}{n-i} \right)$$

Proof. The proof is similar to one of Theorem 3 but we differentiate k times

$$\sum_{i=0}^{n} K_i(j)z^{n-i} = (z + (q-1))^{n-j}(z-1)^j, \qquad j = 0, 1, 2, \ldots, n \qquad \square$$

Corollary 7. $\mathbf{V}_n\widehat{\mathbf{K}} = \mathbf{B}\mathbf{U}_n$, *where* $\mathbf{B} = diag(1, q, \ldots, q^n)$.

Proof. Multiply $\mathbf{U}\widehat{\mathbf{K}} = \widehat{\mathbf{D}}\mathbf{V}$ by $\widehat{\mathbf{K}}$ from the right and use that $\widehat{\mathbf{K}}^2 = q^n\mathbf{I}_{n+1}$. $\square$

The reader can prove that $\mathbf{V}_n^{-1} = \left((-1)^{i-j}\binom{n-j}{n-i} \right)$ and $\mathbf{U}_n^{-1} = \left((-1)^{n-i-k}\binom{n-i}{k} \right)$ with arguments similar to ones used in Lemma 2.

Theorem 8. $\mathbf{W}_n\widehat{\mathbf{K}} = \widehat{\mathbf{D}}\mathbf{V}_n$, *where* $\widehat{\mathbf{D}} = diag(q^n, q^{n-1}, \ldots, q, 1)$,

$$\mathbf{W}_n = (w_{ki}) = \left(\binom{i}{n-k} \right); \qquad \mathbf{V}_n = (v_{ij}) = \left(\binom{n-j}{n-i} \right)$$

for $k, i, j = 0, 1, \ldots, n$. *($\mathbf{W}_n$ is flip horizontally $\mathbf{V}_n$).*

Corollary 9. $\mathbf{K} = \widetilde{\mathbf{W}}_n\mathbf{D}\mathbf{V}_{n-1}$, *where* $\widetilde{\mathbf{W}}_n$ *is* $\mathbf{W}_n = \left((-1)^{k-i}\binom{i}{n-k} \right)$ *with deleted first row and column.*

4   How to Compute Effectively Distance Distributions

Theorem 10. *Let C be $OA(M, n, q, t)$ and $\mathbf{v} \in \mathbb{Z}_q^n$. If $\mathbf{p}(\mathbf{v}) = (p_0, p_1, \ldots, p_n)$ is the distance distribution of C with respect to $\mathbf{v}$ then for any polynomial $f(x)$ of degree $\deg f \leq t$ the following hold*

$$\sum_{i=0}^{n} p_i f(i) = f_0 M, \qquad f_0 = \frac{1}{q^n} \sum_{i=0}^{n} f(i) K_i(0) = \frac{1}{q^n} \sum_{i=0}^{n} \binom{n}{i} (q-1)^i f(i) \quad (10)$$

where $f(x) = f_0 + \sum_{j=1}^{t} f_j K_j(x)$.

Proof. The value of f_0 is given by Theorem 1. Substituting $x = i$ and multiplying $f(i)$ by p_i we get

$$p_i f(i) = f_0 p_i + \sum_{j=1}^{t} f_j p_i K_j(i), \qquad \text{for } i = 0, 1, \ldots, n.$$

Summarizing on i we obtain

$$\sum_{i=0}^{n} p_i f(i) = f_0 \sum_{i=0}^{n} p_i + \sum_{j=1}^{t} \left(f_j \sum_{i=0}^{n} p_i K_j(t_i) \right) = f_0 M + \sum_{j=1}^{t} \left(f_j \sum_{i=0}^{n} p_i K_j(i) \right)$$

Now applying Lemma 1 using that C has strength t we obtain the assertion. □

The above simple corollary of Delsarte's lemma is a very useful tool for studying orthogonal arrays and partially their distance distributions. Its significance is due to the large freedom we have to choose the polynomial $f(x)$.

Setting $f(x) = x^k$ for $k = 0, 1, \ldots, t$ in Theorem 10 we obtain

Theorem 11. *Let C be $OA(M, n, q, t)$ and $\mathbf{v} \in \mathbb{Z}_q^n$. If $\mathbf{p}(\mathbf{v}) = (p_0, p_1, \ldots, p_n)$ is the distance distribution of C with respect to $\mathbf{v}$ then for $k = 0, 1, \ldots, t$*

$$\sum_{i=0}^{n} p_i i^k = \frac{M}{q^n} \sum_{i=0}^{n} \binom{n}{i} i^k (q-1)^i \quad (11)$$

Equation (11) shows that $(p_0, p_1, \ldots, p_n)$ is a solution of a linear systems with nonnegative integer coefficients. Our task is to find all its nonnegative integer solutions. It is well known that the space of solutions of a linear system $\mathbf{A}\mathbf{x}^\tau = \mathbf{b}$ is the coset $\mathbf{x}_0 + \mathbf{U}$, where $\mathbf{x}_0$ is a partial solution and $\mathbf{U}$ is the null space of $\mathbf{A}$. In our case $\text{rank } \mathbf{A} = t + 1$ thus $\dim \mathbf{U} = n + 1 - (t + 1) = n - t$. Hence $\mathbf{U}$ is generated by the rows of $(n - t) \times (n + 1)$ matrix $\mathbf{A}^\perp$ with rank $n - t$ that satisfies $\mathbf{A}(\mathbf{A}^\perp)^\tau = \mathbf{O}$.

A partial solution $\mathbf{x}_0$ can be easily computed by setting $n - t$ of variable equal to zero and solving the obtained determined system with $t + 1$ equation and $t + 1$ unknowns.

Theorem 12 gives an explicit form for $\mathbf{A}^\perp$. Its proof is based on the following lemma.

Lemma 3. *For any* $k = 0, 1, 2, \ldots, n$ *and* s *nonnegative integer*

$$\sum_{i=0}^{n} \binom{n}{i} (i+s)^k x^{i+s} = (1+x)^{n-k} g_k(x), \qquad \deg g_k(x) = k + s \qquad (12)$$

and the leading coefficient of $g_k(x)$ *is* $(n+s)^k$.

Proof. We prove the lemma by mathematical induction. The Newton binomial gives

$$\sum_{i=0}^{n} \binom{n}{i} x^{i+s} = x^s (1+x)^n.$$

Differentiating and multiplying by x we get

$$\sum_{i=0}^{n} \binom{n}{i} (i+s) x^{i+s} = (1+x)^{n-1} x^s [(n+s)x + s] = (1+x)^{n-1} g_1(x),$$

where $\deg g_1(x) = s + 1$ and its leading coefficient is $(n + s)$.

Now we have a base for induction. Assume that (12) is true. We prove it for $k + 1$. Differentiating and multiplying by x we get

$$\sum_{i=0}^{n} \binom{n}{i} (i+s)^{k+1} x^{i+s} = x \left[(n-k)(1+x)^{n-k-1} g_k(x) + (1+x)^{n-k} g_k'(x) \right]$$

$$= (1+x)^{n-k-1} x \left[(n-k) g_k(x) + (1+x) g_k'(x) \right]$$

$$= (1+x)^{n-k-1} g_{k+1}(x),$$

It is easy to check that the leading coefficient of $g_{k+1}(x)$ is $(n-k)(n+s)^k + (k+s)(n+s)^k = (n+s)^{k+1}$ and $\deg g_{k+1} = k + s + 1$. $\qquad \square$

Theorem 12. *Let* $\mathbf{A} = (a_{ij}) = (j^i)$, $i = 0, 1, \ldots, t$, $j = 1, 2, \ldots, n$. *If* $t < m \leq n$ *the vector*

$$\left(1, \; -\binom{m}{1}, \; \binom{m}{2}, \ldots, (-1)^j \binom{m}{j}, \ldots, (-1)^m, 0, \ldots, 0 \right)$$

and all $n - m - 1$ *its cyclic right shifts are linear independent and belong to the null-space of* $\mathbf{A}$. *In partial for* $m = t + 1$ *they form a basis of the null-space.*

Proof. Setting $x = -1$ and $n = m$ in (12) we obtain for $k = 0, 1, \ldots, m - 1$

$$\sum_{i=0}^{m} (-1)^{i+s} \binom{m}{i} (i+s)^k = 0.$$

This proves the theorem. $\qquad \square$

5   Conclusion

The contributions of this paper are as follows:

In Sect. 3 we give Smith normal forms of Krawtchouk matrix $\mathbf{K}$ and its extended matrix $\hat{\mathbf{K}}$. The explicit form of transformation matrices enables to facilitate computation of all nonnegative integer solutions of systems of linear equations and inequalities whose matrices are Krawtchouk matrix or part of Krawtchouk matrix. In Sect. 4 we prove that the distance distribution of an orthogonal array is a nonnegative integer solutions of systems of linear equations with integer coefficients and give an explicit form of the null space of the matrix of the linear system (Theorem 12).

The obtained results give useful tools to researchers for solving existence and classification problems in theory of codes and orthogonal arrays.

Acknowledgments. This work has been accomplished with the financial support of the Ministry of Education and Science of Bulgaria by the Grant No. D01-221/03.12.2018 for National Centre of High-performance and Distributed Computing—part of the Bulgarian National Roadmap on RIs.

References

1. Boyvalenkov, P., Kulina, H.: Investigation of binary orthogonal arrays via their distance distributions. Probl. Inf. Transm. **49**(4), 320–330 (2013)
2. Boyvalenkov, P., Marinova, T., Stoyanova, M.: Nonexistence of a few binary orthogonal arrays. Discret. Appl. Math. **217**(2), 144–150 (2017)
3. Boumova, S., Marinova, T., Stoyanova, M.: On ternary orthogonal arrays. In: Proceedings of 16th International Workshop on Algebraic and Combinatorial Coding Theory (ACCT-XVI), Svetlogorsk, Russia, 2–8 September 2018, pp. 102–105 (2018). https://www.dropbox.com/s/h7u89lh8vyirww9/Proceedings%20final.pdf?dl=0
4. Delsarte, P.: Bounds for unrestricted codes by linear programming. Philips Res. Rep. **27**, 272–289 (1972)
5. Delsarte, P.: Four fundamental parameters of a code and their combinatorial significance. Inform. Control **23**, 407–438 (1973)
6. Delsarte, P.: An algebraic approach to the association schemes of coding theory. Philips Res. Rep. Suppl. (10) (1973)
7. Hedayat, A., Sloane, N.J.A., Stufken, J.: Orthogonal Arrays: Theory and Applications. Springer, New York (1999). https://doi.org/10.1007/978-1-4612-1478-6
8. Krawtchouk, M.: Sur une généralisation des polynômes d'Hermite. Compt. Rend. **189**, 620–622 (1929)
9. Levenshtein, V.I.: Krawtchouk polynomials and universal bounds for codes and designs in hamming spaces. IEEE Trans. Inform. Theory **41**(5), 1303–1321 (1995)
10. MacWilliams, F.J., Sloane, N.J.A.: The Theory of Error-Correcting Codes. North Holland, Amsterdam (1977)
11. Riordan, J.: Combinatorial Identities. Wiley, Hoboken (1968)
12. Sloane, N.J.A.: http://neilsloane.com/oadir/index.html
13. https://store.fmi.uni-sofia.bg/fmi/algebra/stoyanova/toa.html
14. Szego, G.: Orthogonal Polynomials, vol. 23. AMS Col. Publ., Providence (1939)

Performance Effects of Running Container-Based Open-MPI Cluster in Public Cloud

Teodor Simchev(✉) and Emanouil Atanassov(✉)

Institute of Information and Communication Technologies (IICT)
at the Bulgarian Academy of Sciences, Sofia, Bulgaria
teo.tanin@gmail.com, emanouil@parallel.bas.bg, iict@bas.bg
http://www.iict.bas.bg

Abstract. The vast majority of HPC users are heavily leveraging MPI middleware for their applications needs. For almost two decades, providing an infrastructure that constantly answers the increasing demand, security standards, software interoperability, and the ineffective resources utilization are the challenges placing HPC administrators between the overhead of the virtualization and the manual tuning of the performance pick, forcing them to find the edge of the consensus on their own.

Recently, developments like Linux Containers, Infrastructure as Code, Public Cloud opened a new horizon in front of the industry, by redefining the engineering roles and providing tools and practices for solving some major caveats from the past.

This paper presents three architectures for setting up Open-MPI cluster in a Linux Container-Based environment and explains how these architectures can be implemented across private and public cloud with the main focus of the performance effects in the public cloud.

Keywords: Linux · Containers · Public cloud · HPC · Open-MPI

1 Introduction

Linux Containers have been threaded as immature and insecure technology in the past, but for the last couple of years, they have shown serious growth [1], mainly because of the evolution of the public cloud and the cloud-native applications. In a nutshell, this lightweight operating-system-level virtualization technology provides a mechanism to set up an application in an isolation from the underlying operating system. Thus it makes it portable across the variety of Linux distributions and provide a resource-controlled sandbox runtime environment with

Research described in this article was partially supported by the National Scientific Program "Information and Communication Technologies for a Single Digital Market in Science, Education and Security (ICTinSES)," financed by the Ministry of Education and Science.

I. Lirkov and S. Margenov (Eds.): LSSC 2019, LNCS 11958, pp. 254–262, 2020.
https://doi.org/10.1007/978-3-030-41032-2_29

almost neglectable performance overhead. All these characteristics made application developers and operations teams start trying to leverage this technology
in all the aspects where such issues appear.

Setting up an Open-MPI cluster could be a relatively simple or very complex
task depending on the level of integration. Keeping it healthy, secured and utilized will be another challenge. Finally extending, recreating or replicating its
setup will be the way to the theoretically unlimited resources of the Public Cloud.
All these challenges could be addressed by the Linux Containers technology and
Infrastructure as Code principles.

1.1 Generic MPI Cluster Architecture

The most common architecture of High-Performance Computing System consists of MPI cluster running an MPI middleware, an implementation of Remote
Direct Memory Access (RDMA) through one of the OpenFabrics network technologies, a Job Scheduler to plan and distribute the workloads depicted at Fig. 1
and variety of hardware specific accelerators in face of GPUs, Co-processors
contributing to the performance pitch. All of these exposed as a highly-coupled
compute resource in a private datacenter.

This architecture has been proven to serve well when it is frequently-enough
highly utilized, and when there is no need to introduce changes in a rapid manner. But dealing with system idle periods, making the latest developments from
the space of the emerging technologies available in the cluster or adjusting the
capacity-on-demand in a matter of minutes are the areas where the traditional
HPC architectures suffer most due to its static setup.

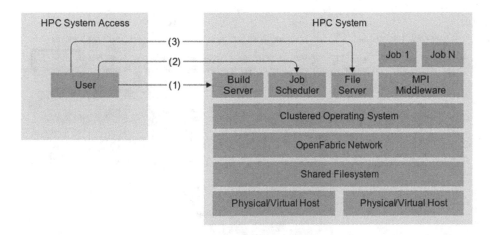

Fig. 1. MPI system architecture.

1.2   MPI Cluster Architectures in Public Cloud

There are many techniques that could be applied in order to overcome the static nature of the HPC setup, each emphasizing on a particular aspect and subdomain of use cases. Using HPC as a service in a public cloud is one of the use cases recently gaining popularity mainly because of the standard set of provided capabilities, its pay-as-you-go model and the multi-region coverage of the cloud providers.

Designing an Open-MPI cluster in the public cloud could be implemented in three ways depending on the capabilities of the provider Fig. 2.

– Bare-metal—this approach is close to the traditional private datacenter setup where hardware is maintained by a 3rd party and the heavy work on setting up the HPC system is in the hands of the user. The benefit of this approach is the performance pitch whether the downsides are the self-management, the non-utilized system idle time and system portability.
– Virtualized—with this approach cloud providers can remove significant part of the user management by templating the setup into set of virtual machines which could be placed in a most effective way on the physical hosts and improve significantly the portability. The downside of the approach is the performance overhead of the virtualization and still the limited portability due to the variety of non-compatible implementations of the hypervisors.
– Containerized—this approach is very lightweight and by its nature. It does not bring any additional computational overhead [2], allows providers and users to cooperate by enforcing infrastructure as code principles. The main disadvantage of this approach comes from the fact that it does not allow

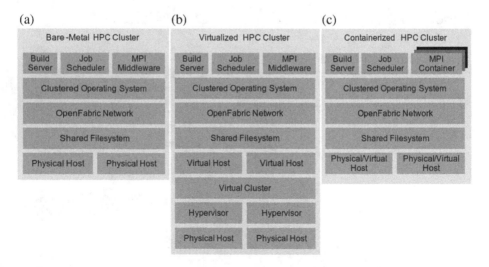

Fig. 2. Generic architectures of MPI based HPC system in public cloud (a) Bare-metal, (b) Virtualized, (c) Containerized architectures

dynamic loading of kernel modules affecting mainly the offloading to the hardware accelerators.

Comparing the containerized approach with the others clearly shows its benefits for both the users and cloud providers and it looks like that it is just a matter of time for hardware vendors to make their solutions securely accessible from the Linux containers [3,4].

2 Experimental Procedures

2.1 Kubernetes-Based MPI Cluster Architectures

As useful as the containers are, they are still only building blocks of the solution, thus the need for container orchestrator is more than obvious. For the last couple of years, there have been plenty of projects targeting Linux container orchestration but one raises above the others becoming the de-facto standard for container orchestration. Kubernetes is the orchestrator used by 32.2% of the companies leveraging the Linux container technology [5]. Today this development is an intrinsic part of the service portfolio for every public cloud provider and this is not accidental. Kubernetes is a desire-driven framework, allowing users to define what they want to achieve and leaving the details to the orchestrator. It offers a rich set of capabilities for containers, network and storage management, ability to place workloads in the best way for maximum performance and vast extensibility, like hooks and custom operators allowing to easily integrate Kubernetes with practically everything.

2.2 Method for Implementing Kubernetes-Based MPI Cluster

The implementation of an Open-MPI cluster on top of Kubernetes could benefit from all of these features at once. The approach taken for this study follows the principles of minimal footprint and maximum reusability. The outlined architecture consists of several generally reusable orchestrator-agnostic containers and the concrete service implementation on top of Kubernetes.

Base Components of the Architecture—the basic building blocks of the cluster consists of the stacked docker containers.

openmpi-base—the fundamental container image of the cluster, it is based on the bitnami/miniben [6] image, providing a Debian OS and Open-MPI (version 4.0.0) bundle with a very small footprint.

openmpi-cluster—built on top of the openmpi-base image with a preconfigured user profile for MPI related tasks, public key authentication, and SSH service. During the instantiation of this container, it allows a user to inject an SSH key in order to communicate with the container SSH daemon.

openmpi-cluster-app—built-on top of the openmpi-cluster image. This image is expected to be installed with the user's MPI program target of execution and all its dependencies.

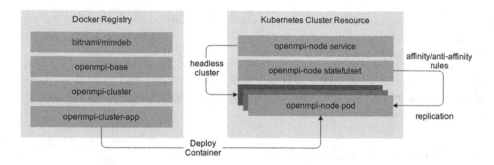

Fig. 3. Open-MPI cluster as Kubernetes resource

Kubernetes Components of the Architecture [7] (see Fig. 3).

openmpi-node pod—a pod-based on openmpi-cluster-app image where a pod is a group of one or more containers, with shared storage/network, and a specification for how to run the containers.

openmpi-node service—a headless service logically grouping openmpi-node pods where service is an abstraction which defines a logical set of pods and a policy by which to access them — sometimes called a micro-service.

openmpi-node statefulset—a stateful placement strategy for openmpi-node pods where statefulset is an abstraction managing the deployment and scaling of a set of pods and provides guarantees about the ordering and uniqueness of these pods.

2.3   MPI Benchmarks on Kubernetes-Based MPI Cluster

Analyzing the performance effects of running MPI Cluster in a public cloud requires a solid cloud provider platform and an industry-standard MPI benchmark. Google Kubernetes Engine (GKE) [8] and Intel MPI Benchmarks [9] were the two choices made for this experiment. GKE is a managed, production-ready environment for deploying containerized applications. Intel MPI Benchmarks provide a set of benchmarks that conform to MPI-1, MPI-2, and MPI-3 standards.

Container Platform Setup—the cluster used for the experiments consists of four n1-standard-1 nodes (2vCPU and 4.0 GB of memory) version 11.11.7-gke.12, each running Container Optimized OS (cos), interconnected with Ethernet achieving 1.95 Gbits/s in a bandwidth test between two instances.

MPI Container Cluster Setup—the Open-MPI cluster specification was implemented following the design outlined in Kubernetes-Based MPI Cluster Architectures. The Intel MPI benchmark has been templated as openmpi-cluster-app image used as target image for the experiment.

MPI Benchmarks Selection—the outlined data in the results section is only a subset of the executed benchmarks, emphasizing mainly on MPI point-to-point and MPI collective types of operations.

Experiment Running Container-Based MPI Cluster on shared hosts—the MPI cluster consist of four container nodes each running in compliance with host-bound anti-affinity rule guaranteeing that the Kubernetes scheduler will place and maintain each one of the nodes on a separate container platform host.

Experiment Running Container-Based MPI Cluster on exclusive hosts—the MPI cluster consist of four container nodes running in compliance with host-bound affinity rule guaranteeing that the Kubernetes scheduler will place and maintain every two of the nodes on a same container platform host.

3   Results

The results in this section are outlined in two categories first relates to the deployment time of the cluster and the second to the behavior of the MPI benchmarks.

3.1   MPI Cluster Setup Time

The time of setting up a Kubernetes-Based Open-MPI cluster in a completely automated manner, for four nodes, in a vanilla GKE cluster resulted in 14 s. This time could be further reduced for the subsequent runs due to the local caching of the base containers for each Kubernetes node. The provisioning flow for each container deployment begins right after the previous one completed successfully. This behavior is conducted by the Kubernetes StatefulSet scheduling system, which follows the master-worker architecture where master initialization must happen before the initialization of every subsequent worker node. The Open-MPI cluster could also be deployed in a headless mode where all its nodes could be provisioned simultaneously. In such a case, the total provisioning time will be 6 s when a single container node will be placed on a single host.

3.2   MPI Benchmarks—Time and Bandwidth Results

Running a workload in the cloud cannot be always very deterministic mainly because of the hidden layer of the providers and the way they manage their resources. Thus, the results outlined in this section represent the average number of the experiments' executions for 1000 subsequent iterations, as the final effect the numbers should be pretty close to reality.

MPI Ping-Pong and Ping-Ping benchmarks show the performance achieved in the communication between any two nodes of the Container-Based MPI cluster. It looks like that time for processing a message remains constant between the shared and exclusive host implementations, while constantly exceeding the message size. This is not true when it comes to the bandwidth, which progresses linearly for the Ping-Pong operation in Fig. 4(a) and much faster for the Ping-Ping at Fig. 4(b). Both figures Figs. 4 and 5 clearly shows that using shared Kubernetes hosts for running MPI cluster nodes have better overall performance

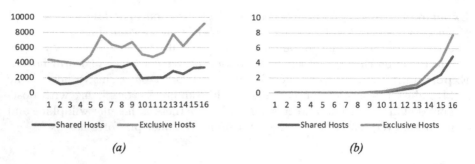

Fig. 4. MPI Ping-Pong—(a) Time/Message Size 2^k, (b) Bandwidth/Message Size 2^k

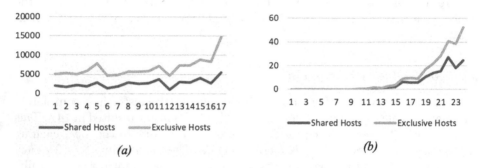

Fig. 5. MPI Ping-Ping—(a) Time/Message Size 2^k, (b) Bandwidth/Message Size 2^k

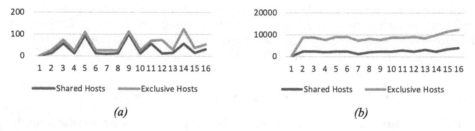

Fig. 6. MPI Scatter—(a) Time/ Min-Message Size 2^k, (b) Time/Max-Message Size 2^k

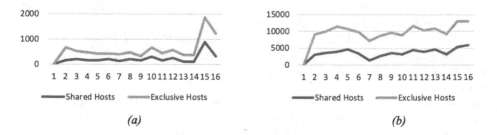

Fig. 7. MPI Gather—(a) Time/Min-Message Size 2^k, (b) Time/Max-Message Size 2^k

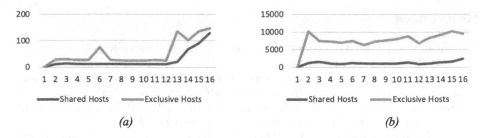

Fig. 8. MPI Bcast—(a) Time/Min-Message Size 2^k, (b) Time/Max-Message Size 2^k

compared to the exclusive hosts' scenario due to the low network latency behavior of the shared hosts.

MPI Scatter, Gather and Bcast benchmarks show the performance results of collective operations between all the nodes of the MPI cluster. Figures 6, 7 and 8 outline the deviations between the minimum (a) and maximum (b) time required to process a message, for messages with an average size between 1 byte and 216 bytes. Again, the overall performance is determined by the connectivity latency between the hosts.

4 Summary

Implementing MPI Cluster as Container-Based solution could be very useful mainly due to its standard packaging and portability, and secondary for achieving better utilization of the underlying resources by mixing HPC and distributed computing workloads. The overall performance of the cluster is conducted by the container system provider's networking, storage, and device-accelerator capabilities.

The results of the presented experiments showed that the overall performance of MPI operations is mainly determined by the networking implementation. In the case of the Ethernet-based networking stack the shared host cluster architecture provides better performance than the exclusive hosts due to the fewer network operations leaving the host boundaries.

Without any extensions both solutions architectures are applicable to the HPC workloads hosted on Ethernet enabled platforms not exposing hardware specific accelerators. For all other cases, the architectures could be enhanced with the available user space libraries for InfiniBand, Omnibus, Nvidia GPUs, Xeon Phi, etc.

A Appendix

Method Implementation Source Code available at https://github.com/tsimchev/k8s-openmpi

Method Experiments Results available at https://github.com/tsimchev/k8s-openmpi-experiments.

References

1. Bernstein, D.: Containers and cloud: from LXC to Docker to Kubernetes. IEEE Cloud Comput. **1**(3), 81–84 (2014)
2. Yong, C., Lee, G.-W., Huh, E.-N.: Proposal of container-based HPC structures and performance analysis. J. Inf. Process. Syst. **14**(6), 1398–1404 (2018)
3. Build and run Docker containers leveraging NVIDIA GPUs. NVIDIA (c2017–2019). https://github.com/NVIDIA/nvidia-docker. Accessed Feb 2019
4. Intel. Building containers for Intel Omni-Path fabrics using docker and singularity. Document number: J57474-4.0 (2017). Accessed Feb 2019
5. Add It Up: Enterprise adoption of Kubernetes is growing. TheNewStack (c2018). https://thenewstack.io/add-it-up-enterprise-adoption-of-kubernetes-is-growing. Accessed Feb 2019
6. A small image based on Debian designed for use in containers. Bitnami (c2016–2017). https://github.com/bitnami/minideb. Accessed Jan 2019
7. Beda, J., Burns, B., Hightower, K.: Kubernetes Up and Running, p. 36, p. 44 (2017). ISBN 9781491935668
8. Containerized Application Management at Scale (c2019). https://cloud.google.com/kubernetes-engine/. Accessed Feb 2019
9. Intel(R) MPI Benchmarks. Intel (c2019). https://github.com/intel/mpi-benchmarks. Accessed Feb 2019

Impact of Data Assimilation on Short-Term Precipitation Forecasts Using WRF-ARW Model

Evgeni Vladimirov[1,2]($\boxtimes$) (ID), Reneta Dimitrova[1] (ID), and Ventsislav Danchovski[1] (ID)

[1] Sofia University "St. Kliment Ohridski", Sofia, Bulgaria
evgeniv@uni-sofia.bg
[2] Bulgarian Air Traffic Services Authority, Sofia, Bulgaria

Abstract. In spite of efforts made by the scientific community during the last decades on the weather forecast improving, prediction of precipitation systems and fogs is still considered to be a difficult challenge. The main reason for the difficulties in prediction of these phenomena is the complexity of their formation, such as orography dependence, spatio-temporal inhomogeneity of land use and large scale synoptic conditions. Remote sensing and in-situ data assimilation have been applied to a number of studies in recent years, demonstrating significant improvements of the model results.

The objective of this study is to evaluate the performance of Weather Research and Forecasting (WRF) model, and assess the improvement in the short-term precipitation forecast, using high-resolution data assimilation of satellite and in-situ measurements. The study case is specific weather phenomenon for the Eastern parts of Balkan Peninsula - passing winter Mediterranean cyclone causing excessive amounts of rainfall in Bulgaria. A three-dimensional variational (3D-Var) data assimilation system is used in this study. The model results obtained using or not data assimilation procedure, are compared to demonstrate the impact of this method on the start time of precipitation, rainfall spacial distribution and amount.

Keywords: WRF · 3D-VAR · Data assimilation · Weather forecast

1   Introduction

The comprehensive understanding of the physical phenomena and their interactions is of key importance for solving theoretical and practical problems that are relevant to the human safety and comfort, and is also very essential for generating weather and climate change forecasts. Terrain and land-use inhomogeneity induce meso-scale flows with thermal circulation domination under quiescent conditions, or significant modification of the large-scale synoptic flow [1].

Huge diversity of processes is presented in complex terrain, such as up/downslope and valley flows; katabatic pooling of cold air in valleys during the night and associated exclusive phenomena like entrainment into, and

The original version of this chapter was revised: an acknowledgement has been added. The correction to this chapter is available at https://doi.org/10.1007/978-3-030-41032-2_73

I. Lirkov and S. Margenov (Eds.): LSSC 2019, LNCS 11958, pp. 263–271, 2020.
https://doi.org/10.1007/978-3-030-41032-2_30

detrainment from, slope and valley flows; intermittent release of air from mountain canyons; gap flows; lee waves. The great variability in spatial and temporal scales, involved in complex terrain phenomena, makes their study very complicated as both scales, meso and micro, become significant, as does as their interaction with each other. Despite of efforts of the scientific community over the past three decades, the gap in knowledge continues to challenge the accuracy of meso and smaller scale weather predictions in complex terrains, as existing sub-grid parametrization (especially for microphysics and turbulence) fail to describe the rapid spatial and temporal variability and intricate dynamics.

Sofia city is surrounded by mountains and all effects described above affect the flow dynamics leading to difficulty in weather forecast. The prediction of the cloud formation and precipitation is a great challenge in meso-scale models. One method to improve the accuracy of short-term precipitation forecast is data assimilation. This method is attractive during the last decade due to meteorological data available from different sources and increasing power of modern supercomputers. The impact of high-resolution data assimilation on short-term mesoscale numerical weather prediction using the Weather Research and Forecasting model (WRF) and its data assimilation module (WRFDA) in a winter cyclone passing over Bulgaria was investigated. The objective of the study is to assess the impact of in-situ and remote sensing data assimilation to the forecast.

2   Model Set Up for the Sofia Region

2.1   WRF Model Set up

The WRF model, version 3.8.1 is used for the numerical experiments. High resolution numerical modelling in both directions - horizontal (500 m grid) and vertical (50 irregular stretched vertical levels with greater density in the PBL) is required for this study. Detailed representation of topography and land cover for Sofia region is very important with the fine resolution used in this study. Two datasets are implemented in WRF - for topography with 1-arc-second resolution (SRTM, NASA; https://lta.cr.usgs.gov/SRTM1Arc), and more accurate physical surface properties via CORINE 2012 landuse with 3-arc-second resolution (CLC2012, EEA; https://land.copernicus.eu/pan-european/corine-land-cover/clc-2012) [9].

Domains used in simulations are shown in Fig. 1. Four nested domains are used based on a Lambert Projection (Fig. 1), which essentially covered Balkan Peninsula (Domain 1, D1), Bulgaria (Domain 2, D2), Western part of Bulgaria (Domain 3, D3) and Sofia Valley (Domain 4, D4). The most inner domain has 157×129 cells with resolution of 500 m. The initial and boundary conditions are 6 h forecast from NCEP GSF 27.11.2015 06 UTC run (for the parent domain D1) and are derived from the 0.25° NCEP GFS Global Forecast Grids Historical Archive (http://rda.ucar.edu/datasets/ds084.1/) on every 6 h.

The WRF physics package includes: a Lin et al. microphysics scheme [2], the Rapid Radiative Transfer Model (RRTM) longwave radiation parameterization [3], Dudhia shortwave radiation parameterization [4], Noah land surface

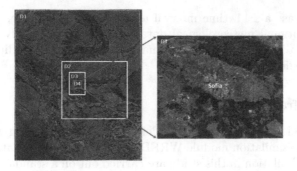

Fig. 1. Domains used in the model simulations. D1 domain includes Balkan Peninsula, D2 covers Bulgaria. D3 and D4 domains cover Sofia region.

model [5]. Simplified Arakawa - Schubert cumulus parameterization [6] is used only for D1 and D2. For high resolution domains D3 and D4 cumulus formation is resolved explicitly by the microphysics. Yonsei University - YSU [7] was selected based on previous comparison [8,9].

2.2   WRFDA 3D-var Set Up

There are a number of data assimilation techniques used in weather forecasting. One of the most prominent are the three- and four-dimensional variational data assimilation methods (3D-var and 4D-var). 3D-var incorporates meteorological data only within a time window around the initialization moment and in this method the analysis increment (an increment is introduced due to the actual observations) does not evolve in time, e.g. it has effect only at the beginning of the simulation. On the other hand 4D-var method uses tangent linear and adjoint models which model the propagation of analysis increment and more computing time is needed [12]. The 3D-var data assimilation method [11] from WRFDA [10] module version 3.8.1. is exploited with the simulations.

The 3D-var data assimilation method represents the process of combining observations and short-range forecasts to obtain initial conditions for the weather forecast simulations at set time intervals.

$$J(x) = (x - x_b)^T \mathbf{B}^{-1}(x - x_b) + (y - H[x])^T \mathbf{R}^{-1}(y - H[x]) = J_b - J_o \qquad (1)$$

In (1) J(x) is called cost function of the analysis (penalty function); J_b is the background term and J_o is the observation term. With data assimilation implementation the initial and boundary conditions at the starting time are corrected so that the cost function of the given element has minimum value.

We apply in this study the standard background error statistics **B** from generic background error data file, provided with the WRFDA module, and the standard variational bias correction. WRFDA is capable of using two radiative transfer models for retrieving meteorological data from remote sensing satellite observations - RTTOV and CRTM. The last one is exploited in this work. For the particular case a ±1 h time interval around the initialization of the model is used for additional meteorological data assimilation. The advantage of this methodology is to provide the best estimation of the initial conditions by gathering meteorological observations.

2.3 HPC Infrastructure

The WRF model is designed to be parallel computing code along with its corresponding data assimilation module WRFDA [13]. Weather simulations and variational data assimilation in this study are carried out on a standard HPC infrastructure - the PHYSON cluster (http://physon.phys.uni-sofia.bg/hardware-en). It is a compact 216 core high performance linux cluster. The system has a 524 GiB of RAM and 6.5 TB disk space needed to store the output of the simulations that are usually large - ranging from few to several tens of gigabytes in size. Most computing nodes consist of 8-core SMP platforms. PHYSON is installed in Sofia University and dedicated to support scientific research and education.

3   Conventional and Nonconventional Observations for Data Assimilation

There are two types of data typically assimilated - conventional and nonconventional. The difference is that conventional are provided in GTS (Global Telecommunication System) and nonconvenitonal could be local, for example satellite, radar, rain gauges, automated weather stations and other. Due to large spatial coverage satellite data from a number of space based sensors are chosen to be assimilated in this particular study. The conventional data from GTS (included in Table 1) and observations from instruments on sun-synchronous orbiting satellites (included in Table 2), available in the time interval around noon (from 11:00 UTC to 13:00 UTC) and thereafter, have been assimilated. The observations used in this work are presented in Tables 1 and 2.

4   Case Study

27.11.2015 (Synoptic analysis)
The case study is well-defined low pressure system above Ionian sea, with center situated west of Bulgaria (see Fig. 2). The south-western flow transported moist and warm air over western Balkans. A warm front and a cold front has consecutively passed over Bulgaria during the next few days followed by an occlusion. The system has provoked intensive precipitation over the Sofia region, started as rain from occasional thunderstorms, and turned into snow with the temperature decrease. Bad weather conditions have caused difficulties in traffic and electricity provision.

Table 1. Number of conventional observations assimilated in each domain

Conventional observations	D1	D2	D3	D4
Sounding reports	9	1	1	1
Synoptic reports	359	58	4	2
Geostationary satellite atmospheric motion vectors	480	90	3	0
GPS Refractivities	300	0	0	0
METAR reports	99	15	1	1
Ship reports	7	0	0	0

Table 2. Data source for nonconventional observations assimilated in each domain

D1	D2	D3	D4
noaa19-amsua	noaa19-amsua	noaa19-amsua	noaa19-amsua
eos2-airs	eos2-airs	-	-
eos2-amsua	eos2-amsua	eos2-amsua	eos2-amsua
jpss0-atms	jpss0-atms	jpss0-atms	jpss0-atms
noaa19-mhs	noaa19-mhs	noaa19-mhs	-

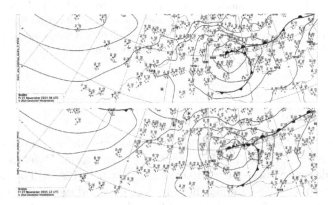

Fig. 2. Analysis from DWD (taken from wetter3.de) for 27.11.2015 of surface pressure (hPa) and frontal systems. The upper is for 06 UTC and the lower - 12UTC

5   Results and Discussion

5.1   Numerical Experiments

Several sources of observations are used in this study - surface observations (Synoptic, METAR and Ship reports, Table 1), upper air observations (Sounding reports, Table 1) and satellite data (Geostationary satellite atmospheric motion vectors and GPS Refractivities, Table 1 and all instruments, Table 2). Observational data are named satellite and non-satellite (surface and upper air observations) for further convenience. Four different numerical experiments are performed – (1) simulation without data assimilation; (2) simulation with only satellite data assimilated; (3) simulation with only non-satellite data assimilated; (4) simulation with satellite and non-satellite data assimilated. The effect on different type data assimilation on short-term local forecast is estimated by plotting differences in fields of temperature and water vapor mixing ratio.

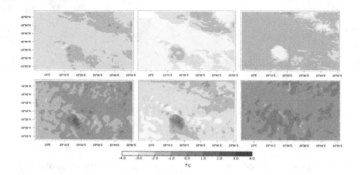

Fig. 3. Temperature (T) field differences at first sigma model level ($\sim$10 m) - (a), (b), (c); and at the 30-th sigma model level ($\sim$1500 m) - (d), (e), (f). T field difference between the case with all data assimilation and the field without assimilation (a, d); between satellite observations assimilation and the field without assimilation (b, e); between non-satellite data assimilation and the field without assimilation

5.2 Temperature

The correct analyses of the temperature fields near the surface and aloft is important, especially for assessment of the type of precipitation. Differences between results from described above experiments are shown in Fig. 3. The assimilation of non-satellite data is less significant (Fig. 3c, f), providing cooling effect $\sim$1 °C at first model level ($\sim$10 m) and do not affect the upper levels (the main reason is that only 1 measurement per day at one location is available from the sounding reports in this area). Satellite data assimilation has meaningful effect at all levels, leading to cooling effect near the ground ($\sim$3–4 °C) which is extended in PBL above the valley floor, but in opposite show warming effect at the higher levels above the Vitosha mountain.

5.3 Water Vapor Mixing Ratio

Water vapor mixing ratio (WVMR) is used in synoptic analysis to provide information on the air mass moisture content above the area of interest. High WVMR and low temperatures are a sign for a possible precipitation. Differences between results from described above experiments are shown in Fig. 4. Again the effect of

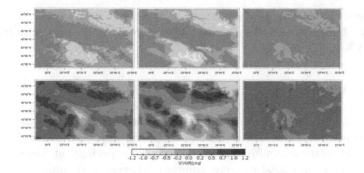

Fig. 4. WVMR field differences at first sigma model level (~10 m) - (a), (b), (c); and at the 30-th sigma model level (~1500 m) - (d), (e), (f). WVMR difference between assimilated all data and without assimilated data (a, d); between satellite observations assimilation and without assimilation (b, e); between non-satellite data assimilation and without assimilation (c, f)

satellite data assimilation is more significant. The model output with assimilation provide higher moisture inside the valley and drier air above the mountains at the near surface level (Fig. 4a, b). The moisture augmentation due to satellite assimilation is more significant at higher level (Fig. 4d, e).

6   Vertical Profiles of Temperature and Relative Humidity

A comparison between vertical profiles of temperature and relative humidity extracted from simulations with and without data assimilation is shown in Fig. 5. The effect of satellite data assimilation is very significant for the relative humidity. Only surface data assimilation is not enough to correct deficit in model

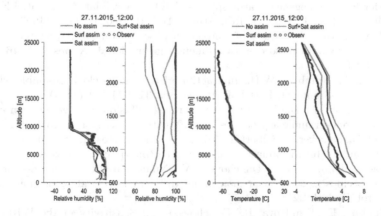

Fig. 5. Vertical profiles of relative humidity (left) and temperature (right). Different altitudes are shown, the right parts of both plots are zoomed to the 2500 m to emphasize on the differences in the PBL

results. Better agreement with observations is registered in both vertical profiles inside PBL. Using satellite data assimilation increase the relative humidity with ~10% and reduce temperature with ~4 °C.

7 Conclusions

Conventional and nonconventional meteorological data had been assimilated in this case study. Satellite data assimilation showed improved prediction of temperature and relative humidity for Sofia region, especially at lower altitudes. Meteorological characteristics were simulated better with only satellite data assimilation, moreover including non-satellite observations in assimilation process diverted results from the actual observations. The case study showed that 3D-var data assimilation in WRF could be used for improving prediction of temperatures and humidity, that are crucial for the precipitation forecasts in Sofia region.

Acknowledgements. This work has been supported by Research Fund at the Bulgarian Ministry of Education and Science, grant number DN4/7 (Study of the PBL structure and dynamics over complex terrain and urban area). We acknowledge also the provided access to the e-infrastructure of the NCDSC - part of the Bulgarian National Roadmap on RIs, with the financial support by the Grant No D01-221/03.12.2018.

References

1. Bodine, D., Klein, P.M., Arms, S.C., Shapiro, A.: Variability of surface air temperature over gently sloped terrain. Appl. Meteorol. Climatol. **48**, 1117–1141 (2009)
2. Lin, Y.L., Farley, R.D., Orville, H.D.: Bulk parametrization of the snow field in a cloud model. J. Appl. Meteorol. **22**, 1065–1092 (1983)
3. Mlawer, E.J., Taubman, S.J., Brown, P.D., Iacono, M.J., Clough, S.A.: Radiative transfer for inhomogeneous atmospheres: RRTM, a validated correlated-k model for the longwave. J. Geophys. Res. Atmos. **102**(4), 16,663–16,682 (1997)
4. Dudhia, J.: Numerical study of convection observed during the winter monsoon experiment using a mesoscale two-dimensional model. J. Atmos. Sci. **46**, 3077–3107 (1989)
5. Arakawa, A., Schubert, W.H.: Interaction of a cumulus cloud ensemble with the large-scale environment, Part I. J. Atmos. Sci. **31**, 674–701 (1974)
6. Hong, S., Noh, Y., Dudhia, J.: A new vertical diffusion package with an explicit treatment of entrainment processes. Mon. Weather Rev. **134**(9), 2318–2341 (2006)
7. Arnold, D., Schicker, I., Seibert, P.: High-resolution atmospheric modelling in complex terrain for future climate simulations (HiRmod). VSC report (2010)
8. Egova, E., Dimitrova, R., Danchovski, V.: Numerical study of meso-scale circulation specifics in the Sofia region under different large-scale conditions. Bul. J. Meteorol. Hydrol. **22**(3–4), 54–72 (2017)
9. Vladimirov, E., Dimitrova, R., Danchovski, V.: Sensitivity of the WRF model results to topography and land cover: study for the Sofia region, Annuaire de l'Université de Sofia "St. Kliment Ohridski", Faculté de Physique **111**, 87–101

10. Barker, D., et al.: The weather research and forecasting model's community variational/ensemble data assimilation system: WRFDA. Bull. Am. Meteorol. Soc. **93**, 831–843 (2012)
11. Barker, D.M., Huang, W., Guo, Y.-R., Bourgeois, A.J., Xiao, Q.N.: A three-dimensional (3DVAR) data assimilation system for use with MM5: implementation and initial results. Mon. Weather Rev. **132**, 897–914 (2004)
12. Mazzarella, V., Maiello, I., Capozzi, V., Budillon, G., Ferretti, R.: Comparison between 3D-Var and 4D-Var data assimilation methods for the simulation of a heavy rainfall case in central Italy. Adv. Sci. Res. **14**, 271–278 (2017)
13. Shainer G., et al.: Weather research and forecast (WRF) model performance and profiling analysis on advanced multi-core HPC clusters. Conference. linuxclusterinstitute.org (2017)

Large-Scale Models: Numerical Methods, Parallel Computations and Applications

An Introduction and Summary of Use of Optimal Control Methods for PDE's

Owe Axelsson[1,2]([⊠])([iD])

[1] Institute of Geonics, The Czech Academy of Sciences, Ostrava, Czech Republic
[2] Department of Information Technology, Uppsala University, Uppsala, Sweden
owe.axelsson@it.uu.se

Abstract. In optimal control formulations of partial differential equations the aim is to find a control function that steers the solution to a desired form. A Lagrange multiplier, i.e. an adjoint variable is introduced to handle the PDE constraint. One can reduce the problem to a two-by-two block matrix form with square blocks for which a very efficient preconditioner, PRESB can be applied. This method gives sharp and tight eigenvalue bounds, which hold uniformly with respect to regularization, mesh size and problem parameters, and enable use of the second order inner product free Chebyshev iteration method, which latter enables implementation on parallel computers without any need to use global data communications. Furthermore this method is insensitive to round-off errors. It outperforms other earlier published methods. Implementational and spectral properties of the method, and a short survey of applications, are given.

Keywords: Optimal control · Preconditioner · Inner product free

1 Introduction

Optimal control problem formulation are fundamental for the construction and test of many equipments in engineering and elsewhere. In a mathematical formulation of them, one considers a domain of definition, Ω which covers the machine or other equipment. The main idea is to control the performance of the machine by use of a control function. This can be a distributed control, (v) that is, defined on the whole of Ω or only on part (Ω_C) of Ω, frequently (part of) the boundary $\partial\Omega$. The solution (u) is normally a solution of a partial differential equation defined on the whole of Ω, but frequently measured, i.e. observed only on a subdomain, Ω_0 or part of the boundary $\partial\Omega$. One has then a target solution defined there and wants to compute the control function so that the computed solution is as close as possible to that desired function.

The work is supported by The Ministry of Education, Youth and Sports of the Czech Republic from the National Programme of Sustainability (NPU II), project "IT4Innovations excellence in science - LQ1602".

© Springer Nature Switzerland AG 2020
I. Lirkov and S. Margenov (Eds.): LSSC 2019, LNCS 11958, pp. 275–283, 2020.
https://doi.org/10.1007/978-3-030-41032-2_31

Since such a problem is of inverse type, i.e. ill-posed, it must be regularized, i.e. a Tichonov type of penalty term is added to the functional to be minimized. One uses then mostly the square of the $L_2(\Omega_C)$-norm of the control function. The paper is structured as follows. In Sect. 2 the optimal control framework is presented followed by the preconditioning method in Sect. 3. Inner product free acceleration methods are then shortly presented in Sect. 4 and the paper ends with some concluding remarks.

2   An Optimal Control Framework

The optimal control framework leads to a linear or nonlinear algebraic equation to be solved. We present a general framework and give some examples of constrained PDE problems.

2.1   The Optimal Control Formulation

The functional to be minimized is

$$J(u,v) = \frac{1}{2}\|u - u_d\|_{\Omega_0}^2 + \frac{1}{2}\beta\|v\|_{L_2(\Omega_C)}^2$$

subject to a state partial differential equation,

$$\mathcal{L}(u) = v + g \quad \text{in} \quad \Omega \quad \text{or} \quad \mathcal{L}(u) = g \quad \text{in} \quad \Omega, \quad u|_{\partial\Omega} = v|_{\partial\Omega},$$

where g is a given source function.

The functional is extended to include the constraint by use of a Lagrange multiplier w, to form

$$F(u,v,w) = J(u,v) + \int_{\Omega} w\mathcal{L}(u) \tag{1}$$

for which we seek the $\inf_{u,v}\sup_{w}$ solution. If $\mathcal{L}(u) = Ku$ for some operator K, then

$$\int_{\Omega} w\mathcal{L}(u) = \int_{\Omega} wKu = \int_{\Omega} uK^*w,$$

where K^* is the adjoint operator to K, that is, the Lagrange multiplier plays the rule of an adjoint function to u.

2.2   Examples of State Differential Equations

The simplest example is when

$$\mathcal{L}(u) = -\Delta u + cu, \quad c \geq 0 \quad \text{in} \quad \Omega$$

i.e. a Poisson equation, which is completed with proper boundary conditions. Another example, see [1] is where

$$\mathcal{L}(u) = \begin{cases} -\Delta \mathbf{u} + \nabla p = f \\ \nabla \cdot \mathbf{u} \qquad\quad = 0 \text{ in } \Omega, \end{cases}$$

which is the Stokes equation with pressure p, also completed with boundary conditions for the vectorial function $\mathbf{u}$. In these problems we can use standard finite element approximations. Frequently one imposes a time-harmonic constraint on the solution, see [2–4]. Take as an example, see [2,4], the electromagnetic equation,

$$\sigma \frac{\partial u(\mathbf{x},t)}{\partial t} + \mathbf{curl}(v\,\mathbf{curl}(\mathbf{u}(\mathbf{x},t))) + \delta \mathbf{u}(\mathbf{x},t) = \mathbf{v}(\mathbf{x},t) \quad \text{in } Q_T,$$
$$\mathbf{u}(\mathbf{x},t) \times \mathbf{n} = \mathbf{0} \qquad \text{on } \Sigma_T, \qquad (2)$$
$$\mathbf{u}(\mathbf{x},0) = \mathbf{v}(\mathbf{x},T) \quad \text{in } \Omega, \quad \mathbf{v}(\mathbf{x},0) = \mathbf{v}(\mathbf{x},T) \text{ in } \Omega,$$

where $Q_T = \Omega \times (0,T)$ is the space-time cylinder and $\Sigma_T = \Gamma \times (0,T)$ is its lateral surface, $\Sigma_0 = \Gamma \times \{0\}$, Ω is an open and bounded domain in $\mathbb{R}^d$ for $d \in 2,3$ with Lipschitz-continuous boundary Γ, and $\mathbf{n}$ is the unit outward normal vector to $\partial \Omega$. Here, σ and v denote the electrical conductivity and magnetic reluctivity, respectively and δ is a small positive parameter. The conductivity $\sigma \in L^\infty(\Omega)$ is a positive constant, the reluctivity $v \in L^\infty(\Omega)$ is uniformly positive and independent on $\mathbf{u}(x,t)$.

Here the control function $\mathbf{v}$ is distributed in the whole domain. Under the assumption that the target solution and the control function are time-harmonic, i.e.,

$$\mathbf{u}_d(\mathbf{x},t) = \widehat{u}(\mathbf{x})e^{i\omega t} \quad \text{and} \quad \mathbf{v}(\mathbf{x},t) = \widehat{v}(\mathbf{x})e^{i\omega t}$$

then $\widehat{u}, \widehat{v}$ are the solutions of the stationary control problem,

$$\min_{\mathbf{u},\mathbf{v}} \frac{1}{2} \int_\Omega |\widehat{u}(\mathbf{x}) - u_d^2(\mathbf{x})|^2 \, dx + \frac{1}{2}\beta \int_\Omega |\widehat{u}(\mathbf{x})|^2 dx,$$

subject to the **curl-curl** operator state equation,

$$i\omega\sigma\widehat{\mathbf{u}}(\mathbf{x}) + \mathbf{curl}(v\,\mathbf{curl}(\mathbf{u}(\mathbf{x}))) + \varepsilon\widehat{\mathbf{u}}(\mathbf{x}) = \widehat{\mathbf{v}}(\mathbf{x}) \text{ in } \Omega,$$
$$\widehat{\mathbf{u}}(\mathbf{x}) \times \mathbf{n} = \mathbf{0} \qquad \text{on } \Gamma.$$

Thus for time-harmonic problems the time-dependent optimal control problem can be transformed to the numerical solution of a time-independent problem. Here one can use the Nédélec **curl** conforming edge finite element basis functions.

2.3   Bound Constrained Solutions or Control Functions

In many practical problems one must impose bounds on the solution to avoid that it reaches values where the equipment or its surrounding can be damaged. Assume then that for such safety reasons the solution $\mathbf{u}$ must be found in an interval $[a, b]$, that is, $a \leq u \leq b$. To impose this additional constraint one can add an extra penalty function with a small parameter $\varepsilon \geq 0$,

$$
\begin{aligned}
J(u, v) = {} & \frac{1}{2}\|u - u_d\|^2_{L^2(\Omega_0)} + \frac{\beta}{2}\|v\|^2_{L^2(\Omega)} + \frac{1}{2\varepsilon}\|\max 0, u - \overline{u}\|^2_{L^2(\Omega_0)} \\
& + \frac{1}{2\varepsilon}\|\min 0, u - \underline{u}\|^2_{L^2(\Omega_0)}
\end{aligned}
\tag{3}
$$

This is the Moreau-Yosida approach, see [5] and the references therein.

Other applications of the optimal control framework are for the solution of time-dependent problems by use implicit Runge-Kutta methods of Radau types, see [6], and solving inverse problems with missing boundary data or missing interior coefficients in elliptic partial differential equations, see [7].

2.4   The First Order Optimality Equations

To compute the optimal solution to (1) one applies the K-K-T first order necessary conditions. Due to the regularization term, these conditions lead also to a unique solution. This leads to a block system of equations. It is easier to write the corresponding matrix equations in the block matrix equation form. After discretization procedure it results to,

$$
\begin{bmatrix} M_0 & 0 & K^T \\ 0 & \beta M_C & -M \\ K & -M & 0 \end{bmatrix} \begin{bmatrix} \mathbf{u} \\ \mathbf{v} \\ \mathbf{w} \end{bmatrix} = \begin{bmatrix} M_0 \mathbf{u}_d \\ 0 \\ \mathbf{g} \end{bmatrix}.
\tag{4}
$$

Here M, M_0, M_C are the mass matrices corresponding to the chosen FEM basis functions for the whole domain Ω and for Ω_0 and Ω_C, respectively. Further K is the FEM representation of the operator K. (For simplicity we keep the same notation for the corresponding matrix.), and $\mathbf{g}$ is the FEM form of the source function g. Here K^T stands for the transpose of K in case the differential equation is non-selfadjoint, such as a convection-diffusion equation. For notational simplicity, we have assumed that there are no bound constraints on the solution. For the **curl-curl** operator problem (2), the block system takes the form

$$
\begin{bmatrix} M & 0 & K - i\omega\sigma M \\ 0 & \beta M & -M \\ K + i\omega\sigma M & -M & 0 \end{bmatrix} \begin{bmatrix} u \\ v \\ w \end{bmatrix} = \begin{bmatrix} M u_d \\ 0 \\ 0 \end{bmatrix}
\tag{5}
$$

where w is the Lagrange multiplier for imposing the state equation constraint. Here, $M = [M_{ij}]$ and $K = [K_{ij}]$ where

$$
M_{ij} = \int_\Omega \varphi_j \varphi_i d\mathbf{x} \quad \text{and} \quad K_{ij} = \int_\Omega v\,\mathbf{curl}(\varphi_j)\,\mathbf{curl}(\varphi_i) + \varepsilon\varphi_j\varphi_i d\mathbf{x}.
$$

Note that here K^T is replaced by the complex conjugate matrix K^*.

Both systems (4) and (5) can be reduced by elimination of the control functions, which for (5) leads to the system,

$$\begin{bmatrix} M & \widehat{K}^* \\ \widehat{K} & -\frac{1}{\beta}M \end{bmatrix} \begin{bmatrix} \mathbf{u} \\ \mathbf{w} \end{bmatrix} = \begin{bmatrix} M & K - i\omega\sigma M \\ K + i\omega\sigma M & -\frac{1}{\beta}M \end{bmatrix} \begin{bmatrix} \mathbf{u} \\ \mathbf{w} \end{bmatrix} = \begin{bmatrix} M_0\mathbf{u}_d \\ 0 \end{bmatrix}. \tag{6}$$

Here M does not have to be regular, because even if it is singular, the relation $\mathbf{v} = \frac{1}{\beta}\mathbf{w}$ holds. One can form the corresponding Schur complement system to be solved by a preconditioned iteration method, see [1,8,9]. For instance for (6) we get

$$\mathcal{S}\mathbf{u} := (M + \beta\widehat{K}^*M^{-1}\widehat{K})\mathbf{u} = M_0\mathbf{u}_d,$$

where $\widehat{K} = K + i\omega\sigma M$. The Schur complement system is solved by a Krylov subspace method, with

$$\mathcal{P} = (M + \sqrt{\beta}\widehat{K}^*)M^{-1}(M + \sqrt{\beta}\widehat{K}).$$

as preconditioner. By use of Cauchy-Schwarz inequality, it is readily seen that the eigenvalues of $\mathcal{P}^{-1}\mathcal{S}$ are contained in the interval $[\frac{1}{2}, 1]$. Hence the method converges rapidly. Each iteration needs solution of arising linear systems with matrices $M + \sqrt{\beta}\widehat{K}^*$ and $M + \sqrt{\beta}\widehat{K}$, and with M to form the corresponding iterative residual, $\mathcal{S}u^{(k)} - M_0\mathbf{u}_d$ at iteration step k. In some problems M is replaced by a singular matrix and it can be advantageous, also computationally, instead to use a preconditioning for the two-by-two block matrix in (6) which does not need any solution with matrix M and which still gives the favourable eigenvalue bounds $[1/2, 1]$ for the correspondingly preconditioned matrix. Such a method will be presented in the next section. This method can also be used if one rewrites the complex valued system, and similarly $M + \sqrt{\beta}\widehat{K}^*$,

$$M + \sqrt{\beta}\widehat{K} = M + \sqrt{\beta}K + i\sqrt{\beta}\omega\sigma M,$$

in two-by-two block real valued form, see [1,9] and references therein.

3   The PRESB Preconditioning Method

The PRESB, preconditioned square block matrix, can be applied for the matrix in (6). We scale this system by the factor $\sqrt{\beta}$ and introduce the scaled control variable, $\widehat{w} = -\frac{1}{\sqrt{\beta}}w$ to obtain

$$\begin{bmatrix} M & -\sqrt{\beta}\widehat{K}^* \\ \sqrt{\beta}\widehat{K} & M \end{bmatrix} \begin{bmatrix} \mathbf{u} \\ \widehat{\mathbf{w}} \end{bmatrix} = \begin{bmatrix} M\mathbf{u}_d \\ 0 \end{bmatrix}, \tag{7}$$

where $\widehat{K} = K + i\omega\sigma M$. To solve this system by iteration we use the PRESB preconditioner

$$\begin{bmatrix} M & -\sqrt{\beta}\widehat{K}^* \\ \sqrt{\beta}\widehat{K} & M + \sqrt{\beta}(\widehat{K} + \widehat{K}^*) \end{bmatrix} \tag{8}$$

which, as will be remarked below, is applicable even if M is singular. These matrices have the form

$$\mathcal{A} = \begin{bmatrix} W & -Z^* \\ Z & W \end{bmatrix} \quad \text{and} \quad \mathcal{B} = \begin{bmatrix} W & -Z^* \\ Z & W + Z + Z^* \end{bmatrix}, \quad \text{respectively.} \tag{9}$$

We assume that W is real, symmetric and that $W + Z$, i.e. also $W + Z^*$ is nonsingular.

We show first how actions of $\mathcal{B}^{-1}$ can be executed. Note that $\mathcal{B}$ can be factorized as

$$\mathcal{B} = \begin{bmatrix} I & 0 \\ -I & I \end{bmatrix} \begin{bmatrix} I & 0 \\ 0 & W + Z \end{bmatrix} \begin{bmatrix} I & -Z^* \\ 0 & I \end{bmatrix} \begin{bmatrix} W + Z^* & 0 \\ 0 & I \end{bmatrix} \begin{bmatrix} I & 0 \\ I & I \end{bmatrix}.$$

Hence, $\mathcal{B}$ is nonsingular and

$$\mathcal{B}^{-1} = \begin{bmatrix} I & 0 \\ -I & I \end{bmatrix} \begin{bmatrix} (W + Z^*)^{-1} & 0 \\ 0 & I \end{bmatrix} \begin{bmatrix} I & Z^* \\ 0 & I \end{bmatrix} \begin{bmatrix} I & 0 \\ 0 & (W + Z)^{-1} \end{bmatrix} \begin{bmatrix} I & 0 \\ I & I \end{bmatrix}.$$

It follows that, besides a matrix vector multiplication with Z^* and vector additions, an action of $\mathcal{B}^{-1}$ involves solving systems with matrices $W + Z$ and $W + Z^*$ but no system with W.

To compute the eigenvalues of $\mathcal{B}^{-1}\mathcal{A}$ we consider the generalized eigenvalue problem

$$\lambda \mathcal{B} \begin{bmatrix} \xi \\ \eta \end{bmatrix} = \mathcal{A} \begin{bmatrix} \xi \\ \eta \end{bmatrix}, \quad \|x\| + \|y\| \neq 0, \quad \text{i.e.} \quad (1 - \lambda)\mathcal{B} \begin{bmatrix} \xi \\ \eta \end{bmatrix} = \begin{bmatrix} 0 \\ (Z + Z^*)\eta \end{bmatrix}. \tag{10}$$

Theorem 1. *Let $\mathcal{A}$ and $\mathcal{B}$ be defined in (9), where W is real, symmetric $\mathcal{N}(W) \neq \{0\}$ and $Z + Z^*$ is positive semidefinite and consider the generalized eigenvalue problem (10). Then the eigenvalues are real and $\lambda = 1$ for $\eta \in \mathcal{N}(Z + Z^*)$, any ξ. Further $1/2 \leq \lambda \leq 1$ for eigenvalues corresponding to eigenvector components η where $\eta^T W \eta > 0$ and $1 \leq \lambda \leq \frac{1}{1-\gamma}$ for eigenvalues corresponding to eigenvector components η where $\eta^T W \eta < 0$, and $\gamma = \max_\eta \frac{\eta^T(\widehat{Z} + \widehat{Z}^*)\eta}{\eta^T(I + \widehat{Z}\widehat{Z}^*)\eta}$, $\widehat{Z} = (-W)^{-1/2}Z(-W)^{-1/2}$ where $\gamma < 1$.*

Proof. It follows from (10) that $\lambda = 1$ for $\eta \in \mathcal{N}(Z + Z^*)$, any ξ, that is, the multiplicity of the unit eigenvalue is at least equal to n if W and Z have order $n \times n$.

For $\lambda \neq 1$ we get $W\xi - Z^*\eta = 0$, and $(1 - \lambda)(Z\xi + (W + Z + Z^*)\eta) = (Z + Z^*)\eta$. Hence

$$(1 - \lambda)(W + Z)(\xi + \eta) = (Z + Z^*)\eta$$

so

$$(1 - \lambda)(W + Z^*)\eta = W(W + Z)^{-1}(Z + Z^*)\eta \tag{11}$$

if $\eta^T W \eta > 0$. Then for such eigenvectors η we can transform (11) by a generalized square root matrix, $W^{-1/2}$, to get

$$(1 - \lambda)(I + \widehat{Z}^*)\widehat{\eta} = (I + \widehat{Z})^{-1}(\widehat{Z} + \widehat{Z}^*)\widehat{\eta},$$

where $\widehat{Z} = W^{-1/2} Z W^{-1/2}$, $\widehat{\eta} = W^{1/2}\eta$. It follows that

$$(1 - \lambda)(I + \widehat{Z})(I + \widehat{Z}^*)\widehat{\eta} = (\widehat{Z} + \widehat{Z}^*)\widehat{\eta}.$$

Clearly $0 \leq \lambda \leq 1$. Since $(I - \widehat{Z})(I - \widehat{Z}^*) \geq 0$ i.e. $\widehat{Z} + \widehat{Z}^* \leq I + \widehat{Z}\widehat{Z}^*$, $(1 - \lambda) \leq \lambda$,   that is $\frac{1}{2} \leq \lambda \leq 1$.

Assume now that $\eta^T W \eta < 0$. Working in a corresponding vector subspace then we multiply (11) with (-1) to get

$$(1 - \lambda)(-W - Z^*)\eta = (-W)(-W - Z)^{-1}(-Z - Z^*)\eta,$$

and a transformation matrix with $(-W)^{-1/2}$ gives then

$$(1 - \lambda)(I - \widehat{Z})(I - \widehat{Z}^*)\widehat{\eta} = -(\widehat{Z} + \widehat{Z}^*)\widehat{\eta},$$

where now $\widehat{Z} = (-W)^{-1/2}Z(-W)^{-1/2}$, $\widehat{\eta} = (-W)^{1/2}\eta$.
From

$$(1 - \lambda)(I + \widehat{Z}\widehat{Z}^* - (\widehat{Z} + \widehat{Z}^*))\widehat{\eta} = -(\widehat{Z} + \widehat{Z}^*)\widehat{\eta}$$

follows now that $1 \leq \lambda \leq \frac{1}{1-\gamma}$.

In [9] it has been shown, also numerically, that the PRESB method outperforms other methods such as those presented in [10].

4   An Inner Product Free Iterative Acceleration Methods

When solving coupled inner-outer iteration methods, i.e. where the outer iteration method involves inner systems that are also solved by iterations, one must use a variable preconditioned outer iteration method, see [11,12] or the flexible version of GMRES [13]. This involves use of several search direction vectors, which are anyway necessary to use when solving non-symmetric equations, such as arises for convection-diffusion problems. If one uses q search vectors, at each iteration one must perform $q(q + 1)/2$ inner products. These vectors must be stored and re-orthogonalized at each iteration step, because exact orthogonalization is lost due to not exact inner solvers and rounding errors during the computation.

Such methods are based on iterative approximations $x^{(k)}$ at each iteration taken from the Krylov subspace

$$K_k(\mathcal{B}^{-1}\mathcal{A}, r^{(0)}) = \text{span}\{r^{(0)}, \mathcal{B}^{-1}\mathcal{A} r^{(0)}, \cdots, (\mathcal{B}^{-1}\mathcal{A})^{(k)} r^{(0)}\},$$

where $r^{(0)}$ is the initial preconditioned residual, $r^{(0)} = \mathcal{B}^{-1}(\mathcal{A} x^{(0)} - b)$.

A conjugate gradient method for an SPD matrix $\mathcal{A}$ satisfies the following equivalent conditions,

(i) $\tilde{x}^{(k)} \in x^{(0)} + K_k(\mathcal{B}^{-1}\mathcal{A}, r^{(0)})$, $x^{(k)} = \text{argmin}\, \|x - \tilde{x}^{(k)}\|_{\mathcal{A}}$

(ii) $r^{(k)} \in K_k(\mathcal{B}^{-1}\mathcal{A}, r^{(0)})^{\perp}$

where part (ii) explains the need to orthogonalize, i.e. perform inner products.

There exists however an alternative, namely the classical Chebyshev iteration method., see e.g. [12, 14]. Here only two vectors must be stored and there are no inner products to be computed which saves both arithmetic costs and time for global communication. Furthermore, this method is not sensitive to rounding errors. Therefore, as shown e.g. in [9], it can outperform GMRES type methods and be competitive even on a single computer machine. To be efficient the method needs sharp eigenvalue bounds of the preconditioned matrix, but as we have seen, such bounds are available for the PRESB method for the classes of problems dealt with here.

The computationally most efficient form of the Chebyshev iteration method can be found in [12]: Given a current approximation $x^{(k)}$ of the previous approximation $x^{(k-1)}$, of the solution vector the iterative recursion can be written,

$$x^{(k+1)} = \alpha_k(x^k - x^{k-1} - \frac{2}{a+b}r^{(k)}) - x^{(k-1)}, \qquad k = 1, 2, \cdots .$$

Here $r^{(k)} = \mathcal{A}x^{(k)} - b$ is the residual vector and $\alpha_k = 1/(1 - (\frac{b-a}{2(b+a)})^2\alpha_{k-1})$, $k = 1, 2, \cdots$ with $\alpha_0 = 1$, where a, b are the eigenvalue bounds.

5   Concluding Remarks

It has been shown that by use of a special preconditioning method for matrices of two-by-two block form such as arises in various optimal control problems for partial differential equations, there exists a very efficient preconditioning method which outperforms other methods. It is parameter free and has fixed given accurate eigenvalue bounds which can be used to apply an inner-product free iterative acceleration method.

References

1. Axelsson, O., Farouq, S., Neytcheva, M.: Comparison of preconditioned Krylov subspace iteration methods for PDE-constrained optimization problems: stokes control. Numer. Algorithms **74**, 19–37 (2017)
2. Axelsson, O., Lukáš, D.: Preconditioning methods for eddy-current optimally controlled time-harmonic electromagnetic problems. J. Numer. Math. **27**(1), 1–21 (2019). https://doi.org/10.1515/jnma-2017-0064
3. Liang, Z.-Z., Axelsson, O., Neytcheva, M.: A robust structured preconditioner for time-harmonic parabolic optimal control problems. Numer. Algorithms **79**, 575–596 (2018)
4. Axelsson, O., Liang, Z.-Z.: A note on preconditioning methods for time-periodic eddy current optimal control problems. J. Comput. Appl. Math. **352**, 262–277 (2019)

5. Axelsson, O., Neytcheva, M., Ström, A.: An efficient preconditioning method for state box-constrained optimal control problems. J. Numer. Math. **26**(4), 185–207 (2018)
6. Axelsson, O., Blaheta, R., Kohut, R.: Preconditioning methods for high-order strongly stable time integration methods with an application for a DAE problem. Numer. Linear Algebra Appl. **22**(6), 930–949 (2015)
7. Axelsson, O., Liang, Z.-Z.: An optimal control framework for the iterative solution of a missing boundary data problem. Work in Progress
8. Pearson, J.W., Wathen, A.J.: A new approximation of the Schur complement in preconditioners for PDE-constrained optimization. Numer. Linear Algebra Appl. **19**(5), 816–829 (2012)
9. Axelsson, O., Salkuyeh, D.K.: A new version of a preconditioning method for certain two-by-two block matrices with square blocks. BIT Numer. Math. **59**(2), 321–342 (2019)
10. Bai, Z.Z., Benzi, M., Chen, F., Wang, Z.Q.: Preconditioned MHSS iteration methods for a class of block two-by-two linear systems with applications to distributed control problems. IMA J. Numer. Anal. **33**(1), 343–369 (2012)
11. Axelsson, O., Vassilevski, P.S.: Algebraic multilevel preconditioning methods, II. SIAM J. Numer. Anal. **27**, 1569–1590 (1990)
12. Axelsson, O.: Iterative Solution Methods. Cambridge University Press, Cambridge (1994)
13. Saad, Y.: A flexible inner-outer preconditioned GMRES algorithm. SIAM J. Sci. Comput. **14**(2), 461–469 (1993)
14. Varga, R.S.: Matrix Iterative Analysis. Springer, Heidelberg (2000). https://doi.org/10.1007/978-3-642-05156-2. Originally published by Prentice-Hall 1962 edition

Parallel BURA Based Numerical Solution of Fractional Laplacian with Pure Neumann Boundary Conditions

Gergana Bencheva, Nikola Kosturski, and Yavor Vutov[(✉)]

Institute of Information and Communication Technologies,
Bulgarian Academy of Sciences, Sofia, Bulgaria
{gery,kosturski,yavor}@parallel.bas.bg

Abstract. The study is motivated by the increased usage of fractional Laplacian in the modeling of nonlocal problems like anomalous diffusion. We present a parallel numerical solution method for the nonlocal elliptic problem: $-\Delta^\alpha u = f$, $0 < \alpha < 1$, $-\partial u(x)/\partial n = g(x)$ on $\partial\Omega$, $\Omega \subset \mathbb{R}^d$. The Finite Element Method (FEM) is used for discretization leading to the linear system $A^\alpha \mathbf{u} = \mathbf{f}$, where A is a sparse symmetric and positive semidefinite matrix. The implemented method is based on the Best Uniform Rational Approximation (BURA) of degree k, $r_{\alpha,k}$, of the scalar function t^α, $0 \le t \le 1$. The related approximation of $A^{-\alpha}\mathbf{f}$ can be written as a linear combination of the solutions of k local problems. The latter are found using the preconditioned conjugate gradient method. The method is applicable to computational domains with general geometry. Linear finite elements on unstructured tetrahedral meshes with local refinements are used in the presented numerical tests. The behavior of the relative error, the number of Preconditioned Conjugate Gradient (PCG) iterations, and the parallel time is analyzed varying the parameter $\alpha \in \{0.25, 0.50, 0.75\}$, the BURA degree $k \in \{5, 6, \ldots, 12\}$, and the mesh size.

Keywords: BURA · Fractional diffusion · Neumann boundary conditions · Unstructured meshes · Parallel algorithm

1 Introduction

The recent advancement in fractional calculus and the progress towards extreme scale computing create possibilities for computer simulation and investigation of more complicated real life nonlocal phenomena. Fractional Laplacian is used to model anomalous diffusion, which appears in applications like turbulent fluid motion, material transport in fractured media, underground flow. These are just some examples of nonlocal problems, where the fractional diffusive flux at a certain location is affected by the state of the field in the entire space. An introduction to the fractional Laplacian with some emphasis on fundamental ideas and

© Springer Nature Switzerland AG 2020
I. Lirkov and S. Margenov (Eds.): LSSC 2019, LNCS 11958, pp. 284–291, 2020.
https://doi.org/10.1007/978-3-030-41032-2_32

model numerical computations is given in [1]. During last years, several numerical methods for fractional diffusion problems assuming general domain were proposed (e.g. [2–4]), following the common idea of transforming the problem to some auxiliary local differential equation in a computational domain of a higher dimension. The alternative approach proposed in [5] (see also [6]) is devoted to solution of linear systems with fractional powers of sparse SPD matrices. The developed methods are based on the best uniform rational approximations (BURA). A unified view of some numerical methods for fractional diffusion is recently published in [7], showing that the methods from [2–4] are equivalent to certain rational approximations. This means that when applicable, the BURA methods are expected to be the best. The analysis of some first parallel implementations of the methods from [2,4,5] (see [5,8] and the references there in) also confirms the advantages of BURA methods. The discussed methods consider the case of fractional diffusion problems with homogeneous Dirichlet boundary conditions, where the numerical tests are mostly in domains like $\Omega = (0,1)^d$.

Our goal is to generalize the improved BURA method from [6] to the case of pure Neumann boundary conditions. The matrix A in the related linear system $A^\alpha \mathbf{u} = \mathbf{f}$ is sparse symmetric and positive semidefinite. The domain has a nontrivial geometry. Linear finite elements on unstructured tetrahedral meshes with local refinement are used in the presented numerical tests. The remainder of the paper is organized as follows. The fractional diffusion problem in terms of spectral decomposition is introduced in the next section. The main idea of the BURA method is presented briefly in Sect. 3. The numerical tests are presented and analyzed in Sect. 4. Some concluding remarks and notes on the further steps are given at the end.

2   Fractional Diffusion Problem

The definition of a fractional diffusion problem based on the spectral decomposition is used in this work. Let us consider the elliptic boundary value problem

$$-\Delta u(x) = f(x), \quad x \in \Omega,$$
$$-\frac{\partial u(x)}{\partial \mathbf{n}} = g(x), \quad x \in \partial\Omega \tag{1}$$

in $\Omega \subset \mathbb{R}^d$ with $\mathbf{n}$ denoting the outward normal unit vector for $\partial\Omega$. The weak formulation (see [9]) of (1) is: *given $f \in L^2(\Omega)$ and $g \in L^2(\partial\Omega)$ find $u \in H^1(\Omega)$ such that*

$$\int_\Omega \nabla u(x) \cdot \nabla v(x) dx = \int_\Omega f(x)v(x)dx + \int_{\partial\Omega} g(\gamma)v(\gamma)d\gamma, \qquad \forall v \in H^1(\Omega),$$

where $d\gamma$ denotes the surface measure of $\partial\Omega$. This weak formulation is used to define the fractional power operator Δ^α, $0 < \alpha < 1$, through its spectral decomposition

$$\Delta^\alpha u = f, \ \Delta^\alpha u(x) = \sum_{i=1}^\infty \lambda_i^\alpha c_i \psi_i(x), \quad \text{where} \quad u(x) = \sum_{i=1}^\infty c_i \psi_i(x), \tag{2}$$

$\{\psi_i(x)\}_{i=1}^{\infty}$ are the L_2-orthonormal eigenfunctions of Δ, the eigenvalue $\lambda_1 = 0$ corresponds to the constant eigenfunction $\psi_1(x)$, and the rest eigenvalues $\{\lambda_i\}_{i=2}^{\infty}$ are real and positive. Similar definition of the fractional power of the related symmetric and positive semidefinite matrix is assumed.

3   Parallel BURA Based Solution Method

We generalize the method from [6] to solve in parallel the pure Neumann fractional diffusion problem (2). The essential steps are briefly presented below.

3.1   Best Uniform Rational Approximation

The element of best uniform rational approximation (BURA) of t^α, $0 < \alpha < 1$ is a rational function $r_{\alpha,k}$ of polynomials of degree k that minimizes the error

$$\|r_{\alpha,k} - t^\alpha\|_{C[0,1]}.$$

The modified Remez algorithm is used to compute the parameters of $r_{\alpha,k}$ (see e.g. [5]). Now, the rational function $\widetilde{r}_{\alpha,k}(\xi) = r_{\alpha,k}(1/t), \xi = 1/t \in [1, +\infty)$ is introduced and the coefficients $c_i > 0$ and $d_i < 0$ of the partial fraction representation

$$\widetilde{r}_{\alpha,k}(\xi) = c_0 + \sum_{i=1}^{k} \frac{c_i}{\xi - d_i}$$

are computed.

3.2   Discrete Problem

The initial (local) problem (1) is discretized by linear finite elements on an unstructured (tetrahedral in the 3D case) mesh. The resulting system of linear algebraic equations (with imposed boundary conditions) can be written as

$$A\mathbf{u} = \mathbf{f},$$

$A = M^{-1}S$, where S and M are the stiffness and the lumped mass matrices respectively. Following the approach in [6], the solution of the nonlocal problem (2) is approximated by

$$\mathbf{u} = A^{-\alpha}\mathbf{f} \approx \lambda_2^{-\alpha} \left(c_0\mathbf{f} + \sum_{i=1}^{k} ((\lambda_2 c_i)(A - \lambda_2 d_i I)^{-1})\mathbf{f} \right) \tag{3}$$

where λ_2 is the smallest positive eigenvalue of A. A is symmetric with respect to the dot product generated by the diagonal (lumped) mass matrix M. It is important to note that A is positive definite in the subspace orthogonal to the constant vectors. The expression (3) means, that in order to find the BURA approximation of $\mathbf{u}$, one has to compute a linear combination of the solutions of k local problems with matrices $A_i = A - \lambda_2 d_i I$ scaled by $(\lambda_2 c_i)$. A parallel PCG solver is applied to these auxiliary sparse symmetric and positive definite systems.

3.3 Solution Steps

The tetrahedral mesh of the Ω is distributed among processors using ParMETIS [10]. The coefficients c_i, d_i of the BURA approximation with polynomials of degree k are computed in advance and read by the program. Each of the k linear systems of algebraic equations are solved using the Preconditioned Conjugate Gradient (PCG) method (see e.g. [11] for details) with a parallel multigrid implementation BoomerAMG from the library $HYPRE$ [12] as the preconditioner. The same preconditioner, constructed from the linear system with the smallest root d_1, is used for the solution of all systems. The approximation of the solution is calculated using (3). More details on the computational setting and the results of the performed numerical tests are presented in the next section.

4   Numerical Experiments

We are solving the linear system $A^{\alpha}\mathbf{u} = \mathbf{f}$, where $0 < \alpha < 1$, and A and $\mathbf{f}$ correspond to FEM discretization of the following 3D Laplace problem with pure Neumann boundary conditions:

$$-\Delta u = 0 \text{ in } \Omega,$$

$$-\frac{\partial u}{\partial \mathbf{n}} = 0 \text{ on } \Gamma_R,$$

$$-\frac{\partial u}{\partial \mathbf{n}} = g_I \text{ on } \Gamma_I,$$

$$-\frac{\partial u}{\partial \mathbf{n}} = g_O \text{ on } \Gamma_O.$$

The computational domain consists of two cylinders (see Fig. 1), where $\partial\Omega = \Gamma_I \cup \Gamma_O \cup \Gamma_R$, Γ_I and Γ_O are the left and right bases of the larger and smaller cylinders respectively. The functions g_I and g_O satisfy the equation

$$\int_{\Gamma_I} g_I d\gamma + \int_{\Gamma_O} g_O d\gamma = 0. \tag{4}$$

More precisely, Γ_I and Γ_O are circles, g_O is a parabolic function vanishing at $\partial\Gamma_O$, with a value of g_O equal to 1 at the center of Γ_O, and g_I is a constant determined by (4). Using Netgen [13], the computational domain is discretized by tetrahedral elements, applying local refinement near the boundaries with nonzero boundary conditions. The resulting mesh is illustrated in Fig. 1. It consists of 109 385 nodes and 572 794 tetrahedral elements. This initial mesh $\mathcal{M}_1$ is further uniformly refined three times to get the meshes $\mathcal{M}_i$ for $i \in \{2, 3, 4\}$. Let us denote by N_i the number of nodes (number of unknowns of the FEM system) corresponding to $\mathcal{M}_i$. Then, $N_{i+1} \approx 8N_i$, and $N_4 \approx 5 \times 10^7$.

The presented numerical experiments are split in three parts. The first of them is devoted to the convergence rate of the FEM discretization with respect to the mesh size. After that, accuracy of BURA approximation on the finest

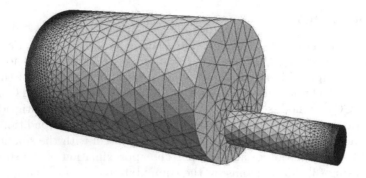

Fig. 1. Computational domain with locally refined unstructured mesh

mesh is investigated, varying the degree k. The last experiments illustrate the overall performance of the developed solver.

Further, the solution on mesh $\mathcal{M}_i$ with order of BURA k is denoted with $\mathbf{u}_i^k$. Since the exact solution of the test problem is unknown, to investigate the rate of convergence, we solve the problem on all available meshes and consider the solution, obtained on the finest mesh as a reference solution. The relative error

$$\frac{\|\hat{\mathbf{u}}_i^{12} - \hat{\mathbf{u}}_4^{12}\|_M}{\|\hat{\mathbf{u}}_4^{12}\|_M}$$

is used for that purpose, where $\hat{\mathbf{u}}_i^k$ is the restriction of the numerical solution $\mathbf{u}_i^k$ to the nodes of the mesh $\mathcal{M}_1$. For this set of experiments, PCG tolerance of $\varepsilon = 10^{-12}$ is used to make sure the PCG solver accuracy does not interfere with the analyzed results. For a similar purpose, the largest considered value of $k = 12$ is used for the BURA approximation.

Here and in what follows $\|\mathbf{u}\|_M$ stands for the energy norm $(\mathbf{u}^T M \mathbf{u})^{\frac{1}{2}}$ associated with the matrix M. Since M is the lumped mass matrix, $\mathbf{u}^T M \mathbf{u}$ is a quadrature formula for the integral $\int_\Omega u^2(x)dx$. Therefore $\|\cdot\|_M$ is approximately equal to the L_2 norm in the related FEM space.

The obtained results are presented in Fig. 2(a). The general conclusion is that the convergence rate decreases for smaller values of α indicating some behaviour of the presented relative errors like $O(h^{2\alpha})$.

Next, we turn our attention to the BURA approximation and the influence of its degree k to the accuracy of the solution. Here, we consider only the solutions obtained on the finest mesh $\mathcal{M}_4$. Again, the PCG tolerance is set to $\varepsilon = 10^{-12}$. In this case, we consider the solution with $k = 12$ as a reference one, and compare the other solutions using a similar relative error in the form

$$\frac{\|\mathbf{u}_4^k - \mathbf{u}_4^{12}\|_M}{\|\mathbf{u}_4^{12}\|_M}.$$

The related results are plotted on Fig. 2(b). According to the general theory (see [6]) the BURA methods have an exponential convergence rate with respect to k, which is confirmed by the presented results.

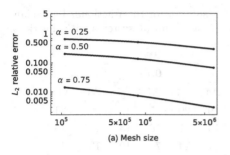
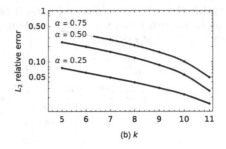

(a) Mesh size   (b) k

Fig. 2. Relative errors: $\dfrac{\|\hat{u}_i^{12}-\hat{u}_4^{12}\|_M}{\|\hat{u}_4^{12}\|_M}$ (a) and $\dfrac{\|u_4^{k}-u_4^{12}\|_M}{\|u_4^{12}\|_M}$ (b).

Here, it is worth to remember that the introduced relative errors use reference solutions instead of the exact one. In general, the conducted 3 consecutive mesh refinements could not be enough for reliable quantitative conclusions. In this sense, the analysis of the presented results is most likely qualitative.

Lastly, we investigate the performance of the developed solver for $k = 12$. Based on the previous numerical tests and the observed behavior of the relative errors, we set $\varepsilon = 10^{-6}$ for the PCG tolerance. In this case, the approximate solution of the considered fractional diffusion problem involves solving 12 linear systems with the matrices $A_i = (A - \lambda_2 d_i I)/(\lambda_2 c_i)$, $i = 1, \ldots, 12$. One can observe that they are quite similar to matrices arising from normal time-dependent diffusion problems. This allows us to use any efficient preconditioner for such problems. In our case, we have chosen BoomerAMG – a parallel algebraic multigrid implementation from LLNL's HYPRE library [12]. The matrices A_i are differently conditioned. The first one always has the highest condition number, and in the presented numerical results, the AMG preconditioner for A_1 is used for all systems. As expected, different number of iterations are needed to converge to the set tolerance for the systems with different matrices A_i. The PCG iterations for each of the systems in the BURA approximation (3), the total number of iterations N_{tot}^{it}, the solution time T_{sol} and the total time T_{tot} are presented in Table 1, for all mesh refinements $\mathcal{M}_i$, $i = 1, 2, 3, 4$ varying also $\alpha \in \{0.25, 0.50, 0.75\}$.

The computations are performed on the Avitohol supercomputer [14] located at IICT-BAS. It consists of 16 core nodes with Intel XeonE5-2650 v2 CPU, running at 2.60 GHz, interconnected with InfiniBand FDR network. All runs were performed on 64 cores using 4 nodes.

The reported total times include the solution time as well as the time for discretization of the problem.

The finer meshes require more PCG iterations for all α. This is due to the aggressive coarsening used in the BoomerAMG setting in order to get a better parallel efficiency. For all meshes $\mathcal{M}_i$, the iteration counts and the solution times decrease with the decrease of α. Let us denote by T_{tot}^i the time corresponding to the mesh $\mathcal{M}_i$. Let us consider the efficiency ratio $E_i = 8 T_{tot}^{i-1}/T_{tot}^i$ to illustrate the total time scalability. Then $E_4 \approx 91\%$ for all α.

Table 1. PCG iterations and parallel times for solution of the fractional Laplacian problem with $k = 12$, $\varepsilon = 10^{-6}$, including the auxiliary linear systems with matrices $A_i = (A - \lambda_2 d_i I)/(\lambda_2 c_i)$.

α	0.25				0.50				0.75			
Mesh	$\mathcal{M}_1$	$\mathcal{M}_2$	$\mathcal{M}_3$	$\mathcal{M}_4$	$\mathcal{M}_1$	$\mathcal{M}_2$	$\mathcal{M}_3$	$\mathcal{M}_4$	$\mathcal{M}_1$	$\mathcal{M}_2$	$\mathcal{M}_3$	$\mathcal{M}_4$
A_1	11	14	17	19	13	16	19	20	15	18	20	21
A_2	7	9	12	15	8	12	14	17	10	13	16	18
A_3	5	7	9	11	6	8	11	14	7	10	13	16
A_4	3	4	6	8	5	6	8	11	6	8	10	13
A_5	2	3	4	5	3	4	6	8	4	6	8	11
A_6	3	3	2	3	2	3	4	6	3	4	6	8
A_7	3	3	3	2	3	2	3	4	2	3	4	6
A_8	2	2	2	2	2	3	3	2	3	2	3	4
A_9	2	2	2	2	3	2	2	2	3	3	2	3
A_{10}	2	2	2	2	2	2	2	2	2	3	3	2
A_{11}	2	2	2	2	2	2	2	2	2	2	2	2
A_{12}	2	2	2	2	2	2	2	2	2	2	2	2
N_{tot}^{it}	44	53	63	73	51	62	76	90	59	74	89	106
T_{sol}[s]	0.20	0.69	4.8	45	0.24	0.86	5.9	55	0.29	1.01	7.0	65
T_{tot}[s]	0.26	1.07	7.7	67	0.30	1.24	8.8	77	0.35	1.39	9.8	86

5   Concluding Remarks

The recently introduced improved BURA method [6] is generalized to the case of fractional diffusion problems with pure Neumann boundary conditions. The considered test problem concerns FEM discretization on unstructured tetrahedral meshes in realistic computational domain with general geometry. The presented large-scale (up to $O(10^7)$ degrees of freedom) numerical results provide some promising proofs of concept of the proposed approach. The following open questions are derived.

The theoretical error estimates of the FEM numerical solutions of fractional diffusion problems with pure Neumann boundary conditions are beyond the scope of this study. However, they are strongly required for future development of the discussed solution methods. Then, a more accurate reference solution will be needed to get some reliable quantitative results analyzing the experimental data. The accuracy (when applicable) of the gradient of BURA computed approximation is the next important question, taking into account the lower regularity of the solution for smaller values of α.

In many of the currently available papers, when comparing some methods for numerical solution of fractional diffusion problems, the number of auxiliary local systems needed to get a certain accuracy is accepted as a measure of the related computational complexity. However, the results presented in Table 1 show rather different numbers of iterations to solve the systems with different matrices A_i. The conclusion is that some more involved study at this point is required, including the reasonable stopping criteria for the PCG iterations.

Acknowledgments. We acknowledge the provided access to the e-infrastructure and support of the Centre for Advanced Computing and Data Processing, with the financial support by the Grant No BG05M2OP001-1.001-0003, financed by the Science and Education for Smart Growth Operational Program (2014–2020) and co-financed by the European Union through the European structural and Investment funds.

The presented work is partially supported by the Bulgarian National Science Fund under grant No. DFNI-DN12/1.

References

1. Pozrikidis, C.: The Fractional Laplacian. CRC Press, Taylor & Francis Group, Boca Raton, Routledge (2016)
2. Bonito, A., Pasciak, J.: Numerical approximation of fractional powers of elliptic operators. Math. Comput. **84**(295), 2083–2110 (2015)
3. Chen, L., Nochetto, R., Enrique, O., Salgado, A.J.: Multilevel methods for nonuniformly elliptic operators and fractional diffusion. Math. Comput. **85**, 2583–2607 (2016)
4. Vabishchevich, P.N.: Numerically solving an equation for fractional powers of elliptic operators. J. Comput. Phys. **282**, 289–302 (2015)
5. Harizanov, S., Lazarov, R., Margenov, S., Marinov, P., Vutov, Y.: Optimal solvers for linear systems with fractional powers of sparse SPD matrices. Numer. Linear Algebra Appl. **25**(5), e2167 (2018). https://doi.org/10.1002/nla.2167
6. Harizanov, S., Lazarov, R., Marinov, P., Margenov, S., Pasciak, J.: Analysis of numerical methods for spectral fractional elliptic equations based on the best uniform rational approximation. arXiv preprint arXiv:1905.08155, (https://arxiv.org/abs/1905.08155) (2019)
7. Hofreither, C.: A unified view of some numerical methods for fractional diffusion. Comput. Math. Appl. (2019). https://doi.org/10.1016/j.camwa.2019.07.025
8. Čiegis, R., Starikovičius, V., Margenov, S., Kriauzienė, R.: Scalability analysis of different parallel solvers for 3D fractional power diffusion problems. Concurr. Computat Pract. Exper. e5163 (2019). https://doi.org/10.1002/cpe.5163
9. Quarteroni, A., Valli, A.: Numerical Approximation of Partial Differential Equations. Springer Series in Computational Mathematics, vol. 23. Springer, Heidelberg (1997). https://doi.org/10.1007/978-3-540-85268-1
10. ParMETIS (2019). http://glaros.dtc.umn.edu/gkhome/metis/parmetis/overview
11. Axelsson, O.: Iterative Solution Methods. Cambridge University Press, New York (1996)
12. HYPRE Library (2019). https://computation.llnl.gov/projects/hypre-scalable-linear-solvers-multigrid-methods
13. Netgen mesher (2019). https://ngsolve.org/
14. Supercomputer System Avitohol (2019). http://iict.bas.bg/avitohol/

Bias Correcting of Selected ETCCDI Climate Indices for Projected Future Climate

Hristo Chervenkov[✉] and Valery Spiridonov

National Institute of Meteorology and Hydrology,
Tsarigradsko Shose blvd. 66, 1784 Sofia, Bulgaria
hristo.tchervenkov@meteo.bg
http://www.meteo.bg

Abstract. Regional climate models (RCMs) have been developed and extensively applied in the recent decades for dynamically downscaling coarse resolution information from different sources, for various purposes, including past climate simulations and future climate projections. Due to systematic and random model errors, however, RCM simulations often show considerable deviations from observations. This has led to the development of a number of correction approaches, which lately become known with the common name bias correction. Although some criticism exists, the general view in the expert community is that the bias-corrected climate change signal is more reliable compared to the uncorrected one and thus is more suitable for impact assessments. In the present study, which is part of more general work, outputs from simulations for the present-day (1961–1990) climate, as well as for the near future scenario (2021–2050), performed with the model ALADIN-Climate, are used for calculation of selected ETCCDI climate indices. The same subset, but based on observational database E-OBS, is taken from the open archive ClimData and used as reference. The results of the computations, performed over the interior of the Balkan Peninsula, demonstrates the possibilities of the selected bias correction technique and its modifications.

Keywords: ETCCDI climate indices · ALADIN-Climate · Bias correction · Linear transformation · E-OBS · ClimData

1 Introduction

Global Circulation Models (GCMs) are the most widespread and successful tools employed for both numerical weather forecast and climate research since the 1980s [15,18]. Regional climate models (RCMs) have been developed and extensively applied in the recent decades for dynamically downscaling coarse resolution information from different sources, such as GCMs and reanalysis, for various purposes, including past climate simulations and future climate projections

© Springer Nature Switzerland AG 2020
I. Lirkov and S. Margenov (Eds.): LSSC 2019, LNCS 11958, pp. 292–299, 2020.
https://doi.org/10.1007/978-3-030-41032-2_33

[1,17]. Due to systematic and random model errors, which are partly inherited from the driving GCMs, RCM simulations often show considerable deviations from observations [10,14]. This has led to the development of a number of correction approaches, which lately become known with the common name bias correction (BC). BC first of all aims to adjust selected statistics of a climate model simulation to better match observed statistics over the present-day reference period. The basic assumption is that bias changes are negligible compared to climate change or, equivalently, that the bias itself is time-invariant [2,8]. Although some criticism exists, the general view in the expert community is that the bias-corrected climate change signal is more reliable compared with the uncorrected one and thus is more suitable for impact assessments.

Over recent years, many different methods have been developed and widely applied to post-process climate projections (see, for instance, [6,7,17] and references therein). A concise and clear description of these methods is listed also in Table 4 of [16]. The aim of this study is to assess the sensitivity of a number of climate indices (CIs) from the Expert Team on Climate Change Detection and Indices (ETCCDI) suite from the calculation method for projected future climate, rather than to give comprehensive review of the various aspects of the BC. A concise description of the theoretical background and the conceptional aspects of the BC can be found in [12] and more detailed presentation of specific methods - in [5,6,17]. In this paper, which is part of more general work, outputs from simulations for the present-day (1961–1990) climate, as well as for the near future scenario (2021–2050), performed with the model ALADIN-Climate, are used for calculation of selected ETCCDI CIs. The same subset, but based on observational database E-OBS, is taken from the open archive ClimData and used as reference. The results of the computations, performed over the interior of the Balkan Peninsula, demonstrates the possibilities of the selected bias correction technique, namely the linear transformation and its modifications.

The paper is structured as follows. Concise description of the ALADIN simulation, as well as the reference data, is in Sect. 2. The selected ETCCDI CIs are addressed shortly in Sect. 3. The main part of the article is Sect. 4, where the used methodology, the performed calculations and obtained results are described. The question how the applied BC affects the resulting time averaged distributions of the selected CIs, which is of primary importance from end-user point of view, is also addressed in this section. Concise conclusion remarks are placed in Sect. 5.

2   ALADIN Simulation and Reference Data

The climate simulations with model system ALADIN-Climate with focus on average precipitation and 2 m temperature were performed in the Bulgarian National Institute of Meteorology and Hydrology in the frame of the EU Framework-supported CECILIA (Central and Eastern Europe Climate Change Impact and Vulnerability Assessment, http://www.cecilia-eu.org/, see [9] for details) project. The used version of ALADIN-Climate corresponds to cycle 24 of the ARPEGE/IFS code, which physical parameterization package is derived directly from the one used in GCM ARPEGE-CLIMAT 4 [1]. The model was driven by the boundary condition of 50 km horizontal resolution coming from a "stretch mesh" version of ARPEGE-CLIMAT 4 GCM. This version of the GCM has a variable horizontal resolution being around 50 km over Southern Europe and decreasing to approximately 300 km at the antipode. The runs are performed for three time slices: 1961–1990 (present climate control run, CR), 2021–2050 (near future run, NF), and 2071–2100 (far future run, FF) at grid spacing of 10 km. All future simulations were carried out using CO_2 concentrations as described by the IPCC A1B scenario [13]. The model domain is centered over Bulgaria, but accommodates significant part of the Balkan Peninsula.

The well-known and freely available for the research community database E-OBS version 16.0 of the European Climate Assessment & Dataset (ECA&D) project [11] is used as reference.

3   Selected ETCCDI Indices

The climate analysis of extreme events for past, present and projected future climate, which is based on CIs, is one of the most widely used non-parametric approaches. The ETCCDI indices have been chosen to sample a wide variety of climates and included indicators such as the total number of days annually with frost and the maximum number of consecutive dry days in a year. The wide applicability of the CIs-based approach was the major motivator for the creation by the corresponding author of the open database, named ClimData (barrier free access on https://repo.vi-seem.eu/handle/21.15102/VISEEM-343). This database is intended to serve as a convenient, barrier free and versatile tool for research and includes datasets of gridded time series of the selected ETCCDI CIs, based on E-OBS [3,4]. The list of indices includes three main classes: absolute-thresholds indices, percentile-based indices, and indices based on the duration of an event. From all 29 ETCCDI-indices, we select subset of the 19 absolute-thresholds and based on the duration of an event CIs. For sake of brevity, however, we present results in this paper only for the following: Frost days, Icing days, Summer days, Tropical nights, Growing season length, Monthly maximum 1-day precipitation, Monthly maximum consecutive 5-day precipitation, Annual count of days when precip. sum ≥ 10 mm, Maximum length of dry spell, Maximum number of consecutive days with precip. sum ≥ 1 mm, Annual total precipitation in wet days, which are traditionally noted as **FD, ID, SD, TR, GSL, RX1DAY, RX5DAY, R10MM, CDD, PRCPTOT** correspondingly. Descriptive list of all 29 ETCCDI CIs could be found on http://etccdi.pacificclimate.org/list_27_indices.shtml.

Depending of the method, these indices are calculated from the uncorrected or corrected ALADIN CR- and NF-output, as demonstrated in the next section.

4 Methodology, Performed Calculations and Obtained Results

Following the notation in [12], the simulated present-day model (predictor) time series of length N of chosen variable will be denoted as x_i^p, the corresponding reference (predictand) time series as y_i^p. The mean of the uncorrected model over the considered present period (i.e. 1961–1990) μ_{raw}^p can be estimated as $\hat{\mu}_{raw}^p = \overline{x_i^p}$ (where the hat denotes traditionally the estimator and the bar averaging in time), the corresponding real mean μ_{real}^p as $\hat{\mu}_{real}^p = \overline{y_i^p}$. An estimator of the model bias for present conditions is then given as

$$\widehat{Bias}(\mu^p) = \overline{x_i^p} - \overline{y_i^p}. \tag{1}$$

Correspondingly, the relative bias might be estimated as

$$\widehat{Rel.Bias}(\mu^p) = \overline{x_i^p}/\overline{y_i^p}. \tag{2}$$

The precipitation (which assumes positive values only) is typically corrected with a factor according Eq. 2 and temperature with an additive term according Eq. 1 [16]. The simple mean bias correction is mathematically similar to the so called delta-change approach, but conceptually different. It generates a future time series by subtracting the present-day model bias from the simulated future time series:

$$x_{i,corr}^f = x_{i,raw}^f - \widehat{Bias}(\mu^p) = x_{i,raw}^f - \left(\overline{x_i^p} - \overline{y_i^p}\right) \tag{3}$$

or equivalently for precipitation

$$x_{i,corr}^f = \frac{x_{i,raw}^f}{\widehat{Rel.Bias}(\mu^p)} = x_{i,raw}^f \times \frac{\overline{y_i^p}}{\overline{x_i^p}}. \tag{4}$$

The latter formulation, expressed with Eqs. 3 and 4, is known as linear transformation (LT or linear scaling) [12,16] and adjusts both mean and variance (but keeps their ratio constant). The LT belongs to the class of the direct approaches and is used as BC technique in the present work.

When dealing with CIs, two possibilities of applying the LT exist. In the first case, which is the most common one, the timeseries of the parameters, necessary for the computation of the indices, are corrected first and the indices are obtained subsequently. All ETCCDI CIs are calculated from the minimum and maximum daily temperature and the daily precipitation sum. Thus, the extreme temperatures are corrected according to Eq. 3 and the precipitation according to Eq. 4. In the second case, as our original proposal, the input parameters are not corrected before the computation of the indices; the indices are computed from the ALADIN-output for the NF and CR and the reference present-day CIs-dataset is taken from ClimData. Then, the LT is applied on the timeseries of these CIs-datasets. The first approach will be noted for conciseness hereafter as 'method 1' and the second—'method 2'.

In all cases the indices are calculated by means of the ETCCDI-supplied software, integrated in a program written specifically for this study. The calculations are performed for each year of the both simulation periods, on every grid cell of the domain and are subsequently time averaged.

CIs, applied without any BC, are most frequently used in studies for projected future climate. The considered indices for the future scenario, obtained with the two methods, together with these, calculated directly from the ALADIN-NF output, are intercompared below.

Figure 1 shows the distribution of the thermal CIs for the near future scenario (averaged over the whole period 2021–2050), calculated directly from the ALADIN-NF output and with the aforementioned two methods.

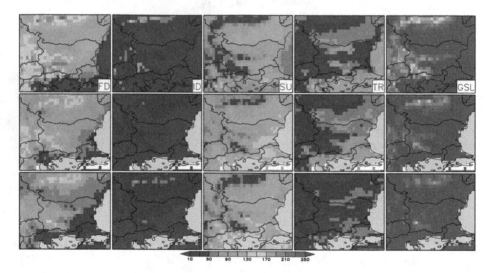

Fig. 1. Thermal CIs for the NF, calculated directly from the ALADIN-NF output (first row), method 1 (second row) and additive variant of method 2 (third row). The units are days. See Sect. 3 for the CIs meaning.

It is well known, that the changes in the occurrence of TR, in smaller extent also of SU, are substantial only in low-elevation areas (below 800 m), which are particularly exposed to persistent and intense warm spells in summer [4]. Generally, TR are not characteristic to the mountain climate of the considered domain. Over many pixels there CI and SU are constantly zero and the proportional variant of method 2 (see Eq. 4 again) is not applicable.

Overall, the distribution patterns of the corresponding CIs are very similar. The vertical gradient and some specific aspects of the regional climate are well reproduced. The corrected "cold" indices (i.e. FD and ID) are generally smaller, especially over the south Carpathian ridge and the Rila mountain; the "hot" indices (SU, TR and GSL) are bigger except TR, where the differences between the methods seems most significant.

Figure 2 shows the distribution of the precipitation-related CIs for the near future scenario, calculated directly from the ALADIN-NF output, and the two methods, were, for conciseness, only the proportional variant of method 2 is demonstrated.

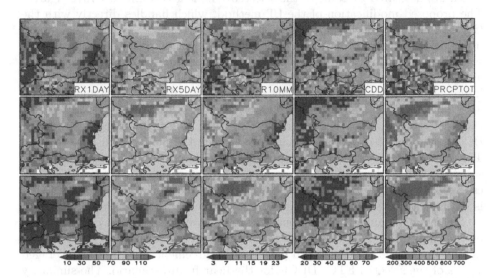

Fig. 2. Precipitation-related CIs for the NF, calculated directly from the ALADIN-NF output (first row), method 1 (second row) and proportional variant of method 2 (third row). The units of RX1DAY, RX5DAY and PRCPTOT are mm; these of R10MM and CDD—days. See Sect. 3 for the CIs meaning.

The significantly higher spatial inhomogeneity in ALADIN-CR appears as main difference between the distributions of the both groups of CIs. It is well known, however, that the precipitation is significantly weaker spatially correlated in comparison with the temperature. The direct incorporation of the E-OBS in 'method 1' leads to overall smoothing. The reason could be rooted in the fact that E-OBS, due to the embedded interpolation procedure, oversmooths the precipitation field [11]. The general distribution patterns of the uncorrected fields and these obtained with 'method 1' and 'method 2', are very similar, as in the case of the thermal CIs. There are not, at least apparent, principal disagreements with the uncorrected CIs. Nevertheless, the impact of 'method 2' appears stronger. A common sign of the impact of the applied BCs, both 'method 1' and 'method 2', which is valid for all precipitation-related CIs over the whole domain, is also absent. Exception is the PRCPTOT, which is the most important indicator of the mean climate state, for the both methods leads to increase.

5   Conclusion

It is known that the BC may alter the mean climate signal of the adjusted variable; however, the effect on the projected occurrence of climate extremes, which are indicated by some of the selected CIs, is less commonly investigated. The proposed modification of the LT method, which handles directly with the CIs, rather than the input parameters, seems promising. As the other direct methods, it is, first, significantly easier for implementation than the others, and, second, is applicable even if only the CIs-datasets are available (which is not a rare case). It has to be kept in mind, however, that according the in-depth intercomparison study of the recent BC methods [16], the direct methods are least able to correct for overall model errors in the validation period and are the least reliable under changed conditions. The study [16] concludes that the BC method called distribution mapping, showed the best overall performance. This method, however, is much more complicated. The implementation of more sophisticated methods increases also the risk of loss of climate change signal, especially when the reference dataset is based on a measurement network that is significantly coarser than the model grid, as in the present case.

The main outcome of the present study is the overall consistency of the results of the application of the considered methods. This consistency is expressed mainly in absence of general and principal disagreements for the time averaged values of the selected ETCCDI CIs for the near future scenario. The similarity of the present results is stronger then these from the delta-change approach, obtained (and not published yet) in the frame of the same project. The research could continue applying other BC-techniques. It is worth emphasizing, however, that all these methods cannot correct for the model's own deficiencies (e.g., dynamics or physical parameterization). As such, the projections of a model that misrepresents some fundamental processes will remain unreliable, even after bias correction [7,12].

Acknowledgment. The authors would like to express their deep gratitude to the projects, organizations and institutes (ClimData, ECA&D, ETCCDI, UNI-DATA and others), which provides free of charge software and data. ClimData is hosted by the repository service of the EC-funded VI–SEEM project (https://vi-seem.eu/. This work was partially supported by the Bulgarian National Science Fund (grant DN-14/3/13.12.2017) and the project "NATIONAL GEO-INFORMATION CENTER", subject of the National Road Map for Scientific Infrastructure 2017–2023, funded by Contr. No D01-161/28.08.2018. Personal thanks to I. Tsonevsky from European Centre for Medium-Range Weather Forecasts for the cooperation.

References

1. Belda, M., et al.: CECILIA regional climate simulations for future climate: analysis of climate change signal. Adv. Meteorol. **2015**, 13 (2015). https://doi.org/10.1155/2015/354727. Article ID 354727

2. Buser, C.M., Künsch, H.R., Lüthi, D., Wild, M., Schär, C.: Bayesian multi-model projection of climate: bias assumptions and interannual variability. Clim. Dyn. **33**, 849–868 (2009). https://doi.org/10.1007/s00382-009-0588-6
3. Chervenkov, H., Slavov, K., Ivanov, V.: STARDEX and ETCCDI climate indices based on E-OBS and CARPATCLIM; part one: general description. In: Nikolov, G., Kolkovska, N., Georgiev, K. (eds.) NMA 2018. LNCS, vol. 11189, pp. 360–367. Springer, Cham (2019). https://doi.org/10.1007/978-3-030-10692-8_40
4. Chervenkov, H., Slavov, K., Ivanov, V.: STARDEX and ETCCDI climate indices based on E-OBS and CARPATCLIM; part two: ClimData in use. In: Nikolov, G., Kolkovska, N., Georgiev, K. (eds.) NMA 2018. LNCS, vol. 11189, pp. 368–374. Springer, Cham (2019). https://doi.org/10.1007/978-3-030-10692-8_41
5. Dosio, A., Paruolo, P.: Bias correction of the ENSEMBLES high-resolution climate change projections for use by impact models: evaluation on the present climate. J. Geophys. Res. **116**, D16106 (2011). https://doi.org/10.1029/2011JD015934
6. Dosio, A., Paruolo, P., Rojas, R.: Bias correction of the ENSEMBLES high resolution climate change projections for use by impact models: analysis of the climate change signal. J. Geophys. Res. **117**, D17110 (2012). https://doi.org/10.1029/2012JD017968
7. Dosio, A.: Projections of climate change indices of temperature and precipitation from an ensemble of bias-adjusted high-resolution EURO-CORDEX regional climate models. J. Geophys. Res. Atmos. **121**, 5488–5511 (2016). https://doi.org/10.1002/2015JD024411
8. Haerter, J.O., Hagemann, S., Moseley, C., Piani, C.: Climate model bias correction and the role of timescales. Hydrol. Earth Syst. Sci. **15**, 1065–1079 (2011). https://doi.org/10.5194/hess-15-1065-2011
9. Halenka, T.: Regional climate modeling activities in CECILIA project: introduction. Időjárás **112**, III–IX (2008)
10. Hall, A.: Projecting regional change. Science **346**(6216), 1461–1462 (2014)
11. Haylock, M.R., Hofstra, N., Klein Tank, A.M.G., Klok, E.J., Jones, P.D., New, M.: A European daily high-resolution gridded dataset of surface temperature and precipitation. J. Geophys. Res (Atmos.) **113**, D20119 (2008). https://doi.org/10.1029/2008JD10201
12. Maraun, D.: Bias correcting climate change simulations - a critical review. Curr. Clim. Change Rep. **2**, 211–220 (2016). https://doi.org/10.1007/s40641-016-0050-x
13. Nakicenovic, N.: Intergovernmental Panel on Climate Change: Emission Scenarios, A Special Report of Working Group III of the Intergovernmental Panel on Climate Change. Cambridge University Press, Cambridge (2000)
14. Rummukainen, M.: State-of-the-art with regional climate models. WIREs Clim. Change **1**, 82–96 (2010). https://doi.org/10.1002/wcc.8
15. Spiridonov, V., Déqué, M., Somot, S.: ALADIN-CLIMATE: from the origins to present date. ALADIN Newslett. **29**, 89–92 (2005)
16. Teutschbein, C., Seibert, J.: Is bias correction of regional climate model (RCM) simulations possible for non-stationary conditions? Hydrol. Earth Syst. Sci. **17**, 5061–5077 (2013). https://doi.org/10.5194/hess-17-5061-2013
17. Teutschbein, C., Wetterhall, F., Seibert, J.: Evaluation of different downscaling techniques. Dyn. Clim. (2011). https://doi.org/10.1007/s00382-010-0979-8
18. Xue, Y., Janjic, Z., Dudhia, J., Vasic, R., De Sales, F.: A review on regional dynamical downscaling in intraseasonal to seasonal simulation/prediction and major factors that affect downscaling ability. Atm. Res. **147–148**, 68–85 (2014). https://doi.org/10.1016/j.atmosres.2014.05.001

Project for an Open Source GIS Tool for Visualization of Flood Risk Analysis After Mining Dam Failures

Nina Dobrinkova[1,2]([✉]), Alexander Arakelyan[3,4], Aghavni Harutyunyan[3], and Sean Reynolds[3]

[1] Institute of Information and Communication Technologies,
Bulgarian Academy of Sciences, Sofia, Bulgaria
ninabox2002@gmail.com
[2] Center for National Security and Defence Research,
Bulgarian Academy of Sciences, Sofia, Bulgaria
[3] AUA Center for Responsible Mining,
American University of Armenia, Yerevan, Armenia
{alexander.arakelyan,a.harutyunyan,sreynolds}@aua.am
[4] Institute of Geological Sciences of National Academy of Sciences,
Yerevan, Armenia

Abstract. Under DG ECHO funded project with acronym: ALTER there has been initiated an effort to support the Armenian Ministry of Emergency Situations in establishment of public-private partnerships to understand and address flood risks that may occur after mining dam failures. The project focus on three pilot areas where dams and other activities present risks to local communities: Akhtala and Teghut areas of Lori Marz along the Shamlugh river; the Vorotan Cascade and its associated dams in the Syunik region; and the Voghji river basin of Syunik region. In our article data collection, analysis and the results of dam break modelling for the Geghi reservoir and Geghanoush tailing dam located in Voghji river basin are presented. All collected data from hydro-meteorological sources, elevation, geologic, geomorphological and land use data have been processed in a way that Flood Hazard Index (FHI) Map of the studied area has been developed. This information is combined in GIS (Geographic Information System) layers. Those layers are being uploaded in specifically designed open source GIS tool in order to assist the end users on the field or in the operational room to rapidly assess the risks associated with flood occurred in a result of dam break and to better plan and visualize their activities.

Keywords: Dam break · GIS · Data collection and analysis · Open source software · Flood risk maps

1 Introduction

The Alliance for Disaster Risk Reduction project (ALTER) has its main scope to understand and address flood risks that may stem from water and mining dam

© Springer Nature Switzerland AG 2020
I. Lirkov and S. Margenov (Eds.): LSSC 2019, LNCS 11958, pp. 300–308, 2020.
https://doi.org/10.1007/978-3-030-41032-2_34

failures. Know-how, technologies and experience from European Union countries have been transferred to Armenia capitalizing on the consortia previous experiences. The project is focused on three pilot areas where dams and other activities are presenting the risks to local communities: Akhtala and Teghut areas of Lori Marz along the Shamlugh river; the Vorotan Cascade and its associated dams in the Syunik region; and the Voghji river basin of Syunik region. In this paper the data collection and preliminary flood hazard assessment method is described on example of one of Voghji river basin, within which our objects of study are Geghi Water Reservoir and Geghanoush Tailing Storage Facility (TSF). After all results are summarized and elaborated in flood risk maps, they have been prepared for upload to a specifically designed Open Source GIS (Geographic Information System). The GIS system is in its testing and validation phase at the time of the paper writing. The system is fully based on open source tools in order to be sustainable after the project end. Its main users will be civil protection and crisis management departments of the Ministry of Emergency Situations (MES) in Armenia. Thus, the system is not going to be distributed in any other structures except MES Intranet in Armenia.

2   Study Area

2.1   Geghi Reservoir

The Geghi reservoir is located in Syunik, the southernmost province of Armenia (Fig. 1). The reservoir is situated on the Geghi river, the left-bank tributary of the river Voghji. The maximum water level discharge occurs during the spring. Due to the high altitude nature of the area, snow melt increases gradually as does the level of the river and the reservoir. Snow melt typically lasts from March to August (Armenian State Hydrometeorological and Monitoring Service officially used sources).

The surface of the Geghi reservoir is 50 ha and the elevation above sea level is nearly 1400 m. The height of the dam is 70 m and the length along the crest is 270 m (Fig. 2). The total volume of reservoir is 15 million cubic meters, but the effective volume is about 12 million cubic meters [1]. Nearly 4,300 people would be affected by in a case of a dam break of the reservoir [2].

2.2   Geghanoush Tailing Storage Facility (TSF)

Geghanoush TSF is located in the gorge of the Geghanoush River, in the southern part of Kapan (Fig. 3). The difference of relative heights between the tailing dam, on one hand, and city buildings and transport infrastructure, on the other hand, is 75 m. In case the reservoir dam is broken due to an earthquake, the sliding mass could cover industrial and residential buildings, and as a result of barrage, the polluted water could flood central quarters of the city.

The existing Geghanoush Tailings Repository was designed in early 1960's and had been operated between 1962 and 1983, when the Kajaran Tailings

Fig. 1. The location of Geghi reservoir. The inset shows its location within Armenia. Background image: Sentinel-2, RGB composite (source: AUA).

Fig. 2. Geghi reservoir, Photo credit: S. Schlaffer

Repository at Artsvanik was commissioned. The Geghanoush tailings repository was re-commissioned in 2006 after the completion of the diversion works and continues to be used today along with an upstream extension currently under construction. The volume of the tailing is 5.4 millions m^3 and the dam height is 21.5 m [1].

3   Methodology

Despite their many beneficial uses and value, dams also considered as a hazardous infrastructure due to their possible failure and massive flooding consequences. To mitigate these risks, potential dam failure events need to be modelled by analyzing of dam breach properties and possible extent of the flooding formed in a result of dam break. The two primary tasks in the analysis of a potential dam failure are the prediction of the reservoir outflow hydrograph and the routing of that hydrograph through the downstream valley to determine dam failure consequences. When population is at risk located close to a dam, it is important to accurately predict the breach outflow hydrograph and its timing relative to events in the failure process that could trigger the start of evacuation efforts [3]. In our paper we used empirical data that is collected for the test area and simulated using well-known regression equations for breach characteristics and peak flow calculation described in details in [8–12] and [3,4] with the available tools like HEC-RAS. As for the tailing dams, these equations and models can't be directly applied. There are several scientific papers on the methods for the calculation of TSF failure outflow characteristics and maximum distance travelled by tailings. One of these methods developed by [5] who combined the lists of TSF failures (more information can be found at [6]) and Chambers and Bowker (TSF

Fig. 3. The location of Geghanoush Tailing Dam. The inset shows its location within Armenia. Background image: Sentinel-2, RGB composite (source: AUA).

Fig. 4. Geghanoush Tailing Dam, photo credit: Haekshin Company.

Failures 1915–2017 as of 16 August 2017) and compared the results of the original linear regressions done in [6] with the results using the updated dataset. The regression equations on dam breach and maximum outflow characteristics both for water reservoirs and TSFs were generally developed based on the statistical analysis of above-mentioned approaches in past dam break events. In our paper, TR-60 and TR-66 simplified dam breach outflow and routing models developed by the Engineering division of Soil Conservation Service of US Department of Agriculture (SCS) in 1981 have been used for Geghi dam break analysis. The method developed by Larrauri and Lall in 2018 [5] was used for Geghanoush TSF dam failure analysis. Mapping of potentially flooded zones due to the dam break were conducted in GIS environment using spatial analysis tools (Fig. 4).

4   Required Data

4.1   Hydro-Meteorological Observation Data

Flood formation and its behavior highly depend to the hydro-meteorological conditions of the territory. Rainfall intensity and duration, snow melt, air temperature and other meteorological factors are key drivers in flood development process. Hydro-meteorological monitoring within the territory of Armenia is conducted by Hydromet Service of the Ministry of Emergency Situations of Armenia with 2 operational stations within Voghji River Basin: Kajaran and Kapan (Fig. 5).

The data collected by the stations gives information about: annual average air temperature, average annual relative humidity, snow cover and its potential melted values. Each of the data sets was giving the potential conditions for possible high waves and thus dam break possibility.

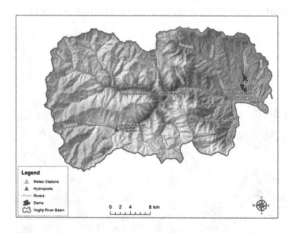

Fig. 5. Hydro-meteorological monitoring posts within Voghji River Basin.

Fig. 6. DEM - 5 m, of studied area (Source: Georisk CJSC)

4.2   Elevation Data and Its Derivatives

Elevation data has a crucial meaning in each flood modelling process. There are various free digital elevation models (DEMs) available online (SRTM, ASTER, ALOS), the spatial resolution of which is 30 m. This resolution is not enough for detailed flood mapping in mountainous areas. From the linearshapefile of elevation isolines of 1:10,000 scale the 5 m DEM of studied area was calculated using Topo to Raster interpolation tool of ArcGIS Spatial Analyst toolbox (Fig. 6):

Geomorphometric parameters (slope, aspect and shaded relief) were derived from DEM. Using ArcHydro Tools, following raster layers were calculated: Flow Direction; Flow Accumulation; Streams; Catchments. From these layers, catchment polygon and drainage line vector layers were obtained which are needed for the modelling purposes.

4.3   Land-Cover and Land-Use

A detailed land-cover and land-use maps were an important component for flood modeling in order to understand the extent of the flood and vulnerability from it, decision-making, as well as a source of baseline information for environmental research. The American University of Armenia GIS and Remote Sensing Lab developed LULC layer for the Voghji River basin based on freely available data from the novel Sentinel-1 and Sentinel-2 missions operated jointly by the European Space Agency (ESA) and the European Commission [7]. For open water (including Geghi reservoir) and tailing ponds Sentinel-1 (SAR) data was used. After obtaining the results of open water and tailing ponds then they were superimposed on the other classes. The final map is shown in the Fig. 7. Additional GIS layers available in AUA and Institute of Geological Sciences geodatabases (infrastructure, buildings, administrative units, water objects, monitoring sites location, etc.) were used to enhance the accuracy of LULC map.

5   Results and Conclusions

Using the data sets presented above, as well as flood hazard, dam break and flood modelling algorithms and statistical tools, as well as GIS spatial analysis and mapping capabilities, flood hazard analysis and dam break flood modelling were

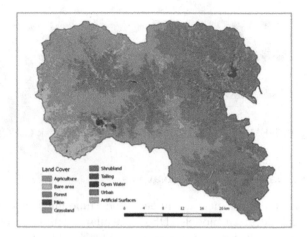

Fig. 7. Land-cover and land-use map of Voghji river basin

Fig. 8. Flood Hazard Index (FHI) Map of studied area.

implemented. Particularly, flood hazard index map for study area were developed and extent and depth of flood formed in a result of Geghi and Geghanoush dam break were modelled (Figs. 8, 9, and 10). Detailed description of dam break flood modelling will be presented in next papers of authors.

All the data collected and presented in the previous sections have as main idea to create algorithm for rapid flood hazard and risk assessment and decision making by the responsible authorities in the form of web-GIS maps available any time. Putting together all missing pieces of data was extensive time consuming work which the Armenian team in the ALTER project has done in the best possible way. Based on the achieved results open source GIS tool has been elaborated and after its testing and validation phase is done it will be installed to dedicated Armenian hosting where the responsible authorities can use it. Initial screen of the tool interface can be seen at Fig. 11.

Fig. 9. Flood extent and depth formed from Geghi reservoir dam break (full failure).

Fig. 10. Flood extent and depth formed from Geghanoush TSF dam break (full failure).

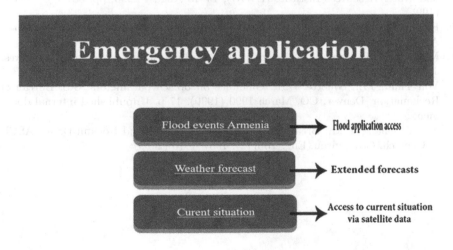

Fig. 11. Algorithm used for data processing and its final application in WEB-GIS.

Acknowledgements. This paper has been supported partially by the Bulgarian National Science Fund project number DN 12/5 called: Efficient Stochastic Methods and Algorithms for Large-Scale Problems and the DG ECHO project called: "Alliance for disaster Risk Reduction in Armenia" with acronym: ALTER and Grand Number: 783214.

References

1. Georisk, C.J.S.C.: Assessment of the Multi-Component Risk Determined by the Maximum Seismic Impact on the Kapan City (Multi-Hazard City Scenario). Project ARM 10–0000005849, Final Report (2017)
2. Gevorgyan, A., Minasyan, R., Khondkaryan, V., Antonyan, A.: The Prediction of Possible Flooding of the Territory as a Result of the Accident of the Geghi Reservoir Dam (2014)
3. Wahl, T.L.: Dam breach modeling—an overview of analysis methods. In: Joint Federal Interagency Conference on Sedimentation and Hydrologic Modeling, Las Vegas, NV, 27 June–1 July 2010
4. Using HEC-RAS for Dam Break Studies. Compiled by Hydrologic Engineering Center of US Army Corps (2014)
5. Concha Larrauri, P., Lall, U.: Tailings dams failures: updated statistical model for discharge volume and runout. Environments **5**, 28 (2018)
6. Rico, M., Benito, G., Diez-Herrero, A.: Floods from tailings dam failures. J. Hazard. Mater. **154**, 79–87 (2008)
7. Schlaffer, S., Harutyunyan, A.: Working Paper: LCLU Voghji River Basin AUA Acopian Center for the Environment. AUA GIS and Remote Sensing Lab (2018)
8. Froehlich, D.C.: Embankment dam breach parameters revisited. In: Proceeding of the First International Conference, Water Resources Engineering, Environmental and Water Resources Institute (EWRI), 14–18 August 1995, pp. 887–891. ASCE (1995)
9. Froehlich, D.C.: Embankment dam breach parameters and their uncertainties. ASCE J. Hydraul. Eng. **134**(12), 1708–1721 (2008)
10. MacDonald, T., Langridge-Monopolis, J.: Breaching characteristics of dam failures. J. Hydraul. Eng. **110**, 567–586 (1984)
11. Von Thun, J.L., Gillette, D.R.: Guidance on breach parameters. U.S. Bureau of Reclamation, Denver, CO, March 1990 (1990). 17 p. Unpublished internal document
12. Xu, Y., Zhang, L.M.: Breaching Parameters for Earth and Rockfill Dams. ASCE J. Geotech. Geoenviron. Eng. **135**(12), 1957–1970 (2009)

Open Source GIS for Civil Protection Response in Cases of Wildland Fires or Flood Events

Nina Dobrinkova[✉] and Stefan Stefanov

Institute of Information and Communication Technologies,
Bulgarian Academy of Sciences, Acad. Georgi Bonchev bl. 2, 1113 Sofia, Bulgaria
ninabox2002@gmail.com, stefans.stefanov303@gmail.com

Abstract. The article describes the capabilities of the open source GIS (Geographic Information Systems) and other Free and Open Source Softwares (FOSS) for building desktop application that can support firefighting and volunteer groups in cases of wildland fires or flood events reactions. The desktop application have two main modules as design. The first module is based on open source GIS software. The second is the server software, database and visualization environment for the application. The main goal of the tool is to visualize administrative and vulnerable objects and POI's (Points of Interests) like logistic centres for water supplies, tools and supplies from where the firefighting and volunteer groups can take what they need on the field work. The idea is to be visualized detailed information about logistic centres and what kind of equipment is stored inside. This is needed, because there aren't implemented modern ICT (Information and Communication Technologies) tools in the field work. The current situation is such that the groups are using instructions written on paper in most of the cases. Our article presents a desktop application that can be used on the field and in an operational rooms by firefighting and volunteer groups acting in cases of wildland fires or flood events. In our application different open source software solutions as Geoserver, Qgis, Web App Builder, Boundless WEBSDK, PostgreSQL and OpenLayers are used:

Geoserver allows the user to display spatial information to the world;

QGIS is a professional GIS (Geographic Information System) cross-platform application that is Free and Open Source Software (FOSS);

Web App Builder is a plugin for QGIS that allows easy creation of web applications;

Boundless WEBSDK which provides tools for easy-to-build JavaScript-based web mapping applications;

PostgreSQL is a powerful, open source object-relational database system;

OpenLayers is an open-source JavaScript library for displaying map data in web browsers.

Keywords: Wildland fires · Flood events · Open source software · Qgis · Geoserver

© Springer Nature Switzerland AG 2020
I. Lirkov and S. Margenov (Eds.): LSSC 2019, LNCS 11958, pp. 309–314, 2020.
https://doi.org/10.1007/978-3-030-41032-2_35

1   Introduction

We are using free data and open source software solutions for developing our application [3,4] for support of volunteer and firefighter groups in cases of wildland fires or flood events. Improving accessibility, time of response and understanding of the disaster in support of volunteer groups on the field. The free sources of data and the open source software solutions give us a lot of opportunities and possibilities to build application that can be used in the operational rooms in cases of wildland fires or flood events. The application can visualize Points of Interest (POIs) which this groups need to know like logistic centers for water supplies and firefighting tools, which are usually well done instructions on a paper documents. We are using basic layers from these data sources that will visualize the needed information in a way that can be easily understood by users of the desktop application.

In order to build our Desktop application we implement only free and open source software for processing the data such as: Qgis [2], Web App Builder, Boundless WEBSDK, Geoserver [1], PostgreSQL and OpenLayers. Qgis [2] is a free open source professional GIS software with which the data is processed. Web app builder makes the data ready to be implemented in the Boundless WEBSDK by which we are building the main core of the application. Geoserver [1] provides the opportunity of using our layer data dynamically or to upload or download new layer data via the application. OpenLayers open source library is used of visualization of the data through the browser.

2   Application Usage and Visualization

The Desktop application has two modules. The first one is for wildland fires and the second one is for flood events [5]. The two modules can operate like two separate applications but also can be combined in one fully operational system. Brief description of each of the modules will be given in the following subsections.

2.1   Wildland Fires Module

The wildland fires module (Fire Module) (Fig. 1) of the desktop application has predefined layers and base map layer based on OpenStreetMaps (OSM). It represents the fire zones and POI's on the territory of Zlatograd forestry department covering the municipalities of Zlatograd, Madan and Nedelino. This module of the desktop application have the ability to show any active fires on the area of interest. It has in addition information about logistic centers for water supplies and firefighting tools. The module is on its validation phase at the time of writing this manuscript. Targeted users are working with it for evaluation and feedback about adding extra features covering their needs.

The Fire Module has different features that can be used by firefighters and volunteer groups in operational room or on the field in case of wildland fires. The module supports Geolocation feature that can help the field work when the

Fig. 1. Wildland fires module main screen

groups want to locate themselves near by the fire source. This will give immediate information in the operational room where exactly the fire is and how far the group is from the nearest logistic center. By using the Draw feature of the tool every user can mark the location of the fire with a sign which will be visualized in real time and will pop up at the operational room monitors. Draw feature has function to draw not only signs but also polygons with the area of the fire.

Measure the distance feature can be used for measuring the distance between the fire and the nearest POI's and also can measure the area of the fire zone.

The module has ability of switching the predefined layers and also the base map layers. The base map layers are including Street map, Satellite map, Shaded relief map and NatGeo map which can help in operational room analysis.

The Pop up feature (Fig. 2) visualizes information about the number and type of tools stored in the logistic centers including their location. The export feature can safe the maps with the new data as picture format files. Which can be used in further data analysis.

Fig. 2. Wildland fires module POI's information

The application has as additional functionality current weather forecast visualization via openweather service connection. It gives detailed information about

Fig. 3. Flood events module main screen

the current or forecast weather conditions. It is also connected to EFFIS emergency management service which provides extra satellite data about the local area hot spots and possible active fire conditions.

2.2   Flood Events Module

The flood events module (Flood Module) (Fig. 3) of the application is designed to support teams that operate on flood events in Armenia. It is based on data coming from the project "Alliance for Disaster Risk Reduction project" with acronym - ALTER. That project focus on establishment of public-private partnerships to understand and address flood risks that may occur in dam failures. The project has three pilot areas in Armenia where dams and other activities present risks to local communities. The areas are the Akhtala and Teghut areas of Lori Marz along the Shamlugh river, the Vorotan Cascade and its associated dams in the Syunik region, and the Kapan and Voghji river basin of Syunik region. The module has been designed to cover data and flood risk maps for one of the potential dam failures. It is under its testing phase with calibrations from the field observations during the time of writing this paper. The end users of the tool in Armenia have the ability to collect data from the field and visualize it with the tool after it is processed to flood risk maps.

The module has the ability of switching the predefined layers and also the base map layers. The predefined layers have a very rich data by turning them off or on. The users can easily make analysis of the risks in cases of flood events by uploading pre-calculated flood risk maps from past events and estimating what is the current situation of the observed area. Layers can be downloaded as geojson files. They can be easily geo-located and their parameters can be changed in addition. The base map layers are including Street map, Satellite map, Shaded relief map and NatGeo map which could support operational teams analysis.

Geolocation feature can easily locate the operators by their GPS of the used device or via network location. Draw feature can be utilized by marking the vulnerable zone with polygon or draw a line marking the danger border visible in operational room. The Pop up feature (Fig. 4) visualizes information about the most vulnerable buildings as schools, kindergartens and others. The export feature can safe the maps with the new data as picture format files. Which can be used in further data analysis. Measurements of distance are available as feature in the tool and can be used to measure the distances within the affected zone.

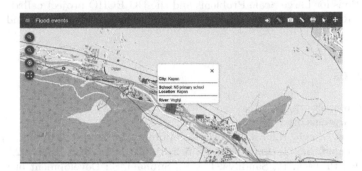

Fig. 4. Flood events module Pop up information

The application provides weather forecast via openweather of current weather conditions. It has the EFAS emergency management service embedded as additional resource of information for the operational teams. The EFAS tool is an EU service that provide extra satellite data about floods in Europe.

3 Conclusion

This article presents a desktop tool with its web application [3–5]. It can be used in cased of wildland fires and flood events. Its potential users are volunteer groups, firefighting teams and civil protection teams. The tool can be used as decision support tool in operational room and navigation app on the field. This kind of ICT solutions are necessary for the growing needs in the context of wildland fires and flood monitoring activities. At this stage we are considering to use QGIS [2] as main GIS processing software, QGIS plugin called Web App Builder for building the application, and for the server part GeoServer [1,3]. PostgreSQL is our database and for the web browser visualization we are using OpenLayers. We are applying services based on GIS technology to build the platform for management large data sets. The tool is designed to deliver knowledge in a timely manner to fire departments and volunteers located on the field or in operational rooms. Its modules are applicable in cases of wildland fires and flood events. The main goal of the Fire and Flood Modules are to deliver information about the location and storage of equipment in Points of Interest (POIs) needed to the field teams. This kind of Information and Communication Technologies (ICT) can meliorate the time of reaction on the field operations, improve the orientation of the teams where the needed equipment is located. The Flood Module has the function to visualize the most vulnerable buildings. It includes different scenarios that can be analysed in operational room and by its tools can support better management of the current and future situation in cases of flood event.

Acknowledgement. This paper has been supported partially by the Bulgarian National Science Fund project number DN 12/5 called: Efficient Stochastic Methods and Algorithms for Large-Scale Problems and the DG ECHO project called: "Alliance for disaster Risk Reduction in Armenia" with acronym: ALTER and Grand Number: 783214.

References

1. http://geoserver.org/about/
2. https://www.qgis.org/
3. Gambhir, D., Singh, H.: An open source approach to build a web GIS application. Int. J. Comput. Sci. Technol. (IJCST) **5**(2–3), 323–325 (2012). ISSN 2229-4333
4. Das, A.K., Prakash, P., Sandilya, C.V.S., Subhani, S.: Development of web-based application for generating and publishing groundwater quality maps using RS/GIS technology and P. Mapper in Sattenapalle, Mandal, Guntur District, Andhra Pradesh. In: Satapathy, S., Avadhani, P., Udgata, S., Lakshminarayana, S. (eds.) ICT and Critical Infrastructure: Proceedings of the 48th Annual Convention of Computer Society of India - Vol II. AISC, vol. 249, pp. 679–686. Springer, Cham (2014). https://doi.org/10.1007/978-3-319-03095-1_74
5. García, V.G., Perotto-Baldivieso, H.L., Hallett, S.: A prototype design for a Web-GIS disaster support system: the Bolivia Amazon case study (2010)

PDE-Constrained Optimization: Matrix Structures and Preconditioners

Ivo Dravins⬥ and Maya Neytcheva⁽✉⁾⬥

Department of Information Technology,
Uppsala University, Box 337, 75105 Uppsala, Sweden
{ivo.dravins,maya.neytcheva}@it.uu.se

Abstract. In this paper we briefly account for the structure of the matrices, arising in various optimal control problems, constrained by PDEs, and how it can be utilized when constructing preconditioners for the arising linear systems to be solved in the optimization framework.

Keywords: PDE-constrained optimal control problems · Numerical solution methods · Preconditioners · Sparse control

1 Introduction

Numerical solution methods for optimal control problems with partial differential equations as constraints (OPT-PDEs) have attracted significant attention since long. Such problems, also with additional constraints on the control and/or state are among the biggest challenges in industry, life sciences and economy. The efficient numerical treatment of such optimization problems includes methods for both optimization and numerical simulations. In this work we address issues related to the efficiency of the numerical solution methods - nonlinear and linear, and the construction of preconditioners, studying their convergence with respect to the large problem size of the arising linear systems and various regularization parameters. For the successful accomplishment of such a task, utilizing the specific algebraic structure of the discrete OPT-PDE problems turns out to be crucial.

The paper is organized as follows. In Sect. 2 we briefly describe the algebraic structures, arising in discrete OPT-PDE problems, corresponding to distributed control (i) without any additional state or control constraints, (ii) with state constraints, (iii) with control constraints and (iv) sparsity constraints on the control. Section 3 describes the chronological development of a particular preconditioning technique, *Preconditioning with square blocks* (PRESB), cf. [1], and its variants, applicable to the above listed problems. The applicability of PRESB for the problems in the case (iii) is analysed. Section 4 introduces a new approach to manage the sparsity of the control, case (iv). Section 5 provides some numerical illustrations and outlook to further research.

Supported by VR Grant 2017-03749 *Mathematics and numerics in PDE-constrained optimization problems with state and control constraints*, 2018–2022.

© Springer Nature Switzerland AG 2020
I. Lirkov and S. Margenov (Eds.): LSSC 2019, LNCS 11958, pp. 315–323, 2020.
https://doi.org/10.1007/978-3-030-41032-2_36

2   OPT-PDEs with State and Control Constraints

Consider problems with distributed control, where the usual functional to be minimized is of the form

$$\mathcal{J}(y, u) = \frac{1}{2}\|y - y_d\|^2_{L^2(\Omega)} + \frac{\alpha}{2}\|u\|^2_{L^2(\Omega)},$$

for simplicity, subject to $-\Delta y = u$ in some domain Ω with $y = 0$ on its boundary $\partial\Omega$. Here α is a regularization parameter. We follow the 'discretize-then-optimize' approach in finite element setting. The discrete constraint equation is then $Ky = Mu + b$. Here K represents the stiffness matrix, M is the mass matrix and b contains boundary terms. To solve the optimization problem, we formulate the corresponding Lagrangian functional, discretize and construct the first order necessary (Karush-Kuhn-Tucker, KKT) conditions. The Lagrangian multiplier to handle the state equation is denoted by p. The discrete version of the Lagrangian functional reads

$$L(y, u, p) = \frac{1}{2}(y - y_d)^T M(y - y_d) + \frac{\alpha}{2}u^T Mu + p^T(Ky - Mu). \qquad (1)$$

We assume here that all three variables are discretized using the same finite element spaces, thus, the mass matrices, corresponding to y and u are the same.

2.1   Distributed Control Problems

Among the most well-studied OPT-PDE formulations is the distributed control problem, i.e., we seek y and u, defined on the whole domain Ω. The first order (uncompressed) KKT system in matrix-vector form reads as follows,

$$\mathcal{A}_f \begin{bmatrix} y \\ u \\ p \end{bmatrix} = \begin{bmatrix} My_d \\ d \\ 0 \end{bmatrix}, \text{ where } \mathcal{A}_f = \begin{bmatrix} M & 0 & K^T \\ K & -M & 0 \\ 0 & \alpha M & -M \end{bmatrix}. \qquad (2)$$

From the third equation we express the control via the adjoint variable, $u = \frac{1}{\alpha}p$, and obtain the reduced system $\begin{bmatrix} M & K^T \\ K & -\frac{1}{\alpha}M \end{bmatrix}\begin{bmatrix} y \\ p \end{bmatrix} = \begin{bmatrix} My_d \\ d \end{bmatrix}$. In order to ensure that the computed state is as close as possible to the desired state y_d, the regularization parameter $0 < \alpha < 1$ is supposed to be small, typically of order $10^{-6} - 10^{-8}$. After scaling and replacing p by $-\sqrt{\alpha}\hat{p}$, the system becomes

$$\mathcal{A}\begin{bmatrix} y \\ \hat{p} \end{bmatrix} = \begin{bmatrix} My_d \\ \sqrt{\alpha}d \end{bmatrix}, \text{ where } \mathcal{A} = \begin{bmatrix} M & -\sqrt{\alpha}K^T \\ \sqrt{\alpha}K & M \end{bmatrix}. \qquad (3)$$

2.2   Distributed Control Problems with State Constraints

Include now box constraints on the state, i.e., impose $y_a \le y \le y_b$ to hold in Ω. In practice the box constraints could be imposed only on a part of the domain,

$\Omega_0 \subset \Omega$, however we assume here that $\Omega_0 = \Omega$. State constraints can be handled in various ways. As in [2], we use the Moreau-Yosida penalty function method [3], where we modify the cost functional and minimize

$$\frac{1}{2}\|y - y_d\|_{L^2(\Omega)}^2 + \frac{\alpha}{2}\|u\|_{L^2(\Omega)}^2 +$$
$$\frac{1}{2\varepsilon}\|\max\{0, y - y_b\}\|_{L^2(\Omega)}^2 + \frac{1}{2\varepsilon}\|\min\{0, y - y_a\}\|_{L^2(\Omega)}^2.$$

Here $0 < \varepsilon < 1$ is another small regularization parameter.

Denote by $\mathcal{I}_i$ and $\mathcal{I}_a$ the sets of inactive and active points, respectively, where *active* are the points, for which the box constraint is violated. The corresponding dimensions, $n_{\mathcal{I}_i}$ and $n_{\mathcal{I}_a}$ satisfy $n = n_{\mathcal{I}_i} + n_{\mathcal{I}_a}$ with n being the degrees of freedom in Ω. The KKT system becomes

$$\begin{bmatrix} M + \varepsilon^{-1} M_a^{(y)} & 0 & -K^T \\ 0 & \alpha M & M \\ -K & M & 0 \end{bmatrix} \begin{bmatrix} \boldsymbol{y} \\ \boldsymbol{u} \\ \boldsymbol{p} \end{bmatrix} = \begin{bmatrix} \boldsymbol{c} \\ \boldsymbol{0} \\ \boldsymbol{d} \end{bmatrix}, \tag{4}$$

where M is the lumped (diagonal) mass matrix (as in [2]), $M_a^{(y)}$ is a part of M with elements set to zero in $\mathcal{I}_i$ and $\boldsymbol{c}$ is of the form $\boldsymbol{c} = M\boldsymbol{y}_d + \varepsilon^{-1}(M_+^{(y)} \boldsymbol{y}_b + M_-^{(y)} \boldsymbol{y}_a)$. Here $M_+^{(y)}$ and $M_-^{(y)}$ are parts of M corresponding to the current active sets, i.e., $M_a^{(y)} = M_+^{(y)} + M_-^{(y)}$.

Solving the above problem has two aspects: we seek the control that would ensure a state as close as possible to the desired state but also we want to minimize the number of elements in the set of active points. Because we minimize a set of points and this affects the system matrix, the problem is nonlinear with a non-differentiable functional. Therefore, we utilize a nonlinear solution method, referred to as the *semi-smooth Newton method* (cf. e.g. [4,6,7]). Scaling (4) analogously to (3) and introducing $\widehat{\boldsymbol{p}} = -\sqrt{\alpha}\boldsymbol{p}$ we obtain

$$\mathcal{A}^s \begin{bmatrix} \boldsymbol{y}^{(k)} \\ \widehat{\boldsymbol{p}}^{(k)} \end{bmatrix} = \begin{bmatrix} \boldsymbol{c} \\ -\sqrt{\alpha}\boldsymbol{d} \end{bmatrix}, \text{ where } \mathcal{A}^s = \begin{bmatrix} M + \frac{1}{\varepsilon}M_a^{(y)} & -\widehat{K}^T \\ \widehat{K} & M \end{bmatrix}, \tag{5}$$

where $\widehat{K} = \sqrt{\alpha}K$. The superscripts $^{(k)}$ in (5) indicate that this system is solved at each nonlinear step, until a certain convergence criterion is met. The term that changes with k is $M_a^{(y)}$. We see that $\mathcal{A}^s$ in (5) is a perturbation of $\mathcal{A}$ in (3).

2.3   Distributed Control Problems with Control Constraints

Consider next box constraints to the control, $u_a \le u \le u_b$. Let λ_a, λ_b be the Lagrange multipliers, related to the control constraints. The Lagrangian functional takes the form $\mathcal{L}(y, u, p, \lambda_a, \lambda_b) = \frac{1}{2}\|y - y_d\|_{L^2(\Omega)}^2 + \frac{\alpha}{2}\|u\|_{L^2(\Omega)}^2 + p^*(\Delta y - u) + \lambda_b(u - u_b) - \lambda_a(u - u_a)$. Usually the multipliers λ_a and λ_b are unified as

$\lambda = \lambda_b - \lambda_a$ (cf. [5]) and, after discretization, the first order necessary conditions become:

(1c) $My + K^T p = My_d,$ (2c) $Ky - Mu = 0,$ (3c) $\alpha Mu - Mp + M\lambda = 0$
(4c) $-\lambda + \max(0, \lambda + c(u - u_b)) + \min(0, \lambda + c(u - u_a)) = 0$ for all $c > 0$.

(We note that the choice of $c > 0$ in (4c) and also in (4s) has an impact on the performance of the Newton iterations and the solution found.) In matrix form the system reads

$$
\begin{bmatrix}
M & 0 & K^T & 0 \\
K & -M & 0 & 0 \\
0 & \alpha M & -M & M \\
0 & cM_a^{(u)} & 0 & -M_i^{(u)}
\end{bmatrix}
\begin{bmatrix}
y \\ u \\ p \\ \lambda
\end{bmatrix}
=
\begin{bmatrix}
b_1 \\ b_2 \\ 0 \\ b_3
\end{bmatrix}.
$$

Here $M_a^{(u)}$, $M_i^{(u)}$ denote lumped mass matrices with nonzero elements, matching active and inactive points. We eliminate $u = \frac{1}{\alpha}(p - \lambda)$, scale and obtain

$$
\mathcal{A}^c
\begin{bmatrix}
y \\ \widehat{p} \\ \lambda
\end{bmatrix}
=
\begin{bmatrix}
b_1 \\ \sqrt{\alpha}b_2 \\ -\alpha b_3
\end{bmatrix},
\quad \text{where } \mathcal{A}^c =
\begin{bmatrix}
M & -\widehat{K}^T & 0 \\
\widehat{K} & M & \frac{1}{\sqrt{\alpha}}M \\
0 & -cM_a^{(u)} & cM_a^{(u)} + \alpha M_i^{(u)}
\end{bmatrix}. \quad (6)
$$

A computation reveals that the Schur complement with respect to the top pivot block can be computed exactly and is of the form

$$
S_{\mathcal{A}^c} =
\begin{bmatrix}
M & -\widehat{K}^T \\
\widehat{K} & M_i^{(u)}
\end{bmatrix}. \quad (7)
$$

In detail, $\begin{bmatrix} 0 \\ \frac{1}{\sqrt{\alpha}}M \end{bmatrix} \left[cM_a^{(u)} + \alpha M_i^{(u)} \right]^{-1} \begin{bmatrix} 0 & -cM_a^{(u)} \end{bmatrix} = \begin{bmatrix} 0 & 0 \\ 0 & M_a^{(u)} \end{bmatrix}$, and we use the
fact that $M_a^{(u)} + M_i^{(u)} = M$, $M_a^{(u)} * M_i^{(u)} = 0$, $M_a^{(u)}M^{-1} = I_a$, $M_i^{(u)}M^{-1} = I_i$
and $I_i * M_a^{(u)} = 0$. Thus, $S_{\mathcal{A}^c}$ is yet another perturbation of $\mathcal{A}$ in (3).

In the numerical experiments, system (6) is solved in its reduced Schur complement form (7).

2.4   Distributed Control Problems with Sparse Control

Next, we add to the cost functional a term, imposing L^1-regularization on the control,

$$
\mathcal{J}(y, u) = \frac{1}{2}\|y - y_d\|^2_{L^2(\Omega)} + \frac{\alpha}{2}\|u\|^2_{L^2(\Omega)} + \beta\|u\|_{L^1(\Omega)}. \quad (8)
$$

Following [8], the first order necessary conditions read as follows:

(1s) $My + K^T p = My_d,$ (2s) $Ky - Mu = 0,$ (3s) $\alpha Mu - Mp + M\lambda = 0$
(4s) $u - \max(0, u + c_1(\lambda - \beta)) - \min(0, u + c_1(\lambda + \beta)) + \max(0, c_2(u - u_b) + c_1(\lambda - \beta)) + \min(0, c_2(u - u_a) + c_1(\lambda + \beta)) = 0$ for all $c_{1,2} > 0$.

After reducing $\boldsymbol{u} = 1/\alpha(\boldsymbol{p} - \boldsymbol{\lambda})$, substituting $\widehat{\boldsymbol{p}} = -\sqrt{\alpha}\boldsymbol{p}$ and scaling, we obtain the same matrix structure as in (6). The system can be further reduced by eliminating $\boldsymbol{\lambda}$ to the corresponding Schur complement, again of the form (7),

$$S_{\mathcal{A}^{cs}} \begin{bmatrix} \boldsymbol{y} \\ \widehat{\boldsymbol{p}} \end{bmatrix} = \begin{bmatrix} \widetilde{\boldsymbol{b}}_1 \\ \sqrt{\alpha}\widetilde{\boldsymbol{b}}_2 \end{bmatrix}, \text{ where } S_{\mathcal{A}^{cs}} = \begin{bmatrix} M & -\widehat{K}^T \\ \widehat{K} & M_a^{(\widehat{p})} \end{bmatrix}. \tag{9}$$

Here $M_a^{(\widehat{p})}$ is a part of M with nonzero entries, corresponding to condition (4s).

We see that when imposing mixed state, control or sparsity constraints, apart from (1c), the first order necessary conditions are identical to those in Sect. 2.4. The Schur-complement reads,

$$S_{\mathcal{A}^{scs}} \begin{bmatrix} \boldsymbol{y} \\ \widehat{\boldsymbol{p}} \end{bmatrix} = \begin{bmatrix} \widetilde{\boldsymbol{b}}_1 \\ \sqrt{\alpha}\widetilde{\boldsymbol{b}}_2 \end{bmatrix}, \text{ where } S_{\mathcal{A}^{scs}} = \begin{bmatrix} M + \frac{1}{\varepsilon}M_a^{(y)} & -\widehat{K}^T \\ \widehat{K} & M_a^{(\widehat{p})} \end{bmatrix}. \tag{10}$$

3   Preconditioning

In a number of papers, cf. [1,9,10], a very efficient preconditioner for the matrix $\mathcal{A}$ in (3) has been derived and tested, namely the PRESB preconditioner

$$\mathcal{P}_{\text{PRESB}} = \begin{bmatrix} M & -\widehat{K}^T \\ \widehat{K} & M + \sqrt{\alpha}(K + K^T) \end{bmatrix}. \tag{11}$$

For brevity we denote $\mathcal{P}_{\text{PRESB}} \equiv \mathcal{P}$. It is shown that if M is symmetric positive definite (spd) and $K + K^T$ is positive semidefinite, all the eigenvalues of the preconditioned matrix $\mathcal{P}^{-1}\mathcal{A}$ are real and belong to the interval $[0.5, 1]$. PRESB has been implemented and compared with several other preconditioners of block-diagonal and block-triangular form, showing robust convergence behavior for a wide range of the parameters h and α, and fastest execution time. In [11] a modified version of PRESB has been used to precondition the matrix $\mathcal{A}^c$ in (5),

$$\mathcal{P}^s = \begin{bmatrix} X + \widehat{K} + \widehat{K}^T & -\widehat{K}^T \\ \widehat{K} & X \end{bmatrix}, \quad X = M + \frac{\sigma}{\varepsilon}M_a^{(y)}. \tag{12}$$

Here σ is a method parameter, chosen slightly larger than 1, say $\sigma = 1.1$. This preconditioner has also shown a very robust convergence behavior with respect to h, α and ε. Based on the latter derivations, we investigate the possibility to apply PRESB-type preconditioning to the matrix block $S_{\mathcal{A}^c}$. Namely, we seek a matrix Y, such that

$$\mathcal{P}^c = \begin{bmatrix} Y & -\widehat{K}^T \\ \widehat{K} & Y + \widehat{K} + \widehat{K}^T \end{bmatrix} \tag{13}$$

would be a good preconditioner to $S_{\mathcal{A}^c}$, respectively, for $S_{\mathcal{A}^{cs}}$. In other words, the matrix $\Pi^c = \begin{bmatrix} Y & -\widehat{K}^T \\ \widehat{K} & Y \end{bmatrix}$ should approximate well $S_{\mathcal{A}^c}$. We analyze $\Pi^c S_{\mathcal{A}^c}^{-1}$

and obtain

$$
\Pi^c S_{A^c}^{-1} = \begin{bmatrix} YM^{-1} - (I - YM^{-1})\widehat{K}^T S^{-1}\widehat{K}M^{-1} & (YM^{-1}\widehat{K}^T - \widehat{K}^T)S^{-1} \\ (I - (\widehat{K}M^{-1}\widehat{K}^T + Y)S^{-1})\widehat{K}M^{-1} & (\widehat{K}M^{-1}\widehat{K}^T + Y)S^{-1} \end{bmatrix}.
$$
(14)

Considering the second block row in (14), we see that $Y = M_i$ is the ideal choice for obtaining a block-row of the identity matrix, $[0\ I]$. However, the first block row becomes then $\left[I_i + (I - I_i)S^{-1}\widehat{K}M^{-1}\ (I_i\widehat{K}^T - \widehat{K}^T)S^{-1}\right]$, showing that the PRESB framework cannot be straightforwardly applied in this case and some further regularization is needed. Here I_i is a part of the identity matrix with nonzero elements in the set of inactive points.

For testing purposes we choose $Y = (1 + h^2)M$. A computation shows that the eigenvalues of $(\mathcal{P}^c)^{-1}S_{A^c}$ lie in the interval $(C\sqrt{\alpha}, 1]$, for some constant C, independent of the discretization parameter h, revealing that the lower bound diminishes when α decreases. The estimate matches the observed increase in the number of linear iterations for fixed h and α - decreased, see Table 1(a).

Table 1. Numerical tests: *Size* denotes the size of the system matrix solved

Size	Problem 1		Problem 2		Problem 3	
	Nonlin. iter.	Av. lin. iter.	Nonlin. iter.	Av. lin. iter.	Nonlin. iter.	Av. lin. iter.
	$\alpha = 10^{-4}$					
8450	4	11	5	13	1	11
33282	4	11	5	13	1	11
132098	4	11	6	13	1	11
	$\alpha = 10^{-5}$					
8450	6	15	7	19	7	17
33282	6	15	8	18	7	17
132098	6	15	8	18	7	17
	$\alpha = 10^{-6}$					
8450	8	24	13	39	8	27
33282	7	25	11	38	8	26
132098	7	25	14	38	9	26
	(a)		(b)		(c)	

An alternative approach to solve the system in (10) is to switch the rows, apply the boundary conditions appropriately and use a preconditioner from [12],

$$
\mathcal{P}_r = \begin{bmatrix} \widehat{K} + M + \frac{1}{\varepsilon}M_a^{(y)} + M_a^{(\widehat{p})} & M_a^{(\widehat{p})} \\ M + \frac{1}{\varepsilon}M_a^{(y)} & -\widehat{K}^T \end{bmatrix} \sim \begin{bmatrix} \widehat{K} + M + \frac{1}{\varepsilon}M_a^{(y)} & M_a^{(\widehat{p})} \\ 0 & \widehat{K} + M_a^{(\widehat{p})} \end{bmatrix}.
$$
(15)

This is applicable when $K = K^T$. The diagonal blocks are spd and can be solved efficiently with multigrid methods.

4 Simulating Directional Sparsity via Variable Regularization Parameter

In [13], using special mathematics tools, a method to impose structure in the sparsity of the control is proposed. We recreate analogous sparsity structure by treating the L^1-regularization parameter β in (8) as a function. This is by no means an equivalent formulation, the pattern of β is decided explicitly in advance. However, the suggested formulation is simple, yet it allows to design a desired sparsity pattern. Problem 3 and Figs. 1(c), (d) illustrate the idea.

5 Numerical Illustrations and Outlook

We illustrate the performance of the involved nonlinear and linear solvers with some numerical experiments. The tests are performed in `Matlab` (Table 1(a)) and in `Julia` [14] (Table 1(b, c)).

Problem 1. Desired state $y_d(x_1, x_2) = \sin(2\pi x_1)\sin(2\pi x_2)e^{2x_1}/6$, $-30 \leq \boldsymbol{u} \leq 30$, $c = \sqrt{\alpha}$, $Y = (1 + h^2)M$. Initial guess for the nonlinear solver - the solution on the previous coarser mesh. Solve (7), preconditioned by P^c in (13);

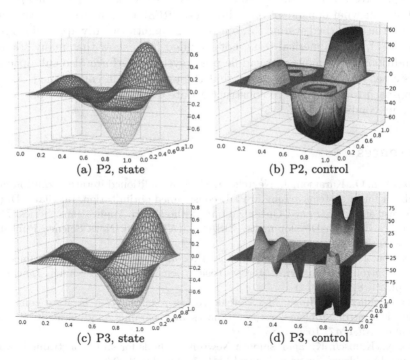

(a) P2, state

(b) P2, control

(c) P3, state

(d) P3, control

Fig. 1. Problems 2 and 3: $\alpha = 10^{-6}$: left: *red* - achieved state, *blue* - desired state (Color figure online)

Problem 2. Desired state as in Problem 1, $-20-50x_1 \leq u \leq 20+50x_2$, $-0.2 \leq y$, $\beta = 10^{-4}$. Initial guess for the nonlinear solver - the solution to the unconstrained problem (3) with $\alpha = 10^{-2}$. Solve (10) preconditioned by (15).

Problem 3. Desired state as in Problem 1, $-100 \leq u \leq 100$, $-0.5 \leq y$. Initial guess for the nonlinear solver as in Problem 2. Solve (10) preconditioned by (15). The L^1-regularization parameter β in (8) is

$$\beta(x_1, x_2) = \begin{cases} 10^{-8} \; ; \; x_1 \in [0.2, 0.4] \cup [0.7, 0.9], \\ 0.99 \; ; \; \text{elsewhere.} \end{cases}$$

For Problems 2 and 3: $c_1 = c_2 = 1/\alpha$, $\varepsilon = \alpha^{\frac{1}{4}}$. The discretization is with square mesh and bilinear finite elements. The outer linear solver is the Generalized Conjugate Residual (GCR) method with relative tolerance 10^{-8}. The inner solver is AMG-preconditioned GCR with relative stopping tolerance 10^{-5}. For all problems and parameter values the inner iterations vary between 5 and 19. Some numerical results are presented in Table 1, and illustrations – in Fig. 1. (In Problem 3, $\alpha = 10^{-4}$, the only active constraint is the sparsity on u, satisfied by the initial guess.)

In conclusion, the tested preconditioners show well-controlled behavior of the nonlinear solver. The performance of the linear solver is relatively independent on h but somewhat dependent on α. Further, PRESB exhibits its attractive properties for the perturbed system (5), but is not straightforwardly applicable for the matrices (7), (9). Numerical tests, not included here, show that many standard preconditioning techniques for saddle point systems perform also sub-optimally in this case. We point out, however, that the problem is ill-conditioned. A possible approach to consider is to construct Monte Carlo-based sparse approximate inverse preconditioning, cf. [15].

References

1. Axelsson, O., Karatson, J., Neytcheva, M.: Preconditioned iterative solution methods for linear systems arising in PDE-constrained optimization. In: Clark, D. (ed.) Robust and Constrained Optimization: Methods and Applications. Series: Mathematics Research Developments. BISAC: MAT042000. Nova Science Publishers, New York (2019)
2. Pearson, J.W., Stoll, M., Wathen, A.J.: Preconditioners for state-constrained optimal control problems with Moreau-Yosida penalty function. Numer. Linear Alg. Appl. **21**, 81–97 (2014)
3. Hintermüller, M., Hinze, M.: Moreau-Yosida regularization in state constrained elliptic control problems: error estimates and parameter adjustment. SIAM J. Numer. Anal. **47**, 1666–1683 (2009)
4. Ito, K., Kunisch, K.: Semi-smooth Newton methods for state-constrained optimal control problems. Systems Control Lett. **5**, 221–228 (2003)
5. Herzog, R., Kunisch, K.: Algorithms for PDE-constrained optimization. GAMM Mitteilungen **33**(2), 163–176 (2010)

6. Porselli, M., Simoncini, V., Tani, M.: Preconditioning of active-set Newton method for PDE-constrained optimal control problems. SIAM J. Sci. Comput. **37**, 472–502 (2015)
7. Herzog, R., Sachs, E.W.: Preconditioned conjugate gradient method for optimal control problems with control and state constraints. SIAM J. Matrix Anal. Appl. **31**, 2291–2317 (2010)
8. Stadler, G.: Elliptic optimal control problems with L1-control cost and applications for the placement of control devices. Comput. Optim. Appl. **44**, 159–181 (2009)
9. Axelsson, O., Boyanova, P., Kronbichler, M., Neytcheva, M., Wu, X.: Numerical and computational efficiency of solvers for two-phase problems. Comput. Math. Appl. **65**, 301–314 (2013)
10. Axelsson, O., Farouq, S., Neytcheva, M.: Comparison of preconditioned Krylov subspace iteration methods for PDE-constrained optimization problems. Poisson and convection-diffusion control. Numer. Algorithms **73**, 631–663 (2016)
11. Axelsson, O., Neytcheva, M., Ström, A.: An efficient preconditioning method for state box-constrained optimal control problems. J. Numer. Math. **26**, 185–207 (2018)
12. Axelsson, O., Neytcheva, M., Liang, Z.: Parallel solution methods and preconditioners for evolution equations. Math Model. Anal. **23**(2), 287–308 (2018)
13. Herzog, R., Stadler, G., Wachsmuth, G.: Directional sparsity in optimal control of partial differential equations. SIAM J. Control Optim. **50**(2), 943–963 (2012)
14. Bezanson, J., Edelman, A., Karpinski, S., Shah, V.: Julia: a fresh approach to numerical computing. SIAM Rev. **50**, 65–98 (2017)
15. Alexandrov, V., Esquivel-Flores, O.A.: Towards Monte Carlo preconditioning approach and hybrid Monte Carlo algorithms for matrix computations. Comput. Math. Appl. **70**(11), 2709–2718 (2015)

One Approach of Solving Tasks in the Presence of Free Surface Using a Multiprocessor Computing Systems

Valentin A. Gushchin[1]([⊠]) [iD] and Vasilii G. Kondakov[2] [iD]

[1] Institute for Computer Aided Design of Russian Academy of Sciences,
Moscow, Russia
gushchin@icad.org.ru
[2] Nuclear Safety Institute of Russian Academy of Sciences, Moscow, Russia
kondakov@ibrae.ac.ru

Abstract. The task about motion of a pair of vortices under a free surface for different Froude numbers and the problem of free oscillations of fluids in a rectangular container are considered. It is assumed that the liquid is weakly compressible and homogeneous. Comparative analysis with analytical and numerical solutions obtained using incompressible approach in the author's previous works. To solve the system of equations obtained in curvilinear coordinates with appropriate boundary and initial conditions the explicit scheme of second order approximation by the method CABARET is used. Also includes parallel version of the algorithm of calculation using Descartes cell decomposition. Evaluation of parallelization on supercomputing facility with distributed memory was performed. The results give way to further generalize this approach for solving problems with a free surface in a three-dimensional setting. The author's plan to construct an effective method for investigation of a non homogeneous fluid flows through the further development of this approach. Such explicit techniques offer the possibility of efficient use of multiprocessor systems (clusters) for solving problems, which previously dominated by models of incompressible medium.

Keywords: CABARET scheme · Weakly compressible medium · Viscous fluid flows

1 Introduction

In previous works [1–6] incompressible fluid model with open boundary is considered. In works [3–6] method based on CABARET scheme with addition of conjugate gradients method for solving Laplace operator for pressure pulsations was introduced. Acquired results showed good agreement with results obtained in works [1,2] using method based on SMIF scheme with splitted physical processes. Using rectangular container problem and arising pair of vortexes as example satisfactory flow pattern was achieved. For first test conforming with analytical solution of experiment were received. For second test satisfactory results

© Springer Nature Switzerland AG 2020
I. Lirkov and S. Margenov (Eds.): LSSC 2019, LNCS 11958, pp. 324–331, 2020.
https://doi.org/10.1007/978-3-030-41032-2_37

of vortex pair velocities were obtained, as well as correct flow pattern of open boundary.

In this work new mathematical model of fluid was suggested, specifically weakly compressible media with linear dependence of pressure pulsations and density. Value of velocity of pressure pulsations propagation is considered arbitrarily, in this method this value is taken from foundation of the problem. For example, in test of floating vortex pair the sound speed is estimated (varied) from assumption that the maximum velocity in calculated domain is 1/10 of sound speed. Aforementioned assumption leads to conclusion that pressure pulsations are less than 1%.

The aim of this work was to build and test new difference scheme using Cabaret method. In this work the equations for Riemann invariants are given in curvilinear reference system. The time step is estimated given CFL number. Results of floating vortex pair test and sinus disturbed open surface in glass test calculations will be shown.

2   Mathematical Model

Let's consider system of equation from [2]:

$$\begin{cases} \frac{\partial \rho}{\partial t} + \frac{1}{R}\frac{\partial R\rho u}{\partial x} + \frac{1}{R}\frac{\partial R\rho(Av+(\xi B+C))u}{\partial \xi} = 0, \\ \frac{\partial u}{\partial t} + \frac{1}{R}\frac{\partial Ru^2}{\partial x} + \frac{1}{R}\frac{\partial R(Av+(\xi B+C))u^2}{\partial \xi} + \frac{1}{\rho}\left[\frac{\partial p}{\partial x} + (\xi B+C)\frac{\partial p}{\partial \xi}\right] = \frac{1}{Re}\triangle u, \\ \frac{\partial v}{\partial t} + \frac{1}{R}\frac{\partial Ruv}{\partial x} + \frac{1}{R}\frac{\partial R(Av+(\xi B+C))uv}{\partial \xi} + \frac{1}{R\rho}\frac{\partial p}{\partial \xi} = \frac{1}{Re}\triangle v. \end{cases} \quad (1)$$

here $R = H + \eta$, $A = \frac{1}{R}$, $B = -AR_x$, $C = AH_x$, $D = -AR_t$ (Fig. 1).

Let's transform the Eq. (1) into so-called divergent form:

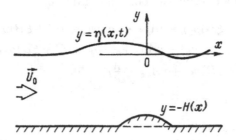

Fig. 1. 2D fluid with free surface.

$$R\frac{\partial \mathbf{U}}{\partial t} + \frac{\partial \mathbf{F}}{\partial x} + \frac{\partial \mathbf{G}}{\partial \xi} = \mathbf{Q},$$

$$\mathbf{U} = \begin{pmatrix} \rho \\ \rho u \\ \rho v \end{pmatrix}, \ \mathbf{F} = \begin{pmatrix} R\rho u \\ R(\rho u^2 + p) \\ R\rho uv \end{pmatrix},$$

$$\mathbf{G} = \begin{pmatrix} \rho v + R(\xi B + C)\rho u \\ \rho uv + R(\xi B + C)(\rho u^2 + p) \\ \rho v^2 + p + R(\xi B + C)\rho uv \end{pmatrix}, \ \mathbf{Q} = \begin{pmatrix} 0 \\ \frac{\rho \triangle u}{Re} \\ \frac{\rho \triangle v}{Re} \end{pmatrix} \quad (2)$$

Now consider the characteristic form of the equations. To do this, let us imagine how the equations should be modified to account for the transition to a curvilinear coordinate system:

$$\begin{cases} f = f(x,y) = \phi(\chi,\xi) \\ (x,y) \rightarrow (\chi,\xi) \\ \frac{\partial f(x,y)}{\partial x} = \frac{\partial \phi(\chi,\xi)}{\partial x} = \frac{\partial \phi}{\partial \chi}\frac{\partial \chi}{\partial x} + \frac{\partial \phi}{\partial \xi}\frac{\partial \xi}{\partial x}, \\ \frac{\partial f(x,y)}{\partial y} = \frac{\partial \phi(\chi,\xi)}{\partial y} = \frac{\partial \phi}{\partial \chi}\frac{\partial \chi}{\partial y} + \frac{\partial \phi}{\partial \xi}\frac{\partial \xi}{\partial y}. \end{cases} \quad (3)$$

In our case, the transformation matrix looks like:

$$\begin{pmatrix} \frac{\partial f}{\partial x} \\ \frac{\partial f}{\partial y} \end{pmatrix} = \begin{pmatrix} 1 & C + \xi B \\ 0 & A \end{pmatrix} \begin{pmatrix} \frac{\partial \phi}{\partial \chi} \\ \frac{\partial \phi}{\partial \xi} \end{pmatrix} \quad (4)$$

Take the equation of state of a weakly compressible medium and substitute continuity into the equation. Next, combine this equation with the equations for the pulse without taking into account the derivatives of the above first order. Substitute the expression for the derivatives by the formula for the transformation of derivatives in a curvilinear coordinate system:

$$\begin{cases} p_t + u\left(p_x + (C + \xi B)p_\xi\right) + vAp_\xi + \rho c^2\left(u_x + (C + \xi B)u_\xi + Av_\xi\right) = 0, \\ u_t + u\left(u_x + (C + \xi B)u_\xi\right) + vAu_\xi + \frac{1}{\rho}\left(p_x + (C + \xi B)p_\xi\right) = 0, \\ v_t + u\left(v_x + (C + \xi B)v_\xi\right) + vAv_\xi + \frac{A}{\rho}p_\xi = 0. \end{cases} \quad (5)$$

In the matrix record we get:

$$\begin{cases} \varphi_t + \mathbf{A_x}\varphi_x + \mathbf{A_\xi}\varphi_\xi = 0, \\ \varphi = \begin{pmatrix} p \\ u \\ v \end{pmatrix}, \ \mathbf{A_x} = \begin{pmatrix} u & \rho c^2 & 0 \\ \frac{1}{\rho} & u & 0 \\ 0 & 0 & u \end{pmatrix}, \ \mathbf{A_\xi} = \begin{pmatrix} w & (C + \xi B)\rho c^2 & A\rho c^2 \\ \frac{C+\xi B}{\rho} & w & 0 \\ \frac{A}{\rho} & 0 & w \end{pmatrix}, \\ w = Av + (C + \xi B)u \end{cases} \quad (6)$$

Find the eigenvalues of matrices A_x, A_ξ:

$$\begin{cases} det\left(\mathbf{A_x} - \lambda\mathbf{E}\right) = 0, \\ det\left(\mathbf{A_\xi} - \mu\mathbf{E}\right) = 0, \end{cases} \Rightarrow \begin{cases} \lambda_{1,3} = u \mp c, \ \lambda_2 = u, \\ \mu_{1,3} = w \mp c\sqrt{A^2 + (C + \xi B)^2}, \ \mu_2 = w. \end{cases} \quad (7)$$

As we can see by two eigenvalues have constant signs $\lambda_1 < 0, \lambda_3 > 0$ and $\mu_1 < 0, \mu_3 > 0$.

Find the proper left vectors of the matrices A_x, A_ξ and compose of them the Riemann invariants:

$$
\begin{cases}
I_1 = u - \frac{p}{\rho c}, I_2 = v, I_3 = u + \frac{p}{\rho c}, \\
J_1 = w_n - \frac{p}{\rho c}, J_2 = w_\tau, J_3 = w_n + \frac{p}{\rho c}, \\
w_n = (Av + (C + \xi B)u)/\sqrt{A^2 + (C + \xi B)^2}, \\
w_\tau = (Au - (C + \xi B)v)/\sqrt{A^2 + (C + \xi B)^2}.
\end{cases}
\tag{8}
$$

Thus, the characteristic system of equations can be written as follows:

$$
\begin{cases}
\frac{\partial I_k}{\partial t} + \lambda_k \frac{\partial I_k}{\partial x} = q_k, \ k = 1, 2, 3, \\
\frac{\partial J_l}{\partial t} + \mu_l \frac{\partial J_l}{\partial \xi} = r_l, \ l = 1, 2, 3.
\end{cases}
\tag{9}
$$

3 Algorithm of Calculation

3.1 CABARET Scheme

First of all we calculate distribution level of free surface on new time layer t_{n+1}:

$$
\frac{\eta_i^{n+1} - \eta_i^n}{\tau} = v_{i,M-1/2}^n - u_{i,M-1/2}^n \frac{\eta_{i+1}^n - \eta_{i-1}^n}{x_{i+1} - x_i},
\tag{10}
$$

Then can be found the values of auxiliary variables A, B, C, D. In cycle by cells we obtain the new conservative variables on half time layer $t_{n+1/2}$:

$$
R_{i+1/2,j+1/2}^n \frac{\mathbf{U}_{i+1/2,j+1/2}^{n+1/2} - \mathbf{U}_{i+1/2,j+1/2}^{n-1/2}}{\tau} + \frac{\mathbf{F}_{i+1,j+1/2}^n - \mathbf{F}_{i,j+1/2}^n}{x_{i+1} - x_i}
$$
$$
+ \frac{\mathbf{G}_{i+1/2,j+1}^n - \mathbf{G}_{i+1/2,j}^n}{\xi_{j+1} - \xi_j} = \mathbf{Q}_{i+1/2,j+1/2}^n,
\tag{11}
$$

Now to complete one time step we must know flux variables on new time layer t_{n+1}. For that there are few equations (9) for Invariants:

$$
\begin{cases}
(I_1)_{i,j+1/2}^{n+1} = 2(I_1)_{i+1/2,j+1/2}^{n+1/2} - (I_1)_{i+1,j+1/2}^n, \\
(I_2)_{i,j+1/2}^{n+1} = 2(I_2)_{i+1/2,j+1/2}^{n+1/2} - (I_2)_{i+1,j+1/2}^n, & \text{if}(\lambda_2)_{i,j+1/2}^{n+1} < 0 \\
(I_2)_{i,j+1/2}^{n+1} = 2(I_2)_{i-1/2,j+1/2}^{n+1/2} - (I_2)_{i-1,j+1/2}^n, & \text{if}(\lambda_2)_{i,j+1/2}^{n+1} > 0 \\
(I_3)_{i,j+1/2}^{n+1} = 2(I_3)_{i-1/2,j+1/2}^{n+1/2} - (I_3)_{i-1,j+1/2}^n,
\end{cases}
\tag{12}
$$

$$\Downarrow$$

$$
\begin{cases}
p_{i,j+1/2}^{n+1} = \frac{\rho c}{2}\left((I_3)_{i,j+1/2}^{n+1} - (I_1)_{i,j+1/2}^{n+1}\right) \\
u_{i,j+1/2}^{n+1} = \frac{1}{2}\left((I_3)_{i,j+1/2}^{n+1} + (I_1)_{i,j+1/2}^{n+1}\right) \\
v_{i,j+1/2}^{n+1} = (I_2)_{i,j+1/2}^{n+1}.
\end{cases}
$$

$$
\begin{cases}
(J_1)_{i+1/2,j}^{n+1} = 2(J_1)_{i+1/2,j+1/2}^{n+1/2} - (J_1)_{i+1/2,j+1}^n \\
(J_2)_{i+1/2,j}^{n+1} = 2(J_2)_{i+1/2,j+1/2}^{n+1/2} - (J_2)_{i+1/2,j+1}^n, & \text{if}(\mu_2)_{i+1/2,j}^{n+1} < 0 \\
(J_2)_{i+1/2,j}^{n+1} = 2(J_2)_{i+1/2,j-1/2}^{n+1/2} - (J_2)_{i+1/2,j-1}^n, & \text{if}(\mu_2)_{i+1/2,j}^{n+1} > 0 \\
(J_3)_{i+1/2,j}^{n+1} = 2(J_3)_{i+1/2,j-1/2}^{n+1/2} - (J_3)_{i+1/2,j-1}^n
\end{cases}
$$

$$\Downarrow \qquad (13)$$

$$
\begin{cases}
p_{i+1/2,j}^{n+1} = \frac{\rho c}{2}\left((J_3)_{i+1/2,j}^{n+1} - (J_1)_{i+1/2,j}^{n+1}\right) \\
w_n = \frac{1}{2}\left((J_3)_{i+1/2,j}^{n+1} + (J_1)_{i+1/2,j}^{n+1}\right) \\
w_\tau = (J_2)_{i+1/2,j}^{n+1}, \\
u_{i+1/2,j}^{n+1} = \frac{(C+\xi B)w_n + Aw_\tau}{A^2+(C+\xi B)^2}, \\
v_{i+1/2,j}^{n+1} = \frac{Aw_n-(C+\xi B)w_\tau}{A^2+(C+\xi B)^2}.
\end{cases}
$$

3.2   Summary

In new scheme the further described optimization is suggested: at starting point in time two layers of time are initialized: at the same time conservative variables at half-full step $t_{1/2}$ and flux variables at zero step are initialized. Further the calculation of new level layer at new time layer takes place. After that the auxiliary variables A, B, C, D are calculated in nodes and at the center of axis X. With all the coefficients in conservative variables equations known, new values at the next half-full step $t_{n+1/2}$ value are calculated. Using Riemann invariants' interpolation ratios new values of streaming variables at full step are calculated using aforementioned equations.

4   Parallelization

Since the obtained difference scheme is explicit, the method of parallelization used in program allows arbitrary domain decomposition into connected sub domains of cells. Flux values will be used as a boundary between neighbor processes. Hence for establishing parallel calculation the values of Riemann invariants are ought to be sent in faces of border cells using values from adjacent sub domain. It is important to provide values of sub domain levels in a way that all the necessary for auxiliary variables arrays are included. To simplify this logic every process can be used to solve the problem of new layer values calculation. Because the number of operations in this procedure depends only on number of mesh divisions along the axis X.

Current algorithm was realized in Fortran90 code with MPI exchange protocol. Part of the computation was done at cluster in Nuclear Safety Institute.

5   Test Section

5.1   Oscillations of Liquid in a Container

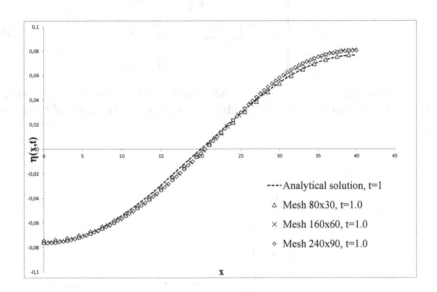

Fig. 2. Comparison with analytic solution.

Let the rectangular container be partially filled with a liquid at rest. At the initial time t = 0, an instantaneous pressure pulse $\Phi = A\sigma(t)cos(kx)$ is applied to the free surface, after which the free surface begins to vibrate. From a linear analysis for the shape of a free surface:

$$\eta(x,t) = -A\sqrt{\frac{\xi}{gH}} \sin\left(\sqrt{\frac{\xi}{gH}}t\right) \cos(kx),\ \xi = kH\,\text{th}(kH). \qquad (14)$$

In the considered variant, $A = 11.78, k = 2\pi/\lambda$, the perturbation wavelength $\lambda = 80$, the number $Re = 10$, and the initial depth of the basin $H = 15$. The calculation was carried out on area of 40×15. The comparison with analytical solution on three meshes was shown in Fig. 2.

5.2   The Interaction of Vortex Pair with a Free Surface

Let's consider the dynamics of vortex pairs and its interaction with a free surface. To simplify the task, we assume that fluid is non-viscous and homogeneous. Let us assume that two vortexes of equal intensity and with opposite direction of rotation are located at a depth $z = -H_0$. It is anticipated that at the initial time, the distance between the centers of the vortexes as well b and vorticity is concentrated in the nuclei of target size with radius r_0. Radial velocity profile for one of the vortices in a polar coordinate system, situated at the center of the vortex has the form:

$$U(r) = \begin{cases} U_0 \cdot \dfrac{r}{r_0}, & r < r_0; \\[2mm] U_0 \cdot \dfrac{(2r_0 - r)}{r_0}, & r_0 < r < 2r_0; \\[2mm] 0, & r > 2r_0; \end{cases} \tag{15}$$

where U_0 - maximum rotation velocity in a vortex. Fluid movement is characterized by two parameters: Froude number: $F = \frac{U}{\sqrt{gr_0}}$ and the ratio of the scales $a = \frac{b}{r_0}$.

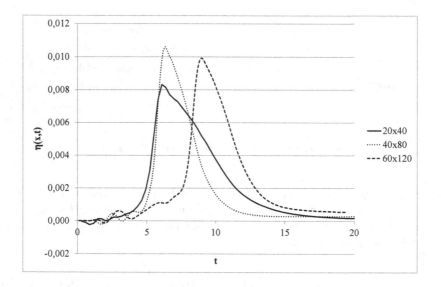

Fig. 3. Comparison of solutions on set of meshes in greater area.

Assuming the symmetry relative to the plane $y = 0$, the solution is searched in the half plane $y = 0$ with size $0 \le y \le L = 180 \cdot r_0$, $-10 \cdot r_0 \le z \le 0$. At $y = 0$ we assume conditions of symmetry and on the boundaries $y = L$ and $z = Z$ the radiation conditions. At the top ($z = 0$) - the conditions on the free surface. The solution domain is covered by uniform grid cells in z direction with step $h_z = 0.2 \cdot r_0$, and on the axis y with $0 \le y \le 18 \cdot r_0$ uses a uniform grid with step $h_y = 0.2 \cdot r_0$, but when $y > 18 \cdot r_0$ grid step increases exponentially. Calculations are made on the grid (120×50) with a time step $t = 0.05$. The results of simulations on area 50×20 in Fig. 3. It was shown that the solution is similar on three meshes with reducing spacing step.

6   Conclusion

New finite difference second order scheme is suggested for system of equations in curvilinear reference system. Divergent form of equations was obtained for conservative variables and continuity equation. Characteristic form of equation was obtained for flux variables, Riemann invariants were calculated using weak compressible approximation given linear system was hyperbolic in reference to first derivatives. Test calculations were carried out successfully.

Acknowledgment. This work was performed in frame of State Assignment of ICAD RAS.

References

1. Belotserkovskii, O.M., Gushchin, V.A., Konshin, V.N.: The splitting method for investigating flows of a stratified liquid with a free surface. USSR Comput. Math. Math. Phys. **27**(2), 181–196 (1987)
2. Gushchin, V.A., Konshin, V.N.: Computational aspects of the splitting method for incompressible flow with a free surface. J. Comput. Fluids **21**(3), 345–353 (1992)
3. Gushchin, V.A., Kondakov, V.G.: On CABARET scheme for incompressible fluid flow problems with free surface. In: International Multidisciplinary Scientific Geo-Conference, SGEM, vol. 17, pp. 485–492. Surveying Geology & Mining Ecology Management, Sofia (2017). https://doi.org/10.5593/sgem2017/21
4. Gushchin, V.A.E., Kondakov, V.G.: On CABARET scheme for incompressible fluid flow problems with a free surface. J. Matematicheskoe Modelirovanie **30**(11), 75–90 (2018)
5. Gushchin, V.A., Kondakov, V.G.: On some approaches for a free surface fluid flows modeling. In: AIP Conference Proceedings, vol. 2025, no. 1, p. 020003. AIP Publishing, October 2018. https://doi.org/10.1063/1.5064876
6. Gushchin, V.A., Kondakov, V.G.: On one method for solving of a non-stationary fluid flows with free surface. In: Dimov, I., Faragó, I., Vulkov, L. (eds.) FDM 2018. LNCS, vol. 11386, pp. 274–280. Springer, Cham (2019). https://doi.org/10.1007/978-3-030-11539-5_30

In Silico Study on the Structure of Novel Natural Bioactive Peptides

Nevena Ilieva[1,2](✉) ⓘ, Peicho Petkov[3] ⓘ, Elena Lilkova[1] ⓘ, Tsveta Lazarova[3],
Aleksandar Dolashki[4], Lyudmila Velkova[4] ⓘ, Pavlina Dolashka[4],
and Leandar Litov[3] ⓘ

[1] Institute of Information and Communication Technologies at the Bulgarian
Academy of Sciences, Acad. G. Bonchev Str., Block 25A, 1113 Sofia, Bulgaria
nevena.ilieva@parallel.bas.bg
[2] Institute of Mathematics and Informatics at the Bulgarian Academy of Sciences,
Acad. G. Bonchev Str., Block 8, 1113 Sofia, Bulgaria
[3] Faculty of Physics, Atomic Physics Department,
Sofia University "St. Kliment Ohridski", 5 J. Bouchier Blvd, 1164 Sofia, Bulgaria
[4] Institute of Organic Chemistry with Centre of Phytochemistry at the Bulgarian
Academy of Sciences, Acad. G. Bonchev Str., Block 9, 1113 Sofia, Bulgaria

Abstract. Antimicrobial peptides (AMPs) are an abundant and diverse
group of molecules produced by many tissues and cell types in a variety of invertebrate, plant and animal species in contact with infectious
microorganisms. They play a crucial role as mediators of the primary
host defense against microbial invasion. The characteristics, the broad
spectrum and largely nonspecific activity of the antimicrobial peptides
qualify them as possible candidates for therapeutic alternatives against
multi-resistant bacterial strains.

AMPs come in nature in the form of multicomponent secretory fluids that exhibit certain biological activity. For development of biologicals with some predesignated properties separation of the individual
components, their purification and activity analysis are needed. *In silico*
experiments are designed to speedup the identification of the active components in these substances, understanding of their structural specifics
and biodynamics.

Here we present the first results of a pilot *in silico* study on the primary structure formation of newly identified in the mucus of molluscs
representatives peptides, as a prerequisite for understanding the possible
role of complexation for their biological activity.

Keywords: Antimicrobial peptides · Mass spectrometry · Primary
structure · Molecular modelling · Folding

1 Introduction

The increased emergence of multi-resistant bacterial strains renders inefficient
the existing traditional antibiotics [31]. Seen from a wider perspective, antibiotic

I. Lirkov and S. Margenov (Eds.): LSSC 2019, LNCS 11958, pp. 332–339, 2020.
https://doi.org/10.1007/978-3-030-41032-2_38

resistance is furthermore threatening to human health since the safety of many medical interventions as major surgeries, transplantations, aggressive treatment of cancer, and other advanced procedures is assured by the protective umbrella of effective antibiotics [4]. The situation is enforced by a substantial decline in the development of new antibacterial agents [18]. The broad spectrum and the largely nonspecific character of the activity of the antimicrobial peptides (AMPs), both natural and synthetic, qualify them as possible candidates for therapeutic alternatives [22] and their potential against multi-drug resistant pathogen infections reinforces the importance of studying their biological properties [14].

AMPs are essential components of innate immunity in most multicellular organisms and represent an ancient nonspecific host defense mechanism against infectious pathogens, including viruses, bacteria, and fungi [14,21], that complements the highly specific cell-mediated immune response [2]. In addition, they also have anticancer [19], antiinflammatory and immunomodulatory role [12]. These peptides vary significantly in composition and size (from 6 to 100 aminoacid residues). Nonetheless, generally they are cationic and amphiphilic, which is considered to be essential for their antibiotic activity [6,14]. Even though bacteria have been exposed to AMPs for millions of years during their co-evolution, they have yet to develop wide-spread resistance [14,28]. This feature of natural AMPs makes them a prime target for research and an ideal template for the design of sustainable antibiotic biologicals.

It has been proven that peptides isolated from the mucus of molluscs and arthropods can be used against viruses, bacteria, fungi and even cancer cells [5,8,29]. Here we present the first results of a pilot *in silico* study on ten bioactive peptides from the mucus of the snail *Cornu aspersum*. The researched sample natural substances were newly identified and have no homologies with any known experimental structure in the PDB [15]. We employ molecular dynamics (MD) simulations to develop 3D structural models of these newly discovered peptides.

2   Materials and Methods

2.1   Mucus Collection and Separation of Fractions

Mucus was collected and purified from *Cornu aspersum* snails grown in Bulgarian farms. The extract was separated to different fractions using Milipore filters. A 3 kDa fraction (masses below 3 kDa) was lyophilized and then applied on Milipore filters 1 kDa. A fraction with peptides with masses in the range 1–3 kDa was obtained and reconstituted in Milli Q water containing 0.10% TFA (v/v) for the analyses.

2.2   Mass Spectrometry Analysis

The molecular masses of isolated fractions were measured by an Autoflex™III, High-Performance MALDI-TOF&TOF/TOF System (Bruker Daltonics) which uses a 200 Hz frequency-tripled Nd-YAG laser operating at a wavelength of

355 nm. A fraction (50 pmol) was dissolved in 0.1% (v/v) TFA and mixed with 3 μl matrix (α-cyano-4-hydroxycinnamic acid) and was applied to the target. A total of 3500 shots were acquired in the MS mode and a collision energy of 4200 was applied. A solution of protein standards was used to calibrate the mass scale. The mass values assigned to the amino acid residues are average masses. *De novo* sequencing of the peptides was performed by MS/MS in a 4700 proteomics analyzer with TOF-TOF optics (Applied Biosystems). The MS/MS spectra were carried out in reflector mode with external calibration, using the 4700 calibration mixture kit (Applied Biosystems). Peptide *de novo* sequencing was performed by precursor ion fragmentation.

2.3   Molecular Modeling Protocol

Starting molecular models were developed for the ten isolated novel peptides, in which the sequences were generated in completely extended conformation. These models were subjected to folding simulations using molecular dynamics (MD).

All simulations were performed with the MD simulation package GROMACS 2016.3 [1]. The latest version of the CHARMM 36 force field was used for parameterization of the peptides [20] in combination with the modified TIP3PS water model for the solvent [23]. The peptides were solvated in cubic boxes with a minimal distance to the box walls of 1.2 nm under periodic boundary conditions. Sodium and chlorine ions with a 0.15 mol/l concentration were added to all systems to neutralize their net charge and to ensure physiological salinity of the solution. Note, that the side-chain protonation corresponded to neutral pH, while the N- and C-termini were not ionized, to avoid charge-interaction artefacts due to the small size of the peptides. The systems were energy-minimized using the steepest descent with a maximum force tolerance of 20 kJ/(mol nm), followed by short 20 ps position-restraint simulations to equilibrate the solvent. Then 1 ns canonical simulations were performed, in which the temperature was gradually increased to 310 K using v-rescale thermostat [3] with a coupling constant of 0.1 ps.

The production MD simulations were run in the isothermal-isobaric ensemble at 310 K temperature and 1 atm pressure, maintained by a v-rescale thermostat [3] with a coupling constant of 0.25 ps and a Parrinello-Rahman barostat [25, 26] with a coupling constant of 1 ps. The leapfrog integrator [17] was used with a time-step of 2 fs, whereas constraints were imposed on bonds between heavy atoms and hydrogens using the PLINCS algorithm [16]. Van der Waals interactions were smoothly switched off from a distance of 1.0 nm and truncated at 1.2 nm. Electrostatic interactions were treated using the smooth PME method [13] with a direct PME cut-off of 1.2 nm. The simulations had a duration of 100 ns. Trajectory frames were recorded every 200 ps.

3   Results and Discussion

Peptides from the mucus of the garden snails *H. lucorum* and *H. aspersa* have been shown to exhibit a broad spectrum of antimicrobial activity against

S. aureus, *S. epidermidis* and *P. acnes* [9, 10]. Recently, a series of novel proline- and glycin-rich antimicrobial peptides from the extracts of snails *Cornu aspersum* were also identified [11, 30]. It has been found that the fraction containing peptides with masses below 10 kDa demonstrated strong antibacterial activity against a pathogen Gram-negative bacterial strain – *Escherichia coli* NBIMCC 878. Therefore, in this work we focused our efforts on the identification, characterization and modelling of peptides with lower molecular weights – less than 3 kDa.

Several peptides were purified from the mucus of *Cornu aspersum* and their MALDI-TOF/MS/MS spectra were analyzed in order to determine their primary structures. As an example, *de novo* sequencing of the peptide detected at m/z 1795.95 Da [M+H]$^+$ is shown in Fig. 1. The amino acid sequence of the peptide was determined by its MALDI-MS/MS spectrum. Following the series of y- and b-ions, the sequence IIIDGFGGGIIVEHDPGS was deduced.

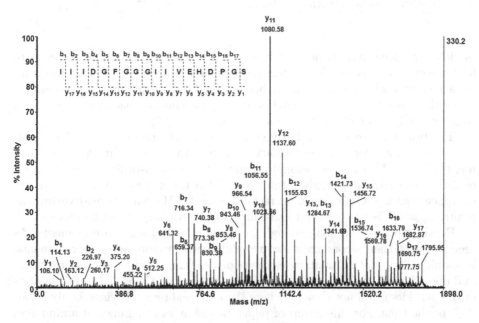

Fig. 1. MALDI-MS/MS spectrum of the peptide at m/z 1795.95 Da (positive ion mode). Standard peptide solution was used to calibrate the mass scale of the AutoflexTM III, High Performance MALDI-TOF & TOF/TOF Systems (Bruker Daltonics).

Along the same procedure, a subset of glycine- and proline- reach peptides in the extract of garden snail Helix aspersa have been confirmed, Table 1.

There was no *a priori* knowledge on the 3D structure of the ten isolated novel peptides. Since no homologies with known experimental structures could be identified in the PDB with a BLASTP search, we could not rely on homology

Table 1. Newly identified low-molecular-weight peptides from the hemolymph of the snail *Cornu aspersum*.

ID	Sequence	$[M+H]^+$ MALDI-MS/MS [Da]	Mol. mass monoisotipic [Da]	Length [#aa]	Net charge [e]
p1	VGCIHEGI	827.41	826.40	8	−1
p2	KKDVGIGIGG	943.60	942.55	10	+1
p3	RVIGNWIGLGL	1197.72	1196.70	11	+1
p4	WHSEGNVGINA	1183.55	1182.54	11	−1
p5	KVKDNQWRP	1170.65	1169.63	9	+2
p6	PRGSGGRGGSHGGGGIPP	1559.76	1558.77	18	+2
p7	VNVVGGGGGIVGGGIGGGGM	1570.78	1569.79	20	0
p8	IIIDGFGGGIIVEHDPGS	1795.95	1794.92	18	−3
p9	GVSIIIGGNHGIIQGIEI	1790.02	1789.01	18	−1
p10	MPEGINPGGIIGGGACIGERP	1994.96	1993.97	21	−1

modeling to develop a 3D model for any of the peptides. Therefore, in order to fold the generated completely extended peptide chains we resorted to the computationally more expensive but methodologically better justifiable alternative – molecular modeling by means of MD simulations. This approach has been shown to successfully yield adequate 3D models for AMPs [27].

The first five peptides are fairly short – up to 11 amino acid residues. This length does not allow for the formation of any stable secondary structure elements (Fig. 2). There are occasionally some α-turns and β-bridges formed, which could involve up to five residues (on average two), but they are short-lived and disappear quickly. On average, there are about 1-2 H-bonds formed within the peptides, which is not enough to sustain stable secondary structure elements.

Peptides p6–p10 are long enough to form secondary structure elements. As seen in Fig. 2, their secondary structure plots contain more and larger elements. It should be noted, that in all cases the peptides tend to adopt β-like structures, and not α-helical conformations. This is also evident on the Ramachandran plots of the peptides (data not shown), where the α-helical region is visited only about 20% of the time. For this group of peptides the average number of amino acid residues in a defined secondary structure is between 4 and 5 with 3-4 H-bonds formed within the peptide. All peptides in this group tend to form a bend in the middle of the chain. Peptides p6 and p7 adopt conformations, which resemble a β-hairpin, but only p10 is stable enough to actually maintain this structural element.

Overall, all peptides but p10 are very flexible and their structure is not well defined. This corresponds to the findings in [7]. They performed long-scale folding simulations of a few α-helical peptides in water and on a water–air (vacuum) interface and showed that the peptides did not adopt a stable α-helical conformations in bulk water and were partially or even fully intrinsically disordered.

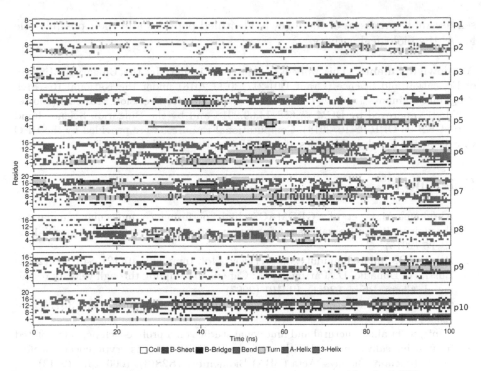

Fig. 2. Secondary structure plots of the ten peptides, as assigned by the DSSP program.

Once placed on an amphiphilic interface, the conformational equilibria are shifted towards α-helical conformations and the peptides' structure stabilises.

We acknowledge that our sampling is limited and probably insufficient to fully characterize the conformational ensembles of the investigated peptides. However, the results in [7] demonstrate that extending the simulation time in bulk water does not improve convergence and that the peptides are likely to remain disordered even if the simulations had been extended to several hundred nanoseconds.

4 Conclusions

This work is only the first step in studying the antimicrobial properties of novel bioactive peptides, isolated from the mucus of the garden snails *H. lucorum* and *H. aspersa*. The primary structure of ten newly identified peptides was determined on the basis of their MALDI-MS/MS spectra, while for the development of the corresponding 3D structural models MD folding simulations were employed. We demonstrated that in bulk water all investigated peptides are flexible and do not form stable secondary structure elements. Thus, the peptides can be characterized as somewhat disordered and favouring β-like structures. In a previous study, we showed that another AMP – indolicidin – self assembles in solution and forms aggregates [24]. Our future efforts will be focused on studying the self-assembly processes of these newly identified peptides and their possible role for AMPs biological activity.

Acknowledgements. This work was supported in part by the Bulgarian Ministry of Education and Science (Grant D01-217/30.11.2018) under the National Research Programme "Innovative Low-Toxic Bioactive Systems for Precision Medicine (BioActiveMed)" approved by DCM # 658/14.09.2018 and by the Bulgarian Science Fund (Grant KP-06-OPR 03-10/2018). Computational resources were provided by the HPC Cluster at the Faculty of Physics at Sofia University "St. Kl. Ohridski".

References

1. Abraham, M.J., et al.: GROMACS: high performance molecular simulations through multi-level parallelism from laptops to supercomputers. SoftwareX **1–2**, 19–25 (2015)
2. Beutler, B.: Innate immunity: an overview. Mol. Immunol. **40**(12), 845–859 (2004)
3. Bussi, G., Donadio, D., Parrinello, M.: Canonical sampling through velocity rescaling. J. Chem. Phys. **126**(1), 014101 (2007)
4. Cars, O., et al.: Meeting the challenge of antibiotic resistance. BMJ **337**, a1438 (2008)
5. Conti, S., et al.: Structural and functional studies on a proline-rich peptide isolated from swine saliva endowed with antifungal activity towards cryptococcus neoformans. Biochim. Biophys. Acta (BBA) Biomembr. **1828**(3), 1066–1074 (2013)
6. Copolovici, D.M., Langel, K., Eriste, E., Langel, U.: Cell-penetrating peptides: design, synthesis, and applications. ACS Nano **8**(3), 1972–1994 (2014)
7. Dalgicdir, C., Globisch, C., Peter, C., Sayar, M.: Tipping the scale from disorder to alpha-helix: folding of amphiphilic peptides in the presence of macroscopic and molecular interfaces. PLoS Comput. Biol. **11**(8), e1004328 (2015)
8. Defer, D., et al.: Antimicrobial peptides in oyster hemolymph: the bacterial connection. Fish Shellfish Immunol. **34**(6), 1439–1447 (2013)
9. Dolashka, P., Dolashki, A., Voelter, W., Beeumen, J.V., Stevanovic, S.: Antimicrobial activity of peptides from the hemolymph of helix lucorum snails. Int. J. Curr. Microbiol. Appl. Sci. **4**(4), 1061–1071 (2015)
10. Dolashka, P., et al.: Antimicrobial proline-rich peptides from the hemolymph of marine snail rapana venosa. Peptides **32**(7), 1477–1483 (2011)
11. Dolashki, A., et al.: Structure and antibacterial activity of isolated peptides from the mucus of garden snail cornu aspersum. Bul. Chem. Commun. **50**(Spec. Issue C), 195–200 (2018)
12. Easton, D.M., Nijnik, A., Mayer, M.L., Hancock, R.E.: Potential of immunomodulatory host defense peptides as novel anti-infectives. Trends Biotechnol. **27**(10), 582–590 (2009)
13. Essmann, U., Perera, L., Berkowitz, M.L., Darden, T., Lee, H., Pedersen, L.G.: A smooth particle mesh ewald method. J. Chem. Phys. **103**(19), 8577–8593 (1995)
14. Fjell, C.D., Hiss, J.A., Hancock, R.E.W., Schneider, G.: Designing antimicrobial peptides: form follows function. Nat. Rev. Drug Discov. **11**, 37–51 (2012)
15. Gilliland, G., et al.: The protein data bank. Nucleic Acids Res. **28**(1), 235–242 (2000). http://www.rcsb.org/
16. Hess, B.: P-LINCS: a parallel linear constraint solver for molecular simulation. J. Chem. Theory Comput. **4**(1), 116–122 (2008)

17. Hockney, R., Goel, S., Eastwood, J.: Quiet high-resolution computer models of a plasma. J. Comput. Phys. **14**(2), 148–158 (1974)
18. Högberg, L.D., Heddini, A.: The global need for effective antibiotics: challenges and recent advances. Trends Pharmacol. Sci. **31**(11), 509–515 (2010)
19. Hoskin, D.W., Ramamoorthy, A.: Studies on anticancer activities of antimicrobial peptides. Biochim. Biophys. Acta (BBA) Biomembr. **1778**(2), 357–375 (2008)
20. Huang, J., et al.: CHARMM36m: an improved force field for folded and intrinsically disordered proteins. Nat. Methods **14**, 71–73 (2016)
21. Kang, H.K., Kim, C., Seo, C.H., Park, Y.: The therapeutic applications of antimicrobial peptides (AMPs): a patent review. J. Microbiol. **55**(1), 1–12 (2017)
22. López-Meza, J.E., Ochoa-Zarzosa, A., Barboza-Corona, J.E., Bideshi, D.K.: Antimicrobial peptides: current and potential applications in biomedical therapies. BioMed Res. Int. **2015**, 367243 (2015)
23. MacKerell, A.D., et al.: All-atom empirical potential for molecular modeling and dynamics studies of proteins. J. Phys. Chem. B **102**(18), 3586–3616 (1998)
24. Marinova, R., Petkov, P., Ilieva, N., Lilkova, E., Litov, L.: Molecular dynamics study of the solution behaviour of antimicrobial peptide indolicidin. In: Georgiev, K., Todorov, M., Georgiev, I. (eds.) BGSIAM 2017. SCI, vol. 793, pp. 257–265. Springer, Cham (2019). https://doi.org/10.1007/978-3-319-97277-0_21
25. Parrinello, M., Rahman, A.: Crystal structure and pair potentials: a molecular-dynamics study. Phys. Rev. Lett. **45**, 1196 (1980)
26. Parrinello, M., Rahman, A.: Polymorphic transitions in single crystals: a new molecular dynamics method. J. Appl. Phys. **52**, 7182 (1981)
27. Passarini, I., Rossiter, S., Malkinson, J., Zloh, M.: In silico structural evaluation of short cationic antimicrobial peptides. Pharmaceutics **10**(3), 72 (2018)
28. Peschel, A., Sahl, H.G.: The co-evolution of host cationic antimicrobial peptides and microbial resistance. Nat. Rev. Microbiol. **4**, 529–536 (2006)
29. Reddy, K., Yedery, R., Aranha, C.: Antimicrobial peptides: premises and promises. Int. J. Antimicrob. Agents **24**(6), 536–547 (2004)
30. Velkova, L., Nissimova, A., Dolashki, A., Daskalova, E., Dolashka, P., Topalova, Y.: Glycine-rich peptides from cornu aspersum snail with antibacterial activity. Bul. Chem. Commun. **50**(Spec. Issue C), 169–175 (2018)
31. World Health Organization: Antimicrobial resistance: global report on surveillance (2014)

Sensitivity of the Simulated Heat Risk in Southeastern Europe to the RegCM Model Configuration—Preliminary Results

Vladimir Ivanov[1](✉), Georgi Gadzhev[1], Kostadin Ganev[1], and Hristo Chervenkov[2]

[1] National Institute of Geophysics, Geodesy and Geography – Bulgarian Academy of Sciences, Acad. G. Bonchev Str., bl. 3, 1113 Sofia, Bulgaria
vivanov@geophys.bas.bg
[2] National Institute in Meteorology and Hydrology, 66, Tsarigradsko Shose blvd, 1784 Sofia, Bulgaria

Abstract. The spatial distribution of the biometeorological conditions is a topic of many studies in different countries. One of the most important aspects of the weather adverse effect on the human beings is the consequences from too much exposure to the heat conditions. The human body can adapt to temperatures, but to some extent. If the air temperatures become too high, human beings at first feel uncomfortable, but the consequences can be a serious threat to health and even life. The main reasons for this threat are related to the lack of perspiration and cardiovascular problems. Atmospheric numerical models for simulating the heat stress is used in many studies. One of the most affected region in the near past, but also most likely in the future, is the Southeastern Europe, including Bulgaria. Global models are with too low resolution, but still they suggest very strong heat stress especially at the end of the 21th century. According to other studies, results from regional meteorological models suggest similar conclusions. The current research is about the heat stress conditions in the Balkan Peninsula, evaluated from ten–year simulations. They are performed with regional climate model RegCM. The model is run many times with different combinations of physics parameterization of some processes. The aim is to compare the heat stress simulated by different model configurations for the Balkan Peninsula and so to reveal the dependence of heat stress evaluation on the model configuration. That would answer the question of the sensitivity of the model to the parameterization schemes from a biometeorological point of view.

Keywords: Regional climate simulation · RegCM4.4 · Heat index · Heat stress · High performance computing

I. Lirkov and S. Margenov (Eds.): LSSC 2019, LNCS 11958, pp. 340–347, 2020.
https://doi.org/10.1007/978-3-030-41032-2_39

1   Introduction

According to the fifth assessment report (AR5) of the United Nations Inter-governmental Panel on Climate Change (IPCC), globally there is a probability above 90% that there is an increasing of the high temperature events both in the day and in the night between 1951 and 2010 [1]. The future projections of the climate models show that the increasing trend will continue, and the high temperatures in the summer will grow faster than the average ones. According to many studies [2], there is an increased risk of heat-related diseases for the people from cities with lower city gross domestic product and age at least 65. In many locations, the risk of mortality is rising above 1%, with every degree of air temperature increase.

The human organism relies on its thermoregulatory system [3], to maintain the heat balance with the environment by – conduction, convection, evaporation, perspiration, and breathing. Their function is to take the excessive heat away in warm and hot conditions. The main environmental factors in sultry conditions are the air temperature and the air humidity. The human body is cooling in a hot environment mainly by evaporation of the sweat. If the humidity is too high, it impedes the evaporation, which additionally increases the skin and the body core temperature. High ambient temperatures provoke dizziness, nausea, weakness and fatigue. In more severe conditions, the human organism may suffer dangerous body core temperature increasing, heat cramps, heat stroke, sunstroke, which can eventually lead to death.

The aim of the current research is to study the behavior of a regional climate model in different combinations of parameterization schemes in relation to the spatial distribution of the heat conditions in the summer. For this purpose, a characteristic called heat index (HI), which combines the influence of the temperature and the humidity is used. It is a reliable characteristic of the hot weather negative impact [4].

2   Methods

The assessment of the influence of heat weather conditions is done by the so-called indices, which are integral measures of the human perception. The "heat index", which is based on the heat balance model between the human body and the air environment [5] is used. It is defined as temperature of the human individual, situated in a real shady environment with certain temperature and relative humidity, that would feel in reference conditions. For simplifying the calculation, the regression formula was developed [6] with some assumptions of the physiological and environmental parameters. The temperature and relative humidity are predictors and the heat index is the dependent variable in the form of single number in temperature units originally in degree of Fahrenheit. The heat index is calculated with the NCAR Command Language software [7]. The heat stress is classified in five categories, according to the severity of the air environment impact on the human beings Table 1 [8]. The heat index values are

Table 1. Considered model configurations and their notations

Interval	Category name	Physiological response
Below 26.7 °C	No stress	No
26.7–32.2 °C	Caution	Fatigue is possible with prolonged exposure and activity. Continuing activity could result in heat cramps
32.2–40.5 °C	Extreme caution	Heat cramps and heat exhaustion are possible. Continuing activity could result in heat stroke
40.5–54.4 °C	Danger	Heat cramps and heat exhaustion are likely; heat stroke is probable with continued activity
$\geq$ 54.4 °C	Extreme danger	Heat stroke is imminent

Table 2. Model configurations under consideration and their notation.

Notation	ICBC	PBL-scheme	M–scheme	CC–scheme
r11122	EIN15	Holtslag	SUBEX	Grell/FC
r11133	EIN15	Holtslag	SUBEX	Emanuel
r11144	EIN15	Holtslag	SUBEX	Tiedtke
r11221	EIN15	Holtslag	Nogherotto/Tompkins	Grell/AS
r11222	EIN15	Holtslag	Nogherotto/Tompkins	Grell/FC
r11233	EIN15	Holtslag	Nogherotto/Tompkins	Emanuel
r11255	EIN15	Holtslag	Nogherotto/Tompkins	Kain-Fritsch
r12121	EIN15	UW	SUBEX	Grell/AS
r12122	EIN15	UW	SUBEX	Grell/FC
r12133	EIN15	UW	SUBEX	Emanuel
r12144	EIN15	UW	SUBEX	Tiedtke
r12155	EIN15	UW	SUBEX	Kain-Fritsch
r12222	EIN15	UW	Nogherotto/Tompkins	Grell/FC
r12233	EIN15	UW	Nogherotto/Tompkins	Emanuel
r12244	EIN15	UW	Nogherotto/Tompkins	Tiedtke
r12255	EIN15	UW	Nogherotto/Tompkins	Kain-Fritsch

valid for shady conditions, and does not consider the wind speed. The exposure to solar radiation can increase the values by up to 15 °F.

The numerical modelling of the heat stress conditions for Southeastern Europe is performed with the regional climate model RegCM version 4.4 [9]. The domain area covers the Balkan Peninsula and parts of Italy and the Asia Minor Peninsula. 16 numerical simulations scenarios for different model configuration (Table 2) with model grid in Lambert Conformal Conic projection were defined. The RegCM model simulations are done with spatial resolution 10 km, time step 25 s and 27 vertical levels in hydrostatical mode. The simulation period is ten years from 30.11.1999 to 30.11.2009. The model is driven by initial and boundary conditions from the ERA-Interim Reanalysis data with horizontal resolution $1.5° \times 1.5°$ with time step 6 h and 37 vertical levels [10]. The data set is evaluated as good for the European region [11]. The model uses different parameterzitaion schemes to simulate the physical processes in sub-grid scales. The detailed description of the model parametrization schemes is presented on [12].

The calculations were implemented on the Supercomputer System "Avitohol" at the Institute of Information and Communication Technologies at the Bulgarian Academy of Sciences (IICT-BAS). The simulations for the selected domain were organized in separate jobs, which again make the jobs run time for 3 months real time fairly reasonable [13].

3 Results

The relative frequency of occurring of cases with heat index category Caution for different model configurations are given at Fig. 1. The simulations r11122, r11133, r11144, r11233, r11255 are characterized by relatively more cases with Caution heat index, especially in the lower terrain parts and the Aegean Sea and Adriatic Sea. The lower terrain forms in the domain have 10% to 20% frequency of Caution heat index, except of the most northern parts where the percentage fall to the interval from 5% to 10%. The Danube plain and the Great Hungarian plain are places with 20% to 30% of cases with Caution HI. The same inference can be made for some spots in the southern parts if the Balkan Peninsula, especially nearby the coastal areas. The southern parts of the Asia

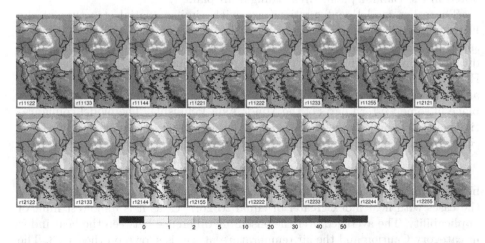

Fig. 1. The relative frequency of the heat index in category Caution for the model configurations.

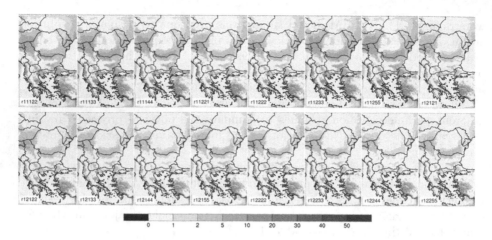

Fig. 2. The relative frequency of the heat index in category Extreme Caution for the model configurations.

Minor Peninsula also get into that interval of Caution index cases, and in some coastal areas the percentage is from 30% to 40%.

The spatial distribution of the relative frequency in the other model simulations is similar, but the percentages of the cases with Caution HI is smaller as a whole, including the marine areas. The cases r12144 and r12244 are the coldest ones having most areas with relative frequency of Caution HI below 10%. The relative frequency of occurring of cases with heat index category Extreme Caution for the different model configurations is given at Fig. 2. The model configurations r11122, r11133, r11144, r11233, r11255 have relatively bigger frequency of the Extreme caution cases in comparison to the other ones. That difference can be noted in the Danube plain, Great Hungarian plain.

The other model configurations are with similar spatial structure of the Extreme Caution relative frequency, but the places with one above 5% are a smaller number and with not so large spatial extent. The places with those conditions are in southern parts of the Great Hungarian plain, Greece and Turkey. However, the spatial extent with relative frequency between 10% and 20% in although smaller than in r11122, r11133, r11144, r11233 and r11255, also takes place in some western parts of the Minor Asia Peninsula. The model configurations r12144 and r12244 have the smallest areas with frequency of Extreme Caution with percentage more than 2%, especially in the Danube plain for r12244.

It is interesting to study the influence of the humidity represented as a relative humidity on the behavior of the heat index. For that purpose the difference between the index and the real air temperature, was calculated, but only for the cases with heat index greater or equal to 26.7 °C, as it is its lowest limit of applicability. The averaged over the ensemble difference between the heat index in category Caution and the air temperature at 2 m is shown on the Fig. 3. The average difference is zero in the higher parts of the mountain areas. On the most

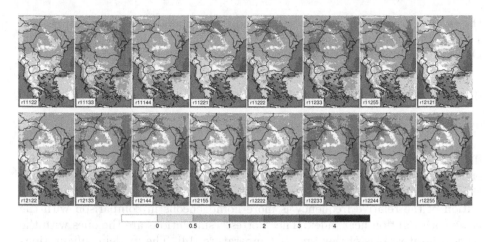

Fig. 3. The average difference between the heat index and the air temperature at 2 m in category Caution for the model configurations.

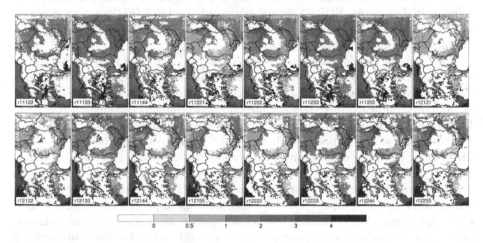

Fig. 4. The average difference between the heat index and the air temperature at 2 m in category Extreme Caution for the model configurations.

part of the domain the difference is between 0.5 °C and 1 °C, but in some places goes up to 2 °C. However, the model configurations r11122, r12121, r12122, and r12222 do not have locations with average difference between the index and the air temperature more than 1 °C, except in the marine areas. There are also many areas with difference between the air temperature and the heat index in the cases with Extreme Caution conditions, shown on the Fig. 4. Its spatial structure is much more diverse than for the cases with Caution conditions. It can be seen that the model configurations r11133, r11233, r11255 and r11222 to some extent are the most notable with the biggest difference between the heat index and the air temperature. The model configurations r12121, r12122 and r12222 are with the smallest difference between the HI and the temperature between 0.5 °C and 1 °C on the most places, and between 1 °C and 2 °C mainly in the northeast. Other model configurations are somewhere between these two groups.

4   Discussion and Conclusion

The demonstrated results show that when the heat index is in the category Caution, most of the simulations with Holtslag PBL scheme produce the hottest conditions. The simulations with UW PBL–scheme and cumulus convection parameterization scheme Tiedtke are the "coldest" ones. The cases with Extreme Caution heat index have a similar spatial distribution. However, the spatial distribution of the relative frequency is more homogeneous in comparison with the cases with Caution heat index. The "hottest" simulations are the ones with the biggest positive bias of the 2-m air temperature [14]. The model configurations with UW PBL–scheme and cumulus convection scheme of Tiedtke, have particularly negative temperature biases among others [14]. The configuration with Holtslag PBL–scheme, SUBEX M–scheme, and the Grell/FC cumulus convection scheme can be taken as a reference concerning the temporal variability and the bias of the air temperature [12,14].

The changing of the model configuration imply a little influence of the humidity on the heat discomfort in Caution heat conditions. The model results with Extreme Caution cases however, are not so similar. The ones with the highest humidity influence in Extreme Caution conditions are the simulations with Holtslag PBL scheme and Emanuel CC–scheme, and they are in the group of configurations with wet bias [14]. It is probably due to the increased soil moisture because of enhanced precipitations in the periods preceding these high index cases.

The study demonstrates that the calculated HI is sensitive to the RegCM configuration, so the proper choice of a combination of parametrization schemes is of importance. More detailed studies for particular periods of the summer season and comparison with observation data could be the key for improving of the model capability to simulate the extreme high–temperature events.

Acknowledgments. This work has been accomplished thanks to the computational capabilities, created in the framework of the MES Grant No. D01–221/03.12.2018 for NCDSC—part of the Bulgarian National Roadmap on RIs.

This work was partially supported by the Bulgarian Ministry of Education and Science under the National Research Programme "Young scientists and postdoctoral students" approved by DCM №577/17.08.2018 and by the Bulgarian National Science Fund (DN–14/3 13.12.2017).

This work has been carried out in the framework of the National Science Program "Environmental Protection and Reduction of Risks of Adverse Events and Natural Disasters", approved by the Resolution of the Council of Ministers №577/17.08.2018 and supported by the Ministry of Education and Science (MES) of Bulgaria (Agreement DO-230/06-12-2018).

Deep gratitude to the organizations and institutes (ICTP, ECMWF, NCEP–NCAR, ECA&D, Unidata, MPI–M and all others), which provide free of charge software and data. Without their innovative data services and tools this study would not be possible.

References

1. Stocker, T.F., et al.: Technical summary. In: Stocker, T.F., et al. (eds.) Climate Change 2013: The Physical Science Basis. Contribution of Working Group I to the Fifth Assessment Report of the Intergovernmental Panel on Climate Change. Cambridge University Press, Cambridge, and New York (2013)
2. Hajat, S., Kosatky, T.: Heat-related mortality: a review and exploration of heterogeneity. J. Epidemiol. Commun. Health **64**(9), 753–760 (2010). https://doi.org/10.1136/jech.2009.087999
3. Starr, C., McMillan, B.: Human Biology. Brooks/Cole Cengager Learning (2010)
4. Monteiro, A., Carvalho, V., Velho, S., Sousa, C.: The accuracy of the heat index to explain the excess of mortality and morbidity during heat waves – a case study in a mediterranean climate. In: Szymańska, D., Chodkowska-Miszczuk, J. (eds.) Bulletin of Geography. Socio-Economic Series, no. 20, pp. 71–84. Nicolaus Copernicus University Press, Toruń (2013). https://doi.org/10.2478/bog-2013-0012
5. Steadman, R.G.: The assessment of sultriness. Part I: a temperature-humidity index based on human physiology and clothing science. J. Appl. Meteor. **18**, 861–873 (1979)
6. Rothfusz, L.P.: The Heat Index "Equation" (or, More Than You Ever Wanted to Know About Heat Index), Scientific Services Division (NWS Southern Region Headquarters) (1990)
7. The NCAR Command Language (Version 6.4.0) [Software]. Boulder, Colorado: UCAR/NCAR/CISL/VETS (2017). http://dx.doi.org/10.5065/D6WD3XH5
8. https://www.weather.gov/safety/heat-index . Accessed 20 Feb 2019
9. Giorgi, F., et al.: RegCM model description and preliminary tests over multiple CORDEX domains. Clim. Res. **52**, 7–29 (2012). https://doi.org/10.3354/cr01018
10. Dee, D.P., et al.: The ERA-interim reanalysis: configuration and performance of the data assimilation system. Q. J. R. Meteorol. Soc. **137**, 553–597 (2011). https://doi.org/10.1002/qj.828
11. Brands, S., Gutiérrez, J.M., Herrera, S., Cofiño, A.S.: On the use of reanalysis data for downscaling. J. Climate **25**, 2517–2526 (2012). https://doi.org/10.1175/JCLI-D-11-00251.1
12. Gadzhev, G., et al.: Climate applications in a virtual research environment platform. Scalable Comput. **19**(2), 107–118 (2018). https://doi.org/10.12694/scpe.v19i2.1347
13. Atanassov, E., Gurov, T., Karaivanova, A., Ivanovska, S., Durchova, M., Dimitrov, D.: On the parallelization approaches for intel MIC architecture. In: AIP Conference Proceedings, vol. 1773, p. 070001 (2016). http://dx.doi.org/10.1063/1.4964983
14. Gadzhev, G., Ivanov, V., Ganev, K., Chervenkov, H.: TVRegCM numerical simulations - preliminary results. In: Lirkov, I., Margenov, S. (eds.) LSSC 2017. LNCS, vol. 10665, pp. 266–274. Springer, Cham (2018). https://doi.org/10.1007/978-3-319-73441-5_28

Large-Scale Prediction of the ARS Family Inhibitors of the Oncogenic KRAS$^{\text{G12C}}$ Mutant

Anna M. Kulakova[1] (ID), Anna V. Popinako[2]($\boxtimes$), and Maria G. Khrenova[1,2]($\boxtimes$) (ID)

[1] Department of Chemistry, Lomonosov Moscow State University,
Moscow 119991, Russia
{kulakova,wasabiko}@lcc.chem.msu.ru

[2] Bach Institute of Biochemistry, Federeal Research Center "Fundamentals of
Biotechnology" of the Russian Academy of Sciences, Moscow 119071, Russia
popinakoav@gmail.com, khrenova.maria@gmail.com

Abstract. The KRAS protein is a molecular switch that activates cellular processes, like cell growth and differentiation. The G12C point mutation of the KRAS is found in various cancer cells. It results in the accretion of the GTP-bound active form thus accelerating downstream signalling pathways. Recently ARS family of compounds was suggested as selective covalent inhibitors of the KRAS$^{\text{G12C}}$. The most prospective ARS-853 has $IC_{50} = 1.6\,\mu M$ that is too large for the medicinal applications. We demonstrate that calculated dissociation constants K_d are proportional to the experimental IC_{50} values and can be utilized as a measure of the inhibitor potency. Using molecular modeling tools we suggest a set of novel compounds with the predicted IC_{50} values more than an order of magnitude lower than that of the ARS-853.

Keywords: KRAS$^{\text{G12C}}$ · Oncogenic mutation · Covalent inhibitor · Molecular docking · ARS.

1 Introduction

The KRAS protein is a member of the small GTPase family that is involved in the transmission of cellular signals. In living cells the KRAS may be presented in either GTP or GDP-bound forms [1,3,4,11]. The first one is supposed to be active, i.e. it transmits signals for the cell growth and differentiation. The GDP-bound state is inactive. Mutations of the KRAS are associated with various human cancers [5]. The oncogenic mutations result in the shift of the cellular equilibrium between the inactive and active states of the KRAS. The active state fraction becomes larger in cancer cells resulting in the faster cell growth and differentiation. Many efforts are already made to find compounds that can stabilize the mutated KRAS in the inactive form. Although, this protein is called "undruggable" as it has a flat surface without pronounced binding pockets [2,10]. Recently, a novel binding pocket in the oncogenic G12C mutant of the KRAS

I. Lirkov and S. Margenov (Eds.): LSSC 2019, LNCS 11958, pp. 348–355, 2020.
https://doi.org/10.1007/978-3-030-41032-2_40

was discovered [8]. It opened new opportunities in the drug discovery and novel covalent inhibitors of the so-called ARS family were suggested [6,9]. Those are bound selectively to the complex of the KRAS^{G12C} with the GDP but not GTP and demonstrate IC$_{50}$ values in the micromolar range. The ARS compounds have activated terminal carbon-carbon double bond and readily react according to the Michael mechanism with the thiolate of the Cys12 residue. Even being covalent inhibitors, those have different IC$_{50}$ values depending on the particular substituent on the opposite side of the molecule from the reactive double bond. In other words not only the chemical reaction, but also initial noncovalent binding contributes to the effective macroscopic parameter IC$_{50}$. Here we focus on the initial stage of the ARS interaction with the KRAS^{G12C}-GDP complex, i.e. the formation of the noncovalent complex. We vary substituents responsible for the noncovalent binding and analyze their impact. Finally, we suggest novel members of the ARS family with the reduced IC$_{50}$ values.

2   Methods and Computations

We start with the crystal structure of the covalent complex between the KRAS^{G12C}-GDP and the ARS-853, PDB ID: 5F2E (Fig. 1) [9]. The local search procedure in the Autodock4 program [7] was utilized to evaluate the dissociation constants K$_d$. The protein and ligands for docking were prepared using AutodockTools package [7]. Ligands were firstly optimized using the semi-empirical method PM6 to better reproduce the interatomic distances. During the protein-ligand complexes search the protein was supposed to be rigid and ligand molecules were flexible with the 4 to 7 degrees of freedom of rotation around dihedrals. The local search procedure was performed in a $45 \times 45 \times 45$ Å^3 cube comprising binding pocket. The influence of different substituents at the hydrophobic binding moiety was studied. We checked around 100 compounds with different carbon chains including methylcyclopropyl (MecPr), methylcyclobutyl (MecBu) and tert-butyl (tBu) and examined 200 conformations of protein-ligand complexes. The hydrogen atoms at all positions were sequentially changed to halogen atoms including F, Cl, Br and I, amino, alcohol and thiol groups.

The mechanism of interaction between the ARS compound and the KRAS^{G12C}-GDP complex is the following: the non-covalent complex KRAS^{G12C}-GDP-ARS formation on the first stage and the formation of the C-S covalent bond ARS-C-S-KRAS^{G12C}-GDP on the second stage. Both of these steps can be characterized by the equilibrium constants, K$_d$ and K$_r$, respectively:

$$K_d = \frac{[ARS][KRAS^{G12C} - GDP]}{[KRAS^{G12C} - GDP - ARS]}$$

$$K_r = \frac{[ARS - C - S - KRAS^{G12C} - GDP]}{[KRAS^{G12C} - GDP - ARS]}$$

Then the overall inhibition constant can be written as

$$K_i = K_d \cdot K_r^{-1} \tag{1}$$

The K_i equilibrium constant corresponds to experiments *in vitro,* where only the $KRAS^{G12C}$, the GDP and the ARS exist. The IC_{50} value is measured *in vivo* and therefore it comprises contributions from all equilibria between the ARS, the $KRAS^{G12C}$, the GDP and the GTP as well as certrain cellular concentrations of protein and cofactors. Therefore the relation for the IC_{50} can be written as

$$IC_{50} = a \cdot K_i, \tag{2}$$

where a is an effective constant that comprises all above mentioned equilibria and certain cellular concentrations of the $KRAS^{G12C}$, the GDP and the GTP. Thus we arrive to the equation

$$IC_{50} = a \cdot K_d \cdot K_r^{-1} \tag{3}$$

The K_r value should be the same for all compounds under considerations as the chemical reaction takes place on the opposite side of the molecule from the substituents that are varied. We can rewrite the equation as follows:

$$IC_{50} = b \cdot K_d \tag{4}$$

where $b = a \cdot K_r^{-1}$. This relation demonstrates that the experimental IC_{50} is in the direct ratio to the calculated K_d value. Thus, we can range the ARS compounds according to their inhibition potency using calculated dissociation constants, K_d.

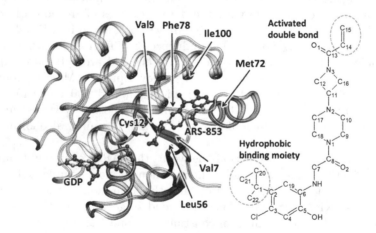

Fig. 1. The complex between the $KRAS^{G12C}$-GDP and the ARS-853 (PDB ID: 5F2E) [9]. Protein is shown in cartoon representation, the ARS-853, the side chain of Cys12 and the GDP are shown in balls and sticks. Residues that forms hydrophobic binding moiety are shown with arrows. Here and in other figures green, red, blue, white, dark green, yellow and ochre colors correspond to carbon, oxygen, nitrogen, hydrogen, chlorine, sulfur and phosphorus atoms, respectively. (Color figure online)

3   Results and Discussion

We start with analysis of the available experimental data on the IC$_{50}$ of the ARS compounds. The inhibitor potency decreases with the decrease of the size of the hydrophobic binding moiety in series MecPr > cPr > Br > Cl > H. The ARS-853 with the MecPr substituent has the lowest IC$_{50} = 1.6\,\mu$M among the experimentally considered species [9]. We estimated the K$_d$ values for all these compounds and plotted them against experimental IC$_{50}$ (Fig. 2). In previous section we demonstrated that the relation between the calculated and experimental values should be $IC_{50} = b \cdot K_d$. Indeed, we found a linear relationship between the calculated and experimental values. The error of these estimates is around 15% (Fig. 2, red line). We understand that the molecular docking procedure has uncertainties in determination of the equilibrium constants due to the fast and simple estimates of the scoring function. Therefore we tried other dependencies that might be senseless from the point of the mechanism of the process, but can improve the correlation between the calculated and experimental values (Fig. 2, blue curve). The nonlinear curve fitting demonstrates better results and is more preferable for the quantitative analysis. Thus, K$_d$ calculations can be utilized for the further search of novel prospective compounds of the ARS family.

The hydrophobic binding moiety of inhibitor (Fig. 1) is surrounded by the side chains of the Val7, Val9, Leu56, Met72, Phe78 and Ile100 residues. This hydrophobic binding pocket is quite large and may accommodate even larger substituent than methylcyclopropyl of ARS-853. Therefore in our further analysis we consider larger non-carbon substituents of the same MecPr core and also examine substituents with the different carbon skeletons.

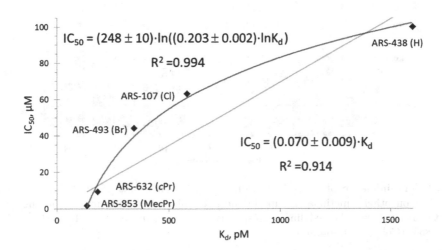

Fig. 2. Dependencies between the experimental IC$_{50}$ (μM) values [9] and the calculated K$_d$ (pM) values. Each point is marked with the compound name and substituent in the hydrophobic binding moiety (in parenthesis). (Color figure online)

Let us first consider the influence of the non-carbon substituents on the inhibitor potency of ARS-853 (Fig. 3). Substitution at the H^{11} either slightly decrease the K_d value or increase up to 2.6 times. An order of magnitude increase is observed when substituting hydrogen atom to the iodine. The K_d value decrease from F to Cl with the increase of the atomic radius. Then the K_d increase in series of Cl < Br << I. This might be due to the steric hindrance between the larger substituents and the side chain of Ile100. Similar dependencies are observed in case of H^{21} substituents; the smallest K_d value is obtained for the chlorine containing compound. The most prospective position for substitution was found to be H^{22}. Substitution of H^{22} to iodine results in the three-fold reduction of K_d.

Next, we analyze two different groups of compounds with *tert*-butyl (*t*Bu) and methylcyclobutyl (Me*c*Bu) in the hydrophobic binding moiety (Figs. 4 and 5). Substitution of Me*c*Pr to both *t*Bu and Me*c*Bu results in the decrease of K_d values. This effect is more pronounced in case of the ARS compound with the Me*c*Bu that has the K_d value three times lower than the ARS-853. Let us consider the ARS compounds with the substituted *t*Bu and Me*c*Bu fragments.

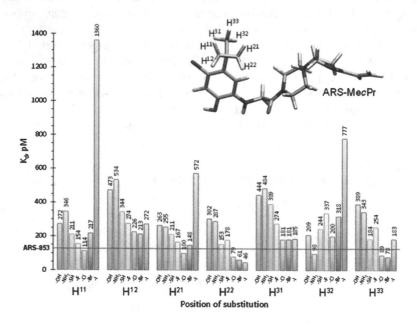

Fig. 3. The influence of the substitutions of hydrogen atoms of methylcyclopropyl (Me*c*Pr) on other functional groups in the hydrophobic binding moiety on the calculated K_d values. The red line corresponds to the calculated $K_d = 135$ pM for the ARS-853. (Color figure online)

The most prospective position for substitutions in the ARS-*t*Bu compounds were found at the H^{13} atom (Fig. 4). Hydrogen substitution results in more than an order of magnitude decrease of the K_d value compared with the ARS-853. Here we should mention that the tBu group can freely rotate around the single carbon-carbon bond between the benzene ring and tBu group, the methyl groups can freely rotate as well. Thus Fig. 4 presents only 7 different compounds with a single substitution of the hydrogen atom to the other groups. The reason of different calculated dissociation constants for the same compounds is different spacial orientations of substituent in the hydrophobic binding moiety. Taking the smallest values among complexes with different conformations of the same substituents in ARS-tBu family, we can conclude that monosubstituted tBu derivatives are more preferable than ARS-tBu or ARS-853 from the point of binding.

Contrary to the ARS-tBu, there are several non-equivalent hydrogen positions in the methylcyclobuthyl (MecBu) group (Fig. 5). According to our calculations the most prospective positions for the substitutions are H^{12} and H^{32} that are located symmetrically. The most prospective candidates contain halogens Cl, Br or I. Such substitutions results in an order of magnitude decrease of the K_d values compared with the ARS-853.

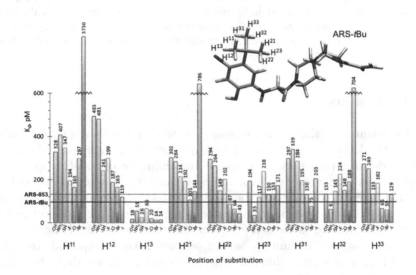

Fig. 4. The influence of the substitutions of hydrogen atoms on other functional groups in the *tert*-butyl (tBu) hydrophobic binding moiety on the calculated K_d values. The red line corresponds to the calculated $K_d = 135$ pM for the ARS-853 and black line for the ARS compound with the unsubstituted tBu hydrophobic binding moiety ($K_d = 99$ pM). (Color figure online)

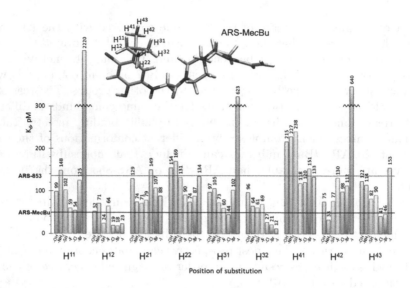

Fig. 5. The influence of the substitutions of hydrogen atoms on other functional groups in the methylcyclobutyl (MecBu) hydrophobic binding moiety on the calculated K_d values. The red line corresponds to the calculated $K_d = 135$ pM for the ARS-853 and black line for the ARS compound with the unsubstituted MecBu hydrophobic binding moiety ($K_d = 50$ pM). (Color figure online)

4   Conclusions

Using molecular modeling tools we demonstrate that the hydrophobic binding pocket of the KRAS can accommodate large molecular fragments. We utilize molecular docking procedure to evaluate the influence of substituents of the hydrophobic binding moiety on IC_{50} values of the ARS compounds. We demonstrate that stronger binding can be achieved if substitute methylcyclopropyl group of ARS-853 with the more bulky *tert*-butyl or methylcyclobutyl groups. Further substitutions of hydrogen atoms to large halogens (Br, I) decrease the dissociation constants. To sum up, we suggest novel ARS compounds that have estimated IC_{50} values more than an order of magnitude lower than the experimentally studied ARS-853.

Acknowledgments. M.G. Khrenova and A.M. Kulakova acknowledge financial support from the RFBR according to the research project № 18-29-13006. The research is carried out using the equipment of the shared research facilities of HPC computing resources at Lomonosov Moscow State University.

References

1. Bourne, H.R., Sanders, D.A., McCormick, F.: The GTPase superfamily: conserved structure and molecular mechanism. Nature **349**, 117–127 (1991)

2. Cox, A.D., Fesik, S.W., Kimmelman, A.C., Luo, J., Der, C.J.: Drugging the undruggable RAS: mission possible? Nat. Rev. Drug Discov. **13**, 828–851 (2014)
3. Downward, J.: The Ras superfamily of small GTP-binding proteins. Trends Biochem. Sci. **15**, 469–472 (1990)
4. Grand, R.J., Owen, D.: The biochemistry of Ras P21. Biochem. J. **279**, 609–631 (1991)
5. Karnoub, A.E., Weinberg, R.A.: Ras oncogenes: split personalities. Nat. Rev. Mol. Cell Biol. **9**, 517–531 (2008)
6. Lito, P., Solomon, M., Li, L.-S., Hansen, R., Rosen, N.: Allele-apecific inhibitors inactivate mutant KRAS G12C by a trapping mechanism. Science **351**, 604–608 (2016)
7. Morris, G.M., et al.: AutoDock4 and AutoDockTools4: automated docking with selective receptor flexibility. J. Comput. Chem. **30**, 2785–2791 (2009)
8. Ostrem, J.M., Peters, U., Sos, M.L., Wells, J.A., Shokat, K.M.: K-Ras(G12C) inhibitors allosterically control GTP affinity and effector interactions. Nature **503**, 548–551 (2013)
9. Patricelli, M.P., et al.: Selective inhibition of oncogenic KRAS output with small molecules targeting the inactive state. Cancer Discov. **6**, 316–329 (2016)
10. Sogabe, S., et al.: Crystal structure of a human K-Ras G12D mutant in complex with GDP and the cyclic inhibitory peptide KRpep-2d. ACS Med. Chem. Lett. **8**, 732–736 (2017)
11. Wittinghofer, A., Pal, E.F.: The structure of Ras protein: a model for a universal molecular switch. Trends Biochem. Sci. **16**, 382–387 (1991)

Identification of Heat Conductivity in (2+1)D Equation as a Function of Time

Tchavdar T. Marinov[1] and Rossitza S. Marinova[2](✉)

[1] Southern University at New Orleans,
6801 Press Drive, New Orleans, LA 70126, USA
tmarinov@suno.edu
[2] Concordia University of Edmonton,
7128 Ada Boulevard, Edmonton, AB T5B-4E4, Canada
rossitza.marinova@concordia.ab.ca

Abstract. The considered problem for identifying the time–dependent heat conductivity coefficient from over–posed boundary data belongs to a class of inverse problems. The proposed solution uses a variational approach for identifying the coefficient. The inverse problem is reformulated as a higher–order elliptic boundary–value problem for minimization of a quadratic functional of the original equation. The resulting system consists of a well–posed fourth–order boundary-value problem for the temperature and an explicit equation for the unknown heat conductivity coefficient. The obtained boundary–value problem is solved by means of an iterative procedure, which is thoroughly validated.

Keywords: Heat conductivity · Inverse problem · Variational method · Boundary data

1 Introduction

This work deals with heat conductivity identification from the heat conduction equation satisfying specific boundary and initial conditions. The general differential equation of heat conduction within a solid is [1]:

$$\frac{\partial T(\boldsymbol{r}, \tau)}{\partial \tau} = \nabla[\lambda \nabla T(\boldsymbol{r}, \tau)] + q(\boldsymbol{r}, \tau), \tag{1}$$

where the variables are: T – the temperature; τ – the time; λ – the heat conductivity coefficient; $\boldsymbol{r}$ – the position vector within the body; q – the heat generation in the medium.

Inverse problems in heat conduction have attracted attention by many researchers in recent year. The problem for heat conductivity coefficient can be determined from the inverse solution to the heat transfer problem, see [3,5–8].

Many practically important problems involving parabolic PDEs are classified as inverse in the sense that the way they are posed is not the standard initial, boundary, or initial–boundary value for which the correctness and well–posedness

© Springer Nature Switzerland AG 2020
I. Lirkov and S. Margenov (Eds.): LSSC 2019, LNCS 11958, pp. 356–364, 2020.
https://doi.org/10.1007/978-3-030-41032-2_41

of the problem has been proved. Clearly, the ill-posed problems are inverse in this sense. The first example for an ill-posed problem was shown by [4] for the initial value problem (i.v.p.) for Laplace equation (the so–called "analytical continuation").

The class of inverse problems is wider than the class of ill-posed problems since the former contains also the problems involving an unknown coefficient in the governing equation to be estimated from additional (overposed) data at the boundary or at some internal points (lines, surfaces) in the domain. In this case, the problem is inverse in the sense that no explicit equation is available to evaluate the unknown coefficient. Intuitively speaking, one should adjust the coefficient in order to make solution meet the overposed data at the boundaries.

The coefficient identification may or may not be incorrect depending on existence and uniqueness of the solution. In most of the situations these questions are hard to answer and any kind of approach capable to shed some light on the problem is welcome. Even if an abstract theorem of uniqueness is available, the actual computation of the unknown coefficient still remains a formidable difficulty and the quest for effective algorithms is still on. At the same time, the estimation of an unknown coefficient from overposed boundary data is of significant practical importance when creating non-invasive methods to identify the material properties of a continuum.

2 The Direct Initial Boundary–Value Problem

We consider the initial boundary–value problem for the heat conduction equation in a bounded domain. The two–dimensional heat conduction equation is

$$\frac{\partial T}{\partial \tau} = \frac{\partial}{\partial x}\left(\lambda \frac{\partial T}{\partial x}\right) + \frac{\partial}{\partial y}\left(\lambda \frac{\partial T}{\partial y}\right), \tag{2}$$

where $\Omega = \{(x, y) : 0 < x < 1;\ 0 < y < 1\} \subset \mathbb{R}^2$ is the domain, $T = T(x, y, \tau)$ is the temperature, and λ is the heat conductivity coefficient. There are no internal heat sources, i.e. $q(x, y, \tau) = 0$.

In this work, the heat conductivity coefficient is considered to be a function of time τ, i.e., $\lambda = \lambda(\tau)$. Equation (2) reduces to

$$\mathcal{R}(x, y, \tau) := -\frac{\partial T(x, y, \tau)}{\partial \tau} + \lambda(\tau)\frac{\partial^2 T(x, y, \tau)}{\partial x^2} + \lambda(\tau)\frac{\partial^2 T(x, y, \tau)}{\partial y^2} = 0. \tag{3}$$

If the coefficient $\lambda = \lambda(\tau)$ is known, an initial condition is needed to make the problem solvable, namely

$$T(x, y, 0) = \phi(x, y), \tag{4}$$

and a boundary condition at each boundary point $(x, y) \in \partial\Omega$ of the body, say

$$T(x, y, \tau)\big|_{(x,y)\in\partial\Omega} = \psi(x, y, \tau). \tag{5}$$

The system of Eqs. (3), (4), and (5) comprises the so–called direct problem. To solve the given problem, which is related to a class of inverse problems, a mathematical approach based on the Calculus of Variations is developed. The inverse problem for the coefficient identification is reformulated as a higher–order elliptic boundary–value problem for minimization of the quadratic functional of the original equation. The system contains a well posed fourth–order boundary–value problem for the sought function T and an explicit equation for the unknown heat conductivity coefficient λ.

3   Inverse Problem Formulation

We now specify the inverse problem we consider in this paper. Suppose that the heat conductivity coefficient $\lambda(\tau)$ is not known. In order to identify it, we need more information for the temperature $T(x, y, \tau)$. In the present work we assume that the temperature field is not only known in the initial time moment $\tau = 0$, but also in a specified final time moment, $\tau = F$,

$$T(x, y, F) = \Phi(x, y). \tag{6}$$

Also, we assume that the heat flux associated with a temperature profile T is given for all $\tau \in [0, F]$ and $(x, y) \in \partial\Omega$, i.e.,

$$-\lambda \frac{\partial T}{\partial \nu}\Big|_{(x,y)\in\partial\Omega} = \Psi(x, y, \tau), \tag{7}$$

where $\dfrac{\partial T}{\partial \nu}$ is the normal derivative of the temperature function T at the boundary point $(x, y) \in \partial\Omega$.

If the heat conductivity coefficient $\lambda(\tau)$ is known, the problem (3)–(7) is over-determined. If the function $\lambda(\tau)$ is not known, it is possible to find the temperature T and the heat conductivity simultaneously. So, we call the pair of functions (T, λ) a solution of the problem (3)–(7). These type of problems are Inverse Problems.

3.1   Variational Approach to Solving the Inverse Problem

Following the idea of the Method of Variational Imbedding (MVI) (see [2, 9, 10]), we replace the problem (3)–(7) with the following minimization problem

$$\mathcal{I}(T, \lambda) = \int_0^F \iint_\Omega [\mathcal{R}(x, y, \tau)]^2 dx dy d\tau \longrightarrow \min, \tag{8}$$

under the conditions (4)–(7).

The functional $\mathcal{I}(T, \lambda)$ is a quadratic and homogeneous function of its argument $\mathcal{R}(x, y, \tau)$. Hence, it attains its minimum if and only if the argument is zero, i.e. $\mathcal{R}(x, y, \tau) = 0$. It follows that there is an one-to-one correspondence between the solution of the original problem (3), (4)–(7) and the minimization problem (8), (4)–(7).

3.2 The "Imbedded" Boundary–Value Problem

Necessary conditions for minimization of the functional $\mathcal{I}(T, \lambda)$ are derived from the Euler–Lagrange equations for the functions $T(x, y, \tau)$ and $\lambda(\tau)$. The equation for the function $T(x, y, \tau)$ is

$$\left(\frac{\partial}{\partial \tau} + \lambda \frac{\partial^2}{\partial x^2} + \lambda \frac{\partial^2}{\partial y^2} \right) \left(-\frac{\partial T}{\partial \tau} + \lambda \frac{\partial^2 T}{\partial x^2} + \lambda \frac{\partial^2 T}{\partial y^2} \right) = 0. \tag{9}$$

If the functions T and λ are as many time differentiable as needed, we can simplify Eq. (9) as follows

$$-\frac{\partial^2 T}{\partial \tau^2} + \lambda^2 \left(\frac{\partial^4 T}{\partial x^4} + \frac{\partial^4 T}{\partial y^4} + 2\frac{\partial^4 T}{\partial y^2 \partial x^2} \right) + \frac{d\lambda}{d\tau} \left(\frac{\partial^2 T}{\partial x^2} + \frac{\partial^2 T}{\partial y^2} \right) = 0. \tag{10}$$

Equation (10) is of second order with respect to the time τ and of fourth order with respect to the spatial variables x and y. There exist sufficient number of initial and boundary conditions (4)–(7) for solving Eq. (10). So, the problem is well–posed if the function $\lambda(\tau)$ is known. Hence, using the MVI, the inverse problem is embedded into a higher–order but well–posed elliptic boundary–value problem. Note that if the coefficient $\lambda(\tau)$ is not consistent with the boundary data, the solution of the obtained via MVI boundary–value problem may not give the desired value of the functional $\mathcal{J}$. In order to achieve the latter, minimization with respect to the function $\lambda(\tau)$ should be considered.

It follows from Eq. (8) that the coefficient $\lambda(\tau)$ can be calculated as

$$\lambda(\tau) = \iint_\Omega \frac{\partial T}{\partial \tau} \left(\frac{\partial^2 T}{\partial x^2} + \frac{\partial^2 T}{\partial y^2} \right) dxdy \bigg/ \iint_\Omega \left(\frac{\partial^2 T}{\partial x^2} + \frac{\partial^2 T}{\partial y^2} \right)^2 dxdy. \tag{11}$$

This approach does not work for stationary fields.

4 Existence and Uniqueness of the Solution

It is important to investigate the individual components of the MVI problem for existence and uniqueness of the solution. Of course, the uniqueness of each subproblem will not automatically bring uniqueness of the full MVI problem. Regardless of the latter, existence and uniqueness of the subproblems are of crucial importance for constructing algorithms for approximating solutions. Because of the limited space, here we present only a brief outline of the proof.

In order to prove the correctness of the fourth–order boundary–value problem (10), (4)–(7), we consider the Hilbert space $\mathcal{H}(\mathcal{D})$, where $\mathcal{D}$ is the domain

$$\mathcal{D} = \{(x, y, \tau) : 0 < x < 1; 0 < y < 1; 0 < \tau < \tau_F\}.$$

Let $\mathcal{H}$ consists of the functions α satisfying the following boundary conditions

$$\alpha|_{\partial\Omega} = \frac{\partial \alpha}{\partial \nu}\bigg|_{\partial\Omega} = \alpha(x, y, 0) = \alpha(x, y, \tau_F) = 0, \tag{12}$$

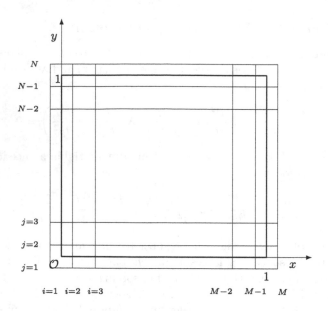

Fig. 1. Grid pattern.

where ν is the outward unit normal. We expect that the functions under consideration are as many time differentiable as necessary.

We also introduce the following scalar product in $\mathcal{H}(\mathcal{D})$

$$[\alpha, \beta] = \iint_{\mathcal{D}} \left(-\frac{\partial \alpha}{\partial \tau} + \lambda \frac{\partial^2 \alpha}{\partial x^2} + \lambda \frac{\partial^2 \alpha}{\partial y^2} \right) \left(-\frac{\partial \beta}{\partial \tau} + \lambda \frac{\partial^2 \beta}{\partial x^2} + \lambda \frac{\partial^2 \beta}{\partial y^2} \right) dxdyd\tau, \quad (13)$$

where $\lambda(\tau) > 0$ is a function defined for $\tau > 0$.

Next, we define a *generalized (weak) solution* of the problem (10), (4)–(7). By the Riesz Representation Theorem for the continuous linear functional on the Hilbert space $\mathcal{H}$, it follows that there exist a unique generalized solution.

Provided that the coefficient $\lambda(\tau) > 0$ is given, we can prove that the Euler–Lagrange Eq. (10) possesses a unique solution satisfying the boundary conditions (4)–(7). Equation (11) is an explicit expression for the coefficient $\lambda(\tau)$; hence, it provides a unique solution for it, if $T(x, y, \tau)$ is known. This allows us to construct a procedure for finding a solution to the nonlinear problem by means of iterations, namely replacing $\lambda(\tau)$ (when calculating T), or $T(x, y, \tau)$ (when calculating λ) with their values calculated at the previous iteration.

5   Numerical Scheme

5.1   Grid and Approximations

As an example, we consider a problem in the unit square $\mathcal{D} = \{(x, y) : 0 < x < 1; 0 < y < 1\}$. We also introduce an orthogonal mesh with a total number of

Fig. 2. Grid nodes in time.

grid lines equal to M and N in the x- and y-directions, respectively. In order to obtain second–order approximation of the derivatives participating in the boundary conditions, we use staggered grid in both directions which overflows the boundaries by half spacing (see Fig. 1).

The spacings are related to the number of points as $h_x \equiv 1/(M-2)$ and $h_y \equiv 1/(N-2)$, and the grid lines are defined by

$$x_i = (i-1.5)h_x \text{ for } i = 1, \ldots, M, \quad y_j = (j-1.5)h_y \text{ for } j = 1, \ldots, N.$$

In order to secure second–order approximation in time, we use a non-staggered grid in time for the temperature $T(x, y, t)$. The grid for the coefficient $\lambda(t)$ is staggered (see Fig. 2).

The total number of grid nodes in the τ–direction for T is equal to L and the total number of grid nodes in the τ–direction for λ is equal to $L-1$. The spacing in the τ–direction is $h_\tau \equiv \tau_F/(L-1)$, and the grid–nodes for T and $\lambda(x, y)$ are defined in the following way: for T: $\tau_l = (l)h_\tau$, for $l = 0, \ldots, L-1$; for λ: $\tau_{l+0.5} = (l+0.5)h_\tau$ for $l = 0, \ldots, L-2$.

The grid described above allows discretization of the derivative in the governing equation and boundary conditions with central differences. After discretization, we obtain a system of linear equations with the following coefficients:

$$T_{i,j,k}: \quad C_k^{00} = \frac{2}{h_\tau^2} + \frac{6l_k^2}{h_x^4} + \frac{8l_k^2}{h_x^2 h_y^2} - \frac{2l_k'}{h_x^2} + \frac{6l_k^2}{h_y^4} - \frac{2l_k'}{h_y^2};$$

$$T_{i,j-1,k}, T_{i,j+1,k}: \quad C_k^{01} = -\frac{4l_k^2}{h_x^2 h_y^2} - \frac{4l_k^2}{h_y^4} + \frac{l_k'}{h_y^2};$$

$$T_{i,j-2,k} T_{i,j+2,k}: \quad C_k^{02} = \frac{l_k^2}{h_y^4};$$

$$T_{i-1,j-1,k}, T_{i-1,j+1,k}, T_{i+1,j-1,k}, T_{i+1,j+1,k}: \quad C_k^{11} = \frac{2l_k^2}{h_x^2 h_y^2};$$

$$T_{i-1,j,k}, T_{i+1,j,k}: \quad C_k^{10} = -\frac{4l_k^2}{h_x^4} - \frac{4l_k^2}{h_x^2 h_y^2} + \frac{l_k'}{h_x^2};$$

$$T_{i-2,j,k}, T_{i+2,j,k}: \quad C_k^{20} = \frac{l_k^2}{h_x^4}; \text{ and } T_{i,j,k-1}, T_{i,j,k+1}: \quad \frac{-1}{h_\tau^2}.$$

We use the extended Midpoint rule to approximate the integrals in (11) of the second–order with respect to all variables.

5.2   Algorithm

The iterations are performed as follows:

(I) With a given initial values for $\lambda_k^{\text{old}} > 0$, the fourth-order boundary value problem Eqs. (10), (5), (7) is solved for the function $T_{i,j,k}$.

(II) With the newly computed values of $T_{i,j,k}$, the function λ_k^{new} is evaluated. If the norm of the difference between the new and the old field for λ is less than ε, i.e. $\max_k |\lambda_k^{\text{new}} - \lambda_{k,l}^{\text{old}}| < \varepsilon$, then the calculations are terminated, otherwise step **(I)** is repeated.

6   Numerical Tests

In order to prove numerically the second–order of approximation, consider the following exact solution of the Eq. (2):

$$T(x, y, t) = (1 + t)^2 e^{-(x+y)}, \qquad \lambda(t) = \frac{1}{1 + t}. \qquad (14)$$

Under proper boundary conditions the numerical solution has to converge to the exact one (14).

Figure 3 shows the point–wise numerical errors for the function $\lambda(\tau)$ calculated with for different spacings $h_x = h_y = h_\tau = 0.1; 0.05; 0.025; 0.0125$.

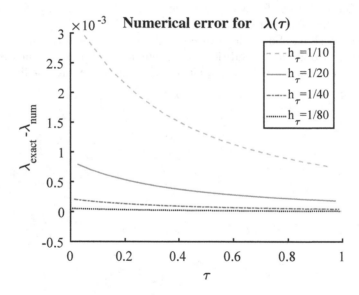

Fig. 3. The difference between numerical and exact values of $\lambda(\tau)$ for $h_x = h_y = h_\tau = 0.1, 0.05, 0.025, 0.0125$.

The rates of convergence are calculated as $\text{rate}_\lambda = \log_2 \dfrac{||\lambda_{2h} - \lambda_{\text{exact}}||}{||\lambda_h - \lambda_{\text{exact}}||}$.

Table 1. The l^2 norm of the difference $\lambda - \lambda_{\text{exact}}$, and the rates of convergence for four different values of the grid spacings $h_x = h_y = h_\tau$.

h_τ	$||\lambda - \lambda_{\text{exact}}||_{l^2}$	rate$_\lambda$
0.100000	0.001657	—
0.050000	0.000416	1.993292
0.025000	0.000104	1.998393
0.012500	0.000026	2.002052

The l^2 norm of the difference between the numerical solution w and the analytical one with four different grid spacings $h_x = h_y = h_\tau = 0.1; 0.05; 0.025; 0.0125$ is given in Table 1 along with the rates of convergence. The presented numerical tests demonstrate the second order rate of convergence.

7   Conclusions

This paper proposes an approach for solving the inverse coefficient problems for the (2+1)D equations of heat conduction based on the measurements of temperature and heat flux at body's boundary. The numerical experiments show that the proposed method gives an accurate simultaneous identification of the temperature and the heat conductivity.

References

1. Kakac, S., Yener, Y., Naveira-Cotta, C.P.: Heat Conduction, 5th edn. CRC Press, Boca Raton (2018)
2. Christov, C.I., Marinov, T.T.: Identification of heat-conduction coefficient via method of variational imbedding. Math. Comput. Model. **27**(3), 109–116 (1998). https://doi.org/10.1016/S0895-7177(97)00269-0
3. Hadała, B., Malinowski, Z., Szajding, A.: Solution strategy for the inverse determination of the specially varying heat transfer coefficient. Int. J. Heat Mass Transf. **104**, 993–1007 (2017). https://doi.org/10.1016/j.ijheatmasstransfer.2016.08.093
4. Hadamard, J.: Le Probleme de Cauchy et les Equations aux Derivatives Partielles Lineares Hyperboliques. Hermann, Paris (1932). https://doi.org/10.1090/S0002-9904-1934-05815-4
5. Kügler, P.: Identification of a temperature dependent heat conductivity from single boundary measurements. SIAM J. Numer. Anal. **41**(4), 1543–1563 (2004). https://doi.org/10.1137/S0036142902415900
6. Lesnic, D., Elliott, L., Ingham, D.B.: Identification of the thermal conductivity and heat capacity in unsteady nonlinear heat conduction problems using the boundary element method. J. Comput. Phys. **126**, 410–420 (1996). https://doi.org/10.1006/jcph.1996.0146
7. Malinowski, Z., Cebo-Rudnicka, A., Hadała, B., Szajding, A.: Inverse method implementation to heat transfer coefficient determination over the plate cooled by water spray. Inverse Prob. Sci. Eng. **23**(3), 518–556 (2014). https://doi.org/10.1080/17415977.2014.923417

8. Nedin, R., Nesterov, S., Vatulyan, A.: Identification of thermal conductivity coefficient and volumetric heat capacity of functionally graded materials. Int. J. Heat Mass Transf. **102**, 213–218 (2016). https://doi.org/10.1016/j.ijheatmasstransfer.2016.06.027

9. Marinov, T.T., Christov, C.I., Marinova, R.S.: Novel numerical approach to solitary-wave solutions identification of Boussinesq and Korteweg-de Vries equations. Int. J. Bifurcat. Chaos **15**(2), 557–565 (2005). https://doi.org/10.1142/S0218127405012211

10. Marinov, T.T., Marinova, R.S., Christov, C.I.: Coefficient identification in elliptic partial differential equation. In: Lirkov, I., Margenov, S., Waśniewski, J. (eds.) LSSC 2005. LNCS, vol. 3743, pp. 372–379. Springer, Heidelberg (2006). https://doi.org/10.1007/11666806_42

Numerical Calculation of Deformations of Composite Material with Fiber Inclusions

Petr V. Sivtsev[✉] and Djulustan Ya. Nikiforov

Ammosov North-Eastern Federal University,
58, Belinskogo, 677000 Yakutsk, Russia
sivkapetr@mail.ru

Abstract. In the numerical simulation of the stress-strain state of a composite material, a problem may arise associated with a large computational complexity due to the grid resolution of a large number of inclusions. It is especially difficult to resolve elongated bodies having linear dimensions that differ by several orders of magnitude, such as fibers. In this paper, we attempt to model fibers in the form of one-dimensional lines, which can significantly reduce the computational complexity of the problem. Comparison of the results for the three-point bending of a concrete block is presented. For the numerical solution, the finite element method was applied using the FEniCS computing platform.

1 Introduction

One of the most striking examples of the use of composite materials is concrete reinforced with inclusions in the form of fibers, which can significantly enhance the strength characteristics of concrete [1]. In recent decades, interest in the study of composite reinforcement by basalt plastic for the subsequent replacement of metal rods in load-bearing reinforced concrete structures in construction has been increased [2]. One of the innovative trends in the development of the North of Russia are the technologies related to the production of basalt continuous fiber and composite materials based on it. The presence of huge stocks of raw materials and the relatively low cost of fibers produced from it makes it possible to consider their prospects in economic terms.

When modeling the problem of calculating the stress-strain state of a composite material with inclusions in the form of fibers, there is a problem associated with a large quantity of the cells needed for grid resolution of each fiber. One way to solve this problem is to use a multiscale method or a method of numerical homogenization. However, in real applications, the number of fibers can be so large that the solution to the problem of constructing local bases for the classical multiscale method will also be quite complex. Certainly, one can use the

The research was supported by mega-grant of the Russian Federation Government (N 14.Y26.31.0013).

I. Lirkov and S. Margenov (Eds.): LSSC 2019, LNCS 11958, pp. 365–372, 2020.
https://doi.org/10.1007/978-3-030-41032-2_42

method of numerical homogenization on the representative element and solve the problem at the macro level using effective coefficients [3,4]. At the same time, it is also worthwhile to take into account that the error of the resulting solution depends on the size of the representative element and one needs to use a large representative element to obtain an accurate solution, which also leads to large expenditures of computing resources. The situation is aggravated by the fact that the difference in the orders of magnitude of the thickness of fibers to their length is at least 2, and often even more. In this paper, we check the accuracy of the calculation of body deformations with the inclusion of fibers in the simulation of fibers in the form of one-dimensional objects as fractures modeled in Discrete Fracture Model [5,6]. We have chosen a three-point bending test as an example [7].

For numerical solution we have used implementation of finite element method using the FEniCS computing platform [8–10]. Results of comparison of deformations between solution with full grid resolution of fibers and solution with one-dimensional fibers are presented. Comparisons include cases with a ratio of fiber thickness to its length equal to 1: 100 and 1: 1000. Concrete with inclusion of basalt or steel fibers was chosen for computational experiment.

2   Problem Statement

Let us consider mathematical model describing stress-strain state of composite concrete under three-point bending test

$$\operatorname{div} \boldsymbol{\sigma} = 0, \quad \boldsymbol{x} \in \Omega = \Omega_1 \cup \sum_{j=1}^{n} \Omega_{2\text{-}j}, \tag{1}$$

where Ω_1 is subdomain of concrete, $\Omega_{2\text{-}j}$, $j = 1...n$ are subdomains of fibers, n is number of fibers, $\boldsymbol{\sigma}$ is stress tensor.

For convenience, we use Voight notation

$$\boldsymbol{\varepsilon} == \begin{pmatrix} \varepsilon_{11} \\ \varepsilon_{12} \end{pmatrix} = \begin{pmatrix} \frac{\partial u_1}{\partial x_1} \\ \frac{\partial u_2}{\partial x_2} \\ \frac{\partial u_2}{\partial x_1} + \frac{\partial u_1}{\partial x_2} \end{pmatrix}, \quad \boldsymbol{\sigma} = \begin{pmatrix} \sigma_{11} \\ \sigma_{22} \\ \sigma_{12} \end{pmatrix} = C\boldsymbol{\varepsilon},$$

here C is elastic tensor, which is represented as follows

$$C = \begin{pmatrix} C_{1111} & C_{1122} & C_{1112} \\ C_{2211} & C_{2222} & C_{2212} \\ C_{1211} & C_{1222} & C_{1212} \end{pmatrix}.$$

In the case of isotropic body, elastic tensor can be expressed by Lame parameters λ, μ, which depend on subdomain and are given as

$$C_i = \begin{pmatrix} \lambda_i + 2\mu_i & \lambda_i & 0 \\ \lambda_i & \lambda_i + 2\mu_i & 0 \\ 0 & 0 & \mu_i \end{pmatrix}.$$

Table 1. Elastic parameters of concrete matrix, basalt and steel fibers

Material	Young modulus E, GPa	Poisson ratio ν
Concrete	40	0.15
Basalt	89	0.26
Steel	200	0.3

where

$$C = C_i, \ \mu = \mu_i, \ \lambda = \lambda_i, \quad x \in \Omega_i \quad i = 1, 2\text{-}j, \quad \forall j = 1...n.$$

Lame parameters can be uniquely determined by Young modulus E and Poisson coefficient ν. Elastic parameters of object under the investigation are presented in Table 1 [11,12].

Equation of solid body is supplemented with boundary conditions related to fixation of vertical displacement on rails and force of press. Rail fixation is defined by Dirichlet boundary condition:

$$u_Y = 0, \quad x \in \Gamma_D, \tag{2}$$

and the press force is defined by Neumann boundary condition

$$\sigma_n = (0, -P), \quad x \in \Gamma_N. \tag{3}$$

To approximate the space, the finite element method is used. The original differential problem is reduced to a discrete variational problem. The numerical implementation is performed using the FEniCS computing platform.

3   Investigation Object

The object of the study is a concrete deep beam with a width of 2 m and a height of 1 m. The included fibers have 2% volume and are located perpendicular to the direction of pressure (Fig. 1).

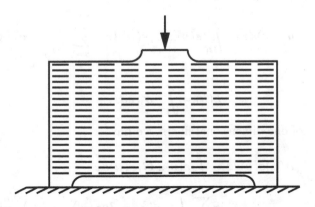

Fig. 1. Deep beam with fiber inclusion under three-point bending test modelling geometry. Rails and press are modeled as concrete inclusions.

Since the object is symmetrical, half of the body is considered with the specification of the condition of symmetry. In the case of fibers with a ratio of thickness to length equal to 1:100, the number of fibers is 1000, while 5000 inclusions are modeled for the 1:1000 ratio. Example of computational grid is presented in Fig. 2.

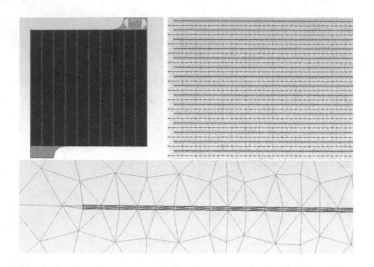

Fig. 2. Example of mesh with grid resolution of fibers. Different levels of zooming: On the left top whole mesh is presented and at the bottom we show zoomed mesh size of fiber.

4 One Dimensional Fiber Model

In the case of the usual finite-element solution of the linear elasticity problem of our object, we have bilinear and linear forms as

$$a(\boldsymbol{u}, \boldsymbol{v}) = \int_{\Omega} \boldsymbol{\sigma}(\boldsymbol{u})\varepsilon(\boldsymbol{v})dx = \int_{\Omega_1} \varepsilon(\boldsymbol{v}) : \boldsymbol{C}_1\varepsilon(\boldsymbol{u})dx + \sum_{j=1}^{n} \int_{\Omega_{2_j}} \varepsilon(\boldsymbol{v}) : \boldsymbol{C}_2\varepsilon(\boldsymbol{u})dx,$$

and

$$L(\boldsymbol{v}) = \int_{\Gamma_N} \boldsymbol{\sigma}_n \boldsymbol{v}dx.$$

But in the case of one-dimensional fibers, we have

$$a(\boldsymbol{u}, \boldsymbol{v}) = \int_{\Omega} \boldsymbol{\sigma}(\boldsymbol{u})\varepsilon(\boldsymbol{v})dx = \int_{\Omega} \varepsilon(\boldsymbol{v}) : \boldsymbol{C}_1\varepsilon(\boldsymbol{u})dx$$
$$+ \sum_{j=1}^{n} \int_{\Gamma_{2\_j}} d(\lambda_2 + 2\mu_2 - \lambda_1 - 2\mu_1)\frac{\partial u_{l\_j}}{\partial x_{l\_j}}\frac{\partial v_{l\_j}}{\partial x_{l\_j}},$$

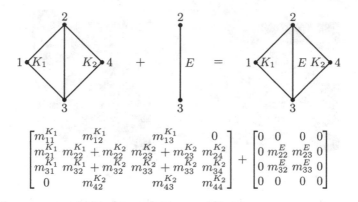

Fig. 3. Discrete fracture model description.

and

$$L(\boldsymbol{v}) = \int_{\Gamma_N} \boldsymbol{\sigma}_n \boldsymbol{v} dx,$$

where d is thickness of fibers and u_{l_j} and v_{l_j} are projections of u and v to unit vector l_j parallel to fiber and $\frac{\partial}{\partial x_{l\_j}}$ is directional derivative in l_j direction. Subdomains Ω_{2_j} are replaced by lines Γ_{2_j}.

Thus, we take into account only longitudinal compression and tension of fibers and neglect other effects. Matrix assembly is similar to Discrete Fracture Model, which is illustrated in Fig. 3. However, in our case we deal with vector values instead of scalars.

5   Comparative Analysis

The example of solution for the case of concrete with 1000 steel fiber inclusions with 1:100 ratio is presented in Fig. 4.

Error of one-dimensional approximation is calculated using following equation

$$\mathrm{ERR}(f) = \left| \frac{f_{\mathrm{fib\_odim}} - f_{\mathrm{fib\_gref}}}{f_{\mathrm{fib\_gref}}} \right|,$$

where $f_{\mathrm{fib\_gref}}$ is solution with grid resolution of included fibers and $f_{\mathrm{fib\_odim}}$ is solution with use of one dimensional approximation.

When we model fibers as one-dimensional object, we can conduct calculations on mesh with significantly less cells and vertices, which leads to lesser cost of calculation and faster solution. Mesh size and comparison of computational time are shown in Table 2. Distribution of the solution error for the case of concrete with 1000 steel fiber inclusion with 1:100 ratio is presented in Fig. 5.

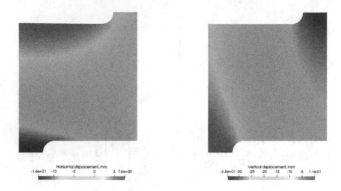

Fig. 4. Horizontal and vertical displacement distribution for the case of concrete with 1000 steel fiber with 1:100 ratio inclusion

Table 2. Mesh size and computational time comparison for different cases

Mesh	1000 fibers with 1:100 ratio		5000 fibers with 1:1000 ratio	
	Grid res.	One dim.	Grid res.	One dim.
Cells	201 390	30 728	4 761 202	587 680
Vertices	100 921	15 590	2 381 707	294 946
Matrix assembly time	2.2	1.3	51	21
System solution time	19.1	3.4	930	86
Total computation time	21.3	4.7	981	107

Table 3. Proposed method error in a case of 1000 basalt fiber with 1:100 ratio

Solution	Grid resolution	One dimensional	Error, %
Max value of $|u_Y|, mm$	34.93	35.11	0.51
Max value of $|u_X|, mm$	14.34	14.30	0.28

Table 4. Proposed method error in a case of 5000 basalt fiber with 1:1000 ratio

Solution	Grid resolution	One dimensional	Error, %
Max value of $|u_Y|, mm$	34.93	35.10	0.48
Max value of $|u_X|, mm$	14.33	14.30	0.21

Results for displacement solution and error of one dimensional approximation for all conducted numerical experiments are shown in Tables 3, 4, 5 and 6. In the case of basalt fibers, we obtain good accuracy for horizontal and vertical displacement. In the case of steel fibers, we recieve results with little more error for horizontal displacement, yet, good accuracy of approximation is still achieved.

Table 5. Proposed method error in a case of 1000 steel fiber with 1:100 ratio

Solution	Grid resolution	One dimensional	Error, %
Max value of $|u_Y|$, mm	34.40	34.58	0.52
Max value of $|u_X|$, mm	13.84	13.70	1.01

Table 6. Proposed method error in a case of 5000 steel fiber with 1:1000 ratio

Solution	Grid resolution	One dimensional	Error, %
Max value of $|u_Y|$, mm	34.36	34.52	0.46
Max value of $|u_X|$, mm	13.77	13.61	1.16

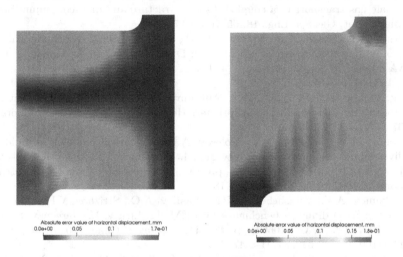

Fig. 5. Absolute values of horizontal and vertical displacement error distribution for the case of concrete with 1000 steel fiber inclusion with 1:100 ratio

6   Conclusion

We made a numerical solution of linear elasticity problem for the three-point bending test of concrete deep beam with fiber inclusion with grid resolution of fibers and using one-dimensional model for fibers. For one-dimensional model we deal with much less number of cells and, therefore, faster solution. Results show good accuracy of proposed method of one-dimensional approximation. In following papers we will perform comparison with numerical homogenization method.

References

1. Smarzewski, P.: Influence of basalt-polypropylene fibres on fracture properties of high performance concrete. Compos. Struct. **209**, 23–33 (2019)

2. Sivtseva, A.V., Sivtsev, P.V.: Numerical simulation of deformations of basalt roving. In: Dimov, I., Faragó, I., Vulkov, L. (eds.) FDM 2018. LNCS, vol. 11386, pp. 501–508. Springer, Cham (2019). https://doi.org/10.1007/978-3-030-11539-5_58
3. Zakharov, P.E., Sivtsev, P.V.: Numerical calculation of the effective coefficient in the problem of linear elasticity of a composite material. Math. Notes NEFU **24**(2), 75–84 (2017)
4. Stepanov, S.P., Vasilyeva, M.V., Vasil'ev, V.I.: Generalized multiscale discontinuous Galerkin method for solving the heat problem with phase change. J. Comput. Appl. Math. **340**, 645–652 (2018)
5. Vasil'ev, V.I., et al.: Numerical solution of a fluid filtration problem in a fractured medium by using the domain decomposition method. J. Appl. Ind. Math. **12**(4), 785–796 (2018)
6. Akkutlu, I.Y., Efendiev, Y., Vasilyeva, M., Wang, Y.: Multiscale model reduction for shale gas transport in a coupled discrete fracture and dual-continuum porous media. J. Nat. Gas Sci. Eng. **48**, 65–76 (2017)
7. Kolesov, A.E., Sivtsev, P.V., Smarzewski, P., Vabishchevich, P.N.: Numerical analysis of reinforced concrete deep beams. In: Dimov, I., Faragó, I., Vulkov, L. (eds.) NAA 2016. LNCS, vol. 10187, pp. 414–421. Springer, Cham (2016). https://doi.org/10.1007/978-3-319-57099-0_46
8. Logg, A., Mardal, K.A., Wells, G.N.: Automated Solution of Differential Equations by the Finite Element Method. Springer, Heidelberg (2012). https://doi.org/10.1007/978-3-642-23099-8
9. Antonov, M.Y., Grigorev, A.V., Kolesov, A.E.: Numerical modeling of fluid flow in liver lobule using double porosity model. In: Dimov, I., Faragó, I., Vulkov, L. (eds.) NAA 2016. LNCS, vol. 10187, pp. 187–194. Springer, Cham (2016). https://doi.org/10.1007/978-3-319-57099-0_18
10. Avvakumov, A.V., Vabishchevich, P.N., Vasilev, A.O., Strizhov, V.F.: Solution of the 3D neutron diffusion benchmark by FEM. In: Lirkov, I., Margenov, S. (eds.) LSSC 2017. LNCS, vol. 10665, pp. 435–442. Springer, Cham (2018). https://doi.org/10.1007/978-3-319-73441-5_47
11. Valentino, P., Furgiuele, F., Romano, M., Ehrlich, I., Gebbeken, N.: Mechanical characterization of basalt fibre reinforced plastic with different fabric reinforcements-Tensile tests and FE-calculations with representative volume elements (RVEs). In: Convegno IGF XXII (2013)
12. Smarzewski, P.: Processes of cracking and crushing in hybrid fibre reinforced high-performance concrete slabs. Processes **7**(1), 49 (2019)

On the Impact of Reordering
in a Hierarchical Semi-Separable
Compression Solver for Fractional
Diffusion Problems

Dimitar Slavchev[(⊠)]

Institute of Information and Communication Technologies
at the Bulgarian Academy of Sciences, Sofia, Bulgaria
dimitargslavchev@parallel.bas.bg

Abstract. The performance of a hierarchical solver for systems of linear algebraic equations arising from finite elements (FEM) discretization of Fractional diffusion problems is the subject of this study. We consider the integral definition of Fractional Laplacian in a bounded domain introduced through the Ritz potential. The problem is non-local and the related FEM system has a dense matrix. We utilize the Structured Matrix Package (STRUMPACK) and its implementation of a Hierarchical Semi-Separable compression in order to solve the system of linear equations. Our main aim is to improve the performance and accuracy of the method by proposing and analyzing 2 schemes for reordering of the unknowns. The numerical tests are run on the high performance cluster AVITOHOL at IICT–BAS.

Keywords: Fractional laplacian · STRUMPACK · Hierarchical Semi-Separable compression · Solving dense systems of linear algebraic equations

1 Intruduction

The fractional in space elliptic operators of power $\alpha \in (0,1)$ are referred to super-diffusion. The related boundary value problems are non-local, and in a very general setting, the numerical solution of such problems is computationally very expensive.

The traditional Gaussian elimination has computational complexity $O(n^3)$, where n is the number of unknowns (degrees of freedom). The methods based on hierarchical compression have complexity $O(r^2 n)$, where r is the maximum rank of the off-diagonal blocks of the matrix. It is calculated during the compression step when the HSS algorithm generates the approximate compressed matrix. Typically r is much smaller than n. For some problems r grows with $O(\ln n)$ leading to nearly optimal overall complexity of $O(n \ln n)$.

However this relation holds true only when the order of the unknowns preserves the *"good"* structure of the matrix. It depends on the ordering of the

© Springer Nature Switzerland AG 2020
I. Lirkov and S. Margenov (Eds.): LSSC 2019, LNCS 11958, pp. 373–381, 2020.
https://doi.org/10.1007/978-3-030-41032-2_43

nodes in the mesh discretization of the problem domain. The ordering coming from the mesh generation algorithm might not provide the desired low-rank structure. This might impede the performance of the Hierarchical based method.

In this paper we examine several strategies for the reordering of unknowns. We compare and analyse the performance of the approximate solutions of the arising systems of linear algebraic equations.

2   Fractional Diffusion Problem Modelled with Fractional Laplacian

In this work we examine a *non-local* diffusion problem modelled with *fractional* Laplacian introduced with Ritz Potential. For $\alpha \in (0, 1)$ the Fractional Laplacian (FL) is defined as

$$(-\Delta)^\alpha u\,(x) = C\,(d, \alpha)\,p.v. \int_{\mathbb{R}^d} \frac{u\,(x) - u\,(y)}{|x - y|^{d+2\alpha}} dy \tag{1}$$

where

$$C\,(d, \alpha) = \frac{2^{2\alpha}\alpha\Gamma\left(\alpha + \frac{d}{2}\right)}{\pi^{d/2}\Gamma\,(1 - \alpha)}$$

is a normalized constant. Here d is the dimension of the problem. We provide the general definition, but the actual numerical tests are done for $d = 2$ dimensions. The FL given by Eq. (1) is one of the simplest pseudo-differential operators and can be regarded as the infinitesimal generator of a α-stable Lévi process. Given a function f, defined on a bounded domain Ω, the homogeneous Dirichlet problem is: find u that satisfies

$$\begin{cases} (-\Delta)^\alpha u = f \text{ in } \Omega, \\ u = 0 \text{ in } \Omega^c. \end{cases} \tag{2}$$

For the Finite Element settings we should consider an admissible triangulation $\mathcal{T}$ of Ω. For a discrete space $\mathbb{V}$ we use continuous piecewise linear elements over $\mathcal{T}$. We also introduce nodal basis $\{\varphi_1, \ldots, \varphi_N\} \in \mathbb{V}$ corresponding to the internal nodes $\{x_1, \ldots, x_N\}$, with $\varphi_i(x_j) = \delta_j^i$.

The system of linear equation is:

$$KU = F, \tag{3}$$

where the unknown is $U = (u_j) \in \mathbb{R}^N$. The coefficient matrix $K = K_{ij} \in \mathbb{R}^{N \times N}$ and the right hand side $F = (f_j) \in \mathbb{R}^N$ are respectively

$$K_{ij} = \frac{C\,(d, \alpha)}{2}\langle\varphi_i, \varphi_j\rangle_{H^\alpha(\mathbb{R})} \quad \text{and} \quad f_j = \int_\Omega f\varphi_j.$$

The *fractional* stiffness matrix K is symmetric and positive and therefore Eq. (2) has a unique solution. The integrals in the inner product used for the computation of K_{ij} are carried over $\mathbb{R}^N$. We need to consider a ball B, that contains the domain Ω, such that the distance between $\overline{\Omega}$ and B^c is positive.

The number of elements on the triangulation of B is denoted with $N_{\tilde{T}}$. For $l, m \in [1, N_{\tilde{T}}]$ we define the elements of the stiffness matrix as

$$K_{ij} = \frac{C(d, \alpha)}{2} \sum_{l=1}^{N_{\tilde{T}}} \left(\sum_{m=1}^{N_{\tilde{T}}} I_{l,m}^{i,j} + 2J_l^{i,j} \right),$$

where the integrals $I_{l,m}^{i,j}$ and $J_l^{i,j}$ are defined as

$$I_{l,m}^{i,j} = \int_{T_l} \int_{T_m} \frac{(\varphi_i(x) - \varphi_i(y))(\varphi_j(x) - \varphi_j(y))}{|x - y|^{2+2\alpha}} dxdy$$

$$J_l^{i,j} = \int_{T_l} \int_{B^c} \frac{\varphi_i(x)\varphi_j(x)}{|x - y|^{2+2\alpha}} dydx.$$

The computation of each integral $I_{l,m}^{i,j}$ and $J_l^{i,j}$ is challenging. The former involves singular integrand when $\overline{T_l} \cap \overline{T_m} \neq \emptyset$, while the latter must be calculated on an unbounded domain.

Numerical results for Eq. (2) as well as a complete n-dimensional finite element analysis for the Fractional Laplacian are available in [1], including regularity of solutions in standard and weighted fractional spaces. In [2] there is a simple FE implementation in MATLAB® code, which serves as complimentary work to [1]. We use this code as a basis for our analysis of the HSS compression preconditioner.

3   Hierarchical Semi-Separable Compression Based Solver

The hierarchical methods for solving *dense* systems of linear equations use the *structure* of the matrix in order to *compress* it into an approximated matrix. This is done by exploiting the low rank nature of the off-diagonal blocks of the matrix. This decomposition is possible for any matrix A, but in practice it is useful (i.e. it lowers the cost of operations and the storage requirements) only when the off-diagonal blocks of A are low-rank.

Matrices without proper *structure* (by which we understand low rank off-diagonal blocks) can also be compressed but that is of little value.

In this work we use the Hierarchically Semi-Separable (HSS) [1,6] compression implemented within the STRUMPACK project [4]. The HSS framework consists of:

1. Hierarchically Semi-Separable compression using random sampling.
2. ULV-like factorization of the compressed matrix and solution.
3. Computing HSS matrix-vector products.

The HSS compression uses a *cluster tree* that defines a hierarchical partitioning of the *dense* matrix A. The root of the tree represents the whole matrix and each leaf corresponds to divisions of the matrix. This is visualized on Fig. 1. This step uses random sampling. The approximation also uses a user defined threshold ε for the calculations. The complexity is $O(r^2n)$, where n is the number of unknowns (nodes) and r is the calculated maximum rank of the matrix. Typically, for well *structured* matrices, r is much smaller than n.

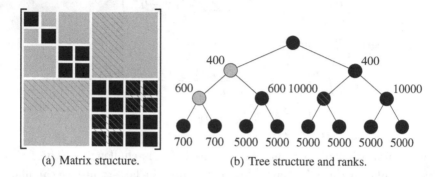

(a) Matrix structure.   (b) Tree structure and ranks.

Fig. 1. A 40000×40000 size matrix compressed using a complete binary tree.

The HSS form of the matrix A can then be factorized by utilizing ULV factorization [3]. The factorization implemented within the STRUMPACK package uses the HSS structure instead of orthogonal transformation (which is used in the classic ULV) and is referred as ULV-like (Fig. 2). The complexity is $O(r^2n)$.

Fig. 2. Illustration of the $ULV - like$ factorization process.

This leaves $O(n-r)$ unknowns which are solved directly with Gaussian elimination. Complexity is $O(rn)$.

4   Numerical Results

The presented numerical results are obtained on the HPC cluster AVITOHOL of the Institute of Information and Communication Technologies, Bulgarian Academy of Sciences. We run the tests on a single node with two Intel Xeon E5-2650v2 8C 2.6 GHz CPUs with 8 cores each. We use the MATLAB® code provided by [2] to generate the system of linear algebraic equation. We then use STRUMPACK HSS solver for *dense* systems.

The HSS algorithm needs two thresholds to be set by the user. These are the relative ε_{rel} and absolute ε_{abs} thresholds. They are used for the calculation of the approximate matrix. In order to test the accuracy of the HSS method we vary $\varepsilon_{rel} = 10^{-2}, 10^{-4}, 10^{-6}, 10^{-8}$. We do not change the absolute threshold $\varepsilon_{abs} = 10^{-8}$.

The times of execution of our tests were much worst than our previous work with a Boundary Element Method in [5]. This prompted us to examine the ordering of the unknowns with respect to their corresponding nodes in the mesh and to develop two alternative reorderings.

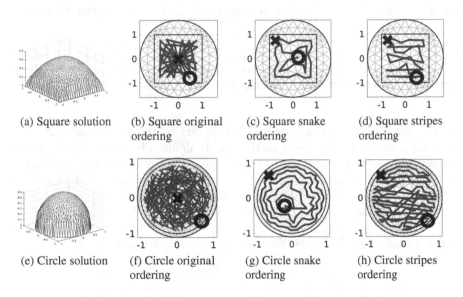

Fig. 3. Solution and node ordering in square (top) and circle (bottom) domain. The dark thick line follows the order of the unknowns corresponding to the nodes in the path of the line. 'X' marks the first and 'O' the last node.

The original ordering of the unknowns is shown on Fig. 3(b) and (f). It comes from the MATLAB®'s `initmesh` function. In this paper we examine two possible reordering schemes.

The "snake" reordering orders the nodes in a spiral-like form, starting from the upper left node and continuing on the next neighbour node with the minimum clockwise angle with the previous node. For the second node only we add an artificial "zeroth" node which is at some distance in $-45°$ from the first. If we come to a node that has no unassigned neighbours we search in the same way among all of the remaining nodes. The resulting reordering is shown on Fig. 3(c) and (g).

The "stripes" reordering orders the nodes in horizontal stripes, starting again from the upper left node and searching for a neighbour that makes the minimum angle with the Y axis within $[0°, 180°]$. When we cannot find any such neighbour the algorithm finds the upper left node of the remaining nodes and continues. This is visualized on Fig. 3(g) and (h). The MATLAB® code for both reorders is provided and described in brief in the Appendix.

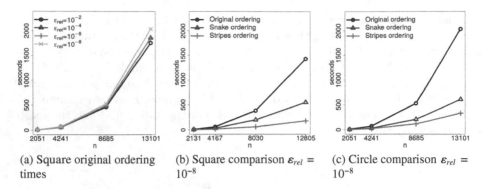

(a) Square original ordering times

(b) Square comparison $\varepsilon_{rel} = 10^{-8}$

(c) Circle comparison $\varepsilon_{rel} = 10^{-8}$

Fig. 4. Solution times of the STRUMPACK HSS solver for square domain with original ordering and varying ε_{rel} (left). Comparison of original, snake and stripes orderings for square (middle) and circle (right) domains with $\varepsilon_{rel} = 10^{-8}$.

The time of execution changes little while varying the relative tolerance ε_{rel}. The results for original ordering in the square domain is shown on Fig. 4(left). The results from the rest of the tests show similar tendency. The original, "snake" and "stripes" orderings are compared on Fig. 4 for the square (center) and circle (right) domain. Both reorderings show improved times to the original. The "snake" reorder improves the time of execution 3× and the "stripes"—6×.

It is important to also analyse the error of the HSS compression and its relation to the error threshold. We calculate the relative error with

$$R_{relative} = \frac{\left| x^{Gauss} - x^{HSS} \right|_{l_2}}{\left| x^{Gauss} \right|_{l_2}} = \frac{\sqrt{\sum_{i=1}^{n} (x_i^{Gauss} - x_i^{HSS})^2}}{\sqrt{\sum_{i=1}^{n} (x_i^{Gauss})^2}}, \qquad (4)$$

where x^{Gauss} is the reference solution and x^{HSS} is the STRUMPACK solution. The calculated $R_{relative}$ values for the different reorderings are presented on Table 1. The results are presented only for one size for each domain, the errors for the other sizes are similar. The lower values of the threshold show marked improvement in the accuracy of the results, while the computational time doesn't

Table 1. The relative error of the solutions obtained with STRUMPACK. Square (left) and circle (right) domain. Results are only for 8030 and 8685 unknowns respectively. The values for the rest of the sizes are similar.

	Square domain. 8030 elements					Circle domain. 8685 elements			
Ordering	\multicolumn{4}{c}{$R_{relative}$ for STRUMPACK with r_{tol}}		Ordering	\multicolumn{4}{c}{$R_{relative}$ for STRUMPACK with r_{tol}}
	10^{-2}	10^{-4}	10^{-6}	10^{-8}			10^{-2}	10^{-4}	10^{-6}	10^{-8}
Original	0.043	0.00042	7.51e-06	5.05e-08		Original	0.259	0.0011	3.85e-06	4.2e-08
Snake	0.2	0.001	2.74e-06	5.34e-08		Snake	0.36	0.0023	8.35e-06	5.15e-08
Stripes	0.29	0.001	7.94e-06	4.42e-08		Stripes	0.33	0.001	6.59e-06	8.67e-08

rise significantly (Fig. 4). The change in the ordering of the unknowns doesn't change the accuracy.

5 Concluding Remarks

The Hierarchical Semi-Separable compression is a powerful method for solving large *dense* systems of linear algebraic equations. However in order to achieve good results the matrix of coefficients should have low rank in it's off-diagonal blocks. This is the "*good* structure" that is exploited in the STRUMPACK *dense* solver [1,6].

In this study we presented two reorderings of the unknowns for a 2d Fractional Laplacian problem that try to achieve such structure and improve the execution times of the algorithm. Numerical results for the original, "snake" and "stripes" reorderings are presented. The "snake" reordering improves the times $3\times$, while the "stripes" achieve a speed-up of $6\times$ compared to the original ordering. At the same time the accuracy of the results doesn't change.

Acknowledgements. We acknowledge the provided access to the e-infrastructure of the Centre for Advanced Computing and Data Processing, with the financial support by the Grant No BG05M2OP001-1.001-0003, financed by the Science and Education for Smart Growth Operational Program (2014–2020) and co-financed by the European Union through the European structural and Investment funds.

This paper is partially supported by the National Scientific Program "Information and Communication Technologies for a Single Digital Market in Science, Education and Security (ICTinSES)", contract No DO1–205/23.11.2018, financed by the Ministry of Education and Science in Bulgaria.

The partial support trough the Bulgarian NSF Grant DN 12/1 is highly acknowledged.

Appendix 1. Snake Reorder

The reorder script should be run after the `main.m` script provided in [2]. The inputs used are:

- `[p,ee,tt]` is the mesh structure, where `p` is the coordinates of the points, `ee`—the edges between the domains and `tt` the triangles.
- `nf` is an array of the IDs of the nodes inside the solution domain $\Omega \backslash B$. Thus `p(nf)` is an array of all nodes within it.

The output of the algorithm is:

- `nff` is the reordered `nf` array. Thus `K(nff,nff)` is the reordered matrix and `b(nff)` is the reordered right hand side.

This algorithm picks from the upper left node of the solution domain $\Omega \backslash B$ as the first node p_1. For the second node p_2 it picks the neighbour node, where the vector $\overrightarrow{p_1 p_2}$ has the minimum clockwise angle with vector that is at $-45°$

from the y axis. For the third node p_3 we pick the neighbour of p_2 that has the minimum angle $\theta = \sphericalangle p_1 p_2 p_3$ and so on. If no neighbours are available (because we picked all of them) we search amongst all of the remaining unordered nodes. The MATLAB® code is below.

```
% Find the index of the point closest to the the upper left
[~,first_point] = max(p(2,nf(:))-p(1,nf(:)));  nff = nf;  no_neighbours = 0;
% Put the next node in it's place
[nff(1), nff(first_point)] = deal(nff(first_point), nff(1));  p1 = [p(1,nff(1))-1, p(2,nff(1))+1];
for i = 2:(length(nff)-1)
    % Find all neighbouring nodes with point nff(i-1)
    neighbour_nodes = tt(1:3,[find(tt(1,:)== nff(i-1)), find(tt(2,:)== nff(i-1)), ...
        find(tt(3,:)== nff(i-1))]);
    % Remove duplicates and nodes outside the solution domain
    neighbour_nodes = intersect(nff(i:length(nff)), neighbour_nodes(neighbour_nodes~=nff(i-1)));
    p0 = p(:,nff(i-1))';
    % Use the previous node as p1. For the first use a pseudo point at (-1,-1 from it.)
    if i == 2,     p1 = [p(1,nff(1))-1, p(2,nff(1))+1];
    else ,         p1 = p(:,nff(i-2))';    end
    % If no neighbour nodes exist look up all remaining nodes.
    if length(neighbour_nodes) <= 0, neighbour_nodes = nff(i:length(nff));  no_neighbours = 1;
    else , no_neighbours = 0; end
    % find the edge with the lowest angle to the previous edge
    for j = 1:length(neighbour_nodes)
        p2 = p(:,neighbour_nodes(j))';  temp = atan2((det([p2-p0; p1-p0])), dot(p1-p0, p2-p0));
        if temp < 0, temp = temp + 2*pi;
        % If there are no neighbours ignore angles below 90 degrees search all remaining nodes.
        if (temp < pi/2) && (no_neighbours ~= 0), temp = temp + 2*pi; end
        if j==1 || temp < min_angle, min_angle=temp; min_node_id=find(nff(:)== neighbour_nodes(j));
        end
    end
    [nff(i), nff(min_node_id)] = deal(nff(min_node_id), nff(i)); % Put the next node in place.
end
```

For the stripes reorder we again pick the first node p_1 as the upper left node of the solution domain $\Omega \backslash B$. For the next p_2 we pick the neighbour node that has the minimum angle with the Y axis $\theta = \sphericalangle (\overrightarrow{Oy}, \overrightarrow{p_1 p_2})$, but ignoring the nodes with angles $\theta \in (\pi, 2\pi)$. When we reach a node with no unordered neighbours, we pick the left up node from the remaining nodes and continue.

```
% Find the index of the point closest to the the upper left
[~,first_point] = max(p(2,nf(:))-p(1,nf(:)));  nff = nf;  no_neighbours = 0;
[nff(1), nff(first_point)] = deal(nff(first_point), nff(1)); % Put the next node in it's place
for i = 2:(length(nff)-1)
    % Find all neighbouring nodes with point nff(i-1)
    neighbour_nodes = tt(1:3,[find(tt(1,:)== nff(i-1)), find(tt(2,:)== nff(i-1)), ...
        find(tt(3,:)== nff(i-1))]);
    % Remove duplicates and nodes outside the solution domain
    neighbour_nodes = intersect(nff(i:length(nff)), neighbour_nodes(neighbour_nodes~=nff(i-1)));
    min_angle = 2*pi; % Initialize minimum angle
    % find the edge with the lowest angle to the previous edge
    for j = 1:length(neighbour_nodes)
        p2 = p(:,neighbour_nodes(j))';
        temp = atan2(p(1,neighbour_nodes(j))-p(1,nff(i-1)), p(2,neighbour_nodes(j))-p(2,nff(i-1)));
        % Remove the points on the left of the Y axis
        if (temp < 0), continue; end
        % find minimum angle
        if j==1 || temp < min_angle , min_angle=temp; min_node_id=find(nff(:)== neighbour_nodes(j));
        end
    end
    % If no neighbours are available search for the upper left one of the remaining nodes
    if min_angle==2*pi
        [~,min_node_id] = max(p(2,nff(i:length(nff))) -p(1,nff(i:length(nff))))
        min_node_id = min_node_id + i -1; % because the id is on the [i,length(nff)]
    end
    [nff(i), nff(min_node_id)] = deal(nff(min_node_id), nff(i)); % Put the next node in it's place
end
```

References

1. Acosta, G., Borthagaray, J.: A Fractional Laplace Equation: Regularity of Solutions and Finite Element Approximations. SIAM Journal on Numerical Analysis **55**(2), 472–495 (2017). https://doi.org/10.1137/15M1033952
2. Acosta, G., Bersetche, F., Borthagaray, J.: A short FE implementation for a 2D homogeneous Dirichlet problem of a fractional Laplacian. Comput. Math. Appl. **74**(4), 784–816 (2017). https://doi.org/10.1016/j.camwa.2017.05.026
3. Chandrasekaran, S., Gu, M., Lyons, W.: A fast adaptive solver for hierarchically semiseparable representations. CALCOLO **42**(3), 171–185 (2005). https://doi.org/10.1007/s10092-005-0103-3
4. Rouet, F.H., Li, X.S., Ghysels, P., Napov, A.: A distributed-memory package for dense hierarchically semi-separable matrix computations using randomization. ACM Trans. Math. Softw **42**(4), 27:1–27:35 (2016). https://doi.org/10.1145/2930660
5. Slavchev, D., Margenov, S.: Analysis of hierarchical compression parallel solver for BEM problems on Intel Xeon CPUs. In: Nikolov, G., Kolkovska, N., Georgiev, K. (eds.) NMA 2018. LNCS, vol. 11189, pp. 466–473. Springer, Cham (2019). https://doi.org/10.1007/978-3-030-10692-8_53
6. Xia, J., Chandrasekaran, S., Gu, M., Li, X.S.: Fast algorithms for hierarchically semiseparable matrices. Numer. Linear Algebra Appl. **17**(6), 953–976 (2010). https://doi.org/10.1002/nla.691

Computer Simulation of a Saline Enhanced Radio-Frequency Hepatic Ablation Process

Yavor Vutov[1], Daniel Nikolov[2], Ivan Lirkov[1]([⊠]),
and Krassimir Georgiev[1]

[1] Institute of Information and Communication Technologies,
Bulgarian Academy of Sciences, Acad. G. Bonchev, bl. 25A, 1113 Sofia, Bulgaria
{yavor,ivan,georgiev}@parallel.bas.bg
[2] Institute of Optics, University of Rochester,
275 Hutchison Road, Rochester, NY 14620, USA
dnikolo2@ur.rochester.edu
http://parallel.bas.bg/~yavor, http://parallel.bas.bg/~ivan/,
http://parallel.bas.bg/~georgiev

Abstract. We consider the simulation of thermal and electrical processes, involved in a radio-frequency ablation procedure. Radio-frequency ablation is a low invasive technique for treatment of hepatic tumors, utilizing AC current to destroy unwanted tissues by heating. We simulate an ablation procedure where the needle is bipolar, i.e. no ground pad is attached. Saline solution is injected through the needle during the procedure, creating a cloud around the tip with higher electrical conductivity. This approach is safer for some patients.

The mathematical model consists of three parts—dynamical, electrical, and thermal. The energy from the applied AC voltage is determined by solving the Laplace equation to find the potential distribution. After that, the electric field intensity and the current density are directly calculated. Finally, the heat transfer equation is solved to determine the temperature distribution.

A 3D image of the patient's liver is obtained from a magnetic resonance imaging scan. Then, the geometry for the needle is added. The CGAL library is used to obtain an unstructured mesh in the computational domain. We use the finite element method in space, to obtain both the current density and the created temperature field. An unstructured mesh parallel solver is developed for the considered problem. The parallelization approach is based on partitioning the meshes using ParMETIS. Numerical tests show good performance of the developed parallel solver.

Keywords: Radio-frequency hepatic ablation · Bio-heat equation · Unstructured mesh · Parallel solver

© Springer Nature Switzerland AG 2020
I. Lirkov and S. Margenov (Eds.): LSSC 2019, LNCS 11958, pp. 382–390, 2020.
https://doi.org/10.1007/978-3-030-41032-2_44

1   Introduction

Radio-frequency ablation (RFA) may be performed to treat tumors in the lung, liver, kidney, and bone, as well as other body organs. Once the diagnosis of tumor is confirmed, a needle-like RFA probe is placed inside the tumor. The radio-frequency waves passing through the probe increase the temperature within tumor tissue and results in destruction of the tumor. RFA can be used with small tumors, whether these arose within the organ (primary tumors) or spread to the organ (metastases). An important advantage of RF current (over previously used low frequency AC or pulses of DC) is that it does not interfere with the muscles and can be used without the need for general anesthesia.

There is an ongoing research in RF probe design. The right procedure parameters are very important for the successful killing of all of the tumor cells with minimal damage on the non-tumor cells.

A comparison of two different RF probe designs is performed in [12]. The first probe design consists of a stainless steel trocar with four nickel-titanium retractable electrodes. Once the probe is in place, the electrodes are deployed and RF current is initiated. Both the surfaces areas of the uninsulated part of the trocar and the electrodes conduct RF current. The second RF probe design has no retractable electrodes. Saline solution is injected through the needle with a constant pressure during the procedure instead, increasing the electrical conductivity of the saturated tissue [14]. A very simple model is considered in [12], which includes a spherical bubble centered around the tip of the needle to be saturated with saline solution throughout the whole procedure.

Computer simulation on geometry obtained from a magnetic resonance imaging (MRI) scan of the patient is performed in [13]. Often, in computer simulations reported in the literature e.g. [5,12,16], the position of the ground pad is neglected and a simple computational domain with a cubic shape is considered. The influence of the position of the ground pad to the ablated volume is studied in [13], verifying the correctness of the assumption that when the pad is *far* from the probe then zero potential condition can be applied on the whole boundary of the domain. A comparison of the resulting ablated volumes, correspond to different positions of the ground pad, is performed in [13].

The simulation of an ablation procedure where the needle is bipolar, i.e. no ground pad is attached, is studied in this paper. An injection of saline solution through the needle is applied during the procedure.

2   The Model, Space, and Time Discretization

The mathematical model consists of three parts—saline infiltration equation, electrical potential derivation, and bio-heat equation.

2.1   Saline Infiltration

The infiltration of sodium chloride solution into the liver tissue during the RFA process is described using the hydraulic conductivity model based on Darcy's law:

$$\frac{\partial}{\partial r}\left(2\pi r k \frac{\partial p}{\partial r}\right) + \frac{\partial}{\partial z}\left(2\pi r k \frac{\partial p}{\partial z}\right) = 2\pi r s_h p + 2\pi r c_h \frac{\partial p}{\partial t}, \tag{1}$$

where p is the pressure, k is hydraulic conductivity coefficient of the tissue, c_h is hydraulic capacity of the porous medium, s_h is hydraulic absorption coefficient, r, z are radial and axial coordinates.

Comsol Multyphysics "Subsurface Flow Module" (see [6]) is applied to solve the infiltration equation. The finite element modeling is based on [1]. We used the necessary physical constants of hydraulic conductivity, capacity, and absorption of liver tissue which have been determined there. From (1) we get the Darcy's velocity $\mathbf{v}$, pressure p, and volumetric saturation fraction γ.

2.2   Electrical Potential Distribution

It is known that when the size of the computational domain is much smaller than the wavelength, we can neglect the contribution from the magnetic field in Maxwell's equation. Thus, the energy from the applied AC voltage is determined by solving the Laplace equation to find the potential distribution V

$$\nabla \cdot \sigma \nabla V = 0, \tag{2}$$

with boundary conditions

$$V = V_0 \text{ at } \partial\Omega_1,$$
$$V = 0 \text{ at } \partial\Omega_2,$$
$$\nabla V \cdot \mathbf{n} = 0 \text{ at } \partial\Omega \backslash \partial\Omega_1 \backslash \partial\Omega_2,$$

where Ω is the entire domain of the model, V is the potential distribution in Ω, σ is the electric conductivity (S/m), V_0 is the applied RF voltage, $\partial\Omega_1$ is the surface of the ablation electrode (anode), $\partial\Omega_2$ is the surface of the ground pad (cathode), $\mathbf{n}$ is the outward facing normal to the boundary.

After determining the potential distribution V, the electric field intensity $\mathbf{E}$ and the current density $\mathbf{J}$ can be computed from

$$\mathbf{E} = -\nabla V, \tag{3}$$
$$\mathbf{J} = \sigma \mathbf{E}. \tag{4}$$

2.3   Bio-Heat Equation

The RF ablation procedure destroys the unwanted tissue by heating, arising when the energy dissipated by the electric current flowing through a conductor is converted to heat. The bio-heat time-dependent partial differential equation

$$\rho c \frac{\partial T}{\partial t} = \nabla \cdot \kappa \nabla T + \mathbf{J} \cdot \mathbf{E} - \mathbf{v} \cdot \nabla T - h_b(T - T_b) \tag{5}$$

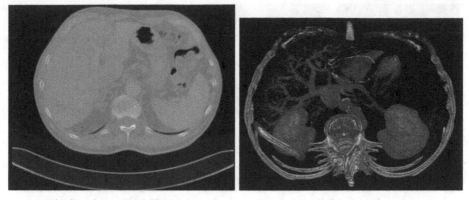

A slice from the MRI image   3D reconstruction

Fig. 1. A slice from the MRI image and 3D reconstruction of the "3Dircadb1.4" data set.

is used to model the heating process during the RFA. The following initial and boundary conditions are applied

$$T = 37\,^{\circ}\text{C} \text{ when } t = 0 \text{ at } \Omega,$$
$$T = 37\,^{\circ}\text{C} \text{ when } t \geq 0 \text{ at } \partial\Omega,$$

where T is the temperature, ρ is the density (kg/m^3), c is the specific heat (J/kg K), κ is the thermal conductivity (W/m K), $\mathbf{J}$ is the current density (A/m), $\mathbf{E}$ is the electric field intensity (V/m), T_b is the blood temperature (37 °C), w_b is the blood perfusion coefficient (1/s), $h_b = \rho_b c_b w_b$ is the convective heat transfer coefficient accounting for the blood perfusion in the model.

3   Numerical Solution

Geometry data from a real patient was used for the computer simulation. The patient's 3D MRI image (see Fig. 1) was taken from "3D Image Reconstruction for Comparison of Algorithm Database" (3D-IRCADb) [10]. The data set used was "3Dircadb1.4". It was already segmented by clinical experts, into different tissues. This segmentation was used in our simulations. Some of the tissues, such as skin and bones, were combined, and not distinguished. The segmentation data was in the form of 3D image, where each voxel was given a number for a particular tissue. The geometry for the RF probe was added directly into that image (see Fig. 2). Then, the unstructured mesh was generated using the CGAL library [4]. The voxel image of the segmentation was directly fed into the library, and a tetrahedral mesh was produced. Local refinement was used near the electro-conducting part of the RF probe.

For the numerical solution of the above discussed partial differential equations the finite element method in space is used [2]. Linear conforming tetrahedral elements are used in this work, directly defined on the elements of the used

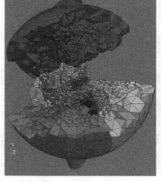

Inserted RF probe   Mesh partitioning

Fig. 2. Inserted RF probe, finite element mesh, and mesh partitioning

unstructured mesh. This additionally provides for an optimal convergence rate and parallel scalability of the applied algebraic multigrid (AMG) preconditioner.

The infiltration equation (1) is solved using Comsol Multiphysics and the velocity of the saline solution is computed from it.

The electrical potential distribution is determined from (2) and the heat source $\mathbf{J} \cdot \mathbf{E}$ is obtained using (3)–(4). To simulate the actual medical equipment, we should determine the potential V_0 for the boundary condition of (2) that will yield a given electrical output power P (W). We use the same approach as in [13]: we solve (2) with a boundary condition $V = 1$ (V) at $\partial \Omega_1$ and then we scale the obtained solution. This adjustment is performed only once in the beginning of the simulation.

To solve the bio-heat equation, after the space discretization, the time derivative is discretized via finite differences and the backward Euler scheme is used [3]. Let us denote with K and M the stiffness and mass matrices from the finite element discretization of (5). Then, the parabolic equation (5) can be written in matrix form as:

$$M \frac{\partial T}{\partial t} + KT = F. \tag{6}$$

If the time-step is denoted by τ, the temperature at the previous time level by T^n, and the temperature at the current time level by T^{n+1}, the approximation of the time derivative in (6) leads to the following system of linear algebraic equations

$$(M + \tau K)T^{n+1} = MT^n + \tau F. \tag{7}$$

The preconditioned biconjugate gradient stabilized (BiPCGstab) method with the BoomerAMG [9] preconditioner, part of the software package hypre [7], is used for the solution of systems of linear algebraic equations in the discrete formulation of (2) and (5). The parallel code is based on a partitioning the meshes using ParMETIS [11] and MPI standard [8,15,17] for the communication

Table 1. The number of finite elements, the number of unknowns, and the number of inner iterations for the used meshes.

Mesh	FEs	Unknowns	Iterations
U1	508219	89169	3035
B1	508219	89169	3928
B2	508636	89084	4236
B3	508050	88995	4217

between processes. Figure 2 shows few parts of the computational domain after using ParMETIS. The partitioning is performed as a separate preprocessing step.

4   Numerical Experiments

The material properties which are used in the simulations are taken from [16]. The blood perfusion coefficient is $w_b = 6.4 \times 10^{-3}\,\mathrm{s}^{-1}$. The applied electrical power is 45 W, saline injection rate is 100 ml/h, and the simulation is done for 10 min. We performed experiments with a set of the RFA probes varying the design.

- All probes have diameter 2 mm.
- Mesh U1 - unipolar probe: length of the anode: 21.7 mm,
- Mesh B1 - bipolar probe: anode–insulator–cathode: 8.5–4.0–9.2 mm,
- Mesh B2 - bipolar probe: anode–insulator–cathode: 8.5–4.5–8.7 mm,
- Mesh B3 - bipolar probe: anode–insulator–cathode: 9.0–3.0–9.7 mm.

We run the simulation with a time-step $\tau = 1\,\mathrm{s}$. The convergence tolerance for the BiPCGstab was set to 10^{-6}. The number of finite elements, the number of unknowns in (7), and the number of inner iterations for all 600 time-steps are presented in Table 1. Figure 3 shows the temperature in a cross-section of the domain for the considered unipolar and bipolar RFA probes.

The cumulative damage integral $\Psi(t)$ is used as a measure of ablated region [5]:

$$\Psi(t) = \ln\left(\frac{C(0)}{C(t)}\right) = A \int e^{-\frac{\Delta E}{RT(t)}}\,dt,$$

where $C(t)$ is the concentration of living cells at a given time, R is the universal gas constant, A is the "frequency" factor for the kinetic expression, ΔE is the activation energy for the irreversible damage reaction. The values used in the simulations are taken from [5]: $A = 7.39 \times 10^{39}\,(\mathrm{s}^{-1})$ and $\Delta E = 2.577 \times 10^5\,(\mathrm{J}\,\mathrm{mol}^{-1})$. As a quantitative criterion of quality of the solution we used two volumes: V_1 ($\Psi > 1$) and $V_{4.6}$ ($\Psi > 4.6$). Tissue damage $\Psi(t) = 4.6$ corresponds to 99% probability of cell death. The value of $\Psi(t) = 1$, corresponding to 63% probability of cell death is significant, because at this point the tissue coagulation first occurs and blood perfusion stops.

Mesh U1   Mesh B1

Mesh B2   Mesh B3

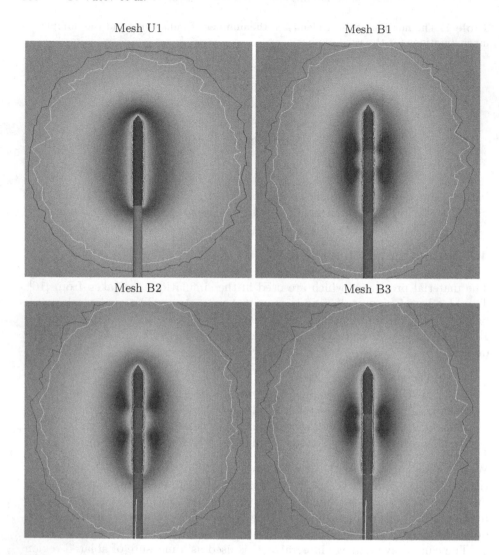

Fig. 3. Temperature field after the RFA procedure ($t = 600\,\mathrm{s}$). Mesh U1 is constructed for the simulation of ablation process using unipolar probe, the rest of the meshes are used for the simulation of the thermal and electrical processes using bipolar probe (varying the size of the anode, insulator, and cathode).

Table 2 shows the ablated volumes for the considered unipolar and bipolar RFA probes. The results from the simulation of the RFA process show that usage of bipolar RFA probe leads to bigger electrical impedance and the unipolar probe with considered size is more efficient in terms of the size of the ablated volume.

Table 2. Simulation results for the used meshes.

Mesh	Electrical impedance (Ω)	Voltage (V)	V_1 (cm^3)	$V_{4.6}$ (cm^3)
U1	59.7	51.8	51.4	39.2
B1	172.6	88.1	41.7	32.0
B2	183.1	90.7	42.1	32.5
B3	161.8	85.3	40.8	31.3

5   Concluding Remarks and Future Directions

In this work we used parallel FE simulations to analyze the thermal and electrical processes, involved in a radio-frequency ablation procedure. An unstructured mesh parallel solver is developed for the considered problem. We performed experiments with a set of the RFA probes varying the design. The numerical results from our simulations show that for the same size of the RFA probe and the same applied electrical power the unipolar probe is more efficient in terms of the size of the ablated volume. The next steps in our work will be to perform the parallel FE simulations taking into account the varying material properties (e.g. destroyed cells have lower heat and electrical conductivity) and to tune the parameters of the parallel solver.

Acknowledgments. We acknowledge the provided access to the e-infrastructure of the NCDSC—part of the Bulgarian National Roadmap on RIs, with the financial support by the Grant No D01-221/03.12.2018. This research was partially supported by grant KP-06-N27/6 from the Bulgarian NSF.

References

1. Barauskas, R., Gulbinas, A., Barauskas, G.: Finite element modeling and experimental investigation of infiltration of sodium chloride solution into nonviable liver tissue. Medicina **43**(5), 399–411 (2007)
2. Brenner, S., Scott, R.: The Mathematical Theory of Finite Element Methods. Texts in Applied Mathematics, vol. 15, 3rd edn. Springer, New York (2008). https://doi.org/10.1007/978-0-387-75934-0
3. Butcher, J.C.: Numerical Methods for Ordinary Differential Equations, 3rd edn. Wiley, Wiley (2016)
4. Computational geometry algorithms library (2012). http://www.cgal.org/
5. Chang, I., Nguyen, U.: Thermal modeling of lesion growth with radiofrequency ablation devices. Biomed. Eng. Online **3**(1), 27 (2004). https://doi.org/10.1186/1475-925X-3-27
6. COMSOL Multiphysics: Earth science module user's guide (2006)
7. Falgout, R.D., Yang, U.M.: *hypre*: a library of high performance preconditioners. In: Sloot, P.M.A., Hoekstra, A.G., Tan, C.J.K., Dongarra, J.J. (eds.) ICCS 2002. LNCS, vol. 2331, pp. 632–641. Springer, Heidelberg (2002). https://doi.org/10.1007/3-540-47789-6_66

8. Gropp, W., Lusk, E., Skjellum, A.: Using MPI: Portable Parallel Programming with the Message-Passing Interface. The MIT Press, Cambridge (2014)
9. Henson, V.E., Yang, U.M.: BoomerAMG: a parallel algebraic multigrid solver and preconditioner. Appl. Numer. Math. **41**(1), 155–177 (2002). http://www.sciencedirect.com/science/article/pii/S0168927401001155
10. IRCAD: 3D image reconstruction for comparison of algorithm database (2012). http://www.ircad.fr/softwares/3Dircadb/3Dircadb1/
11. Karypis, G.: METIS and ParMETIS. In: Padua, D. (ed.) Encyclopedia of Parallel Computing, pp. 1117–1124. Springer, Boston (2011). https://doi.org/10.1007/978-0-387-09766-4_500
12. Kosturski, N., Margenov, S., Vutov, Y.: Comparison of two techniques for radio-frequency hepatic tumor ablation through numerical simulation. In: Todorov, M., Christov, C. (eds.) Applications of Mathematics in Technical and Natural Sciences, AMiTaNS 2011. AIP Conference Proceedings, vol. 1404, pp. 431–437. AIP (2011). https://doi.org/10.1063/1.3659945
13. Kosturski, N., Margenov, S., Vutov, Y.: Computer simulation of RF liver ablation on an MRI scan data. In: Todorov, M. (ed.) Applications of Mathematics in Technical and Natural Sciences. AIP Conference Proceedings, vol. 1487, pp. 120–126. AIP (2012). https://doi.org/10.1063/1.4758949
14. Shimizu, A., et al.: Expansion of radiofrequency ablation volume by saturated NaCl saline injection in the area of vaporization. Acta Radiol. **50**(1), 61–64 (2009). https://doi.org/10.1080/02841850802562071
15. Snir, M., Otto, S., Huss-Lederman, S., Walker, D., Dongarra, J.: MPI: The Complete Reference. Scientific and Engineering Computation Series. The MIT Press, Cambridge (1997). Second printing
16. Tungjitkusolmun, S., et al.: Three-dimensional finite-element analyses for radio-frequency hepatic tumor ablation. IEEE Trans. Biomed. Eng. **49**(1), 3–9 (2002). https://doi.org/10.1109/10.972834
17. Walker, D., Dongarra, J.: MPI: a standard Message Passing Interface. Supercomputer **63**, 56–68 (1996)

Studying the Influence of Climate Changes on European Ozone Levels

Zahari Zlatev[1]🆔, Ivan Dimov[2], István Faragó[3,4]🆔, Krassimir Georgiev[2]🆔, and Ágnes Havasi[3,5(✉)]🆔

[1] Department of Environmental Science, Aarhus University, Roskilde, Denmark
zz@envs.au.dk
[2] Institute of Information and Communication Technologies,
Bulgarian Academy of Sciences, Sofia, Bulgaria
ivdimov@bas.bg, georgiev@parallel.bas.bg
[3] MTA-ELTE Numerical Analysis and Large Networks Research Group,
Budapest, Hungary
{faragois,havasia}@cs.elte.hu
[4] Institute of Mathematics, Budapest University of Technology and Economics,
Budapest, Hungary
[5] Department of Applied Analysis and Computational Mathematics,
Eötvös Loránd University, Budapest, Hungary

Abstract. The large-scale air pollution model UNI-DEM (the Unified Danish Eulerian Model) was used together with several carefully selected climatic scenarios. It was necessary to run the model over a long time-interval (sixteen consecutive years) and to use fine resolution on a very large space domain. This caused great difficulties because it was necessary to (a) perform many runs with different input parameters, (b) use huge input files containing the needed meteorological and emission data, (c) resolve many problems related to the computational difficulties, (d) develop and apply carefully prepared parallel codes, (e) exploit efficiently the cache memories of the available computers and (f) store in a proper way huge output files for visualization and animation. It will be described how these difficult tasks have been resolved and many results related to some potentially harmful ozone levels will be presented.

Keywords: Large-scale air pollution models · Non-linear PDEs · Parallel codes · High-speed computers · Climate changes · AOT40

1 Climatic Scenarios

The impact of the climatic changes on critical pollution levels has been studied by using UNI-DEM (the Unified Danish Eulerian Model) with the following three climatic scenarios.

First Climatic Scenario: The predicted by the IPCC (Intergovernmental Panel on Climate Change) annual changes of the temperature in Europe and

© Springer Nature Switzerland AG 2020
I. Lirkov and S. Margenov (Eds.): LSSC 2019, LNCS 11958, pp. 391–399, 2020.
https://doi.org/10.1007/978-3-030-41032-2_45

its surrounding, presented in Fig. 1 in [15], see also [13], are used in this scenario. Take an arbitrary cell on the surface level of UNI-DEM. If the increase of the temperature in the corresponding cell in Fig. 1 in [15] is $\beta \in [a, b]$, then the temperature in the model cell is set to $\delta = a + \gamma(n)$ at hour n, where $\gamma(n) \in [0, b - a]$ is generated randomly so that the expected value of the increase of the temperature in this cell will be $0.5(b - a)$. Then the annual change of the temperature in each surface cell of UNI-DEM will be the same as the predicted value in the IPCC report [7]. A similar procedure is used to determine the increases of the temperature in all the other horizontal planes. This means that only the temperatures are varied in the first scenario.

Second Climatic Scenario: The temperatures are varied in nearly the same way as in the First Climatic Scenario, but we have taken into account several other predictions of the IPCC specialists: (a) the maximal temperatures and the numbers of hot days in land areas will be increased, (b) the minimal temperatures will become higher and the numbers of cold and frost days over land areas will be decreased and (c) the diurnal range of the temperature over the land areas will be reduced. Therefore, the factors used to increase the temperatures during the night were made greater than the factors used to increase the temperatures during the days to satisfy the requirements (b) and (c). The day-time temperatures during the summer were increased by a larger amount when the days were hot in order to satisfy the requirement (a). We also reduced by 10% the cloud covers during the summer periods. All these changes were carried out in the land areas and the temperatures were varied so that their annual means remained the same as those prescribed in the report of the IPCC specialists.

Third Climatic Scenario: There will be more intense precipitation events, but increased summer drying and risks of drought in the future, see Table 9.6 on p. 575 in [7]. We increased the winter precipitation both over land and over sea, while the precipitation events over the European land areas were reduced during summer. We transformed the humidity data in a similar manner, increased by 10% the cloud covers during winter and kept these covers the same as those in the Second Climatic Scenario during summer. The expected mean values of the temperature changes remained the same as those prescribed in [7].

2   Mathematical Description of the Air Pollution Model

UNI-DEM is based on the system of non-linear partial differential equations

$$\partial_t c_i = -\partial_x(uc_i) - \partial_y(vc_i) - \partial_z(wc_i) + \partial_x(K_x\partial_x c_i) + \partial_y(K_y\partial_y c_i) + \partial_z(K_z\partial_z c_i)$$
$$+ Q_i(t, x, y, z, c_1, c_2, \ldots, c_s) + (k_{1i} + k_{2i})c_i + E_i(t, x, y, z) \tag{1}$$

for $i = 1, 2, \ldots, s$, where $s = 56$; see, [1, 12–14]. The concentrations of the pollutants are denoted by $c_i = c_i(t, x, y, z)$. The wind velocities are denoted by u, v, and w, and the diffusion coefficients by K_x, K_y, and K_z. The chemical reactions are described by the non-linear terms Q_i. The dry and wet deposition coefficients are denoted by k_1 and k_2, respectively. E_i stands for the emissions.

The space domain is a parallelepiped when a stereographic coordinate system is used. This domain is a part of the domain used in EMEP (the European Monitoring and Evaluation Programme); see [5]. The surface plane is a $(4800 \, \text{km} \times 4800 \, \text{km})$ square. It is discretized by using a fine $(10 \, \text{km} \times 10 \, \text{km})$ grid, which produces 230400 grid-squares. Ten non-equidistant grid points are used in the vertical direction, which means that the total number of grid-squares is 2304000. The time-interval is normally one year when only air pollution is to be studied. A stepsize of 30 s is used. Huge input files containing meteorological and emission data are to be used. The computational and storage problems are further increased when the impact of the climatic changes on the pollution levels is to be investigated, because the model has to be run over long intervals of many consecutive years and with many scenarios. Fourteen scenarios were used in [13] and each scenario was run over a time-period of 16 years.

Sequential Splitting. The direct application of some numerical method in the solution of (1) will result in enormous computational problems. It will be necessary to solve systems of ODEs with $\mathcal{O}(10^9)$ equations. Moreover, systems of linear algebraic equations are to be handled at every time-step and the number of equations in each of these systems is $\mathcal{O}(10^8)$ when a run over one year is to be carried out. This task is impossible for existing computers when executed over many consecutive years and with different scenarios. It is necessary to split (1). Sequential splitting is used and it is giving some advantages, because the huge computational problem is reduced to several simpler problems, and parallel tasks appear in a natural way. Moreover, the different physical processes involved in UNI-DEM can be handled with different numerical methods. However, the order of accuracy of the splitting procedure is only one and we should avoid the introduction of artificial boundary conditions. That can be achieved if (1) is split into three sub-models, to be handled successively:

$$\partial_t c_i^{[1]} = -\partial_x(uc_i) - \partial_y(vc_i) + \partial_x(K_x \partial_x c_i) + \partial_y(K_y \partial_y c_i), \ i = 1, 2, \ldots, s \quad (2)$$

$$\partial_t c_i^{[2]} = Q_i(t, x, y, z, c_1, c_2, \ldots, c_s) + (k_{1i} + k_{2i})c_i + E_i(t, x, y, z), \ i = 1, 2, \ldots, s \quad (3)$$

$$\partial_t c_i^{[3]} = -\partial_z(wc_i) + \partial_z(K_z \partial_z c_i), \ i = 1, 2, \ldots, s \quad (4)$$

The boundary conditions on the vertical sides of the space domain of (1) are used as boundary conditions of (2), no boundary conditions are needed in (3), and the boundary conditions on the top and on the bottom of the space domain of (1) are used as boundary conditions of (4). This means that there is no need to introduce artificial boundary conditions.

Semi-discretization and Parallel Tasks. Semi-discretization of the space derivatives of (2) and (4) can be performed by using central differences and a first order finite element method, respectively, while (3) does not contain space derivatives. Assume that $N_1 = N_2 = 480$ and $N_3 = 10$. Then the semi-discretization results in the following three systems of ordinary differential equations (ODEs):

$$\frac{dg^{[1]}}{dt} = f^{[1]}(t, g^{[1]}) \quad g^{[1]} \in \mathbb{R}^{N_1 \times N_2 \times N_3 \times s} \quad (5)$$

$$\frac{dg^{[2]}}{dt} = f^{[2]}(t, g^{[2]}) \quad g^{[2]} \in \mathbb{R}^{N_1 \times N_2 \times N_3 \times s} \tag{6}$$

$$\frac{dg^{[3]}}{dt} = f^{[3]}(t, g^{[3]}) \quad g^{[3]} \in \mathbb{R}^{N_1 \times N_2 \times N_3 \times s} \tag{7}$$

Each of the systems (5), (6) and (7) contains 129024000 equations, and these systems must be handled successively at each time-step. The number of time-steps in a one-year run is 1051200. The computational work seems to be enormous. However, parallel tasks appear in a natural way. The computations related to (5) are independent for each of the horizontal planes and for each of the chemical species. Thus, 560 parallel tasks are to be carried out at every time-step and each of these tasks contains a system of 230400 ODEs. The computations related to (6) are independent for each of the 2304000 spatial grid-points, which means that the number of parallel tasks at every time-step is 2304000 and each of these tasks contains a system of 56 ODEs. The computations involved in the treatment of (7) along the vertical grid-lines, are independent. Therefore, 12902400 parallel tasks appear at every time-step and each of these tasks contains a system of 10 ODEs. The appearance of many parallel tasks is useful when parallel computers are available, but that is not enough. The problem is that the parallel tasks appearing in (5), (6) and (7) are different in size and the requirement to keep the data participating in the computations related to each of these tasks as long as possible in the cache memory of the available computer will not be satisfied when the parallel tasks are treated directly. The parallel tasks in (5) are very large, while the parallel tasks in both (6) and (7) are too small. The problems related to the achievement of optimal treatment of the parallel tasks in (6) and (7) can easily be resolved by uniting several of the small tasks in a larger task.

Horizontal Advection and Diffusion. The systems of ODEs in (5) are linear and non-stiff. Explicit methods for solving ODEs can successfully be used, but large values of u and v may cause computational instability. Predictor-corrector schemes [10] can be used in the attempts to preserve the stability. The parallel tasks in (5) are too large and should be split into smaller tasks. That is relatively easy, because basic linear algebra operations (mainly matrix-vector multiplications) are the most time-consuming part of the computations when explicit methods for solving ODEs are used and software for performing such operations on parallel computers is easily available; [2] and [3].

Vertical Advection and Diffusion. The systems of ODEs involved in (7) are mildly stiff, and it is necessary to treat these systems with implicit numerical methods. The Trapezoidal Rule was successfully applied. Systems of algebraic equations are to be solved when implicit methods for solving ODEs are used and this is normally causing computational difficulties, but not in this case, because these systems are **linear** and their coefficient matrices are **tri-diagonal**.

Treatment of the Chemical Sub-model. The systems of ODEs involved in (6) are non-linear, very stiff and badly scaled. Therefore, the treatment of (6) is the greatest challenge in the solution of (1). The condition numbers of the Jacobians involved in (6) vary in the range $[4.66 \cdot 10^8, 9.27 \cdot 10^{12}]$ when one system is

Table 1. Typical diurnal variation of several chemical species.

Chemical species	Minimal values	Maximal values
Nitrogen monoxide	8.4E+04	3.5E+09
Ozone	1.2E+12	1.4E+12
Hydroxyl radical	3.3E+04	2.3E+07
$O(^1D)$	3.4E−29	2.6E−02

run over 24 h. Furthermore, the results in Table 1 show that the systems in (6) are badly scaled. Implicit algorithms are to be applied because of the stiffness, which implies that sparse but very small, 56×56, systems of linear algebraic equations are to be solved in the inner loop of the iteration. The application of general methods for sparse matrices, [8,9,11], will be very inefficient. The major problems are related to (a) the indirect addressing, (b) the use of many integer arrays the contents of which should very often be updated, (c) the performance of many short loops and (d) the need to search for pivotal elements at every stage of the Gaussian elimination. The tasks (a), (b), (c), and (d) are expensive when the matrix is small. This is why a special sparse matrix algorithm has been developed and used for the chemical part, [6]. This algorithm is based on four steps: (A) reordering based on the Markowitz pivotal strategy [8,10,11] is performed to determine the pivotal elements, to move these elements to the main diagonal and to remove all small non-zero elements which will never be used in the computations, (B) finding the positions in which new non-zero elements will be created and reservation of places for all such elements in the arrays where the non-zero elements obtained during the LU factorization are to be stored, (C) preparation of a loop-free code for the numerical calculation of the LU factorization and (D) preparation of a loop-free code for the numerical calculation of the back-substitution (based on the LU factorization of the previous step). So the disadvantages (a), (b), (c), and (d) are replaced by four advantages: (i) no indirect addressing, (ii) no integer array is used, (iii) the code is loop-free, and (iv) the pivotal search is avoided. The implicit Backward Differentiation Formula was used in the runs. It is also necessary to combine several systems (6), because the parallel tasks are very small.

3   Results Related to AOT40 Values

The effects of long-term exposures to high ozone concentrations are measured in terms of AOT40 (Accumulated exposure Over Threshold of 40 ppb):

$$AOT40 = \sum_{j=1}^{N} \max(c_j - 40, 0), \tag{8}$$

where N is the number of day-time hours in the studied period and c_j is the ozone concentration in hour j, measured in ppb. The period is May, June and July when damaging effects on crops are studied. Three extra months

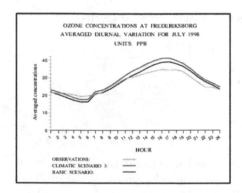
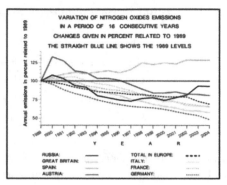

Fig. 1. Diurnal variation of the O_3 concentrations in Frederiksborg and the NO emissions in some European countries and in Europe as a whole during a 16-year period.

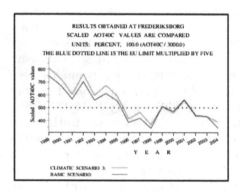
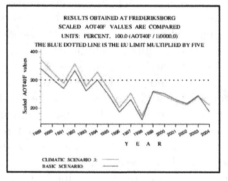

Fig. 2. AOT40C/F values obtained by two scenarios scaled with the EU critical values.

(April, August and September) are to be added when damages on forests are to be investigated. AOT40C and AOT40F will be respectively used. It is desirable to keep $AOT40C \leq 3000$ ppb and $AOT40F \leq 10000$ ppb in order to avoid damages on crops and forests, [4]. In the left-hand-side plot of Fig. 1 diurnal variation of the ozone concentrations obtained by the Basic Scenario and the Third Climatic Scenarios are compared with measurements. On the right the decreasing trend of the human-made emissions of nitrogen oxides is shown. The decrease of these emissions should lead to some decrease of the ozone concentrations (and especially to the AOT40C and AOT40F values), because the nitrogen oxide participates in the chemical reactions producing ozone. The two plots in Fig. 2 show the AOT40C and AOT40F values in Frederiksborg (Denmark). These values are decreasing (because the human-made emissions are decreasing), but the climatic changes lead often to higher values in comparison with the Basic Scenario. The critical level of AOT40C are greatly exceeded in the South-eastern part of Europe (by greater than 500% in the Western parts of the Balkan Peninsula) (Fig. 3). The climatic changes will cause additional increase of AOT40C (in some areas the increases are higher than 15%). The left-hand-side plot in Fig. 4 shows

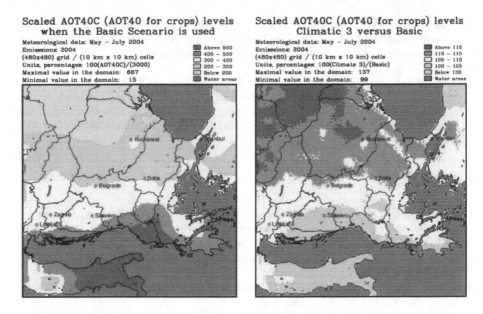

Fig. 3. Comparing the AOT40C levels in South-eastern Europe with the EU critical level (left) and the increases in % when the Third Climatic Scenario is used (right).

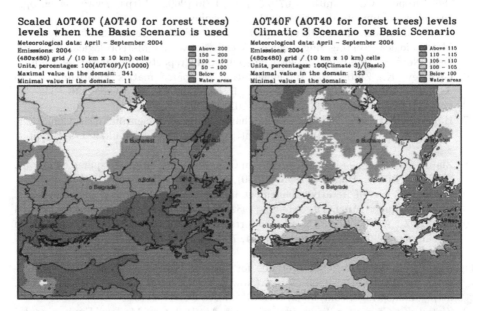

Fig. 4. AOT40F levels in the South-eastern part of Europe vs the EU critical level (left) and the increases in percent when the Third Climatic Scenario is used (right).

that the critical levels of AOT40F are exceeded very much in the South-eastern part of Europe (at places by greater than 200%), but not as much as the values of the AOT40C. The climatic changes will cause additional increase in AOT40F.

Acknowledgments. Project no. ED_18-1-2019-0030 (Application-specific highly reliable IT solutions) has been implemented with the support provided from the National Research, Development and Innovation Fund of Hungary, financed under the Thematic Excellence Programme funding scheme.

The project partially has been supported by the European Union, and co-financed by the European Social Fund (EFOP-3.6.3-VEKOP-16-2017-00002). The work is also partially funded by the Ministry of Education and Science of Bulgaria under the National Scientific Program "ICT in SES" and by the Bulgarian NSF project DN 12/5-2017.

References

1. Alexandrov, V., Owczarz, W., Thomsen, P.G., Zlatev, Z.: Parallel runs of large air pollution models on a grid of SUN computers. Math. Comput. Simul. **65**, 557–577 (2004). https://doi.org/10.1016/j.matcom.2004.01.022
2. Anderson, E., et al.: LAPACK: Users' Guide. SIAM, Philadelphia (1992). http://www.netlib.org/lapack/lug/
3. Barker, V.A., et al.: LAPACK95: Users' Guide. SIAM, Philadelphia (2001). http://www.netlib.org/lapack95/lug95/
4. European Parliament: Directive 2002/3/EC of the European Parliament and the Council of 12 February 2002 relating to ozone in ambient air. Official Journal of the European Communities L67 9.3, pp. 14–30 (2002). https://www.eea.europa.eu/policy-documents/directive-2002-3-ec...ozone-in
5. EMEP: Emission data: status report. EMEP/MSC-W report 1/99, July 1999, Meteorological Synthesizing Centre - West, Norwegian Meteorological Institute, Oslo, Norway (1999). http://www.emep.int/publ/reports/1999/note1_99_1.pdf
6. Georgiev, K., Zlatev, Z.: Implementation of sparse matrix algorithms in an advection-diffusion-chemistry module. J. Comput. Appl. Math. **236**, 342–353 (2011). https://doi.org/10.1016/j.cam.2011.07.026
7. Houghton, J.T., et al. (eds.): Climate Change 2001: The Scientific Basis, Cambridge University Press, Cambridge (2001). http://cedadocs.ceda.ac.uk/981/9/Chapter_8.pdf
8. Zlatev, Z.: On some pivotal strategies in Gaussian elimination by sparse technique. SIAM J. Numer. Anal. **17**, 18–30 (1980). www.jstor.org/stable/2156544
9. Zlatev, Z.: Use of iterative refinement in the solution of sparse linear systems. SIAM J. Numer. Anal. **19**, 381–399 (1982). https://www.jstor.org/stable/i337734
10. Zlatev, Z.: Application of predictor-corrector schemes with several correctors in solving air pollution problems. BIT **24**, 700–715 (1984). https://doi.org/10.1007/BF01934925
11. Zlatev, Z.: Computational Methods for General Sparse Matrices. Kluwer Academic Publishers, Dordrech (1991). (Now distributed by Springer-Verlag, Berlin). http://link.springer.com/book/10.1007%2F978-94-017-1116-6
12. Zlatev, Z.: Computer Treatment of Large Air Pollution Models. Environmental and Technology Library, vol. 2. Kluwer Academic Publishers, Dordrech (1995). https://doi.org/10.1007/978-94-011-0311-4. (Now distributed by Springer-Verlag, Berlin)
13. Zlatev, Z.: Impact of future climate changes on high ozone levels in European suburban areas. Clim. Change **101**, 447–483 (2010). https://doi.org/10.1007/s10584-009-9699-7

14. Zlatev, Z., Dimov, I.: Computational and Numerical Challenges in Environmental Modelling. Studies in Computational Mathematics, vol. 13. Elsevier, Amsterdam (2006). https://books.google.dk/books?isbn=0080462480
15. Zlatev, Z., Dimov, I., Faragó, I., Georgiev, K., Havasi, Á.: Large-scale air pollution modeling in Europe under different climatic scenarios. Int. J. Big Data Min. Glob. Warming **1**(2) (2019). 1950009 (28 pages). https://doi.org/10.1142/S2630534819500098

Monte Carlo Algorithms: Innovative Applications in Conjunctions with Other Methods

A Revised Wigner Function Approach for Stationary Quantum Transport

Robert Kosik[✉], Johann Cervenka, Mischa Thesberg, and Hans Kosina

Institute for Microelectronics, TU Wien, Vienna, Austria
{kosik,cervenka,thesberg,kosina}@iue.tuwien.ac.at
http://www.iue.tuwien.ac.at

Abstract. The Wigner equation describing stationary quantum transport has a singularity at the point $k = 0$. Deterministic solution methods usually deal with the singularity by just avoiding that point in the mesh (e.g., Frensley's method). Results from such methods are known to depend strongly on the discretization and meshing parameters.

We propose a revised approach which explicitly includes the point $k = 0$ in the mesh. For this we give two equations for $k = 0$. The first condition is an algebraic constraint which ensures that the solution of the Wigner equation has no singularity for $k = 0$. If this condition is fulfilled we then can derive a transport equation for $k = 0$ as a secondary equation.

The resulting system with two equations for $k = 0$ is overdetermined and we call it the constrained Wigner equation. We give a theoretical analysis of the overdeterminacy by relating the two equations for $k = 0$ to boundary conditions for the sigma equation, which is the inverse Fourier transform of the Wigner equation.

We show results from a prototype implementation of the constrained equation which gives good agreement with results from the quantum transmitting boundary method. No numerical parameter fitting is needed.

Keywords: Wigner function · Sigma function · Finite difference method · Constrained equation · Quantum transport · Device simulation · Resonant tunneling diode

1 Wigner Function Formalism

An attractive approach to quantum transport simulation is based on the Wigner function formulation of quantum mechanics [8] because it is formally close to a classical phase space description and allows one to use a mixed quantum-classical description of the system. This work deals with the stationary Wigner equation in a single spatial dimension.

© Springer Nature Switzerland AG 2020
I. Lirkov and S. Margenov (Eds.): LSSC 2019, LNCS 11958, pp. 403–410, 2020.
https://doi.org/10.1007/978-3-030-41032-2_46

1.1 Wigner Function

The Wigner function $f(r, k)$ is derived from the von Neumann density function $\rho(x, y)$ as the result of two consecutive transformations.

1. Introduce new coordinates for the quantum density

$$r = \frac{x + y}{2}, \qquad s = x - y.$$

Using these coordinates the density matrix transforms into an intermediate form, which we call the sigma function

$$\sigma(r, s) = \rho(r + \frac{s}{2}, r - \frac{s}{2}). \tag{1}$$

2. The Wigner function $f(r, k)$ is derived from the sigma function $\sigma(r, s)$ via a Fourier transform in coordinate s

$$f(r, k) = \frac{1}{2\pi} \int \sigma(r, s)\, e^{-i k s}\, ds. \tag{2}$$

With these conventions a Schrödinger plane wave $\psi = e^{i k_0 x}$ has a corresponding sigma function $e^{i k_0 s}$ and a Wigner function $\delta(k - k_0)$.

1.2 Wigner Equation

Stationary quantum transport is described by the Liouville-von Neumann equation for the density matrix $\rho(x, y)$

$$-\frac{\hbar^2}{2m} \left(\frac{\partial^2}{\partial x^2} - \frac{\partial^2}{\partial y^2} \right) \rho + \left(V(x) - V(y) \right)\rho = 0 \tag{3}$$

where $V(x)$ is the potential energy. Using coordinates (r, s) the stationary von Neumann equation transforms into the stationary sigma equation

$$\frac{\hbar^2}{m} \frac{\partial^2 \sigma}{\partial r s} = U(r, s)\sigma(r, s) \tag{4}$$

where the potential term $U(r, s)$ is defined by

$$U(r, s) = V\left(r + \frac{s}{2} \right) - V\left(r - \frac{s}{2} \right). \tag{5}$$

In a single spatial dimension equation (4) is the characteristic hyperbolic form of the stationary von Neumann equation (3).

Applying the Fourier transform (2) to the sigma equation (4) gives the stationary Wigner equation

$$\frac{\hbar k}{m} \frac{\partial f(r, k)}{\partial r} = \int f(r, k - k') V_w(r, k') dk'. \tag{6}$$

Here the Wigner potential $V_w(r, k)$ is defined as the Fourier transform of $U(r, s)$ divided by $i\hbar$

$$V_w(r, k) = \frac{1}{i\hbar} \frac{1}{2\pi} \int U(r, s) e^{-iks} ds. \tag{7}$$

For non-zero bias the Wigner potential has a $1/k$-singularity at $k = 0$.

For open systems classical inflow boundary conditions (BCs) are imposed on the stationary Wigner equation (two-point boundary value problem)

$$f(r_{min}, k) = f_L(k) \quad \text{(for } k > 0) \qquad f(r_{max}, k) = f_R(k) \quad \text{(for } k < 0). \tag{8}$$

Here f_L and f_R are prescribed distributions depending on temperature and the doping concentration in the electrodes.

2 Critique of Frensley's Method

In a single space the Wigner equation (6) can be rewritten for $k \neq 0$ as

$$\frac{\partial f(r, k)}{\partial r} = \frac{1}{k} \frac{m}{\hbar} \int f(r, k - k') V_w(r, k') dk'. \tag{9}$$

The form (9) emphasizes that the equation becomes singular at $k = 0$.

In [3] William Frensley proposed a discrete method for the Wigner equation (9). A special feature of the method is that it uses an equi-spaced grid shifted by $\Delta k/2$ excluding the point $k = 0$. Frensley's original discretization solves the Wigner equation (9) using upwinding on a coarse r-grid.

However, the method has been criticized for the results depending strongly on the type of discretization used and its parameters. The upwinding introduces a lot of artificial diffusion and the method breaks down when the grid is refined.

Figure 1 displays numerical results from the simulation of Tsuchiya's resonant tunneling diode [7]. All results were calculated using shooting methods and massive parallelization. The coherence length is kept fixed in this example (fixed k-grid). With refinement of Δr the artificial diffusion is reduced and simulation results using upwinding slowly converge to the numerically exact solution (semi-discrete solution). The upper solid red line was calculated without upwinding using $N_r = 800$ points. It does not change noticeably if the r-grid is refined.

3 Constrained Wigner Equation

Unfortunately, the numerically exact solution appears to be unphysical, showing no negative differential resistance and too high current. Furthermore, on close inspection, numerical solutions $f(r, k)$ show a sharp discontinuity and strong negative values around $k = 0$.

Theoretical analysis motivated by these observations lead to the insight that the breakdown is due to the inadequate treatment of the equation near the singular point $k = 0$.

If we want to avoid a singularity we actually get two equations for $k = 0$ and thus an overdetermined system:

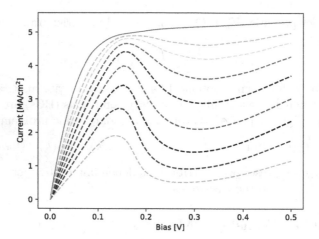

Fig. 1. The dashed lines are I–V curves from Frensley's discretization using upwinding with $N_r = 800$ (orange), $N_r = 1600$ (blue), all the way up to $N_r = 102400$ (cyan). With refinement the dashed lines slowly converge towards the upper solid red line which is the solution without upwinding. (Color figure online)

1. Putting $k = 0$ in (6) gives the following regularity constraint

$$\int f(r, k')V_w(r, k')dk' = 0. \tag{10}$$

In this degenerate case the left hand side in Eq. (6) vanishes and we do not get a differential equation. This special case is called an algebraic constraint in [1,5]. It is needed to avoid poles on the right hand side of (9). The regularity constraint has also a physical interpretation: The total inscattering rate at $k = 0$ must vanish in the steady state.

2. If constraint (10) is fulfilled then (using L'Hospital's rule for a quotient and Leibniz's rule for differentiation under the integral sign) we can take the limit $k \to 0$ in (9). This gives the "transport" equation at $k = 0$

$$\frac{\partial f(r, 0)}{\partial r} = \frac{m}{\hbar} \int f_k(r, -k')V_w(r, k')dk' = -\frac{m}{\hbar} \int f_k(r, k')V_w(r, k')dk'. \tag{11}$$

Here $f_k(r, k) = \frac{\partial f(r,k)}{\partial k}$ denotes the first order k-derivative of $f(r, k)$.

We call the overdetermined system with two equations for $k = 0$ the constrained Wigner equation.

It has to be pointed out, that the zero bias case is special. In this case the Wigner potential is not singular at $k = 0$ and the ansatz $\tilde{f}(r, k) = \frac{h(r,k)}{k}$ gives a well-defined equation for h. The solution $\tilde{f}$ has a pole at $k = 0$ and the regularity constraint (10) is not necessarily fulfilled. In addition, for zero bias the solution may contain contributions $g(r)\delta(k)$.

4   Constrained Sigma Equation

The significance of a parallel investigation of the sigma equation and the Wigner equation is explained by noting that the two equations for $k = 0$ are related to two types of boundary conditions for the sigma function. A constrained sigma equation corresponding to the constrained Wigner equation is derived in this section.

4.1   Goursat Problem

The sigma function has the symmetry property $\sigma(r, -s) = \overline{\sigma(r, s)}$. Its real part is even, the imaginary part b is an odd function in s. This allows one to define a purely real sigma function $\tilde{\sigma}$

$$\tilde{\sigma}(r, s) = a(r, s) + b(r, s) \tag{12}$$

which is useful to avoid complex numbers in the numerical implementation and for visualization. The function $\tilde{\sigma}$ is a real solution to the sigma equation (4).

Integrating both sides of (4) over a rectangular domain gives

$$\sigma(r, s) = \sigma_0(r, s) + \int_0^r \int_0^s \frac{m}{\hbar^2} U(r', s') \sigma(r', s') \, dr' \, ds' \tag{13}$$

where $\sigma_0(r, s)$ is a solution to the homogeneous sigma equation. A homogeneous solution σ_0 is of the form

$$\sigma_0(r, s) = \phi(r) + \psi(s) - \phi(0), \qquad \phi(0) = \psi(0). \tag{14}$$

The solution σ of (13) fulfills $\sigma(0, s) = \psi(s)$ and $\sigma(r, 0) = \phi(r)$, which are boundary conditions of Goursat type. In general, these consist in boundary conditions on an angle formed by two characteristics. Equation (13) is a two-dimensional integral equation of Volterra type. Existence and uniqueness of the solution to the Goursat problem can be proved [2, 6].

Note that inflow boundary conditions as defined in Eq. (8) for the Wigner equation can also be imposed in the sigma equation by calculating the Fourier transform of the sigma function on the boundary s-lines at r_{min}, r_{max}.

In contrast to the Wigner equation, the sigma equation has an additional freedom in the choice of boundary conditions, because boundary conditions $\phi(r)$ on a characteristic r-line have no immediate analogue in the Wigner equation.

4.2   BCs for the Constrained Sigma Equation

The two equations for $k = 0$ in the constrained Wigner equation can be related to boundary conditions for the sigma equation.

Regularity Constraint: Periodic BCs. The regularity constraint is the Wigner equation for $k = 0$. In s-space the regularity constraint (10) becomes

$$\int_{-a}^{a} U(r, s)\sigma(r, s)ds = 0 \tag{15}$$

assuming a symmetric finite s-interval $(-a, a)$. Integrating both sides of the sigma equation (4) over the interval $(-a, a)$ we derive

$$\sigma_r(a) - \sigma_r(-a) = \frac{m}{\hbar^2} \int_{-a}^{a} U(r, s)\sigma(r, s)ds = 0 \tag{16}$$

and hence constraint (15) is related to periodic BCs for σ_r on a symmetric, finite domain.

Transport Equation at $k = 0$: Anti-periodic BCs. To study the transport equation at $k = 0$ in the sigma representation we take the inverse Fourier transform of Eq. (11) which gives

$$\int \frac{\partial \sigma(r, s)}{\partial r} ds = -\frac{m}{\hbar^2} \int s U(r, s)\sigma(r, s)ds. \tag{17}$$

Multiplying the stationary sigma equation (4) with $-s$ and integrating over s gives

$$-\int s \frac{\partial}{\partial r}\frac{\partial}{\partial s}\sigma(r, s)ds = -\frac{m}{\hbar^2} \int s U(r, s)\sigma(r, s)ds. \tag{18}$$

Subtracting the two Eqs. (17) and (18) we get a condition on σ_r which is independent of U

$$\int \frac{\partial}{\partial s}[s \frac{\partial}{\partial r}\sigma(r, s)]ds = 0. \tag{19}$$

On a finite symmetric domain this gives anti-periodic boundary conditions for σ_r, i.e., $\sigma_r(r, -a) = -\sigma_r(r, a)$. The sigma equation with anti-periodic BCs for σ in s-space is related to Frensley's method which uses a shifted k-grid.

Overdetermined Boundary Value Problem. Summarizing we have both periodic and anti-periodic boundary conditions for σ_r. It follows that $\sigma_r = 0$ and σ is constant on the s-boundaries. The only reasonable choice for the integration constant is to set

$$\sigma(r, s_{max}) = \sigma(r, s_{min}) = 0 \tag{20}$$

on a s-domain symmetric around $s = 0$.

The constrained sigma equation consists of double homogeneous boundary conditions (20) plus inflow boundary conditions imposed on the Fourier transform of σ. This system is also overdetermined and corresponds to the constrained Wigner equation.

5   Proof of Concept

Results from a prototype implementation are included down below. This should serve as a proof of concept and back up our claims about the root cause of numerical problems and inconsistencies, which are observed in stationary simulations based on Frensley's method.

The version easiest to implement has been chosen for prototyping. It uses double homogeneous boundary conditions in the sigma equation. We use an orthogrid and a stencil

$$\sigma(0,0) + \sigma(1,1) - \sigma(0,1) - \sigma(1,0) = \frac{1}{4} \sum_{i=0}^{1} \sum_{j=0}^{1} \tilde{U}(i,j)\sigma(i,j) \qquad (21)$$

for the unit square.

Using Lagrange multipliers, inflow boundary conditions are fulfilled exactly and conservation of mass is also exact. The remaining equations of the overdetermined system are only fulfilled approximately. A sparse direct solver is used for the least squares solution of the system.

For a test we simulated a GaAs-AlGaAs double barrier resonant tunneling diode (barrier width 2.8 nm, well width 4.5 nm) as specified in [7]. The coherence length used in the simulation is 36 nm. The simulation is done for two grid sizes. The dotted line is the result for $(N_r = 500, N_s = 400)$. The grid is then refined once in each dimension. The dashed line is the result for $(N_r = 1000, N_s = 800)$. As seen in Fig. 2 the solution from the constrained sigma equation changes

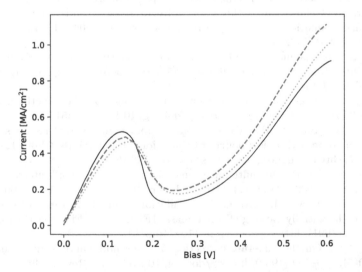

Fig. 2. The solid line is the solution from the QTBM, which is compared with the two solutions from the constrained sigma equation for $N_r = 500$ (dotted) and $N_r = 1000$ (dashed). The resonance from the QTBM is reproduced. No parameter fitting is employed. The method is stable under mesh refinement.

with the refinement but it is quite stable. This should be compared with grid refinement for Frensley's method in Fig. 1. As we cannot use a shooting method for the constrained equation, the use of very fine meshes like in Fig. 1 (up to $N_r = 102400$) is not computationally feasible.

In the same figure the two constrained solutions are compared with the result from the quantum transmitting boundary method (QTBM) [4]. The fit with the QTBM (solid line) is reasonably good for the resonance peak. At higher bias we get a discrepancy, which needs further research.

For non-zero bias, the Wigner transforms of the scattering modes assumed in the QTBM are solutions to the constrained Wigner equation. However, the Wigner function model assumes classical boundary conditions and a finite coherence length, hence a perfect fit with QTBM is not to be expected.

In contrast to the results from Frensley's method (see Fig. 1), the results from the constrained Wigner equation are physically reasonable and consistent when the grid is refined. We believe that initial results for the constrained equation as demonstrated in Fig. 2 are encouraging and that the revised method deserves further in-depth study.

Acknowledgement. This work has been supported in parts by the Austrian Research Promotion Agency (FFG), grant 867997.

References

1. Arnold, A., Lange, H., Zweifel, P.F.: A discrete-velocity, stationary Wigner equation. J. Math. Phys. **41**(11), 7167–7180 (2000). https://doi.org/10.1063/1.1318732
2. Brunner, H.: Collocation Methods for Volterra Integral and Related Functional Equations. Cambridge University Press, Cambridge (2004). https://doi.org/10.1017/cbo9780511543234
3. Frensley, W.R.: Boundary conditions for open quantum systems driven far from equilibrium. Rev. Mod. Phys. **62**(3), 745–791 (1990). https://doi.org/10.1103/RevModPhys.62.745
4. Lent, C.S., Kirkner, D.: The quantum transmitting boundary method. J. Appl. Phys. **67**(10), 6353–6359 (1990). https://doi.org/10.1063/1.345156
5. Li, R., Lu, T., Sun, Z.: Parity-decomposition and moment analysis for stationary Wigner equation with inflow boundary conditions. Front. Math. China **12**(4), 907–919 (2017). https://doi.org/10.1007/s11464-017-0612-9
6. Suryanarayana, M.B.: On multidimensional integral equations of Volterra type. Pac. J. Math. **41**(3), 809–828 (1972). https://doi.org/10.2140/pjm.1972.41.809
7. Tsuchiya, H., Ogawa, M., Miyoshi, T.: Simulation of quantum transport in quantum devices with spatially varying effective mass. IEEE Trans. Electron Devices **38**(6), 1246–1252 (1991). https://doi.org/10.1109/16.81613
8. Wigner, E.P.: On the quantum correction for thermodynamic equilibrium. Phys. Rev. **40**(5), 749–759 (1932). https://doi.org/10.1103/PhysRev.40.749

Techniques for Statistical Enhancement in a 2D Multi-subband Ensemble Monte Carlo Nanodevice Simulator

Cristina Medina-Bailon[1,2]([✉]), Carlos Sampedro[2], Jose Luis Padilla[2],
Luca Donetti[2], ViharGeorgiev[1], Francisco Gamiz[2], and Asen Asenov[1]

[1] School of Engineering, University of Glasgow, Glasgow G12 8LT, Scotland, UK
Cristina.MedinaBailon@glasgow.ac.uk
[2] Nanoelectronics Research Group, Universidad de Granada,
18071 Granada, Spain

Abstract. Novel numerical techniques are needed in advanced simulation tools in order to accurately describe the behavior of nanoelectronic devices. In this work, two different numerical techniques for statistical enhancement are included in a 2D Multi-Subband Ensemble Monte Carlo (MS-EMC) simulator. First, the consideration of the Fermi-Dirac statistics for the boundary conditions in the ohmic contacts instead of the Boltzmann ones provides a more accurate picture of the distribution function. Second, the energy-dependent weight model reduces the stochastic noise that the superparticles with very high energy introduce in the device performance. In this work, we study the impact of both numerical techniques in two of the potential candidates to extend the CMOS technology: the Fully-Depleted Silicon-On-Insulator (FDSOI) and the FinFET devices. We show that the choice of the Fermi-Dirac statistics has the same impact in both the FDSOI and the FinFET, whereas the energy-dependent weight model has more significance in the FDSOI than in the FinFET because the latter has better electrostatic integrity.

Keywords: Fermi-Dirac statistics · Boundary conditions ·
Energy-dependent weight · Stocastic noise · Tail electrons · MS-EMC ·
FDSOI · FinFET

1 Introduction

As the electronic devices have reached the nanoscale, it is mandatory to consider more complex physical phenomena in the corresponding simulation scheme. Accordingly, new important numerical techniques are required to accurately describe the behavior of these advanced architectures [1,2]. One of the most popular approaches is to incorporate them into semi-classical simulators due to

This work was supported by the U.K. EPSRC Projects No. EP/P009972/1 and EP/S001131/1.

© Springer Nature Switzerland AG 2020
I. Lirkov and S. Margenov (Eds.): LSSC 2019, LNCS 11958, pp. 411–419, 2020.
https://doi.org/10.1007/978-3-030-41032-2_47

their lower computational demand in comparison to the purely quantum transport models.

In this work, two different numerical techniques for statistical enhancement are described in order to develop a more realistic Monte Carlo simulator. First, a new method for the boundary conditions in the ohmic contacts is implemented. The superparticles are considered to enter in the device through the source/drain to keep charge neutrality. The injected superparticles obey the Fermi-Dirac (FD) statistics, providing a more accurate picture of the distribution function in comparison to Maxwell-Boltzmann (MB) statistics. Second, an energy-dependent weight for superparticles is considered. The electrons tend to be at the lower energy levels, whereas the high energy superparticles are rare events and so their weight should be reduced. This model dramatically reduces the stochastic noise that high energy superparticles introduce in the device performance because the statistics is dominated by the higher weighted superparticles.

The structure of this work is organized as follows. The main characteristics of the simulation tool as well as the device parameters are reported in Sect. 2. Then, a detailed discussion of the inclusion of both numerical techniques is given in Sects. 3 and 4, respectively, together with the results obtained from two of the potential candidates to extend the CMOS technology beyond the 10 nm node: the Fully-Depleted Silicon-On-Insulator (FDSOI) and FinFET devices. Finally, conclusions are given in Sect. 5.

2   2D Multisubband Ensemble Monte Carlo Tool and Simulated Devices

The starting point of the simulation framework is a 2D Multi-Subband Ensemble Monte Carlo (MS-EMC) code which is based on the space-mode approach for the quantum transport. The tool solves the one dimensional (1D) Schrödinger equation in the confinement direction and the Boltzmann Transport Equation (BTE) in the transport plane. The system is coupled by solving Poisson's equation in the two dimensional (2D) simulation domain. This simulator has already shown its capabilities studying different nano-transistors as well as tunneling phenomena [5]. For this paper, we have activated the S/D tunneling module in the simulations [6] to accurately reproduce the behavior of the electronic devices in the nanometer regime.

Device parameters, effective masses and orientation for the FDSOI and FinFET structures herein analyzed are outlined in Fig. 1. The gate work function is fixed to 4.385 eV. A Back-Bias polarization of 0 V and a Back-Plane work function of 5.17 eV have been chosen for the FDSOI. Moreover, the realistic band structure of the 2D devices has been taken into account by accurately extracting the effective masses (see Fig. 1(c)) using density functional theory (DFT) simulations included in QuantumATK Synopsys [8].

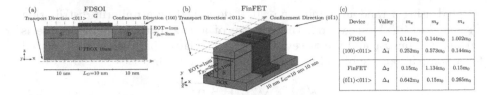

Fig. 1. (a) FDSOI and (b) FinFET structures analyzed in this work including the fixed device parameters and orientations. (c) Calibrated effective masses using DFT simulations in Si for these devices: m_x is the transport mass, m_y is the mass in the direction normal to transport, m_z is the confinement mass, m_0 is the electron free-mass, and the subindex in Δ represents the corresponding degeneracy factor.

3   Fermi-Dirac Injection in the Ohmic Contacts

3.1   Description of the Model

The Monte Carlo method solves the BTE by tracing the motion of particles in the simulation domain. Imposing boundary conditions on the BTE is mandatory when the particles reach interfaces between regions with different physical properties. A mixing of the absorbing/injecting boundary conditions for the ohmic contacts are considered in our MC transport loop [7,9]. First, the free-flight subroutine simulates the carrier motion and the superparticles leaving the drain/source are injected back into the source/drain at the beginning of each time step. Second, when a superparticle is injected, the charge neutrality condition is evaluated in the boundary and, in case it does not fulfill this condition, it is marked to be erased at the end of the loop. Third, when the free-flight is completed, we have to erase the marked superparticles and evaluate again the charge neutrality condition in the contacts. If the number of superparticles injected into the contacts is not enough to fulfill the carrier neutrality condition, more superparticles are injected until that condition is satisfied.

Once the boundary condition procedure has been described, two statistics can be assumed regarding the carrier distribution: the equilibrium MB or the FD statistics. Their carrier distribution function ($f_{MB}(E_k)$ and $f_{FD}(E_k)$, respectively) can be formulated including the kinetic energy (E_k) and the s-th subband energy (E_S):

$$f_{MB}(E_k) = \exp\left(\frac{-(E_k + E_S - E_F)}{k_B T}\right) ; f_{FD}(E_k) = \frac{1}{1 + \exp\left(\frac{E_k + E_s - E_F}{k_B T}\right)} \quad (1)$$

On the one hand, the equilibrium MB statistics describe a thermal isotropic injection. The superparticle must be defined before being injected in a particular subband at the ohmic contacts by means of three parameters: the angle in which the superparticle is going to be injected φ, the kinetic energy E_k, and the velocity in the direction normal to the interface v_x. The angle is randomly calculated in the interval $\varphi \in [0, 2\pi]$. In addition, due to the thermal condition, E_k can be selected using a random number $r \in [0,1]$ described by a uniform distribution $E_k = -k_B T ln(r)$. In general, the velocity of a superparticle in the device is calculated from E_k and the wavevector (k'). The latter parameter is calculated for a non-parabolic subband in the crystal coordinates by:

$$\frac{k'}{\sqrt{m_{eff}}} = \frac{\sqrt{2E_k(1 + \alpha E_k)}}{\hbar} \tag{2}$$

where α is the non-parabolic parameter and m_{eff} is the effective mass that matches $\frac{k'^2}{m_{eff}} = \frac{k_x'^2}{m_x'} + \frac{k_z'^2}{m_z'}$.

Then, k' is divided into its transport and confinement components according to the angle φ:

$$k_x' = \frac{k'}{\sqrt{m_{eff}}} cos(\varphi) \sqrt{m_x'}; \; k_z' = \frac{k'}{\sqrt{m_{eff}}} sin(\varphi) \sqrt{m_z'} \tag{3}$$

Thus, the superparticle velocity in the crystal is given by:

$$v_x' = k_x' \frac{\hbar}{m_x'} \frac{1}{1 + 2\alpha E_k}; \; v_z' = k_z' \frac{\hbar}{m_z'} \frac{1}{1 + 2\alpha E_k} \tag{4}$$

Finally, a change in the coordinates between the crystal and the device orientation is required being θ the angle between them. Assuming that the direction normal to the interface is the x direction in the transport plane, the velocity of a superparticle in the device is calculated as:

$$v_x = v_x' cos(\theta) + v_z' sin(\theta) = \frac{\sqrt{2E_k(1 + \alpha E_k)}q}{1 + 2\alpha E_k} \left[\frac{cos(\varphi)cos(\theta)}{\sqrt{m_x'}} + \frac{sin(\varphi)sin(\theta)}{\sqrt{m_z'}} \right] \tag{5}$$

On the other hand, injecting particles according to an equilibrium distribution may be inconsistent with the out-of-equilibrium regime inside the device. Accordingly, the FD statistics is a more adequate guess but at the expense of introducing higher computational cost. These statistics are also an equilibrium distribution but it is a better conjecture in degenerate or quasi-degenerate systems such as the ohmic regions due to their high doping. In these regions, the Fermi levels are very close or even inside the conduction band. The probability of injecting superparticles at a given state is required in order to determine the superparticle parameters. This probability is proportional to the group velocity in the direction normal to the interface and to $f_{FD}(E_k)$: $p_{FD}(E_k) = f_{FD}(E_k)v_x(E_k)$.

In this approximation, the superparticle angle depends on the angle between the crystal axis and device orientation θ: $\varphi \in [\theta - \frac{\pi}{2}, \theta + \frac{\pi}{2}]$. In consequence, the probability of a superparticle crossing a surface depends on its kinetic energy and its angle of motion and it can be calculated by introducing Eq. 5 and the φ dependence in $p_{FD}(E_k)$:

$$p_{FD}(E_k) = f_{FD}(E_k) \frac{\sqrt{2E_k(1+\alpha E_k)q}}{1+2\alpha E_k} \int_{\theta-\frac{\pi}{2}}^{\theta+\frac{\pi}{2}} \left[\frac{cos(\varphi)cos(\theta)}{\sqrt{m_x'}} + \frac{sin(\varphi)sin(\theta)}{\sqrt{m_z'}} \right] d\varphi$$

$$= f_{FD}(E_k) \frac{\sqrt{2E_k(1+\alpha E_k)q}}{1+2\alpha E_k} \left[\frac{1+cos(2\theta)}{\sqrt{m_x'}} + \frac{1-cos(2\theta)}{\sqrt{m_z'}} \right]$$

(6)

Once this probability is determined, the kinetic energy and the angle φ are randomly chosen using a direct technique in the generation of random numbers with given probability distribution function.

3.2   Results

Figure 2a shows the probability of injecting superparticles in the device given by the MB and FD statistics as a function of the kinetic energy for a given subband. The most likely kinetic energy is around 0 eV using MB statistics, whereas it is shifted to 0.08 eV for the FD ones. As the injection velocity increases with the kinetic energy, the superparticles velocity in the direction normal to the interface (v_x) is also higher for the FD statistics than for the MB ones in the channel (Fig. 2b). In general, the drain current in Monte Carlo simulators is calculated by multiplying the velocity by the number of superparticles in

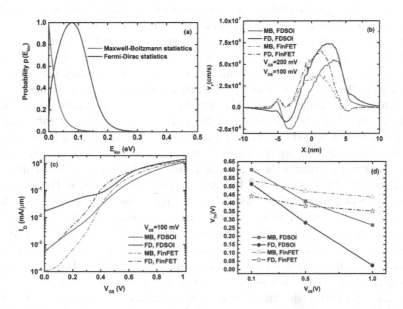

Fig. 2. Comparison between the Maxwell-Boltzmann (MB) and Fermi-Dirac (FD) statistics considering the FDSOI and the FinFET devices (Fig. 1) and $V_{DS} = 100$ mV: (a) Probability of injecting superparticles given by both statistics as a function of the kinetic energy. (b) Average velocity in the direction normal to the interface (v_x). (c) I_D vs. V_{GS}. (d) Threshold voltage (V_{TH}) as a function of the drain bias.

the center of the channel. Consequently, when choosing between both carrier distribution functions, I_D is higher for the FD statistics than for the MB ones as shown in Fig. 2c. Finally, Fig. 2d shows the threshold voltage V_{TH} when both statistics are considered for the FDSOI and the FinFET devices and different drain biases. The impact of choosing the FD statistics instead of MB is similar for the FDSOI and FinFET for low drain bias, whereas it is more remarkable for higher drain biases in the FDSOI.

4   Energy-Dependent Weight for Superparticles

4.1   Description of the Model

In general, small channel devices present higher electric fields and so higher electron energy. Accordingly, these carriers, known as tail electrons, have higher energy than a critical energy level which depends on the voltage bias. They can create reliability problems and have influence over the carrier distribution. Despite the fact that these tail electrons are more unlikely compared to the common ones, they introduce a stochastic noise in MC (like in any other method using random numbers) in predefined regions by maintaining a certain number of particles in these high energy regions.

As a result, a weight redistribution technique [3,4] is needed to improve the statistics of the high energy tails for the simulated particles. In the MS-EMC tool, each superparticle is assigned a weight which denotes the number of electrons comprising the superparticle. It is important to highlight that the weight assignment is only calculated in two situations and it remains constant along its whole life in the device. First, when the superparticles are initialized in the simulation, their weight is assigned according to their initial kinetic energy. Second, when the superparticle is going to be injected in the device because it has reached an ohmic contact, the weight is calculated according to kinetic energy computed by the FD statistics (Sect. 3) for this particular subband.

When a new superparticle in going to be included in the simulation domain with an energy level higher than a critical energy, a lower weight compared to the low energy superparticles is assigned. The critical energy is calculated in consonance with the voltage bias for each subband. In this case, the simulation has two type of superparticles which are energy-dependent for each subband: heavy and light weighted superparticles. In this scenario, a higher number of superparticles but with lower electrons per particle is included in the tail area. Accordingly, the stochastic noise is reduced because the statistical average is calculated including a larger number of samples. Figure 3(a) shows an example of this procedure: in the left side, a large number of superparticles with light weight fills completely the energy tail area and, hence, the statistical average can include different kinetic energy and velocities; whereas in the right side of the figure, only one heavy weighted superparticle is contained in the statistical calculation increasing the stochastic noise.

Apparently, the main drawback of this method is the increase of the computational time by simulating particles with low weight. However, as the injection or initialization of superparticles with high energy are rare events, the number of them is much lower than the heavy weighted superparticles. Therefore, it does not introduce a significant modification of the simulation time allowing in contrast a dramatic enhancement of the system statistics.

4.2   Results

Figure 3b shows the carrier concentration along the transport direction for both FDSOI and FinFET devices and $V_{GS} = 300\,\text{mV}$ when all the superparticles have the same weight (constant weight) and when the energy-dependent weight model is taken into account. The carrier concentration is lower in the center of the device for the energy-dependent weight model because the superparticles located over the potential barrier have higher energy and so its equivalent weight is lower that those located at a lower energy. The influence of this model on the drain current (I_D) is analyzed in Fig. 3c. As already mentioned in Sect. 3.2, the drain current in MC is calculated by multiplying the velocity by the number of superparticles in the center of the device. Accordingly, the drain current is reduced when we consider the energy-dependent weight model due to the lower carrier concentration in the center of the device. Furthermore, the difference in

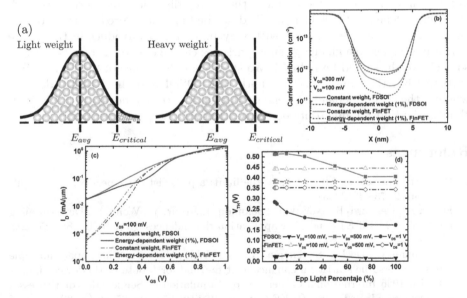

Fig. 3. Comparison between the constant weight and the energy-dependent weight models considering the FDSOI and the FinFET devices (Fig. 1) and $V_{DS} = 100\,\text{mV}$: (a) Schematic representation of an energy tail area which is filled by light (left) and heavy (right) weight superparticles. (b) Electron distribution along the transport direction for $V_{GS} = 300\,\text{mV}$. (c) I_D vs. V_{GS}. (d) Threshold voltage (V_{TH}) as a function of the drain bias ranging the percentage of the light weighted particles with respect to the heavy ones. Consider that 100% represents the constant case.

the I_D between both models is mainly observable for lower gate bias. In the case the potential barrier is tiny, the thermionic current is very high and the light weighted superparticles do not have influence over the stochastic noise.

Finally, the impact of this model on the threshold voltage (V_{TH}) for both devices and different drain biases is shown in Fig. 3d. The percentage of the light weighted superparticles with respect to the heavy ones is ranged from 0.1% to 100%, being the latter percentage the equivalent to the constant weight case. The threshold voltage decreases for increasing percentage but it is more remarkable for lower drain biases. This weight model is noticeable for the FDSOI, whereas there is almost no difference for the FinFET.

5   Conclusions

This work presents the implementation of two numerical techniques for statistical enhancement in a MS-EMC tool and the study of their impact in ultrascaled FDSOI and FinFET devices. First, a new method for the boundary conditions in the ohmic contacts is introduced. The superparticles are considered to enter in the device space for the source/drain if they reach the other contact. The parameters that describe the superparticle motion are calculated using the Maxwell-Boltzmann and the Fermi-Dirac statistics, with the second ones providing a more accurate description of the actual distribution function. Second, the energy-dependent weight model is described in order to reduce the stochastic noise that the superparticles with very high energy introduce in the device performance. These high energy superparticles can be defined as rare events and so their weight should be reduced. We show that the choice of the Fermi-Dirac statistics has the same impact in both the FDSOI and the FinFET devices, whereas the energy-dependent weight model has more significance in the FDSOI than in the FinFET due to its better electrostatic integrity.

References

1. Fischetti, M.: Scaling MOSFETs to the limit: a physicist's perspective. J. Comput. Electron. **2**, 73–79 (2003)
2. Frank, D., Dennard, R., Nowak, E., Solomon, P., Taur, Y., Wong, H.: Device scaling limits of Si MOSFETs and their application dependences. Proc. IEEE **89**, 259–288 (2001)
3. Jungemann, C., Decker, S., Thoma, R., Eng, W.L., Goto, H.: Phase space multiple refresh: a versatile statistical enhancement method for Monte Carlo device simulation. In: 1996 International Conference on Simulation of Semiconductor Processes and Devices, SISPAD 1996 (IEEE Cat. No. 96TH8095), pp. 65–66 (1996)
4. Kim, J., Shin, H., Lee, C., Park, Y.J., Min, H.S.: A new weight redistribution technique for electron-electron scattering in the MC simulation. IEEE Trans. Electron Devices **51**(9), 1448–1454 (2004)
5. Medina-Bailon, C., et al.: Multisubband ensemble Monte Carlo analysis of tunneling leakage mechanisms in ultrascaled FDSOI, DGSOI, and FinFET devices. IEEE Trans. Electron Devices **66**(3), 1145–1152 (2019). https://doi.org/10.1109/TED.2019.2890985

6. Medina-Bailon, C., Padilla, J., Sampedro, C., Godoy, A., Donetti, L., Gámiz, F.: Source-to-drain tunneling analysis in FDSOI, DGSOI and FinFET devices by means of multi-subband ensemble Monte Carlo. IEEE Trans. Electron Devices **65**(11), 4740–4746 (2018). https://doi.org/10.1109/TED.2018.2867721
7. Oriols, X., Fernàndez-Díaz, E., Alvarez, A., Alarcón, A.: An electron injection model for time-dependent simulators of nanoscale devices with electron confinement: application to the comparison of the intrinsic noise of 3D-, 2D- and 1D-ballistic transistors. Solid-State Electron. **51**(2), 306–319 (2007)
8. QuantumATK version O-2018.06. Synopsys, inc. (2018). https://www.synopsys.com/silicon/quantumatk.html
9. Woolard, D.L., Tian, H., Littlejohn, M.A., Kim, K.W.: Efficient ohmic boundary conditions for the Monte Carlo simulation of electron transport. IEEE Trans. Electron Devices **41**(4), 601–606 (1994)

Efficient Stochastic Algorithms for the Sensitivity Analysis Problem in the Air Pollution Modelling

Tzvetan Ostromsky[1]([⊠]), Venelin Todorov[1,2], Ivan Dimov[1], and Zahari Zlatev[3]

[1] Department of Parallel Algorithms, Institute of Information and Communication Technologies, Bulgarian Academy of Sciences (IICT-BAS),
Acad. G. Bonchev 25 A, 1113 Sofia, Bulgaria
{ceco,venelin}@parallel.bas.bg, ivdimov@bas.bg
[2] Department of Information Modelling, Institute of Mathematics and Informatics, Bulgarian Academy of Sciences (IMI-BAS),
Acad. Georgi Bonchev Street, Block 8, 1113 Sofia, Bulgaria
vtodorov@math.bas.bg
[3] National Centre for Environment and Energy, University of Århus,
Frederiksborgvej 399 P. O. Box 358, 4000 Roskilde, Denmark
zz@dmu.dk

Abstract. Sensitivity analysis of the results of large and complicated mathematical models is rather tuff and time-consuming task. However, this is quite an important problem as far as their critical applications are concerned. There are many such applications in the area of air pollution modelling. On the other hand, there are lots of natural uncertainties in the input data sets and parameters of a large-scale air pollution model. Such a model, the Danish Eulerian Model with its up-to-date high-performance implementations, is under consideration in this work. Its advanced chemical scheme (the Condensed CBM IV) takes into account a large number of chemical species and numerous reactions between them.

Four efficient stochastic algorithms have been used and compared by their accuracy in studying the sensitivity of ammonia and ozone concentration results with respect to the input emission levels and some chemical reactions rate parameters. The results of our numerical experiments show that the stochastic algorithms under consideration are quite efficient for the purpose of our sensitivity studies.

1 Introduction

We discuss a systematic approach for sensitivity analysis studies in the area of air pollution modelling. The Unified Danish Eulerian Model (UNI-DEM) [16,17] is used in this particular study. Different parts of the large amount of output data, produced by the model, were used in various practical applications, where the reliability of this data should be properly estimated. Another reason to choose

© Springer Nature Switzerland AG 2020
I. Lirkov and S. Margenov (Eds.): LSSC 2019, LNCS 11958, pp. 420–428, 2020.
https://doi.org/10.1007/978-3-030-41032-2_48

this model as a case study here is its sophisticated chemical scheme, where all relevant chemical processes in the atmosphere are accurately represented.

Four efficient stochastic algorithms (Sobol QMC, Halton QMC, Sobol Scrambled sequence 1 and Sobol scrambled sequence 2) have been applied to sensitivity studies of concentration variations of air pollutants with respect to the emission levels and some chemical reactions rates. More information on Sobol QMC algorithm can be found in [1]. For generating Sobol quasirandom sequences we use an adaptation of INSOBL and GOSOBL routines, implemented respectively in ACM TOMS Algorithm 647 [5] and ACM TOMS Algorithm 659 [2]. The original code can only compute the "next" element of the sequence. The adapted code allows the user to specify the index of the desired element. The Halton sequence is completely described in [6,7]. For the next two algorithms we use two types of Sobol sequences, implemented in Matlab, combined with a random linear scramble of J described by Matousek in [11]. We use the Matlab function $p = sobolset(d)$, which constructs a d-dimensional point set p of the sobolset class, with default property settings. Implementation of the Scrambled Digital Sequences is discussed in [9] and in [10].

The object p returned by the function *sobolset* encapsulates properties of a specified quasi-random sequence. The point set is finite, with a length determined by the Skip and Leap properties and by the limits on the size of point set indices (maximum value of 2^{53}). The point set values are not generated and not stored in memory until p is accessed by using net or parenthesis indexing. For the first sequence (SobolSet1) we generate a 3-D Sobol point set, skip the first 100 values, and then retain every 11th point. For the second sequence (SobolSet2) we generate a 3-D Sobol point set, skip the first 1000 values, and then retain every 101st point.

2   An Overview of UNI-DEM and Its Sensitivity Analysis Version

UNI-DEM is a powerful large-scale air pollution model for calculation the concentrations of a large number of pollutants and other chemical species in the air. The calculations are done in a large spatial domain, which covers completely the European region and the Mediterranean, for certain time period. The huge amount of temporary results produced by the model can hardly be stored and used directly in most practical applications. That is why they are averaged (daily, monthly, yearly) to form the main output data sets. The mean monthly concentrations are one of the most commonly used. In this particular study we use them for two of the most dangerous pollutants: the ozone (O_3) and the ammonia (NH_3). Other accumulative functions related to some specific applications, maximal values, etc. are also calculated, exported and used in various application areas (environmental protection, agriculture, health care, etc.).

UNI-DEM is mathematically represented by a large PDE system, in which the main physical and chemical processes (advection, diffusion, chemical reactions, emissions and deposition) are represented. For the purpose of its easier numerical treatment, certain splitting procedure is applied, so that the model is split into 3 relatively independent modules (submodels): Advection–diffusion, Chemistry–deposition and Vertical transport.

The above submodels, especially the Chemistry-deposition one, are rather tuff computational tasks even for the most advanced supercomputers. Efficient parallelization has always been very helpful for the efficient computer implementation of UNI-DEM. The task became much more challenging with development of the sensitivity analysis version of the code, SA-DEM [3,4]. It consists of the following three parts:

- A modification of UNI-DEM with ability to modify certain parameters, subject to SA study (for instance, some chemical rate parameters, or the input data stream for the anthropogenic emissions). A small number of input parameters is reserved for this purpose.
- A driver routine that automatically generates a set of tasks to produce the necessary results for a particular SA study. It allows to perform in parallel a large number of runs with common input data (reusing it), producing at once a whole set of values on a regular mesh (used later for calculating the sensitivity indices).
- An additional program for extracting the necessary part of the output data and computing the normalised ratios (to be used on a later stage).

Significant improvements of the earlier versions of SA-DEM were made by introducing two additional levels of parallelism: top-level (MPI) and bottom-level (OpenMP). They allow us to use efficiently the computational power of the contemporary cluster supercomputers with multicore nodes.

3 Sensitivity Studies with Respect to Emission Levels

Results for the sensitivity of UNI-DEM output (in particular, the ammonia mean monthly concentrations) with respect to the anthropogenic emissions input data variation are shown and discussed in this section. The anthropogenic emissions input consists of 4 different components $\mathbf{E} = (\mathbf{E^A}, \mathbf{E^N}, \mathbf{E^S}, \mathbf{E^C})$:

$\mathbf{E^A}$ – ammonia (NH_3); $\mathbf{E^S}$ – sulphur dioxide (SO_2);
$\mathbf{E^N}$ – nitrogen oxides ($NO + NO_2$); $\mathbf{E^C}$ – anthropogenic hydrocarbons.

The domain under consideration is the 4-dimensional hypercube $[0.5, 1]^4$. Polynomials of second degree have been used as an approximation tool [4]. The input data have been generated by the improved SA-DEM version, developed for the purpose of our sensitivity studies (see the previous section).

Results of the relative error estimation for the quantities f_0, the total variance $\mathbf{D}$, first-order (S_i) and total (S_i^{tot}) sensitivity indices are given in Tables 1, 2, 3, respectively. f_0 is presented by a 4-dimensional integral, while the rest of the above quantities are presented by 2-dimensional integrals, following the ideas of *correlated sampling* technique to compute sensitivity measures in a reliable

Table 1. Relative error estimation for calculating $f_0 \approx 0.048$.

# of samples n	SobolACM	Halton	SobolSet1	SobolSet2
	Relative error	Relative error	Relative error	Relative error
2^{10}	5.56e−04	3.15e−05	3.24e−04	3.93e−03
2^{12}	1.16e−04	1.14e−04	2.11e−04	1.49e−04
2^{14}	3.14e−05	1.27e−05	6.05e−05	2.44e−04
2^{16}	8.78e−06	8.20e−06	9.59e−06	5.15e−05
2^{18}	1.75e−06	2.40e−06	6.39e−06	7.41e−06
2^{20}	4.97e−07	1.03e−06	4.44e−06	4.60e−07

Table 2. Relative error for the evaluation of the total variance $\mathbf{D} \approx 0.0002$.

# of samples n	SobolACM	Halton	SobolSet1	SobolSet2
	Relative error	Relative error	Relative error	Relative error
2^{10}	2.28e−03	1.40e−02	6.24e−02	3.20e−02
2^{12}	9.38e−04	7.81e−03	2.40e−02	3.20e−03
2^{14}	1.92e−04	1.77e−03	8.70e−03	1.24e−03
2^{16}	5.86e−05	5.96e−04	2.68e−03	1.28e−03
2^{18}	8.61e−06	1.48e−04	1.46e−04	1.88e−04
2^{20}	1.60e−06	4.77e−05	8.94e−05	4.12e−05

way (see [8,15]). The four different stochastic approaches used for numerical integration are presented in separate columns of the tables.

The particular case study confirms that these algorithms are suitable and more efficient for smooth functions with comparatively low dimensions. From Tables 1 and 2 we can conclude that all stochastic approaches under

Table 3. Relative error estimation of sensitivity indices for some input parameters, obtained by using various MC and QMC approaches ($n = 2^{16} = 65536$).

Est. quantity	Ref. value	SobolACM	Halton	SobolSet1	SobolSet2
S_1	9e−01	5.78e−06	2.95e−04	4.54e−03	2.40e−03
S_2	2e−04	1.52e−03	3.49e−02	6.08e−01	4.52e−01
S_3	1e−01	4.39e−05	2.30e−03	1.82e−02	2.03e−02
S_4	4e−05	2.87e−03	1.21e−01	7.48e−01	2.13e−01
S_1^{tot}	9e−01	5.19e−06	2.97e−04	2.24e−03	1.35e−03
S_2^{tot}	2e−04	1.36e−04	3.24e−02	7.83e−01	1.72e−01
S_3^{tot}	1e−01	4.65e−05	2.25e−03	3.08e−02	2.01e−02
S_4^{tot}	5e−05	1.57e−03	1.20e−01	6.10e−01	4.96e−01

consideration give reliable relative errors for sufficiently large number of samples. The most efficient in terms of computational complexity is the SobolACM algorithm. The algorithms using SobolSets are characterized with error of the same order as the Halton sequence for small in value sensitivity measures. From these tables one can see that the SobolSet 2 gives more reliable results.

We study the computational efficiency of the stochastic algorithms under consideration for evaluating sensitivity measures presented by multidimensional integrals (total variance) or a ratio of multidimensional integrals (Sobol global sensitivity indices). Not surprisingly, most influential emissions about ammonia output concentrations are ammonia emissions themselves (about 89% for Milan). The second most influential emissions about ammonia output are sulphur dioxide emissions (about 11%). See [4] for more detailed analysis.

4   Sensitivity Studies with Respect to Chemical Reactions Rates

Another part of our research was to study the sensitivity of the ozone concentration values in the air over Genova with respect to the rate variation of some chemical reactions of the condensed CBM-IV scheme [16], namely: # 1, 3, 7, 22 (time-dependent) and # 27, 28 (time independent). The simplified chemical equations of those reactions are:

[#1]	$NO_2 + h\nu \Longrightarrow NO + O$;	[#22]	$HO_2 + NO \Longrightarrow OH + NO_2$;
[#3]	$O_3 + NO \Longrightarrow NO_2$;	[#27]	$HO_2 + HO_2 \Longrightarrow H_2O_2$;
[#7]	$NO_2 + O_3 \Longrightarrow NO_3$;	[#28]	$OH + CO \Longrightarrow HO_2$.

The domain under consideration is the 6-dimensional hypercube $[0.6, 1.4]^6$. Polynomials of second degree have been used for approximation again (see [3]).

Homma and Saltelli discuss in [8] which is the better estimation of $f_0^2 = \left(\int_{U^d} f(\mathbf{x}) d\mathbf{x} \right)^2$ in the expression for total variance and Sobol global sensitivity measures. The first formula is

$$f_0^2 \approx \frac{1}{n} \sum_{i=1}^{n} f(\mathbf{x}_{i,1}, \ldots, \mathbf{x}_{i,d}) \, f(\mathbf{x}'_{i,1}, \ldots, \mathbf{x}'_{i,d})$$

and the second one is

$$f_0^2 \approx \left\{ \frac{1}{n} \sum_{i=1}^{n} f(\mathbf{x}_{i,1}, \ldots, \mathbf{x}_{i,d}) \right\}^2$$

where $\mathbf{x}$ and $\mathbf{x}'$ are two independent sample vectors. In case of estimating sensitivity indices of a fixed order, the first formula is better (as recommended in [8]).

Table 4. Relative error for the evaluation of $f_0 \approx 0.27$.

# of samples n	SobolACM	Halton	SobolSet1	SobolSet2
	Relative error	Relative error	Relative error	Relative error
2^{10}	1.62e−04	1.60e−04	1.69e−03	5.92e−03
2^{12}	4.54e−05	5.55e−05	5.74e−03	1.75e−03
2^{14}	3.59e−06	2.70e−05	5.74e−04	7.01e−04
2^{16}	4.70e−06	1.60e−06	2.63e−04	1.31e−04
2^{18}	5.90e−07	1.02e−06	3.72e−05	1.43e−05
2^{20}	1.36e−07	5.56e−07	5.20e−06	3.48e−06

Table 5. Relative error for the evaluation of the total variance $\mathbf{D} \approx 0.0025$.

# of samples n	SobolACM	Halton	SobolSet1	SobolSet2
	Relative error	Relative error	Relative error	Relative error
2^{10}	5.75e−03	4.86e−02	8.32e−02	3.89e−02
2^{12}	2.43e−03	1.25e−03	5.35e−02	1.61e−02
2^{14}	9.90e−05	1.65e−03	3.59e−02	1.38e−02
2^{16}	5.81e−05	4.34e−04	9.67e−03	1.38e−03
2^{18}	7.71e−06	3.79e−04	4.18e−04	1.81e−04
2^{20}	1.75e−06	3.34e−05	2.01e−05	1.89e−05

Table 6. Relative error estimation of sensitivity indices for some internal parameters, obtained by using various MC and QMC approaches ($n = 2^{16} = 65536$).

Est. quantity	Ref. value	SobolACM	Halton	SobolSet1	SobolSet2
S_1	4e−01	1.83e−04	2.87e−03	2.75e−02	4.23e−02
S_2	3e−01	2.69e−05	3.76e−03	3.34e−02	1.40e−02
S_3	5e−02	1.08e−04	7.27e−03	3.73e−02	3.35e−02
S_4	3e−01	1.37e−04	2.19e−03	4.74e−02	1.75e−02
S_5	4e−07	2.69e−01	3.68e+01	4.14e+01	1.20e+01
S_6	2e−02	2.81e−03	1.30e−02	1.08e−01	3.59e−02
S_1^{tot}	4e−01	1.39e−04	4.05e−02	2.02e−02	2.03e−02
S_2^{tot}	3e−01	4.32e−05	3.26e−03	3.51e−02	1.86e−02
S_3^{tot}	5e−02	1.08e−04	6.43e−03	6.03e−01	4.38e−01
S_4^{tot}	3e−01	3.77e−04	2.11e−03	4.88e−02	2.19e−02
S_5^{tot}	2e−04	1.40e−03	1.38e−02	1.87e−01	1.87e−01
S_6^{tot}	2e−02	1.29e−05	1.04e−02	8.02e−01	7.62e−01
S_{12}	6e−03	6.03e−04	7.92e−03	1.09e−02	5.36e−02
S_{14}	5e−03	2.17e−03	9.12e−03	4.39e−01	1.90e−01
S_{15}	8e−06	9.33e+02	9.36e+02	9.56e+02	9.56e+02
S_{24}	3e−03	4.97e−04	1.83e−02	8.32e−01	2.48e−01
S_{45}	1e−05	1.48e−02	9.08e−01	3.99e−01	1.52e−01

Table 7. Relative error estimation of sensitivity indices for some internal parameters, obtained by using various MC and QMC approaches ($n = 2^{20} = 1048576$).

Est. quantity	Ref. value	Sobol	Halton	SobolSet1	SobolSet2
S_1	4e−01	5.21e−06	1.65e−04	7.78e−04	2.82e−03
S_2	3e−01	1.14e−06	2.01e−04	1.91e−03	2.33e−03
S_3	5e−02	8.89e−06	4.90e−04	2.19e−04	3.65e−03
S_4	3e−01	9.23e−06	1.06e−04	1.53e−02	3.49e−03
S_5	4e−07	1.28e−01	9.92e−01	6.73e−01	6.98e−01
S_6	2e−02	1.34e−05	3.01e−04	1.23e−03	9.99e−03
S_1^{tot}	4e−01	5.69e−06	1.65e−04	7.66e−04	1.37e−03
S_2^{tot}	3e−01	8.40e−07	1.81e−04	7.61e−03	3.30e−03
S_3^{tot}	5e−02	7.48e−06	4.63e−04	2.75e−03	5.77e−03
S_4^{tot}	3e−01	7.38e−06	9.42e−05	1.79e−04	1.41e−03
S_5^{tot}	2e−04	2.75e−04	2.29e−03	3.64e−02	3.70e−02
S_6^{tot}	2e−02	1.61e−05	4.44e−04	3.86e−03	1.88e−02
S_{12}	6e−03	2.81e−05	8.54e−04	3.40e−02	3.37e−02
S_{14}	5e−03	5.24e−05	1.34e−04	1.71e−02	6.84e−02
S_{15}	8e−06	9.33e+02	9.34e+02	9.34e+02	9.35e+02
S_{24}	3e−03	2.85e−05	1.27e−04	3.68e−02	2.81e−01
S_{45}	1e−05	2.21e−03	6.20e−02	7.59e−01	9.92e−02

The relative error estimation for the quantities f_0, the total variance **D** and some sensitivity indices are given in Tables 4, 5 and 6 respectively. The four different stochastic approaches used for numerical integration are presented in separate columns of these tables. The quantity f_0 is presented by 6-dimensional integral, while the rest are presented by 12-dimensional integrals, following the ideas of *correlated sampling*.

Table 7 is similar to Table 6, with the only difference – the increased number of samples $n = 2^{20}$ (instead of $n = 2^{16}$ in Table 6). In general, this increases the accuracy of the estimated quantities. Exceptions are S_5 and S_{15}, which have extremely small reference values. None of the 4 methods estimates them reliably (in terms of relative error). This natural "size effect" does not destroy the accuracy of the corresponding total sensitivity indices (which are much larger, so the influence of S_5 and S_{15} is negligible).

From these tables we can see that SobolACM gives better results than Halton and the difference is 1–2 orders. The Sobol sets produce better results for 4 and 6-dimensional integrals in comparison with 8 and 12-dimensional integrals. In some cases the results for the Sobol scrambled sequences are better than those for the Halton sequence - see the value for S_{45} in Table 6.

Acknowledgements. The authors would like to thank Rayna Georgieva for her help. The work is supported in parts by the Bulgarian NSF under Projects DN 12/5-2017 "Efficient Stochastic Methods and Algorithms for Large-Scale Problems" and DN 12/4-2017 "Advanced Analytical and Numerical Methods for Nonlinear Differential Equations with Applications in Finance and Environmental Pollution", and the Bilateral Project Bulgaria-Russia DNTS 02/12-2018 "Development and investigation of finite-difference schemes of higher order of accuracy for solving applied problems of fluid and gas mechanics and ecology", by the NSP "Information and Communication Technologies for a Single Digital Market in Science, Education and Security" (ICTinSES), financed by the Ministry of Education and Science.

References

1. Antonov, I., Saleev, V.: An economic method of computing LP_τ-sequences. USSR Comput. Math. Phy. **19**, 252–256 (1979)
2. Bratley, P., Fox, B.: Algorithm 659: implementing Sobol's quasirandom sequence generator. ACM Trans. Math. Softw. **14**(1), 88–100 (1988)
3. Dimov, I., Georgieva, R., Ostromsky, T., Zlatev, Z.: Variance-based sensitivity analysis of the unified Danish Eulerian model according to variations of chemical rates. In: Dimov, I., Faragó, I., Vulkov, L. (eds.) NAA 2012. LNCS, vol. 8236, pp. 247–254. Springer, Heidelberg (2013). https://doi.org/10.1007/978-3-642-41515-9_26
4. Dimov, I.T., Georgieva, R., Ostromsky, T., Zlatev, Z.: Sensitivity studies of pollutant concentrations calculated by UNI-DEM with respect to the input emissions. Central Eur. J. Math. Numer. Methods Large Scale Sci. Comput. **11**(8), 1531–1545 (2013)
5. Fox, B.: Algorithm 647: implementation and relative efficiency of quasirandom sequence generators. ACM Trans. Math. Softw. **12**(4), 362–376 (1986)
6. Halton, J.: On the efficiency of certain quasi-random sequences of points in evaluating multi-dimensional integrals. Numer. Math. **2**, 84–90 (1960)
7. Halton, J., Smith, G.B.: Algorithm 247: radical-inverse quasi-random point sequence. Commun. ACM **7**, 701–702 (1964)
8. Homma, T., Saltelli, A.: Importance measures in global sensitivity analysis of nonlinear models. Reliab. Eng. Syst. Saf. **52**, 1–17 (1996)
9. Hong, H.S., Hickernell, F.J.: ALGORITHM 823: implementing scrambled digital sequences. ACM Trans. Math. Softw. **29**(2), 95–109 (2003)
10. Kocis, L., Whiten, W.J.: Computational investigations of low-discrepancy sequences. ACM Trans. Math. Softw. **23**(2), 266–294 (1997)
11. Matousek, J.: On the L2-discrepancy for anchored boxes. J. Complex. **14**(4), 527–556 (1998)
12. Ostromsky, T., Dimov, I., Georgieva, R., Zlatev, Z.: Parallel computation of sensitivity analysis data for the Danish Eulerian model. In: Lirkov, I., Margenov, S., Waśniewski, J. (eds.) LSSC 2011. LNCS, vol. 7116, pp. 307–315. Springer, Heidelberg (2012). https://doi.org/10.1007/978-3-642-29843-1_35

13. Ostromsky, T., Dimov, I.T., Georgieva, R., Zlatev, Z.: Air pollution modelling, sensitivity analysis and parallel implementation. Int. J. Environ. Pollut. **46**(1/2), 83–96 (2011)
14. Ostromsky, Tz., Dimov, I.T., Marinov, P., Georgieva, R., Zlatev, Z.: Advanced sensitivity analysis of the Danish Eulerian model in parallel and grid environment. In: Proceedings of the 3rd International Conference on AMiTaNS 2011, AIP Conference Proceedings, vol. 1404, pp. 225–232 (2011)
15. Sobol, I.M., Tarantola, S., Gatelli, D., Kucherenko, S., Mauntz, W.: Estimating the approximation error when fixing unessential factors in global sensitivity analysis. Reliab. Eng. Syst. Saf. **92**, 957–960 (2007)
16. Zlatev, Z.: Computer Treatment of Large Air Pollution Models. KLUWER Academic Publishers, Dorsrecht (1995)
17. Zlatev, Z., Dimov, I.T.: Computational and Numerical Challenges in Environmental Modelling. Elsevier, Amsterdam (2006)

Kinetic Monte Carlo Analysis of the Operation and Reliability of Oxide Based RRAMs

Toufik Sadi[1][(✉)], Oves Badami[2], Vihar Georgiev[2], and Asen Asenov[2]

[1] Engineered Nanosystems Group, School of Science, Aalto University,
P.O. Box 12200, 00076 Aalto, Finland
toufik.sadi@aalto.fi
[2] School of Engineering, Electronic and Nanoscale Engineering,
University of Glasgow, Glasgow G12 8LT, Scotland, UK

Abstract. By using a stochastic simulation model based on the kinetic Monte Carlo approach, we study the physics, operation and reliability of resistive random-access memory (RRAM) devices based on oxides, including silicon-rich silica (SiO_x) and hafnium oxide – HfO_x – a widely used transition metal oxide. The interest in RRAM technology has been increasing steadily in the last ten years, as it is widely viewed as the next generation of non-volatile memory devices. The simulation procedure describes self-consistently electronic charge and thermal transport effects in the three-dimensional (3D) space, allowing the study of the dynamics of conductive filaments responsible for switching. We focus on the study of the reliability of these devices, by specifically looking into how oxygen deficiency in the system affects the switching efficiency.

Keywords: Kinetic Monte Carlo · RRAM reliability · Nano-devices · Transport phenomena

1 Introduction

We investigate, by means of a unique numerical simulator, the switching behaviour and reliability of resistive random-access memory (RRAM) devices. Memristors, such as RRAMs, were suggested theoretically almost 50 years ago [1], but their realization remained elusive for decades. After their first experimental demonstration 11 years ago [2], the interest in these devices has been increasing steadily, with a variety of research work being published on the topic [3–7]. Nowadays, RRAMs are widely believed to be the next generation of non-volatile memory devices; e.g. in its 2013 report [8], the 'International Technology Roadmap for Semiconductors' (ITRS) cites a multitude of incentives for developing RRAM technology, such as low cost, low power dissipation, high endurance and three-dimensional (3D) crossbars integration. The potential applications of RRAMs are also numerous, ranging from high-density memories and novel processor architectures to neuromorphic computing and neural networks [9–11].

© Springer Nature Switzerland AG 2020
I. Lirkov and S. Margenov (Eds.): LSSC 2019, LNCS 11958, pp. 429–437, 2020.
https://doi.org/10.1007/978-3-030-41032-2_49

We employ a kinetic Monte Carlo (KMC) simulator to study RRAM structures based on two promising oxide materials: (i) the widely used transition metal oxide (TMO) material – HfO_x – and (ii) the less studied SiO_x. SiO_x has promising potential in nanoelectronics, as it offers Si integration advantages. RRAMs are characterized by a strong memristive behavior, and hence are best simulated using a stochastic 'microscopic' method such as KMC. Also, the full potential of RRAMs can only be fully uncovered when using physical models instead of the widely used empirical approximations [7,12]. The simulation framework describes self-consistently charge transport, via ions and electrons, and thermal effects in the three-dimensional (3D) space using a procedure coupling a KMC model for charge carrier dynamics to self-heating. The KMC solver correctly describes vacancy generation and recombination, but also includes all relevant electron trapping and tunneling mechanisms [13,14]. It allows the study of the dynamics of conductive filaments (CFs), and reconstructs all the resistance switching regimes, including CF electroforming, set and reset processes.

This work explores the details of the stochastic simulation procedure for the analysis of RRAM structures, emphasizing the distinctive peculiarities of the numerical models incorporated within the simulator. We discuss the switching characteristics of the RRAMs, and highlight the need for using 3D electrothermal models to capture accurately device switching. We then show how the loss of oxygen ions from the device contacts can degrade the switching efficiency.

2   State-of-the-Art and Beyond

The memristive behaviour of RRAMs is a direct consequence of the formation and destruction of CFs, i.e. direct electrical conductive paths between the cathode and anode [13,15,16]. Such filaments are created from the generated oxygen ion-vacancy pairs whose dynamics are governed by the local electric field and temperature distributions. Previous work on RRAMs consisted mainly of studying TMO based devices [6,17], which are highly suitable for high-density integration due to their high dielectric constants. TMOs, however, are not easily integrated into Si chips, unlike SiO_x based RRAMs which can potentially lead to cheap Si electronics integration. For this reason, our work also looks into SiO_x devices aiming to unlock their potential in prospective applications. Previous modelling work on RRAMs has relied mostly on phenomenological models, such as the resistor breaker network [7,17], which do not calculate in a self-consistent fashion the local electric fields and temperatures. Most models also rely on 2D approximations [6,12] which can lead to unreliable results [18].

To provide a complete picture of the microscopic behavior of RRAMs based on oxide materials, we developed a unique 3D simulator based on the KMC method for particle transport. The simulator has several features and capabilities distinguishing it from other phenomenological models [6,7,12]. The simulator uses a powerful combination of tools, including KMC particle (ion and electron) transport, Poisson's and heat diffusion equations solvers, as discussed in Sect. 3. It is able to describe electron-ion interactions and reconstruct realistically the CF

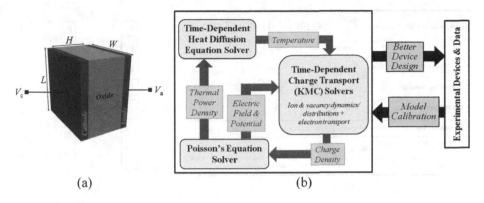

Fig. 1. (a) The studied RRAM, with an oxide thickness $H = 10$ nm located between two contacts with an area $L \times W = 20$ nm $\times$ 20 nm. (b) The simulator, coupling the KMC description of electron and ion transport to the temperature and electric fields.

formation and rupture in the 3D real space. It provides a time-domain description of transport, by coupling self-consistently electron and oxygen ion KMC trajectory simulations to the local electric field and temperature distributions. The dynamic nature of the vacancy generation and electron trapping is considered accurately, as discussed in detail in Refs. [14,16,19]. In general, our work is supported by experimental data [3,20], which are necessary to calibrate the simulator and increase its predictability.

The studied structures are illustrated in Fig. 1(a), consisting of an oxide (SiO_x or HfO_x) layer with a typical thickness $T \sim 10$ nm, sandwiched between two electrodes (a cathode and an anode) made of a titanium nitride (TiN) layer. The experimental devices used to calibrate our simulator have contacts with typical areas as large as $100\,\mu m \times 100\,\mu m$ [3]. However, the simulations can be limited to a much smaller area (e.g. $L \times W = 20$ nm $\times$ 20 nm, as used here), where for example a grain boundary may be present. This is common practice in Monte Carlo modeling, in general, to minimize simulation time while maintaining reasonable accuracy [6,13,16]. This shrinking of the studied domain is also justified by experimental observations, suggesting the existence of only one dominating CF per contacted structure [3]. Figure 1(b) summarizes the main components of the simulator, which are discussed in more detail below.

3 Numerical Simulation Method

Figure 1(b) is a flowchart illustrating the simulation framework. A rigorous simulation procedure is implemented to couple self-consistently time-dependent electron and oxygen ion dynamics to the local temperature and electric field distributions in the simulated oxide volume, as obtained by numerically solving Poisson's and the time-dependent heat diffusion equations using the finite-volume discretisation method [21]. The KMC algorithm is employed to describe ion-vacancy pair

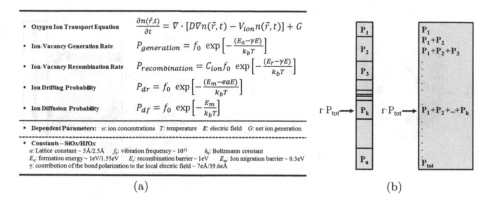

- **Oxygen Ion Transport Equation** $\dfrac{\partial n(\vec{r},t)}{\partial t} = \nabla \cdot [D\nabla n(\vec{r},t) - V_{ion}n(\vec{r},t)] + G$

- **Ion-Vacancy Generation Rate** $P_{generation} = f_0 \ \exp\left[-\dfrac{(E_a - \gamma E)}{k_b T}\right]$

- **Ion-Vacancy Recombination Rate** $P_{recombination} = C_{ion}f_0 \ \exp\left[-\dfrac{(E_r - \gamma E)}{k_b T}\right]$

- **Ion Drifting Probability** $P_{dr} = f_0 \ \exp\left[-\dfrac{(E_m - eaE)}{k_b T}\right]$

- **Ion Diffusion Probability** $P_{df} = f_0 \ \exp\left[-\dfrac{E_m}{k_b T}\right]$

- **Dependent Parameters:** n: ion concentrations T: temperature E: electric field G: net ion generation

- **Constants – SiOx/HfOx**
  a: Lattice constant ~ 5Å/2.5Å f_0: vibration frequency ~ 10^{13} k_b: Boltzmann constant
  E_a: formation energy ~ 1eV/1.55eV E_r: recombination barrier ~ 1eV E_m: Ion migration barrier ~ 0.3eV
  γ: contribution of the bond polarization to the local electric field ~ 7eÅ/39.6eÅ

(a)   (b)

Fig. 2. (a) Ion-vacancy dynamics equations and relevant parameters. (b) The KMC procedure for selecting a process k from n processes with probabilities P_i.

generation and recombination processes, as well as the drifting and diffusion of ions between interstitial sites and vacancies. The KMC simulator directly solves for the ionic transport equation, as shown in Fig. 2(a) along with other important formulas and useful parameters used here. We use the established vacancy generation model for hafnia [6,22] and the refined model for SiO_x RRAM, as detailed in Refs. [13,16]. As is standard in Monte Carlo transport models, the field and temperature distributions are updated regularly as particles (electrons or ions) move, and important physical quantities are re-calculated. These include mainly the ion-vacancy generation rate $P_{generation}$, and the probability of ion-vacancy recombination $P_{recombination}$, as summarized in Fig. 2(a). The generated ions travel through lattice sites (vacancies or interstitials), either by drifting with an average velocity V_{ion} and probability P_{dr}, or diffusing according to the diffusion constant D and probability P_{df} [13].

The general concept of the KMC algorithm is illustrated in Fig. 2(b), and is applied to simulate ion-vacancy generation and recombination events, as well as predicting the movements of the ions. The simulation process starts by building the device geometry, assuming a 3D uniform matrix of oxide molecules or oxygen vacancies at lattice sites, with an average effective lattice constant. As the practice in oxide RRAM modelling [6] is, we use uniform meshing with the mesh size corresponding to the lattice constant. The number of initial vacancies are calculated assuming a typical vacancy concentration (e.g. 2×10^{19} cm^{-3}) with the vacancy x, y and z coordinates being calculated using three corresponding random numbers. Two electrodes limit the structure, from both sides, where the Dirichlet boundary condition is imposed to bias the structure. As ion-vacancy generation events are selected (in time) according to the probability $P_{generation}$ using random numbers, the generated ions move between neighboring lattice points, in the form of vacancies and interstitials, or leave the oxide through an electrode. The trajectory of an ion is also selected using KMC, by constructing cumulative ladders from drifting and diffusion probabilities (P_{dr}

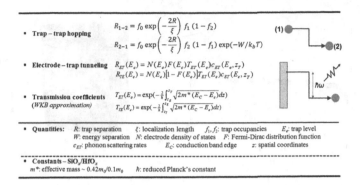

Fig. 3. Trap-assisted electron tunneling equations, the relevant parameters used here, and representations of trap-trap and electrode-trap tunneling mediated by phonons.

and P_{df}), considering all possible neighboring lattice sites and electrodes, and using a random number to choose the ion subsequent destination. Similarly, an ion-vacancy recombination process is selected randomly according to the probability $P_{recombination}$.

All the important processes contributing to electron transport are included in the simulation [13,18], including trap-assisted tunneling (electrode-trap, trap-trap, and trapped electron to the conduction band (CB) tunneling mechanisms), Fowler-Nordheim tunneling, Poole-Frenkel emission, Schottky emission, and direct electron tunneling [14]. Trap-assisted tunneling mechanisms, as summarized in Fig. 3, are the dominant transport effects needing special attention in oxides [13,23,24]. The KMC algorithm is applied to simulate the evolution of the electron population trapped in the available vacancies, providing a more realistic description of trap occupancies compared to other simpler steady-state current solvers [6]. Electron trapping events are modelled according to the rates provided in Fig. 3. The KMC modelling process progresses as follows. For every electron located in the oxide, a cumulative tunneling rate ladder is generated including all possible final destinations (vacancies or electrodes). The final electron position (trapped in a vacancy or leaving through an electrode) is chosen from the ladder using a generated random number. The process of electron injection from the contacts is implemented using the same cumulative ladder approach, with the injected carrier jumping to occupy a vacancy or tunnel through to the conduction band or the other electrode.

4   Results, Analysis and Discussion

The basic characteristics of SiO_x and HfO_x RRAMs have been discussed in our previous work [13,18]. Here, we demonstrate the impact of oxygen ion leakage through the RRAM electrodes on the switching efficiency. First, we run a simulation for a device with an arbitrary initial vacancy distribution for the geometry shown in Fig. 1(a), to generate a CF to be used for our tests. Figure 4 shows the

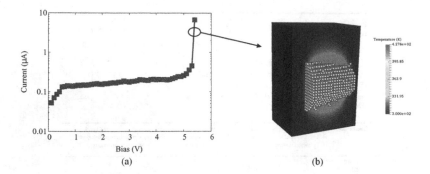

Fig. 4. (a) The $I - V$ characteristics during electroforming. (b) The fully-formed CF (vacancies shown as spheres) and the corresponding temperature distribution, from the cathode (left) to the anode (right). We apply a current compliance limit $\sim 10^{-5}$ A.

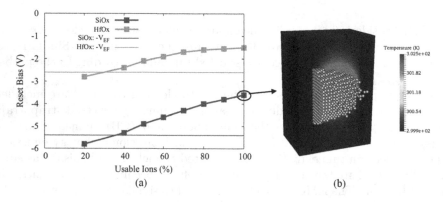

Fig. 5. (a) Reset bias as a function of the ion percentage stored in the anode, for SiO_x and HfO_x RRAMs. (b) The broken CF and the temperature map in SiO_x.

$I - V$ characteristics during electroforming and the corresponding fully-formed CF, for the SiO_x device, as obtained for a bias ramp rate of 0.1 V/ns. As can be seen, CFs form a direct path between the two electrodes, via a continuous chain of traps (conducting centers). The rupture and reconstruction of the filament is responsible for the memristive behaviour of oxide RRAMs [13,18]. It is of note that in real devices, the CFs are of a 3D nature justifying the use of a (computationally costly) 3D model to reflect the full physics of RRAMs. The temperature distribution is superimposed on top of the 3D mapping of the CF in Fig. 4(b) to highlight the importance of thermal effects during filament forming.

Once the reference CF is formed, we apply a current compliance limit of 10^{-5} A, at which the applied bias is progressively reduced to zero. We then study the switching efficiency during the reset process, as bias is reduced further to negative values (RRAM bipolar operation mode), inciting the oxygen ions trapped in the anode to move back to the oxide and recombine with CF vacancies until the CF is ruptured. Figure 5(a) illustrates how the average reset bias [at which the device switches from a high current state (low resistance state – LRS) to a low current state (high resistance state – HRS)] varies as the number of ions is reduced from the nominal number (100%), assuming a bias ramp rate of 0.1 V/0.1 ns. Figure 5(b) shows, for the 100% case, the broken filament after a LRS-to-HRS transition at the reset bias, and the corresponding temperature map showing a negligible temperature increase at the HRS; the CF breaks as ions recombine with vacancies, especially near the anode where most of the ions are stored. Clearly, as the percentage of available oxygen ions is reduced, the reset bias increases in magnitude. This reduces the probability of a proper LRS-to-HRS switching process, as more vacancies may be generated in the device at high (biases) fields, resulting e.g. in the reconstruction of the CF or the creation of parasitic transport channels outside the CF location. For the SiO_x (HfO_x) device for example, below a percentage of 30%, the LRS-to-HRS transition does not occur even at a bias $-V_{EF} = -5.4$ V (-2.6 V), where V_{EF} is the electroforming bias. At reset biases with a magnitude much higher than the forming biases V_{EF}, an acceleration of ion-vacancy generation may occur resulting in the reset process failure, which may also lead to device breakdown unless the device is disconnected. This specific study illustrates, using an atomistic physical view, one of the main challenges facing RRAM technology: the design of reliable oxygen storage or supply systems to increase the device reliability and endurance.

5   Conclusion

We apply a KMC simulation framework to study the switching characteristics and the reliability of oxide RRAM devices based on the mainstream materials SiO_x and HfO_x. We discussed the need for using 3D models accounting self-consistently for self-heating. Most importantly, we presented a specific study demonstrating how oxygen ion leakage from the contacts affects the switching behaviour. The study illustrates one of the main bottlenecks of RRAM technology development, mainly the need for the design of reliable oxygen storage or supply systems to increase the RRAM reliability and endurance. The simulation framework is well-suited for exploring the physics, operation and reliability of RRAM devices, providing a reliable computational tool for the optimization of existing device technologies and the development of new RRAM designs.

Acknowledgment. The authors thank the Engineering and Physical Sciences Research Council (EPSRC–UK) for funding under grant agreement EP/K016776/1.

References

1. Chua, L.: Memristor - the missing circuit element. IEEE Trans. Circuit Theory **18**, 507–519 (1971)
2. Strukov, D.B., Snider, G.S., Stewart, D.R., Williams, R.S.: The missing memristor found. Nature **453**(43), 80–83 (2008)
3. Mehonic, A., et al.: Resistive switching in silicon sub-oxide films. J. Appl. Phys. **111**, 074507 (2012)

4. Chua, L.: Resistance switching memories are memristors. Appl. Phys. A **102**, 765–783 (2011)
5. Yao, J., Zhong, L., Natelson, D., Tour, J.M.: In situ imaging of the conducting filament in a silicon oxide resistive switch. Sci. Rep. **2**, 242 (2012)
6. Yu, S., Guan, X., Wong, H.-S. P.: On the stochastic nature of resistive switching in metal oxide RRAM: physical modeling, Monte Carlo simulation, and experimental characterization. In: 2011 IEEE International Electron Devices Meeting (IEDM), p. 17.3.1, 5–7 December 2011, Washington DC, USA (2011)
7. Chae, S.C., et al.: Random circuit breaker network model for unipolar resistance switching. Adv. Mater. **20**, 1154–1159 (2008)
8. The ITRS Report 2013. http://www.itrs2.net/2013-itrs.html. Accessed 5 June 2018
9. Jo, S.H., Chang, T., Ebong, I., Bhadviya, B.B., Mazumder, P., Lu, W.: Nanoscale memristor device as synapse in neuromorphic systems. Nano Lett. **10**, 1297–1301 (2010)
10. Pershin, Y.V., Di Ventra, M.: Experimental demonstration of associative memory with memristive neural networks. Neural Netw. **23**, 881–886 (2010)
11. Mehonic, A., Kenyon, A.J.: Emulating the electrical activity of the neuron using a silicon oxide RRAM cell. Front. Neurosci. **10**, 1–10 (2016)
12. Kim, S., et al.: Physical electro-thermal model of resistive switching in bi-layered resistance-change memory. Sci. Rep. **3**, 1680 (2013)
13. Sadi, T., Mehonic, A., Montesi, L., Buckwell, M., Kenyon, A., Asenov, A.: Investigation of resistance switching in SiO_x RRAM cells using a 3D multi-scale kinetic Monte Carlo simulator. J. Phys. Condens. Matter **30**(8), 084005 (2018)
14. Jegert, G.C.: Modeling of leakage currents in high-k dielectrics. Ph.D. dissertation, Technical University of Munich, Germany (2011). http://www.iaea.org/inis/collection/NCLCollectionStore/_Public/44/011/44011419.pdf. Accessed 5 June 2018
15. Buckwell, M., Montesi, L., Hudziak, S., Mehonic, A., Kenyon, A.J.: Conductance tomography of conductive filaments in intrinsic silicon-rich silica RRAM. Nanoscale **7**(43), 18030–18035 (2015)
16. Sadi, T., et al.: Advanced physical modeling of SiO_x resistive random access memories. In: International Conference on Simulation of Semiconductor Processes and Devices (SISPAD), 6–8 September 2016, Nuremberg, Germany, pp. 149–152 (2016)
17. Brivio, S., Spiga, S.: Stochastic circuit breaker network model for bipolar resistance switching memories. J. Comput. Electron. **16**(4), 1154–1166 (2017)
18. Sadi, T., Asenov, A.: Microscopic KMC modeling of oxide RRAMs. In: Nikolov, G., Kolkovska, N., Georgiev, K. (eds.) NMA 2018. LNCS, vol. 11189, pp. 290–297. Springer, Cham (2019). https://doi.org/10.1007/978-3-030-10692-8_32
19. Vandelli, L., Padovani, A., Larcher, L., Southwick, R.G., Knowlton, W.B., Bersuker, G.: A physical model of the temperature dependence of the current through SiO_2/HfO_2 stacks. IEEE Trans. Electron Devices **58**, 2878–2887 (2011)
20. Mehonic, A., et al.: Structural changes and conductance thresholds in metal-free intrinsic SiO_x resistive random access memory. J. Appl. Phys. **117**, 124505 (2015)
21. Sadi, T., Thobel, J.-L., Dessenne, F.: Self-consistent electrothermal Monte Carlo simulation of single InAs nanowire channel metal-insulator field-effect transistors. J. Appl. Phys. **108**, 084506 (2010)
22. McPherson, J., Kim, J.-Y., Shanware, A., Mogul, H.: Thermochemical description of dielectric breakdown in high dielectric constant materials. Appl. Phys. Lett. **82**, 2121–2123 (2003)

23. Medina-Bailon, C., et al.: Multisubband ensemble Monte Carlo analysis of tunneling leakage mechanisms in ultrascaled FDSOI, DGSOI, and FinFET devices. IEEE Trans. Electron Devices **66**, 1145–1152 (2019)
24. Medina-Bailon, C., et al.: Impact of the trap attributes on the gate leakage mechanisms in a 2D MS-EMC nanodevice simulator. In: Nikolov, G., Kolkovska, N., Georgiev, K. (eds.) NMA 2018. LNCS, vol. 11189, pp. 273–280. Springer, Cham (2019). https://doi.org/10.1007/978-3-030-10692-8_30

Multi-Subband Ensemble Monte Carlo Simulator for Nanodevices in the End of the Roadmap

Carlos Sampedro[1][✉] , Cristina Medina-Bailon[1,2] , Luca Donetti[1] ,
Jose Luis Padilla[1] , Carlos Navarro[1] , Carlos Marquez[1] ,
and Francisco Gamiz[1]

[1] Nanoelectronics Research Group, Departamento de Electrónica y Tecnología de los
Computadores, Universidad de Granada, 18071 Granada, Spain
csampe@ugr.es
[2] Device Modelling Group, School of Engineering, University of Glasgow,
Glasgow G12 8LT, UK

Abstract. As the scaling of electronic devices approaches to the end of
the roadmap quantum phenomena play an important role not only in the
electrostatics but also in the electron transport. This work presents the
capabilities of a novel implementation of Multi-Subband Ensemble Monte
Carlo simulators (MS-EMC) including transport quantum phenomena.
In particular, an effective computational scheme of tunneling mechanisms
(including S/D tunneling, GLM and BTBT) is shown taking advantage
of the main features of semi-classical transport models which are the
reduction of the computational requirements and a higher flexibility in
comparison to purely full quantum codes.

Keywords: MS-EMC · FDSOI · FinFET · End of the roadmap ·
Tunneling

1   Introduction

As the scaling of electronic devices approaches to the end of the roadmap,
their performance is degraded due to the appearance of the short-channel effects
(SCEs). Classically, the loss of gate terminal control over the channel and the
increase of the influence of source and drain regions have been the reasons of
the degradation of threshold voltage and the subthreshold characteristics [27]. In
this way, device architecture optimizations and material development efforts are
mainly focused on the reduction of SCEs. To accomplish such extreme scaling

This work has been supported in part by the European Community's Seventh Framework Programme Marie Curie Action (Programme Andalucía Talent Hub) under Grant
291780, in part by the Horizon 2020 projects REMINDER under Grant 687931 and
WAYTOGO-FAST under Grant 662175, and in part by the Spanish Ministry of Economy, Industry and Competitivity under Grant TEC2017-89800-R.

I. Lirkov and S. Margenov (Eds.): LSSC 2019, LNCS 11958, pp. 438–445, 2020.
https://doi.org/10.1007/978-3-030-41032-2_50

and obtain circuits with a reduced impact of variability [18], two are the main proposed solutions based on standard silicon CMOS process: the use of multiple gate devices (MuGFETs) and the extension of planar technology by means of SOI. The first option features an outstanding SCEs control being the most promising candidate to further extend the end of the roadmap [2,10]. The second scaling path extends planar technology taking advantage of the benefits provided by Ultra Thin Fully Depleted SOI devices (UTBSOI) with a good SCEs control and a simpler fabrication process compared to 3D devices. This fact allows a reduction in the overall cost and an almost straightforward layout transfer from original bulk designs to SOI [9]. This technology also provides extra options thanks to the possibility of taking advantage of ultrathin buried oxide, and back plane in order to enhance SCE immunity or to implement non conventional devices like 1T-DRAM cells. However, at such small dimensions quantum phenomena play an important role in the behavior of the transistors not only in the electrostatics due to confinement but also in the transport. In particular, direct Source-to-Drain tunneling (S/D tunneling) through the narrow potential barrier, gate leakage mechanisms (GLM) in ultrathin insulators and band-to-band tunneling (BTBT) at high drain bias conditions and for TFET applications have to be taken in to account. Within this framework, where manufacturing costs grow exponentially as device dimensions are aggressively scaled down, advance device simulators are powerful tools that can elucidate, from an *a priori* device optimization strategy, the optimal configuration for future technologies reducing the design cost.

In this work, a novel implementation of a Multi-Subband Ensemble Monte Carlo simulator (MS-EMC) is proposed to include the aforementioned quantum phenomena that limit the scaling at the end of the roadmap. In particular, an effective computational scheme of tunneling mechanisms (including S/D tunneling, GLM and BTBT) is shown for a better understanding of the physical limitations and required optimizations of future devices in terms of: geometry, channel orientation, doping profiles, and mobility boosters. Taking advantage of the main features of semi-classical transport models which are the reduction of the computational requirements and a higher flexibility in comparison to purely full quantum codes.

2 Simulation Approach: The Multi-Subband Method

To face the challenge of simulating nanodevices in the end of the roadmap, different methods are available ranging from classical to full quantum approaches. As aforementioned, confinement determines the electrostatic in these structures being necessary to include quantum models in the simulation framework. Full quantum simulators based on numerical solutions of the Schrödinger equation or the Non-Equilibrium Green's Functions theory (NEGF) are then, of especial interest in this case [24]. In a quantum model, the transport of charged particles is treated coherently according to a quantum wave equation. However, the introduction of scattering is very demanding from a computational point of view.

440   C. Sampedro et al.

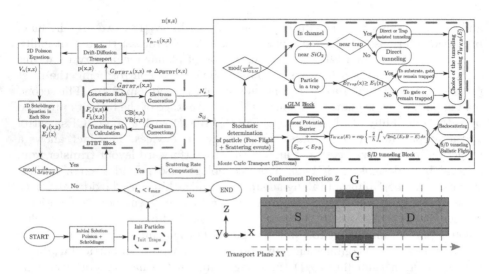

Fig. 1. Flowchart of the MS-EMC presented in this work including Tunneling mechanisms. Bottom-right, schematic representation of the simulation domain for a DGSOI device.

Ensemble Monte Carlo (EMC) simulators present several advantages compared to full quantum approximations, especially for the straightforward implementation of scattering mechanisms and the reduced computational cost. In order to include quantum confinement the easiest solution is to add a correction term to the electrostatic potential. The objective of this strategy is to mimic the carrier profile [1,5,23]. The main drawback of this solution is the need of performing a calibration process since the models include a set of fitting parameters.

A more accurate approach is obtained from the coupling of the Monte Carlo solution of the Boltzmann Transport equation and the 1D solution of the Schrödinger equation. From the simulation point of view, our transistor is considered as a stack of slices perpendicular to the confinement direction z (Fig. 1 bottom-right). This method, the Multi-Subband Ensemble Monte Carlo (MS-EMC) [7,19–21], is based on the mode-space approach of quantum transport [26]. The electrostatics of the system is calculated from the self-consistent solution of the 2D Poisson's equation in the xz plane and the 1D Schrödinger equation solved for each slice and conduction band valley. As a result, the evolution along the transport direction, x, for the i-th valley and the ν-th subband of the eigen-energies, $E_{i,\nu}(x)$, and the wave functions, $\xi_{i,\nu}(x,z)$ are obtained. The Boltzmann Transport equation (BTE) is solved in the xy plane using the EMC method and to evaluate the transport properties along the Source/Drain axis [21]. Non-parabolic conduction band approximation is included in both confinement [7] and transport approaches. According to the mode-space approach, the driving field undergone by a simulated super-particle belonging to a subband is calculated from the derivative of $E_{i,\nu}(x)$, as a consequence, the driving force is different for each of the subbands, in opposition to standard EMC simulators where the band-edge is used to obtain the driving field. The subband population is obtained from a re-sampling of the super-particles using the cloud-in-cell method. This population is used to weight the corresponding distribution function $|\xi_{i,\nu}(x,z)|^2$ to calculate the electron density, $n(x,z)$. Finally, the electrostatic potential is updated by solving the 2D Poisson equation using the previous $n(x,z)$ as input. This approach is especially appropriate for the study of 1D confinement in nanoscale devices. The full flowchart of the proposed implementation is shown in Fig. 1. The increase in the computational cost of this implementation is partially overcome thanks to an efficient parallel implementation. Concerning scattering models, acoustic and intervalley phonons are included [7] whereas surface roughness scattering is described in [6] and Coulomb interaction in [8]. In order to catch the local particularities of the wavefunctions, a different scattering rate table is calculated for each slice i.

2.1 MS-EMC Capabilities

In order to extend Moore's Law, geometrical scaling is not enough to fulfill the requirements demanded by the industry. Therefore, it is necessary to implement technology boosters to increase the general performance of next generation devices. Such phenomena must be included in the simulation frame to keep predictive capabilities. In particular, arbitrary confinement and transport directions are needed for technology optimization [21], statistical enhancement techniques extend MS-EMC application to low power-subthreshold operations [22], source and drain doping engineering allow a better control of SCEs [3], arbitrary strain profiles are needed for the optimization of future architectures [12] and interface traps have an important impact into the general device performance [17]. Finally, the transition from diffusive to ballistic transport has to be characterized in order to understand the physics behind electron transport in ultra-scaled devices [11].

2.2 Tunneling Models

The main limitation of the MS-EMC method is the impossibility of including quantum transport phenomena in a direct way due to the particle description of the mobile carriers. However, it is possible to include tunneling mechanisms as separate blocks in the MS-EMC scheme obtaining very good results with a small increase in the computational cost as will be shown in the following section. This implementation gives a higher flexibility, since the different mechanisms can be activated or deactivated at will, allowing studies concerning the impact of each of them separately which is not always possible to perform in other implementations. S/D Tunnel, GLM, and BTBT are the three selected mechanisms. As it can be observed in Fig. 1, S/D Tunnel and GLM are inside the MC block whereas BTBT is embedded in the Poisson, drift-diffusion loop. This means that the probability of a S/D Tunnel or a GLM event is evaluated for each superparticle at the end of a flight. In both cases WKB approach is considered considering a ballistic flight inside the barrier for S/D Tunneling and direct and trap assisted tunneling in the case of GLM. A thorough description of each implementation can be found in [16] and [14] respectively. Concerning BTBT, after the solution of Poisson equation which uses as inputs the electron concentration from the MC block and the holes concentration from a drift-diffusion solution, The number of electron-hole pairs generated is determined from Kane's model including corrections arising from bound states. An in-depth description of the implementation can be found in [15].

3   Validation and Scaling Results

To validate the MS-EMC simulator for ultrashort devices, different comparisons were performed in three different ways. In a first approach a set of experimental data has been compared to our simulations. For a fair comparison it is necessary an in depth knowledge of the technological parameters. A detailed enough description of UTBSOI devices is presented in [4] where a SGSOI with $T_{Si} = 8\,nm$ and $L_G = 33\,nm$ is characterized. I_D-V_{GS} curves for $V_{DS} = 1.1\,V$ (solid) and $100\,mV$ (dashed) are shown in Fig. 2 left. Our simulations (symbols) show a good agreement with experimental data (lines) in both subthreshold and conduction regimes using the same set of scattering parameters for all the calculations. Once the code was compared to available experimental results, the next step was to go further into the scaling and to compare a double gate structure with a different solver of the BTE, in particular a deterministic one. A thorough study of this comparison can be found in [25]. Simulation results show an excellent agreement with the two implementations with a great advantage in terms of computational cost of the MS-EMC code. Finally, the above described tunneling mechanisms were compared to quantum codes as a way to established the MS-EMC capabilities in ultimated scaled devices. In particular, a comparison

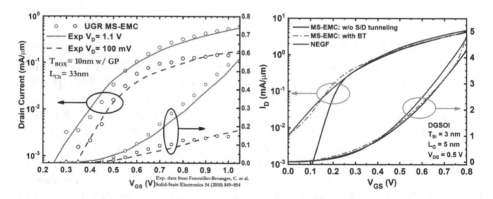

Fig. 2. Left. MS-EMC comparison with experimental results obtained from [4] for a UTBSOI device. Right. MS-EMC simulation of quasiballistic transport in a DGSOI device compared to NEGF calculations. Notice the impact of S/D tunneling in the subthreshold region of operation.

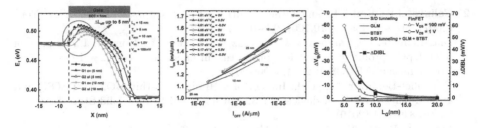

Fig. 3. Left. Impact of doping profile variation on device electrostatics. Center. I_{ON}/I_{OFF} ratio for different gate lengths and metal work-function and back bias combinations for UTBSOI devices. Right. V_{TH} and DIBL variation as a function of the gate length in FinFETs considering different tunnel mechanisms.

with NEGF simulators is shown in [13] for ultrashort DGSOI devices where S/D tunneling is switched on and off to determine the impact on transport behavior in the quasiballistic regime. As shown in Fig. 2 right, it is not possible to reproduce the degradation appearing in the subthreshold regime as a consequence of direct S/D tunneling (dashed line). These three examples demonstrate the capabilities of the MS-EMC simulator under very different geometries and transport conditions.

As mentioned above, this MS-EMC code has been extensively used for the study of scaled device for future technology nodes. Figure 3 left shows the variation in the subband profile for a UTBSOI device considering different types of doping profiles including abrupt, with gate overlap and gate underlap. It can be observed how the effective channel length can varies up to 5 nm depending on the doping profile, which implies important variations in device characteristics. In Fig. 3 center, I_{ON} *vs.* I_{OFF} plots are presented for UTBSOI devices considering different metal work-functions and back bias conditions. Finally, in Fig. 3 right the threshold voltage and DIBL variations are plotted as a function of the gate length considering different drain bias conditions and tunnel mechanisms. From the simulations it can be inferred that S/D tunneling dominates the observed degradation in the characteristics for devices shorter than 7.5 nm.

4   Conclusions

This work presents a review of the different capabilities and implemented models in the MS-EMC simulator developed at the University of Granada. The simulation frame presents a high flexibility to study different technological choices including tunnel mechanisms for the optimization of ultra-scaled nanodevices in the end of the roadmap.

References

1. Asenov, A., Brown, A.R., Watling, J.R.: Quantum corrections in the simulation of decanano MOSFETs. Solid State Electron. **47**(7), 1141–1145 (2003)

444   C. Sampedro et al.

2. Colinge, J.P.: FinFETs and Other Multi-Gate Transistors. Springer, New York (2007). https://doi.org/10.1007/978-0-387-71752-4
3. Diaz-Llorente, C., Sampedro, C., Gamiz, F., Godoy, A., Donetti, L.: Impact of S/D doping profile into electrical properties in nanoscaled UTB2SOI devices. In: Proceedings of EUROSOI 2014, O06 (2014)
4. Fenouillet-Beranger, C., et al.: Impact of a 10 nm ultra-thin BOX (UTBOX) and ground plane on FDSOI devices for 32 nm node and below. Solid-State Electron. **54**(9), 849–854 (2010)
5. Ferry, D., Ramey, S., Shifren, L., Akis, R.: The effective potential in device modeling: the good, the bad and the ugly. J. Comput. Electron. **1**, 59–65 (2002)
6. Fischetti, M.V., Gamiz, F., Hänsch, W.: On the enhanced electron mobility in strained-silicon inversion layers. J. Appl. Phys. **92**(7320), 7320–7324 (2002). https://doi.org/10.1063/1.1521796
7. Fischetti, M.V., Laux, S.: Monte Carlo study of electron transport in silicon inversion layers. Phys. Rev. B **48**(4), 2244–2274 (1993)
8. Jiménez-Molinos, F., Gamiz, F., Donetti, L.: Coulomb scattering in high-κ gate stack silicon-on-insulator metal-oxide-semiconductor field effect transistors. J. Appl. Phys. **104**(6), 063704 (2008). https://doi.org/10.1063/1.2975993
9. Khakifirooz, A., et al.: Fully depleted extremely thin SOI for mainstream 20 nm low-power technology and beyond. In: 2010 IEEE International on Solid-State Circuits Conference Digest of Technical Papers (ISSCC), pp. 152–153, February 2010
10. Kuhn, K., Liu, M., Kennel, H.: Technology options for 22 nm and beyond. In: 2010 International Workshop on Junction Technology (IWJT), pp. 1–6, May 2010
11. Mangla, A., Sallese, J.M., Sampedro, C., Gamiz, F., Enz, C.: Modeling the channel charge and potential in quasi-ballistic nanoscale double-gate MOSFETs. IEEE Trans. Electron Devices **61**(8), 2640–2646 (2014)
12. Medina-Bailon, C., Sampedro, C., Gamiz, F., Godoy, A., Donetti, L.: Impact of non uniform strain configuration on transport properties for FD14+ devices. Solid-State Electron. **115**, 232–236 (2016)
13. Medina-Bailon, C., et al.: MS-EMC vs. NEGF: a comparative study accounting for transport quantum corrections. In: 2018 Joint International EUROSOI Workshop and International Conference on Ultimate Integration on Silicon (EUROSOI-ULIS), pp. 1–4. IEEE, March 2018. https://doi.org/10.1109/ulis.2018.8354758
14. Medina-Bailon, C., et al.: Multi-subband ensemble Monte Carlo study of tunneling leakage mechanisms. In: 2017 International Conference on Simulation of Semiconductor Processes and Devices (SISPAD), pp. 281–284. IEEE, September 2017. https://doi.org/10.23919/sispad.2017.8085319
15. Medina-Bailon, C., Padilla, J.L., Sampedro, C., Alper, C., Gamiz, F., Ionescu, A.M.: Implementation of band-to-band tunneling phenomena in a multisubband ensemble Monte Carlo simulator: application to silicon TFETs. IEEE Trans. Electron Devices **64**(8), 3084–3091 (2017). https://doi.org/10.1109/ted.2017.2715403
16. Medina-Bailon, C., Padilla, J.L., Sampedro, C., Godoy, A., Donetti, L., Gamiz, F.: Source-to-drain tunneling analysis in FDSOI, DGSOI, and FinFET devices by means of multisubband ensemble Monte Carlo. IEEE Trans. Electron Devices **65**(11), 4740–4746 (2018). https://doi.org/10.1109/ted.2018.2867721
17. Medina-Bailon, C., et al.: Impact of the trap attributes on the gate leakage mechanisms in a 2D MS-EMC nanodevice simulator. In: Nikolov, G., Kolkovska, N., Georgiev, K. (eds.) NMA 2018. LNCS, vol. 11189, pp. 273–280. Springer, Cham (2019). https://doi.org/10.1007/978-3-030-10692-8_30

18. Millar, C., Reid, D., Roy, G., Roy, S., Asenov, A.: Accurate statistical description of random dopant-induced threshold voltage variability. IEEE Electron Device Lett. **29**(8), 946–948 (2008)
19. Riolino, I., et al.: Monte-Carlo simulation of decananometric double-gate SOI devices: multi-subband vs. 3D-electron gas with quantum corrections. In: Proceedings of the 36th European Solid-State Device Research Conference, ESSDERC 2006, Montreux (2006)
20. Saint-Martin, J., Bournel, A., Monsef, F., Chassat, C., Dollfus, P.: Multi sub-band Monte Carlo simulation of an ultra-thin double gate MOSFET with 2D electron gas. Semicond. Sci. Tech. **21**(4), 29–31 (2006)
21. Sampedro, C., Gámiz, F., Godoy, A., Valín, R., García-Loureiro, A., Ruiz, F.: Multi-subband Monte Carlo study of device orientation effects in ultra-short channel DGSOI. Solid-State Electron. **54**(2), 131–136 (2010)
22. Sampedro, C., Gamiz, F., Godoy, A., Valin, R., Garcia-Loureiro, A.: Improving subthreshold MSB-EMC simulations by dynamic particle weighting. In: 2013 International Conference on Simulation of Semiconductor Processes and Devices (SISPAD), pp. 276–279. IEEE, September 2013. https://doi.org/10.1109/sispad.2013.6650628
23. Sampedro-Matarin, C., Gamiz, F.J., Godoy, A., Garcia-Ruiz, F.: The multivalley effective conduction band-edge method for Monte Carlo simulation of nanoscale structures. IEEE Trans. Electron Devices **53**(11), 2703–2710 (2006)
24. Tsuchiya, H., Svizhenko, A., Anatram, M.P., Ogawa, M., Miyoshi, T.: Comparison of non-equilibrium Green's function and quantum-corrected Monte Carlo approaches in nano-MOS simulation. J. Comput. Electron. **4**, 35–38 (2005)
25. Vecil, F., Mantas, J.M., Caceres, M.J., Sampedro, C., Godoy, A., Gamiz, F.: A parallel deterministic solver for the Schrödinger-Poisson-Boltzmann system in ultra-short DG-MOSFETs: comparison with Monte-Carlo. Comput. Math. Appl. **67**(9), 1703–1721 (2014). https://doi.org/10.1016/j.camwa.2014.02.021
26. Venugopal, R., Ren, Z., Datta, S., Lundstrom, M.S., Jovanovic, D.: Simulating quantum transport in nanoscale transistors: real versus mode-space approaches. J. Appl. Phys. **92**(7), 3730–3739 (2002). https://doi.org/10.1063/1.1503165
27. Wong, H.S.P.: Beyond the conventional transistor. IBM J. Res. Dev. **46**(2.3), 133–168 (2002). https://doi.org/10.1147/rd.462.0133

A Monte Carlo Evaluation of the Current and Low Frequency Current Noise at Spin-Dependent Hopping

Viktor Sverdlov[1(✉)] and Siegfried Selberherr[2]

[1] Christian Doppler Laboratory for Nonvolatile Magnetoresistive Memory and Logic, Institute for Microelectronics, TU Wien, Gußhausstraße 27-29, 1040 Vienna, Austria
sverdlov@iue.tuwien.ac.at
[2] Institute for Microelectronics, TU Wien, Gußhausstraße 27-29, 1040 Vienna, Austria
selberherr@iue.tuwien.ac.at

Abstract. Monte Carlo methods are convenient to model the electron transport due to single electron hopping. The algorithm allows to incorporate a restriction that due to the Coulomb repulsion each trap can only be occupied by a single electron. With electron spin gaining increasing attention, the trap-assisted electron transport has to be generalized to include the electron spin, especially in the presence of an external magnetic field and with transport between ferromagnetic contacts. An innovative Monte Carlo method to deal with the spin-dependent hopping is presented. When the electron spin is taken into account, the escape transition rates are described by transition matrices which describe the coupled spin and occupation relaxation from the trap. The transport process is represented by a cyclic repetition of consecutive electron hops from the source to a trap and from the trap to the drain. The rates do not depend on the previous hops nor on time. The method allows to evaluate the electron current as well as the low frequency current noise at spin-dependent hopping. Our Monte Carlo approach resolves a controversy between theoretical results found in literature.

1 Introduction

An elementary particle, the electron, plays the most important role in improving the human life. The property of the electron charge to interact with the electric field is exploited in every electric device from energy generation to microelectronics. As the transistor is currently approaching its smallest ultimate limits, another electron intrinsic characteristic, the electron spin, attracts increasing attention as a supplementary degree of freedom to be used in upcoming nanoelectronic devices. Spin-dependent transport properties play increasingly important role in applications. Recently, an extremely large magnetic response on light emission caused by spin-charge correlated transport was observed at room temperature [1]. Resonant spin-dependent tunneling plays an important role in

© Springer Nature Switzerland AG 2020
I. Lirkov and S. Margenov (Eds.): LSSC 2019, LNCS 11958, pp. 446–453, 2020.
https://doi.org/10.1007/978-3-030-41032-2_51

defining the large resistance modulation with magnetic fields observed in three-terminal spin accumulation experiments [2]. However, the expressions for the magnetoresistance dependencies obtained in [2] were challenged [3]. To resolve the controversy, we developed a numerical Monte Carlo approach for the trap-assisted spin tunneling in tunnel junctions.

2   Method

To develop the Monte Carlo approach for spin-dependent trap-assisted transport, we at first briefly outline the algorithm for spin-independent hopping. Single electron hopping between the trap levels is the main transport mechanism in non-degenerate semiconductors. In the case of spin-independent hopping the master equation for the trap occupations is conveniently solved by a Monte Carlo method. The transition rate of hopping between two given sites defines the frequency of an electron to travel between the two sites. Importantly, before the transition the initial site must be occupied by an electron while the final site is empty. The fact that the final site must be empty for a successful transition is the manifestation that each site can only be occupied by a single electron. The single occupation is a consequence of the Coulomb blockade, when the strong on-site Coulomb repulsion prevents two charged electrons to occupy the same site. Knowing the transition rate Γ between the two sites, the *random* time t distribution of an electron hop is determined by the exponential probability $P(t) = \exp(-\Gamma t)$. Using a random number r uniformly distributed between zero and one, the random time t is conveniently found [4] as

$$t = \frac{-\ln(r)}{\Gamma}. \tag{1}$$

Given the transition rates between the traps, the rate of an electron to escape from a certain trap i is the sum $\sum_j \Gamma_{ij}$ of the rates Γ_{ij} to all the traps j which are empty [5]. The transport process is then conveniently modeled as follows. For given sites' occupations the sum of all possible transition rates $\Gamma = \sum_{ij} \Gamma_{ij}$ is computed. The sum of all rates Γ is substituted into (1) to determine the transition time for an electron to perform a hop. Which particular transition ij happens is determined by the probability

$$P_{ij} = \frac{\Gamma_{ij}}{\Gamma}. \tag{2}$$

The approach described above also can treat contacts. The source contact is modeled as a site which always supplies an electron for hopping, while the drain contact is modeled as a site where an electron can always escape. In order to do so it is sufficient to lift the restriction of single occupancy of the drain site.

In the case of single electron hopping through a trap between the metal source and ferromagnetic drain, the escape rates from the trap depend on the spin orientation of the electron on the trap relative to the drain magnetization direction. When a voltage between the electrodes is applied, current flows, and an average spin at the trap appears. This spin influences the trap occupation $n(t)$ and the current. The average spin $\mathbf{s}(t)$ at the trap is determined by the drain magnetization orientation. It is built up slowly as a result of many electron hops from the trap to the drain. It then appears that both probabilities of an electron, to hop from the source to the trap and to escape from the trap to the drain, depend on the history of the previous hops. This violates the picture of the spin-independent charge transfer as a series of consecutive *independent* hops from the source to the trap and further to the drain each described by a time-independent transition rate and inhibits using traditional Monte Carlo techniques to evaluate the current.

The master equation for the spin density matrix at the trap can be derived from the stochastic Liouville equation [6]. In the basis with the quantization axis chosen along the magnetization direction (Fig. 1) in the ferromagnetic contact the corresponding equations for the trap occupation $n(t)$ and the spin $\mathbf{s}(t)$ are [7]:

$$\frac{dn(t)}{dt} = \Gamma_N(1 - n(t)) - \Gamma_F n(t) - \Gamma_F \mathbf{p}\mathbf{s}(t) \tag{3}$$

$$\frac{d\mathbf{s}(t)}{dt} = -\Gamma_F \mathbf{s}(t) - \Gamma_F \mathbf{p} n(t) + [\mathbf{s}(t) \times \omega_{\mathbf{L}}] \tag{4}$$

Here Γ_N is the tunneling rate from the metal source to the trap and $\Gamma_F = (\Gamma_+ + \Gamma_-)/2$ is the average tunneling rate from the trap to the ferromagnetic drain with a polarization $p \leq 1$. Electrons with spins parallel/antiparallel to the drain polarization vector $\mathbf{p}$ tunnel with the rates $\Gamma_\pm = \Gamma_F(1 \pm |\mathbf{p}|)$, correspondingly. Although the particular expressions for the transition rates depend on the microscopic transport mechanism, the use of the transition rates as parameters of the problem allows to describe both the resonant tunneling [2] and the single-electron hopping [8] on equal footing. The Larmor frequency vector $\omega_{\mathbf{L}} = e\mathbf{B}/(mc)$ direction is defined by the magnetic field $\mathbf{B}$ which forms an angle

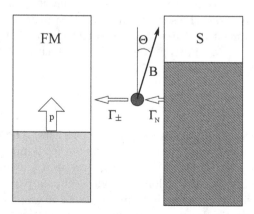

Fig. 1. An electron tunnels with the rate Γ_N on the trap and $\Gamma_\pm$ to the ferromagnet. A magnetic field $\mathbf{B}$ forms the angle Θ with the ferromagnetic drain polarization $\mathbf{p}$.

Θ with $\mathbf{p}$ (Fig. 1). Equation (3) determining $n(t)$ contains the influx contribution and the escape term. The influx term from the normal source does not depend on the spin and can be treated in a way similar to the spin-independent hopping. Namely, the random time distribution to jump from the normal source on the empty trap is determined by the exponential distribution (1) with the transition rate Γ_N.

The escape rate depends also on the spin $\mathbf{s}(t)$. In order to find the escape rate we assume that the probability $P_{out}(t)$ to escape from the occupied trap is equal to

$$P_{out}(t) = 1 - n(t), \tag{5}$$

where the probability $n(t)$ of the trap to be occupied at the time t is determined by

$$\begin{pmatrix} \frac{dn(t)}{dt} \\ \frac{ds_x(t)}{dt} \\ \frac{ds_y(t)}{dt} \\ \frac{ds_z(t)}{dt} \end{pmatrix} = - \begin{pmatrix} \Gamma_F & p\Gamma_F \sin(\Theta) & 0 & p\Gamma_F \cos(\Theta) \\ p\Gamma_F \sin(\Theta) & \Gamma_F & \omega_L & 0 \\ 0 & -\omega_L & \Gamma_F & 0 \\ p\Gamma_F \cos(\Theta) & 0 & 0 & \Gamma_F \end{pmatrix} \cdot \begin{pmatrix} n(t) \\ s_x(t) \\ s_y(t) \\ s_z(t) \end{pmatrix}. \tag{6}$$

This is the first important assumption.

Equation (6) must be complemented with an initial condition. Since electrons are tunneling on the trap from a non-magnetic source, they have an equal probability to have their spin projection up or down on any axis, so their initial spin before tunneling to the drain is zero. This is the second non-trivial assumption which contradicts the intuition that an average spin at the trap depends on the drain magnetization polarization and thus must be finite. We now demonstrate that the results obtained with this assumption are correct.

The transport process is represented as a cyclic repetition of the two tunneling processes from the source to the trap and from the trap to the drain. The first process is described by a random time defined with the help of Eq. (1) with the replacement of Γ by Γ_N. The second tunneling process from the trap to the drain is described by the tunneling time found with the help of Eqs. (5) and (6). Therefore, Eq. (6) is applicable, if the trap is occupied by an electron. Equation (6) is then solved with the initial conditions

$$n(t = 0) = 1; \mathbf{s}(t = 0) = 0. \tag{7}$$

3   Results

The numerical solution for $n(t)$ is shown in Fig. 2. In contrast to tunneling to a normal electrode, the dependence is more complex as it is not determined by an exponential dependence with a single rate. By generating a random number r uniformly distributed between zero and one, the random tunneling time t_F is found by solving $n(t_F) = r$. The current I is evaluated with respect to N transport cycles as

$$I = e \frac{N}{\sum_{i=1}^{N}(t_N + t_F)}. \tag{8}$$

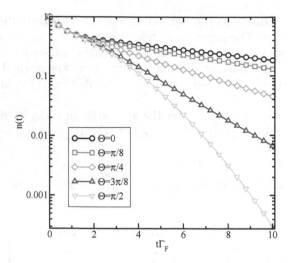

Fig. 2. Probability of trap occupancy. $p = 0.9$, $\omega_L = \Gamma_F$.

The results of the current I are compared with the current computed as a stationary solution of (3, 4) [2] (solid lines) in Fig. 3. The perfect agreement between the results proves that the Monte Carlo algorithm suggested to treat the spin-dependent tunneling is correct. Figure 4 demonstrates the comparison of the current Eq. (8) with the results obtained in [3]. The reason for the discrepancy is clarified in Fig. 5 where the dependence of the occupation $n(t)$ defining the

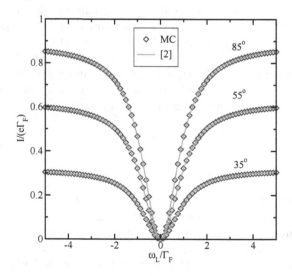

Fig. 3. Comparison of the current I computed as the stationary solution [2] (solid lines) and by the suggested Monte Carlo method using Eq. (8) (symbols). $p = 1$, $\Gamma_N = 8\Gamma_F$.

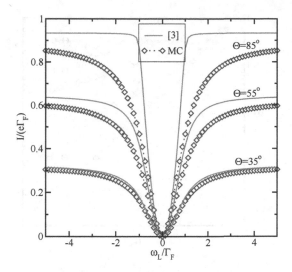

Fig. 4. The current I computed with Eq. (8) is compared with the results from [3], for several angles Θ. A large discrepancy is observed if the magnetic field **B** is not parallel to **p**. $p = 1$, $\Gamma_N = 8\Gamma_F$.

escape probability and the escape tunneling time computed with the method from [3] (solid lines) are compared with $n(t)$ evaluated from Eq. (6). Therefore, the assumption that the tunneling rates from the trap are determined by the two Zeeman spin levels adopted in [3] is valid only, if the magnetic field **B** is parallel to the ferromagnetic drain polarization **p**. In a general case of an arbitrary orientation between **B** and **p** the tunneling rates must be evaluated from the more general expression Eq. (6) which contains a 4×4 relaxation matrix. Shorter tunneling times obtained by considering only two Zeeman levels result in the larger current observed in Fig. 4.

At spin-independent single-electron tunneling the charge is transferred by instantaneous electron hops between the electrodes and the traps separated by long waiting times. The discreteness of the charge transfer is conveniently described by current fluctuations. The low frequency current noise is called the shot noise. To quantitatively characterize the charge transfer discreteness, the ratio of the spectral density of the current fluctuations to the current, or the Fano factor F [5] is introduced. If the transport is due to consecutive single electron hops between the two contacts, the charge transfer resembles shots of single electrons. The charge transfer is due to discrete electrons, and the Fano factor equals to one. If the charge transfer between the electrodes is due to trap-assisted hopping via a single trap, the charge transfer is performed in two steps, the transport is less discrete, and the Fano factor is less than one [5].

The Fano factor for the case of spin-dependent trap-assisted hopping between the normal metal source and the ferromagnetic drain is shown in Fig. 6. The results indicate that, in contrast to the spin-independent hopping, the shot noise

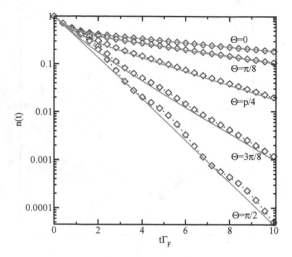

Fig. 5. Time dependence of $n(t)$ evaluated by using the two escape rates from the Zeeman levels to the drain [3] (solid lines) and as a result of numerical solution of Eq. (6) (symbols). $p = 0.9$, $\omega_L = 2\Gamma_F$.

is enhanced above one at small magnetic fields. The maximal value of the Fano factor equals three. It implies that the electrons are transferred in bunches of three electrons in average separated by longer waiting times. A Fano factor larger than one is characteristic for spin-dependent trap-assisted hopping.

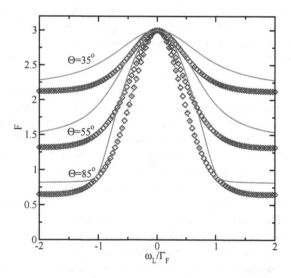

Fig. 6. Fano factor F at spin-dependent trap-assisted tunneling evaluated by using the escape rates from the two Zeeman levels [3] (solid lines) and by the suggested Monte-Carlo method (symbols). $p = 1$, $\Gamma_N = 8\Gamma_F$.

4   Summary and Conclusion

A Monte Carlo method describing spin-dependent trap-assisted hopping is developed. Peculiarities of the current and the shot noise at spin-dependent trap-assisted hopping are investigated. It is shown that the escape probability from a trap to a ferromagnetic electrode is determined by a 4×4 matrix. In contrast to spin-independent hopping, the Fano factor characterizing the charge transfer discreteness can be larger than one. This implies that due to the spin correlations the electrons are transferred in bunches separated by longer waiting times. The results are important for evaluating the role of oxide defects in magnetic tunnel junctions used in modern nonvolatile magnetoresistive random access memory.

Acknowledgements. The financial support by the Austrian Federal Ministry for Digital and Economic Affairs and the National Foundation for Research, Technology and Development is gratefully acknowledged.

References

1. Wang, Y., Sahin-Tiras, K., Harmon, N.J., Wohlgenannt, M., Flatt, M.E.: Immense magnetic response of exciplex light emission due to correlated spin-charge dynamics. Phys. Rev. X **6**, 011011 (2016)
2. Song, Y., Dery, H.: Magnetic-field-modulated resonant tunneling in ferromagnetic-insulator-nonmagnetic junctions. Phys. Rev. Lett. **113**, 047205 (2014)
3. Yue, Z., Prestgard, M.C., Tiwari, A., Raikh, M.E.: Resonant magnetotunneling between normal and ferromagnetic electrodes in relation to the three-terminal spin transport. Phys. Rev. B **91**, 195316 (2015)
4. Wasshuber, C., Kosina, H., Selberherr, S.: SIMON - a simulator for single-electron tunnel devices and circuits. IEEE Trans. Comput. Aided Des. Integr. Circuits Syst. **16**, 937–944 (1997)
5. Korotkov, A.N., Likharev, K.K.: Shot noise suppression at one-dimensional hopping. Phys. Rev. B **61**, 15975–15987 (2000)
6. Halbekorn, R.: Density matrix description of spin-selective radical pair reactions. Molecular Phys. **32**, 1491–1493 (1976)
7. Sverdlov, V., Weinbub, J., Selberherr, S.: Spin-dependent trap-assisted tunneling in magnetic tunnel junctions: a Monte Carlo study. In: Abstract Book International Workshop on Computational Nanotechnology, pp. 88–90 (2017)
8. Sverdlov, V.A., Korotkov, A.N., Likharev, K.K.: Shot noise suppression at two-dimensional hopping. Phys. Rev. B **63**, 081302(R)1–4 (2001)

Efficient Stochastic Approaches for Multidimensional Integrals in Bayesian Statistics

Venelin Todorov[1,2(✉)] and Ivan Dimov[2]

[1] Department of Information Modeling, Institute of Mathematics and Informatics, Bulgarian Academy of Sciences,
Acad. Georgi Bonchev Street, Block 8, 1113 Sofia, Bulgaria
venelin@parallel.bas.bg, vtodorov@math.bas.bg
[2] Department of Parallel Algorithms, Institute of Information and Communication Technologies, Bulgarian Academy of Sciences,
Acad. G. Bonchev Street, Block 25 A, 1113 Sofia, Bulgaria
ivdimov@bas.bg

Abstract. A fundamental problem in Bayesian statistics is the accurate evaluation of multidimensional integrals. A comprehensive experimental study of quasi-Monte Carlo algorithms based on Sobol sequence combined with Matousek linear scrambling and a comparison with adaptive Monte Carlo approach and a lattice rule based on generalized Fibonacci numbers has been presented. The numerical tests show that the stochastic algorithms under consideration are efficient for multidimensional integration and especially for computing high dimensional integrals. It is a crucial element since this may be important to be estimated in order to achieve a more accurate and reliable interpretation of the results in Bayesian statistics which is foundational in applications such as machine learning.

Keywords: Monte Carlo and quasi-Monte Carlo algorithms · Multidimensional integrals · Bayesian statistics · Machine learning

1 Introduction

Stochastic techniques have been developed over many years in a range of different fields, but have only recently been applied to the problems in Bayesian statistics [12]. As well as providing a consistent framework for statistical pattern recognition, the stochastic approach offers a number of practical advantages including a solution to the problem for higher dimensions [11]. Multidimensional integrals arise in algebraic analysis for nonidentifiable learning machines [19]. The accurate evaluation of marginal likelihood integrals is a difficult fundamental problem in Bayesian inference that has important applications in machine learning [17]. Conventional approaches to network training are based on the minimization of

© Springer Nature Switzerland AG 2020
I. Lirkov and S. Margenov (Eds.): LSSC 2019, LNCS 11958, pp. 454–462, 2020.
https://doi.org/10.1007/978-3-030-41032-2_52

an error function, and are often motivated by some underlying principle such as maximum likelihood [3].

The Monte Carlo method is known to be only accurate with a tremendous amount of scenarios since its rate of convergence is $O(1/\sqrt{N})$ [5]. In the last few years new approaches have been developed that outperform standard Monte Carlo in terms of numerical efficiency. It has been found that there can be efficiency gains in using deterministic sequences rather than the random sequences which are a feature of standard Monte Carlo [4]. These deterministic sequences are carefully selected so that they are well dispersed throughout the region of integration. Sequences with this property are known as low discrepancy sequences. Quasi-Monte Carlo methods use deterministic sequences that have better uniform properties measured by discrepancy. They are usually superior to the Monte Carlo method as they have a convergence rate of $O((\log N)^s/N)$, where N is the number of samples and s is the dimensionality of the problem.

2   Formulation of the Problem

A fundamental problem in neural networks is the accurate evaluation of multi-dimensional integrals. We will primarily be interested in two kinds of integrals. The first has the form

$$\int_\Omega p_1^{u_1}(x) \dots p_s^{u_s}(x) dx, \tag{1}$$

where $\Omega \subseteq \mathcal{R}^s$, $x = (x_1, \dots, x_s)$, $p_i(x)$ are polynomials and u_i are integers. The second kind of integrals has the form

$$\int_\Omega e^{-Nf(x)}\phi(x)dx, \tag{2}$$

where $f(x)$ and $\phi(x)$ are s-dimensional polynomials and N is a natural number. These integrals are investigated by Lin in [11,12]. The asymptotics of such integrals is well understood for regular statistical models, but little was known for singular models until a breakthrough in 2001 due to Watanabe [19]. His insight was to put the model in a suitable standard form by employing the technique of resolution of singularities from algebraic geometry. To apply the Monte Carlo method we will map the domain Ω into the s dimensional hypercube $[0,1]^s$. There is always such a transformation, for example $2/\pi \arctan(x)$ maps $(0, \infty)$ to $(0, 1)$.

Consider the problem of approximate integration of the multiple integral

$$\int_{[0,1)^s} f(\mathbf{x})d\mathbf{x} = \int_0^1 dx^{(1)} \int_0^1 dx^{(2)} \dots \int_0^1 dx^{(s)} f(x^{(1)}, x^{(2)}, \dots, x^{(s)}) = \theta \tag{3}$$

where $x = (x^{(1)}, \dots, x^{(s)}) \in [0, 1)^s$ and $|\theta| < 1$. Since the variance is finite, the function f must be square-integrable in $[0, 1)^s$.

For small values of s, numerical integration methods such as Simpson's rule or the trapezoidal rule can be used to approximate the integral. These methods, however, suffer from the so-called curse of dimensionality and become impractical as s increases beyond 3 or 4. One viable technique for larger values of s is to use sampling methods such that the estimator of θ becomes $\hat{\theta} = \frac{1}{N} \sum_{n=0}^{N-1} f(x_n)$ where $P_N = \{x_0, x_1, \ldots, x_{N-1}\} \in [0,1)^s$ is some point set. Different techniques are available for selecting these point sets.

When the integration nodes P_N are N independently and identically distributed random points in $[0,1)^s$, the above sampling method becomes the standard Monte Carlo integration method and the resulting estimator $\hat{\theta}^{MC} \equiv \theta^{MC}$ is known as the Monte Carlo estimator. Important properties of $\hat{\theta}^{MC}$ are as follows:

- It is an unbiased estimator of θ with variance σ^2/N; i.e.

$$\mathbb{E}[\hat{\theta}^{MC}] = \theta \text{ and } Var[\hat{\theta}^{MC}] = \sigma^2/N$$

- The Strong Law of Large Numbers asserts that $\hat{\theta}^{MC}$ converges to θ almost surely.
- The Central Limit Theorem guarantees that the distribution of $\hat{\theta}$ converges asymptotically to a normal distribution with mean θ and variance σ^2/N as $N \to \infty$. In other words, the error $|\theta - \hat{\theta}^{MC}|$ converges probabilistically at a rate of $O(N^{-1/2})$.
- The rate of convergence $O(N^{-1/2})$ is independent of s.

3   Description of the Stochastic Methods

3.1   Scrambled Sobol Sequence

Much of the efforts to improve Monte Carlo methods are in construction of variance reduction methods which speed up the computation or to use quasirandom sequences. A quasirandom or low discrepancy sequence, such as the Faure, Halton, Hammersley, Niederreiter, or Sobol sequences, is "less random" than a pseudorandom number sequence, but more useful for such tasks as approximation of integrals in higher dimensions, and in global optimization. This is because low discrepancy sequences tend to sample space "more uniformly" than random numbers. The Sobol sequence [1] is the most widely deployed low-discrepancy sequence, and is used for calculating multi-dimensional integrals. For example, Paskov uses a quasi-Monte Carlo sequence - the Sobol sequence - to find the present value of securities which involves up to 360-dimensional integrals [15]. Owen first proposed the idea of scrambling this sequence in a manner that maintained its low discrepancy [14]. One of his motivations was to use these scrambled sequences to provide quasi-Monte Carlo methods with simple error estimates like those in normal Monte Carlo. In fact, it is now common for the Sobol sequence as well as (t, m, s)-nets and (t, s)-sequences to be used with scrambling. However, many have pointed out that scrambling is often difficult to implement and time consuming [2]. Implementing scrambled digital sequences is discussed in [9]. We use a random linear scramble combined with a random digital shift, described by Matousek in [13]. Generally this scrambling improves the results produced by the Sobol sequence.

3.2   Adaptive Algorithm

The adaptive algorithm [7] has higher accuracy and faster convergence than the plain Monte Carlo integration as can be seen from the tables below. The only drawback is the higher computational time. The algorithm is described below [6].

Algorithm

1. **Input data:** *number of points N, constant ε (estimation for the variance), constant δ (stop criterion; estimation for the length of subintervals on every coordinate).*
2. **For** $j = 1$, M^s:
   - **2.1. Calculate** *the approximation of I_{Ω_j} and the variance D_{Ω_j} in subdomain Ω_j based on N independent realizations of random variable θ_N;*
   - **2.2. If** $(D_{\Omega_j} \geq \varepsilon)$ **then**
     - **2.2.1. Choose** *the axis direction on which the partition will perform,*
     - **2.2.2. Divide** *the current domain into two (G_{j_1}, G_{j_2}) along the chosen direction,*
     - **2.2.3. If** *the length of obtained subinterval is less than δ* **then go to** *step 2.2.1* **else** $j = j_1$ (G_{j_1} *is the current domain) and* **go to step** *2.1;*
   - **2.3. Else if** $(D_{\Omega_j} < \varepsilon)$ *but an approximation of $I_{G_{j_2}}$ has not been calculated yet,* **then** $j = j_2$ (G_{j_2} *is the current domain along the corresponding direction) and* **go to step** *2.1;*
   - **2.4. Else if** $(D_{\Omega_j} < \varepsilon)$ *but there are subdomains along the other axis directions,* **then go to** *step 2.1;*
   - **2.5. Else** *Accumulation in the approximation I_N of I.*

3.3   Lattice Rules

Let n be an integer, $n \geq 2$ and $a = (a_1, a_2, \ldots a_s)$ be an integer vector modulo n. A set of the form [18]

$$P_n = \left\{ \left\{ \frac{ak}{n} \right\} = \left(\left\{ \frac{a_1 k}{n} \right\}, \ldots, \left\{ \frac{a_s k}{n} \right\} \right) \mid k = 1, \ldots, n \right\} \tag{4}$$

is called a lattice point set, where $\{x\}$ denotes the fractional part of x. The vector a is called a lattice point or generator of the set. This article restricts itself to sets of the form (4), which are also called node sets of rank-1 lattices [16]. The earlier development of these lattices is covered in detail in the monograph of Hua and Wang [8]. As one can see, the formula for the lattice point set is simple to program. The difficulty lies in finding a good value of a, such that the points in the set are evenly spread over the unit cube. The choice of good generating vector, which leads to small errors, is not trivial. Complicated methods from theory of numbers are widely used, for example Zaremba's index or error of the worst function. Korabov [10] consider the following vectors: $g = (1, a, a^2, \ldots, a^{s-1}) \bmod N, 1 \leq a \leq N - 1, gcd(a, N) = 1$.

This method can be applied only for number of points $n_l = F_l^{(s)}$, i.e., only for generalized Fibonacci number of points. This set used the generating vector [18]

$a = (1, F_{l+1}^{(s)}, ..., F_{l+s-1}^{(s)}))$, $n_l = F_l^{(s)}$, where $F^{(s)}$ is the corresponding generalized Fibonacci number of dimensionality s: $F_{l+s}^{(s)} = F_l^{(s)} + F_{l+1}^{(s)} + ... + F_{l+s-1}^{(s)}, l = 0, 1, ...$ with initial conditions: $F_0^{(s)} = F_1^{(s)} = ... = F_{s-2}^{(s)} = 0, F_{s-1}^{(s)} = 1$, for $l = 0, 1, ... $.

4 Numerical Examples

We considered three different examples of 4,7,10 and 30-dimensional integrals, respectively, for which we have computed their reference values.

Example 1. s = 4.

$$\int_{[0,1]^4} x_1 x_2^2 e^{x_1 x_2} \sin(x_3) \cos(x_4) \approx 0.108975. \tag{5}$$

Example 2. s = 7.

$$\int_{[0,1]^7} e^{1 - \sum_{i=1}^{3} \sin(\frac{\pi}{2}.x_i)} \times arcsin \left(\sin(1) + \frac{\sum_{j=1}^{7} x_j}{200} \right) \approx 0.7515. \tag{6}$$

Example 3. s = 10.

$$\int_{[0,1]^{10}} \frac{4x_1 x_3^2 e^{2x_1 x_3}}{(1 + x_2 + x_4)^2} e^{x_5 + \cdots + x_{10}} \approx 14.808435. \tag{7}$$

Example 4. s= 30.

$$\int_{[0,1]^{30}} \frac{4x_1 x_3^2 e^{2x_1 x_3}}{(1 + x_2 + x_4)^2} e^{x_5 + \cdots + x_{20}} x_{21} \ldots x_{30} \approx 3.244. \tag{8}$$

The results are given in the tables below. We make a comparison between plain Monte Carlo (CRUDE), Adaptive Monte Carlo approach (ADAPT), Fibonacci lattice sets (FIBO), Sobol sequence (SOBOL) and Matousek scrambling for Sobol sequence (SCRAMBLE). Each table contains information about the stochastic approach which is applied, the obtained relative error (RE), the needed CP-time in seconds and the number of points. Note that when the FIBO method is tested, the number of sampled points are always generalized Fibonacci numbers of the corresponding dimensionality.

Table 1. Algorithm comparison of the rel.errors for the 4-dimensional integral.

# of points	Crude	t,s	Adapt	t,s	Fibo	t,s	Sobol	t,s	Scramble	t,s
1490	5.25e−3	0.002	2.08e−4	0.07	1.01e−3	0.004	9.46e−4	0.43	3.78e−3	0.47
10671	1.83e−3	0.01	2.98e−4	1.09	8.59e−5	0.02	5.28e−4	1.4	6.10e−4	1.59
20569	6.59e−4	0.02	2.44e−4	1.74	3.89e−5	0.03	3.52e−5	4.32	1.97e−5	4.54
39648	1.04e−3	0.06	8.26e−5	4.58	3.01e−5	0.07	2.68e−5	7.77	9.67e−6	8.26
147312	3.78e−3	0.15	7.03e−5	11.98	3.71e−6	0.24	2.29e−6	23.7	1.40e−6	27.91

Table 2. Algorithm comparison of the rel.errors for the 7-dimensional integral.

# of points	Crude	t,s	Adapt	t,s	Fibo	t,s	Sobol	t,s	Scramble	t,s
2000	6.39e−3	0.14	4.44e−4	1.62	2.81e−3	0.23	5.45e−3	1.04	2.51e−3	1.42
7936	8.51e−3	0.64	8.04e−4	6.90	1.38e−3	0.87	1.28e−3	2.08	1.16e−3	3.08
15808	2.58e−3	0.95	1.98e−4	11.26	9.19e−4	1.73	9.65e−4	3.26	7.58e−4	5.89
62725	2.55e−3	2.54	2.38e−4	29.27	2.78e−5	3.41	5.18e−4	12.3	3.11e−4	15.64
124946	2.22e−3	6.48	1.47e−4	76.46	6.87e−5	6.90	1.09e−4	25.4	8.22e−5	31.41

Table 3. Algorithm comparison of the rel.errors for the 10-dimensional integral.

# of points	Crude	t,s	Adapt	t,s	Fibo	t,s	Sobol	t,s	Scramble	t,s
1597	2.38e−2	0.002	2.43e−3	1.18	4.39e−3	0.003	6.31e−3	0.02	1.46e−3	0.05
17711	1.61e−2	0.02	8.27e−4	1.07	1.81e−3	0.04	5.31e−4	0.11	1.83e−4	0.21
121393	8.84e−3	0.15	4.42e−4	9.45	1.20e−3	0.16	1.78e−4	1.21	3.12e−5	1.47
832040	3.74e−3	0.75	5.48e−5	77.21	1.19e−5	0.70	3.24e−5	12.1	8.25e−6	14.41
3524578	5.12e−3	6.35	8.33e−6	256.37	2.63e−6	6.45	4.57e−6	121.5	7.71e−7	139.1

Numerical results show essential advantage for the lattice sets algorithm based on Fibonacci generalized numbers (in 2–4 orders) and Sobol scramble sequence in comparison with Crude algorithm and Adaptive algorithm for the lower dimensional cases. The results for relative errors corresponding to FIBO and Sobol are similar especially for higher sample number (see Tables 1, 2 and 3). If the computational time is fixed the advantage of Fibonacci lattice sets in terms of relative error in comparison with Adaptive Monte Carlo and Crude Monte Carlo is clearly seen (see Figs. 1, 2 and 3). For 30 dimensional integral the scramble sequence outperforms the FIBO method and Sobol sequence by at least 2 orders - see Table 4. The experiments show that the Matousek linear scrambling for Sobol sequence is the best method in terms of lower relative errors with increasing the dimensionality of the integral.

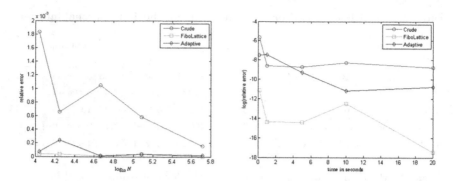

Fig. 1. Comparison of the RE for the 4-dimensional integral with different stochastic methods.

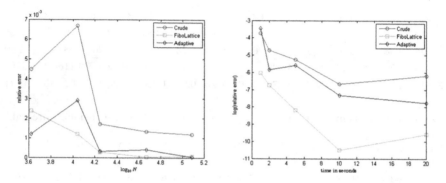

Fig. 2. Comparison of the RE for the 7-dimensional integral with different stochastic methods.

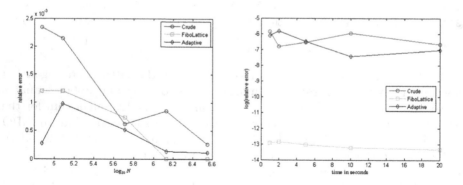

Fig. 3. Comparison of the RE for the 10-dimensional integral with different stochastic methods.

Table 4. Algorithm comparison of the rel.errors for the 30-dimensional integral.

# of points	Scramble	t,s	Sobol	t,s	Fibo	t,s
1024	5.78e−2	0.53	1.18e−1	0.42	8.81e−1	0.02
16384	1.53e−2	5.69	8.40e−2	4.5	6.19e−1	0.14
131072	1.35e−3	42.1	1.18e−2	30.2	2.78e−1	1.16
1048576	6.78e−4	243.9	9.20e−3	168	9.86e−2	8.61

5   Conclusion

In this paper we compare the performance of different quasi-Monte Carlo and Monte Carlo algorithms for multidimensional integrals connected with Bayesian statistics used in machine learning. A comprehensive experimental study of Crude Monte Carlo, Adaptive Monte Carlo algorithm, Fibonacci lattice sets, Sobol sequence and Matousek scrambling for Sobol sequence has been done. All algorithms under consideration are efficient for evaluation the problem under consideration. These approaches are the only possible algorithms for high dimensional integrals because the deterministic algorithms need a very large amount of time for the evaluation of the integral. Adaptive algorithm is a useful Monte Carlo technique which needs very small number of points and its strength shows when the integrand is not smooth. This study shows that quasi-Monte Carlo algorithms outperform the Monte Carlo methods for smooth functions. The Matousek scrambling for Sobol sequence gives better results compared to the Sobol sequence with increasing dimensionality of the multiple integral. Clearly, the progress in the area of artificial neural networks and machine learning is closely related to the progress in reliable algorithms for multidimensional integration.

Acknowledgement. The first author Venelin Todorov is supported by the Bulgarian National Science Fund under Projects DN 12/5-2017 "Efficient Stochastic Methods and Algorithms for Large-Scale Problems", DN 12/4-2017 "Advanced Analytical and Numerical Methods for Nonlinear Differential Equations with Applications in Finance and Environmental Pollution" and KP-06-M32/2-17.12.2019 "Advanced Stochastic and Deterministic Approaches for Large-Scale Problems of Computational Mathematics" and by the National Scientific Program "Information and Communication Technologies for a Single Digital Market in Science, Education and Security" (ICTinSES), contract No. D01–205/23.11.2018, financed by the Ministry of Education and Science.

References

1. Antonov, I., Saleev, V.: An economic method of computing LP tau-sequences. USSR Comput. Math. Math. Phys. **19**, 252–256 (1980)
2. Atanassov, E.I.: A new efficient algorithm for generating the scrambled Sobol' sequence. In: Dimov, I., Lirkov, I., Margenov, S., Zlatev, Z. (eds.) NMA 2002. LNCS, vol. 2542, pp. 83–90. Springer, Heidelberg (2003). https://doi.org/10.1007/3-540-36487-0_8

3. Bendavid, J.: Efficient Monte Carlo integration using boosted decision trees and generative deep neural networks. arXiv preprint arXiv:1707.00028 (2017)
4. Boyle, P., Lai, Y., Tan, K.: Using lattice rules to value low-dimensional derivative contracts (2001)
5. Dimov, I.: Monte Carlo Methods for Applied Scientists, 291 p. World Scientific, Singapore (2008)
6. Dimov, I., Georgieva, R.: Monte Carlo algorithms for evaluating Sobol' sensitivity indices. Math. Comput. Simul. **81**(3), 506–514 (2010)
7. Dimov, I., Karaivanova, A.: Error analysis of an adaptive Monte Carlo method for numerical integration. Math. Comput. Simul. **47**, 201–213 (1998)
8. Hua, L.K., Wang, Y.: Applications of Number Theory to Numerical analysis. Springer, Heidelberg (1981)
9. Hong, H.S., Hickernell, F.J.: ALGORITHM 823: implementing scrambled digital sequences. ACM Trans. Math. Softw. **29**(2), 95–109 (2003)
10. Korobov, N.M.: Number-Theoretical Methods in Approximate Analysis. Fizmatgiz, Moscow (1963)
11. Lin, S.: Algebraic methods for evaluating integrals in Bayesian statistics. Ph.D. dissertation, UC Berkeley, May 2011
12. Lin, S., Sturmfels, B., Xu, Z.: Marginal likelihood integrals for mixtures of independence models. J. Mach. Learn. Res. **10**, 1611–1631 (2009)
13. Matousek, J.: On the L2-discrepancy for anchored boxes. J. Complex. **14**(4), 527–556 (1998)
14. Owen, A.: Variance and discrepancy with alternative scramblings. ACM Trans. Comput. Logic **13**, 1–16 (2002)
15. Paskov, S.: Computing high dimensional integrals with applications to finance. Columbia University (1994, preprint)
16. Sloan, I.H., Kachoyan, P.J.: Lattice methods for multiple integration: theory, error analysis and examples. SIAM J. Numer. Anal. **24**, 116–128 (1987)
17. Song, J., Zhao, S., Ermon, S.: A-NICE-MC: adversarial training for MCMC. In: Advances in Neural Information Processing Systems, pp. 5140–5150 (2017)
18. Wang, Y., Hickernell, F.J.: An historical overview of lattice point sets. In: Fang, K.T., Niederreiter, H., Hickernell, F.J. (eds.) Monte Carlo and Quasi-Monte Carlo Methods 2000. Springer, Heidelberg (2002). https://doi.org/10.1007/978-3-642-56046-0_10
19. Watanabe, S.: Algebraic analysis for nonidentifiable learning machines. Neural Comput. **13**, 899–933 (2001)

Parallel Multilevel Monte Carlo Algorithms for Elliptic PDEs with Random Coefficients

Petr Zakharov[1]([✉])[iD], Oleg Iliev[2,4][iD], Jan Mohring[2][iD], and Nikolay Shegunov[3]

[1] North-Eastern Federal University, Yakutsk, Russia
`zapetch@gmail.com`
[2] Fraunhofer ITWM, Kaiserslautern, Germany
`{iliev,mohring}@itwm.fraunhofer.de`
[3] Sofia University, Sofia, Bulgaria
`nshegunov@fmi.uni-sofia.bg`
[4] Institute of Mathematics and Informatics,
Bulgarian Academy of Science, Sofia, Bulgaria

Abstract. In this work, we developed and investigated Monte Carlo algorithms for elliptic PDEs with random coefficients. We considered groundwater flow as a model problem, where a permeability field represents random coefficients. The computational complexity is the main challenge in uncertainty quantification methods. The computation contains generating of a random coefficient and solving of partial differential equations. The permeability field was generated using the circulant embedding method. Multilevel Monte Carlo (MLMC) simulation can be based on different approximations of partial differential equations. We developed three MLMC algorithms based on finite volume, finite volume with renormalization and renormalization approximation. We compared numerical simulations and parallel performance of MLMC algorithms for 2D and 3D problems.

Keywords: Monte Carlo method · Stochastic PDE · Renormalization

1 Introduction

In mathematical modeling, there are a lot of uncertain parameters which can not be defined exactly. Uncertain parameters can highly impact on the results of simulations. In groundwater flow simulations it is not possible or requires too many efforts to define the permeability field in the whole simulation domain. Groundwater flow is described by Darcy's Law [25], which contains hydraulic conductivity (permeability). Usually, soil permeability measurement is given by values in very sparse space points, and for the rest of domain, permeability is uncertain. To handle with this there are uncertainty quantification methods and one of is Monte Carlo method.

To use the Monte Carlo method it is necessary to consider a large number of different permeability realizations. To generate geostatistically relevant random

© Springer Nature Switzerland AG 2020
I. Lirkov and S. Margenov (Eds.): LSSC 2019, LNCS 11958, pp. 463–472, 2020.
https://doi.org/10.1007/978-3-030-41032-2_53

permeability there are different approaches [6,7]. In Monte Carlo simulations the computational complexity contains permeability generating and solving of a partial differential equation. The computational cost is the main challenge in uncertainty quantification methods.

Multilevel Monte Carlo (MLMC) method recomended as faster method than standard Monte Carlo [2,13,14]. Groundwater flow MLCM simulation can be based on different spatial approximations: finite element [1,3], mixed finite method [5], multiscale finite element [20], finite volume [4,18]. In this work we used finite volume method for PDE problem approximation and also used simplified renormalization method [19] for a total flux approximation.

In this paper, we considered only one type of quantity of interest: the expectation of a total flux through the domain. We developed three MLMC algorithms based on finite volume, finite volume with renormalization and renormalization approximation. In the first section we gave a description of the dimensionless model problem. In Sect. 2 we described random permeability properties and used generation method. In the next two sections, finite volume approximation and the renormalization method are described. In Sect. 3 we gave a short description of the Multilevel Monte Carlo method. In Sect. 3.2 we described the parallel algorithm of MLMC. And in Sect. 3.3 we defined three MLMC algorithms with a different approximation of total flux. In the last two sections, we showed numerical simulations and compared MLMC algorithms for 2D and 3D problem respectively.

2   Model Problem and Discretization

2.1   Model Problem

We consider model problem in a unit cube domain $x = (x_1, \ldots, x_d) \in D = [0,1]^d$ with the boundary $\Gamma = \partial D$. Let denote the left boundary of the domain by $\Gamma_l = \{x \in \Gamma : x_1 = 0\}$ and the right boundary by $\Gamma_r = \{x \in \Gamma : x_1 = 1\}$. Stationary single phase flow in porous media is described by Darcy's law and incompressible condition [5,25] and is combined to equation

$$- \nabla (k \nabla p) = 0, \quad x \in D, \tag{1}$$

where $k = k(x, \omega)$ is the random scalar permeability, which is defined by random vector ω. On the left and right boundary we fix pressure and on other boundary use no flux condition

$$p = 1, \quad x \in \Gamma_l, \quad p = 0, \quad x \in \Gamma_r, \quad \frac{\partial p}{\partial n} = 0, \quad x \in \Gamma \setminus (\Gamma_l \cup \Gamma_r). \tag{2}$$

A typical quantity of interest in subsurface flow with random permeability is a total flux through the domain. But in the more general case, it can be any functional of pressure and random permeability. We restrict ourselves just to considering the total flux

$$Q(\omega) = - \int_{\Gamma_l} k \frac{\partial p}{\partial n} \, ds, \tag{3}$$

The total flux also can be considered as an effective permeability of a whole domain, i.e. $k_e = Q$.

2.2 Random Field

Random field should describe the real soil permeability but relatively simple to numerically solve the problem. We use extensively studied random permeability with a lognormal distribution, i.e. $K(\boldsymbol{x}, \boldsymbol{\omega}) = \log k(\boldsymbol{x}, \boldsymbol{\omega})$ is the logarithm of the permeability. We assume that its expected value and spatial covariance are shift invariant

$$E\left[K(\boldsymbol{x}, \cdot)\right] = 0, \quad E\left[K(\boldsymbol{x}, \cdot)K(\boldsymbol{y}, \cdot)\right] = C(\boldsymbol{x}, \boldsymbol{y}) = C(\boldsymbol{y}, \boldsymbol{x}), \quad \boldsymbol{x}, \boldsymbol{y} \in D. \quad (4)$$

In this work we use the following practically relevant two-point covariance function [17]

$$C(\boldsymbol{x}, \boldsymbol{y}) = \sigma^2 \exp\left(\frac{-\|\boldsymbol{x} - \boldsymbol{y}\|_2}{\lambda}\right), \quad \boldsymbol{x}, \boldsymbol{y} \in D, \quad (5)$$

where σ^2 is the variance, λ is the correlation length. Typical values in subsurface flow applications are $1 \leq \sigma \leq 2.5$ and $0.05 \leq \lambda \leq 0.3$.

In the literature, there are available several approaches to generate random permeability, i.e. circulant embedding [8,15,16], Karhunen-Loève expansion [4, 12]. In this work, we use the circulant embedding method, which is based on Fourier transformation over a circulant covariance matrix, more information can be found in the paper [20]. Circulant embedding generation is implemented using FFTW library [11].

2.3 Finite Volume Method

Each realization of random permeability $k(\boldsymbol{x}, \boldsymbol{\omega})$ we numerically solve single phase flow problem. To construct discrete problem we use finite volume method on uniform cell-centered grid with $M = m^d$ cells. We describe discretization on $d = 3$, for $d = 2$ it is simpler and similar. To approximate permeability on the cell edge we use harmonic average (for simplicity of notation we skip subindex if it is not changed)

$$\overline{k}_{i_j + \frac{1}{2}} = 2(k_{i_j}^{-1} + k_{i_j+1}^{-1})^{-1}.$$

After integration equation (1) over cell we obtain standard seven-point schemes and apply it for each cell in the grid

$$-\sum_{j=1}^{d}\left(k_{i_j+\frac{1}{2}}\left(p_{i_j+1} - p_{i_j}\right) - k_{i_j-\frac{1}{2}}\left(p_{i_j} - p_{i_j-1}\right)\right) = 0, \quad i_1, i_2, i_3 = 1, \ldots, m.$$

Zero-valued Neumann boundary condition is accounted in the scheme by default. To describe Dirichlet boundaries we replace harmonic average $\overline{k}$ by value in the cell k and use an one-sided difference instead of the central difference.

2.4 Simplified Renormalization

Renormalization is the recursive algorithm for calculating effective coefficient, more details about this method can be found in the following papers [21,24]. In this work, we use a simplified version of renormalization [19], which assumes only horizontal flow direction.

The main idea of simplified renormalization is using harmonic average μ_h with respect to flow direction and arithmetic average μ_a with respect to perpendicular of flow direction. After calculating of two variants of combination arithmetic and harmonic average order, it is applied geometric mean μ_g. Let consider domain with 2^d cells and coefficients $k_i, i = 1, \ldots, 2^d$. Simplified renormalization have the following form for 2D and 3D respectively

$$k_r = \mu_g \left(\mu_a(\mu_h(k_1, k_2), \mu_h(k_3, k_4)), \ \mu_h(\mu_a(k_1, k_3), \mu_a(k_2, k_4)) \right),$$
$$k_r = \mu_g \left(\mu_a(\mu_h(k_1, k_2), \mu_h(k_3, k_4), \mu_h(k_5, k_6), \mu_h(k_7, k_8)) \right),$$
$$\mu_a(k_1, k_3, k_5, k_7), \ \mu_a(k_2, k_4, k_6, k_8)) \right).$$

One time renormalization gives averaged coefficients in 2 times coarser grid than initial coefficient grid. If grid size is a power of two $M = 2^g$, recursive using of renormalization until 1 value gives effective permeability of the whole domain.

3 Multilevel Monte Carlo Algorithms

3.1 Multilevel Monte Carlo

In the literature Multilevel Monte Carlo methods for stochastic PDEs are extensively investigated [1,3,4,16,18,20,23]. Here we give an only brief description of Multilevel Monte Carlo method. Let $\omega : \Omega \to \mathbb{R}^M$ be a random vector over probability space (Ω, F, P) and Q_M is the approximation of quantity of interest Q. We assume that as $M \to \infty$ the expected value $\mathrm{E}[Q_M] \to \mathrm{E}[Q]$ and have the order of convergence α, i.e.

$$|\mathrm{E}[Q_M - Q]| \leq M^{-\alpha}.$$

Also we introduce $\{M_l : l = 0, \ldots, L\}$ an increasing sequence of levels, i.e. $M_0 < M_1 < \cdots < M_{L-1} < M_L = M$. The main idea of multilevel Monte Carlo calculation is estimating of $\mathrm{E}[Q]$ on the coarsest level $l = 0$ and correcting on other finer levels. Final expectation is described by the following telescopic sum

$$\mathrm{E}[Q_M] = \mathrm{E}[Q_{M_0}] + \sum_{l=1}^{L} \mathrm{E}[Q_{M_l} - Q_{M_{l-1}}] = \sum_{l=0}^{L} \mathrm{E}[Y_l],$$

where we denote $Y_0(\omega) = Q_{M_0}(\omega)$ and $Y_l(\omega) = Q_{M_l}(\omega) - Q_{M_{l-1}}(\omega)$ for $l = 1, \ldots, L$. For each level l let consider N_l different random vectors ω_l^i and use standard estimator for the expectations and the multilevel estimator

$$\widehat{Y_l} := \frac{1}{N_l} \sum_{i=1}^{N_l} Y_l(\omega_l^i), \quad \widehat{Q} = \sum_{l=0}^{L} \widehat{Y_l}.$$

We calculate all the estimators $\widehat{Y}_l$ independently and use mean square error to estimate the accuracy

$$e\left(\widehat{Q}\right)^2 = \mathrm{E}\left[\left(\widehat{Q} - \mathrm{E}[Q]\right)^2\right] = \sum_{l=0}^{L}\frac{\mathrm{V}[Y_l]}{N_l} + \mathrm{E}[Q_M - Q]^2, \qquad (6)$$

where $\mathrm{V}[Y_l] = \mathrm{E}[Y_l^2] - \mathrm{E}[Y_l]^2$ is the variance. First term of the error represents the sampling error and linearly decreases with the number of samples. The second term is the square error of approximation Q_M. To achieve the error ε it is sufficient that both terms in (6) are less than $\varepsilon^2/2$. It means that we need to choose sufficiently large $M = M_L \gtrsim \varepsilon^{-1/\alpha}$ and $N_l \gtrsim \varepsilon^{-2}, l = 0, \ldots, L$.

The number of samples N_l can be chosen in optimal way, when computational time is minimized [4,9,18,20]. Treating the N_l as continues values the optimal number of samples are given by

$$N_l = \varepsilon^{-2}\left(\sum_{j=0}^{L}\sqrt{\mathrm{V}[Y_j]\, t_j}\right)\sqrt{\frac{\mathrm{V}[Y_l]}{t_l}}, \qquad (7)$$

where t_l is the average computing time of one sample $Y_l(\omega_l^i)$.

3.2 Parallel Algorithm

We use static load balancing for Monte Carlo simulations, which is simple for implementation and showed good performance [22]. To minimize unused processor time we use homogeneous bulk synchronous model [10], where all tasks execute on the same level and with the same number of processes.

Algorithm. Parallel MLMC algorithm

1: Set initial samples $N_l, l = 0, \ldots, L$
2: **while** $e > \varepsilon$ **do**
3:     Compute Y_l until N_l, $l = 0, \ldots, L$ in parallel
4:     Synchronize and update $\widehat{Y}_l, \widehat{V}_l, e_l, t_l$, $l = 0, \ldots, L$
5:     Select level j with the maximum $e_j/(N_j\, t_j)$
6:     Calculate N_j^1 using (7)
7:     **if** $e - e_j < \varepsilon$ **then**
8:         Calculate N_j^2 giving $e \leq \varepsilon$
9:     Set $N_j = \min(N_j^1, N_j^2, 2\, N_j)$

In large scale parallel MLMC computations, using the exact optimal number of samples (7) leads to processes idling or parallelization of levels. To avoid these situations we round up the optimal number of samples to utilize all processes, i.e. always $N_l \vdots g_l$. And at the end of MLMC computation, we can reduce the accuracy of some levels using over-computed accuracy. It means we only compute the required number of samples to achieve the defined tolerance ε and the number of samples N_l is close to optimal.

3.3 MLMC Algorithms

Let we have uniformly refining set of grids $\{M_l : M_l = m_l^d = 2^{(l+s)d}, l = 0, \ldots, L\}$, where $M_0 = 2^{sd}$ is the minimal grid size which resolves the correlation length λ. In the MLMC method for each level, except the coarsest, we need to solve a couple of problems: fine and coarse. It is assumed that a fine problem has a higher accuracy but more computationally costly than a coarse problem. Fine and coarse problems use the same random permeability field but have different grid size. We are considering two approaches of coarsening permeability field: skipping values and renormalization.

Skipping values is the simplest approach of discrete field coarsening: we evaluate coefficient with two times larger spatial step and skip every second cell in all dimension directions. For the coarse problem with the grid size $M = (m/2)^3$ we used values of the permeability k on the fine grid $M = m^3$ in the following cells

$$k_{2i_1, 2i_2, 2i_3}, \quad i_1, i_2, i_3 = 1, \ldots, m/2.$$

In this approach part of the information from permeability is not used but it does not influence the accuracy of MLMC simulations, only on the number of samples N_l. And the main advantage of this approach is the possibility to generate random permeability on a level grid. Using averaging approaches, like renormalization, requires a generation of a random field on the finest grid to satisfy the telescopic sum used in MLMC.

Combining finite volume method and described coarsening approaches we have the following three MLMC algorithms based on: (1) finite volume with skipping values, (2) finite volume with renormalization, and (3) renormalization with skipping values.

4 Numerical Results

4.1 2D MLMC Simulations

Let denote the mean and variances of the algorithms by $\widehat{Q}^i, \widehat{V}_l^i, l = 0, \ldots, L, i = 1, 2, 3$, where i is the number of algorithm. Algorithm 1 gives the same result as Algorithm 2 due to the finest problems in both simulations are the same. But Algorithm 1 requires more samples to achieve the same tolerance. Algorithm 3 gives a different quantity of interest from other and to investigate the accuracy we use a solution of Algorithm 1 as a reference solution.

To minimize approximation and sampling error we set $\varepsilon = 0.001$ and $M_L = 2^{10} \times 2^{10}$. Also we set the number of levels $L = 6$ which is motivated by the correlation length $m_0^{-1} = 2^{-5} < \lambda_{min} = 0.05$. In Fig. 1 we showed the mean of the total flux $\widehat{Q}$ and difference between Algorithms 1 and 3. MLMC based on renormalization with skipping values shows very good accuracy and relative error of the mean less than 2%.

To figure out the influence of an approximation error we made simulations for different grid sizes $m = 2^s, s = 4, \ldots, 10$. We used following parameters of

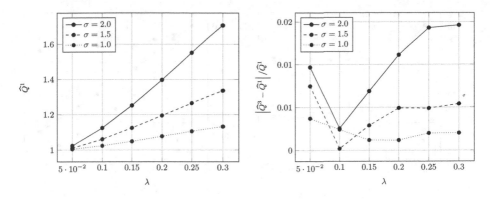

Fig. 1. Mean of Algorithm 1 and mean relative difference of Algorithms 1 and 3

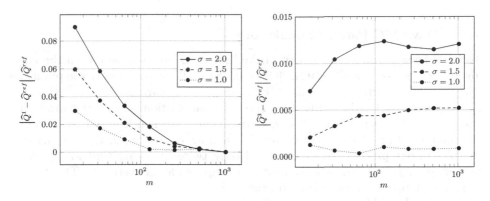

Fig. 2. Relative error of Algorithms 1 and 3 for $\lambda = 0.2$ and different grid size m

simulations: $\lambda = 0.2, \varepsilon = 0.001, L = s - 3$. To compare the approximation error of Algorithms 1 and 3 we used the reference solution $\widehat{Q}^{ref}$, which is the solution of Algorithm 1 on the finest grid.

In Fig. 2 we see that the results of Algorithm 1 highly depend on grid size. On the smallest grid $m = 2^4$, the relative error is near to 9%. Also, the approximation error of Algorithm 1 is sensitive to the total flux magnitude. The results of Algorithm 3 almost do not depend on grid size. It means that there is no need to consider very fine grids for Multilevel Monte Carlo method. For considered simulations, the maximum relative error of Algorithm 3 is quite small and equal to 1.5%.

To compare the efficiency of the algorithms, we used $\sigma = 2.0$ and $\lambda = 0.2$, which give relatively large total flux and variance. For this simulations we used the tolerance $\varepsilon = 0.005$ and the grid size $M = 2^{10} \times 2^{10}$. In Fig. 3 we compare the total computational time depending on the number of levels L and the average solution time of sample depending on level for $L = 8$. For all algorithms, there is a number of levels from which computation time does not decrease.

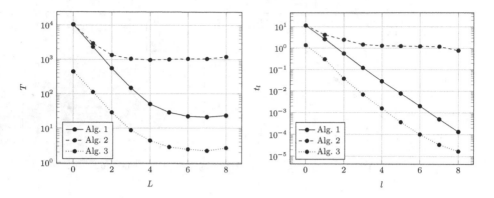

Fig. 3. Comparison of total time for different levels and average time for $L = 8$

4.2   3D MLMC Parallel Simulations

To investigate parallel efficiency of MLMC for a 3D problem we ran on the following processes count $P = 1024, 2048, 4096, 8192$. We consider only the parallel efficiency of Algorithm 1. We used the next problem parameters: $m = 8^2, \sigma = 2.0, \lambda = 0.2, \varepsilon = 0.001$. In Fig. 4 we showed computation and synchronization time for a different number of levels. Correlation of the synchronization time to the number of processes is noticeable. In each synchronization, the number of samples in one process can be increased only twice. It means that for a large number of processes, less synchronization is required for convergence. This leads to the reduction of synchronization time.

For the 3D problem, the parallel efficiency almost does not depend on a number of levels. Iterations count of linear solver in the 3D problem for considered parameters mostly the same, which leads to small idling time of processes.

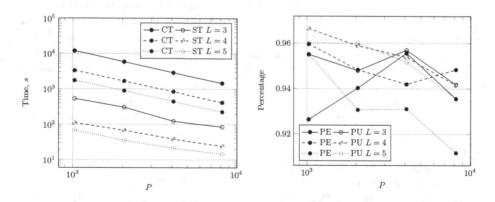

Fig. 4. Algorithm 1: computation time (CT), synchronization time (ST) on the left side and processes usage (PU), parallel efficiency (PE) on the right side

5 Conclusion

In this work, we investigated three algorithms of MLMC based on finite volume, finite volume with renormalization and renormalization. MLMC based on finite volume showed good accuracy and acceleration depending on a number of levels. The second algorithm based on finite volume and renormalization gives the same accuracy as first algorithm, but it is much slower and bounded by the generation of permeability on the finest grid. The advantage of the second algorithm is the least number of samples compared to other algorithms. The last algorithm based on only renormalization approximation shows the lowest computational time and weak dependence on grid size. For MLMC simulations which do not requires precise results (the relative error less than 4%) algorithm based on renormalization will be convenient. The parallel algorithm based on homogeneous bulk synchronous showed good efficiency for 3D MLMC problem.

References

1. Barth, A., Schwab, C., Zollinger, N.: Multi-level Monte Carlo finite element method for elliptic PDEs with stochastic coefficients. Numer. Math. **119**(1), 123–161 (2011)
2. Brandt, A., Galun, M., Ron, D.: Optimal multigrid algorithms for calculating thermodynamic limits. J. Stat. Phys. **74**(1–2), 313–348 (1994)
3. Charrier, J., Scheichl, R., Teckentrup, A.L.: Finite element error analysis of elliptic PDEs with random coefficients and its application to multilevel Monte Carlo methods. SIAM J. Numer. Anal. **51**(1), 322–352 (2013)
4. Cliffe, K.A., Giles, M.B., Scheichl, R., Teckentrup, A.L.: Multilevel Monte Carlo methods and applications to elliptic PDEs with random coefficients. Comput. Vis. Sci. **14**(1), 3 (2011)
5. Cliffe, K., Graham, I.G., Scheichl, R., Stals, L.: Parallel computation of flow in heterogeneous media modelled by mixed finite elements. J. Comput. Phys. **164**(2), 258–282 (2000)
6. De Marsily, G., Delay, F., Gonçalvès, J., Renard, P., Teles, V., Violette, S.: Dealing with spatial heterogeneity. Hydrol. J. **13**(1), 161–183 (2005)
7. Delhomme, J.: Spatial variability and uncertainty in groundwater flow parameters: a geostatistical approach. Water Resour. Res. **15**(2), 269–280 (1979)
8. Dietrich, C.R., Newsam, G.N.: Fast and exact simulation of stationary Gaussian processes through circulant embedding of the covariance matrix. SIAM J. Sci. Comput. **18**(4), 1088–1107 (1997)
9. Dimov, I., Georgieva, R., Todorov, V.: Balancing of systematic and stochastic errors in Monte Carlo algorithms for integral equations. In: Dimov, I., Fidanova, S., Lirkov, I. (eds.) NMA 2014. LNCS, vol. 8962, pp. 44–51. Springer, Cham (2015). https://doi.org/10.1007/978-3-319-15585-2_5
10. Drzisga, D., Gmeiner, B., Rüde, U., Scheichl, R., Wohlmuth, B.: Scheduling massively parallel multigrid for multilevel Monte Carlo methods. SIAM J. Sci. Comput. **39**(5), S873–S897 (2017)
11. Frigo, M., Johnson, S.G.: The design and implementation of FFTW3. Proc. IEEE **93**(2), 216–231 (2005)

12. Ghanem, R.G., Spanos, P.D.: Stochastic finite element method: response statistics. In: Ghanem, R.G., Spanos, P.D. (eds.) Stochastic Finite Elements: A Spectral Approach, pp. 101–119. Springer, New York (1991). https://doi.org/10.1007/978-1-4612-3094-6_4

13. Giles, M.B.: Multilevel Monte Carlo path simulation. Oper. Res. **56**(3), 607–617 (2008)

14. Giles, M.: Improved multilevel Monte Carlo convergence using the milstein scheme. In: Keller, A., Heinrich, S., Niederreiter, H. (eds.) Monte Carlo and Quasi-Monte Carlo Methods, pp. 343–358. Springer, Heidelberg (2008). https://doi.org/10.1007/978-3-540-74496-2_20

15. Graham, I.G., Kuo, F.Y., Nuyens, D., Scheichl, R., Sloan, I.H.: Analysis of circulant embedding methods for sampling stationary random fields. SIAM J. Numer. Anal. **56**(3), 1871–1895 (2018)

16. Graham, I.G., Kuo, F.Y., Nuyens, D., Scheichl, R., Sloan, I.H.: Quasi-Monte Carlo methods for elliptic PDEs with random coefficients and applications. J. Comput. Phys. **230**(10), 3668–3694 (2011)

17. Hoeksema, R.J., Kitanidis, P.K.: Analysis of the spatial structure of properties of selected aquifers. Water Resour. Res. **21**(4), 563–572 (1985)

18. Iliev, O., Mohring, J., Shegunov, N.: Renormalization based MLMC method for scalar elliptic SPDE. In: Lirkov, I., Margenov, S. (eds.) LSSC 2017. LNCS, vol. 10665, pp. 295–303. Springer, Cham (2018). https://doi.org/10.1007/978-3-319-73441-5_31

19. Lunati, I., Bernard, D., Giudici, M., Parravicini, G., Ponzini, G.: A numerical comparison between two upscaling techniques: non-local inverse based scaling and simplified renormalization. Adv. Water Resour. **24**(8), 913–929 (2001)

20. Mohring, J., et al.: Uncertainty quantification for porous media flow using multilevel Monte Carlo. In: Lirkov, I., Margenov, S.D., Waśniewski, J. (eds.) LSSC 2015. LNCS, vol. 9374, pp. 145–152. Springer, Cham (2015). https://doi.org/10.1007/978-3-319-26520-9_15

21. Renard, P., De Marsily, G.: Calculating equivalent permeability: a review. Adv. Water Resour. **20**(5–6), 253–278 (1997)

22. Šukys, J., Mishra, S., Schwab, C.: Static load balancing for multi-level Monte Carlo finite volume solvers. In: Wyrzykowski, R., Dongarra, J., Karczewski, K., Waśniewski, J. (eds.) PPAM 2011. LNCS, vol. 7203, pp. 245–254. Springer, Heidelberg (2012). https://doi.org/10.1007/978-3-642-31464-3_25

23. Teckentrup, A.L., Scheichl, R., Giles, M.B., Ullmann, E.: Further analysis of multilevel Monte Carlo methods for elliptic PDEs with random coefficients. Numer. Math. **125**(3), 569–600 (2013)

24. Wen, X.H., Gómez-Hernández, J.J.: Upscaling hydraulic conductivities in heterogeneous media: an overview. J. Hydrol. **183**(1–2), ix–xxxii (1996)

25. Whitaker, S.: Flow in porous media I: a theoretical derivation of Darcy's law. Transp. Porous Media **1**(1), 3–25 (1986)

Application of Metaheuristics to Large-Scale Problems

Generalized Nets Model of Data Parallel Processing in Large Scale Wireless Sensor Networks

Alexander Alexandrov[✉], Vladimir Monov, and Tasho Tashev

Institute of Information and Communication Technologies,
Bulgarian Academy of Sciences, Sofia, Bulgaria
akalexandrov@iit.bas.bg
http://www.iict.bas.bg

Abstract. The Generalized Nets (GN) approach is an advanced way of parallel processes modeling and analysis of complex systems as Large-scale Wireless Sensor Networks (LWSN). The LWSN such as meteorological and air quality monitoring systems could generate a large amount of data that can reach petabytes per year. The sensor data-parallel processing is one of the possible solutions to reduce inter-node communication to save energy. At the same time, the on-site parallel processing requires additional energy, needed for computational data processing. Therefore, the development of a realistic model of the process is critical for the optimization analysis of every large scale sensor network.

In the proposed paper, a new developed GN based model of a sensor nodes data-parallel processing of LWSN with cluster topology is presented. The proposed model covers all the aspects of the inter-node sensor data integration and the cluster-based parallel processes specific for large scale amounts of sensor data operations.

Keywords: Generalized Nets · Data parallel processing · LSWSN

1 Introduction

1.1 Introduction to Large Scale Wireless Sensor Networks (LWSN)

Recent advances in wireless communication, embedded computation, and Micro-electromechanical Systems (MEMS) technologies have enabled large-scale wireless sensor networks (LWSN) to come to fruition. More and more, LWSNs are changing the way that people cognize the physical world, and they will be an infrastructure for future security systems. The concept of LWSNs was described in [7,8]: an LWSN is a sensor network that contains thousands, or even tens of thousands of small sensors, which are distributed over a vast field to obtain fine-grained, high-precision sensing data. LWSNs are used in many areas [4], ranging from ecological and precision agriculture information monitoring to intrusion detection, surveillance, and structural integrity monitoring etc.

© Springer Nature Switzerland AG 2020
I. Lirkov and S. Margenov (Eds.): LSSC 2019, LNCS 11958, pp. 475–483, 2020.
https://doi.org/10.1007/978-3-030-41032-2_54

Fig. 1. Summary of the research problems and their relationships in distributed and parallel data processing in LWSN.

However, sensors in LWSNs are typically resource-limited; they are powered by batteries and can only communicate with neighbors using short-range radio. For the purpose of massive data collection and processing, an important problem to address in LWSN is how to store data and subsequently conduct computation in a distributed fashion and in parallel. In practice, an LWSN could yield data in amounts approaching or exceeding petabytes each year. The storage, query, and computation of such amounts of data by resource-limited sensors are highly challenging tasks. If the (massive amount of) data is processed centrally, all data needs to be transmitted to a central server using multi-hop transmissions. In such cases, an LWSN will suffer high communication costs. A promising solution is to exploit the advantages of the distributed storage and parallel processing capabilities of an LWSN. Instead of transmitting data to a central server, data is stored and processed in-network. This can markedly reduce communication costs. The intensive computational task is decomposed into many small tasks, each of which is affordable to a single sensor, and computation is executed in parallel by the distributed sensors. Figure 1 summarizes these sub-problems and their relationships.

The distributed storage and parallel computing problem can be decomposed into three subproblems—system architecture design, distributed data storage, and data-parallel processing.

System Architecture Design. The fundamental problem with distributed storage and parallel data processing is system architecture design [7, 8, 10], which concentrates on energy-efficient topology control and sensor management. Both distributed storage and parallel processing depend heavily on the type of network organization (topology, architecture, etc.)

Distributed Data Storage. Many researchers have presented the sensor network as a distributed database. Distributed data storage not only saves the cost of data collection and transmission but also forms the foundation for parallel processing as a general basis for computation task decomposition.

The Parallel Data Processing. The Data Parallel processing methods concentrate on how to divide a computationally intensive task into many small tasks and how to execute these tasks locally on the distributed sensors in parallel. The minimization of the communication cost and the execution time is the general consideration in the design of the sensor data-parallel processing.

1.2   Introduction to GN

The Generalized Nets (GNs, [1–3]) appear as extensions of the regular Petri Nets (PNs) and all their modifications. In principle, the GNs are different from the ways of defining the other types of PNs. The components in the typical GN-definition provide more and better modeling capabilities and therefore determine the GNs among the separate types of PNs. Similarly to the PNs, GNs contain places, transitions, and tokens, but their transitions have a much more complex structure.

In GNs every transition is described by a three-tuple:

$$Z = \langle L', L'', r \rangle, \tag{1}$$

where L' and L'' are non-empty sets of places (the transition's input and output places, respectively); for the transition Z these are:

$$L' = \{l'_1, l'_2..........l'_i\} \text{ and } L'' = \{l''_{i+1}, l''_{i+2}..........l''_j\}$$

r is the transition's condition determining which tokens will pass (or transfer) from the transition's inputs to its outputs; it has the form of an Index Matrix (IM) (Fig. 2):

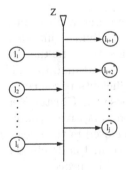

Fig. 2. GN transition example

The GN-tokens enter the network with initial predefined parameters. After the move to the new place, the GN-tokens can change their parameters or save the initial ones. The biggest difference between PNs and the Predicate-Transition Nets, GN-tokens can keep all their own characteristics and during the process, they can be used for evaluation of the transition condition predicates. The second big difference to the remaining types of PNs, the GNs contain a global temporal scale. The GNs can have more than 20 conservative extensions (i.e., extensions for which their functioning and the results of their work can be represented by an ordinary GN). Some of them are: GNs with global memory; GNs with optimization components; GNs with complex transition type; GNs with characteristic functions of the places and arcs.

In the current paper we will be focused on the GNs with Global Memory as the most appropriate to the data parallel processing in the LSWSN. Based on [1,2] the ordered 4-tuple

$$E^* = \langle\langle A, \rangle, \langle K \rangle, \langle T \rangle, \langle B, X, \Phi, b \rangle\rangle \tag{2}$$

is called a Generalized Net with Global Memory where:

- A is the set of transitions;
- K is the set of the GN's tokens;
- T is the time moment when GN starts to function;
- B is a Global Memory which stores parameters related to the specific processes modeled by GN;
- X is the set of all initial characteristics which the tokens can obtain on entering the net;
- Φ is the characteristic function that assigns new characteristics to every token when it makes the transfer from an input to an output place of a given transition.
- b is a function which specifies the maximal number of the token's characteristics.

2 Sensor Node Clustering Parallel Processing in LSWSN

The process of sensor node clustering in different topologies [4,5] requires a parallel data exchange and can be divided into 3 main stages—discovery stage, assigning stage and monitoring stage. The discovery stage starts a parallel process of neighbor nodes discovery and mapping. The task of the assigning stage is to assign special weight coefficients to every sensor node depending on their specific parameters and to choose the Cluster Head (CH). The main role of the monitoring stage is to ensure an adaptive dynamical reconfiguration of the sensor network. All the stages are closed in the cycle and are executed in fixed time periods. All the stages of the parallel node clustering are described in details in [7] and here we will only resume the process:

Discovery Stage. The discovery stage process is executed on every sensor node in the LSWSN in parallel. The process begins for neighbor nodes discovery by transmitting a broadcast message and answering of the messages of the neighbor nodes. Based on the received answers with node coordinates and the signal level, it starts a process that includes an analysis of the node parameters and calculation of the node weight coefficient. The weight coefficient depends on the number of directly answered neighbor nodes and the received signal level.

The parameters based on which we calculate the weight coefficient of K_{weight} for every sensor node N_i are as follows:

– C_i represents the number of neighbor sensor nodes in the communication distance of node N_i

$$C_i = |N(i)| = \sum_{j \in N(i), i \neq j} \{dist(i,j) < S_{range}\} \tag{3}$$

Where
– $dist(i,j)$ is the distance between a couple of nodes in communication distance,
– S_{range} is a coefficient who represents the maximum communication distance between two nodes and depends on the current hardware implementation of the network.
– D_i represents the average distance between node N_i and the neighbor nodes j. For every node, we calculate D_i by the Eq. (3)

$$D_i = 1/C_i \sum_{j \in N(i)} \{dist(i,j)\} \tag{4}$$

– M_i is a coefficient representing the mobility of the sensor node, e.g. the probability that this node to change its coordinates during the specified period.

$$Mi = 1/T \sum_{(t=1)}^{T} \sqrt{(X_t - X_{t-1})^2 + (Y_t - Y_{t-1})^2} \tag{5}$$

Where (X_t, Y_t) and $(X_{t-1}, Yt - 1)$ are the coordinates of the node i in time t and $t - 1$.
– $E_{current}$ - represents the current amount of energy of node N_i
Generally

$$E_{current} = E_i - (E_{rx}.t_1 + E_{tx}.t_2 + E_{comp}.t_3 + E_{sensor}.t_4) \tag{6}$$

Where E_i is the initial amount of energy of the node i ;
  E_{rx} is the amount of energy needed for the receiving signals mode;
  E_{tx} is the amount of energy needed for the transmitting mode of the sensor node;
  E_{comp} is the amount of energy needed for the work of the microcontroller block for the clusters generation operations;
  E_{sensor} is the amount of energy needed for the sensor node coordinates calculation;
  $t_1 - t_4$ time intervals related to the sensor blocks energy consumption;

The weight coefficient P_i is calculated by the equation:

$$P_i = \omega_1.C_i + \omega_2.D_i + \omega_3.M_i + \omega_4.E_{current} \tag{7}$$

where $\omega_1 \div \omega_4$ are correction coefficients depending of specific requirements.

$$\omega_1 + \omega_2 + \omega_3 + \omega_4 = 1 \tag{8}$$

Assigning Stage. In the assigning phase the process of CH choice starts. On the basis of the already calculated weight coefficient, we choose the sensor node with the maximal weight coefficient as a cluster head and the nodes connected to this node are excluded from the process of other CH choice. After the first CH choice, the procedure is repeated with the rest nodes until the final clustering of the sensor network.

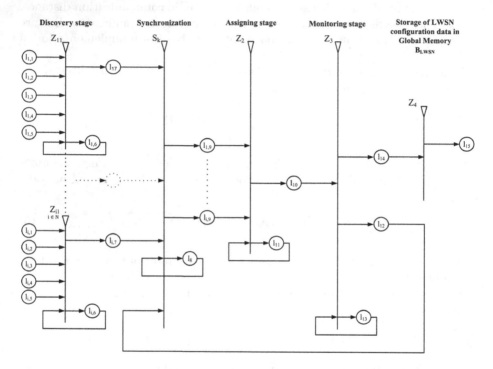

Fig. 3. GN model of parallel sensor data clustering process in LWSN

Monitoring Stage. The monitoring stage in the LSWSNs is a very important phase during the process of network adaptation. On the basis of the monitoring, results have executed a process of adaptive reconfiguration and redistribution of the communication nodes. In the proposed method in the monitoring phase, we analyze the following 4 situations leading to adaptive reconfiguration.

- sensor node's battery capacity near to critical minimum;
- add a new sensor node to the cluster (network);
- movement of the sensor node outside of the current CH distance (typical for mobile sensor networks);
- the crash of the sensor node;

3   Generalized Nets Model of LSWSN Sensor Node Clustering Parallel Processing

A sample GN model of the sensor node clustering parallel data exchange process is presented in Fig. 3. The transition Z_{i1} represents the sensor node input parameters needed for the clustering process described in detail in [7].

The token α enters GN in place l_{i1} with characteristic "C_i - number of neighbor sensor nodes in the communication distance N_i"

The token β enters GN in place l_{i2} with characteristic S_{range} - maximum communication distance between two nodes.

The token γ enters GN in place l_{i3} with characteristic "D_i - average distance between node N_i and the neighbor nodes j".

The token δ enters GN in place l_{i4} with characteristic "M_i - mobility of the sensor node"

The token ϵ enters GN in place l_{i5} with characteristic "$E_{current}$ - current amount of energy of node N_i"

$$Z_{i1} = <\{l_{i1}, l_{i2}, l_{i3}, l_{i4}, l_{i5}, l_{i6}\}, \{l_{i6}, l_{i7}\}, r_{i,1}> \qquad (9)$$

$$r_{i,1} = \begin{array}{c|cc} & l_{i,6} & l_{i,7} \\ \hline l_{i,1} & true & true, \wedge(l_{i1}, l_{i6}) \\ l_{i,2} & true & true \\ l_{i,3} & true & true \\ l_{i,4} & true & true \\ l_{i,5} & true & true \\ l_{i,6} & true & W_{i6,i7}, \wedge l_{i6} \end{array} \qquad (10)$$

Where $W_{i6,i7}$ is "finished calculation of weighting coefficient P_i".

The transition $S_k, k \in N$ represents the synchronization point of the discovery stage parallel process, executed in sensor nodes $i, i \in N$.

$$S_k = <\{(l_{i7}, i \in N), l_8, l_{12}\}, \{(l_{i9}, i \in N), l_8, l_{12}\} r_k, k \in N> \qquad (11)$$

$$r_k = \begin{array}{c|ccccc} & l_{1,9} & .... & l_{i,9} & l_8 & l_{12} \\ \hline l_{1,7} & true & & true & true & true \\ . & . & . & . & . & . \\ . & . & . & . & . & . \\ . & . & . & . & . & . \\ l_{i,7} & true & & true & true & true \\ l_8 & true & & true & W_{i7,8} & true \\ l_{12} & true & & true & true & W_{8,12} \end{array} \qquad (12)$$

Where $W_{i7,8}$ is "finished synchronization process".

The transition Z_2 represents the assigning stage of the parallel processing executed in sensor nodes $i, i \in N$.

$$Z_2 = <\{(l_{i,9}, i \in N), l_{11}\}, \{l_{10}, l_{11}\}, r_2> \qquad (13)$$

$$r_2 = \begin{array}{c|cc} & l_{10} & l_{11} \\ \hline l_{1,9} & true & true \\ & \vdots & \\ & \vdots & \\ l_{i,9} & true & true \\ l_{11} & true & W_{i9,11} \end{array} \tag{14}$$

Where $W_{i9,11}$ is "calculated and assigned Cluster Head (CH) role".

The transition Z_3 represents the monitoring stage of the sensor data-parallel process executed in sensor nodes i, $i \in N$.

$$Z_3 = <\{l_{10}, l_{13}\}, \{l_{12}, l_{13}, l_{14}\}, r_3> \tag{15}$$

$$r_3 = \begin{array}{c|ccc} & l_{12} & l_{13} & l_{14} \\ \hline l_{10} & true & true & true \\ l_{13} & true & true & W_{13,14} \end{array} \tag{16}$$

Where $W_{13,14}$ is "finished period of the Monitoring stage".

$$Z_4 = <\{(l_{14}\}, \{l_{15}\}, r_4> \tag{17}$$

$$r_4 = \begin{array}{c|c} & l_{15} \\ \hline l_{14} & W_{14,15} \end{array} \tag{18}$$

Where $W_{14,15}$ is "received token in l_{12}".

As is shown on Fig. 3 the transition Z_4 and output l_{15} represents the Global Memory component of the presented GN model B_{LWSN}.

4   Conclusion

The paper presents a new concept for modeling a sensor data-parallel clustering process in LWSN, based on Generalized Nets with Global Memory component. The advantages of the new concept are:

– the information collected during the model execution process is stored and can be used for parametrization and adaptive dynamic change of the parallel process key parameters.
– the proposed GN model is a very good start point for LWSN parallel processes analysis and simulation by Ns-3 and/or Omnet++ simulators and can reduce sensitively the cost of the LWSN system architecture design.

The future step will be to apply the proposed new concept in the area of real LWSN design.

References

1. Atanassov, K.: Generalized Nets. World Scientific, Singapore (1991)
2. Fidanova, S., Atanasov, K., Marinov, P.: Generalized Nets and Ant Colony Optimization. Publisher Prof. Marin Drinov Academic Publishing House, Sofia (2011). ISBN 978-954-322-473-9
3. Sotirov, S., Atanasov, K.: Generalized Nets and Supervised Neural Networks. Prof. Marin Drinov Academic Publishing House, Sofia (2011). ISBN 978-954-322-623-8
4. Balabanov, T., Zankinski, I., Barova, M.: Strategy for individuals distribution by incident nodes participation in star topology of distributed evolutionary algorithms. Cybern. Inf. Technol. **16**(1), 80–88 (2016)
5. Balabanov, T., Sevova, J., Kolev, K.: Optimization of string rewriting operations for 3D fractal generation with genetic algorithms. In: International Conference on Numerical Methods and Applications, pp. 48–54 (2018)
6. Alexandrov, A., Monov, V.: Method for adaptive node clustering in AD HOC wireless sensor networks. DCCN 2018 **99**(110), 99–110 (2016)
7. Wang, Y., Wang, Y.: Distributed storage and parallel processing in large-scale wireless sensor networks, pp. 288–305. Springer, Heidelberg (2016). https://doi.org/10.3233/978-1-60750-803-8-288. https://doi.org/10.10007/1234567890
8. Wang, X., Zhang, R.: Parallel processing for large-scale fault tree in wireless sensor networks. J. Netw. **8**(5), 1160–1167 (2013)
9. Tcheshmedjiev, P.: Synchronizing parallel processes using generalized nets. NT J. "Bioautomation" **14**(1), 69–74 (2010)
10. Atanasova, T.: Modelling of complex objects in distance learning systems. In: Proceedings of the First International Conference "Innovative Teaching Methodology", 25–26 October 2014, Tbilisi, Georgia, pp. 180–190 (2014). ISBN 978-9941-9348-7-2

Modeling Block Structured Project Scheduling with Resource Constraints

Amelia Bădică[1], Costin Bădică[1(✉)], Doina Logofătu[2], Ion Buligiu[1], and Liviu Ciora[1]

[1] University of Craiova, Craiova, Romania
cbadica@software.ucv.ro
[2] University of Applied Sciences, Frankfurt, Germany

Abstract. We propose a formal model of block-structured project scheduling with resource constraints, with the goal of designing optimization algorithms. We combine block structured modeling of business processes with results from project scheduling literature. Differently from standard approaches, here we focus on block structured scheduling processes. Our main achievement is the formulation of an abstract mathematical model of block-structured resource-constrained scheduling processes. We tested the correctness and feasibility of our approach using an initial experimental prototype based on Constraint Logic Programming.

Keywords: Project scheduling · Process algebra · Ordering and resource constraints · Constraint Logic Programming

1 Introduction

In this work we are interested to derive a formal model of block-structured project scheduling with resource constraints, with the goal of designing optimization algorithms. The starting point of our work is two fold: (i) we reuse ideas and results from project scheduling literature regarding the design of benchmarks for optimization algorithms, in particular some of the results already incorporated into PSPLIB [4]; (ii) we reuse block structured models of business processes introduced in [5].

For example, in manufacturing there is interest for automated synthesis of flexible and correct process models from declarative ordering constraints. Correctness can be ensured by synthesizing a block-structured process. One approach uses standard project scheduling algorithms [4] and then synthesizes a process from the schedule. This might have drawbacks, by leading to unstructured and overly constrained processes [6].

Differently from standard approaches [4] and previous works [1,6], here we focus on the synthesis of block structured scheduling processes with both resource and ordering constraints. Our main achievement is the formulation of an abstract model of block-structured resource-constrained scheduling processes. The model has two components for activities and resources modeling. Scheduling processes

© Springer Nature Switzerland AG 2020
I. Lirkov and S. Margenov (Eds.): LSSC 2019, LNCS 11958, pp. 484–492, 2020.
https://doi.org/10.1007/978-3-030-41032-2_55

must satisfy ordering constraints stating the precedence relations for executing pairs of activities. Following the proposal of [4], processes are constrained by availability of resources.

We are also interested in computational experiments for testing the correctness and feasibility of our approach. Differently from [6] and [1], we have developed a mathematical programming optimization model for our problem.

The general scheduling problem with ordering and resource constraints originates from the areas of multiprocessor and project scheduling. According to the early result [10], scheduling with precedence constraints is NP-complete. Moreover, the problems of scheduling with precedence and resource constraints are included into the standard catalogue [2] of NP-complete problems (problems SS9 and SS10).

Therefore in this work we were interested in exploring a subset of the space of feasible solutions representing hierarchical decomposition processes, initially introduced in [1]. We have used Constraint Logic Programming – CLP for building our experimental prototype [8, 11].

2   Modeling Block Structured Resource Constrained Processes

2.1   General Model

Process Trees. Let us consider a finite nonempty set Σ of activities. We focus on process models that represent sets of admissible schedules. A schedule is a process trace that contains exactly one instance of each activity. Block structured scheduling processes are defined as algebraic terms formed using sequential ($\rightarrow$) and parallel ($\parallel$) operators.

Let $supp(P)$ be the support set (or alphabet) of process P. It represents the set of activities occurring in P. In what follows we denote activities of Σ with $a, b, c, \ldots$ and process terms with $P, Q, R, \ldots$.

Block structured scheduling process are represented as tree structured terms (or process trees) recursively defined as follows:

- If $a \in \Sigma$ then a is a process such that $supp(a) = \{a\}$.
- If P and Q are processes such that $supp(P) \cap supp(Q) = \emptyset$ then $P \rightarrow Q$ and $P \parallel Q$ are processes with $supp(P \rightarrow Q) = supp(P \parallel Q) = supp(P) \cup supp(Q)$.

The semantics of a process is given by its set of traces (or language). The language $\mathcal{L}(P)$ of process P is recursively defined as follows:

- $\mathcal{L}(a) = \{a\}$
- $\mathcal{L}(P \rightarrow Q) = \mathcal{L}(P) \rightarrow \mathcal{L}(Q)$
- $\mathcal{L}(P \parallel Q) = \mathcal{L}(P) \parallel \mathcal{L}(Q)$

It is not difficult to observe that if P is a well-formed block-structured scheduling process then all its traces $t \in L(P)$ have the same length $|t| = |supp(P)|$.

Ordering Graph. We can impose ordering constraints of the activities of a process, based on domain-specific semantics. These constraints are specified using an *activity ordering graph* $\mathcal{G} = \langle \Sigma, E \rangle$ [6] such that:

- Σ is the set of nodes and each node represents an activity in Σ.
- $E \subseteq \Sigma \times \Sigma$ is the set of edges. Each edge represents an ordering constraint. If $(u, v) \in E$ then in each acceptable schedule activity u must precede activity v.

Observe that for an activity ordering graph $\mathcal{G} = \langle \Sigma, E \rangle$, set E defines a partial ordering relation on Σ, i.e. it is transitive and antisymmetric, so it cannot define cycles. In standard project scheduling terminology, graph $\mathcal{G}$ is known as activity-on-node network [4] and it is a directed acyclic graph (DAG hereafter).

Let $\mathcal{G} = \langle \Sigma, E \rangle$ be an ordering graph and let t be a trace containing all the activities of Σ with no repetition. Then t *satisfies* $\mathcal{G}$, written as $t \models \mathcal{G}$, if and only if trace t does not contain activities ordered differently than as specified by $\mathcal{G}$.

The language $\mathcal{L}(\mathcal{G})$ of an ordering graph $\mathcal{G}$ is the set of all traces that satisfy $\mathcal{G}$, i.e:

$$\mathcal{L}(\mathcal{G}) = \{t \mid t \models \mathcal{G}\}$$

Let P be a scheduling process and let $\mathcal{G} = \langle \Sigma, E \rangle$ be an ordering graph. P *satisfies* $\mathcal{G}$ written as $P \models \mathcal{G}$, if and only if:

- $\mathcal{L}(P) \subseteq \mathcal{L}(\mathcal{G})$, i.e. each trace of P satisfies $\mathcal{G}$, and
- $supp(P) = \Sigma$, i.e. all the activities of Σ are relevant and occur in P.

The set of processes P such that $P \models \mathcal{G}$ is nonempty, as it contains at least one sequential process defined by the topological sorting of $\mathcal{G}$.

Resources. Processes are constrained by availability of the resources required for executing their activities. According to standard project scheduling literature [4], resources can be classified as: renewable, nonrenewable, and doubly constrained.

Renewable resources are available on a period-by-period basis. Per-period available quantity is assumed constant. Examples are: manpower, machines, fuel flow, space.

Nonrenewable resources are limited on a total project basis. There is a limited overall consumption quantity of a nonrenewable resource for the entire project. Examples are: money, energy, raw material.

Doubly constrained resources are limited on a total project basis, as well as per-period basis. Examples are: money if both project budget and per-period cash flow are limited; manpower if a skilled worker can spend only a limited number of periods on the project. Note that doubly constrained resources can be taken into account by appropriately extending sets of renewable and nonrenewable resources.

Let $\mathcal{R}$ and $\mathcal{N}$ be the sets of renewable and nonrenewable resources. We assume that:

- For each renewable resource $r \in \mathcal{R}$ its per period capacity is ρ_r and each activity $a \in \Sigma$ consumes $\rho_{a,r}$ units of r.
- For each nonrenewable resource $n \in \mathcal{N}$ its overall capacity is ν_n and each activity $a \in \Sigma$ consumes $\nu_{a,n}$ units of n.

Each process P consumes $\rho(P, r)$ units of renewable resource r and $\nu(P, n)$ units of nonrenewable resource n. Functions ρ and ν can be defined compositionally as follows:

- If $a \in \Sigma$ then $\rho(a, r) = \rho_{a,r}$ and $\nu(a, n) = \nu_{a,n}$.
- $\rho(P \to Q, r) = \max(\rho(P, r), \rho(Q, r))$
  $\nu(P \to Q, n) = \nu(P, n) + \nu(Q, n)$
- $\rho(P \parallel Q, r) = f_r^{\parallel}(\rho(P, r), \rho(Q, r))$
  $\nu(P \parallel Q, n) = f_n^{\parallel}(\nu(P, n), \nu(Q, n))$

Functions $f_r^{\parallel}$ and $f_n^{\parallel}$ describe resource consumption of processes executed in parallel. Typically, they are resource specific and generally they are sub-additive. This means that when several processes are grouped together in parallel they could consume at most (sometimes strictly less) resources than the sum of their individual consumptions. For example, when several virtual machines are packed on a server, their total memory requirement could decrease due to pages shared by all of them that need to be stored once [9]. Typical examples are:

- If a resource $r \in \mathcal{R} \cup \mathcal{N}$ is not shared at all when processes are grouped in parallel then its consumption can be described by an additive function:
  $f_r^{\parallel}(q_1, q_2) = q_1 + q_2$
- Time can be also considered a (nonrenewable) resource. If two processes are not constrained in any way and can be grouped in parallel then duration of the resulted process is equal to the maximum of the durations of each process, i.e.:
  $f_{time}^{\parallel}(t_1, t_2) = \max(t_1, t_2)$

For each $r \in \mathcal{R}$ and $n \in \mathcal{N}$, resource constraints for a process P can be now defined by the following inequalities:
$$\rho(P, r) \le \rho_r$$
$$\nu(P, n) \le \nu_n$$

Optimal Process. Each activity execution consumes a positive real time, so "time" can be considered a nonrenewable resource. The duration of execution $d(P)$ of a process P is defined as follows:
$$d(P) = \nu(P, time)$$

The *minimum duration of execution* of a process that satisfies a given ordering graph $\mathcal{G}$, as well as a given set of resource constraints is denoted with $d_{MIN}(\mathcal{G})$. The corresponding process P^* is called *optimal scheduling process* and we have:
$$d(P^*) = d_{MIN}(\mathcal{G})$$

In what follows we consider a single nonrenewable resource – "time" that is actually used for defining the optimization criteria. So $\mathcal{N} = \{time\}$ and our process is constrained only by renewable resources $\mathcal{R}$.

2.2 Hierarchical Decomposition Processes

We follow the idea of hierarchical decomposition of the ordering graph from [1]. However, instead of defining a single hierarchical decomposition process, we define the subspace of all hierarchical decomposition processes that are "consistent" with the hierarchical decomposition of the ordering graph and then we explore it to pickup the optimal process, actually obtaining a suboptimal solution for our problem.

Let $\mathcal{G} = \langle \Sigma, E \rangle$ be an ordering graph.

– For each node $v \in \Sigma$ we define the set $I(v)$ of *input neighbors* of v as $I(v) = \{u \in \Sigma \mid (u, v) \in E\}$, and the set $O(v)$ of *output neighbors* of v as $O(v) = \{u \in \Sigma \mid (v, u) \in E\}$.
– For each node $v \in \Sigma$ we recursively define its *level* $\ell(v)$ as function $\ell : \Sigma \to \mathbb{N}$:

$$(\forall v \in \Sigma)\, \text{if}\ I(v) = \emptyset \ \text{then}\ \ell(v) = 0$$
$$(\forall v \in \Sigma)\, \text{if}\ I(v) \neq \emptyset \ \text{then}\ \ell(v) = 1 + \max_{u \in I(v)} \{l(u)\}$$

– Let $h(\mathcal{G})$ be the *height* of graph $\mathcal{G}$, defined as $h(\mathcal{G}) = \max_{v \in \Sigma} \{\ell(v)\}$.

Now, rather than defining a single hierarchical decomposition of $\mathcal{G}$, induced by mapping l, we define the nonempty space of hierarchical decompositions of $\mathcal{G}$.

A hierarchical decomposition mapping of ordering graph $\mathcal{G}$ is a function $p : \Sigma \to \mathbb{N}$ such that:

$$(\forall v \in \Sigma)\, \text{if}\ O(v) = \emptyset \ \text{then}\ p(v) \leq h(\mathcal{G})$$
$$(\forall v \in \Sigma)\, \text{if}\ I(v) \neq \emptyset \ \text{then}\ p(v) \geq 1 + \max_{u \in I(v)} \{p(u)\}$$

Note that the set $\mathcal{H}(\mathcal{G})$ of hierarchical decomposition mappings p satisfying these equations is not empty, as obviously mapping ℓ is an element of this set.

For each mapping $p \in \mathcal{H}(\mathcal{G})$ we can define a scheduling process $P_{HD}(\mathcal{G}, p)$ that satisfies $\mathcal{G}$. This result is stated by the following proposition.

Proposition 1 *(Hierarchical Decomposition Process). Let $\mathcal{G} = \langle \Sigma, E \rangle$ be an ordering graph and let $p \in \mathcal{H}(\mathcal{G})$. The hierarchical decomposition process $P_{HD}(\mathcal{G}, p)$ associated to $\mathcal{G}$ and p is defined as:*

– $\Sigma_i = \{v \mid p(v) = i\}$ *for all* $i = 0, 1, \ldots, h(\mathcal{G})$.
– $P_i = \|_{v \in \Sigma_i} v$ *for all* $0 \leq i \leq h(\mathcal{G})$.
– $P_{HD}(\mathcal{G}, p) = P_0 \to P_1 \to \cdots \to P_{h(\mathcal{G})}$.

Then $P_{HD}(\mathcal{G}, p) \models \mathcal{G}$.

We are interested to determine the optimal hierarchical decomposition process:

$$p^* = \arg \min_{p \in \mathcal{H}(\mathcal{G})} d(P_{HD}(\mathcal{G}, p))$$
$$P_{HD}(\mathcal{G}) = P_{HD}(\mathcal{G}, p^*)$$
$$d_{HD}(\mathcal{G}) = d(P_{HD}(\mathcal{G}))$$

Assuming that $h = h(\mathcal{G})$ is known, an hierarchical decomposition mapping (and process) can be represented with a sequence H of n decision variables with values in the set $\{0, 1, \ldots, h\}$. The optimal hierarchical decomposition process can be determined by minimizing variable CHD defined by:

$$(\forall i : 1 \ldots n)\,((O(i) = \emptyset) \Rightarrow (H_i \leq h))$$
$$(\forall i : 1 \ldots n)\,((I(i) \neq \emptyset) \Rightarrow (H_i \geq 1 + \max_{j \in I(i)} \{H_j\}))$$
$$CHD = \sum_{i=0}^{h} \max\{D_j \mid 1 \leq j \leq n \wedge H_j = i\}$$

Note that solving this optimization problem is intuitively more simple than solving the original problem of computing the optimal scheduling process. Nevertheless, its solution will only provide a suboptimal scheduling process.

Moreover, note that process $P_{HD}(\mathcal{G}, p)$ might violate resource constraints. Fortunately, we can transform $P_{HD}(\mathcal{G}, p)$ into a process $P'_{HD}(\mathcal{G}, p)$ that satisfies both ordering and resource constraints using a variant of the well known bin-packing problem, as described below [2] (problem SR1).

Let $\Sigma_0, \Sigma_1, \ldots \Sigma_h$ be the optimal hierarchical decomposition of Σ, i.e. $\Sigma_l = \{a \in \Sigma | p^*(a) = l\}$ for all $l = 0, 1, \ldots, h$. Activities of Σ_i are items that must be placed in bins representing a partition of Σ_i such that the cost of the partition must be minimized. Each bin is multiply constrained by the upper bounds of the available renewable resources.

If $|\Sigma_l| = n_l$ then a nontrivial partition of Σ_i will contain at most n_l subsets. It can be represented using a vector H^l of n_l decision variables in range $1 \ldots n_l$. So we obtain a series of $i = 0, 1, \ldots h$ bin packing problems with constraints defined as:

$$\forall l = 0 \ldots h \ \forall i = 1 \ldots n_l \ \forall r \in \mathcal{R} \ \sum_{a \in \Sigma_l} (H_a^l = i)\rho_{a,r} \leq \rho_r$$

and the bins optimization cost defined as:

$$\forall l = 0 \ldots h \ Cost_l = \sum_{i=1}^{n_l} \max_{a \in \Sigma_l} (H_a^l = i)\rho_{a,time}$$

3   Computational Experiments

We have performed computational experiments for assessing the correctness and feasibility of our approach by exploring the subspace of hierarchical decomposition processes defined by an ordering graph and satisfying the resource constraints.

We have used the 64-bit version of ECLiPSe-CLP ([11]) 7.0 #44 on an $x64$-based PC with a 2 cores / 4 threads Intel© Core™ i7-5500U CPU at 2.40 GHz running Windows 10.

We have developed an experimental CLP program[1] based on our proposed models and using the following programming techniques:

(i) *Declarative loops* for implementing model formulas with universal quantifiers.

---

[1] The complete ECLiPSe-CLP code, the data sets that we have used in our experiments, as well as the experimental results obtained can be downloaded from http://software.ucv.ro/~cbadica/lssc2019.zip.

(ii) *Reified constraints* that allow to mix integer constraints with Boolean constraints by reifying truth values as 0 and 1.

Our heuristic search algorithm uses branch-and-bound method [7] incorporated into Gecode and performs more search steps as follows:

- A search step to determine the unconstrained optimal hierarchical decomposition process. The output consists of the graph height and the hierarchical decomposition subsets.
- A sequence of search steps for solving a series of bin packing problems for each hierarchical decomposition subset of activities, by minimizing the execution time of the activities of each subset.

We have used Gecode [12] constraint solver version 4.4.0 that is incorporated into ECLiPSe-CLP as an external library. We extracted the timing information using *statistics(hr_time, Time)* system predicate that determines the value of a high-resolution timer in seconds [11].

We have applied our prototype CLP program to the *j30* data set from [13]. This benchmark set contains 480 resource-constrained project scheduling problems, each problem involving the optimization of the total makespan of projects with 30 activities and 4 renewable constraints.

Each data set was converted from .*RCP* format into Prolog with schema:

Listing 1.1. Resource constraint scheduling problem given as a set of Prolog facts
```
number_of_renewable_resources(4).
% available_renewable_resource(Resource, ResourceQty).
available_renewable_resource(1, 12).
available_renewable_resource(2, 13).
...
number_of_activities(32).
% activity(Activity,Duration,ActivityResources,ListOfSuccesors).
activity(1, 0, [0, 0, 0, 0], [2, 3, 4]).
activity(2, 8, [4, 0, 0, 0], [6, 11, 15]).
...
activity(31, 2, [0, 0, 2, 0], [32]).
activity(32, 0, [0, 0, 0, 0], []).
```

The total time for processing our data set was 342.068 s. The searches used a timeout of 120 s. This timeout was exceeded for a single problem, while for 479 problems resulted an average processing time 0.462 s, with minimum 0.286 s and maximum of 11.29 s. Note that for 5 problems the processing time was above 1 s.

Taking into account that we did not have the optimal makespan values for our sample data set (PSPLIB contains optimal values for the provided data sets, but only for unstructured optimal schedules), we compared our results with the following measures (see Fig. 1 that presents the results obtained for problems 200 − 299 of *j30* data set):

- The critical path of the set of activities [3] denoted with CP.
- The costs associated to the hierarchical decomposition processes defined by mappings ℓ and p^* denoted with HD and $HDOpt$.
- The subptimal cost obtained using our heuristic approach, denoted with $Cost$.
- The lower and upper bounds of the costs, representing the sum of durations of all the activities (Max) and the maximum duration of activities (Min).

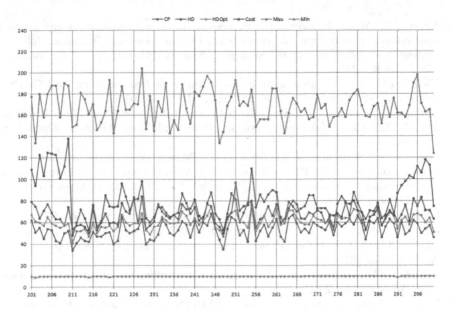

Fig. 1. Experimental results for problems 200–299 of the *j30* data set showing problem (*X* axis) vs project makespan (*Y* axis).

4   Conclusions and Future Works

In this paper we have introduced a new formal model of block structured scheduling processes with ordering and resource constraints. The model is suitable for optimization task. We have presented experimental results obtained using a Constraint Logic Programming prototype and an heuristic search algorithm inspired by hierarchical decomposition of directed acyclic graphs. We have use a standard benchmark data set from the project scheduling literature.

References

1. Bădică, A., Bădică, C., Dănciulescu, D., Logofătu, D.: Greedy heuristics for automatic synthesis of efficient block-structured scheduling processes from declarative specifications. In: Iliadis, L., Maglogiannis, I., Plagianakos, V. (eds.) AIAI 2018. IAICT, vol. 519, pp. 183–195. Springer, Cham (2018). https://doi.org/10.1007/978-3-319-92007-8_16
2. Garey, M.R., Johnson, D.S.: Computers and Intractability: A Guide to the Theory of NP-Completeness. W. H. Freeman and Company, San Franisco (1979)
3. Kelley Jr., J.E.: Critical-path planning and scheduling: mathematical basis. Oper. Res. **9**(3), 296–320 (1961). https://doi.org/10.1287/opre.9.3.296. Informs
4. Kolisch, R., Sprecher, A.: PSPLIB - a project scheduling library. Eur. J. Oper. Res. **96**(1), 205–216 (1997). https://doi.org/10.1016/S0377-2217(96)00170-1. Elsevier
5. Pesic, M., van der Aalst, W.M.P.: A declarative approach for flexible business processes management. In: Eder, J., Dustdar, S. (eds.) BPM 2006. LNCS, vol. 4103, pp. 169–180. Springer, Heidelberg (2006). https://doi.org/10.1007/11837862_18

6. Mrasek, R., Mülle, J., Böhm, K.: Process synthesis with sequential and parallel constraints. In: Debruyne, C., et al. (eds.) On the Move to Meaningful Internet Systems, vol. 10033, pp. 43–60. Springer, Cham (2016). https://doi.org/10.1007/978-3-319-48472-3_3

7. Niederliński, A.: A Gentle Guide to Constraint Logic Programming via ECLiPSe, 3rd edn. Jacek Skalmierski Computer Studio, Gliwice (2014)

8. Schimpf, J., Shen, K.: ECLiPSe - from LP to CLP. Theor. Pract. Log. Program. **12**(1–2), 127–156 (2012). https://doi.org/10.1017/S1471068411000469. Cambridge University Press

9. Sindelar, M., Sitaraman, R.K., Shenoy, P.: Sharing-aware algorithms for virtual machine colocation. In: Proceedings of 23rd ACM Symposium on Parallelism in Algorithms and Architectures (SPAA), pp. 367–378. ACM (2011). https://doi.org/10.1145/1989493.1989554

10. Ullman, J.D.: NP-complete scheduling problems. J. Comput. Syst. Sci. **10**(3), 384–393 (1975). https://doi.org/10.1016/S0022-0000(75)80008-0. Academic Press

11. The ECLiPSe Constraint Programming System. http://www.eclipseclp.org/. Accessed Mar 2019

12. Gecode - Generic Constraint Development Environment. https://www.gecode.org/. Accessed Mar 2019

13. Project Scheduling Problem Library - PSPLIB. http://www.om-db.wi.tum.de/psplib/. Accessed Mar 2019

Solving Combinatorial Puzzles with Parallel Evolutionary Algorithms

Todor Balabanov$^{(\boxtimes)}$ (iD), Stoyan Ivanov, and Rumen Ketipov

Institute of Information and Communication Technologies, Bulgarian Academy of Sciences, acad. Georgi Bonchev Str., Block 2, 1113 Sofia, Bulgaria
todorb@iinf.bas.bg
http://iict.bas.bg/

Abstract. Rubik's cube is the most popular combinatorial puzzle. It is well known that solutions of the combinatorial problems are generally hard to find. If 90° clockwise rotations of the cube's sides are taken as operations it will give a minimal cube's grammar. By building formal grammar sentences with the usage of the six operations ([L]eft, [R]ight, [T]op, [D]own, [F]ront, [B]ack) all cube's permutations can be achieved. In an evolutionary algorithms (like genetic algorithms for example) set of formal grammar sentences can be represented as population individuals. Single cut point crossover can be efficiently applied when population individuals are strings. Changing randomly selected operation with another randomly selected operation can be used as efficient mutation operator. The most important part of such global optimization is the fitness function. For better individuals fitness value evaluation a combination between Euclidean and Hausdorff distances is proposed in this research. The experiments in this research are done as parallel program written in C++ and Open MPI.

Keywords: Distributed evolutionary algorithms · Combinatorial puzzles · Integer optimization

1 Introduction

A parallel implementation of a genetic algorithm-based solver of the Rubik's cube was implemented by Balabanov in [1] and it was presented in [2]. Rubik's cube was invented and introduced by Erno Rubik in the 70s of the 20th century. After its creation the cube became the most popular combinatorial puzzle all over the world. In its original version it has 3×3×3 cubical segments. There are stickers in six different colors on each subcube square of the exposed sides. Each of the six planes (3×3×1) can be rotated in 90, 180, 270 or 360°, relative to the other part of the puzzle. In the original initial state all sides of the cube are in single color. Scumbling of the puzzle is done by many random rotations of the (3×3×1) sides. The optimization task aims to restore the cube in its original

This work was supported by a private funding of Velbazhd Software LLC.

I. Lirkov and S. Margenov (Eds.): LSSC 2019, LNCS 11958, pp. 493–500, 2020.
https://doi.org/10.1007/978-3-030-41032-2_56

state. Such combinatorial optimization problem is quite difficult because there are billions of combinations. The real number of combinations is $4.3252 * 10^{19}$ [3] and all of them can be reached from any starting combination. The puzzle is successfully resolved when a sequence of moves is applied such that all subcubes are matched to each other by their color on each side of the cube. According to an estimation in [3] resolutions sequences variate from 50 to 100 moves when the cube is well scrambled.

When there is an optimization problem with a sequence of commands it is a perfect candidate for evolutionary algorithms as optimizers. This research addresses the application of parallel genetic algorithms for Rubik's cube optimal or suboptimal solutions findings. The source code of the experiments is written in C++ with OpenMPI for parallel calculations and it can be found in a public source code repository [1]. Modification of the evaluation function presented in [2] is upgraded by addition of Hausdorff distance component.

The rest of this paper is organized as follows: Sect. 2 briefly describes theoretical details. Hence, Sect. 3 presents the proposed modifications into a practical software example and Sect. 4 is devoted to some experiments and results. Finally, Sect. 5 concludes and presents some ideas for further research.

2   Parallel Genetic Algorithms

Genetic algorithms are global optimization strategy inspired from the evolution process in the Biology theories. Place of the genetic algorithms and the genetic programming in the family of the metaheuristics is well presented in Fig. 1.

Solutions of a particular problem are represented as vectors of values into the solution space. All selected solution vectors are the population of the algorithm. The most common way of initial population establishment is by generation of random vectors. Each new generation appears in the population after recombination of selected individuals. In genetic algorithms recombination is done by two consequent operators - crossover and mutation. Which individuals to participate in the recombination process is decided by application of selection operator. It is very common during selection process elitism rule to be applied. Elitism means that some percent of the best found solutions survive to the real end of the optimization process. Because genetic algorithms based optimization is an iterative optimization a stopping criteria is needed. The most used stopping criteria is initially given number of genetic algorithm generations.

Genetic algorithms are the base of the genetic programming which is used in this research. Each element of the solution vector actually is an operation applied over the state of the Rubik's cube. Ordered set of such instructions is actually an algorithmic program. Because there is no direct intermediate relation between the individuals in a particular population genetic algorithms are highly appropriate for implementation in parallel computing or distributed computing. Population of the genetic algorithm can be easily divided in many sub-population and it can be distributed on many processors/cores or even heterogeneous computers in a cluster. Separation of the global population is the preferred approach,

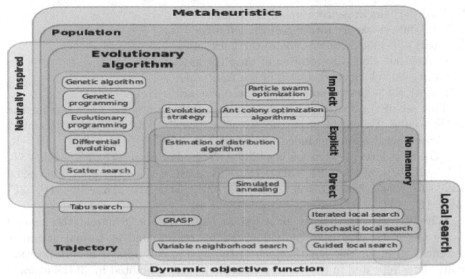

Fig. 1. Euler diagram of the different classifications of metaheuristics.

but in cases where only the fitness value calculation is time consuming, population is kept in the central processor/computer and only fitness value calculation is sent to the other contributing processors/computers.

When sub-populations distribution calculation scheme is selected some strategy for individual migration should be applied [2]. Migration between different islands is needed in order best found solutions to be available in some or in all sub-populations. When the implementation of the calculation is organized as donated distributed computing project in the inclusion of a new remote contributing computer fresh subset of the global population can be supplied. With such strategy solutions space is much better investigated.

3   Modified Rubik's Cube Solver

The core of the optimization code is Rubik's cube representation into the computer memory. For the needs in this research the cube is presented as six (one for each side) two-dimensional (3×3) arrays. Values in these arrays are integer numbers which correspond to cube's colors. There are better ways for digital representation [3], but it is much more practical in this way from algorithmic aspect.

Data structures are the first side of the modeling process. the algorithmic operations done over the data structures are the second side. The cube has six sides that is why the minimum number of operations over the cube is six. Six capital letters are used for 90° clockwise rotations, as proposed in [2, 4]:

T (Top) -90° clockwise rotation of the top side;
L (Left) -90° clockwise rotation of the left side;
B (Back) -90° clockwise rotation of the back side;
R (Right) -90° clockwise rotation of the right side;
F (Front) -90° clockwise rotation of the front side;
D (Down) -90° clockwise rotation of the down side.

This set of six operations is the minimal fully functional grammar for the Rubik's cube. Extended grammars are also possible, for example if counter-clockwise operators are included (+T, +L, +B, +R, +F, +D, -T, -L, -B, -R, -F, -D). Next level of extension is addition as number of turns (+1T, +2T, +3T, +1L, +2L, +3L, +1B, +2B, +3B, +1R, +2R, +3R, +1F, +2F, +3F, +1D,+2D, +3D, -1T, -2T, -3T, -1L, -2L, -3L, -1B, -2B, -3B, -1R, -2R, -3R, -1F, -2F, -3F, -1D, -2D, -3D) [2].

With the presented ideas for a formal Rubik's cube grammar the neutral choice is genetic algorithm individuals to be represented as formal grammar sentences with variable length. Each of the letters can appear at any position many times repeated in the chromosome. As it was appointed in [3] the average expected length of the chromosomes can be between 50 and 100.

```
double hausdorff(const RubiksCube &cube) const {
        /* Minimums should be found for each side. */
        double min[] = {INT_MAX, INT_MAX, INT_MAX, INT_MAX, INT_MAX, INT_MAX};

        /* Check all sides in pairs. */
        for(int s1=0; s1<6; s1++) {
                for(int s2=0; s2<6; s2++) {
                        double distance
                                = euclidean(*sides[s1], *(cube.sides)[s2]);

                        /* Keep track for the minimum distance. */
                        if(min[s1] > distance) {
                                min[s1] = distance;
                        }
                }
        }

        /* Find the maximum between the minimums. */
        double result = min[0];
        for(int s1=0; s1<6; s1++) {
                if(result < min[s1]) {
                        result = min[s1];
                }
        }

        return(result);
}
```

Fig. 2. Fitness value evaluation by combination between Euclidean and Hausdorff distance.

Table 1. Genetic algorithm parameters.

Parameter	Value
Generation gap	0.93
Crossover rate	0.98
Mutation rate	0.01
Maximum generations	10000
Number of individuals	37
Number of variables	Floating
Inserted rate	100 %

Single cut point is selected as crossover population, but other options [5] are also applicable. As mutation operator random change of a single instruction is selected. Selection is done by randomly selected parents, but elitism rule is applied. For the evaluation of the newly created individuals instructions encoded in the individual are applied over the scrambled cube. After that the state of the cube is compared with the target state (cube in the solved state). The listing in Fig. 2 shows the proposed in this paper modification of fitness evaluation function. For each pairs of cube's sides Euclidean distance is calculated. After that according to Hausdorff distance rules the maximum of the minimums is found. Evaluated fitness value is positive because the Euclidean distance is calculated with positive integers (cube's colors are mapped to integers) and the Hausdorff distance is a calculation of a maximum of the minimums. The puzzle is as better solved as the fitness value is smaller.

4   Experiments and Results

All experiments were done on a single processor desktop machine - Intel Core i5, 2.3 GHz, 2 Cores, 8 GB RAM and Mac OS X 10.13.6, Apple LLVM version 9.1.0. For the parallel implementation Open MPI is used.

Experiments are done in two groups with 30 independent runs for each. The source code originally is divided for test with star topology and incident nodes participation as migration strategies. That is why there are two groups of experiments. Each experiment compares pure Euclidean distance implementation and the proposed Hausdorff distance modification. Parameters of the genetic algorithm are listed in Table 1.

Figure 3 shows that when star topology is used the advantage of Hausdorff modification is not so great, but as it is shown in Fig. 4 when an incident nodes participation is used the proposed modification leads to convergence seep-up. Calculation of an Euclidean distance between two cubes uses six calculations of the sides for the cube (Listing 1.1). In the case of Hausdorff distance there are six times more calls of a single Euclidean distance calculation (Listing 1.2).

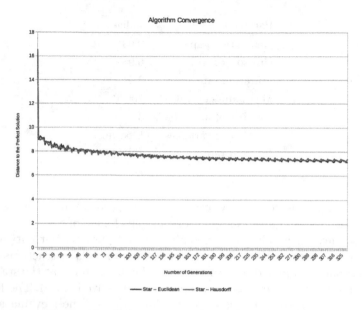

Fig. 3. Algorihthm convergence with star topology.

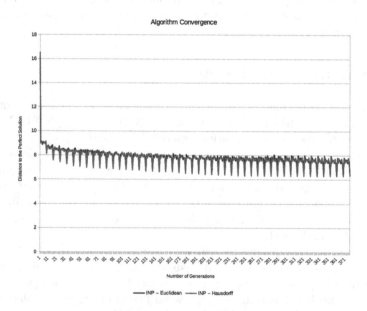

Fig. 4. Algorihtm convergence with incident nodes participation.

Listing 1.1. Euclidean distance.

```
double euclidean(const int side1[3][3],
                 const int side2[3][3]) const {
  double distance = 0.0;

  for(int i=0; i<3; i++)
    for(int j=0; j<3; j++)
      distance += (side1[i][j]-side2[i][j]) *
                  (side1[i][j]-side2[i][j]);

  return sqrt(distance);
}
```

Listing 1.2. Hausdorff distance.

```
double hausdorff(const RubiksCube &cube) const {
  double min[] = {INT_MAX, INT_MAX, INT_MAX,
                  INT_MAX, INT_MAX, INT_MAX};

  for(int s1=0; s1<6; s1++)
    for(int s2=0; s2<6; s2++) {
      double distance =
      euclidean(*sides[s1], *(cube.sides)[s2]);

      if(min[s1] > distance)
        min[s1] = distance;
    }

  double result = min[0];
  for(int s1=0; s1<6; s1++)
    if(result < min[s1])
      result = min[s1];

  return(result);
}
```

5   Conclusions

The experiments show that the addition of Hausdorff distance component improves the performance of the genetic algorithm. A calculation of the Hausdorff distance is a little bit slower than the calculation of the Euclidean distance, but better solution fitness estimation generally leads to genetic algorithm convergence improvement. Further investigations in the field of the soft computing can be done for the proposed fitness value evaluation as it was done in [6].

As further research it will be interesting an evaluation of the fitness value to be additionally filtered with Kalman filter [7], for example. Another interesting direction would be an involvement of the artificial neural networks such as [8,9] for preliminary solutions evaluation.

References

1. MPI Parallel Implementation of Genetic Algorithm Based Rubik's Cube Solver. http://github.com/TodorBalabanov/RubiksCubeGeneticAlgorithmsSolver. Accessed 10 Feb 2019
2. Balabanov, T., Zankinski, I., Barova, M.: Strategy for individuals distribution by incident nodes participation in star topology of distributed evolutionary algorithms. Cybern. Inf. Technol. **16**(1), 80–88 (2016)
3. Korf, R.: Finding optimal solutions to Rubik's cube using pattern databases. In: AAAI-1998 Proceedings, pp. 700–705. AAAI Press, Menlo Park (1998)
4. Randall, K.: Cilk - Efficient Multithreaded Computing. Doctor of Philosophy Thesis in Computer Science and Engineering, Massachusetts Institute of Technology, USA (1998)
5. Poli, R., Kozak, J.: Genetic programming. In: Burke, E.K., Kendall, G. (eds.) Search Methodologies, pp. 143–185. Springer, Boston (2014). https://doi.org/10.1007/978-1-4614-6940-7_6
6. Angelova, V.: Investigations in the area of soft computing targeted state of the art report. Cybern. Inf. Technol. **9**(1), 18–24 (2009)
7. Alexandrov, A.: Ad-hoc Kalman filter based fusion algorithm for real-time wireless sensor data integration. Flexible Query Answering Systems 2015. AISC, vol. 400, pp. 151–159. Springer, Cham (2016). https://doi.org/10.1007/978-3-319-26154-6_12
8. Tashev, T., Hristov, H.: Modeling of synthesis of information processes with generalized nets. Cybern. Inf. Technol. **3**(2), 92–104 (2003)
9. Atanasova T., Barova M.: Exploratory analysis of time series for hypothesize feature values. In: UniTech 2017 Proceedings, vol. 16, no. 2, pp. 399–403 (2017)

Multi-objective ACO Algorithm for WSN Layout: InterCriteria Analisys

Stefka Fidanova[1](✉) and Olympia Roeva[2]

[1] Institute of Information and Communication Technologies,
Bulgarian Academy of Sciences, Sofia, Bulgaria
stefka@parallel.bas.bg
[2] Institute of Biophysics and Biomedical Engineering,
Bulgarian Academy of Sciences, Sofia, Bulgaria
olympia@biomed.bas.bg

Abstract. One of the key objectives during wireless sensor networks deployment is full coverage of the monitoring region with a minimal number of sensors and minimized energy consumption of the network. In this paper we apply multi-objective Ant Colony Optimization (ACO) to solve this hard, from the computational point of view telecommunication problem. The number of ants is one of the key algorithm parameters in the ACO and it is important to find the optimal number of ants needed to achieve good solutions with minimal computational resources. The InterCriteria Analisys is applied in order to study the influence of ants number on the algorithm performance.

1 Introduction

Initial deployments of wireless sensor networks (WSN) were completed by the military, for reconnaissance and surveillance [1]. Examples of other possible applications of WSN's are: forest fire prevention, volcano eruption study [8], health data monitoring [9], civil engineering [7] and others.

The energy for collecting data and its transmission comes from the battery of a node. One of the WSN nodes has special role. It is a High Energy Communication Node (HECN), which collects data from across the network and transmits it to the "main computer" to be processed. The sensors transmit their data to the HECN, either directly or via hops, using closest sensors as communication relays. The WSN can have large numbers of nodes and the problem can be very complex. Thus, one of the best choice is to apply some metaheuristic method.

The problem of designing a WSN is multi-objective, with two objective functions. These are (1) minimize the energy consumption of the nodes in the network, and (2) minimize the number of nodes. The full coverage of the network and connectivity are considered as constraints. In our work we propose a multi-objective ant colony optimization (ACO).

In the past, [15] solved an instance of the WSN layout using a multi-objective genetic algorithm. In their formulation, a fixed number of sensors had to be

I. Lirkov and S. Margenov (Eds.): LSSC 2019, LNCS 11958, pp. 501–509, 2020.
https://doi.org/10.1007/978-3-030-41032-2_57

placed in order to maximize the coverage. However, in some applications the most important is the network energy. In this context, in [4] an ACO algorithm was proposed, but it is applicable to a special case when the sensors are antennas and the work concerns only energy minimization. In [20] an evolutionary algorithm was applied to this variant of the problem. In [6] several evolutionary algorithms to solve the problem were proposed. Finally, in [5] a genetic algorithm, which achieves similar solutions as the algorithms in [6] was studied, but tested only on small test problems.

In this paper we study the influence of the number of ants to the algorithm performance and quality of the achieved solutions. The computational resources, which the algorithm needs, are not negligible. The computational resources depends on the size of the solved problem and on the number of ants. Our aim in this work is to find a minimal number of ants which allow the algorithm to find good solution. Moreover, the recently proposed approach InterCriteria Analisys (ICrA) is applied for further investigation of the influence of the ants number on ACO algorithm.

ICrA, proposed by [13], is a recently developed approach for evaluation of multiple objects against multiple criteria and thus discovering existing correlations between the criteria themselves. It is based on the apparatus of the index matrices (IMs) [10], and the intuitionistic fuzzy sets [11] and can be applied to decision making in different areas of knowledge [16–19].

2   Theoretical Background

2.1   Multi-objective ACO for WSN Layout

We apply multi-objective ACO to solve the WSN problem. The ACO algorithm uses a colony of artificial ants that behave as cooperating agents. With the help of the pheromone and the heuristic information they try to construct better solutions and to find the optimal ones. The pheromone corresponds to the global memory of the ants and the heuristic information is a some preliminary knowledge of the problem. The problem is represented by a graph and the solution is represented by a path in the graph or by tree in the graph. Ants start from random nodes and construct feasible solutions. When all ants construct their solution the pheromone is updated. The new, added, pheromone depends to the quality of the solution. The elements of the graph, which belong to better solutions will receive more pheromone and will be more desirable in the next iteration.

In our implementation, we use the MAX-MIN Ant System (MMAS) which is one of the most successful ant approaches originally presented in [2].

In our case, the graph of the problem is represented by a square grid. The nodes of the graph are enumerated. The ants will deposit their pheromone on the nodes of the grid. We will deposit the sensors on the nodes of the grid too. The solution is represented by tree. An ant starts to create a solution starting from random node, which communicates with the HECN. Construction of the heuristic information is a crucial point in the ant algorithms. Our heuristic information is a product of three values (Eq. 1).

$$\eta_{ij}(t) = s_{ij} l_{ij} (1 - b_{ij}), \tag{1}$$

where s_{ij} is the number of the new points (nodes of the graph) which the new sensor will cover, and which are not covered by other sensors, and

$$l_{ij} = \begin{cases} 1 \text{ if communication exists}; \\ 0 \text{ if there is not communication}. \end{cases} \tag{2}$$

Here, b_{ij} is the solution matrix and the matrix element $b_{ij} = 1$ when there is sensor on this position otherwise $b_{ij} = 0$. With s_{ij} we try to increase the number of points covered by one sensor and thus to decrease the number of sensors we need. With l_{ij} we guarantee that all sensors will be connected. With b_{ij} we guarantee that maximum one sensor will be mapped on the same point. The search stops when transition probability $p_{ij} = 0$ for all values of i and j. It means that there are no more free positions, or that all area is fully covered.

At the end of every iteration the quantity of the pheromone is updated. The pheromone trail update rule is given by:

$$\tau_{ij} \leftarrow \rho \tau_{ij} + \Delta \tau_{ij}, \tag{3}$$

$$\Delta \tau_{ij} = \begin{cases} 1/F(k) \text{ if } (i,j) \in \{\text{non-dominated solution constructed by ant } k\}, \\ 0 \qquad \text{otherwise}. \end{cases}$$

We decrease the pheromone with a parameter $\rho \in [0,1]$. This parameter models evaporation in the nature and decreases the influence of old information on the search process. After that, we add the new pheromone, which is proportional to the value of the fitness function. The fitness function is constructed as follows:

$$F(k) = \frac{f_1(k)}{\max_i f_1(i)} + \frac{f_2(k)}{\max_i f_2(i)} \tag{4}$$

Where $f_1(k)$ is the number of sensors proposed by the k-th ant and $f_2(k)$ is the energy of the solution of the k-th ant. These are also the objective functions of the WSN layout problem. We normalize the values of two objective functions with their maximal achieved values from the first iteration.

2.2   InterCriteria Analysis

InterCriteria analysis, based on the apparatuses of Index Matrices (IM) [10] and Intuitionistic Fuzzy Sets (IFS) [12], is given in details in [13].

In order to find the agreement between two criteria, the vectors of all internal comparisons for each criterion are constructed, which elements fulfill one of the three relations R, $\overline{R}$ and $\tilde{R}$. The nature of the relations is chosen such that for a fixed criterion C and any ordered pair $\langle x, y \rangle \in C^*(O)$:

$$\langle x, y \rangle \in R \Leftrightarrow \langle y, x \rangle \in \overline{R}, \langle x, y \rangle \in \tilde{R} \Leftrightarrow \langle x, y \rangle \notin (R \cup \overline{R}), R \cup \overline{R} \cup \tilde{R} = C^*(O).$$

When comparing two criteria the degree of "agreement" $(\mu_{C,C'})$ is usually determined as the number of matching components of the respective vectors. The degree of "disagreement" $(\nu_{C,C'})$ is usually the number of components of opposing signs in the two vectors. From the way of computation it is obvious that $\mu_{C,C'} = \mu_{C',C}$ and $\nu_{C,C'} = \nu_{C',C}$. Moreover, $\langle \mu_{C,C'}, \nu_{C,C'} \rangle$ is an Intuitionistic Fuzzy Pair.

There may be some pairs $\langle \mu_{C,C'}, \nu_{C,C'} \rangle$, for which the sum $\mu_{C,C'} + \nu_{C,C'}$ is less than 1. The difference

$$\pi_{C,C'} = 1 - \mu_{C,C'} - \nu_{C,C'} \tag{5}$$

is considered as a degree of "uncertainty".

3   Experimental Results

3.1   ACO Application on Various Sizes of Problem

We have implemented software, which realizes our ant algorithm. Our software can solve the problem at any rectangular area, the communication and the coverage radius can be different and can have any positive value. We can have regions in the area. The program was written in C language, and the tests were run on computer with an Intel Pentium 2.8 GHz processor. In our tests we use an example where the area is square. The coverage and communication radii cover 30 points. The HECN is fixed in the centre of the area. For the tests we have used areas with three sizes: 350×350 points, 500×500 points, and 700×700 points.

In our previous work [3], we showed that our ant algorithm outperforms the existing algorithms for this problem. There, after several runs of the algorithm we were able to specify the most appropriate values of its parameters: $\alpha = \beta = 1$, $\rho = 0.5$, $\tau_0 = 0.5$. We study the influence of the number of ants on the quality of the solutions. We fixed the number of the iterations to be 60 (about 3 h per ant) and the number of ants to have following values $\{1, 2, 3, 4, 5, 6, 7, 8, 9, 10\}$.

We run our ACO algorithm 30 times for each number of ants. We extract the Pareto front from the solutions of these 30 runs. In Tables 1, 2, and 3 we show the achieved non dominated solutions (approximate Pareto fronts) for case 350×350, 500×500, and 700×700, respectively.

The left column represents the number of sensors and in other columns we present the energy corresponding to this number of sensors and the number of ants. Analyzing the Table 1 (case 350×350) we observe that the best algorithm performance in the case 350×350 is achieved by 7 ants, more ants leads to more computational time. From Table 2 (case 500×500) we observe that the

Table 1. Approximate Pareto fronts, example 350×350

Sensors	Ants									
	1	2	3	4	5	6	7	8	9	10
111	30	36	30	30	30	30	30	30	30	30
112	30	36	30	30	30	30	30	30	30	30
113	28	35	28	30	30	30	28	28	28	28
114	26	26	26	26	26	26	26	26	26	26
115	26	26	26	26	26	26	26	26	26	26
116	26	26	26	26	26	26	25	25	26	25

Table 2. Approximate Pareto fronts, example 500×500

Sensors	Ants									
	1	2	3	4	5	6	7	8	9	10
223	90	96	90	90	89	81	90	90	90	90
224	61	96	89	89	88	65	61	59	57	71
225	61	96	74	58	60	58	57	58	57	57
226	59	95	73	57	59	57	56	58	57	57
227	60	57	57	57	57	56	56	57	57	57
228	60	57	57	57	57	56	56	57	54	57
229	58	57	57	55	57	56	56	56	54	56
230	57	57	57	55	57	52	56	54	54	56
231	57	55	57	55	55	52	56	54	54	56
232	57	55	55	51	54	50	52	51	54	48
233	57	55	55	51	54	50	51	51	54	48
234	57	55	55	51	53	50	51	48	53	48
235	57	55	54	51	53	50	51	48	50	48
236	57	55	54	51	53	50	51	48	50	48
237	57	55	54	51	53	50	51	48	50	48
238	57	55	53	51	53	50	51	48	50	48
239	56	55	53	50	53	50	51	48	50	48
240	53	53	53	50	53	50	51	48	50	48
241	53	53	53	50	53	50	51	48	50	48
242	53	53	53	50	53	50	51	48	50	48
243	53	53	53	50	53	50	51	48	50	48
244	53	53	53	50	52	50	51	48	50	48

approximate Pareto front achieved by 6 ants dominates others. Analyzing the Table 3 (case 700 × 700) we observe that the approximate Pareto front achieved by 6 ants again dominates others. In all discussed cases the approximate Pareto fronts achieved by 6 and 7 ants outperform others. Thus it is the best number of ants for our sensor layout problem.

3.2 ICrA Results

In case of size 350 × 350, in order to apply the ICrA the IM based on the results presented in Table 1 is constructed. The cross-platform software for ICrA approach, ICrAData, is used [14]. After the application of ICrA the following IM of values of degrees of "agreement" $\mu_{C,C'}$ are obtained (Table 4). In the table, as well as in the Tables 5 and 6, in bold are the estimations that show high correlation between the considered ACO algorithms.

In case of size 500 × 500 again IM based on the results presented in Table 2 is constructed. The obtained degrees of "agreement" are as presented in Table 5.

In case of size 700 × 700 the IM based on the results presented in Table 3 is constructed. The obtained degrees of "agreement" are as presented in Table 6.

Table 3. Approximate Pareto fronts, example 700 × 700

Sensors	Ants									
	1	2	3	4	5	6	7	8	9	10
437	173	173	173	173	173	118	168	172	261	172
438	173	173	173	173	173	118	112	117	260	172
439	172	173	173	173	140	93	110	115	131	172
440	172	173	173	173	115	93	110	114	111	162
441	172	173	173	122	111	93	110	114	111	110
442	172	173	173	114	111	93	110	112	111	110
443	172	150	123	114	111	93	110	112	111	110
444	124	112	112	106	107	93	110	102	111	105
445	117	112	112	106	107	93	110	102	108	105
446	117	112	105	105	105	93	107	102	104	105
447	117	112	105	105	105	93	105	102	102	105
448	115	111	105	105	105	93	105	102	102	105
449	115	111	105	105	105	93	102	99	102	105
450	113	111	105	105	105	93	102	99	102	105
451	113	109	105	105	105	93	102	99	97	105
452	113	109	105	105	105	93	99	99	97	104
453	113	109	105	105	105	93	99	99	97	104
454	113	109	105	105	96	93	96	96	96	104
455	106	106	105	105	96	93	96	96	96	97

Table 4. Obtained degrees of "agreement" $\mu_{C,C'}$ - problem size 350×350

$\mu_{C,C'}$	ACO_1	ACO_2	ACO_3	ACO_4	ACO_5	ACO_6	ACO_7	ACO_8	ACO_9	ACO_{10}
ACO_1		1	1	0.87	0.87	0.87	0.87	0.87	1	0.87
ACO_2	1		1	0.87	0.87	0.87	0.87	0.87	1	0.87
ACO_3	1	1		0.87	0.87	0.87	0.87	0.87	1	0.87
ACO_4	0.87	0.87	0.87		1	1	0.73	0.73	0.87	0.73
ACO_5	0.87	0.87	0.87	1		1	0.73	0.73	0.87	0.73
ACO_6	0.87	0.87	0.87	1	1		0.73	0.73	0.87	0.73
ACO_7	0.87	0.87	0.87	0.73	0.73	0.73		1	0.87	1
ACO_8	0.87	0.87	0.87	0.73	0.73	0.73	1		0.87	1
ACO_9	1	1	1	0.87	0.87	0.87	0.87	0.87		0.87
ACO_{10}	0.87	0.87	0.87	0.73	0.73	0.73	1	1	0.87	

Table 5. Obtained degrees of "agreement" $\mu_{C,C'}$ – problem size 500×500

$\mu_{C,C'}$	ACO_1	ACO_2	ACO_3	ACO_4	ACO_5	ACO_6	ACO_7	ACO_8	ACO_9	ACO_{10}
ACO_1		**0.89**	0.78	**0.9**	0.71	0.71	0.68	0.73	0.7	0.7
ACO_2	**0.89**		0.8	**0.87**	0.78	0.76	0.73	0.74	0.71	0.73
ACO_3	0.78	0.8		**0.87**	0.83	0.75	0.79	0.82	0.82	0.73
ACO_4	**0.9**	**0.87**	**0.87**		0.79	0.79	0.78	0.81	0.76	0.81
ACO_5	0.71	0.78	0.83	0.79		0.84	**0.87**	**0.93**	0.84	0.81
ACO_6	0.71	0.76	0.75	0.79	0.84		**0.9**	**0.89**	0.77	**0.96**
ACO_7	0.68	0.73	0.79	0.78	**0.87**	0.9		0.89	0.81	**0.9**
ACO_8	0.73	0.74	0.82	0.81	**0.93**	0.89	0.89		0.87	0.88
ACO_9	0.7	0.71	0.82	0.76	0.84	0.77	0.81	**0.87**		0.79
ACO_{10}	0.7	0.73	0.73	0.81	0.81	**0.96**	**0.9**	**0.88**	0.79	

Table 6. Obtained degrees of "agreement" $\mu_{C,C'}$ – problem size 700×700

$\mu_{C,C'}$	ACO_1	ACO_2	ACO_3	ACO_4	ACO_5	ACO_6	ACO_7	ACO_8	ACO_9	ACO_{10}
ACO_1		**0.88**	0.72	0.72	0.8	0.35	0.84	0.85	0.85	0.78
ACO_2	**0.88**		0.77	0.71	0.74	0.28	0.77	0.82	0.81	0.8
ACO_3	0.72	0.77		**0.94**	0.82	0.46	0.64	0.7	0.68	0.7
ACO_4	0.72	0.71	**0.94**		**0.87**	0.46	0.64	0.74	0.7	0.74
ACO_5	0.8	0.74	0.82	**0.87**		0.4	0.76	0.85	0.84	0.83
ACO_6	0.35	0.28	0.46	0.46	0.4		0.36	0.33	0.32	0.39
ACO_7	0.84	0.77	0.64	0.64	0.76	0.36		0.81	**0.89**	0.73
ACO_8	0.85	0.82	0.7	0.74	0.85	0.33	0.81		0.84	0.82
ACO_9	0.85	0.81	0.68	0.7	0.84	0.32	**0.89**	0.84		0.78
ACO_{10}	0.78	0.8	0.7	0.74	0.83	0.39	0.73	0.82	0.78	

Based on the ICrA outcomes it is shown that the ACO algorithms with very close number of ants (e.g. ACO_1 and ACO_2, ACO_3 and ACO_4 or ACO_7 and ACO_8) perform in similar way. The high correlation between such pairs is preserved regardless the problem size. Such relation is obvious. According to the results in Table 4 (case 350×350) very high correlation is observed for the ACO_9 and ACO_1, ACO_2, ACO_3. These relations are not observed in the other two cases. In case of problem size 350×350 the existing many very high correlations are explained with the fact the most of the considered ACO algorithms can solve the problem with good solution quality. Whereas, in the case of size 500×500 or 700×700 only few ACO algorithms perform very well. So, if we considered results in case of larger problem sizes, the ICrA results show that the number of ans has the significant influence on the obtained results.

4   Conclusion

In this paper we have studied the influence of the number of ants on the performance of the ACO algorithm, applied to the wireless sensor network. Smaller number of ants leads to the shorter running time and minimizes memory use, which is important for complex/large cases. We varied the number of ants, while fixing the number of iterations. Furthermore, we included the concept of an Extended front, as an additional tool to compare approximate Pareto fronts that do not dominate each other. The best approximate Pareto front and the best performance were achieved when the number of ants was equal to 6 in the cases 700×700 and 500×500, and 7 in the case 350×350. The results are analysed based on ICrA, too. The analysis confirms considerable influence of the ants number on the quality of the decision, especially in the case of bigger problem sizes.

Acknowledgment. This work is partially supported by the Projects: KP-06-N22/1 "Theoretical Research and Applications of InterCriteria Analysis" and by the Bulgarian Scientific Fund by the granr DN 12/5.

References

1. Deb, K., Pratap, A., Agrawal, S., Meyarivan, T.: A fast and elitist multi-objective genetic algorithm: nsga-ii. IEEE Trans. Evol. Comput. **6**(2), 182–197 (2002)
2. Dorigo, M., Stutzle, T.: Ant Colony Optimization. MIT Press, Cambridge (2004)
3. Fidanova, S., Shindarov, M., Marinov, P.: Multi-objective ant algorithm for wireless sensor network positioning. Comptes Randus de l'Academie Bulgare des Sciences **66**(3), 353–360 (2013)
4. Hernandez, H., Blum, C.: Minimum Energy Broadcasting in Wireless Sensor Networks: An ant Colony Optimization Approach for a Realistic Antenna Model. J. of Applied Soft Computing **11**(8), 5684–5694 (2011)
5. Konstantinidis, A., Yang, K., Zhang, Q., Zainalipour-Yazti, D.: A multi-objective Evolutionary Algorithm for the deployment and Power Assignment Problem in Wireless sensor Networks. J. of Computer networks **54**(6), 960–976 (2010)

6. Molina, G., Alba, E., El-G, Talbi: Optimal Sensor Network Layout Using Multi-Objective Metaheuristics. Universal Computer Science **14**(15), 2549–2565 (2008)
7. Paek J., Kothari N., Chintalapudi K., Rangwala S. and Govindan R. (2005), The Performance of a Wireless Sensor Network for Structural Health Monitoring, In Proc. of 2nd European Workshop on Wireless Sensor Networks, Istanbul, Turkey
8. Werner-Allen, G., Lorinez, K., Welsh, M., Marcillo, O., Jonson, J., Ruiz, M., Lees, J.: Deploying a Wireless Sensor Network on an Active Volcano. IEEE Internet Computing **10**(2), 18–25 (2006)
9. Yuce, M.R., Ng, S.W., Myo, N.L., Khan, J.Y., Liu, W.: Wireless Body Sensor Network Using Medical Implant Band. Medical Systems **31**(6), 467–474 (2007)
10. K. Atanassov, Index Matrices: Towards an Augmented Matrix Calculus, Studies in Computational Intelligence, 573, 2014
11. K. Atanassov, Intuitionistic Fuzzy Sets, VII ITKR Session, Sofia, 20–23 June 1983, Reprinted: Int J Bioautomation, 20(S1), 2016, S1–S6
12. K. Atanassov, Review and New Results on Intuitionistic Fuzzy Sets, Mathematical Foundations of Artificial Intelligence Seminar, Sofia, 1988, Preprint IM-MFAIS-1-88, Reprinted: Int J Bioautomation, 20(S1), 2016, S7–S16
13. Atanassov, K., Mavrov, D., Atanassova, V.: Intercriteria Decision Making: A New Approach for Multicriteria Decision Making. Based on Index Matrices and Intuitionistic Fuzzy Sets, Issues in IFSs and GNs **11**, 1–8 (2014)
14. Ikonomov, N., Vassilev, P., Roeva, O.: ICrAData - Software for InterCriteria Analysis. Int J Bioautomation **22**(1), 1–10 (2018)
15. D.B. Jourdan, Wireless Sensor Network Planning with Application to UWB Localization in GPS-denied Environments, Massachusets Institute of Technology, PhD thesis, 2000
16. S. Ribagin, Shannon, A., Atanassov, K., Intuitionistic fuzzy evaluations of the elbow joint range of motion, Advances in Intelligent Systems and Computing, Volume 401, 2016, 225–230
17. Todinova, S., Mavrov, D., Krumova, S., Marinov, P., Atanassova, V., Atanassov, K., Taneva, S.G.: Blood plasma thermograms dataset analysis by means of InterCriteria and correlation analyses for the case of colorectal cancer. Int J Bioautomation **20**(1), 115–124 (2016)
18. V. Traneva, Atanassova V., Tranev S. Index matrices as a decision-making tool for job appointment, Springer Nature Switzerland AG, G. Nikolov et al. (Eds.): NMA 2018, LNCS 11189, 1–9, 2019
19. P. Vassilev, L. Todorova, V. Andonov, An auxiliary technique for InterCriteria Analysis via a three dimensional index matrix, Notes on Intuitionistic Fuzzy Sets, Vol. 21, 2015, No. 2, 71–76
20. Wolf, S., Mezz, P.: Evolutionary Local Search for the Minimum Energy Broadcast Problem. In: Cotta, C., van Hemezl, J. (eds.) VOCOP 2008. Lecture Notes in Computer Sciences, vol. 4972, pp. 61–72. Springer, Germany (2008)

Reachable Sets of Nonlinear Control Systems: Estimation Approaches

Tatiana F. Filippova[1,2](✉) iD

[1] Department of Optimal Control,
Krasovskii Institute of Mathematics and Mechanics, Russian Academy of Sciences,
16 S. Kovalevskaya Street, Ekaterinburg 620108, Russian Federation
ftf@imm.uran.ru
[2] Ural Federal University, 19 Mira street, Ekaterinburg 620002, Russian Federation

Abstract. The dynamical control systems of a special structure with a combined nonlinearity of quadratic and bilinear kinds presenting in state velocities are studied. The uncertainty in initial states and in system parameters is also assumed and it has a set-membership type when only the bounding sets for unknown items are given. The ellipsoidal estimates of reachable sets are derived using the special structure of studied control system. The techniques of generalized solutions of Hamilton-Jacobi-Bellman (HJB) equations and HJB inequalities together with previously established results of ellipsoidal calculus are applied to find the set-valued estimates of reachable sets as the level sets of a related cost functional. The computational algorithms and related numerical examples are also given.

Keywords: Control system · Nonlinearity · Reachable set · Uncertainty · State estimation

1 Introduction

The paper is devoted to the study of control systems with nonlinearity and uncertainty in related dynamical equations. The case of a set-membership description of uncertainty [19, 22, 27] is studied here when only bounds on uncertain items are done and any additional information (e.g. probability characteristic) is unknown. The main goal here is to construct for such control systems related reachable sets or, if it is difficult to find the reachable sets precisely, to construct their outer (external) estimates.

The state estimation approach which uses the special bilinear–quadratic structure of nonlinearity of studied control system and uses also the advantages of ellipsoidal calculus [19, 22, 25, 26] is further developed for a different class of uncertain nonlinear systems. Here techniques related to constructing external set-valued estimates of reachable sets for nonlinear control systems and based on results and on related techniques of the theory of generalized solutions of Hamilton - Jacobi - Bellman (HJB) equations and inequalities are developed.

© Springer Nature Switzerland AG 2020
I. Lirkov and S. Margenov (Eds.): LSSC 2019, LNCS 11958, pp. 510–517, 2020.
https://doi.org/10.1007/978-3-030-41032-2_58

Solutions to equations of the HJB type are rather difficult to calculate, and the design of related computational algorithms is important. However, for many applied problems one may be satisfied with approximate solutions that may be achieved by substituting the original HJB equations with variational inequalities due to certain comparison principles [15, 16, 20, 21]. Based on this key idea, it turns out to be possible to obtain estimates for the solutions of a nonlinear controlled system of the class under consideration.

The paper is organized as follows. After introducing some notations and definitions, the main problem is formulated in Sect. 2. The approaches related to estimates of reachable sets in nonlinear case and based on results of the theory of generalized solutions of Hamilton - Jacobi - Bellman inequalities are given in Sect. 3. Finally, some concluding remarks are given.

This study continues the researches presented in [9–13] but here a more complicated case is considered, when the dynamical equations contain a nonlinearity of quadratic type and also contain bilinear terms defined by an uncertain matrix with common quadratic constraints on its elements. This case is both of theoretical and of applied importance, in particular such problems may arise in modeling and identification for mechatronic systems (e.g., in robotics, in problems of motor actuation, hydraulic actuation and others applied fields), the approaches developed here may be used in model-based advanced control of complex systems, such as adaptive control, robust control, sliding-mode control, H-infinite control, etc. [1–6, 17, 18, 24].

2   Problem Formulation

2.1   Basic Notations

Let $\mathbb{R}^n$ denote the n–dimensional Euclidean space and $x'y$ is the usual inner product of $x, y \in \mathbb{R}^n$ with the prime as a transpose and with $\|x\| = (x'x)^{1/2}$. We use the symbol comp $\mathbb{R}^n$ for the variety of all compact subsets $A \subset \mathbb{R}^n$ and the symbol conv $\mathbb{R}^n$ for the variety of all compact convex subsets $A \subset \mathbb{R}^n$.

Let us denote the set of all closed convex subsets $A \subseteq \mathbb{R}^n$ by the symbol clconv $\mathbb{R}^n$. Let $\mathbb{R}^{n \times m}$ stands for the set of all real $n \times m$-matrices, diag $\{v\}$ denotes a diagonal matrix with the elements of vector v on the main diagonal. Denote by $I \in \mathbb{R}^{n \times n}$ the identity matrix and by Tr (A) the trace of $n \times n$-matrix A (the sum of its diagonal elements).

We denote also by $B(a, r) = \{x \in \mathbb{R}^n : \|x - a\| \le r\}$ the ball in $\mathbb{R}^n$ with a center $a \in \mathbb{R}^n$ and a radius $r > 0$ and denote by

$$E(a, Q) = \{x \in \mathbb{R}^n : \ (Q^{-1}(x - a), (x - a)) \le 1\}$$

the ellipsoid in $\mathbb{R}^n$ with a center $a \in \mathbb{R}^n$ and with a symmetric positive definite $n \times n$-matrix Q.

2.2 Problem Description

Consider the following nonlinear control system

$$\dot{x} = A(t)x + f(x)d + u(t), \quad x_0 \in X_0, \quad t \in [t_0, T], \tag{1}$$

where $x, d \in \mathbb{R}^n$, $\|x\| \leq K$ $(K > 0)$, $f(x)$ is the nonlinear function, which is quadratic in x, that is $f(x) = x'Bx$, with a given symmetric and positive definite $n \times n$-matrix B.

Control function $u(t)$ is assumed to be Lebesgue measurable on $[t_0, T]$ and it satisfies the constraint $u(t) \in U$ for a.e. $t \in [t_0, T]$ where U is a given set belonging to comp $\mathbb{R}^n$. We will assume further that $U = E(\hat{a}, \hat{Q})$.

We assume that the $n \times n$-matrix function $A(t)$ in (1) has the form

$$A(t) = A^0 + A^1(t). \tag{2}$$

Here A^0 is a given constant $n \times n$-matrix, the measurable and $n \times n$-matrix $A^1(t)$ is unknown but bounded, $A^1(t) \in \mathcal{A}^1$ $(t \in [t_0, T])$.

Therefore we have the constraint

$$A(t) \in \mathcal{A} = A^0 + \mathcal{A}^1, \tag{3}$$

where we assume that

$$\mathcal{A}^1 = \left\{ \begin{array}{l} A = \{a_{ij}\} \in R^{n \times n} : a_{ij} = 0 \text{ for } i \neq j, \text{ and} \\ a_{ii} = a_i, \quad i = 1, \ldots, n, \quad a = (a_1, \ldots, a_n), \quad a'Da \leq 1 \end{array} \right\}, \tag{4}$$

with $D \in \mathbb{R}^{n \times n}$ being a symmetric and positive definite matrix.

We assume that X_0 in (1) is an ellipsoid, $X_0 = E(a_0, Q_0)$, with a symmetric and positive definite matrix $Q_0 \in \mathbb{R}^{n \times n}$ and with a center $a_0 \in \mathbb{R}^n$.

The main problem studied here is to find external ellipsoidal estimates for reachable sets $X(t)$ $(t_0 < t \leq T)$ basing on results and on related techniques of the theory of generalized solutions of Hamilton - Jacobi - Bellman equations and inequalities. We investigate a more complicated case than in [10] and use here the technique recently developed in [11–13].

3 Main Results

3.1 Dynamic Programming Approach in General Case

Let us mention first some important results from the optimal control theory received in [7, 14–16, 20, 21, 23, 28] that relate to this issue.

Consider the control system described by the ordinary differential equation

$$\dot{x} = f(t, x, u(t)), \quad t \in [t_0, T] \tag{5}$$

with a function $f : [t_0, T] \times \mathbb{R}^n \times \mathbb{R}^m \to \mathbb{R}^n$ measurable in t and continuous in other variables. Here x stands for the state vector, t stands for time and control $u(\cdot)$ is a measurable function satisfying the constraints

$$u(\cdot) \in \mathcal{U} = \{u(\cdot) : u(t) \in U, \quad t \in [t_0, T]\} \tag{6}$$

where $U \in \mathrm{comp}\mathbb{R}^m$.

Let us assume that the initial condition $x(t_0)$ to the system (5) is unknown but bounded

$$x(t_0) = x_0, \quad x_0 \in X_0 \in \mathrm{comp}\mathbb{R}^n. \tag{7}$$

Let the absolutely continuous function

$$x(t) = x(t, u(\cdot), t_0, x_0)$$

be a solution to (5) with initial state x_0 satisfying (7) and with control function $u(t)$ satisfying (6).

Consider the control system (5)–(7) and assume in this Section that the function $f(t, x, u)$ in (5) is continuous in all variables and has continuous partial derivatives with respect to x. Suppose also that conditions providing the extendability of solutions to (5)–(7) on the interval $[t_0, T]$ are satisfied.

Denote by $X(t) = X(t; t_0, X_0)$ the reachable set of the system (5)–(7) at time t. It is known that the reachable set may be expressed as a level set of a value function for an auxiliary control problem [20]. The value function for the auxiliary problem is the solution to the following Hamilton - Jacobi - Bellman (HJB) equation

$$V_t(t, x) + \max_{u \in U} (V_x, f(t, x, u)) = 0. \tag{8}$$

In the common situation the value function may be not differentiable, in this case a solution to the HJB equation is treated as the viscosity (or minmax) solution [14,23,28]. The precise solutions to such equations of the HJB type are rather difficult to calculate. The use of corresponding variational HJB inequalities and related comparison theorems instead makes it possible to obtain approximate estimates of reachable sets (e.g., [16,20,22]).

Consider the following auxiliary result.

Lemma 1 ([20]). *Assume that there exists a function $\mu(t)$ integrable on $[t_0, T]$ and such that*

$$V_t(t, x) + \max_{u \in U} (V_x, f(t, x, u)) \leq \mu(t), \quad t_0 \leq t \leq T. \tag{9}$$

Then the following external estimate of the reachable set $X(t)$ of the system (5)–(7) is true

$$X(t) \subseteq \left\{ x : V(t, x) \leq \int_{t_0}^{t} \mu(s)ds + \max_{x \in X_0} V(t_0, x) \right\}, \quad t_0 \leq t \leq T. \tag{10}$$

Note that, without loss of generality, it is possible to take $\mu(s) = 0$ in (9) [16].

Instead of (9), consider now the following inequality of a more general type

$$V_t(t, x) + \max_{u \in U} (V_x, f(t, x, u)) \leq g(t, V(t, x)), \quad t_0 \leq t \leq T, \tag{11}$$

where $g(t, V)$ is integrable in $t \in [t_0, T]$ and is continuously differentiable in variable V.

Consider the following ordinary differential equation

$$\dot{U}(t) = g(t, U), \quad U(t_0) = U_0, \quad t_0 \leq t \leq T, \tag{12}$$

which is called a *comparison equation* for (5)–(7).

Theorem 1 ([15, 16]). *Assume the relations (11) and (12) are fulfilled. Assume also that*

$$\max_{x \in X_0} V(t_0, x) \leq U_0. \tag{13}$$

Then the following upper estimate is valid

$$X(t) \subseteq \{x : V(t, x) \leq U(t)\}, \quad t_0 \leq t \leq T. \tag{14}$$

The above results will be used further, in estimating the attainability sets of the system (1)–(3) with uncertainty and nonlinearity.

3.2   Main Theorem: HJB-Estimate of Reachable Set

Now rewrite the studied system (1)–(3) in the form of the corresponding differential inclusion

$$\dot{x} \in \mathcal{A}x + f(x)d + U, \quad x_0 \in X_0, \quad t \in [t_0, T], \tag{15}$$

and assume further that

$$U = E(\hat{a}, \hat{Q}), \tag{16}$$

with $\hat{a} \in \mathbb{R}^n$ and a symmetric and positive definite $n \times n$-matrix $\hat{Q}$.

The solution of the problem of estimating the unknown states of nonlinear differential inclusion (15) and the study of related problems of control synthesis may be reduced to the investigation of first order PDEs of the Hamilton-Jacobi-Bellman (HJB) type and of their modifications and generalizations. This approach was outlined earlier in [8, 11], where it was studied however for simpler class of systems. The control system of type (15)–(16) corresponds to a more complicated case for the analysis, since there are two nonlinear constraints simultaneously, namely we have here a bilinear-quadratic dynamics with an additional assumption on quadratic constraints for unknown matrix elements.

Consider the following HJB-type inequality

$$V_t(t, x) + \max_{u \in E(\hat{a}, \hat{Q})} \max_{A \in \mathcal{A}} (V_x, Ax + f(x)d + u) \leq 0 \tag{17}$$

with the boundary condition

$$V(t_0, x) = \phi(x) \leq 0 \tag{18}$$

where $\phi(x)$ is a given continuously differentiable function.

Denote by $k_0 > 0$ the minimal positive number k for which the inclusion

$$X_0 = E(a_0, Q_0) \subseteq E(a_0, k^2 B^{-1}) $$

is true.

Define the functions $a^+(t)$ and $r^+(t)$ as the solutions of the following nonlinear ordinary differential equations,

$$\dot{a}^+(t) = A^0 a^+(t) + ((a^+(t))'Ba^+(t) + r^+(t))d + \hat{a}, \quad t_0 \le t \le T, \qquad (19)$$

$$\dot{r}^+(t) = \max_{\|l\|=1} \left\{ l'\left(2r^+(t)B^{1/2}(A^0 + 2d(a^+(t))'B)B^{-1/2} \right. \right. \\ \left. \left. + q^{-1}(r^+(t))B^{1/2}\hat{Q}^*B^{1/2}))l \right\} + q(r^+(t))r^+(t), \qquad (20)$$

$$q(r) = ((nr)^{-1} Tr(B\hat{Q}^*))^{1/2}, \qquad (21)$$

where the positive definite matrix $\hat{Q}^*$ is such that

$$A^1 a_0 + E(0, \hat{Q}) + kD^{1/2}B^{1/2}B(0,1) \subset E(0, \hat{Q}^*), \qquad (22)$$

and initial states for $a^+(\cdot)$ and $r^+(\cdot)$ are

$$a^+(t_0) = a_0, \quad r^+(t_0) = k^2. \qquad (23)$$

Theorem 2. *Let the function $V(t,x)$ be defined as follows*

$$V(t,x) = (x - a^+(t))'(r^+(t))^{-1}B(x - a^+(t)) - 1 \qquad (24)$$

with $a^+(t)$ and $r^+(t)$ defined in (19)–(23). Then $V(t,x)$ satisfies the HJB inequality (17) and the following boundary condition of type (18) is valid

$$V(t_0, x) = (x - a_0)'k^{-2}B(x - a_0) - 1 \le 0. \qquad (25)$$

Moreover, the following inclusion is true

$$X(t) \subseteq \{x : V(t,x) \le 0\}, \quad t_0 \le t \le T. \qquad (26)$$

Proof. The proof of the theorem is based on results of [11] and is carried out with necessary corrections due to the more complicated structure of constraints on the initial data and parameters. Note here also that the existence of solutions of the system (19)–(23) follows from the classical results of the differential equations theory and may be established also similar to the reasonings given in [8, 11]. □

Theorem 2 allows to find the solution of HJB inequality (17)–(18) explicitly. It follows from the special form of the chosen initial function $V(t_0, x)$ (25) and from a special type of studied control system. In more general cases the use of appropriate approximations gives the way to establish a similar connection between the techniques of ellipsoidal calculus for dynamic control systems with uncertainties and results based on comparison theorems of the theory of Hamilton-Jacobi-Bellman equations and inequalities.

4 Conclusion

The paper deals with the problems of state estimation for nonlinear dynamical control systems under set-membership description of system uncertainties. The class of nonlinear control systems for which bilinear and quadratic elements can be simultaneously present in the state velocities of a dynamical system is investigated. Here the techniques based on recent results of the theory of generalized solutions of HJB equations (or related HJB inequalities) are further developed to obtain new ellipsoidal estimates for the tubes of solutions of the studied control system. The results obtained here may be used in further theoretical and applied researches in optimal control problems and in state estimation for dynamical systems with more complicated classes of uncertainty of set-membership and other types, in particular for a class of impulsive control problems under uncertainty in initial states and other parameters.

References

1. Asselborn, L., Groß, D., Stursberg, O.: Control of uncertain nonlinear systems using ellipsoidal reachability calculus. In: Proceedings of the 9th IFAC Symposium on Nonlinear Control Systems, Toulouse, France, 4–6 September 2013, IFAC, pp. 50–55 (2013)
2. August, E., Lu, J., Koeppl, H.: Trajectory enclosures for nonlinear systems with uncertain initial conditions and parameters. In: Proceedings of the 2012 American Control Conference, Fairmont Queen Elizabeth, Montréal, Canada, pp. 1488–1493, June 2012
3. Blanchini, F., Miani, S.: Set-Theoretic Methods in Control. Systems & Control: Foundations & Applications. Birkhäuser, Basel (2015)
4. Boscain, U., Chambrion, T., Sigalotti, M.: On some open questions in bilinear quantum control. In: European Control Conference (ECC), Zurich, Switzerland, July 2013, pp. 2080–2085 (2013)
5. Ceccarelli, N., Di Marco, M., Garulli, A., Giannitrapani, A.: A set theoretic approach to path planning for mobile robots. In: Proceedings of the 43rd IEEE Conference on Decision and Control, Atlantis, Bahamas, pp. 147–152, December 2004
6. Chernousko, F.L., Rokityanskii, D.Ya.: Ellipsoidal bounds on reachable sets of dynamical systems with matrices subjected to uncertain perturbations. J. Optimiz. Theory Appl. **104**(1), 1–19 (2000)
7. Crandall, M.G., Evans, L.C., Lions, P.-L.: Some properties of solutions of Hamilton-Jacobi equations. Trans. Am. Math. Soc. **282**, 487–502 (1984)
8. Filippova, T.F.: State estimation for a class of nonlinear dynamic systems with uncertainty through dynamic programming technique. In: Proceedings of the 6th International Conference "Physics and Control - 2013", PhysCon2013, San Lois Potosi, Mexico, 26–29 August 2013, pp. 1–6 (2013)
9. Filippova, T.F.: Ellipsoidal estimates of reachable sets for control systems with nonlinear terms. In: Proceedings of the IFAC-PapersOnLine: 20th World Congress of the International Federation of Automatic Control (IFAC-2017), Toulouse, France, 9–14 July 2017. **50**(1), 15925–15930 (2017)
10. Filippova, T.F.: Estimation of star-shaped reachable sets of nonlinear control systems. In: Lirkov, I., Margenov, S. (eds.) LSSC 2017. LNCS, vol. 10665, pp. 210–218. Springer, Cham (2018). https://doi.org/10.1007/978-3-319-73441-5_22

11. Filippova, T.F.: The HJB approach and state estimation for control systems with uncertainty. IFAC-PapersOnLine **51**(13), 7–12 (2018)
12. Filippova, T.F.: Differential equations for ellipsoidal estimates of reachable sets for a class of control systems with nonlinearity and uncertainty. IFAC-PapersOnLine **51**(32), 770–775 (2018)
13. Filippova, T.F.: Description of dynamics of ellipsoidal estimates of reachable sets of nonlinear control systems with bilinear uncertainty. In: Nikolov, G., Kolkovska, N., Georgiev, K. (eds.) NMA 2018. LNCS, vol. 11189, pp. 97–105. Springer, Cham (2019). https://doi.org/10.1007/978-3-030-10692-8_11
14. Fleming, W.H., Soner, H.M.: Controlled Markov Processes and Viscosity Solutions, 2nd edn. Springer, New York (2006)
15. Gurman, V.I.: The Extension Principle in Problems of Control. Fizmatlit, Moscow (1997). (in Russian)
16. Gusev, M.I., Kurzhanski, A.B.: On the hamiltonian techniques for designing nonlinear observers under set-membership uncertainty. In: Preprints of the 7-th IFAC Symposium on Nonlinear Control Systems, Pretoria, South Africa, 21–24 August 2007, pp. 343–348 (2007)
17. Kishida, M., Braatz, R.D.: Ellipsoidal bounds on state trajectories for discrete-time systems with linear fractional uncertainties. Optim. Eng. **16**, 695–711 (2015)
18. Kuntsevich, V.M., Volosov, V.V.: Ellipsoidal and interval estimation of state vectors for families of linear and nonlinear discrete-time dynamic systems. Cybern. Syst. Anal. **51**(1), 64–73 (2015)
19. Kurzhanski, A.B.: Control and Observation under Conditions of Uncertainty. Nauka, Moscow (1977). (in Russian)
20. Kurzhanski, A.B.: Comparison principle for equations of the Hamilton-Jacobi type. Proc. Steklov Inst. Math. **253**(Suppl. 1), 185–195 (2006)
21. Kurzhanski, A.B.: Hamiltonian techniques for the problem of set-membership state estimation. Int. J. Adapt. Control Signal Process. **25**(3), 249–263 (2010)
22. Kurzhanski, A.B., Varaiya, P.: Dynamics and Control of Trajectory Tubes: Theory and Computation. Systems & Control, Foundations & Applications, vol. 85. Birkhäuser, Basel (2014)
23. Lions, P.L.: Generalized Solutions of Hamilton-Jacobi Equations. Research Notes in Mathematics, vol. 69. Pitman Advanced Publishing Program, Boston (1982)
24. Malyshev, V.V., Tychinskii, Yu.D.: Construction of attainability sets and optimization of maneuvers of an artificial Earth satellite with thrusters in a strong gravitational field. Proc. RAS Theory Control Syst. **4**, 124–132 (2005)
25. Mazurenko, S.S.: A differential equation for the gauge function of the star-shaped attainability set of a differential inclusion. Doklady Math. **86**(1), 476–479 (2012)
26. Sinyakov, V.V.: Method for computing exterior and interior approximations to the reachability sets of bilinear differential systems. Differ. Equ. **51**(8), 1097–1111 (2015)
27. Schweppe, F.: Uncertain Dynamic Systems. Prentice-Hall, Englewood Cliffs (1973)
28. Subbotin, A.I.: Generalized Solutions of First-order PDE's. The Dynamic Optimization Perspective. Birkhauser, Boston (1995)

Jumping Average Filter Parameter Optimization for Pulsar Signal Detection

Ivan Garvanov[1](✉) and Vladimir Ivanov[2]

[1] University of Library Studies and Information Technologies,
Sofia, Bulgaria
i.garvanov@unibit.bg
[2] Institute of Information and Communication Technologies,
Acad. G. Bonchev bl 2, Sofia, Bulgaria
Ivanov.vladi@gmail.com

Abstract. The paper studies the parameters of an average jumping window algorithm to improve the signal-to-noise ratio while retaining the signal characteristics. The studies were conducted with an FPGA device for processing and detecting a real pulsar signal B0329+54.

Keywords: Jumping Average Filter · FPGA device · Pulsar signal detection

1 Introduction

In practice, the moving average algorithm is applied for processing and analyzing data samples by creating a series of averages of different subsets of the complete data set. This algorithm is called a moving mean or moving average and is a type of final pulse response filter. The variations of this filter are different, and in practice the most common is the averaging with: simple and cumulative or weighted values. The moving window may be sliding or jumping.

As a result of the use of a sliding window, the data is smoothed while the application of a jumping window causes the signal to be silenced. The jumping average filter (JAF) averaging window size is essential in the processing of the signals. With a larger window size, a greater signal smoothing or better noise in a jumping window occurs. As a result of the use of an average jumping window, the frequency of the signal changes and the number of samples in the sample is reduced.

The influence of the size of the jumping window on the processing and detection of pulsar signal, which is characterized by a signal-to-noise ratio of about -60 dB, has been investigated in [1]. As a result of this study, dependence is drawn on the relationship between the sampling frequency of the signal and the new frequency of the signal obtained after processing. The research is done in the development environment of MATLAB.

Pulsars are fast rotating neutron stars that emit radio waves, which is received on earth as a series of very stable fast periodic pulses [2]. Different

© Springer Nature Switzerland AG 2020
I. Lirkov and S. Margenov (Eds.): LSSC 2019, LNCS 11958, pp. 518–523, 2020.
https://doi.org/10.1007/978-3-030-41032-2_59

applications of pulsar signals have been available in recent years. They can be used to create a navigation system similar to GNSS or to be used to create early warning systems from falling ground targets [3–5]. The problem of using them is the low power of grounded pulsar signals. One way to increase the noise signal ratio is to use JAF [1].

In this article, a research will be conducted to optimize the algorithm parameter with an average jumping window in the pulsar signal processing with an FPGA device. Optimizing this parameter is essential for both the performance of the algorithm and the quality of the detection and evaluation of the pulsar signal parameters.

2   Average Filter with a Jumping Window

The Jumping Average Filter (JAF) is a modified version of the Moving Average Filter (MAF). The input data of the filter is divided into M non-overlapping segments (windows), each of which contains the N samples. The data from each window is averaged and the resulting value used to form the new output sequence containing the M samples.

$$y(i) = \frac{1}{N} \sum_{k=1}^{N} x((i-1)N + k), i\epsilon\,[1, M] \tag{1}$$

The SNR of the new sequence $y(i)$ will be times larger than of the input of the sequence $x(i)$. This processing results in a N -fold decrease in sampling frequency $f_{s,new}$ compared to sampling frequency of the input f_s. Therefore, the JAF acts not only as a low- pass filter but a decimator as well. When the signal processing is carried out in the time domain, the use of the JAF can be very useful in the sense of reducing the processing time. The key problem concerned with the Jumping Average Window (JAW) is the optimal choice of the jumping window length. When choosing the window length of the JAW we must take into account not only the level of suppression of the noise variance, but the degree of distortion of the useful signal immersed in noise. The optimal window size of the JAW can be determined only in cases where the spectrum of the signal is known Δf and bounded by a certain frequency and the noise power does not exceed a certain level. The maximum number of samples that can be used in the jumping window are [1]:

$$N_{max} = \frac{F_s}{F_{s,new}} \tag{2}$$

where fs is a sampling frequency, $f_{s,new}$ is a new sampling frequency. In order not to disturb the Nyquist theorem is necessary $f_{s,new} \geq \Delta f$.

3   FPGA Implementation of Jumping Average Filter

Implementation of Jumping Average Filter in FPGA device [6] is shown in Fig. 1, where the input data to be processed is input to $DataINNinput(17:0)$. They

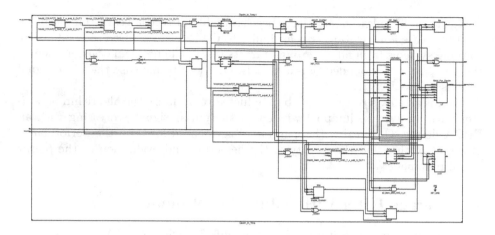

Fig. 1. Jumping average filter implemented in FPGA

are in the form of an additional code that allows you to work with whole numbers with a sign. The data is perceived by the front-cluster device of the clk clock signal after an old impulse is given at the start input.

The Debounce block is used to start the system. It allows the operation of the epouch counter, the purpose of which is to control the number of data averaged by the jumping window. For this time, the data inn (17:0) inputs arrive at the input of the arithmetic module realized on the DSP48A1 built-in FPGA DSP module. This module works in cumulative add-on mode [7]. When the epoch counter value reaches the specified value corresponding to the size of the jump window, the device performs the following operations.

– Records the result of the cumulative adder in the memory.
– Increases by 1 the contents of the address generator that is responsible for the memory address where the next average value is to be recorded.
– Resets the contents of the cumulative adder.
– This process is repeated until the authorized memory entry is depleted, and then the device completes its work.

4 Pulsar Signal

Pulsars are rotating neutron stars (Fig. 2a) that emit broadband electromagnetic signals [1]. The period of repetition of pulsar signals is the same as the pulsar rotation period. The periodic repetition of pulsar signals is stable over time and is comparable to the accuracy of atomic clocks. The signals from the pulsars differ from one another by the type of their profiles (Fig. 2b).

The main limitation for the use of pulsar signals in practice is the very low signal-to-noise ratio (SNR) from -40 dB to -90 dB [1–5]. This is due to long distances from the ground to the pulsars, which are in the order of several light-years. These signal-to-noise ratios require long pulsar monitoring time to detect the signal [1].

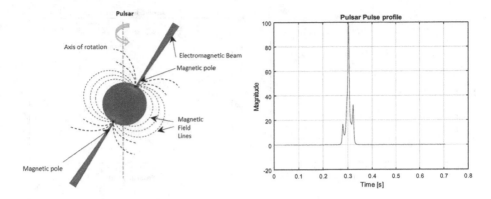

Fig. 2. (a) Model of pulsar, (b) Profile of pulsar B0329+54

5   Experimental Results

Jumping Averaging Filter Parameter Optimization has been used FPGA implementation of Jumping Average Filter and using real signal of pulsar. The experimental data contain the noisy signal received from pulsar B0329+54 at the Westerbork radio observatory (Fig. 3a). The experimental data are sampled at a frequency of $f_s = 40$ MHz, and the number of samples of the input signal within a repetition period is $28582316 = 2.8e^7$. The specter of pulsar signal $\Delta f = 400$ Hz is shown on Fig. 3b.

Table 1. SNR for different values of window length

N - window cells	fs, new in [Hz]	SNR in [dB]
$1e^3$	40 000	7.45
$1e^4$	4 000	10.32
$1e^5$	400	16.23
$1e^6$	40	17.05

The maximum number of samples that can be used in the jumping window is $Nmax = 1e^5$. Increasing the SNR to increase the detection probability of the pulsar signal is possible by increasing the size of the jumping window, but the signal at the output of the filter will be distorted. The results of processing the pulsar signal of Fig. 4a with JAF at the size of the jumping window $N=1e^3$, $1e^4$, $1e^5$ and $1e^6$ are shown from Fig. 4(a) to (d). From this figures it can be seen that by increasing the size of the jumping window N from $1e^3$ to $1e^6$, it results in an increase in the signal-to-noise ratio. This dependence is also shown in Table 1. It is noteworthy that after the value of $N=1e^5$ the increase in SNR is not very high, while the quality of the pulsar signal profile is impaired.

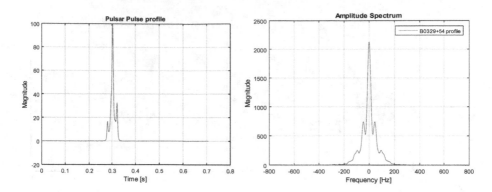

Fig. 3. (a) Pulsar signal (1 period), (b) Specter of pulsar B0329+54

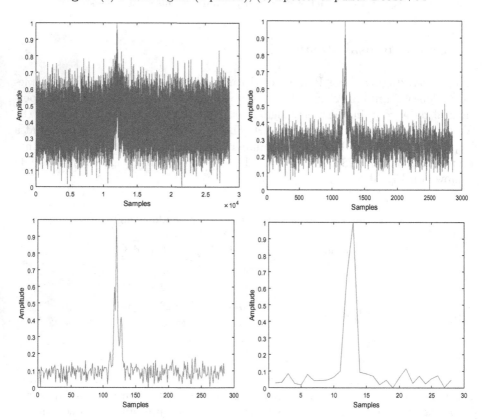

Fig. 4. (a) JAF output $N=1e^3$, (b) JAF output $N=1e^4$, (c) JAF output $N=1e^5$, (d) JAF output $N=1e^6$

6   Conclusions

The obtained results show that the presented algorithm can be successfully used for processing and detection of pulsar signals. Using Jumping Average Filter in time domain we increase the signal to noise ratio and reduce the detect time. A mathematical dependence is proposed to select the size of JAW. Examples and illustrations are based on pulsar signal from pulsar B0329+54.

Acknowledgments. The research has been carried out under the Scientific Research Fund under the Contest for the Financing of Scientific Research of Young Scientists and Postdoctoral Students - 2018, Contract KP-06-M27/9 of 2018 "Contemporary digital methods and tools for exploring and modeling transport flows" and a project BG05M2OP001-1.001-0003-C01, "Center of Excellence for Informatics and Information and Communication Technology", 2018–2023.

References

1. Garvanov, I., Kabakchiev, Ch., Behar, V., Garvanova, M.: The experimental study of possibility for pulsar signal detection. In: The Second International Conference Engineering Telecommunications - EnT 2016, Moscow/Dolgoprudny, pp. 68–71 (2016)
2. Lorimer, D., Kramer, M.: Handbook of Pulsar Astronomy. Cambridge University Press, New York (2005)
3. Buist, P., Engelen, S., Noroozi, A., Sundaramoorthy, P., Verhagen, S., Verhoeven, C.: Principles and potential of pulsar navigation. In: 24 ON Conference, Portland (2011)
4. Garvanov, I., Kabakchiev, C., Behar, V., Garvanova, M.: Target detection using a GPS forward-scattering radar. In: International Conference Engineering Telecommunications - EnT 2015, Moscow/Dolgoprudny, pp. 29–33 (2015)
5. Kabakchiev, C., Behar, V., Garvanov, I., Kabakchieva, D., Garvanova, M., Rohling, H.: Air target detection in pulsar FSR system. In: International Conference Engineering Telecommunications - EnT 2018, Moscow/Dolgoprudny (2018)
6. Ivanov, V., Garvanov, I.: Implementing of average jumping window with FPGA. In: Engineering Technologies Education Security, pp. 194–197. Veliko Tarnovo (2018)
7. Garvanova, M., Slavova, S.: Mathematical statistics and data processing with SPSS, vol. 2, no. 5, p. 234. Publishing house, Sofia (2015). ISBN 978-619-185-183-6

Precision in High Dimensional Optimisation of Global Tasks with Unknown Solutions

Kalin Penev[✉]

School Media Arts and Technology, Solent University, East Park Terrace,
Southampton SO14 0YN, UK
Kalin.Penev@solent.ac.uk

Abstract. High dimensional optimisation is a challenge for most of the available search methods. Resolving global and constrained task seems to be even harder and exploration of tasks with unknown solutions can be seen very rare in the literature and requires more research efforts. This article analyses optimisation of high dimensional global, including constrained, tasks with unknown solutions. Reviewed and analysed are experimental results precision, possibilities for trapping in local sub-optima and adaptation to unknown search spaces.

Keywords: Free Search · Multidimensional global optimisation

1 Introduction

Research efforts in the area of multidimensional search and optimisation generate different questions [1,4–6,8,11,13,20,21] and needs more fundamental research in order to build knowledge sufficient for resolving various tasks. A dilemma rose by optimisation of global multidimensional problems with non-uniformly and remotely distributed local suboptimal solutions, could be formulated as precision versus correctness. Precision is understood as a measure of valid numbers after the decimal coma. Correctness is understood as identification of exact global optimum amongst many local sub optima.

Investigations on multidimensional tests suggest that an increase the number of dimensions leads to inability of the search methods to identify the optimum. This is particularly highlighted by the results achieved on global tasks.

Review of recent publications [4,7,12,15,17] suggests that for tasks within the range of 20–50 dimensions, methods can easily distinguish global optimum from local sub-optima. This is still possible for global tasks within the range of 100–400 dimensions. However for tasks within the range of 1000–10000 and above dimensions this becomes almost impossible. The question is: What are the reasons for this limitation? More detailed observation identifies that each variable has its own specific area which play a role for forming global optimum. If one variable is outside of this area the solution is sub-optimal.

© Springer Nature Switzerland AG 2020
I. Lirkov and S. Margenov (Eds.): LSSC 2019, LNCS 11958, pp. 524–529, 2020.
https://doi.org/10.1007/978-3-030-41032-2_60

For 20–50 dimensions if one variable is outside of its optimal area the difference between this sub-optimum and global optimum is typically in the range of several percents. Methods can easily identify this difference and then distinguish global optimum.

For 100–400 dimensions if one or two variables are outside of their optimal areas the difference between this sub-optimum and global optimum is in the range of one percent. Some methods still can identify this difference and then distinguish global optimum.

For 1000–10000 and more dimensions if five or ten variables are outside of their optimal areas the difference between this sub-optimum and global optimum is below one percent. Only few methods can identify this difference and then distinguish global optimum [1, 18].

The article presents an investigation on optimisation of several multidimensional heterogeneous real-value numerical tests. These are used - Ackley [2], Griewank [10], Keane's Bump [14], Michalewicz [14], Norwegian [3], Rastrigin [16], Step [9] and Rosenbrock [19], test functions. Experimental results discussed in this article are achieved by Free Search (FS) [18].

2 Analysis and Discussion

This section will review within the first part result on optimisation of tasks with below hundreds dimensions. Second part will focus on hundreds dimensional task. Third part will introduce result on thousand dimensional tasks.

2.1 Low Dimensional Tasks

Optimisation problems with low number of parameters below one hundred are relatively simple and can be easily resolved by most of the optimisation methods. A numerical test which is classified as a hard on low dimensions is constrained Keane's Bump test. Particular example is its 50 dimensional version.

Achieved by Free Search result on Bump test, which identifies the optimal values with precision 10^{-11} is $F_{max50} = 0.835262348358115$ with constraint value $p = 0.75000000000000155$.

Corresponding variables for this solution are presented in Table 1. Due the heuristic approach implemented in algorithm Free Search there is no guarantee that it is the global optimum. It will be nice to see improved by other methods result. Exhaustive search which could guarantee possible optimum with the same precision should explore 50 dimensional search space from 0 to 10 with granularity at least 10^{-12} per dimension, which in total equates to 10^{600} locations.

2.2 Hundred Dimensional Tasks

This section summarises results on optimisation of 100 dimensional Norwegian and Michalewicz test functions limited to low, medium, and high number of iterations and updated with extra search starting from best achieved location.

Table 1. Variables for Bump test $F_{max50} = 0.835262348358115$

x0 = 6.2835797902617516	x17 = 2.9524114588141508	x34 = 0.46001886537952297
x1 = 3.1699376777500143	x18 = 2.9379900975870918	x35 = 0.45827603976373454
x2 = 3.156074749723996	x19 = 2.9232836057447771	x36 = 0.45656222211455522
x3 = 3.1423609878041932	x20 = 0.48823744173286926	x37 = 0.45487684374388804
x4 = 3.1287695107543283	x21 = 0.48593392519529544	x38 = 0.45321821190663503
x5 = 3.1152747643628493	x22 = 0.4836826364813	x39 = 0.45158651639926856
x6 = 3.1018528645810473	x23 = 0.48148246973308972	x40 = 0.449980222959319
x7 = 3.088480538514534	x24 = 0.47932981475899472	x41 = 0.44839856026986158
x8 = 3.0751349167360189	x25 = 0.47722236395944401	x42 = 0.44684046137453542
x9 = 3.0617943894947892	x26 = 0.47515900821764157	x43 = 0.44530576420283136
x10 = 3.0484368235138755	x27 = 0.4731373982323247	x44 = 0.44379365517281105
x11 = 3.0350390366956366	x28 = 0.47115575813689387	x45 = 0.44230323452275311
x12 = 3.0215778555508499	x29 = 0.46921217893825617	x46 = 0.44083365158292653
x13 = 3.0080295243393778	x30 = 0.46730534146908231	x47 = 0.43938498943233062
x14 = 2.9943676920815716	x31 = 0.46543440391236818	x48 = 0.43795641918838452
x15 = 2.9805647610851183	x32 = 0.46359705504397125	x49 = 0.43654683784954496
x16 = 2.9665903794608957	x33 = 0.46179196398120126	

Table 2. Optimal results for 100 dimensional Norwegian test.

Iterations	Result	
Low	0.750627	–
Medium	0.967082	22.382279%
High	1.00004	3.295668%
Extra	1.000056278217909	0.000162%

On Table 2 in first column number of iteration are shown qualitatively. Second column contains best achievements. Third column indicates improvement in %.

Presented in Table 2 results, for 100 dimensional Norwegian test, show that for low and medium number of iterations correct optimum cannot be achieved. Identification how many variables for sub-optimal solution are outside of their optimal area could be a subject of further research.

For high number of iterations method reached near optimal region. Difference for sub-optimal and near optimal solution is 3%. Last row presents accepted as correct optimum with improved precision. Due the heuristic nature of Free Search there is no 100% guarantee that this is correct global optimum.

Table 3 Optimal results for 100 dimensional Michalewicz test.

On Table 3 number of iteration are shown qualitatively in the first column. Second column contains best achievements. Third column indicates improvement in %. Presented in Table 3 results for 100 dimensional Michalewicz test suggests that for low, medium, and high number of iterations Free Search reached near

Table 3. Optimal results for 100 dimensional Michalewicz test.

Iterations	Result	
Low	99.5808	–
Medium	99.6157	0.350346%
High	99.6191	0.034130%
Extra	99.620193836	0.000010%

optimal region. Difference between solutions is below 1%. Last row presents accepted as correct optimum with improved precision. Due the heuristic nature of Free Search there is no 100% guarantee that this is correct global optimum. It will be of interest to see whether other methods can disprove or confirm the results presented in this section.

2.3 Thousands Dimensional Tasks

Evaluation of thousands dimensional tasks approaching a new phase of extensive use of computational resources based on parallel processing and using GPU accelerated computing, which decrease the time for calculations but does not always lead to appropriate results [6]. This section discusses results of optimisation of 1000 dimensional Bump test function and 2000 and 10000 dimensional versions of Ackley [2], Griewank [10], Michalewicz [14], Rastrigin [16], Step [9] and Rosenbrock [19], test functions. Bump test although could be classified as a scalable test if explored for more than 440 dimensions faced limitation regarding the requirement to start from one location $x_i = 5$ and constraint $\prod_0^n x_i > 0.75$. For $n \geq 440$ product constraint $\prod_0^n x_i$ exceeds maximal value which could be presented in 64 bit floating point format.

New maximal value for 1000 dimensional version on Keane bump test is identified $F_{1000\ Bump} = 0.85285332941$. Disproof or confirmation of correctness and precision assessment of this result could be a subject of further research.

Evaluation of Ackley, Griewank, Michalewicz, Rastrigin, Step tests, is based on experiments limited to 2.10^9 functions evaluations. Rosenbrock test function is explored for 2.10^{10} function evaluations.

All experiments for 10000 dimensions are limited to 10^9 objective function evaluations. Results for 2000 and 10000 dimensional experiments suggests that the correct optimum for Step test can be achieved with high precision. Optimal area for Michalewicz and Rosenbrock tests is identified. Due to the specific landscape of Ackley, Griewank and Rastrigin, tests achieved results could be classified as near optimal sub-optima. Better precision and correctness on 2000 and 10000 dimensional tests requires more objective function evaluations, however this may not be feasible due to time delays. Better precision and correctness could be achieved by algorithms' ability for orientation within multidimensional search space and ability to distinguish small differences in optimal results (Tables 4 and 5).

Table 4. Optimal results for 2000 dimensional test.

Ackley	−0.00020573
Griewank	−0.02460318
Michalewicz	1999.48
Rastrigin	−0.00000328
Rosenbrock	−0.00448202
Step	4000

Table 5. Optimal results for 10000 dimensional test.

Ackley	−0.000707076
Michalewicz	9999.25
Rastrigin	−0.000571037
Step	20000.0000

3   Conclusion

This article distinguishes and defines more precisely criteria precision and correctness in assessment of optimisation results. This could support improvement of optimisation methods. It discusses the dilemma precision versus correctness in optimisation of global multidimensional problems with non-uniformly and remotely distributed local suboptimal solutions, in particular on test functions with unknown solutions.

Experimental results for various tasks divided in three groups by number of parameters namely 20–50 dimensions, 100–400 dimensions, and 1000–10000 dimensions archived by Free Search optimisation method are summarized and analysed. The analysis identifies and highlights possible precision and correctness and in general possible quality of the results in high-dimensional optimisation.

Firm generalisation of these initial highlights needs further fundamental research. More algorithms should be tested since different techniques explore the search space in specific manner.

Further research should focus also on development of new tests (possibly with unknown optimal solution), improvements of search methods orientation and ability to distinguish small differences within multidimensional search space.

References

1. Abiyev, R.H., Tunay, M.: Optimization of high-dimensional functions through hypercube evaluation. Comput. Intell. Neurosci. **2015**, 967320 (2015)
2. Ackley, D.H.: A Connectionist Machine for Genetic Hillclimbing. Kluwer, Boston (1987)

3. Brekke E.F.: Complex Behaviour in Dynamical Systems. The Norwegian University of Science and Technology, pp. 37–38 (2004). http://www.academia.edu/545835/COMPLEXBEHAVIORINDYNAMICALSYSTEMS. Accessed 29 May 2014

4. Cano, A., Garcia-Martinez, C., Ventura, S.: Extremely high-dimensional optimization with MapReduce: scaling functions and algorithm. Inf. Sci. **415–416**, 110–127 (2017)

5. Caraffini, F., Neri, F., Iacca, G.: Large scale problems in practice: the effect of dimensionality on the interaction among variables. In: Squillero, G., Sim, K. (eds.) EvoApplications 2017, Part I. LNCS, vol. 10199, pp. 636–652. Springer, Cham (2017). https://doi.org/10.1007/978-3-319-55849-3_41

6. Cao, B., et al.: Distributed parallel particle swarm optimization for multi-objective and many-objective large-scale optimization. IEEE Access **5**, 8214–8221 (2017)

7. Chu, X., Hu, M., Wu, T., Weir, J., Lu, Q.: AHPS2: an optimizer using adaptive heterogeneous particle swarms. Inf. Sci. **280**, 26–52 (2014). https://doi.org/10.1016/j.ins.2014.04.043

8. Grosan, C., Abraham, A., Hassinen, A.: A line search approach for high dimensional function optimization. Telecommun. Syst. **46**(3), 217–243 (2011)

9. De Jung K.A.: An Analysis of the Behaviour of a Class of Genetic Adaptive Systems, Ph.D. thesis, University of Michigan (1975)

10. Griewank, A.O.: Generalized decent for global optimization. J. Optim. Theory Appl. **34**, 11–39 (1981)

11. Kotsialos, A.: Nonlinear optimisation using directional step lengths based on RPROP. Optim. Lett. **8**(3), 1401–1415 (2014)

12. Liang, J., Baskar, S., Suganthan, P., Qin, A.: Performance evaluation of multiagent genetic algorithm. Nat. Comput. **5**(1), 83–96 (2006)

13. Macnish, C., Yao, X.: Direction Matters in High-Dimensional Optimisation, pp. 2372–2379. IEEE (2008)

14. Michalewicz, Z.: Genetic Algorithms + Data Structures = Evolution Programs. Springer, Heidelberg (1992). https://doi.org/10.1007/978-3-662-03315-9

15. Montes De Oca, M., Aydin, D., Stutzle, T.: An incremental particle swarm for large-scale continuous optimization problems: an example of tuning-in-the-loop (re)design of optimization algorithms. Soft Comput. **15**(11), 2233–2255 (2011)

16. Mühlenbein, H., Schomisch, D., Born, J.: The parallel genetic algorithm as function optimizer. Parallel Comput. **17**, 619–632 (1991)

17. Nesmachnow, S.: An overview of metaheuristics: accurate and efficient methods for optimisation. Int. J. Metaheuristics **3**(4), 320–347 (2014)

18. Penev, K.: Free search - comparative analysis 100. Int. J. Metaheuristics (IJMHEUR) **3**(2), 118–132 (2014)

19. Rosenbrock, H.H.: An automate method for finding the greatest or least value of a function. Comput. J. **3**(1960), 175–184 (1960)

20. Yin, J., Wang, Y., Hu, J.: Free search with adaptive differential evolution exploitation and quantum-inspired exploration. J. Netw. Comput. Appl. **35**(3), 1035–1051 (2012)

21. Yang, Z., Tang, K., Yao, X.: Differential Evolution for High-Dimensional Function Optimization, pp. 3523–3530. IEEE (2007)

An Intuitionistic Fuzzy Approach to the Travelling Salesman Problem

Velichka Traneva[✉][iD] and Stoyan Tranev[iD]

"Prof. Asen Zlatarov" University, "Prof. Yakimov" Bourgas, 8000 Bourgas, Bulgaria
veleka13@gmail.com, tranev@abv.bg
http://www.btu.bg

Abstract. The travelling salesman problem (TSP) is a classical problem in the combinatorial optimization. Its objective is to find the cheapest route of a salesman starting from a given city, visiting all other cities only once and finally come to the same city where he started. There are different approaches for solving travelling salesman problems with clear data. In real life in one situation there may be not possible to get the delivery costs as a certain quantity. To overcome this Zadeh introduce fuzzy set concepts to deal with an imprecision. There exist algorithms for solution of this problem based on fuzzy or triangular intuitionistic fuzzy numbers (private case of intuitionistic fuzzy sets (IFSs)). But many times the degrees of membership and non-membership for certain element are not defined in exact numbers. Atanassov and Gargov in 1989 first identified it in the concept of interval-valued intuitionist fuzzy sets (IVIFS) which is characterized by sub-intervals of unit interval. In this paper, a new type of TSP is formulated, in which the travelling cost from one city to another is interval-valued intuitionistic fuzzy number (IVIFN), depending on the availability of the conveyance, condition of the roads, etc. We propose for the first time the Hungarian algorithm for finding of an optimal solution of TSP using the apparatuses of index matrices (IMs), introduced in 1984 by Atanassov, and of IVIFSs. The example shown in this paper guarantees the effectiveness of the algorithm. The presented approach for solving a new type of TSP can be applied to problems with imprecise parameters and can be extended in order to obtain the optimal solution for other types of multidimensional TSPs.

Keywords: Decision making · Hungarian algorithm · Index matrix · Interval-Valued Intuitionistic fuzzy pair · Salesman problem

1 Introduction

The TSP was investigated by Hamilton [8]. The basic polynomial time algorithm is the Hungarian method, which was developed by Kuhn in 1955 [9]. In real life

Supported by the project of Asen Zlatarov University under Ref. No. NIX-423/2019 "Innovative methods for extracting knowledge management".

I. Lirkov and S. Margenov (Eds.): LSSC 2019, LNCS 11958, pp. 530–539, 2020.
https://doi.org/10.1007/978-3-030-41032-2_61

there are situations related to imperfect or unknown information on transport costs. Therefore the use of intuitionistic fuzzy logic proposed by Atanassov [1] as an extension of Zadeh's fuzzy logic [16] provides us with tools for modeling in an uncertain environment. The TSP has been considered firstly with fuzzy and next with intuitionistic fuzzy parameters. A method for solving intuitionistic fuzzy TSP (IFTSP) by using similarity measures and score function has been developed in [10]. The optimal solution of IFTSP with triangular intuitionistic fuzzy costs has been solved in [11] using the fuzzy Hungarian method. In [14] we proposed an intuitionistic fuzzy Hungarian method, based on the IFSs and IMs concepts, for solving an intuitionistic fuzzy assignment problem. The fuzzy and intuitionistic fuzzy approach to the TSP cannot be handled with uncertainty in determining the transport costs for the travelling of the salesman. Atanassov and Gargov [4] generalized IFS as IVIFS. We have already used this apparatus in [13] to model and solve the interval-valued assignment problem. In this paper, we model by the concepts of IVIFSs and IMs [1,2] the TSP, in which the transport costs are considered as IVIF numbers. We propose an interval-valued intuitionistic fuzzy Hungarian algorithm to find the optimal solution.

The rest of this paper is structured as follows: Sect. 2 describes the related concepts of the IMs and IVIFPs. In Sect. 3, we propose an algorithm for IVIFTSP, based on the Hungarian algorithm, by using the concepts of IMs and IVIFSs. Effectiveness of proposed method is demonstrated by an example. Section 4 offers the conclusion and outlines some aspects for future research.

2   Basic Definitions

2.1   Short Notes on Interval-Valued Intuitionistic Fuzzy Pairs

The concept of IVIFPs was introduced in [7]. The **IVIFP** is an object of the form $\langle M, N \rangle$, where $M, N \subseteq [0,1]$, $M = [\inf M, \sup M]$, $N = [\inf N, \sup N]$ and $\sup M + \sup N \leq 1$, that are used as an evaluation of some object or process.

The IVIFP x is an **"interval valued inuitionistic fuzzy false pair"** (**IVIFFP**) if and only if $\inf M \leq \sup N$, while x is a **"false pair"** (**IVFP**) iff $M = [0,0]$, $N = [1,1]$. Let us have two IVIFPs $x = \langle M, N \rangle$ and $y = \langle P, Q \rangle$.

In [5,7] are defined the operations

$$\neg x = \langle N, M \rangle;$$

$$x \wedge_1 y = \langle [\min(\inf M, \inf P), \min(\sup M, \sup P)], [\max(\inf N, \inf Q), \max(\sup N, \sup Q)] \rangle;$$

$$x \vee_1 y = \langle [\max(\inf M, \inf P), \max(\sup M, \sup P)], [\min(\inf N, \inf Q), \min(\sup N, \sup Q)] \rangle;$$

$$x \wedge_2 y = x + y = \langle [\inf M + \inf P - \inf M \inf P, \sup M + \sup P - \sup M \sup P], [\inf N \inf Q, \sup N \sup Q] \rangle;$$

$$x \vee_2 y = x.y = \langle [\inf M \inf P, \sup M \sup P], [\inf N + \inf Q - \inf N \inf Q, \sup N + \sup Q - \sup N \sup Q] \rangle;$$

$$x - y = \langle [\max(0, \min(\inf M - \sup P, 1 - \sup N + \sup Q)), \max(0, \min(\sup M - \inf P, 1 - \sup N + \sup Q))], [\min(1, \min(\inf N + \inf Q, 1 - \sup M + \inf P)), \min(1, \sup N + \sup Q, 1 - \sup M + \inf P)] \rangle$$

and the relations

$$
\begin{array}{lll}
x \leq y & \text{iff} & \inf M \leq \inf P \text{ and } \sup M \leq \sup P \\
& & \text{and } \inf N \geq \inf Q \text{ and } \sup N \geq \sup Q \\
x \leq_\square y & \text{iff} & \inf M \leq \inf P \text{ and } \sup M \leq \sup P \\
x \leq_\diamond y & \text{iff} & \inf N \geq \inf Q \text{ and } \sup N \geq \sup Q \\
x = y & \text{iff} & \inf M = \inf P \text{ and } \sup M = \sup P \\
& & \text{and } \inf Q = \inf N \text{ and } \sup Q = \sup N \\
x =_\square y & \text{iff} & \inf M = \inf P \text{ and } \sup M = \sup P \\
x =_\diamond y & \text{iff} & \inf N = \inf Q \text{ and } \sup N = \sup Q.
\end{array}
\tag{1}
$$

2.2   Definition of 2D-IVIFIM, Operations and Relations

Let $\mathcal{I}$ be a fixed set. By two-dimensional interval-valued intuitionistic fuzzy index matrix (2D-IVIFIM) [6] with index sets K and L $(K, L \subset \mathcal{I})$, we denote the object $[K, L, \{\langle M_{k_i,l_j}, N_{k_i,l_j}\rangle\}]$

$$
\equiv \begin{array}{c|cccccc}
 & l_1 & \cdots & l_j & \cdots & l_n \\
\hline
k_1 & \langle M_{k_1,l_1}, M_{k_1,l_1}\rangle & \cdots & \langle M_{k_1,l_j}, N_{k_1,l_j}\rangle & \cdots & \langle M_{k_1,l_n}, N_{k_1,l_n}\rangle \\
\vdots & \vdots & \ddots & \vdots & \ddots & \vdots \\
k_m & \langle M_{k_m,l_1}, N_{k_m,l_1}\rangle & \cdots & \langle M_{k_m,l_j}, N_{k_m,l_j}\rangle & \cdots & \langle M_{k_m,l_n}, N_{k_m,l_n}\rangle
\end{array},
$$

where for every $1 \leq i \leq m, 1 \leq j \leq n$:

$$
M_{k_i,l_j} \subseteq [0,1], N_{k_i,l_j} \subseteq [0,1], \sup M_{k_i,l_j} + \sup N_{k_i,l_j} \leq 1.
$$

Let "$*$" and "$\circ$" be two fixed operations over IVIFPs and let $\langle M, N\rangle * \langle P, Q\rangle = \langle M *_l P, N *_r Q\rangle$, where "$*_l$" and "$*_r$" are determined by the form of the operation "$*$". Following [3,6,12], we recall some operations over two 2D-IVIFIMs $A = [K, L, \{\langle M_{k_i,l_j}, N_{k_i,l_j}\rangle\}]$ and $B = [P, Q, \{\langle R_{p_r,q_s}, S_{p_r,q_s}\rangle\}]$:

Negation: $\neg A = [K, L, \{\langle N_{k_i,l_j}, M_{k_i,l_j}\rangle\}]$

Addition-(*): $A \oplus_{(*_l, *_r)} B = [K \cup P, L \cup Q, \{\langle \Phi_{t_u,v_w}, \Psi_{t_u,v_w}\rangle\}]$, where

$$
\langle \Phi_{t_u,v_w}, \Psi_{t_u,v_w}\rangle = \begin{cases}
\langle M_{k_i,l_j}, N_{k_i,l_j}\rangle, & \text{if } t_u = k_i \in K, v_w = l_j \in L - Q \\
& \text{or } t_u = k_i \in K - P, v_w = l_j \in L \\
\langle R_{p_r,q_s}, S_{p_r,q_s}\rangle, & \text{or } t_u = p_r \in P, v_w = q_s \in Q - L \\
& \text{or } t_u = p_r \in P - K, v_w = q_s \in Q. \\
\langle *_l(M_{k_i,l_j}, R_{p_r,q_s}), & \text{if } t_u = k_i = p_r \in K \cap P, \\
\quad *_r(N_{k_i,l_j}, S_{p_r,q_s})\rangle, & v_w = l_j = q_s \in L \cap Q \\
\langle [0,0], [1,1]\rangle, & \text{otherwise}
\end{cases}
$$

Termwise multiplication-(*): $A \otimes_{(*_l, *_r)} B = [K \cap P, L \cap Q, \{\langle \Phi_{t_u,v_w}, \Psi_{t_u,v_w}\rangle\}]$, where $\langle \Phi_{t_u,v_w}, \Psi_{t_u,v_w}\rangle = \langle *_l(M_{k_i,l_j}, R_{p_r,q_s}), *_r(N_{k_i,l_j}, S_{p_r,q_s})\rangle$.

Projection: Let $W \subseteq K$, $V \subseteq L$. Then, $pr_{W,V}A = [W, V, \{\langle R_{p_r,q_v}, S_{p_r,q_v}\rangle\}]$, where for each $k_i \in W, l_j \in V$ $\langle R_{p_r,q_v}, S_{p_r,q_v}\rangle = \langle M_{k_i,l_j}, N_{k_i,l_j}\rangle$.

Substitution: Let the IM $A = [K, L, \{a_{k,l}\}]$ be given. Local substitution over the IM A is defined for the pair of indices (p, k) by $\left[\frac{p}{k}; \perp\right] A = [(K - \{k\}) \cup \{p\}, L, \{a_{k,l}\}]$.

Index type operations: $AGIndex_{\{(\min)/(\min_\square)/(\min_\circ)\}(\nmid)}(A) = \langle k_i, l_j\rangle$, which finds the index of the minimum element of A that has no empty value [12] according to (1). If $AGIndex_{(\min,\max),(\nmid)}(A)$ can not be determined, then its value is equal to "$\perp$".

$Index_{(\nmid)/(1)}(A) = \{\langle k_{i_1}, l_{j_1}\rangle, \ldots, \langle k_{i_x}, l_{j_x}\rangle, \ldots, \langle k_{i_u}, l_{j_u}\rangle\}$, where $\langle k_{i_x}, l_{j_x}\rangle$ (for $1 \leq x \leq u$) is the index of the element of A, whose cell is full (or the value 1).

$Index_{(\max/\min\{M \text{ or } N\}),k_i}(A) = \{\langle k_i, l_{v_1}\rangle, \ldots, \langle k_i, l_{v_x}\rangle, \ldots, \langle k_i, l_{v_V}\rangle\}$, where $\langle k_i, l_{v_x}\rangle$ (for $1 \leq i \leq m, 1 \leq v \leq n, 1 \leq x \leq V$) are the indices of the IFFP of k_i-th row of A, for which $M_{k_i,l_{v_x}}$ or $N_{k_i,l_{v_x}}$ is maximum/minimum [14].

$Index_{(\max/\min\{M \text{ or } N\}),l_j}(A) = \{\langle k_{w_1}, l_j\rangle, \ldots, \langle k_{w_y}, l_j\rangle, \ldots, \langle k_{w_W}, l_j\rangle\}$, where $\langle k_{w_y}, l_j\rangle$ (for $1 \leq j \leq n, 1 \leq y \leq W, 1 \leq w \leq m$) are the indices of the IFFP of l_j-th column of A, for which $M_{k_{w_y},l_j}$ or $N_{k_{w_y},l_j}$ is maximum/minimum.

Aggregate global internal operation: $AGIO_{\oplus_{(\max,\min)}}(A)$.
This operation finds the "$\oplus_{(\max,\min)}$"-operation of all the matrix elements.

Internal Subtraction of IMs' Components [12]
$IO_{-_{(\min,\max)}}(\langle k_i, l_j, A\rangle, \langle p_r, q_s, B\rangle) = [K, L, \{\langle \gamma_{t_u,v_w}, \delta_{t_u,v_w}\rangle\}]$, where $k_i \in K$, $l_j \in L$; $p_r \in P$, $q_s \in Q$ and $\langle \gamma_{t_u,v_w}, \delta_{t_u,v_w}\rangle$

$$= \begin{cases} \langle M_{t_u,v_w}, N_{t_u,v_w}\rangle, & \text{if } t_u \neq k_i \in K, \\ & v_w \neq l_j \in L, \\ \langle[\max(0, \inf M - \sup P), \max(0, \sup M - \inf P)]\rangle, & \text{if } t_u = k_i \in K \\ \langle[\min(1, \inf N + \inf Q, 1 - \sup M + \inf P), & v_w = l_j \in L. \\ \min(1, \sup N + \sup Q, 1 - \inf M + \sup P)]\rangle, \end{cases}$$

The non-strict relation "inclusion about value" is defined by:
$A \subseteq_v B$ iff $(K = P)\&(L = Q)\&(\forall k \in K)(\forall l \in L)$
$(\langle M_{k,l}, N_{k,l}\rangle \leq \langle R_{k,l}, S_{k,l}\rangle)$.

3   Interval-Valued Intuitionistic Fuzzy Approach to the Travelling Salesman Problem

In this section, we formulate and solve the following new type of IVIFTSP by the Hungarian algorithm, based on IMs concept: A salesman has to visit m cities $K = \{k_1, \ldots, k_i, \ldots, k_m\}$. He wishes to start from a particular city, visit each city once, and then return to his starting point. The objective is to select the sequence in which the cities are visited in such a way that his total cost is minimized. The costs c_{k_i,l_j} (for $1 \leq i, j \leq m, i \neq j$) of going of the k_i -th city to the l_j -th city are an IVIFP, which are calculated on the basis of expert knowledge, are given.

Let us be given the following IVIFIMs, in accordance with the problem:

$$C[K, L] = \begin{array}{c|cccc} & l_1 & \cdots & l_n & R \\ \hline k_1 & \langle M_{k_1,l_1}, N_{k_1,l_1} \rangle & \cdots & \langle M_{k_1,l_n}, N_{k_1,l_n} \rangle & \langle M_{k_1,R}, N_{k_1,R} \rangle \\ \vdots & \vdots & \ddots & \vdots & \vdots \\ k_m & \langle M_{k_m,l_1}, N_{k_m,l_1} \rangle & \cdots & \langle M_{k_m,l_n}, N_{k_m,l_n} \rangle & \langle M_{k_m,R}, N_{k_m,R} \rangle \\ Q & \langle M_{Q,l_1}, N_{Q,l_1} \rangle & \cdots & \langle M_{Q,l_n}, Nu_{Q,l_n} \rangle & \langle M_{Q,R}, N_{Q,R} \rangle \end{array},$$

where $K = \{k_1, k_2, \ldots, k_m, Q\}$, $L = \{l_1, l_2, \ldots, l_n, R\}$, and for $1 \leq i \leq m, 1 \leq j \leq n$: $\{c_{k_i,l_j}, c_{k_i,R}, c_{Q,l_j}\}$ are IVIFPs. The costs $c_{k_i,k_i} = \langle [\perp, \perp], [\perp, \perp] \rangle$ (for $1 \leq i \leq m$). We can see, that $|K| = m + 1$ and $|L| = n + 1$;

$$X[K*, L*, \{x_{k_i,l_j}\}],$$

where $K* = \{k_1, k_2, \ldots, k_m\}$, $L* = \{l_1, l_2, \ldots, l_n\}$ and for $1 \leq i \leq m$, $1 \leq j \leq n$:

$$x_{k_i,l_j} = \langle R_{k_i,l_j}, S_{k_i,l_j} \rangle = \begin{cases} \langle [1,1], [0,0] \rangle, & \text{if the salesman travels from} \\ & k_i\text{-th city to } l_j\text{-th city } (k_i \neq l_j) \\ \langle [\perp, \perp], [\perp, \perp] \rangle, & \text{if } k_i = l_j \\ \langle [0,0], [1,1] \rangle, & \text{otherwise.} \end{cases}$$

Let us define the following auxiliary matrices:

(1) $D[K*, L*]$ where for $1 \leq i \leq m$, $1 \leq j \leq n$: $d_{k_i,l_j} \in \{1, 2\}$, if the element s_{k_i,l_j} of S is crossed out with 1 or 2 lines respectively;

(2) $RC[K*, e_0] = \begin{array}{c|c} & e_0 \\ \hline k_1 & rc_{k_1,e_0} \\ \vdots & \vdots \\ k_m & rc_{k_m,e_0} \end{array}$, where for $1 \leq i \leq m$: rc_{k_i,e_0} is equal to 0 or 1,

depending on whether the k_i-th row of $K*$ of the matrix S is crossed out;

(3) $CC[r_0, L*] = \begin{array}{c|ccccc} & l_1 & \cdots & l_j & \cdots & l_n \\ \hline r_0 & cc_{r_0,l_1} & \cdots & cc_{r_0,l_j} & \cdots & cc_{r_0,l_n} \end{array}$, where for $1 \leq j \leq m$:

cc_{k_i,l_j} is equal to 0 or 1, depending on whether the l_j-th row of $K*$ of the matrix S is crossed out.

Let in the begining $rc_{k_i,e_0} = cc_{r_0,l_j} = 0$. We propose an algorithm for finding the optimal solution of the IVIFTSP, based on the Hungarian algorithm and on the concepts of IMs and of IVIFSs. A part of Microsoft Visual Studio.NET 2010 C project's program code [17] is used in the algorithm. The software "IndMat-Calc v 0.9" [15] is used to implement the IMs operations.

Step 1. Check whether the IM C is square, if not, make it square by similar operations to those in [13]. Let us create IM $S = [K, L, \{s_{k_i,l_j}\}]$ such that $S = C$.

Step 2. In each row k_i of K of S, the smallest element is found among the elements s_{k_i,l_j} $(j = 1, \ldots, m)$ and it is subtracted from all elements s_{k_i,l_j}, for $j = 1, 2, \ldots, m$. Go to *Step 3*.

Step 2.1. For each row k_i of K of S, the smallest element is found and is recorded as the value of the element $s_{k_i,R}$:

for (int $i = 0; i < m; i + +$)
for (int $j = 0; j < m; j + +$) $\{AGIndex_{\{(\min)/(\min_\square)/(\min_\diamond)\}}(\not L)\,(pr_{k_i,L}S) = \langle k_i, l_{v_j}\rangle$; If $AGIndex_{\{(\min)/(\min_\square)/(\min_\diamond)\}}(\not L)\,(pr_{k_i,L}S) = \bot$ then execute $Index_{(\max M),k_i}\,(pr_{k_i,L}S)$;

We create S_1 and $S_2 : S_1[k_i, l_{v_j}] = pr_{k_i,l_{v_j}}S; S_2 = \left[\bot; \frac{R}{l_{v_j}}; \bot\right]S_1;$

$S := S \oplus_{(\max,\min)} S_2.\}$

Step 2.2. The smallest element $s_{k_i,l_{v_j}}$ is subtracted from the elements s_{k_i,l_j} $(j = 1, \ldots, m)$. We create IM $B = pr_{K,R}S$.

for (int $i = 0; i < m; i + +$)
for (int $j = 0; j < m; j + +$)

If $s_{k_i,l_j} \neq \bot$, then $\{IO_{-(\max,\min)}\,(\langle k_i, l_j, S\rangle, \langle k_i, R, B\rangle)\}$.

Step 3. For each index l_j of L of S, the smallest element is found among the elements s_{k_i,l_j} $(i = 1, \ldots, m)$ and it is subtracted from all elements s_{k_i,l_j}, for $i = 1, 2, \ldots, m$. Go to *Step 4*.

Similar operations to those in *Step 2*. are executed. They are presented in [14].

Step 4. Cross out all elements s_{k_i,l_j} for $\langle k_i, l_j\rangle \in \{Index_{(\max N),k_i/l_j}(S)\}$ or equal to $\langle[0,0],[1,1]\rangle$ in S with the minimum possible number of lines (horizontal, vertical or both). If the number of these lines is m, go to *Step 6*. If the number of lines is less than m, go to *Step 7*.

This step introduces IM $D[K*, L*]$, which has the same structure as the IM X. We use to mark whether an element in S is crossed out with a line.

If $d_{k_i,l_j} = 1$, then the element s_{k_i,l_j} is covered with one line;

If $d_{k_i,l_j} = 2$, then the element s_{k_i,l_j} is covered with two lines.

We create two IMs $CC[r_0, L*]$ and $RC[K*, e_0]$, in which is recorded that the element is covered by a line in a row or column in the S matrix.

for (int $i = 0; i < m; i + +$)
for (int $j = 0; j < m; j + +$)

If $s_{k_i,l_j} = \langle [0,0], [1,1] \rangle$ (or $\langle k_i, l_j \rangle \in Index_{(\max N),k_i/l_j}(S)$) and $d_{k_i,l_j} = 0$, then $\{rc_{k_i,e_0} = 1;$ for (int $i = 0; i < m; i + +$) $d_{k_i,l_j} = 1; S_{(k_i,\perp)}\}$.

If $s_{k_i,l_j} = \langle [0,0], [1,1] \rangle$ (or $\langle k_i, l_j \rangle \in Index_{(\max N),k_i}(S)$) and $d_{k_i,l_j} = 1$, then $\{d_{k_i,l_j} = 2; cc_{r_0,l_j} = 1;$ for (int $j = 0; j < n; j + +$) $d_{k_i,l_j} = 1; S_{(\perp,l_j)}\}$.

Then we count the covered rows and columns in CC and RC by:

$$Index_{(1)}(RC) = \{\langle k_{u_1}, e_0 \rangle, \ldots, \langle k_{u_i}, e_0 \rangle, \ldots, \langle k_{u_x}, e_0 \rangle\};$$
$$Index_{(1)}(CC) = \{\langle r_0, l_{v_1} \rangle, \ldots, \langle r_0, l_{v_j} \rangle, \ldots, \langle r_0, l_{v_y} \rangle\}.$$

If count($Index_{(1)}(RC)$)+count($Index_{(1)}(CC)$) $= m$, then to *Step 6*, otherwise to *Step 5*.

Step 5. We find the smallest element in the IM S that it is not crossed by the lines in *Step 4*, and subtract it from any uncovered element of S, and we add it to each element, which is covered by two lines. We return to *Step 4*.

The operation $AGIndex_{\{(\min)/(\min_\square)/(\min_\circ)\}(\measuredangle)}(S) = \langle k_x, l_y \rangle$ finds the smallest element index of the IM S. The operation $IO_{-(\max,\min)}(\langle S \rangle, \langle k_x, l_y, S \rangle)$ subtract it from any uncovered element of S. Then we add it to each element of S, which is crossed out by two lines:

for (int $i = 0; i < m; i + +$)
for (int $j = 0; j < m; j + +$)

$\{$if $d_{k_i,l_j} = 2$, then $S_1 = pr_{k_x,l_y}C; S_2 = pr_{k_i,l_j}C \oplus_{(\max,\min)} \left[\frac{k_i}{k_x}; \frac{l_j}{l_y}\right] S_1;$
$S := S \oplus_{(\max,\min)} S_2;$
if $d_{k_i,l_j} = 1$ or $d_{k_i,l_j} = 2$ then $S := S \oplus_{(\max,\min)} pr_{k_i,l_j}C\}$; Go to *Step 4*.

Step 6. Examine the rows until a row-wise exactly single element, which is IVIFFP, is found. Mark this IVIFFP to make the assignment, then cross out all IVIFFP-elements are lying in the respective column, showing that they cannot be considered for future assignment. Continue this way until all the rows have been examined. If there lie more than one unmarked IVIFFP-elements in any column or row, then mark one of them arbitrary and cross out the remaining IVIFFPs in its row or column. Repeat the process until no unmarked IVIFFP is left in the matrix. Thus exactly one marked IVIFFP in each row and each column of S is obtained. The optimal solution $X_{opt}[K*, L*, \{x_{k_i,l_j}\}]$ has been found, where assignments are located where the elements $\langle[1,1],[0,0]\rangle$ in the X corresponding to the marked elements in the matrix.

{for (int $i = 0; i < m; i++$)
for (int $j = 0; j < n; j++$)
if ($(\langle k_i, l_j \rangle \in Index_{(\max \nu), k_i/l_j}(S)$) and $d_{k_i,l_j} \neq 3$), then $x_{k_i,l_j} = \langle[1,1],[0,0]\rangle$;
for (int $i = 0; i < m; i++$) $d_{k_i,l_j} = 3$; for (int $j = 0; j < m; j++$) $d_{k_i,l_j} = 3$}.

Step 7. If the route conditions are satisfied then the optimal solution X_{opt} is found and the optimal cost is: $AGIO_{\oplus(\max,\min)} \left(C_{(\{Q\},\{R\})} \otimes_{(\min,\max)} X_{opt} \right)$. If not, making adjustments in assignments to satisfy the conditions with minimum increase in total cost and the algorithm consider the "next best solution".

Let us apply the defined algorithm to the following TSP in order to demonstrate its effectiveness: A salesman has to visit 4 cities $K = \{k_1, k_2, k_3, k_4\}$. He wishes to start his visit from his home city A and visits all other cities once and return to his home city. The travel costs c_{k_i,k_j} (for $1 \leq i, j \leq m$) of the k_i-th to the k_j-th city are given in form of IVIFPs and are defined as elements of C, where

$$C[K,L] = \begin{cases} & \begin{array}{c|cc} & l_1 & l_2 \\ \hline k_1 & \langle[\perp,\perp],[\perp,\perp]\rangle & \langle[0.67,0.78],[0.14,0.20]\rangle \\ k_2 & \langle[0.52,0.60],[0.28,0.35]\rangle & \langle[\perp,\perp],[\perp,\perp]\rangle \\ k_3 & \langle[0.62,0.72],[0.20,0.25]\rangle & \langle[0.35,0.45],[0.33,0.43]\rangle \\ k_4 & \langle[0.78,0.85],[0.05,0.10]\rangle & \langle[0.70,0.80],[0.15,0.23]\rangle \\ Q & \langle[\perp,\perp],[\perp,\perp]\rangle & \langle[\perp,\perp],[\perp,\perp]\rangle \end{array} \end{cases}$$

l_3	l_4	R
$\langle[0.50,0.65],[0.25,0.30]\rangle$	$\langle[0.40,0.50],[0.30;0.40]\rangle$	$\langle[\perp,\perp],[\perp,\perp]\rangle$
$\langle[0.65,0.70],[0.20,0.25]\rangle$	$\langle[0.56,0.63],[0.15,0.25]\rangle$	$\langle[\perp,\perp],[\perp,\perp]\rangle$
$\langle[\perp,\perp],[\perp,\perp]\rangle$	$\langle[0.65,0.80],[0.10,0.15]\rangle$	$\langle[\perp,\perp],[\perp,\perp]\rangle$
$\langle[0.60,0.70],[0.18,0.25]\rangle$	$\langle[\perp,\perp],[\perp,\perp]\rangle$	$\langle[\perp,\perp],[\perp,\perp]\rangle$
$\langle[\perp,\perp],[\perp,\perp]\rangle$	$\langle[\perp,\perp],[\perp,\perp]\rangle$	$\langle[\perp,\perp],[\perp,\perp]\rangle$

After application of the algorithm we get the final IM C in the form:

$$
C[K,L] = \begin{cases}
\begin{array}{c|cc}
 & l_1 & l_2 \\
\hline
k_1 & \langle[\perp,\perp],[\perp,\perp]\rangle & \langle[0.12,0.43],[0.57,0.57]\rangle \\
k_2 & \langle[0.00,0.08],[0.92,0.92]\rangle & \langle[\perp,\perp],[\perp,\perp]\rangle \\
k_3 & \langle[0.00,0.20],[0.80,0.80]\rangle & \langle[0.00,0.10],[0.90,0.90]\rangle \\
k_4 & \langle[0.10.0.33],[0.67,0.67]\rangle & \langle[0.15,0.45],[0.55,0.55]\rangle \\
Q & \langle[0.00,0.08],[0.56,0.70]\rangle & \langle[0.00,0.10],[0.66,0.86]\rangle
\end{array}
\end{cases}
$$

$$
\begin{array}{ccc}
l_3 & l_4 & R \\
\langle[0.00,0.15],[0.85,0.85]\rangle & \langle[0.00,0.10],[0.90,0.90]\rangle & \langle[0.40,0.50],[0.30,0.40]\rangle \\
\langle[0.00,0.20],[0.80,0.80]\rangle & \langle[0.00,0.23],[0.77,0.77]\rangle & \langle[0.52,0.60],[0.28,0.35]\rangle \\
\langle[\perp,\perp],[\perp,\perp]\rangle & \langle[0.05,0.40],[0.60,0.60]\rangle & \langle[0.35,0.45],[0.33,0.43]\rangle \\
\langle[0.00,0.20],[0.80,0.80]\rangle & \langle[\perp,\perp],[\perp,\perp]\rangle & \langle[0.60,0.70],[0.18,0.25]\rangle \\
\langle[0.00,0.15],[0.50,0.60]\rangle & \langle[0.00,0.10],[0.60;0.80]\rangle & \langle[\perp,\perp],[\perp,\perp]\rangle
\end{array}
$$

The test for the optimality is satisfied (the number of lines $= m = n = 4$). The optimal route is: $A \longrightarrow D \longrightarrow C \longrightarrow B \longrightarrow A$ and the optimal cost of travelling is $\langle[0.92,0.97],[0.005,0.021]\rangle$.

The example illustrates the efficiency of the algorithm.

4   Conclusion

In the paper we define for the first time an interval-valued intuitionistic fuzzy algorithm for solving IVIFTSP, which is based on the concepts of IMs and of IVIFSs. Its main advantages are that the algorithm can be applied to problems with imprecise parameters and can be extended in order to obtain the optimal solution for other types of multidimensional problems. The example demonstrates the correctness and efficiency of the algorithm. In future the proposed method will be extended for various types TSPs in an uncertain environment.

References

1. Atanassov, K.T.: Intuitionistic Fuzzy Sets, VII ITKR Session, Sofia, 20–23 June 1983. (Deposed in Centr. Sci. Techn. Library of the Bulg. Acad. of Sci. 1697/84) (in Bulgarian)
2. Atanassov, K.: Generalized index matrices. Comptes rendus de l'Academie Bulgare des Sci. **40**(11), 15–18 (1987)
3. Atanassov, K.T.: Index Matrices: Towards an Augmented Matrix Calculus. SCI, vol. 573. Springer, Cham (2014). https://doi.org/10.1007/978-3-319-10945-9
4. Atanassov, K., Gargov, G.: Interval valued intuitionistic fuzzy sets. Fuzzy Sets Syst. **31**(3), 343–349 (1989)
5. Atanassov, K.T.: Interval-Valued Intuitionistic Fuzzy Sets. SFSC, vol. 388. Springer, Cham (2020). https://doi.org/10.1007/978-3-030-32090-4

6. Atanassov, K.: Extended Interval Valued Intuitionistic Fuzzy Index Matrices (2019, in press). (sub-mitted by Springer)
7. Atanassov, K., Vassilev, P., Kacprzyk, J., Szmidt, E.: On interval valued intuitionistic fuzzy pairs. J. Univ. Math. **1**(3), 261–268 (2018)
8. Biggs, L., Lloyd, K., Wilson, R.: Graph Theory 1736–1936. Clarendon Press, Oxford (1986)
9. Kuhn, H.: The Travelling salesman problem. In: Proceedings of Sixth Symposium in Applied Mathematics of the American Mathematical Society. McGraw-Hill, New York (1955)
10. Mukherjee, S., Basum, K.: Solution of a class of Intuitionistic fuzzy assignment problem by using similarity measures. Knowl. Based Syst. **27**, 170–179 (2012)
11. Prabakaran, K., Ganesan, K.: Fuzzy Hungarian method for solving intuitionistic fuzzy travelling salesman problem. J. Phys. Conf. Ser. **1000**, 2–13 (2018)
12. Traneva, V., Tranev, S.: Index Matrices as a Tool for Managerial Decision Making. Publ. House of the Union of Scientists, Bulgaria (2017). (in Bulgarian)
13. Traneva, V., Tranev, S.: An interval-valued intuitionistic fuzzy approach to the assignment problem. In: Kahraman, C., Cebi, S., Cevik Onar, S., Oztaysi, B., Tolga, A.C., Sari, I.U. (eds.) INFUS 2019. AISC, vol. 1029, pp. 1279–1287. Springer, Cham (2020). https://doi.org/10.1007/978-3-030-23756-1_150
14. Traneva, V., Tranev, S., Atanassova, V.: An intuitionistic fuzzy approach to the Hungarian algorithm. In: Nikolov, G., Kolkovska, N., Georgiev, K. (eds.) NMA 2018. LNCS, vol. 11189, pp. 167–175. Springer, Cham (2019). https://doi.org/10.1007/978-3-030-10692-8_19
15. Software for index matrices. http://justmathbg.info/indmatcalc.html. Accessed 1 Feb 2019
16. Zadeh, L.: Fuzzy sets. Inf. Control **8**(3), 338–353 (1965)
17. Munkres' Assignment Algorithm. http://csclab.murraystate.edu/~bob.pilgrim/445/munkres.html. Accessed 15 Feb 2019

Alternatives for Neighborhood Function in Kohonen Maps

Iliyan Zankinski, Kolyu Kolev, and Todor Balabanov[✉] [iD]

Institute of Information and Communication Technologies,
Bulgarian Academy of Sciences, Acad. Georgi Bonchev Street, Block 2,
1113 Sofia, Bulgaria
iliyan@hsi.iccs.bas.bg, todorb@iinf.bas.bg
http://iict.bas.bg/

Abstract. In the field of the artificial intelligence artificial neural networks are one of the most researched topics. Multilayer perceptron has a reputation for the most used type of artificial neural network, but other types such as Kohonen maps, generalized nets [1] or combinations with Kalman filter [2,3] are also very interesting. Proposed by Teuvo Kohonen in the 1980s, self-organizing maps have application in meteorology, oceanography, project prioritization and selection, seismic facies analysis for oil and gas exploration, failure mode and effects analysis, creation of artwork and many other areas. Self-organizing maps are very useful for visualization by data dimensions reduction. Unsupervised competitive learning is used in self-organizing maps and the basic idea is the net to classify input data in predefined number of clusters. When the net has fewer nodes it achieve results similar to K-means clustering. One of the components in the self-organizing maps is the neighborhood function. It gives scaling factor for the distance between one neuron and other neurons in each step. The simplest form of a neighborhood function gives 1 for the closest nodes and 0 for all other, but the most used neighborhood function is a Gaussian function. In this research fading cosine and exponential regulated cosine functions are proposed as alternatives for neighborhood function.

Keywords: Artificial neural networks · Self-organizing maps · Neighborhood functions

1 Introduction

Self-organizing maps or Kohonen Neural Networks (KNNs) are networks with unsupervised training [4]. They are very useful in finding nonlinear dependencies when data are presented in very high dimensional spaces. The projection from the high-dimensional space is usually done in a rectangular lower-dimensional space [5]. The main idea behind KNNs is the organization of unlabeled vectors

This work was supported by a private funding of Velbazhd Software LLC.

© Springer Nature Switzerland AG 2020
I. Lirkov and S. Margenov (Eds.): LSSC 2019, LNCS 11958, pp. 540–544, 2020.
https://doi.org/10.1007/978-3-030-41032-2_62

with particular features in predefined number of groups called clusters [6]. Grid of the self-organizing map is a handy tool for convenient visualization which can reveal different features of the network. SOMs are attractive when there consist of two or more separate regions. The real goal is not to find a perfect clustering but get good idea of the cluster structure.

1.1 Clustering

Clustering means a separation of the data set in set of groups. In separation where each data sample belongs exactly to only one group it is called straight clustering. If each data sample has varying degree of membership to different groups it is called fuzzy clustering.

Generally accepted concept of an optimal clustering is data set separation which minimizes the distance inside the cluster and maximizes the distance between the clusters. The most used form of distance measurement is the Euclidean norm [7].

1.2 SOM Training

The network consists of a grid (usually two dimensional [8]) with units. The units are connected to adjacent units with a neighborhood relation. The amount of grid units, which usually varies from a few dozen up to several thousand, gives the accuracy and generalization possibilities of the KNN. The network forms an elastic mesh that folds as a cloud formed by the input data during training phase. Data samples lying near each other in the input space are mapped into nearby grid units.

The network training is done iteratively. A data sample vector is randomly chosen from the input data set, as first step. As second step, distances between the selected vector and all the prototype vectors are computed. The best matching unit is the grid unit with prototype closest the selected vector. In the third step, the prototype vectors in the grid are updated. The best matching unit and its topological neighbors are moved closer to the input vector in the input space [9,10].

2 Neighborhood Function

The most used KNN's neighborhood function is the Gaussian function. In this research two alternative functions are proposed. The first function is fading cosine, which is shown in Fig. 1-Left. The second function is exponential regulated cosine, which is shown in Fig. 1-Right.

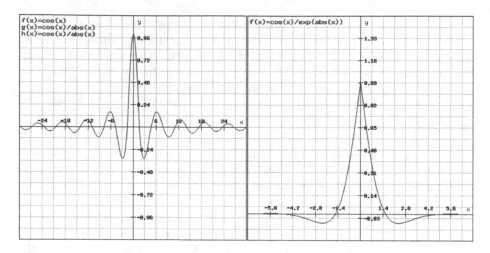

Fig. 1. Left - Fading cosine neighborhood function. Right - Exponential regulated cosine neighborhood function.

The idea for the both functions is to stress grid nodes down and up. The exponential regulated cosine Eq. 2 gives smoother stress than the fading cosine Eq. 1.

$$f(x) = \begin{cases} cos(x) & -\pi/2 < x < \pi/2 \\ \frac{cos(x)}{|x|} & +\pi/2 \geq x \leq -\pi/2 \end{cases} \tag{1}$$

$$f(x) = \frac{cos(x)}{e^{|x|}} \tag{2}$$

3 Experiments and Results

All experiments were done on a single processor desktop machine - Intel Core i5, 2.3 GHz, 2 Cores, 8 GB RAM and Mac OS X 10.13.6, Apple LLVM version 9.1.0.

As experimental data set rents and living area (shown in Fig. 2) are taken from the open source project, which can be found at [11].

Experiments are done with Gausssian neighborhood function Fig. 3-Left, fading cosine neighborhood function Fig. 3-Center and exponential regulated cosine neighborhood function Fig. 3-Right. Results show that fading cosine function performs less effective than exponential regulated cosine, but exponential regulated cosine gives sharper clusters separation than the Gaussian function.

#	Metres quadrats	Habitacions	Preu lloguer	#	Metres quadrats	Habitacions	Preu lloguer	#	Metres quadrats	Habitacions	Preu lloguer	#	Metres quadrats	Habitacions	Preu lloguer
1	60	3	375	33	55	2	450	65	45	1	295	97	70	1	450
2	96	3	650	34	90	3	425	66	43	1	400	98	85	2	550
3	135	4	550	35	120	5	350	67	95	4	415	99	70	3	350
4	90	3	550	36	120	4	600	68	70	2	580	100	183	3	1150
5	72	4	450	37	45	1	450	69	71	2	400	101	40	1	295
6	210	4	1090	38	70	4	550	70	75	3	300	102	60	3	400
7	72	4	475	39	80	4	390	71	70	2	350	103	80	3	525
8	260	4	1000	40	97	3	380	72	60	2	400	104	97	3	625
9	110	3	1000	41	100	4	420	73	83	3	490	105	88	3	580
10	149	4	550	42	100	2	650	74	40	1	460	106	68	2	400
11	75	2	550	43	77	3	625	75	100	4	500	107	102	3	650
12	127	3	700	44	95	3	600	76	65	2	400	108	45	1	375
13	100	4	430	45	90	4	400	77	65	3	330	109	100	4	400
14	90	4	390	46	80	4	450	78	50	1	295	110	90	3	400
15	90	3	400	47	160	4	800	79	50	2	235	111	50	2	400
16	31	1	350	48	80	2	550	80	70	2	280	112	65	3	490
17	77	4	450	49	65	3	250	81	63	2	280	113	40	1	375
18	61	2	350	50	60	2	450	82	97	3	626	114	68	1	450
19	97	3	650	51	74	2	350	83	46	1	300	115	79	1	500
20	73	3	625	52	75	2	450	84	75	2	450	116	45	1	350
21	62	2	380	53	105	4	525	85	75	3	290	117	55	1	375
22	56	3	360	54	95	4	500	86	95	3	450	118	59	2	350
23	55	1	500	55	53	2	500	87	90	4	420	119	71	3	400
24	100	2	600	56	140	2	800	88	95	3	400	120	71	1	400
25	65	2	350	57	72	2	450	89	70	3	400	121	85	3	600
26	89	3	335	58	78	3	450	90	83	4	520	122	108	2	460
27	65	2	425	59	80	2	450	91	70	2	390	123	80	2	750
28	70	3	425	60	240	3	1500	92	90	4	400	124	145	4	675
29	120	4	450	61	149	4	350	93	75	2	250	125	95	4	415
30	40	1	280	62	140	4	600	94	71	3	425	126	90	4	500
31	120	3	475	63	90	3	370	95	70	3	275				
32	90	3	500	64	100	4	650	96	115	4	525				

Fig. 2. Rents and living area data set [11].

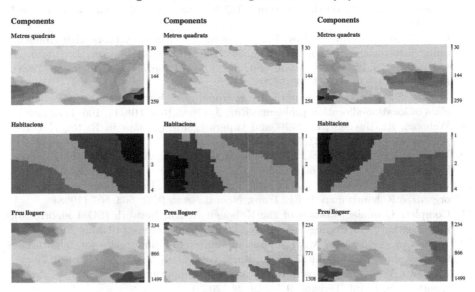

Fig. 3. Left - Gausssian neighborhood function. Center - Fading cosine neighborhood function. Right - Exponential regulated cosine neighborhood function.

4   Conclusions

The proposed neighbor functions give promising results as it is shown in the experimental section. Stressing the neighboring nodes down and up leads to better separation between the formed clusters. As further research it will be interesting the proposed neighborhood functions to be combined with different distance norms. In some problems Hausdorff distance can be used for example. Situations in time series [12] are also interesting for classification with KNN and the capabilities of the soft computing [13].

References

1. Tashev, T., Hristov, H.: Modeling of synthesis of information processes with generalized nets. Cybern. Inf. Technol. **3**(2), 92–104 (2003)
2. Alexandrov, A.: Ad-hoc Kalman filter based fusion algorithm for real-time wireless sensor data integration. FQAS 2015. AISC, vol. 400, pp. 151–159. Springer, Cham (2016). https://doi.org/10.1007/978-3-319-26154-6_12
3. van der Voort, M., Dougherty, M., Watson, S.: Combining Kohonen maps with ARIMA time series models to forecast traffic flow. Transp. Res. Part C: Emerg. Technol. **4**(5), 307–318 (1996)
4. Schreck, T., Bernard, J., von Landesberger, T., Kohlhammer, J.: Visual cluster analysis of trajectory data with interactive Kohonen maps. Inf. Vis. **8**(1), 14–29 (2009)
5. Macq, D., Verleysen, M., Jespers, P., Legat, J.D.: Analog implementation of a Kohonen map with on-chip learning. IEEE Trans. Neural Netw. **4**(3), 456–461 (1993)
6. Cottrell, M., Letremy, P., Roy, E.: Analysing a contingency table with Kohonen maps: a factorial correspondence analysis. In: Mira, J., Cabestany, J., Prieto, A. (eds.) IWANN 1993. LNCS, vol. 686, pp. 305–311. Springer, Heidelberg (1993). https://doi.org/10.1007/3-540-56798-4_164
7. Lozano, S., Guerrero, F., Onieva, L., Larraneta, J.: Kohonen maps for solving a class of location-allocation problems. Eur. J. Oper. Res. **108**(1), 106–117 (1998)
8. Wehrens, R., Buydens, L.: Self- and super-organizing maps in R: the Kohonen package. J. Stat. Softw. **21**(5), 1–19 (2007)
9. Vesanto, J., Alhoniemi, E.: Clustering of the self-organizing map. IEEE Trans. Neural Netw. **11**(3), 586–600 (2000)
10. Amerijckx, C., Verleysen, M., Thissen, P., Legat, J.D.: Image compression by self-organized Kohonen map. IEEE Trans. Neural Netw. **9**(3), 503–507 (1998)
11. Complete C implementation of the Kohonen Neural Network (SOM algorithm). http://github.com/Coding-Sunday-Sofia/Kohonen. Accessed 01 Mar 2019
12. Atanasova, T., Barova, M.: Exploratory analysis of time series for hypothesize feature values. In: UniTech17 Proceedings, vol. 16, no. 2, pp. 399–403 (2017)
13. Angelova, V.: Investigations in the area of soft computing targeted state of the art report. Cybern. Inf. Technol. **9**(1), 18–24 (2009)

Large Scale Machine Learning: Multiscale Algorithms and Performance Guarantees

A Modified Gomory-Hu Algorithm with DWDM-Oriented Technology

Winfried Auzinger[1]($\boxtimes$) ⓘ, Kvitoslava Obelovska[2] ⓘ,
and Roksolyana Stolyarchuk[3] ⓘ

[1] Institute of Analysis and Scientific Computing, TU Wien, Vienna, Austria
`w.auzinger@tuwien.ac.at`
[2] Institute of Computer Science and Information Technologies,
Lviv Polytechnic National University, Lviv, Ukraine
`obelyovska@gmail.com`
[3] Institute of Applied Mathematics and Fundamental Sciences,
Lviv Polytechnic National University, Lviv, Ukraine
`sroksolyana@yahoo.com`
`http://www.asc.tuwien.ac.at/~winfried/`

Abstract. Optimization of the topology of computer networks based
on the classical Gomory-Hu algorithm does not take the specific transfer
technology into account. For WDM technology requirements this leads
to a redundancy of channel capacities.

To reduce the redundancy of allocating network resources, we propose
a modification of the Gomory-Hu algorithm which takes account of the
specifics of DWDM technology – not at the final stage but already at
intermediate stages in the process. The original algorithm proposed by
Gomory and Hu involves the decomposition of the graph of the input network into ring subnets of different dimensions. Our modified algorithm
takes account of the technical parameters of the DWDM technology for
each ring during the decomposition.

We illustrate our method by an example. The technique can be
extended to large networks, which may lead to a significant economic
effect.

Keywords: Network topology · Channel capacity · Dense Wavelength
Division Multiplexing (DWDM) · Gomory-Hu algorithm

1 Introduction

Current developments in the fields of data transmission technology are characterized by intense growth of information flow and increasing requirements for

Supported by the Austrian Federal Ministry of Education, Science and Research and
the Ukrainian Ministry of Science and Education, under the joint Ukraine-Austria
R & D project 'Traffic and telecommunication networks modelling', project No. UA
10/2017/0118U001750, M-130/2018.

I. Lirkov and S. Margenov (Eds.): LSSC 2019, LNCS 11958, pp. 547–554, 2020.
https://doi.org/10.1007/978-3-030-41032-2_63

the quality of transmission. New technologies for various purposes and their further exploitation require significant costs for modern telecommunication equipment and channel resources. Thus, the problem of optimization of data transmission networks, the hardware basis of which are backbone networks, is becoming increasingly important.

Remark 1. The algorithm proposed in this paper has not yet been implemented in software. In the context of the joint Ukraine-Austria R & D project 'Traffic and telecommunication networks modelling', we are preparing an implementation in Maple[1] using the GraphTheory package. As a further step, following ideas from [1], parallelization of the process can be envisaged based on a master/slave model which is convenient to use for prototyping purposes.

2   Problem Setting

One of the major ways to ensure cost-efficient use of Wide and Metropolitan Area Networks relies on optimization of their topology. Many works have been devoted to the design of topologies of main networks, examples of which can be found in [5,6], where different approaches for the choice of network topology are considered and methods and algorithms for optimization are analyzed and systematized.

The cost of using networks is mainly determined by occupying channel resources, which significantly depend on the network capacity. The principles of the Gomory-Hu topological design are described in [2,3,6]. Gomory and Hu proposed an algorithm which enables to provide a synthesis of network topology and choice of channel capacities. The network designed according to this algorithm enables transmission of a maximum given input flow with a minimum required total capacity over the channels. In [9] a simulation model based on the Gomory-Hu algorithm (besides some other algorithms) was implemented. In [11], devoted to the embedding of virtual topologies in network clouds, the algorithmic steps proposed start with building the Gomory-Hu tree.

Optimization via the Gomory-Hu algorithm results in channel capacities which do not take account of particular transmission technologies in the different channels. However, the capacity of the separate channels should be selected in accordance with the requirements of the transfer technology used. Taking into account different capacities of the channels it is to be expected that a modified optimization procedure will lead to an improved performance with the available network resources.

A modified Gomory-Hu-type algorithm for the optimization of networks using SDH (Synchrone Digital Hierarchy) technology was proposed in [7]. The purpose of the present paper is to investigate the possibility of minimizing the excess capacity by modifying the Gomory-Hu algorithm in a way taking account of the available channel capacities in accordance with the requirements of the DWDM (Dense Wavelength Division Multiplexing) technology.

---

[1] Maple is a product by Maplesoft[TM] (www.maplesoft.com).

As a state of the art, the DWDM transport technology provides the highest speed among all other technologies for transmitting data via an optical pair. High speed is provided by *wavelength multiplexing*, where dozens or even hundreds of independent data flows are transmitted through a single optical pair, different flows being transmitted in different optical ranges.

Current commercial DWDM systems use up to 80 transfer channels of capacity up to 40 Gbps, which amounts to a total transfer capacity up to 3.2 Tbps. These systems are able to overcome distances of more than 2000 km without signal renewal [4]. Current experiments enable transferring an even higher flow, but only for distances of a few hundreds km [8, 10]. Recently, a DWDM with 200 transfer channels with a capacity of 40 Gbps per channel was realized, resulting in a total capacity of 8 Tbps per fiber [4]. An example of a system in which each channel carries 100 Gbps and 192 channels per fiber pair, which amounts to a total of 19.2 Tbps per pair, is reported in [12].

3   The Classical Gomory-Hu Algorithm

In the following we first review the details of the classical Gomory-Hu algorithm. The input data is a set of nodes, together with the requirement of exchange of information and the intensity of flows that need to be provided between them. These data are represented in form of an undirected weighted graph, where the weights of the edges represent the flows to be transmitted.

The algorithm is based on certain rules for splitting the given graph into several subnets, with the goal of performance optimization as explained below. All these subnets, except the last one, are weighted ring subnets with constant weight. The last subnet is a direct channel between two nodes or it may be void.

The result of the resulting optimization procedure is again a graph representing the topology of the network after optimization. The resulting weights represent the required channel capacities after optimization. In this way one can find the topology of the network and the capacity of its channels for which transmission with maximum flow is ensured, and at the same time the weights of all edges (i.e., the required capacity of the communication channels) will be minimal.

By superposition of all the resulting subnets one obtains an *optimized network that will feature minimum total capacities of the channels (edges), while providing transmission of maximum flow.*

The Gomory-Hu algorithm consists of two major stages:

(i) decomposition,
(ii) superposition.

ad (i): Decomposition

1. Specification of the input network in form of a weighted non-directed graph $A := G_{\text{in}}$. The weights of the edges represent the required intensities of flows.
2. Decomposition of the graph $A = \{a_{ij}\}$ into

- a ring graph[2] SNk which includes all the nodes of the graph A, and assigning to each edge of the ring the weight $W_{min}/2$, where k is the cycle number and W_{min} is the minimal weight of the edges of the graph A;
- a graph B which is obtained by subtracting the value W_{min} from the weight of each edge of graph A whose weight is greater than zero.

If the number of edges in the resulting graph B is greater than one, then we accept $A = B$ and go back to step 2, repeating the iteration for creating a cycle. Otherwise the decomposition stage is completed. Then, the graph B will consist of one segment with a weight greater than zero, or it may be void.

ad (ii): Superposition

Construction of the output graph by integration of all graphs in which the input graph was decomposed in step **(i)**.

Example 1. Fig. 1 shows the results for the following input data:

$$a_{12} = 1000 \text{ Gbps}, \quad a_{13} = 800 \text{ Gbps}, \quad a_{15} = 800 \text{ Gbps},$$
$$a_{24} = 300 \text{ Gbps}, \quad a_{25} = 500 \text{ Gbps}, \quad a_{45} = 500 \text{ Gbps}.$$

Let us discuss these results. The verification is performed for maximum flow, in our case it is $a_{12} = 1000$ Gbps. In the resulting network, this flow can be transmitted simultaneously in the following way:

$$a_{12} \Rightarrow 600 \text{ Gbps},$$
$$a_{15432} \Rightarrow 250 \text{ Gbps},$$
$$a_{1532} \Rightarrow 150 \text{ Gbps},$$

where a_{15432} corresponds to the path from node 1 to node 2 across the nodes $5, 4, 3$, and a_{1532} to the path from node 1 to node 2 across the nodes $5, 3$. The sum of these flows is 1000 Gbps. Thus, the network is able to transmit the maximum flow without any excess resources, i.e., all network resources are busy for transmission of maximum flow. The total capacity of all channels is 2050 Gbps.

When constructing a network or renting a channel, real channels will be selected taking into account the capabilities of the DWDM technology. Let us denote by C_{ij} the throughput of the channel between nodes i and j. According to the optimized results obtained by the Gomory-Hu algorithm for Example 1 (see Fig. 1), we need channels with capacities

$$C_{12} = 600 \text{ Gbps}, \quad C_{23} = C_{15} = 400 \text{ Gbps}, \quad C_{53} = 150 \text{ Gbps},$$
$$\text{and} \quad C_{54} = C_{43} = 250 \text{ Gbps}.$$

However, for this example we have assumed that the capacity of one optical fiber is 400 Gbps. This means that for further optimization the capacity of each

---

[2] SN is an abbreviation for 'SubNet'.

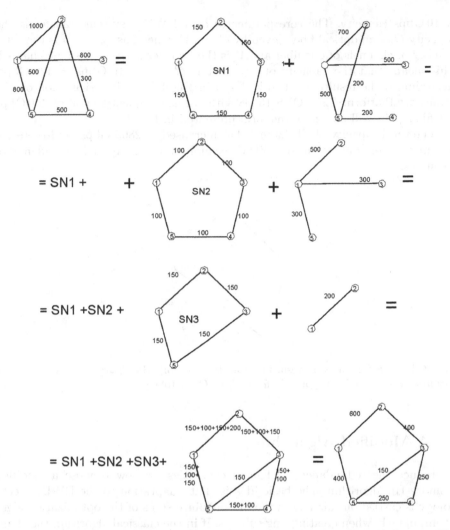

Fig. 1. Example 1: Illustration of the results obtained by the classical Gomory-Hu algorithm.

channel should be a multiple of 400 Gbps. Therefore, in Fig. 2, in the resulting network adapted to the DWDM technology, we increase some of the capacities:

$$C_{12} = 800 \text{ Gbps}, \quad C_{53} = C_{54} = C_{43} = 400 \text{ Gbps}.$$

As a result, the total capacity and hence the cost is higher than for the version obtained by the classical Gomory-Hu algorithm.

Example 2. (based on Example 1): We now assume that the DWDM technology, in particular, the Transport Platform Cisco ONS 15808, is used. For extended-long-haul applications up to 2250 km the Cisco ONS 15808 supports 40 channels of 10 Gbps capacity. The core parameter of a DWDM system transfer is the capacity C of an optical fiber, given by $C = nV$, where, as before, n is the total number of channels of one fiber and V is the transfer speed of a single channel. This means that the capacity of one fiber is $C = 40 \cdot 10$ Gbps $= 400$ Gbps. Accordingly, the resulting network shown in Fig. 1, with its orientation on the Transport Platform Cisco ONS 15808 with transfer capacity equal to 400 Gbps per fiber pair, will now have the form presented in Fig. 2.

The total capacity of all channels has increased to 2800 Gbps, and therefore this method of adaptation to DWDM technology has generated redundancy of resources.

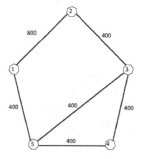

Fig. 2. Example 2: Network resulting from the Gomory-Hu algorithm adapted to the requirements of the Transport Platform Cisco ONS 15808.

4   A Modified Algorithm

To reduce the redundancy of channel capacities we now propose a modified Gomory-Hu algorithm. The basic idea is that adaptation to the DWDM technology is carried out already in the intermediate steps of the optimization algorithm, namely when creating ring subnets. If in the classical algorithm the channel capacity of ring subnets was chosen as $W_{\min}/2$, it is now replaced by the closest higher value jC, where C is the capacity per fiber. Obviously this also increases redundancy, but it may be taken into account in the next steps in the construction of new ring subnets. Their capacity will be chosen smaller taking into account the introduced redundancy and may be smaller compared to the classical Gomory-Hu algorithm.

The modified algorithm can be represented as follows.

1. Specification of the input network in form of a weighted non-directed graph $A := G_{\text{in}}$. The weights of the edges represent the required intensities of flows.
2. Find the minimal weight of the edges of the graph $A - W_{\min}$, and replace $W_{\min}$ by the closest higher value jC for $j = 1, 2, 3, \ldots C$, where C is the capacity per fiber.

3. Decomposition of graph A into
   - a ring graph SNk which includes all the nodes of graph A, and assigning to each edge of the ring the weight $W_{min}/2$ where k is the cycle number;
   - a graph B, which is obtained by subtracting the value of W_{min} from all edges of graph A whose weight is greater than zero, and substituting negative weights by zero.
4. If the number of edges in graph B is greater than one, then we accept $A = B$ and go back to step 2.
5. Replace the non-zero edges of graph B by the nearest higher value jC, $j = 1, 2, 3, \ldots$, where C is the capacity per fiber.
6. Integration of all graphs of SNk and graph B.

Example 3. (based on Example 1): An illustration of the proposed approach is shown in the example of the implementation of the modified algorithm for the same input data as before for the classical version. Fig. 3 shows the process and result of optimization based on the modified Gomory-Hu algorithm.

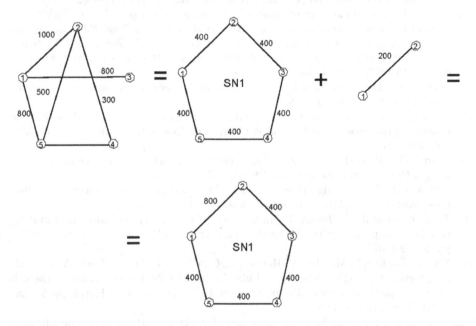

Fig. 3. Example 3: Illustration of the results obtained by the modified Gomory-Hu algorithm

The total required capacity for all channels amounts to 2400 Gbps. When using the classical algorithm with adaptation to DWDM technology, it was 2800 Gbps. So there is a redundancy reduction of 400 Gbps.

The gain in capacities, or its absence, in the transition from the classical algorithm to the modified one, will depend on the intensities of the input flows.

Since an a priori analysis of input data does generally not allow to predict which algorithm will yield better results, it is recommended for each input set to investigate both options (classical and modified), to compare the results and choose the option with minimal redundancy.

References

1. Cohen, J., Rodrigues, L.A., Duarte, E.P.: A parallel implementation of Gomory-Hu's cut tree algorithm. In: Proceedings IEEE 24th International Symposium on Computer Architecture and High Performance Computing, Columbia University, New York, pp. 124–131 (2012)
2. Ford, L.R., Fulkerson, D.R.: Flows in Networks. Princeton University Press, Princeton (1962)
3. Gomory, R.E., Hu, T.C.: Multi-terminal network flows. J. Soc. Ind. Appl. Math. **9**(4), 551–570 (1961)
4. Ivaniga, T., Ivaniga, P.: The development of DWDM using OADM to influence a non-linear effect SBS. ARPN J. Eng. Appl. Sci. **13**(13), 4185–4194 (2018)
5. Kasprzak, A.: Exact and approximate algorithms for topological design of wide area networks with non-simultaneous single commodity flows. In: Sloot, P.M.A., Abramson, D., Bogdanov, A.V., Gorbachev, Y.E., Dongarra, J.J., Zomaya, A.Y. (eds.) ICCS 2003. LNCS, vol. 2660, pp. 799–808. Springer, Heidelberg (2003). https://doi.org/10.1007/3-540-44864-0_82
6. Larsson, C.: Design of Modern Communication Networks. Methods and Applications. Elsevier, Amsterdam (2014)
7. Obelovska, K., Grutsynak, G., Sagajdak, S.: Modified Gomory-Hu algorithm for network optimization based on SDM technology. Comput. Sci. Inf. Technol. **694**, 401–406 (2011)
8. Skorpil, V., Precechtel, R.: Training a neural network for a new node element design. Przegl. Elektrotechniczny **89**(2b), 187–192 (2013)
9. Tapolcai, J.: Routing algorithms in survivable telecommunication networks. PhD thesis summary, Budapest, Hungary (2004)
10. Tóth, J., Ovseník, Ľ., Turán, J.: An overview of various types of waveguide grating based demultiplexors in WDM systems. In: IWSSIP 2015, City University, London, pp. 29–32 (2015)
11. Xin, Y., Baldine, I., Mandal, A., Heermann, C., Chase, J., Yumerefendi, A.: Embedding virtual topologies in networked clouds. In: CFI 2011 Proceedings of the 6th International Conference on Future Internet Technologies, Seoul, Korea, pp. 26–29. ACM New York (2011)
12. Dense wavelength division multiplexing (DWDM). https://searchnetworking. techtarget.com/definition/dense-wavelength-division-multiplexing-DWDM

Additional Contributed Papers

Adaptive Exponential Integrators
for MCTDHF

Winfried Auzinger[1]([envelope])[iD], Alexander Grosz[1][iD], Harald Hofstätter[2],
and Othmar Koch[2][iD]

[1] Vienna University of Technology, Wiedner Hauptstraße 8–10, 1040 Vienna, Austria
`w.auzinger@tuwien.ac.at`, `e1525490@student.tuwien.ac.at`
[2] Institute of Mathematics, University of Vienna, Oskar-Morgenstern-Platz 1,
1090 Vienna, Austria
`hofi@harald-hofstaetter.at`, `othmar@othmar-koch.org`

Abstract. We compare exponential-type integrators for the numerical time-propagation of the equations of motion arising in the multi-configuration time-dependent Hartree-Fock method for the approximation of the high-dimensional multi-particle Schrödinger equation. We find that among the most widely used integrators like Runge-Kutta, exponential splitting, exponential Runge-Kutta, exponential multistep and Lawson methods, exponential Lawson multistep methods with one predictor/corrector step provide optimal stability and accuracy at the least computational cost, taking into account that the evaluation of the non-local potential terms is by far the computationally most expensive part of such a calculation. Moreover, the predictor step provides an estimator for the time-stepping error at no additional cost, which enables adaptive time-stepping to reliably control the accuracy of a computation.

Keywords: Multi-configuration time-dependent Hartree-Fock method · Time integration · Splitting methods · Exponential integrators · Lawson methods · Local error estimators · Adaptive stepsize selection

1 Introduction

We compare time integration methods for nonlinear Schrödinger-type equations

$$i\,\partial_t u(t) = A\,u(t) + B(u(t)) = H(u(t)), \quad t > t_0, \quad u(t_0) = u_0, \tag{1}$$

on the Hilbert space $\mathcal{B} = L^2$. Here, $A: \mathcal{D} \subseteq \mathcal{B} \to \mathcal{B}$ is a self-adjoint differential operator and B a generally unbounded nonlinear operator. Our focus is on the equations of motion associated with the multi-configuration time-dependent Hartree-Fock (MCTDHF) approximation to the multi-particle electronic Schrödinger equation, where the key issue is the high computational effort

Supported by the Vienna Science and Technology Fund (WWTF) grant MA14-002. The computations have been conducted on the Vienna Scientific Cluster (VSC).

I. Lirkov and S. Margenov (Eds.): LSSC 2019, LNCS 11958, pp. 557–565, 2020.
https://doi.org/10.1007/978-3-030-41032-2_64

for the evaluation of the nonlocal (integral) operator B. Thus, in the choice of the most appropriate integrator, we emphasize a minimal number of evaluations of B for a given order and disregard the effort for the propagation of A, which can commonly be realized at essentially the cost of two (cheap) transforms between real and frequency space via fast transforms like [I]FFT. The approaches that we pursue and advocate in this paper are thus based on splitting of the vector fields in (1). It turns out that exponential integrators [6] based on the variation of constants serve our purpose best, as they provide a desirable balance between computational effort and stability.

2   The MCTDHF Method

We focus on the comparison of numerical methods for the equations of motion associated with MCTDHF for the approximate solution of the time-dependent multi-particle Schrödinger equation

$$i \frac{\partial \psi}{\partial t} = H\psi,$$

where the complex-valued wave function $\psi = \psi(x_1, \ldots, x_f, t)$ depends on time t and, in the case considered here, the positions $x_1, \ldots, x_f \in \mathbf{R}^3$ of electrons in an atom or molecule. The time-dependent Hamiltonian reads

$$H = H(t) := \sum_{k=1}^{f} \left(\frac{1}{2} \Delta^{(k)} + U(x_k) + \sum_{\ell < k} V(x_k - x_\ell) \right) + V_{\text{ext}}(x_1, \ldots, x_f, t)$$

$$=: T + W(t, x_1, \ldots, x_f),$$

$$T = \sum_{k=1}^{f} \frac{1}{2} \Delta^{(k)}, \quad U(x) = -\frac{Z}{|x|}, \ Z \in \mathbf{N}, \quad V(x - y) = \frac{1}{|x - y|}.$$

Here $V_{\text{ext}}(x_1, \ldots, x_f, t)$ is a smooth time-dependent function, and $\Delta^{(k)}$ is the Laplace operator with respect to x_k only.

In MCTDHF as put forward in [12], the multi-electron wave function ψ is approximated by a function u living in a manifold $\mathcal{M}$ characterized by the ansatz

$$u = \sum_{(j_1, \ldots, j_f)} a_{j_1, \ldots, j_f}(t) \, \phi_{j_1}(x_1, t) \cdots \phi_{j_f}(x_f, t) =: \sum_J a_J(t) \, \Phi_J(x, t). \tag{2}$$

For the electronic Schrödinger equation, the Pauli principle implies that only solutions u are considered which are antisymmetric under exchange of any pair of arguments x_j, x_k,

Now, the Dirac-Frenkel variational principle [3] in conjunction with orthogonality conditions is used to derive differential equations for the coefficients a_J and the so-called single-particle functions ϕ_j in (2), where we will henceforth tacitly identify u with the vector (a, ϕ) of coefficients and orbitals,

$$i \frac{da_J}{dt} = \sum_K \langle \Phi_J |W| \Phi_K \rangle a_K \quad \forall J, \tag{3}$$

$$i \frac{\partial \phi_j}{\partial t} = T \phi_j + (I - P) \sum_{k=1}^{N} \sum_{\ell=1}^{N} \rho_{j,\ell}^{-1} \overline{W}_{\ell,k} \, \phi_k, \quad j = 1, \ldots, N, \tag{4}$$

where

$$\overline{W}_{j,\ell} = \langle \psi_j |W| \psi_\ell \rangle, \quad \text{with} \quad \psi_j = \langle \phi_j | u \rangle, \quad \rho_{j,\ell} = \langle \psi_j | \psi_\ell \rangle,$$

and where P is the orthogonal projector onto the space spanned by the functions ϕ_j. We will henceforth denote

$$A = \frac{i}{2} \left(0, \Delta^{(1)}, \ldots, 0, \Delta^{(f)} \right)^T, \quad B = B(a, \phi), \tag{5}$$

where B is the vector of the components associated with the potential which constitute the computationally most expensive part.

2.1   Splitting Methods

Popular integrators for quantum dynamics are exponential time-splitting methods which are based on multiplicative combinations of the partial flows $\mathcal{E}_A(t, u)$: $u \mapsto u(t) = e^{tA} u$ and $\mathcal{E}_B(t, u)$: $u \mapsto u(t)$ with $u'(t) = B(u(t))$, $u(0) = u$. For a single step $(t_n, u_n) \mapsto (t_{n+1}, u_{n+1})$ with time-step h, this reads

$$u_{n+1} := \mathcal{S}(h, u_n) = \mathcal{E}_B(b_s h, \cdot) \circ \mathcal{E}_A(a_s h, \cdot) \circ \ldots \circ \mathcal{E}_B(b_1 h, \cdot) \circ \mathcal{E}_A(a_1 h, u_n),$$

where the coefficients $a_j, b_j, j = 1 \ldots s$ are determined according to the requirement that a prescribed order of consistency is obtained [5]. For a convergence analysis of splitting methods in the context of MCTDHF, see for instance [9].

2.2   Exponential Integrators

An approach which also exploits the separated vector fields is given by the class of exponential integrators, which are comprehensively discussed in [6]. Here the variation of constant formula is used to express the solution of (1) for a time-step $t_n \to t_{n+1} = t_n + h$ via the integral equation

$$u(t_n + h) = e^{hA} u_n + \int_0^h e^{(h-\tau)A} B(u(t_n + \tau)) \, d\tau. \tag{6}$$

Different numerical integrators are distinguished depending on how the integral in (6) is approximated.

Exponential Runge-Kutta Methods. When the integral in (6) is approximated by a quadrature formula of Runge-Kutta type, relying on evaluations of the nonlinear operator B at interior points $t_n + h\tau_j$, $\tau_j \in [0,1]$, $j = 1,\ldots,k$, an *exponential Runge-Kutta* method is obtained. This corresponds to replacing $B(\cdot)$ in the integrand by a polynomial interpolant at the points

$$\big(t_n + h\tau_1, B(u(t_n + h\tau_1))\big), \ldots, \big((t_n + h\tau_k, B(u(t_n + h\tau_k))\big).$$

The method is realized by stepping from $t_n + h\tau_j \to t_n + h\tau_{j+1}$ in the same way as for a Runge-Kutta method, with appropriate weights of the stages. For implicit methods, nonlinear systems of equations have to be solved, which is generally considered as prohibitive. Note that after interpolation, the resulting integral can be evaluated analytically by using the φ-functions or alternatively, by numerical quadrature [6]. Such a procedure has first been proposed in [4], for a stiff error analysis, see [6] and references therein. For our comparisons, we use the fourth order Krogstad method mentioned there.

Exponential Multistep Methods. The integral in (6) can be approximated in terms of an interpolation polynomial at previous approximations

$$\big(-(k-1)h, B(u_{n-k+1})\big), \ldots, \big((-h, B(u_{n-1})), (0, B(u_n))\big). \tag{7}$$

This yields an (explicit) exponential Adams-Bashforth multistep method first mentioned in [2], and introduced more systematically in [11], see also for instance [1,6]. If the interpolation also comprises the forward point $(h, B(u_{n+1}))$, an (implicit) exponential Adams-Moulton method is obtained. These two approaches can be combined in a predictor/corrector method in the same way as for linear multistep methods. Exponential multistep methods have first been considered and analyzed in [1] under the assumption of smooth B, and a starting strategy is also given there.

Lawson Methods. In Lawson methods, Eq. (1) is transformed prior to the numerical integration by the substitution $u(t) \to e^{-tA} u(t)$. To the resulting equation

$$u'(t) = e^{-tA} B\left(e^{tA} u(t)\right) =: F(u(t)), \tag{8}$$

any appropriate time-stepping scheme can be applied. The main advantage lies in the fact that the dynamics associated with the non-smooth operator A is separated by the transformation which can be realized cheaply in frequency space, while the problem subjected to the time-stepping scheme is smoother, thus allowing for larger time-steps. This transformation was first introduced in [10] for ordinary differential equations.

In a one-step version, an explicit Runge–Kutta method is employed to solve (8), which is equivalent to interpolation at interior nodes of the whole integrand in (6) by a polynomial in the same fashion as in (7). Reference [7] gives a convergence proof of Lawson Runge-Kutta methods in the stiff case, however under the assumption that the operator B is smooth, which is not the case in the MCTDHF equations we are considering. A convergence proof for Adams-Lawson multistep methods for the MCTDHF equations under minimal regularity requirements is given in the forthcoming work [8]. The proof addresses the transformed equation (8) and combines stability and consistency to conclude convergence. To this end, a boot-strapping argument is employed, first showing convergence in the Sobolev space H^1. Stability in L^2 only holds if the numerical solution is in H^1, which follows from the first argument, whence convergence in L^2 is inferred. Lipschitz conditions for the right-hand side entering the stability arguments can be shown by appropriate Sobolev-type inequalities in both H^1 and L^2. To prove consistency, the norms of derivatives of F in (8) are estimated, which amounts to bounds on commutators of the operators A and B. This implies assumptions on the regularity of the exact solution u.

We will demonstrate that the best approach for our goal is to use exponential Lawson multistep methods in a predictor/corrector implementation, which is shown to increase the accuracy and also provides a local error estimator for adaptive time-stepping at no additional cost. The efficiency of the time discretization can be improved if high-order time propagators are employed. In the multistep approach, this does not imply additional computational cost if no memory limitations have to be taken into account.

Comparisons. To assess the performance of the exponential integration methods described above, we will also show results for the classical explicit Runge-Kutta method of fourth order (RK4) and the second-order Strang splitting.

3   Numerical Results

To illustrate the performance of our numerical methods, we consider MCTDHF with the choice $N = 4$ for a one-dimensional model of a helium atom investigated in [12], where[1]

$$H(t) = H_0 + (x_1 + x_2)\,\mathcal{E}(t),$$
$$H_0 = -\frac{1}{2}(\partial_{x_1}^2 + \partial_{x_2}^2) - \frac{2}{\sqrt{x_1^2 + b^2}} - \frac{2}{\sqrt{x_2^2 + b^2}} + \frac{1}{\sqrt{(x_1 - x_2)^2 + b^2}},$$

with a smoothed Coulomb potential with shielding parameter $b = 0.7408$, which is irradiated by a short, intense, linearly polarized laser pulse

$$\mathcal{E}(t) = \mathcal{E}_0\,g(t)\sin(\omega t).$$

The peak amplitude is set to $\mathcal{E}_0 = 0.1894$, the frequency is $\omega = 0.1837$, and we define the envelope $g(t) = 1.2\exp\left(-5\cdot 10^{-4}\,(t - 6\pi/\omega)^2\right)$. The parameters are taken from [12], and the envelope is a smooth approximation of the

---

[1] Note that in exponential integrators, the explicit time-dependence in the potential does not call for a special treatment in the numerical quadrature, in the splitting methods, the potential is propagated by an explicit Runge-Kutta method of appropriate order.

trapezoidal envelope chosen there. In [12], this model serves to illustrate the effect of correlation on the probability density along the diagonal $x = y$, which implies that the single-configuration Hartree–Fock approximation is insufficient. We first investigate stable long-time propagation in Fig. 1. We monitor norm conservation of the wave function in the propagation of the ground state for the Hamiltonian $H_0 = H(0)$ for different equidistant stepsizes to resolve precisely the onset of instability. For RK4, the number of steps is specified in the plot; for all other methods, the number of steps is in $\{1000, 2000, \ldots, 12000\}$. If norm conservation is violated beyond the effect of numerical accuracy, the method cannot be recommended for physical applications. Indeed, we observe the following: Explicit Runge-Kutta methods only behave in a stable way when the numerical accuracy is already very high, close to round-off error. Exponential multistep methods[2] behave stably only for short times, even when a corrector step is performed. Exponential Runge-Kutta and Runge-Kutta-Lawson methods behave stably, likewise as splitting methods. Adams-Lawson multistep methods behave very stably, a corrector step adds to the accuracy, as well as providing an error estimate as the basis for adaptive time-stepping.

Next, we compare the efficiency of the different integrators. The unstable exponential multistep methods are no longer considered. While showing the same stability behavior, the Yoshida splitting is demonstrated to be less efficient than the Suzuki splitting, and the low order (but popular) Strang splitting is not competitive. High-order multistep methods provide higher accuracy at the same computational effort and are thus also considered for this comparison. To this end, we plot in Fig. 2 the accuracy as compared to a very precise reference solution at $t = 80$ as a function of the number of evaluations of the computationally expensive potential part B (dots on solid lines). Furthermore, we give the CPU time required in a sequential implementation on one thread of the Vienna Scientific Cluster (VSC) 3 comprising one Intel Xeon E5-2650v2 processor with 8 cores of 2.6 gHz (crosses '×'). We note that, as expected, the runtime is proportional to the number of potential evaluations. We observe that high-order Lawson multistep methods perform best, where particularly the high order which can be achieved in the multistep versions without additional evaluations is advantageous. Splitting methods, particularly the low order Strang splitting, are not very efficient due to the high effort for the propagation of the potential.

We stress that this shows only the picture on uniform grids. The multistep versions show their biggest advantage in adaptive time-stepping due to the cheap means of error estimation in the predictor/corrector implementation. To demonstrate that this works reliably for Adams-Lawson methods, we show in Fig. 3 the laser field $\mathcal{E}(t)$ and total energy functional (top) illustrating the local solution smoothness, and the stepsizes (bottom) automatically generated for the Adams-Lawson method of order 6. We see that the adaptively chosen stepsizes reflect the smoothness of the time evolution and the Lawson method enables larger step-

---

[2] In this experiment, all multistep methods are started by the Krogstad exponential Runge-Kutta method with stepsize $h/50$.

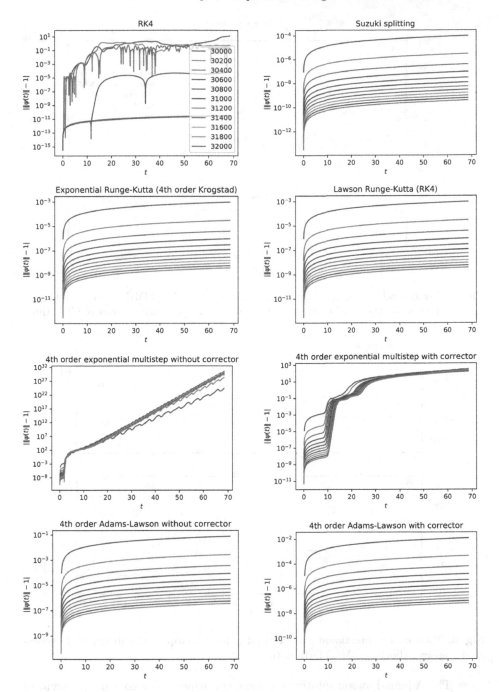

Fig. 1. Comparison of stable long-time integration.

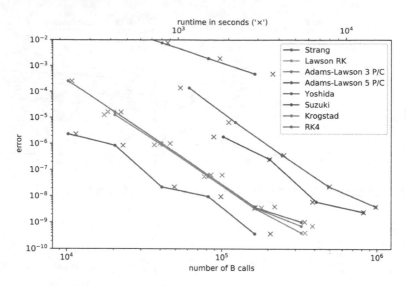

Fig. 2. Work/precision comparison for the helium atom, MCTDHF with $N = 4$. Dots on solid lines show the number of evaluations of B and '$\times$' mark seconds of CPU time.

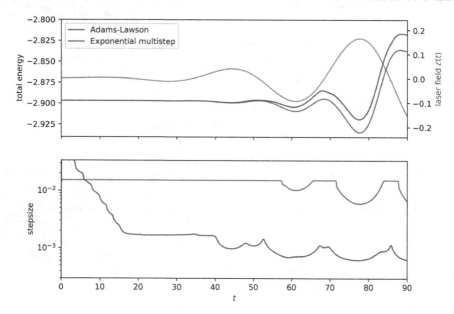

Fig. 3. Total energy functional and external potential (top) and automatically generated stepsizes (bottom), MCTDHF with $N = 4$.

sizes. The Adams-Lawson solution has been confirmed to be converged to within the prescribed tolerance 10^{-5}. On the other hand, the corresponding exponential multistep method (without the Lawson transformation) shows a noticeable deviation in the solution.

References

1. Calvo, M., Palencia, C.: A class of explicit multistep exponential integrators for semilinear problems. Numer. Math **102**, 367–381 (2011)
2. Certaine, J.: The solution of ordinary differential equations with large time constants. In: Ralston, A., Wilf, H. (eds.) Mathematical Methods for Digital Computers, pp. 128–132. Wiley, Hoboken (1960)
3. Frenkel, J.: Advanced General Theory Wave Mechanics. Clarendon Press, Oxford (1934)
4. Friedli, A.: Verallgemeinerte Runge-Kutta Verfahren zur Loesung steifer Differentialgleichungssysteme. In: Bulirsch, R., Grigorieff, R.D. (eds.) Numerical Treatment of Differential Equations. Lecture Notes in Mathematics, vol. 631, pp. 35–50. Springer, Heidelberg (1978). https://doi.org/10.1007/BFb0067462
5. Hairer, E., Lubich, C., Wanner, G.: Geometric Numerical Integration. Springer-Verlag, Heidelberg (2002)
6. Hochbruck, M., Ostermann, A.: Exponential integrators. Acta Numer. **19**, 209–286 (2010)
7. Hochbruck, M., Ostermann, A.: On the convergence of Lawson methods for semilinear stiff problems. CRC Preprint 2017/9, KIT Karlsruhe Institute of Technology (2017). https://www.waves.kit.edu/downloads/CRC1173_Preprint_2017-9.pdf
8. Koch, O.: Convergence of exponential Lawson-multistep methods for the MCTDHF equations, to appear in M2AN. Model. Numer. Anal. **53**, 2109–2119 (2019)
9. Koch, O., Neuhauser, C., Thalhammer, M.: Error analysis of high-order splitting methods for nonlinear evolutionary Schrödinger equations and application to the MCTDHF equations in electron dynamics. M2AN Math. Model. Numer. Anal. **47**, 1265–1284 (2013)
10. Lawson, J.: Generalized Runge-Kutta processes for stable systems with large Lipschitz constants. SIAM J. Numer. Anal. **4**, 372–380 (1967)
11. Norsett, S.P.: An A-stable modification of the Adams-Bashforth methods. In: Morris, J.L. (ed.) Conference on the Numerical Solution of Differential Equations. LNM, vol. 109, pp. 214–219. Springer, Heidelberg (1969). https://doi.org/10.1007/BFb0060031
12. Zanghellini, J., Kitzler, M., Brabec, T., Scrinzi, A.: Testing the multi-configuration time-dependent Hartree-Fock method. J. Phys. B: At. Mol. Phys. **37**, 763–773 (2004)

Convergence Analysis of a Finite Volume Gradient Scheme for a Linear Parabolic Equation Using Characteristic Methods

Fayssal Benkhaldoun[1,2] and Abdallah Bradji[3(✉)]

[1] LAGA, University of Paris 13, Paris, France
`fayssal@math.univ-paris13.fr`
[2] UM6P, Ben Guerir, Morocco
`Fayssal.BENKHALDOUN@um6p.ma`
[3] LMA (Laboratoire de Mathématiques Appliquées), Faculty of Sciences,
University of Annaba, Annaba, Algeria
`abdallah.bradji@gmail.com`, `abdallah.bradji@etu.univ-amu.fr`,
`bradji@math.univ-paris13.fr`
`https://www.math.univ-paris13.fr/~fayssal/`
`https://www.i2m.univ-amu.fr/~bradji/`

Abstract. The first aim of this work is to establish a finite volume scheme using the Characteristic method for non-stationary advection-diffusion equations. The second aim is to analyze the convergence order of this scheme. The finite volume method considered here has been developed recently in [3] to approximate heterogeneous and anisotropic diffusion problems using a general class of nonconforming meshes. The formulation of schemes using the finite volume method of [3] can be obtained by replacing the gradient of the exact solution by a stable and consistent discrete gradient. This work is a continuation of the previous ones [1,2] in which we derived directly a finite volume scheme for the heat equation along with a convergence analysis.

Keywords: Finite volume · Parabolic equations · Characteristics method

1 Description of the Model and Aim of This Note

We are concerned with the following UADP (Unsteady Advection-Diffusion Problem):

$$u_t(\boldsymbol{x},t) - \Delta u(\boldsymbol{x},t) + \mathrm{div}(\mathbf{v}u)(\boldsymbol{x},t) + b(\boldsymbol{x})u(\boldsymbol{x},t) = f(\boldsymbol{x},t), \ \boldsymbol{x} \in \Omega, \ t \in (0,T),$$
$$(1)$$

where Ω is an open bounded connected subset of $\mathbb{R}^d$ $(d \in \mathbb{N}^\star)$, $T > 0$, f is a given function, and $\mathbf{v} = \mathbf{v}(\boldsymbol{x},t) \in \mathbb{R}^d$ is a vector field. We assume here that b is only depending on $\boldsymbol{x}$.

© Springer Nature Switzerland AG 2020
I. Lirkov and S. Margenov (Eds.): LSSC 2019, LNCS 11958, pp. 566–575, 2020.
https://doi.org/10.1007/978-3-030-41032-2_65

Initial conditions are given by:

$$u(0) = u^0. \tag{2}$$

where u^0 is a given function defined on Ω. Dirichlet boundary conditions are given by

$$u(\boldsymbol{x}, t) = 0, \quad (\boldsymbol{x}, t) \in \partial\Omega \times (0, T). \tag{3}$$

For the sake of simplicity, we assume that the following hypotheses are satisfied:

Assumption 1 (Assumptions on v and b). *We assume that the functions* $\boldsymbol{v}$ *and b are satisfying:*

$$\boldsymbol{v} \in \mathscr{C}^1(\overline{\Omega} \times [0, T]), \quad \boldsymbol{v}(\boldsymbol{x}, t) = 0, \quad \forall(\boldsymbol{x}, t) \in \partial\Omega \times [0, T], \tag{4}$$

$$b \in \mathscr{C}^1(\overline{\Omega}), \quad \text{and} \quad b(\boldsymbol{x}) + \operatorname{div}\boldsymbol{v}(\boldsymbol{x}, t) \geq 0, \quad \forall(\boldsymbol{x}, t) \in \Omega \times [0, T]. \tag{5}$$

In this note, we consider SUSHI (Scheme Using Stabilization and Hybrid Interfaces) developed in [3] to approximate UADP (1)–(3) combined with characteristics method. Characteristics method is the replacement of the advective part of the equation by total differentiation along characteristics. Such method is well developed in the context of FEM (Finite Element Method), see [4, Subsection 12.5, Pages 423–427]. However, to the best of our knowledge, the characteristics method has not been attracted the attention it merits in FV (Finite Volume) methods for parabolic equations. This work is a continuation of our previous works [1,2] in which we derived directly schemes using SUSHI for the heat equation $u_t - \Delta u = f$ along with a convergence analysis. However, the equation (that is (1)) we consider in this note is more general. We will derive a FV scheme, using SUSHI combined with characteristics method, for (1)–(3) along with a convergence analysis.

2   Space and Time Discretizations

We consider as discretization in space the mesh of [3] in which a SUSHI is developed. In brief, such mesh is defined as the triplet $\mathscr{D} = (\mathscr{M}, \mathscr{E}, \mathscr{P})$ where $\mathscr{M}$ is the set of cells, $\mathscr{E}$ is the set of edges, and $\mathscr{P}$ is a set of points $\boldsymbol{x}_K$ in each cell K. We assume that, for all $K \in \mathscr{M}$, there exists a subset $\mathscr{E}_K$ of $\mathscr{E}$ such that $\partial K = \cup_{\sigma \in \mathscr{E}_K} \overline{\sigma}$. For any $\sigma \in \mathscr{E}$, we denote by $\mathscr{M}_\sigma = \{K, \sigma \in \mathscr{E}_K\}$. We then assume that, for any $\sigma \in \mathscr{E}$, either $\mathscr{M}_\sigma$ has exactly one element and then $\sigma \subset \partial\Omega$ (the set of these interfaces, called boundary interfaces, denoted by $\mathscr{E}_{\text{ext}}$) or $\mathscr{M}_\sigma$ has exactly two elements (the set of these interfaces, called interior interfaces, denoted by $\mathscr{E}_{\text{int}}$). For all $\sigma \in \mathscr{E}$, we denote by $\boldsymbol{x}_\sigma$ the barycentre of σ. For all $K \in \mathscr{M}$ and $\sigma \in \mathscr{E}$, we denote by $\mathbf{n}_{K,\sigma}$ the unit vector normal to σ outward to K. Denoting by $d_{K,\sigma}$ the Euclidean distance between $\boldsymbol{x}_K$ and the hyperplane including σ, one assumes that $d_{K,\sigma} > 0$. We then denote by $\mathscr{D}_{K,\sigma}$ the cone with vertex $\boldsymbol{x}_K$ and basis σ. Also, h_K is used to denote the diameter of K. For more details on the mesh, we refer to [3, Definition 2.1, Page 1012].

We define the discrete space $\mathscr{X}_{\mathscr{D},0}$ as the set of all $v = ((v_K)_{K \in \mathscr{M}}, (v_\sigma)_{\sigma \in \mathscr{E}})$, where $v_K, v_\sigma \in \mathbb{R}$ and $v_\sigma = 0$ for all $\sigma \in \mathscr{E}_{\mathrm{ext}}$. Let $H_{\mathscr{M}}(\Omega) \subset L^2(\Omega)$ be the space of functions which are constant on each control volume K of the mesh $\mathscr{M}$. For all $v \in \mathscr{X}_{\mathscr{D}}$, we denote by $\Pi_{\mathscr{M}} v \in H_{\mathscr{M}}(\Omega)$ the function defined by $\Pi_{\mathscr{M}} v(\boldsymbol{x}) = v_K$, for a.e. $\boldsymbol{x} \in K$, for all $K \in \mathscr{M}$. In order to analyze the convergence, we need to consider the size of the discretization $\mathscr{D}$ defined by $h_{\mathscr{D}} = \sup\{\mathrm{diam}(K), K \in \mathscr{M}\}$ and the regularity of the mesh given by

$$\theta_{\mathscr{D}} = \max\left(\max_{\sigma \in \mathscr{E}_{\mathrm{int}}, K, L \in \mathscr{M}} \frac{d_{K,\sigma}}{d_{L,\sigma}}, \max_{K \in \mathscr{M}, \sigma \in \mathscr{E}_K} \frac{h_K}{d_{K,\sigma}}\right).$$

The formulation of the scheme we want to consider involves the discrete gradient, denoted by $\nabla_{\mathscr{D}}$, developed in [3]. The value of $\nabla_{\mathscr{D}} u$, where $u \in \mathscr{X}_{\mathscr{D},0}$, is defined by, for all $K \in \mathscr{M}$, for a.e. $\boldsymbol{x} \in \mathscr{D}_{K,\sigma}$

$$\nabla_{\mathscr{D}} u(\boldsymbol{x}) = \frac{1}{\mathrm{m}(K)} \sum_{\sigma \in \mathscr{E}_K} \mathrm{m}(\sigma)(u_\sigma - u_K) \mathbf{n}_{K,\sigma} +$$

$$\left(\frac{\sqrt{d}}{d_{K,\sigma}}(u_\sigma - u_K - \nabla_K u \cdot (\boldsymbol{x}_\sigma - \boldsymbol{x}_K))\right) \mathbf{n}_{K,\sigma}. \quad (6)$$

We introduce now the inner product defined on $\mathscr{X}_{\mathscr{D},0} \times \mathscr{X}_{\mathscr{D},0}$ and given by

$$\langle u, v \rangle_F = \int_\Omega \nabla_{\mathscr{D}} u(\boldsymbol{x}) \cdot \nabla_{\mathscr{D}} v(\boldsymbol{x}) d\boldsymbol{x}. \quad (7)$$

The time discretization is performed with a constant time step $k = \dfrac{T}{N+1}$, where $N \in \mathbb{N}^\star$, and we shall denote $t_n = nk$, for $n \in [\![0, N+1]\!]$. We denote by ∂^1 the discrete first time derivative given by

$$\partial^1 v^{j+1} = \frac{v^{j+1} - v^j}{k}. \quad (8)$$

Throughout this paper, the letter C stands for a positive constant independent of the parameters of the space and time discretizations.

3   Definition of Characteristics

In this section, we summarize some results of the method of characteristics. These results can be found for instance in [4, Section 12.5, Pages 423–427] and references therein. For any $s \in [0, T]$ and $\boldsymbol{x} \in \Omega$, we define the characteristic lines associated to $\mathbf{v} = \mathbf{v}(\boldsymbol{x}, t)$ as the vector functions $\Phi = \Phi(t; \boldsymbol{x}, s) : [0, T] \longrightarrow \Omega$ satisfying the following differential equation:

$$\begin{cases} \dfrac{d\Phi}{dt}(t; \boldsymbol{x}, s) = \mathbf{v}(\Phi(t; \boldsymbol{x}, s), t), \quad t \in (0, T) \\[2mm] \Phi(s; \boldsymbol{x}, s) = \boldsymbol{x}. \end{cases} \quad (9)$$

Let us quote some properties concerning the characteristic lines associated to a function $\mathbf{v} = \mathbf{v}(\boldsymbol{x}, t)$:

– The existence and uniqueness of the characteristic lines for each choice of s and $\boldsymbol{x}$ hold under suitable assumptions on $\mathbf{v}$, for instance $\mathbf{v}$ continuous in $\overline{\Omega} \times [0, T]$ and Lipschitz continuous in $\overline{\Omega}$, uniformly with respect to $t \in [0, T]$. These conditions are satisfied under Assumption 1.
– The uniqueness stated in the previous item implies that

$$\Phi(t; \Phi(s; \boldsymbol{x}, \tau), s) = \Phi(t; \boldsymbol{x}, \tau). \tag{10}$$

Indeed

$$\frac{d\Phi(t; \Phi(s; \boldsymbol{x}, \tau), s)}{dt} = \mathbf{v}(\Phi(t; \Phi(s; \boldsymbol{x}, \tau), s), t) \quad \text{and} \quad \frac{d\Phi(t; \boldsymbol{x}, \tau)}{dt} = \mathbf{v}(\Phi(t; \boldsymbol{x}, \tau), t).$$

In addition to this

$$\Phi(s; \Phi(s; \boldsymbol{x}, \tau), s) = \Phi(s; \boldsymbol{x}, \tau).$$

– Taking $t = \tau$ in (10) yields

$$\Phi(\tau; \Phi(s; \boldsymbol{x}, \tau), s) = \Phi(\tau; \boldsymbol{x}, \tau) = \boldsymbol{x}. \tag{11}$$

– For any t and s, the inverse of the function $\boldsymbol{x} \mapsto \Phi(t; \boldsymbol{x}, s)$ is $\boldsymbol{x} \mapsto \Phi(s; \boldsymbol{x}, t)$.

Let us define

$$\overline{u}(\boldsymbol{x}, t) = u(\Phi(t; \boldsymbol{x}, 0), t). \tag{12}$$

Replacing x by $\Phi(0; \boldsymbol{x}, t)$ in (12) yields

$$u(\Phi(t; \Phi(0; \boldsymbol{x}, t), 0), t) = \overline{u}(\Phi(0; \boldsymbol{x}, t), t). \tag{13}$$

Using (11), (13) implies that

$$u(\boldsymbol{x}, t) = \overline{u}(\Phi(0; \boldsymbol{x}, t), t). \tag{14}$$

We have, using the definition (12)

$$\frac{\partial \overline{u}}{\partial t}(\boldsymbol{x}, t) = \frac{\partial u}{\partial t}(\Phi(t; \boldsymbol{x}, 0), t) + \sum_{i=2}^{d} \frac{\partial u}{\partial x_i}(\Phi(t; \boldsymbol{x}, 0), t)\frac{\partial \Phi_i}{\partial t}(t; \boldsymbol{x}, 0)$$

$$= \frac{\partial u}{\partial t}(\Phi(t; \boldsymbol{x}, 0), t) + \nabla u(\Phi(t; \boldsymbol{x}, 0), t) \cdot \mathbf{v}(\Phi(t; \boldsymbol{x}, 0), t). \tag{15}$$

Replacing x by $\Phi(0; \boldsymbol{x}, t)$ in (1) and using (15) yield

$$\frac{\partial \overline{u}}{\partial t}(\boldsymbol{x}, t) - \nabla u(\Phi(t; \boldsymbol{x}, 0), t) \cdot \mathbf{v}(\Phi(t; \boldsymbol{x}, 0), t) - \overline{\Delta u}(\boldsymbol{x}, t)$$
$$+ \operatorname{div}(\mathbf{v}u)(\Phi(0; \boldsymbol{x}, t), t) + \overline{b}(\boldsymbol{x})\overline{u}(\boldsymbol{x}, t) = \overline{f}(\boldsymbol{x}, t).$$

This is equivalent to

$$\frac{\partial \overline{u}}{\partial t} - \overline{\Delta u} + \left(\overline{b} + \overline{\operatorname{div}\mathbf{v}}\right)\overline{u} = \overline{f}. \tag{16}$$

Taking $t = t_{n+1}$ as argument in Eq. (16) leads to

$$\frac{\partial \overline{u}}{\partial t}(t_{n+1}) - \overline{\Delta u}(t_{n+1}) + \left(\overline{b} + \overline{\mathrm{div} \mathbf{v}}(t_{n+1})\right) \overline{u}(t_{n+1}) = \overline{f}(t_{n+1}). \qquad (17)$$

Let us consider the first order approximation

$$\frac{\partial \overline{u}}{\partial t}(\boldsymbol{x}, t_{n+1}) \approx \frac{\overline{u}(\boldsymbol{x}, t_{n+1}) - \overline{u}(\boldsymbol{x}, t_n)}{k}.$$

This gives, thanks to (12)

$$\frac{\partial \overline{u}}{\partial t}(\boldsymbol{x}, t_{n+1}) \approx \frac{u(\Phi(t_{n+1}; \boldsymbol{x}, 0), t_{n+1}) - u(\Phi(t_n; \boldsymbol{x}, 0), t_n)}{k}.$$

Using (11) (with $\tau = t_{n+1}$ and $s = 0$) and (10) (with $t = t_n$, $s = 0$, and $\tau = t_{n+1}$), we get the following approximation for $\frac{\partial \overline{u}}{\partial t}(\Phi(0; \boldsymbol{x}, t_{n+1}), t_{n+1})$

$$\frac{u(\Phi(t_{n+1}; \Phi(0; \boldsymbol{x}, t_{n+1}), 0), t_{n+1}) - u(\Phi(t_n; \Phi(0; \boldsymbol{x}, t_{n+1}), 0), t_n)}{k}$$

$$= \frac{u(\boldsymbol{x}, t_{n+1}) - u(\Phi(t_n; \boldsymbol{x}, t_{n+1}), t_n)}{k}.$$

Let us set

$$\frac{\partial \overline{u}}{\partial t}(\Phi(0; \boldsymbol{x}, t_{n+1}), t_{n+1})$$
$$= \frac{u(\Phi(t_{n+1}; \Phi(0; \boldsymbol{x}, t_{n+1}), 0), t_{n+1}) - u(\Phi(t_n; \Phi(0; \boldsymbol{x}, t_{n+1}), 0), t_n)}{k} + \mathbb{T}_1^{n+1}(\boldsymbol{x})$$
$$= \frac{u(\boldsymbol{x}, t_{n+1}) - u(\Phi(t_n; \boldsymbol{x}, t_{n+1}), t_n)}{k} + \mathbb{T}_1^{n+1}(\boldsymbol{x}). \qquad (18)$$

Using a Taylor expansion to get

$$|\mathbb{T}_1^{n+1}| \leq Ck\|u\|_{\mathscr{C}^1([0,T]; \mathscr{C}(\overline{\Omega}))}. \qquad (19)$$

Taking $\boldsymbol{x} = \Phi(0; \boldsymbol{x}, t_{n+1})$ in (17), using (14), and gathering the result with (18) yield

$$\frac{u(t_{n+1}) - u(t_n)(\Phi(t_n; \boldsymbol{x}, t_{n+1}))}{k} - \Delta u(t_{n+1}) + (b + \mathrm{div} \mathbf{v}(t_{n+1})) u(t_{n+1})$$
$$= f(t_{n+1}) - \mathbb{T}_1^{n+1}(\boldsymbol{x}). \qquad (20)$$

Let us now look for a suitable approximation for $\Phi(t_n; \boldsymbol{x}, t_{n+1})$. Taking $s = t_{n+1}$ in (9) leads to

$$\frac{d\Phi}{dt}(t; \boldsymbol{x}, t_{n+1}) = \mathbf{v}(\Phi(t; \boldsymbol{x}, t_{n+1}), t) \quad \text{and} \quad \Phi(t_{n+1}; \boldsymbol{x}, t_{n+1}) = \boldsymbol{x}. \qquad (21)$$

Integrating (21) over $t \in (t_n, t_{n+1})$ yields

$$x - \Phi(t_n; x, t_{n+1}) = \int_{t_n}^{t_{n+1}} \mathbf{v}(\Phi(t; x, t_{n+1}), t)dt.$$

This gives

$$\Phi(t_n; x, t_{n+1}) = x - \int_{t_n}^{t_{n+1}} \mathbf{v}(\Phi(t; x, t_{n+1}), t)dt \approx$$

$$x - k\mathbf{v}(\Phi(t_{n+1}; x, t_{n+1}), t_{n+1}) = \omega^{n+1}(x), \quad (22)$$

where, using (11),

$$\omega^{n+1}(x) = x - k\mathbf{v}(x, t_{n+1}). \tag{23}$$

Let us set

$$\Phi(t_n; x, t_{n+1}) = \omega^{n+1}(x) + \mathbb{T}_2^{n+1}(x) \quad \text{and} \tag{24}$$

$$u(t_n)(\Phi(t_n; x, t_{n+1})) = u(t_n)(\omega^{n+1}(x)) + \mathbb{T}_3^{n+1}(x). \tag{25}$$

We can check that ω^{n+1} is a second order accurate approximation for $\Phi(t_n; \cdot, t_{n+1})$. This implies that $\mathbb{T}_3^{n+1}$ is of order two, i.e.

$$|\mathbb{T}_3^{n+1}| \leq Ck^2 \|u\|_{\mathscr{C}^1([0,T]; \mathscr{C}(\overline{\Omega}))}. \tag{26}$$

Under Assumption 1, we have $\mathbf{v}(x, t_{n+1}) = 0$. Let $x^\star(x)$ be the point of $\partial\Omega$ which has minimal distance from x. We have then, using (22)

$$|\omega^{n+1}(x) - x| = k\,|\mathbf{v}(x, t_{n+1})| = k\,|\mathbf{v}(x, t_{n+1}) - \mathbf{v}(x^\star(x), t_{n+1})|$$

$$\leq k|x - x^\star(x)| \sup_{(x,t)\in\overline{\Omega}\times[0,T]} |\nabla\mathbf{v}(x, t)|, \tag{27}$$

where $|\cdot|$ denotes the Euclidean norm in $\mathbb{R}^d$. Let us choose k sufficiently small such that

$$k \sup_{(x,t)\in\overline{\Omega}\times[0,T]} |\nabla\mathbf{v}(x, t)| < 1. \tag{28}$$

Gathering this fact with (27) implies that $|\omega^{n+1}(x) - x| < |x - x^\star(x)|$. This yields $\omega^{n+1}(x) \in \Omega$.

From (20) and (24), we deduce that

$$\Delta u(t_{n+1}) + f(t_{n+1}) = \frac{u(t_{n+1}) - u(t_n)(\omega^{n+1})}{k} +$$

$$(b + \operatorname{div}\mathbf{v}(t_{n+1}))\, u(t_{n+1}) + \mathbb{T}_1^{n+1}(x) - \frac{\mathbb{T}_3^{n+1}(x)}{k}. \tag{29}$$

4   Formulation of an Implicit FV Scheme and Statement of Its Convergence Result

In this section, we apply the SUSHI to UADP (1)–(3). This scheme is implicit and it is based on the approximation (29) of Eq. (1).

Definition 1 (Formulation of an implicit FV scheme for (1)–(3) using characteristics). *Let ω^{n+1} be the function given by (23). We define the following FV scheme as an approximation for the UADP (1)–(3): Find $u_{\mathscr{D}}^0 \in \mathscr{X}_{\mathscr{D},0}$ such that*

$$\langle u_{\mathscr{D}}^0, v \rangle_F = -\left(\Delta u^0, \Pi_{\mathscr{M}} v \right)_{L^2(\Omega)}, \quad \forall v \in \mathscr{X}_{\mathscr{D},0}, \tag{30}$$

and for any $n \in [\![0, N]\!]$, find $u_{\mathscr{D}}^{n+1} \in \mathscr{X}_{\mathscr{D},0}$ such that, for all $v \in \mathscr{X}_{\mathscr{D},0}$

$$\frac{1}{k} \left(\Pi_{\mathscr{M}} u_{\mathscr{D}}^{n+1} - \Pi_{\mathscr{M}} u_{\mathscr{D}}^n (\omega^{n+1}), \Pi_{\mathscr{M}} v \right)_{L^2(\Omega)} + \langle u_{\mathscr{D}}^{n+1}, v \rangle_F$$
$$+ \left((b + \operatorname{div} \boldsymbol{v}(t_{n+1})) \Pi_{\mathscr{M}} u_{\mathscr{D}}^{n+1}, \Pi_{\mathscr{M}} v \right)_{L^2(\Omega)} = (f(t_{n+1}), \Pi_{\mathscr{M}} v)_{L^2(\Omega)}. \tag{31}$$

We state now one of the main results of this work, that is the convergence of the FV scheme given by (30)–(31).

Theorem 1 ($L^\infty(L^2)$-error estimate for scheme (30)–(31)). *Let Ω be a polyhedral open bounded subset of $\mathbb{R}^d$, where $d \in \mathbb{N} \setminus \{0\}$. Assume that the solution of (1)–(3) satisfies $u \in \mathscr{C}^1([0,T]; \mathscr{C}^2(\overline{\Omega}))$ and $\theta_{\mathscr{D}}$ satisfies $\theta \geq \theta_{\mathscr{D}}$. Let $\nabla_{\mathscr{D}}$ be the discrete gradient defined as in (6). Let $k = \frac{T}{N+1}$, with $N \in \mathbb{N}^\star$, and denote by $t_n = nk$, for $n \in [\![0, N+1]\!]$. For any $n \in [\![0, N]\!]$, let ω^{n+1} be the function defined on Ω and given by (23). Assume in addition that the step k is sufficiently small in the sense of (28).*

Then, under Assumption 1, there exists a unique solution $(u_{\mathscr{D}}^n)_{n=0}^{N+1} \in \mathscr{X}_{\mathscr{D},0}^{N+2}$ for scheme (30)–(31) and the following $L^\infty(L^2)$-error estimate holds:

$$\max_{n=0}^{N+1} \| \Pi_{\mathscr{M}} u_{\mathscr{D}}^n - u(t_n) \|_{L^2(\Omega)} \leq C \left(k + h_{\mathscr{D}} + \frac{h_{\mathscr{D}}}{k} \right) \| u \|_{\mathscr{C}^1([0,T]; \mathscr{C}^2(\overline{\Omega}))}. \tag{32}$$

If we assume in addition that for some given positive δ, we have $h_{\mathscr{D}} \leq Ck^{1+\delta}$, then the error estimate (32) becomes as

$$\max_{n=0}^{N+1} \| \Pi_{\mathscr{M}} u_{\mathscr{D}}^n - u(t_n) \|_{L^2(\Omega)} \leq C \left(k + k^\delta + h_{\mathscr{D}} \right) \| u \|_{\mathscr{C}^1([0,T]; \mathscr{C}^2(\overline{\Omega}))}. \tag{33}$$

To prove Theorem 1, we use the following new a priori estimate:

Theorem 2 (A priori estimate for the discrete problem). *Under the same hypotheses of Theorem 1, we assume that there exists $(\eta^n)_{n=0}^{N+1} \in (\mathscr{X}_{\mathscr{D},0})^{N+2}$ such that $\eta_{\mathscr{D}}^0 = 0$ and for all $n \in [\![0, N]\!]$*

$$\frac{1}{k} \left(\Pi_{\mathscr{M}} \eta_{\mathscr{D}}^{n+1} - \Pi_{\mathscr{M}} \eta_{\mathscr{D}}^n (\omega^{n+1}), \Pi_{\mathscr{M}} v \right)_{L^2(\Omega)} + \langle \eta_{\mathscr{D}}^{n+1}, v \rangle_F$$
$$+ \left((b + \operatorname{div} \boldsymbol{v}(t_{n+1})) \Pi_{\mathscr{M}} \eta_{\mathscr{D}}^{n+1}, \Pi_{\mathscr{M}} v \right)_{L^2(\Omega)} = \left(\mathscr{S}^{n+1}, \Pi_{\mathscr{M}} v \right)_{L^2(\Omega)}, \tag{34}$$

where $\mathscr{S}^{n+1} \in L^2(\Omega)$, *for all* $n \in [\![0, N]\!]$. *Then, the following estimate holds:*

$$\max_{n=0}^{N+1} \|\Pi_{\mathscr{M}} \eta_{\mathscr{D}}^n\|_{L^2(\Omega)} \leq C\mathscr{S}. \tag{35}$$

where $\mathscr{S} = \max_{n=0}^{N} \|\mathscr{S}^{n+1}\|_{L^2(\Omega)}$.

An Overview on the Proof of Theorem 2: Taking $v = \eta_{\mathscr{D}}^{n+1}$ in (34) and using hypothesis (5) of Assumption 1 and the Cauchy Schwarz inequality yield

$$\|\Pi_{\mathscr{M}} \eta_{\mathscr{D}}^{n+1}\|_{L^2(\Omega)}^2 + k\|\nabla_{\mathscr{D}} \eta_{\mathscr{D}}^{n+1}\|_{L^2(\Omega)^d}^2$$
$$\leq k\|\mathscr{S}^{n+1}\|_{L^2(\Omega)}\|\Pi_{\mathscr{M}} \eta_{\mathscr{D}}^{n+1}\|_{L^2(\Omega)} + \|\Pi_{\mathscr{M}} \eta_{\mathscr{D}}^n(\omega^{n+1})\|_{L^2(\Omega)}\|\Pi_{\mathscr{M}} \eta_{\mathscr{D}}^{n+1}\|_{L^2(\Omega)}. \tag{36}$$

Using inequality $ab \leq a^2/2 + b^2/2$, estimate (36) implies that

$$\|\Pi_{\mathscr{M}} \eta_{\mathscr{D}}^{n+1}\|_{L^2(\Omega)}^2 \leq 2k\|\mathscr{S}^{n+1}\|_{L^2(\Omega)}\|\Pi_{\mathscr{M}} \eta_{\mathscr{D}}^{n+1}\|_{L^2(\Omega)} + \|\Pi_{\mathscr{M}} \eta_{\mathscr{D}}^n(\omega^{n+1})\|_{L^2(\Omega)}^2. \tag{37}$$

Using inequality $ab \leq \varepsilon a^2 + b^2/\varepsilon$ with $\varepsilon = k/(1+k)$, estimate (37) implies that

$$\|\Pi_{\mathscr{M}} \eta_{\mathscr{D}}^{n+1}\|_{L^2(\Omega)}^2 \leq 4k(1+k)^2\|\mathscr{S}^{n+1}\|_{L^2(\Omega)}^2 + (1+k)\|\Pi_{\mathscr{M}} \eta_{\mathscr{D}}^n(\omega^{n+1})\|_{L^2(\Omega)}^2. \tag{38}$$

We have, thanks to the definition of $\Pi_{\mathscr{M}}$, $\Pi_{\mathscr{M}} \eta_{\mathscr{D}}^n(\omega^{n+1})(\boldsymbol{x}) = \eta_K^n$ if $\omega^{n+1}(\boldsymbol{x}) \in K$. Therefore

$$\|\Pi_{\mathscr{M}} \eta_{\mathscr{D}}^n(\omega^n)\|_{L^2(\Omega)}^2 = \sum_{K \in \mathscr{M}} m\left(\{\boldsymbol{x} \in \Omega : \omega^{n+1}(\boldsymbol{x}) \in K\}\right)(\eta_K^n)^2.$$

Using a change of variable yields $m\left(\{\boldsymbol{x} \in \Omega : \omega^{n+1}(\boldsymbol{x}) \in K\}\right) = \int_{(\omega^{n+1})^{-1}(K)} d\boldsymbol{x} \leq (1+Ck)m(K)$ (Note that $(\omega^{n+1})^{-1}$ exists since it is injective thanks to (28). This gives

$$\|\Pi_{\mathscr{M}} \eta_{\mathscr{D}}^n(\omega^{n+1})\|_{L^2(\Omega)}^2 \leq (1+Ck)\|\Pi_{\mathscr{M}} \eta_{\mathscr{D}}^n\|_{L^2(\Omega)}^2. \tag{39}$$

This with (38) imply that

$$\|\Pi_{\mathscr{M}} \eta_{\mathscr{D}}^{n+1}\|_{L^2(\Omega)}^2 \leq 4k(1+k)^2\|\mathscr{S}^{n+1}\|_{L^2(\Omega)}^2 + (1+Ck)(1+k)\|\Pi_{\mathscr{M}} \eta_{\mathscr{D}}^n\|_{L^2(\Omega)}^2. \tag{40}$$

From (40) and the fact that $\eta_{\mathscr{D}}^0 = 0$, we are able to prove the required estimate (35). □

Sketch of the Proof of Theorem 1

The uniqueness and existence for scheme (30)–(32) stem from the facts that $\|\nabla_{\mathscr{D}}\cdot\|_{L^2(\Omega)^d}$ is a norm on $\mathscr{X}_{\mathscr{D},0}$, a priori estimate (35), and the matrices involved are square. To prove estimate (32), we compare (30)–(31) with the following scheme: For all $n \in [\![0, N+1]\!]$, find $\bar{u}_{\mathscr{D}}^n \in \mathscr{X}_{\mathscr{D},0}$ such that

$$\langle \bar{u}_{\mathscr{D}}^n, v\rangle_F = -(\Delta u(t_n), \Pi_{\mathscr{M}} v)_{L^2(\Omega)}, \quad \forall v \in \mathscr{X}_{\mathscr{D},0}. \tag{41}$$

Taking $n = 0$ in (41), using the fact that $u(0) = u^0$ (subject of (2)), and comparing with scheme (30), we get $\eta_{\mathscr{D}}^0 = 0$, where, for all $n \in [\![0, N+1]\!]$, $\eta_{\mathscr{D}}^n \in \mathscr{X}_{\mathscr{D},0}$ is given by $\eta_{\mathscr{D}}^n = u_{\mathscr{D}}^n - \bar{u}_{\mathscr{D}}^n$.

First step: Comparison between u and $\bar{u}_{\mathscr{D}}^n$. We have (see [3])

$$\|u(t_n) - \Pi_{\mathscr{M}}\bar{u}_{\mathscr{D}}^n\|_{L^2(\Omega)} \leq Ch_{\mathscr{D}}\|u\|_{\mathscr{C}(0,T;\mathscr{C}^2(\overline{\Omega}))}. \tag{42}$$

Second step: Comparison between $\bar{u}_{\mathscr{D}}^n$ and $u_{\mathscr{D}}^n$. Writing (41) in the level $n+1$ and subtracting the result from (31) yield

$$\begin{aligned}
&\frac{1}{k}\left(\Pi_{\mathscr{M}}u_{\mathscr{D}}^{n+1} - \Pi_{\mathscr{M}}u_{\mathscr{D}}^n(\omega^{n+1}), \Pi_{\mathscr{M}}v\right)_{L^2(\Omega)} + \langle \eta_{\mathscr{D}}^{n+1}, v\rangle_F \\
&+ \left((b + \mathrm{div}\mathbf{v}(t_{n+1}))\,\Pi_{\mathscr{M}}u_{\mathscr{D}}^{n+1}, \Pi_{\mathscr{M}}v\right)_{L^2(\Omega)} \\
&= (f(t_{n+1}) + \Delta u(t_{n+1}), \Pi_{\mathscr{M}}v)_{L^2(\Omega)}.
\end{aligned} \tag{43}$$

Replacing $\Delta u(t_{n+1}) + f(t_{n+1})$ by its value of (29) in (43) yields

$$\begin{aligned}
&\frac{1}{k}\left(\Pi_{\mathscr{M}}\eta_{\mathscr{D}}^{n+1} - \Pi_{\mathscr{M}}\eta_{\mathscr{D}}^n(\omega^{n+1}), \Pi_{\mathscr{M}}v\right)_{L^2(\Omega)} + \langle \eta_{\mathscr{D}}^{n+1}, v\rangle_F \\
&+ \left((b + \mathrm{div}\mathbf{v}(t_{n+1}))\,\Pi_{\mathscr{M}}\eta_{\mathscr{D}}^{n+1}, \Pi_{\mathscr{M}}v\right)_{L^2(\Omega)} = \left(\mathscr{S}^{n+1}, \Pi_{\mathscr{M}}v\right)_{L^2(\Omega)},
\end{aligned} \tag{44}$$

where

$$\begin{aligned}
\mathscr{S}^{n+1} =\; &\frac{u(t_{n+1}) - u(t_n)(\omega^{n+1}(\boldsymbol{x}))}{k} - \frac{\Pi_{\mathscr{M}}\left(\bar{u}_{\mathscr{D}}^{n+1} - \bar{u}_{\mathscr{D}}^n(\omega^{n+1})\right)}{k} \\
&+ (b + \mathrm{div}\mathbf{v}(t_{n+1}))\,\Pi_{\mathscr{M}}\left(u(t_{n+1}) - \bar{u}_{\mathscr{D}}^{n+1}\right) + \mathbb{T}_1^{n+1} - \frac{\mathbb{T}_3^{n+1}}{k}.
\end{aligned} \tag{45}$$

From (44) and the fact that $\eta_{\mathscr{D}}^0 = 0$, we deduce that $(\eta^n)_{n=0}^{N+1} \in (\mathscr{X}_{\mathscr{D},0})^{N+2}$ is satisfying the hypotheses of Theorem 2. This allows to apply a priori estimate (35) to get $\max_{n=0}^{N+1}\|\Pi_{\mathscr{M}}\eta_{\mathscr{D}}^n\|_{L^2(\Omega)} \leq C\mathscr{S}$, where $\mathscr{S} = \max_{n=0}^{N}\|\mathscr{S}^{n+1}\|_{L^2(\Omega)}$, and $\mathscr{S}^{n+1}$ is given by (45). Using estimate (42), (39), (19), (26), and Assumption 1 imply that $\max_{n=0}^{N+1}\|\Pi_{\mathscr{M}}\eta_{\mathscr{D}}^n\|_{L^2(\Omega)} \leq C\left(k + h_{\mathscr{D}} + \frac{h_{\mathscr{D}}}{k}\right)\|u\|_{\mathscr{C}^1([0,T];\mathscr{C}^2(\overline{\Omega}))}$. This with (42) and triangle inequality imply the desired estimate (32). Estimate (33) is a straightforward consequence of the proved estimate (32). This completes the proof of Theorem 1. $\qquad\square$

5   Some Concluding Remarks and Perspectives

We applied SUSHI combined with characteristics method to approximate UADP (1)–(3). This model is more general than that we considered in [1,2] in which we derived schemes directly along with a convergence analysis. We proved the $L^\infty(L^2)$–error estimate (32) which is a conditional convergence. This error estimate is proved thanks to the new a prior estimate of Theorem 2. Both, scheme

(30)–(31), Theorem 2, and convergence order (32) are new. The convergence order $k + h_{\mathscr{D}} + \dfrac{h_{\mathscr{D}}}{k}$ of (32) is similar to the one obtained in the context of FEM, that is $k + h + \dfrac{h^2}{k}$, see [4, Page 427] but it is different because of the presence of $\dfrac{h_{\mathscr{D}}}{k}$ instead of $\dfrac{h^2}{k}$. This difference stems from the first order $L^\infty(L^2)$–error estimate (42) which is second order in FEM.

This note is an initiation in the application of FV methods combined with the method of characteristics for UADP. As extension to the present work, there are several tasks to be addressed in the near future. Among them, is to try to prove an unconditional convergence instead of the conditional one stated in (32). The proof of a convergence in the discrete energy norm of $L^\infty(H^1)$ and extension of the present work to semi-linear UADP are also interesting perspectives to work on.

References

1. Bradji, A., Fuhrmann, J.: Some abstract error estimates of a finite volume scheme for a nonstationary heat equation on general nonconforming multidimensional spatial meshes. Appl. Math. **58**(1), 1–38 (2013)
2. Bradji, A., Fuhrmann, J.: Error estimates of the discretization of linear parabolic equations on general nonconforming spatial grids. C. R. Math. Acad. Sci. Paris **348**(19-20), 1119–1122 (2010)
3. Eymard, R., Gallouët, T., Herbin, R.: Discretization of heterogeneous and anisotropic diffusion problems on general nonconforming meshes. IMA J. Numer. Anal. **30**(4), 1009–1043 (2010)
4. Quarteroni, A., Valli, A.: Numerical Approximation of Partial Differential Equations. Springer Series in Computational Mathematics. Springer, Heidelberg (2008). https://doi.org/10.1007/978-3-319-32354-1

Implementing a Mesh-Projection Schemes Using the Technology of Adaptive Mesh Refinement

Dmitry Boykov[✉], Sergey Grigoriev, Olga Olkhovskaya, and Alexey Boldarev

Keldysh Institute of Applied Mathematics (Russian Academy of Sciences),
Moscow, Russia
boykovds@gmail.com, sergejgri@gmail.com, olkhovsk@gmail.com,
boldar@imamod.ru

Abstract. The adaptive mesh refinement (AMR) is a basic method for development of efficient technologies allowing a numerical solution of various problems of continuum mechanics. Numerical modeling of heat-mass transfer, hydrodynamics, structural/fracture mechanics etc. deals with non-linear strongly coupled processes which significantly differ in spatial and temporal scales. Modeling of multiscale correlated phenomena stimulates application of computational technologies using irregular grids, among which the octree meshes are the most known and widely used. Using the created data for tree-structured meshes we developed the dynamic loading balance algorithm aimed at applications to the cluster type parallel computing systems. The developed tools support functionality necessary to implement various numerical models of continuum mechanics. As an example of possible applications we discuss the constructed family of mesh projective approximations to second-order partial differential equations with a variable tensor-type coefficients. The difference operator of the scheme provides energy conservation and possesses the "self-adjoint" property which is inherent to the original differential operator, e.g. in the case of a heat transfer model. We consider numerical results obtained by solution of some model initial boundary value problems for parabolic equations using the developed AMR technique.

Keywords: Adaptive mesh refinement · Load balancing ·
Grid-projection scheme · Message passing interface

1 Introduction

Adaptive Mesh Refinement technology (AMR) is designed to improve the accuracy of computer modeling and reduce the cost of computing resources. The most common is the use of hierarchical octree grids. This approach was proposed more

The work was supported by Russian Science Foundation (project No. 16-11-00100p).

I. Lirkov and S. Margenov (Eds.): LSSC 2019, LNCS 11958, pp. 576–583, 2020.
https://doi.org/10.1007/978-3-030-41032-2_66

than 40 years ago [1] for hydrodynamic problems and is currently being success-fully used both in computer graphics [2] and in computational physics [3]. In particular, AMR is advisable to use for the calculation of non-stationary pro-cesses of heat transfer. Local adaptation of computational grids may be required to allow heat dissipation of compact sources and simulate heat transfer in highly heterogeneous environments, for example, in complex technological structures or anisotropic composite materials [4].

Such calculations are performed on high-performance computing clusters using geometric parallelism (domain decomposition) and MPI technology for organizing interprocessor exchanges. In this connection, there are problems of load balancing, which are characteristic of all dynamic adaptation algorithms, and complicated by the need to maintain the hierarchical structure of the grid when divided into subregions. Traditionally, space filling curves (SFC) [5] are used for this purpose. We have proposed new efficient ways to describe hierar-chical grids that preserve the index structure and provide quick access to an arbitrary element and iterators on adjacent grid elements. New algorithms of static (initial) and dynamic load balancing of computational cores using various types of SFCs have been developed.

Another important problem arising when using AMR for the numerical solu-tion of equations and systems of equations of mathematical physics is the con-struction of difference schemes with specified properties on such grids. In partic-ular, if we are talking about heat transfer problems, grid operators must not only provide an approximation of the initial equations with the necessary accuracy, but also preserve such properties of differential operators as self-adjoint and pos-itive definiteness, continuity of heat fluxes and conservation laws. To construct such schemes, it is convenient to use projection methods and the finite element method [6]. These methods are widely used for irregular grid patterns, to which octree grids can be assigned. A special choice of basis functions allowed us to construct a new formalized procedure for constructing schemes of a given quality on grids of the specified type for the heat equation with coefficients of a tensor type.

2 Detailed Data Structures

The widespread use of the discussed grid technology is mainly due to the simplic-ity of the grid organization (rectangular, with some complication). The following describes the requirements that were used in the development of data structures for working with octree grids within the framework.

When generating the original regular grid, it is convenient to use the three-index (i, j, k) cell numbering. Such indexation allows at the stage of the primary generation of the computational grid to immediately calculate all the neighbors of the considered cell. Such a calculation does not mean the real existence of the cell, but allows the construction of the initial neighborhood graph for the cells. The need to build and store explicitly the neighborhood graph of cells is due to the requirement for fast, beyond $O(1)$, access to an arbitrary neighbor of the cell in question. Storing the cell adjacency graph explicitly allows, among other things, to perform separating and combine operations of cells in the same way as $O(1)$ (indicated without considering the processing of neighbors). Note that the operation of separating a cell, taking into account the separating of adjacent cells with the considered cells, may in accordance with the geometric criterion of separating, may in general $O(N)$, where N is the total number of grid cells.

The main requirements for a data structure that works with octreemesh are: access to an arbitrary grid element for $O(1)$; the organization of the passage in all leaf cells; the organization of the passage in all non-leaf cells; ensuring the possibility of quick access to all grid elements belonging to a particular cell.

As a geometrical criterion for separated adjacent cells, the need to respect the ratio of the linear dimensions of adjacent elements is not more than 1:2. In addition, to create solvers based on dynamic adaptation techniques, as well as the generators of the corresponding grids, we also need separating and reverse combining of cells (they are applied to the set of cells specified by the enumeration or predicate, and change the level of separated by one).

3   The Relationship Between Grid Elements and Stored Values

Except for the trivial case, when the structure of a rectangular grid corresponds exactly to a three-dimensional array, and therefore storing grid values in such an array provides an obvious correspondence of grid values to grid elements: grid values are stored directly in structures describing the grid element. The advantage is that access to grid values is extremely simple and fast, and in addition, the correspondence between the grid and the set of values is not disturbed with changes in the grid. For hierarchical grids, therefore, this method of matching is more attractive - the hierarchical grid is stored as an octal cell tree, and physical data is stored in the leaves. The ordering along the space-filling curve is used for mesh decomposition, load balancing and for some computational purposes, for example, when filling a matrix of coefficients of a system of linear algebraic equations (SLAE)—usually matrix inversion programs work with arrays of coefficients. Thus, we need to store an indication, is element separated or not, and if it is separated, store all child cells, physical attribute, boundary indication attribute and pointer to the parent cell, if it is necessary. The original development is the modified Morton curve for a geometrically arbitrary region is also implemented.

4   Parallel Implementation

The implementation of parallel computing in the MPI paradigm involves the decomposition of adaptive grids, which is associated with certain difficulties because of the need to maintain the correct grid structure on a distributed system for the shortest possible time. In addition, there is the problem of load balancing, because one crushing operation increases the number of cells by 7, which in the worst case gives an increase in the number of cells processed by calculating on one MPI process 7 times.

When implementing load balancing, you must also take into account the need to maintain vertical relationships in the structure. Regarding the construction of fields for interprocessor exchanges at the subdomain boundaries (the so-called fictive, ghost, halo cells), if the primary cell is considered to be a unit of information, then the primary cells should be transferred as a whole, with all their child cells. The width of the fields must correspond to the approximation pattern, taking into account that the primary cells may or may not be fragmented somewhere.

Static initial load balancing is carried out using a spatially filling curve adapted to an arbitrary region. The advantage of the Morton curve is the computability of the ordinal number of an element along the curve depending on the $(i,\ j,\ k)$ - index. The disadvantage of the curve is the nonlocality of the location of elements. The Hilbert curve guarantees the property of the locality of elements, at the cost of not being able to quickly and unambiguously calculate the number of an element when ordered along such a curve. The project uses both options of space-filling curves.

In addition to maintaining the correctness of all calculated values on different processes containing adjacent domains, the fields also serve to comply with the geometric criterion for grid fragmentation, due to the need to verify the topology for adjacent domains. This leads to some complication of the procedure for adapting the grid to the solution: First, the grid is adapted locally on each processor, and then the exchange between fields is performed to confirm the topology. Due to the fact that a priory grid decomposition by processors is unknown, this operation is global, and this approach requires no more than $O(s)$ exchange sessions between processors. The fields themselves are formed (with dynamic balancing, re-formed) only after the load balancing process is completed. By virtue of storing the entire adjacency graph, the task of constructing fields of a given magnitude is reduced to a calculation.

Dynamic balancing is performed by diffuse balancing, with an adjustable percentage redistributed over the data iteration. At the same time, since the grid cell itself contains some calculated values, the size of which is not known in advance, the redistributed cell numbers are first calculated when balancing, and then, for one iteration of the data exchange, the cells and their contents are transferred.

Let's consider this algorithm. For definiteness, let's set maximum allowed imbalance in percent as $maxd$, total number of MPI-processes as P, current process number as i, total number of balanced elements on current process as n_i, number of steps $stp = 0$. In following algorithm values src is temporary value, which is used for store MPI communication partners.

1. [Check if i is even] If process number i, is even, set go to step 2, else go to step 3
2. [Set temporary values] Set $src = i + 1$, go to step 4

3. [Set temporary values] Set $src = i - 1$, go to step 10
4. [Exchange number of elements] Send to src number of elements n_i and receive from n_{src}
5. [Calculate balance necessity: sending] Calculating $n_i - n_{src} - n_{src} * maxd$, if this value is less than zero, go to step 6, else go to step 7
6. [Send values] pack $n_{src} * maxd$ balancing elements and send them to src.
7. [Calculate balance necessity: receiving] Calculating $n_{src} - n_i - n_i * maxd$, if this value is less than zero, go to step 8, else go to 9
8. [Receive values] Receive $n_i * maxd$ balancing elements from src.
9. [Check termination condition] Set $stp = stp + 1$. If $stp = 2$, stop the algorithm, else go to step 3.
10. [Calculate balance necessity: receiving] Calculating $n_{src} - n_i - n_i * maxd$, if this value is less than zero, go to step 11, else go to step 12
11. [Receive values] Receive $n_i * maxd$ balancing elements from src.
12. [Calculate balance necessity: sending] Calculating $n_i - n_{src} - n_{src} * maxd$, if this value is less than zero, go to step 13, else go to step 14
13. [Send values] pack $n_{src} * maxd$ balancing elements and send them to src.
14. [Check termination condition] Set $stp = stp + 1$. If $stp = 2$, stop the algorithm, else go to step 2.

5   Implementing a Mesh-Projection Schemes

Consider the construction of the scheme by the Galerkin method with discontinuous basis functions on the example of a model quasilinear parabolic equation

$$C\frac{\partial u}{\partial t} = \nabla \bullet (k \, \nabla \circ u) \tag{1}$$

where $\bullet$ and $\circ$ are binary operators of scalar multiplication, inner product or outer product of vectors, u is a scalar or vector function. The auxiliary function v and system are written in the form:

$$v = \nabla \circ u \tag{2}$$

$$C\frac{\partial u}{\partial t} = \nabla \bullet kv + fu \tag{3}$$

Using the basis functions and the corresponding integration procedures, we obtain generalized forms for recording final schemes [7]. Finally, for each grid cell i we get:

$$C_i V_i \cdot \frac{\partial u_i}{\partial t} = - \sum_{k \in In30_i} \sum_{j \in In03_k} u_j \cdot \frac{S_j(p_k) \cdot \kappa_k \cdot S_i(p_k)}{V(p_k)} + f_i \cdot u_i \cdot V_i \tag{4}$$

where $InAB_i$ is a set of grid elements of dimension B, incident to element with number i of dimension A, $S(p_k)$ and $V(p_k)$ - face area and volume associated to the node p_k.

The grid pattern of the **A** operator for the ω_i cell includes all the cells that have at least one common node with it, and may consist of several dozen cells (for example, on a tetrahedral mesh) [8]. A variant of the scheme leading to a more compact template can be constructed by choosing another system of basis functions [4]. Consider the heat equation in the following form:

$$\frac{\partial T}{\partial t} = \frac{\partial}{\partial s}\left(\kappa_0 \cdot T^\alpha \cdot \frac{\partial T}{\partial s}\right),$$ (5)

where T – desired function (temperature measured in keV), κ_0, α – free coefficients, $s \equiv x \,|\, y \,|\, z$. This equation, with the following initial and boundary conditions:

$$T(s,0) = \left[\frac{\alpha D}{\kappa_0}(s_0 - s)\right]^{\frac{1}{\alpha}} \quad s \le s_0; \qquad T(s,0) = 0 \qquad s > s_0;$$ (6)

$$T(0,t) = \left[\frac{\alpha D}{\kappa_0}(Dt + s_0)\right]^{\frac{1}{\alpha}} \qquad t > 0.$$ (7)

considered task got an analytical solution in the form of a running wave at a constant speed:

$$T(s,t) = \left[\frac{\alpha D}{\kappa_0}(Dt + s_0 - s)\right]^{\frac{1}{\alpha}} \qquad s < s_0 + Dt;$$ (8)

$$T(s,t) = 0 \qquad s > s_0 + Dt;$$ (9)

where D – wave speed, s_0 – free coefficient.

6   Results

The solution of the nonlinear heat equation was performed in three-dimensional computational domains. For calculations, we used octreemesh and homogeneous computational grids consisting of cubic elements. The sizes of various grids are 64, 128, and 256, the number of cells in one of the directions. For testing purpose we are using running wave (see Fig. 1). When using AMR technology in the calculations, we have achieved increased accuracy in solving the problem, while spending more time on the calculation. At the same time, the initial grid on the graphs(see Figs. 2 and 3) was the same, but when using AMR, the number of cells increased up to 2.5 times. Also, the total execution time was affected by the complication of work with the octreemesh topology, and the change in the connection topology with parallel calculation. To study the approximating properties of the constructed scheme, a projection scheme for the Laplace equation with homogeneous boundary conditions was considered. The decomposition of the required function was substituted into the resulting difference expression in a Taylor series at the centers of mass of the corresponding cells. It was found that on regular grids of homogeneous elements, the scheme approximates the

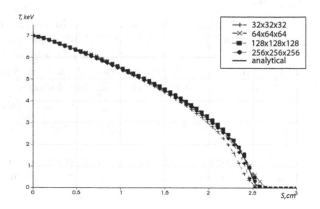

Fig. 1. Test result on the different grid size.

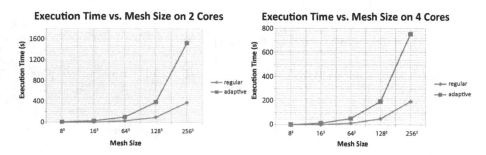

Fig. 2. Execution time vs. mesh size on 2 & 4 processors with regular/adaptive refinement.

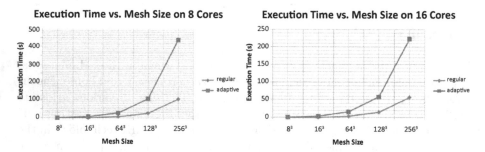

Fig. 3. Execution time vs. mesh size on 8 & 16 processors with regular/adaptive refinement.

Laplace equation with an error of $O(h^2)$. The constructed scheme, due to the continuity of flows and conservative difference schemes, will allow to avoid loss of accuracy at the place of contact of large and small cells. Refinement near the wave front allowed to reduce the grid size up to three times. The following free parameter values were used for the test: $\alpha = 2.0$, $\kappa = 0.5$, $s_0 = 0.5$, $D = 5.0$; model time t varied from 0 to 0.4 with a constant pitch $\tau = 2 \cdot 10^{-4}$.

7   Conclusion and Future Work

The technique presented in this paper provides a strategy for parallelization of adaptive mesh applications. We have presented efficient way of keeping data related to the mesh application, dynamic algorithms for grid adaptive refinement and load balancing. It is relatively easy transition to an application developer from sequential application to MPI parallel application, being just few inputs required by the framework. We demonstrated the performance of our framework with 3 dimensional applications: an application solving second-order Partial Differential Equation with tensor form coefficient. Our load balancing algorithm represents reasonable load balance. We presented results that verify the overall scalability of our code. Thus, our framework allows client-side execution applications improve the accuracy of the solution using adaptive mesh refinement. Main authors contribution consists in implimentation load balancing algorithm, which is described above, inside meshing framework. We believe with very little changes, we can improve the performance of our framework further. Future work may include making the framework enable to plug-in third party load balancing algorithms, and mapping the processor architecture to mesh architecture.

References

1. Berger, M.J., Colella, P.: Local adaptive mesh refinement for shock hydrodynamics. Comput. Phys. **82**, 64–84 (1989)
2. Luebke, D.P.: Level of Detail for 3D Graphics. Morgan Kaufmann Publishers Inc., San Francisco (2003)
3. Peraire, J., Patera, A.T.: Bounds for linear-functional outputs of coercive partial differential equations: local indicators and adaptive refinement. In: Advances in Adaptive Computational Methods in Mechanics 47 Studies in Applied Mechanics, pp. 199–216 (1998)
4. Boyard, N.: Heat Transfer in Polymer Composite Materials: Forming Processes. John Wiley & Sons, Inc., Hoboken (2016)
5. Sagan, H.: Space-Filling Curves. Springer, New York (1994). https://doi.org/10.1007/978-1-4612-0871-6
6. Fletcher, C.A.J.: Computational Galerkin Methods. Springer, Heidelberg (1984). https://doi.org/10.1007/978-3-642-85949-6
7. Olkhovskaya, O.G.: Grid-projection schemes for approximation of the second order partial differential equations on irregular computational meshes. Keldysh Institute Preprints (226) (2018). http://library.keldysh.ru/preprint.asp?id=2018-226
8. Zhukov, V. T.: Numerical solution of parabolic equations on locally-adaptive grids by Chebyshev method. Keldysh Institute Preprints (87) (2015). http://library.keldysh.ru/preprint.asp?id=2015-87
9. Zienkiewicz, O.C.: The Finite Element Method in Engineering Science. McGraw-Hill, UK (1971)

Valuation of European Options with Liquidity Shocks Switching by Fitted Finite Volume Method

Miglena N. Koleva$^{(\boxtimes)}$ and Lubin G. Vulkov

University of Ruse, 8 Studentska str., 7017 Ruse, Bulgaria
{mkoleva,lvalkov}@uni-ruse.bg

Abstract. In the present paper, we construct a *superconvergent* fitted finite volume method (FFVM) for pricing European option with switching liquidity shocks. We investigate some basic properties of the numerical solution and establish superconvergence in maximal discrete norm. An efficient algorithm, governing the degeneracy and exponential non-linearity in the problem, is proposed. Results from various numerical experiments with different European options are provided.

1   Introduction and Problem Formulation

In this paper we propose an FFVM for valuation European option with liquidity shocks, which is described by a system of one parabolic and one ODE equations with exponential non-linear terms [7]. Because the parabolic equation is degenerate when the underlying stock price approaches zero and the domain is a semi-infinite interval, classical methods such as a finite difference, finite volume, and finite element methods usually cannot be used without the truncating (or transforming) the solution domain near the degenerate point and infinity [3,9,10]. FFVM is proposed in [10] for the classical Black-Scholes equation and latter was developed for more complicated models in mathematical finance [1,9].

The FFVM is based on standard primal-dual mesh construction in which the dual nodes are the midpoints of the intervals of the primal mesh. The authors of [11] showed that it is possible to find a point in each subinterval, at which the approximate flux has a higher-order of accuracy. We implement this idea to our model system, without using the logarithmic transformation to truncate the semiinfinite interval $[0, \infty)$ to a finite $[-\ln x, \ln x]$ as it was done in [6].

We consider the parabolic-ordinary system for option buyer's prices $p(S,t)$ and $q(S,t)$, $t \in (0,T]$ (remaining time), $S > 0$ (underlying asset), derived in [7].

$$p_t + \frac{1}{2}\sigma^2 S^2 p_{SS} - \frac{v_{01}}{\gamma}\frac{F_1}{F_0}e^{-\gamma(q-p)} + \frac{(d_0 + v_{01})}{\gamma} - \frac{1}{\gamma}\frac{F_0'}{F_0} = 0,$$

$$q_t - \frac{v_{10}}{\gamma}\frac{F_0}{F_1}e^{-\gamma(p-q)} + \frac{v_{10}}{\gamma} - \frac{1}{\gamma}\frac{F_1'}{F_1} = 0, \quad p(S,T) = q(S,T) = h(S) \geq 0,$$

(1)

© Springer Nature Switzerland AG 2020
I. Lirkov and S. Margenov (Eds.): LSSC 2019, LNCS 11958, pp. 584–592, 2020.
https://doi.org/10.1007/978-3-030-41032-2_67

where σ is the volatility, γ is the investor's risk aversion parameter, $F_j(t) = F_j(t; \nu_{01}, \nu_{10}, d_0)$, $j = \{0, 1\}$ are known function [7], $F_0(T) = F_1(T) = 1$, ν_{01}, ν_{10} are transition intensities, $d_0 = \mu^2/2\sigma^2$, μ is a drift rate and $h(S)$ is the payoff.

Substituting $\tau = T - t$, $u = \gamma R^0$ and $v = \gamma R^1$ [5,6], $R^0(S, t) = p(S, t) - \ln F_0(t)/\gamma$, $R^1(S, t) = q(S, t) - \ln F_1(t)/\gamma$, the system (1) becomes

$$u_\tau - \frac{\sigma^2}{2} S^2 u_{SS} + ae^u e^{-v} - b = 0, \qquad v_\tau + ce^v e^{-u} - c = 0, \tag{2}$$

where $a = \nu_{01}, b = d_0 + \nu_{01}, c = \nu_{10}$ and initial conditions are given by

$$u(S, 0) = u^0(S) = \gamma h(S), \quad v(S, 0) = v^0(S) = \gamma h(S). \tag{3}$$

The authors of [3] studied well-possedness and proved comparison (maximum) principle for the initial-value problem (2), (3). In our previous works, implicit-explicit schemes [8], fully implicit scheme [5] and high-order compact finite difference scheme [6] for the problem (2), (3) are constructed.

The rest of the paper is organized as follows. In the next section, we develop FFVM and establish some theoretical results. Efficient implementation of the discrete scheme and numerical tests are given in Sect. 3. The results are summarized in the Conclusion section.

2   The Fitted Finite Volume Method

In this section, we develop a fitted finite volume method for the model (2), (3). Let us rewrite the first equation in (2) in the divergent form

$$u_\tau - \frac{\sigma^2}{2}(S^2 u_S - 2Su)_S + F(u, v) = 0, \ F(u, v) = f(u, v) - \sigma^2 u, \ f(u, v) = ae^{u-v} - b. \tag{4}$$

Space Discretization. Let divide the space interval $I = (0, S_{max})$ into M subintervals $I_i := (S_i, S_{i+1})$, $i = 0, 1, \ldots, M - 1$, where $0 = S_0 < S_1 < \cdots < S_M = S_{max}$. Then, we set $h_i = S_{i+1} - S_i$ for each $i = 0, \ldots, M - 1$. Further, we define a dual grid, by choosing a set of points $S_{i-1/2}$, $i = 0, \ldots, M + 1$, such that $S_{-1/2} = S_0 < S_{1/2} < S_1 < S_{i+1/2} < S_2 < \cdots < S_{M-1} < S_M = S_{M+1/2}$. Typically for the FVM is to chose the points $\{S_{i-1/2}\}_{i=0}^{M+1}$ to be the midpoint of the interval (S_{i-1}, S_i) for each $i = 1, 2, \ldots, M$. Further, we will determine the grid nodes of the dual mesh just as in [11], in order to attain second order accuracy of the approximation of the computed flux at $S_{i-1/2}$ for any $i = 1, 2, \ldots, M$.

By integrating both sides of (4) over intervals $(S_{i-1/2}, S_{i+1/2})$, we derive

$$\int_{S_{i-1/2}}^{S_{i+1/2}} u_\tau dS - \frac{\sigma^2}{2}[S(Su_S - 2u)]\Big|_{S_{i-1/2}}^{S_{i+1/2}} + \int_{S_{i-1/2}}^{S_{i+1/2}} F(u, v)dS = 0, \ i = 1, 2, \ldots, M - 1.$$

Using the mid-point quadrature rule for the first and the third terms, we get

$$\frac{\partial u_i}{\partial \tau} l_i - \frac{\sigma^2}{2}\left[S_{i+1/2}\rho(u)|_{S_{i+1/2}} - S_{i-1/2}\rho(u)|_{S_{i-1/2}}\right] + F(u_i, v_i)l_i = 0, \tag{5}$$

where $l_0 = S_{1/2}$, $l_i = S_{i+1/2} - S_{i-1/2}$, $i = 1, 2, \ldots, M-1$, $\frac{\partial u_i}{\partial \tau} = \frac{\partial u}{\partial \tau}\big|_{S_i}$, u_i is approximation of the solution at grid node (t, S_i) and $\rho(u)$ is the flux associated with u defined by $\rho(u) = Su_S - 2u$.

In order to obtain the approximation to $\rho(u)$ at the points $S_{i-1/2}$ and $S_{i+1/2}$ for any $i = 1, 2, \ldots, M-1$, we follow [11]. Two cases are considered:

Case 1: i ≥ 1. In this case, ρ is approximated in I_i by a constant ρ_i, defined by the next two-point boundary value problem:

$$(\rho_i)' = (Sw' - 2w)' = 0, \quad S \in I_i, \quad w(S_i) = u_i, \quad w(S_{i+1}) = u_{i+1}. \tag{6}$$

Solving (6) analytically, the following approximations are derived

$$w(S) = \frac{u_{i+1} - u_i}{S_{i+1}^2 - S_i^2} S^2 - \frac{S_i^2 u_{i+1} - S_{i+1}^2 u_i}{S_{i+1}^2 - S_i^2}, \tag{7}$$

$$\rho_i = 2\frac{S_i^2 u_{i+1} - S_{i+1}^2 u_i}{S_{i+1}^2 - S_i^2} = 2\frac{S_i^2}{S_{i+1}^2 - S_i^2} u_{i+1} - 2\frac{S_{i+1}^2}{S_{i+1}^2 - S_i^2} u_i. \tag{8}$$

Case 2: i = 0. Now, the solution to (6) and the associated flux ρ_0 cannot be determined by simply setting $S_0 = 0$ in (7) and (8), because the first equation in (2) and (6) become degenerate at $S = 0$. We consider the asymptotic behavior of ρ_0 when $S_0 \to 0+$. Rewrite (8), for any $S_0 > 0$, as

$$\rho_0 = 2\frac{S_0^2 S_1^{-2} u_1 - u_0}{1 - S_0^2 S_1^{-2}}, \quad \text{to get} \quad \lim_{S_0 \to 0+} \rho_0 = -2u_0. \tag{9}$$

To derive the approximation at inner grid points S_i, $i = 1, 2, \ldots, M-1$, we replace the fluxes in (5) by the approximations (8) and (9). The left boundary condition is obtained using (5) and (9). The resulting semidiscrete system is:

$$\frac{\partial u_i}{\partial \tau} l_i + e_{i,i-1} u_{i-1} + e_{i,i} u_i + e_{i,i+1} u_{i+1} + f_i(u_i, v_i) l_i = 0, \quad i = 0, 1, \ldots, M-1, \tag{10}$$

$$e_{0,-1} = e_{0,1} = e_{0,0} = 0, \quad e_{1,0} = -\sigma^2 \frac{S_1}{2}, \quad e_{1,1} = \sigma^2 \frac{S_2^2 S_{3/2}}{S_2^2 - S_1^2} - \sigma^2 \frac{S_1}{2},$$

$$e_{1,2} = -\sigma^2 \frac{S_1^2 S_{3/2}}{S_2^2 - S_1^2}, \quad e_{i,i-1} = -\sigma^2 \frac{S_i^2 S_{i-1/2}}{S_i^2 - S_{i-1}^2}, \quad e_{i,i+1} = -\sigma^2 \frac{S_i^2 S_{i+1/2}}{S_{i+1}^2 - S_i^2},$$

$$e_{i,i} = \sigma^2 \frac{S_{i-1}^2 S_{i-1/2}}{S_i^2 - S_{i-1}^2} + \sigma^2 \frac{S_{i+1}^2 S_{i+1/2}}{S_{i+1}^2 - S_i^2} - \sigma^2 l_i, \quad 2 \le i \le M-1.$$

Further, the approximation (10) is completed by the boundary condition

$$u_M(\tau) = u_b(\tau), \tag{11}$$

where $u_b(\tau) \ge 0$ is known function and depends on the option. The unknown solution $u(\tau) = (u_1(\tau), u_2(\tau), \ldots, u_M(\tau))^T$, satisfies the system (10), (11).

The grid nodes of the dual mesh are chosen as follows:

$$S_{i+1/2} = 2\frac{S_{i+1}^{-1} - S_i^{-1}}{S_{i+1}^{-2} - S_i^{-2}} = 2\frac{S_i S_{i+1}}{S_{i+1} + S_i}, \quad i = 1, \ldots, M-1. \tag{12}$$

Full Discretization. To obtain the full discretization of the system (2), we define the time mesh τ_n, $n = 0, 1, \ldots, N$, where $0 = \tau_0 < \tau_1 < \cdots < \tau_n < \cdots < \tau_N = T$ and $\Delta\tau_n = \tau_{n+1} - \tau_n$. Consider the weighted approximation of (10), (11)

$$\frac{u_i^{n+1} - u_i^n}{\Delta\tau_n}l_i + E_i u^{n+1} + \theta f_i(u_i^{n+1}, v_i^{n+1})l_i + (1-\theta)f_i(u_i^n, v_i^n)l_i = 0,$$
$$u_M^{n+1} = u_b^{n+1}, \quad i = 0, 1, \ldots, M-1, \tag{13}$$

with initial condition $u^0 = (u_0^0, u_1^0, \ldots, u_M^0)^T$. Here u^n denotes the approximation to $u(\tau_n)$ and $u_i^n = u_i(\tau_n)$, $n = 0, 1, \ldots, N-1$, $\theta \in [0,1]$ and

$$E_0 = (0, 0, \ldots, 0), \quad E_1 = (e_{1,0}, e_{1,1}, e_{1,2}, 0, \ldots, 0),$$
$$E_i = (0, \ldots, 0, e_{i,i-1}, e_{i,i}, e_{i,i+1}, 0, \ldots, 0), \quad i = 2, 3, \ldots, M-2,$$
$$E_{M-1} = (0, \ldots, 0, e_{M-1,M-2}, e_{M-1,M-1}, e_{M-1,M})$$

Next, we rewrite (13) in the following equivalent matrix-vector form:

$$(G^n + E)u^{n+1} + \theta\overline{f}^{n+1} = \overline{G}^n u^n - (1-\theta)\overline{f}^n + \epsilon u_b^{n+1}, \quad n = 0, 1, \ldots, N-1, \tag{14}$$

where $\epsilon = [0, \ldots, 0, 1]^T$ and $\overline{f}^n = \overline{f}(u^n, v^n)$ are vectors with $M+1$ entries, $E = [E_0, E_1, \ldots, E_{M-1}, E_0]^T$, G^n and $\overline{G}^n$ are $(M+1) \times (M+1)$ matrices:

$$G^n = \frac{1}{\Delta\tau_n}\text{diag}\{1, l_1, \ldots, l_{M-1}, \Delta\tau_n\}, \quad \overline{G}^n = \frac{1}{\Delta\tau_n}\text{diag}\{1, l_1, \ldots, l_{M-1}, 0\},$$
$$\overline{f}^n = [\overline{f}_0^n, \overline{f}_1^n, \ldots, \overline{f}_{M-1}^n, 0]^T, \quad \overline{f}_i^n = f_i^n l_i, \quad i = 1, \ldots M-1.$$

Similarly, for the second equation in (2), we have

$$\frac{v_i^{n+1} - v_i^n}{\Delta\tau_n} + \theta g_i(u_i^{n+1}, v_i^{n+1}) + (1-\theta)g_i(u_i^n, v_i^n) = 0, \quad n = 0, 1, \ldots, N-1,$$
$$g_i(u_i^n, v_i^n) = ce^{v_i^n}e^{-u_i^n} - c, \quad i = 0, 1, \ldots, M.$$

The corresponding matrix-vector form is

$$G^n v^{n+1} + \theta g^{n+1} = \overline{G}^n v^n - (1-\theta)g^n, \quad g^n = [g_0^n, g_1^n, \ldots, g_{M-1}^n, 0]^T. \tag{15}$$

Analysis of the Numerical Scheme. Next, we establish the following results.

Theorem 1 (Positive ODE system). *The ODE system (3), (10), (11) is a positive semi-discretization, i.e. $u(\tau) \geq 0$ and $v(\tau) \geq 0$ holds for all $\tau \geq 0$.*

Proof (Outline). We use [2, Lemma 2.1] and [4], taking into account that $u^0 \geq 0$, $v^0 \geq 0$ and $b \geq a > 0$.

It is obvious that G^n and $G^n + E$ in (14), (15) are M-matrices. Indeed, as $\sigma < 1$ (by financial arguments), the condition $\frac{1}{\triangle \tau^n} > \sigma^2$ is fulfilled for each $\triangle \tau^n < 1$. Therefore, considering the coefficients $e_{i,i}$, $e_{i,i\pm 1}$ in (10), we may conclude that $G^n + E$ is strictly diagonal dominant matrix with positive main diagonal elements and non-positive off-diagonal entries. Thus, we are in position to prove the convergence in maximal discrete norm ($\| \cdot \|_\infty$).

Theorem 2 (Convergence). *Let $(u, v) \in C((0, L) \times [0, T)) \cap C^{4,2}((0, L) \times (0, T))$ be classical solutions of (3), (4), (11), and (u^n, v^n) are solutions of (14), (15). Then for sufficiently small h and $\triangle \tau$, the following error estimate holds:*

$$\|u - u^n\|_\infty + \|v - v^n\|_\infty \leq C(\triangle \tau + h^2), \quad h = \max_{0 \leq i \leq M-1} h_i \ \triangle \tau = \max_{0 \leq n \leq N-1} \triangle \tau^n,$$

for constant C, independent on h and $\triangle \tau$.

Proof (Outline). We use Taylor series expansion for the nonlinear terms f and g, [11, Theorems 4.1, 4.2] and discrete maximum principle.

Theorem 3 (Unconditionally weak positivity preserving). *For the solution of the full discrete scheme (3), (14), (15) we have $u^n \geq -\varepsilon$, $v^n \geq -\varepsilon$, where $\varepsilon = O(\triangle \tau^n)$.*

Proof (Outline). The proof is based on Theorems 1, 2 and $u^n = u(\tau_n) + O(\triangle \tau_n)$, $v^n = v(\tau_n) + O(\triangle \tau_n)$, where $u(\tau)$ and $v(\tau)$ satisfy (3), (10), (11).

3 Numerical Implementation and Validation

We consider two difference schemes - fully implicit scheme (FIS), $\theta = 1$ and implicit-explicit scheme (IMEXS), $\theta = 0$. To accelerate the computational process, we solve each discrete system (14) and (15) separately and consequently, updating the solutions and keeping the three-diagonal sparse structure of the coefficient matrices. Namely, for $\theta = 0$ and $n = 0, 1, \ldots, N - 1$, we have

$$\begin{aligned}
(G^n + E)u^{n+1} &= \overline{G}^n u^n - \overline{f}(u^n, v^n) + \epsilon u_b^{n+1}, \\
G^n v^{n+1} &= \overline{G}^n v^n - g(u^{n+1}, v^n).
\end{aligned} \tag{16}$$

In the case of $\theta = 1$, we apply Newton-like method to solve the non-linear systems of algebraic equation. To find u^{n+1} and v^{n+1}, at each time level $n = 0, 1, \ldots, N-1$ we assign a iteration process. Starting with $u^{(0)} := u^n$, $v^{(0)} := v^n$, we compute $u^{(k+1)}$ and $v^{(k+1)}$, $k = 1, 2, \ldots$, solving the system

$$\begin{aligned}
(G^n + E + \overline{f}'_u(u^{(k)}, v^{(k)}))u^{(k+1)} &= \overline{f}'_u(u^{(k)}, v^{(k)})u^{(k)} - \overline{f}(u^{(k)}, v^{(k)}) + \overline{G}^n(u), \\
(G^n + g'_v(u^{(k+1)}, v^{(k)}))v^{(k+1)} &= g'_v(u^{(k+1)}, v^{(k)})v^{(k)} - g(u^n, v^n) + \overline{G}^n(v),
\end{aligned}$$

where $\overline{f}'_u(u^{(k)}, v^{(k)}))$ and $\mathbf{g}'_u(u^{(k+1)}, v^{(k)}))$ are $(M+1) \times (M+1)$ diagonal matrices with entries $\overline{f}'_u(u^{(k)}, v^{(k)})) = \overline{f}(u^{(k)}, v^{(k)})) - b\mathbf{l}$, $\mathbf{l} = [1, l_1, \ldots, l_{M-1}, 0]^T$ and $\overline{G}^n(u) := \overline{G}^n u^n + \epsilon u_b^{n+1}$, $g'_v(u^{(k)}, v^{(k)})) = g(u^{(k)}, v^{(k)})) - c\mathbf{1}$, for unit column vector $\mathbf{1}$ of size $M + 1$.

The iteration process continue up to reaching the desired accuracy in maximal discrete norm (tol). Then we set $u^{n+1} := u^{(k+1)}$ and $v^{n+1} := v^{(k+1)}$.

Next, we will verify the order of convergence and efficiency of the proposed numerical schemes for the model problem (2), (3), (11). The model parameters are $\sigma = 0.2$, $\gamma = 1$, $\mu = 0.06$, $\nu_{01} = 1$, $\nu_{10} = 12$ (i.e. the liquidity shocks occur at a rate of once per year and last an average of one month [7]). The final time is $T = 0.5$ and $S_{\max} = 100$. We give the values of the solution at strike $S = E$ (where the expected error is largest), the corresponding absolute value of the difference (diff$_u$, diff$_v$) between the solutions u^n, v^n at consecutive embedded meshes and convergence (CR_E^u, CR_E^v) at strike point at final time. In order to compare the efficiency of both schemes, we list CPU time (in seconds) and averaging number of iterations (iter) at each time layer for FIS and $tol = 10^{-6}$.

The computations are performed on uniform primal mesh with step size h and dual mesh (12). In view of Theorem 2, the expected order of convergence is $O(\triangle\tau + h^2)$. Therefore to verify the convergence rate both in space and time, we take a fixed uniform time step size $\triangle\tau = h^2$.

Example 1 (*Call option*). In this case $h(S) = \max(S - E, 0)$ and we set $E = 50$. At $S = S_{\max}$ we use the natural boundary condition [5]

$$u_b(\tau, S_{\max}) = \gamma(S_{\max} - E) + b\tau - \frac{aA_2}{Q}\ln|e^{Q\tau} - D_1| - \frac{aA_1}{Q}\ln|1 - D_1 e^{-Q\tau}| + \ln|1 - D_1|,$$

where $\lambda = (c - b)/(2a)$, $P = \lambda^2 + c/a$, $A_1 = \sqrt{P} + \lambda$, $A_2 = \sqrt{P} - \lambda$, $Q = 2a\sqrt{P}$ and $D_1 = (1 - A_2)/(1 + A_1)$.

The results from this test example are given in Tables 1 and 2. We observe second order convergence rate in space and because of the fixed ratio $\triangle\tau/h^2 = 1$, we may conclude that the order of convergence in time is first.

Table 1. Computations with FIS, Call option

N	$u(E,T)$	diff$_u$	CR_E^u	$v(E,T)$	diff$_v$	CR_E^v	iter	CPU
801	2.69190			2.36822			8	0.17
1601	2.69882	6.915e-3		2.38007	1.186e-2		5	0.52
3201	2.70053	1.707e-3	2.0182	2.38303	2.958e-3	2.0028	3	2.23
6401	2.70095	4.250e-4	2.0056	2.38377	7.385e-4	2.0019	3	15.58
12801	2.70106	1.062e-4	2.0003	2.38395	1.846e-4	2.0001	2	77.76
25601	2.70108	2.642e-5	2.0077	2.38400	4.600e-5	2.0048	2	571.74
51201	2.70109	6.622e-6	1.9961	2.38401	1.152e-5	1.9975	2	5082.30

Table 2. Computations with IMEXS, Call option

N	$u(E,T)$	diff$_u$	CR_E^u	$v(E,T)$	diff$_v$	CR_E^v	CPU
801	2.71321			2.44568			0.05
1601	2.70419	9.023e-3		2.39944	4.625e-2		0.11
3201	2.70187	2.318e-3	1.9605	2.38788	1.157e-2	1.9994	0.47
6401	2.70129	5.836e-4	1.9900	2.38498	2.892e-3	1.9997	3.25
12801	2.70114	1.462e-4	1.9974	2.38426	7.231e-4	1.9999	24.01
25601	2.70110	3.656e-5	1.9994	2.38407	1.808e-4	2.0000	189.05
51201	2.70109	9.142e-6	1.9996	2.38403	4.520e-5	2.0000	1593.36

We compute the solutions by IMEXS (16) and IMEX scheme 2 (without Richardson extrapolation), developed in [8], on very fine mesh, such that to obtain one and the same (up to nine digits after the decimal point) numerical approximations of $u(E,T)$ and $v(E,T)$. These values we will call reference values and will denote by U_{ref} and V_{ref}. On Fig. 1 we plot the errors $ER_u = |U_{\text{ref}} - u(E,T)|$ and $ER_v = |V_{\text{ref}} - v(E,T)|$, computed by IMEXS (16) and IMEX scheme 2 [8], on different meshes versus CPU time.

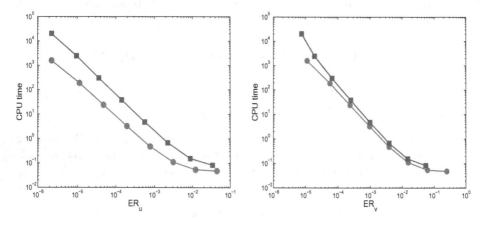

Fig. 1. Errors ER_u (*left*) and ER_v (*right*) for IMEXS (16) (line with circles) and IMEX scheme 2 [8] (line with squares) vs. CPU time

Example 2 (*Butterfly option*). For this option $h(S) = \max(E_1 - S, 0) + \max(E_2 - S, 0) - 2\max(E - S, 0)$, $u_b(\tau, S_{\max}) = 0$ and we set $E_1 = 40$, $E = 50$ and $E_2 = 60$. The results are listed in Tables 3 and 4. The accuracy $O(\triangle\tau + h^2)$ is confirmed.

Table 3. Computations with FIS, Butterfly option

N	$u(E,T)$	diff$_u$	CR_E^u	$v(E,T)$	diff$_v$	CR_E^v	iter	CPU
801	5.00961			5.31060			8	0.18
1601	4.98680	2.276e-2		5.28178	2.882e-2	1.9694	5	0.54
3201	4.98104	5.753e-3	1.9840	5.27453	7.254e-3	1.9901	3.39	2.89
6401	4.97960	1.443e-3	1.9950	5.27271	1.819e-3	1.9953	3	15.96
12801	4.97923	3.611e-4	1.9989	5.27225	4.547e-4	2.0003	3	111.90
25601	4.97914	9.032e-5	1.9992	5.27214	1.137e-4	1.9994	2.12	601.41
51201	4.97912	2.255e-5	2.0019	5.27211	2.840e-5	2.0018	2	5121.35

Table 4. Computations with IMEXS, Butterfly option

N	$u(E,T)$	diff$_u$	CR_E^u	$v(E,T)$	diff$_v$	CR_E^v	CPU
801	4.99225			5.21961			0.06
1601	4.98265	9.602e-3		5.25911	3.950e-2		0.12
3201	4.98001	2.634e-3	1.8663	5.26886	9.753e-3	2.0178	0.51
6401	4.97934	6.728e-4	1.9687	5.27129	2.431e-3	2.0043	3.98
12801	4.97917	1.691e-4	1.9922	5.27190	6.073e-4	2.0011	25.03
25601	4.97913	4.234e-5	1.9980	5.27205	1.518e-4	2.0003	190.45
51201	4.97912	1.059e-5	1.9992	5.27209	3.794e-5	2.0001	1601.12

4   Conclusions

The following conclusions can be drawn from the experiments. The order of convergence in maximal discrete norm for both call and butterfly options, computed by FIS and IMEXS is second in space and first in time.

In the stability regions of the IMEXS, it is faster than FIS.

We observe better efficiency of IMEXS (16) in comparison with IMEX scheme 2, developed in [8]. In contrast to [6], here we overcome the degeneration, dealing with the original variable S. We impose natural boundary conditions on the left boundary exactly on $S = 0$ and the solution can be computed very close to $S = 0$.

Acknowledgments. This research is supported by the Bulgarian National Science Fund under Project DN 12/4 from 2017.

References

1. Chernogorova, T., Valkov, R.: Finite volume difference scheme for a degenerate parabolic equation in the zero-coupon bond pricing. Math. Comput. Model. **54**, 2659–2671 (2011)

2. Gerisch, A., Griffiths, D.F., Weiner, R., Chaplain, M.A.J.: A Positive splitting method for mixed hyperbolic-parabolic systems. Numer. Meth. Part. Differ. Equat. **17**(2), 152–168 (2001)
3. Gyulov, T.B., Vulkov, L.G.: Well posedness and comparison principle for option pricing with switching liquidity. Nonlinear Anal. Real World Appl. **43**, 348–361 (2018)
4. Hundsdorfer, W., Verwer, J.: Numerical Solution of Time-Dependent Advection-Diffusion-Reaction Equations. Springer Series in Computational Mathematics, vol. 33. Springer, Heidelberg (2003). https://doi.org/10.1007/978-3-662-09017-6
5. Koleva, M.N., Vulkov, L.G.: Fully implicit time-stepping schemes for a parabolic-ODE system of european options with liquidity shocks. In: Lirkov, I., Margenov, S.D., Waśniewski, J. (eds.) LSSC 2015. LNCS, vol. 9374, pp. 360–368. Springer, Cham (2015). https://doi.org/10.1007/978-3-319-26520-9_40
6. Koleva, M., Mudzimbabwe, W., Vulkov, L.: Fourth-order compact schemes for a parabolic-ordinary system of European option pricing liquidity shocks model. Numer. Algorithms **74**(1), 59–75 (2017)
7. Ludkovski, M., Shen, Q.: European option pricing with liquidity shocks. Int. J. Theor. Appl. Finance **16**(7), 1350043 (2013)
8. Mudzimbabwe, W., Vulkov, L.: IMEX schemes for a parabolic-ODE system of European options with liquidity shocks. J. Comp. Appl. Math. **299**, 245–256 (2016)
9. Valkov, R.: Convergence of a finite volume element method for a generalized Black-Scholes equation transformed on finite interval. Numer. Algorithms **68**(1), 61–80 (2015)
10. Wang, S.: A novel fitted finite volume method for the Black-Sholes equation governing option pricing. IMA J. Numer. Anal. **24**, 699–720 (2004)
11. Wang, S., Shang, S., Fang, Z.: A superconvergence fitted finite volume method for Black-Sholes equation governing European and American options. Numer. Meth. Part. Differ. Equ. **31**(4), 1190–1208 (2014)

Space-Time Finite Element Methods for Parabolic Initial-Boundary Value Problems with Non-smooth Solutions

Ulrich Langer[1]([✉])[iD] and Andreas Schafelner[2]

[1] Institute for Computational Mathematics, Johannes Kepler University Linz, Altenbergerstr. 69, 4040 Linz, Austria
ulanger@numa.uni-linz.ac.at
[2] Doctoral Program "Computational Mathematics", Johannes Kepler University Linz, Altenbergerstr. 69, 4040 Linz, Austria
andreas.schafelner@dk-compmath.jku.at
http://www.numa.uni-linz.ac.at, https://www.dk-compmath.jku.at

Abstract. We propose consistent, locally stabilized, conforming finite element schemes on completely unstructured simplicial space-time meshes for the numerical solution of parabolic initial-boundary value problems under the assumption of maximal parabolic regularity. We present new a priori discretization error estimates for low-regularity solutions, and some numerical results including results for an adaptive version of the scheme and strong scaling results.

Keywords: Parabolic initial-boundary-value problems · Space-time finite element methods · Unstructured meshes · Adaptivity

1 Introduction

Parabolic initial-boundary value problems of the form

$$\partial_t u - \mathrm{div}_x(\nu \nabla_x u) = f \text{ in } Q, \quad u = 0 \text{ on } \Sigma, \quad u = u_0 \text{ on } \Sigma_0 \tag{1}$$

describe not only heat conduction and diffusion processes but also 2D eddy current problems in electromagnetics and many other evolution processes, where $Q = \Omega \times (0, T)$, $\Sigma = \partial\Omega \times (0, T)$, and $\Sigma_0 = \Omega \times \{0\}$ denote the space-time cylinder, its lateral boundary, and the bottom face, respectively. The spatial computational domain $\Omega \subset \mathcal{R}^d$, $d = 1, 2, 3$, is supposed to be bounded and Lipschitz. The final time is denoted by T. The right-hand side f is a given source function from $L_2(Q)$. The given coefficient ν may depend on the spatial variable x as well as the time variable t. In the latter case, the problem is called non-autonomous. We suppose at least that ν is uniformly positive and bounded almost everywhere. We here consider homogeneous Dirichlet boundary

Supported by the Austrian Science Fund under the grant W1214, project DK4.

I. Lirkov and S. Margenov (Eds.): LSSC 2019, LNCS 11958, pp. 593–600, 2020.
https://doi.org/10.1007/978-3-030-41032-2_68

conditions for the sake of simplicity. In practice, we often meet mixed boundary conditions. Discontinuous coefficients, non-smooth boundaries, changing boundary conditions, non-smooth or incompatible initial conditions, and non-smooth right-hand sides can lead to non-smooth solutions.

In contrast to the conventional time-stepping methods in combination with some spatial discretization method, or the more advanced, but closely related discontinuous Galerkin (dG) methods based on time slices, we here consider space-time finite element discretizations treating time as just another variable, and the term $\partial_t u$ in (1) as a convection term in time. Following [7], we derive consistent, locally stabilized, conforming finite element schemes on completely unstructured simplicial space-time meshes under the assumption of maximal parabolic regularity; see, e.g., [5]. Unstructured space-time schemes have some advantages with respect to adaptivity, parallelization, and the numerical treatment of moving interfaces or special domains. However, the combination of adaptivity and parallelization is still a challenge. We refer the reader to the survey paper [9] that provides an excellent overview of completely unstructured space-time methods and simultaneous space-time adaptivity. In particular, we would like to mention the papers [8] that is based on an inf-sup-condition, [4] that uses mesh-grading in time, and [1] that also uses stabilization techniques. All three papers treat the autonomous case.

We here present new a priori estimates for low-regularity solutions. In order to avoid reduced convergence rates appearing in the case of uniform mesh refinement, we also consider adaptive refinement procedures in the numerical experiments presented in Sect. 5. The adaptive refinement procedures are based on residual a posteriori error indicators. The huge system of space-time finite element equations is then solved by means of the Generalized Minimal Residual Method (GMRES) preconditioned by an algebraic multigrid cycle. In particular, in the 4D space-time case that is 3D in space, simultaneous space-time adaptivity and parallelization can considerably reduce the computational time. The space-time finite element solver was implemented in the framework of MFEM. The numerical results nicely confirm our theoretical findings. The parallel version of the code shows an excellent parallel performance.

2   Weak Formulation and Maximal Parabolic Regularity

The weak formulation of the model problem (1) reads as follows: find $u \in H_0^{1,0}(Q) := \{u \in L_2(Q) : \nabla_x u \in [L_2(Q)]^d, \, u = 0 \text{ on } \Sigma\}$ such that (s.t.)

$$\int_Q (-u\,\partial_t v + \nu\,\nabla_x u \cdot \nabla_x v)\,\mathrm{d}(x,t) = \int_Q f\,v\,\mathrm{d}(x,t) + \int_\Omega u_0\,v|_{t=0}\,\mathrm{d}x \qquad (2)$$

for all $v \in \hat{H}_0^1(Q) = \{v \in H^1(Q) : v = 0 \text{ on } \Sigma \cup \Sigma_T\}$, where $\Sigma_T := \Omega \times \{T\}$. The existence and uniqueness of weak solutions is well understood; see, e.g., [6]. It was already shown in [6] that $\partial_t u \in L^2(Q)$ and $\Delta_x u \in L^2(Q)$ provided that $\nu = 1$, $f \in L^2(Q)$, and $u_0 = 0$. This case is called maximal parabolic regularity. Similar results can be obtained under more general assumptions imposed on the data; see, e.g., [5] for some very recent results on the non-autonomous case.

3 Locally Stabilized Space-Time Finite Element Method

In order to derive the space-time finite element scheme, we need an admissible, shape regular decomposition $\mathcal{T}_h = \{K\}$ of the space-time cylinder $\overline{Q} = \bigcup_{K \in \mathcal{T}_h} \overline{K}$ into finite elements K. On $\mathcal{T}_h$, we define a H^1 - conforming finite element space V_h by means of polynomial simplicial finite elements of the degree p in the usual way; see, e.g., [2]. Let us assume that the solution u of (2) belongs to the space $V_0 = H_{0,\underline{0}}^{\mathcal{L},1}(\mathcal{T}_h) := \{u \in L_2(Q) : \partial_t u \in L_2(K), \mathcal{L}u := \mathrm{div}_x(\nu\nabla_x u) \in L_2(K) \; \forall K \in \mathcal{T}_h, \text{ and } u|_{\Sigma \cup \Sigma_0} = 0\}$, i.e., we only need some local version of maximal parabolic regularity, and, for simplicity, we assume homogeneous initial conditions, i.e., $u_0 = 0$. Multiplying the PDE (1) on K by a local time-upwind test function $v_h + \theta_K h_K \partial_t v_h$, with $v_h \in V_{0h} = \{v_h \in V_h : v_h = 0 \text{ on } \Sigma \cup \Sigma_0\}$, $h_K = \mathrm{diam}(K)$, and a parameter $\theta_K > 0$ which we will specify later, integrating over K, integrating by parts, and summing up over all elements $K \in \mathcal{T}_h$, we arrive at the following consistent space-time finite element scheme: find $u_h \in V_{0h}$ s.t.

$$a_h(u_h, v_h) = l_h(v_h), \quad \forall v_h \in V_{0h}, \tag{3}$$

with $l_h(v_h) = \sum_{K \in \mathcal{T}_h} \int_K f v_h + \theta_K h_K f \partial_t v_h \mathrm{d}(x,t)$ and the bilinear form

$$\begin{aligned} a_h(u_h, v_h) = \sum_{K \in \mathcal{T}_h} \int_K & \left[\partial_t u_h v_h + \theta_K h_K \partial_t u_h \partial_t v_h \right. \\ & \left. + \nu\nabla_x u_h \cdot \nabla_x v_h - \theta_K h_K \mathrm{div}_x(\nu\nabla_x u_h) \partial_t v_h \right] \mathrm{d}(x,t). \end{aligned}$$

The bilinear form $a_h(\,.\,,\,.\,)$ is coercive on $V_{0h} \times V_{0h}$ w.r.t. to the norm

$$\|v\|_h^2 = \frac{1}{2}\|v\|_{L_2(\Sigma_T)}^2 + \sum_{K \in \mathcal{T}_h}\left[\theta_K h_K\|\partial_t v\|_{L_2(K)}^2 + \|\nabla_x v\|_{L_2^\nu(K)}^2\right], \tag{4}$$

i.e., $a_h(v_h, v_h) \geq \mu_c\|v_h\|_h^2, \; \forall v_h \in V_{0h}$, and bounded on $V_{0h,*} \times V_{0h}$ w.r.t. to the norm

$$\|v\|_{h,*}^2 = \|v\|_h^2 + \sum_{K \in \mathcal{T}_h}\left[(\theta_K h_K)^{-1}\|v\|_{L_2(K)}^2 + \theta_K h_K\|\mathrm{div}_x(\nu\nabla_x v)\|_{L_2(K)}^2\right], \tag{5}$$

i.e., $a_h(u_h, v_h) \leq \mu_b\|u_h\|_{h,*}\|v_h\|_h, \; \forall u_h \in V_{0h,*}, \forall v_h \in V_{0h}$, where $V_{0h,*} := H_{0,\underline{0}}^{\mathcal{L},1}(\mathcal{T}_h) + V_{0h}$; see [7, Lemma 3.8] and [7, Remark 3.13], respectively. The coercivity constant μ_c is robust in h_K provided that we choose $\theta_K = \mathcal{O}(h_K)$; see Sect. 5 or [7, Lemma 3.8] for the explicit choice. From the above derivation of the scheme, we get consistency $a_h(u, v_h) = l_h(v_h), \; \forall v_h \in V_{0h}$, provided that the solution u belongs to $H_{0,\underline{0}}^{\mathcal{L},1}(\mathcal{T}_h)$ that is ensured in the case of maximal parabolic regularity. The space-time finite element scheme (3) and the consistency relation immediately yield Galerkin orthogonality

$$a_h(u - u_h, v_h) = 0, \quad \forall v_h \in V_{0h}. \tag{6}$$

We deduce that (3) is nothing but a huge linear system of algebraic equations. Indeed, let $V_{0h} = \mathrm{span}\{p^{(j)}, j = 1, \ldots, N_h\}$, where $\{p^{(j)}, j = 1, \ldots, N_h\}$ is the nodal finite element basis and N_h is the total number of space-time degrees of freedom (dofs). Then we can express each function in V_{0h} in terms of this basis, i.e., we can identify each finite element function $v_h \in V_{0h}$ with its coefficient vector $\mathbf{v}_h \in \mathbb{R}^{N_h}$. Moreover, each basis function $p^{(j)}$ is also a valid test function. Hence, we obtain N_h equations from (3), which we rewrite as a system of linear algebraic equations, i.e. $\mathbf{K}_h \mathbf{u}_h = \mathbf{f}_h$, with the solution vector $\mathbf{u}_h = (u_j)_{j=1,\dots,N_h}$, the vector $\mathbf{f}_h = \left(l_h(p^{(i)})\right)_{i=1,\dots,N_h}$, and system matrix $\mathbf{K}_h = \left(a_h(p^{(j)}, p^{(i)})\right)_{i,j=1,\dots,N_h}$ that is non-symmetric, but positive definite.

4   A Priori Discretization Error Estimates

Galerkin orthogonality (6), together with coercivity and boundedness, enables us to prove a Céa-like estimate, where we bound the discretization error in the $\| \cdot \|_h$-norm by the best-approximation error in the $\| \cdot \|_{h,*}$-norm.

Lemma 1. *Let the bilinear form $a_h(\cdot, \cdot)$ be coercive [7, Lemma 3.8] with constant μ_c and bounded [7, Lemma 3.11, Remark 3.13] with constant μ_b, and let $u \in H_{0,\underline{0}}^{\mathcal{L},1}(\mathcal{T}_h)$ be the solution of the space-time variational problem (2). Then*

$$\|u - u_h\|_h \leq \left(1 + \frac{\mu_b}{\mu_c}\right) \inf_{v_h \in V_{0h}} \|u - v_h\|_{h,*}, \tag{7}$$

where $u_h \in V_{0h}$ is the solution to the space-time finite element scheme (3).

Proof. Estimate (7) easily follows from triangle inequality and Galerkin-orthogonality; see [7, Lemma 3.15, Remark 3.16] for details.

Next, we estimate the best approximation error by the interpolation error, where we have to choose a proper interpolation operator $\mathcal{I}_*$. For smooth solutions, i.e., $u \in H^l(Q)$ with $l > (d+1)/2$, we obtained a localized a priori error estimate, see [7, Theorem 3.17], where we used the standard Lagrange interpolation operator $\mathcal{I}_h$; see e.g. [2]. In this paper, we are interested in non-smooth solutions, which means that we only require $u \in H^l(Q)$, with $(d+1)/2 \geq l > 1$. Hence, we cannot use the Lagrange interpolator. We can, however, use so-called quasi-interpolators, e.g. Clément [3] or Scott-Zhang [2]. For this kind of operators, we need a neighborhood S_K of an element $K \in \mathcal{T}_h$ which is defined as $S_K := \{K' \in \mathcal{T}_h : \overline{K} \cap \overline{K'} \neq \emptyset\}$. Let $v \in H^l(Q)$, with some real $l > 1$. Then, for the Scott-Zhang quasi-interpolation operator $\mathcal{I}_{SZ} : L_2(Q) \to V_{0h}$, we have the local estimate (see e.g. [2, (4.8.10)])

$$\|v - \mathcal{I}_{SZ} v\|_{H^k(K)} \leq C_{\mathcal{I}_{SZ}} h_K^{l-k} |v|_{H^l(S_K)}, \quad k = 0, 1. \tag{8}$$

For details on how to construct such a quasi-interpolator, we refer to [2] and the references therein. For simplicity, we now assume that ν is piecewise constant, i.e., $\nu|_K = \nu_K$, for all $K \in \mathcal{T}_h$. Then we can show the following lemma.

Lemma 2. *Let $v \in V_0 \cap H^l(Q)$ with some $l > 1$, and let $p \geq 1$ denote the polynomial degree of the finite element shape functions on the reference element. Then the following interpolation error estimates are valid:*

$$\|v - \mathcal{I}_{SZ}v\|_{L_2(\Sigma_T)} \leq c_1 \Big(\sum_{\substack{K \in \mathcal{T}_h \\ \partial K \cap \Sigma_T \neq \emptyset}} h_K^{2s-1} |v|_{H^s(S_K)}^2\Big)^{1/2}, \tag{9}$$

$$\|v - \mathcal{I}_{SZ}v\|_h \leq c_2 \Big(\sum_{K \in \mathcal{T}_h} h_K^{2(s-1)} |v|_{H^s(S_K)}^2\Big)^{1/2}, \tag{10}$$

$$\|v - \mathcal{I}_{SZ}v\|_{h,*} \leq c_3 \Big(\sum_{K \in \mathcal{T}_h} h_K^{2(s-1)} \big(|v|_{H^s(S_K)}^2 + \|\mathrm{div}_x(\nu\nabla_x v)\|_{L_2(K)}^2\big)\Big)^{1/2}, \tag{11}$$

with $s = \min\{l, p+1\}$ and positive constants c_1, c_2 and c_3, that do not depend on v or h_K provided that $\theta_K = \mathcal{O}(h_K)$ for all $K \in \mathcal{T}_h$.

Proof. Estimates (9) and (10) are easy to proof by using the scaled trace inequality and quasi-interpolation estimates (8). Estimate (11) contains the term $\theta_K h_K \|\mathrm{div}_x(\nu\nabla_x(v - \mathcal{I}_{SZ}v))\|_{L_2(K)}^2$ that needs a special treatment. The case $p = 1$ is straightforward since $\mathrm{div}_x \mathcal{I}_{SZ}(\nu\nabla_x v) = 0$. Otherwise, adding and subtracting the linear quasi-interpolant $\mathcal{I}_{SZ}^1 v$ of v, then using triangle and inverse inequalities, and finally the quasi-interpolation estimate (8) for $k = 1$, we arrive at the desired estimate for $p > 1$.

Now we are in the position to prove our main theorem.

Theorem 1. *Let $l > 1$ and $p \geq 1$. Let $u \in V_0 \cap H^l(Q)$ be the exact solution, and $u_h \in V_{0h}$ be the approximate solution of the finite element scheme (3). Furthermore, let the assumptions of Lemma 1 (Céa-like estimate) and 2 (quasi-interpolation estimates) hold. Then the a priori error estimate*

$$\|u - u_h\|_h \leq C \Big(\sum_{K \in \mathcal{T}_h} h_K^{2(s-1)} \big(|u|_{H^s(S_K)} + \|\mathrm{div}_x(\nu\nabla_x u)\|_{L_2(K)}^2\big)\Big)^{1/2} \tag{12}$$

holds, with $s = \min\{l, p+1\}$ and a positive generic constant C.

Proof. Choosing $v_h = \mathcal{I}_{SZ}u$ as some approximation in (7), we can apply the quasi-interpolation estimate (11) to obtain

$$\|u - u_h\|_h \leq \Big(1 + \frac{\mu_b}{\mu_c}\Big)\|u - \mathcal{I}_{SZ}u\|_{h,*}$$

$$\leq c_3 \Big(1 + \frac{\mu_b}{\mu_c}\Big)\Big(\sum_{K \in \mathcal{T}_h} h_K^{2(s-1)} \big(|u|_{H^s(S_K)}^2 + \|\mathrm{div}_x(\nu\nabla_x u)\|_{L_2(K)}^2\big)\Big)^{1/2}.$$

We set $C = c_3(1 + \mu_b/\mu_c)$ to obtain (12), which closes the proof.

We again mention that, for $l > (d+1)/2$, we can use the Lagrange interpolation that leads to a completely local estimate [7].

5 Numerical Results

We implemented the space-time finite element scheme (3) in C++, where we used the finite element library MFEM[1] and the solver library *hypre*[2]. The linear system was solved by means of the GMRES method, preconditioned by the algebraic multigrid *BoomerAMG*. We stopped the iterative procedure if the initial residual was reduced by a factor of 10^{-8}. Both libraries are already fully parallelized with the Message Passing Interface (MPI). Therefore, we performed all numerical tests on the distributed memory cluster RADON1[3] in Linz. For each element $K \in \mathcal{T}_h$, we choose $\theta_K = h_K/(\tilde{c}^2 \overline{\nu}_K)$, where $\tilde{c}$ is computed by solving a local generalized eigenvalue problem which comes from an inverse inequality [7].

5.1 Example: Highly Oscillatory Solution

We first consider the unit hypercube $Q = (0,1)^{d+1}$, with $d = 3$, as the space-time cylinder, and set $\nu \equiv 1$. The manufactured function

$$u(x,t) = \sin(1/(1/(10\pi) + (x_1^2 + x_2^2 + x_3^2 + t^2)^{0.5}))$$

serves as the exact solution, where we compute the right-hand side f accordingly. This solution is highly oscillatory. Hence, we do not expect optimal rates for uniform refinement in the pre-asymptotic range. However, using adaptive refinement, we may be able to recover the optimal rates. We use the residual based error indicator proposed by Steinbach and Yang in [9]. For each element $K \in \mathcal{T}_h$, we compute $\eta_K^2 := h_K^2 \|R_h(u_h)\|_{L_2(K)}^2 + h_K \|J_h(u_h)\|_{L_2(\partial K)}^2$, where u_h is the solution of (3), $R_h(u_h) := f + \mathrm{div}_x(\nu \nabla_x u_h) - \partial_t u_h$ in K and $J_h(u_h) := [\nu \nabla_x u_h]_e$ on $e \subset \partial K$, with $[.]_e$ denoting the jump across one face $e \subset \partial K$. Then we mark each element where the condition $\eta_K \geq \sigma \max_{K \in \mathcal{T}_h} \eta_K$ is fulfilled, with an a priori chosen threshold σ, e.g., $\sigma = 0.5$. Note that $\sigma = 0$ results in uniform refinement. In Fig. 1, we observe indeed reduced convergence rates for all polynomial degrees tested. However, using an adaptive procedure, we are able to recover the optimal rates. Moreover, we significantly reduce the number of dofs required to reach a certain error threshold. For instance, in the case $d = 3$ and $p = 2$, we need 276 922 881 dofs to get an error in the $\|.\|_h$-norm of $\sim 10^{-1}$, whereas we only need 26 359 dofs with adaptive refinement. In terms of runtime, the uniform refinement needed 478.57 s for assembling and solving, while the complete adaptive procedure took 156.5 s only. The parallel performance of the code is also shown in Fig. 1, where we obtain a nice strong scaling up to 64 cores. Then the local problems are too small (only $\sim 10\,000$ dofs for 128 cores) and the communication overhead becomes too large. Numerical results for $d = 2$ can be found in [7].

---

[1] http://mfem.org/.
[2] https://www.llnl.gov/casc/hypre/.
[3] https://www.ricam.oeaw.ac.at/hpc/.

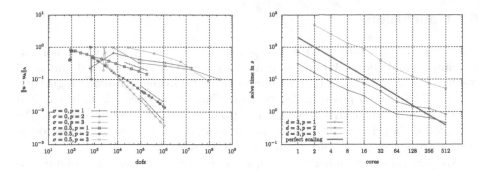

Fig. 1. Example 5.1: Error rates in the $\|\cdot\|_h$-norm (left), the dotted lines indicate the optimal rate; Strong scaling on a mesh with $1\,185\,921$ dofs for $p = 1, 2$ and $5\,764\,801$ dofs for $p = 3$ (right).

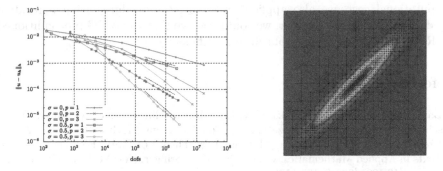

Fig. 2. Example 5.2: Error rates in the $\|\cdot\|_h$-norm for $d = 2$, the dotted lines indicate the optimal rates (left); Diagonal cut through the space-time mesh $\mathcal{T}_h$ along the line from $(0, 0, 0)$ to $(1, 1, 1)$ after 8 adaptive refinements (right).

5.2   Example: Moving Peak

For the second example, we consider the unit-cube $Q = (0, 1)^3$, i.e. $d = 2$. As diffusion coefficient, the choice $\nu \equiv 1$ is made. We choose the function

$$u(x, t) = (x_1^2 - x_1)(x_2^2 - x_2)e^{-100((x_1 - t)^2 + (x_2 - t)^2)},$$

as exact solution and compute all data accordingly. This function is smooth, and almost zero everywhere, except in a small region around the line from the origin $(0, 0, 0)$ to $(1, 1, 1)$. This motivates again the use of an adaptive method. We use the residual based indicator η_K introduced in Example 5.1. In Fig. 2, we can observe that we indeed obtain optimal rates for both uniform and adaptive refinement. However, using the a posteriori error indicator, we reduce the number of dofs needed to reach a certain threshold by one order of magnitude. For instance, in the case $p = 2$, we need $16\,974\,593$ dofs to obtain an error of $\sim 7 \times 10^{-5}$ with uniform refinement. Using adaptive refinement, we need $1\,066\,777$ dofs only.

6 Conclusions

Following [7], we introduced a space-time finite element solver for non-autonomous parabolic evolution problems on completely unstructured simplicial meshes. We only assumed that we have so-called maximal parabolic regularity, i.e., the PDE is well posed in L_2. We note that this property is only required locally in order to derive a consistent space-time finite element scheme. We extended the a priori error estimate in the mesh-dependent energy norm to the case of non-smooth solutions, i.e. $u \in H^{1+\epsilon}(Q)$, with $0 < \epsilon \le 1$.

We performed two numerical examples with known solutions. The first example had a highly oscillatory solution, and the second one was almost zero everywhere except along a line through the space-time cylinder. Using a high-performance cluster, we solved both problems on a sequence of uniformly refined meshes, where we also obtained good strong scaling rates. In order to reduce the computational cost, we also applied an adaptive procedure, using a residual based error indicator. Moreover, we could observe that the AMG preconditioned GMRES method solves the problem quite efficiently.

References

1. Bank, R.E., Vassilevski, P., Zikatanov, L.: Arbitrary dimension convection-diffusion scheme for space-time discretizations. J. Comput. Appl. Math. **310**, 19–31 (2017)
2. Brenner, S.C., Scott, L.R.: The Mathematical Theory of Finite Element Methods. Texts in Applied Mathematics, vol. 15, 3rd edn. Springer, New York (2008). https://doi.org/10.1007/978-0-387-75934-0
3. Clément, P.: Approximation by finite element functions using local regularization. Rev. Française Automat. Informat. Recherche Opérationnelle Sér **9**(R–2), 77–84 (1975)
4. Devaud, D., Schwab, C.: Space-time hp-approximation of parabolic equations. Calcolo **55**(3), 35 (2018)
5. Fackler, S.: Non-autonomous maximal regularity for forms given by elliptic operators of bounded variation. J. Differ. Equ. **263**, 3533–3549 (2017)
6. Ladyzhenskaya, O.A.: The Boundary Value Problems of Mathematical Physics. Applied Mathematical Sciences, vol. 49. Springer-Verlag, New York (1985). https://doi.org/10.1007/978-1-4757-4317-3
7. Langer, U., Neumüller, M., Schafelner, A.: Space-time finite element methods for parabolic evolution problems with variable coefficients. In: Apel, T., Langer, U., Meyer, A., Steinbach, O. (eds.) FEM 2017. LNCSE, vol. 128, pp. 247–275. Springer, Cham (2019). https://doi.org/10.1007/978-3-030-14244-5_13
8. Steinbach, O.: Space-time finite element methods for parabolic problems. Comput. Methods Appl. Math. **15**(4), 551–566 (2015)
9. Steinbach, O., Yang, H.: Space-time finite element methods for parabolic evolution equations: discretization, a posteriori error estimation, adaptivity and solution. In: Langer, U., Steinbach, O. (eds.) Space-Time Methods: Application to Partial Differential Equations, Radon Series on Computational and Applied Mathematics, vol. 25, pp. 207–248. de Gruyter, Berlin (2019)

MATLAB Implementation
of Element-Based Solvers

Leszek Marcinkowski[1] and Jan Valdman[2(✉)]

[1] Faculty of Mathematics, University of Warsaw, Warszawa, Poland
`lmarcin@mimuw.edu.pl`
[2] Faculty of Science, University of South Bohemia,
České Budějovice, and The Czech Academy of Sciences,
Institute of Information Theory and Automation, Prague, Czechia
`jan.valdman@utia.cas.cz`

Abstract. Rahman and Valdman (2013) introduced a vectorized way to assemble finite element stiffness and mass matrices in MATLAB. Local element matrices are computed all at once by array operations and stored in multi-dimensional arrays (matrices). We build some iterative solvers on available multi-dimensional structures completely avoiding the use of a sparse matrix.

Keywords: MATLAB code vectorization · Finite elements · Stiffness and mass matrices · Iterative solvers

1 Motivation Example

We solve a benchmark boundary value problem

$$-\triangle u + \nu u = f \qquad \text{on } x \in \Omega = (0,1) \times (0,1)$$

for given $f \in L^2(\Omega)$ and a parameter $\nu \geq 0$. Nonhomogeneous Dirichlet or homogeneous Neumann boundary conditions are assumed on parts of boundary $\partial\Omega$ and measure of the Dirichlet boundary has to be positive for $\nu = 0$. A finite element method is applied and leads to a linear system of equations

$$Au = (K + \nu M)u = b, \tag{1}$$

for an unknown vector $u \in \mathbb{R}^{n_n}$, where n_n denotes the number of mesh nodes (vertices). Stiffness and mass matrices $K, M \in \mathbb{R}^{n_n \times n_n}$ and the right hand side vector $b \in \mathbb{R}^{n_n}$ are defined as

$$K_{ij} = \int_\Omega \nabla \Phi_i \cdot \nabla \Phi_j \, \mathrm{d}x, \qquad M_{ij} = \int_\Omega \Phi_i \Phi_j \, dx, \qquad b_j = \int_\Omega f \Phi_j \, \mathrm{d}x \tag{2}$$

The work of the 1st author was partially supported by Polish Scientific Grant: National Science Center 2016/21/B/ST1/00350.
The work of the 2nd and the corresponding author was supported by the Czech Science Foundation (GACR), through the grant GA17-04301S.

I. Lirkov and S. Margenov (Eds.): LSSC 2019, LNCS 11958, pp. 601–609, 2020.
https://doi.org/10.1007/978-3-030-41032-2_69

using local basis functions Φ_i for $i = 1, \ldots, n_n$ and ∇ denotes the gradient operator. Figure 1 shows an example of a 2D discretization of Ω. Sparse matrices K, M are generated as

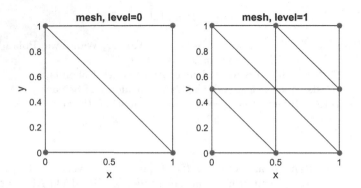

Fig. 1. Two examples of triangular meshes of a unit square domain Ω with $n_e = 2$ elements and $n_n = 4$ nodes (left) and $n_e = 8$ elements and $n_n = 9$ nodes (right).

$$K = \sum_{e=1}^{n_e} C_e^T K_e C_e, \qquad M = \sum_{e=1}^{n_e} C_e^T M_e C_e, \qquad (3)$$

where n_e denotes a number of mesh elements (number of triangles in Fig. 1),

$$K_e, M_e \in \mathbb{R}^{n_b \times n_b}, \qquad e = 1, \ldots, n_e$$

are local element matrices and

$$C_e \in \mathbb{R}^{n_b \times n_n}, \qquad e = 1, \ldots, n_e$$

are Boolean connectivity matrices which distribute the terms in local element matrices to their associated global degrees of freedom. Here, n_b denotes a number of local basic functions. In the simplest case of nodal linear (P_1) finite elements:

$$n_b = 3 \qquad \text{for triangles in 2D,}$$
$$n_b = 4 \qquad \text{for tetrahedra in 3D.}$$

Extensions to higher order isoparametric elements are also possible. All matrices K_e, M_e for $e = 1, \ldots, n_e$ are generated at once using vectorized routines of [3]. They are stored as 3-dimensional full matrices (see Fig. 2) of sizes

$$n_b \times n_b \times n_e.$$

The storage of 3-dimensional matrices contains certain memory overheads in comparison to sparse matrices (which can be automatically generated from

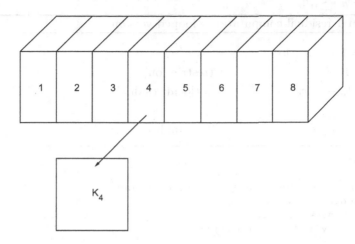

Fig. 2. Example of a 3-dimensional array storing all local stiffness matrices. The matrix corresponds to a triangular mesh with 8 elements displayed on Fig. 1 (right). A particular local stiffness matrix $K_4 \in \mathbb{R}^{3 \times 3}$ is indicated.

them), since local contributions from restrictions of basis functions to shared elements are stored separately. Our aim is to build and explain in detail simple linear iterative solvers based on local element matrices K_e, M_e without assembling the sparse matrices M, K. This is our first attempt in this direction and therefore we show the possibility of this approach rather than efficient implementations and runtimes. The complementary software to this paper is available for download

https://www.mathworks.com/matlabcentral/fileexchange/70255.

2 Element-Based Solvers

Some examples of element-based iterative solvers are provided including their simple MATLAB implementations. All are based on a vectorized computation of a (column) residual vector

$$r := b - Ax \tag{4}$$

for a given approximation (column) vector $x \in \mathbb{R}^{n_n}$. The residual is computed using local matrices and local vectors

$$A_e := K_e + \nu M_e \in \mathbb{R}^{n_b \times n_b}, \quad b_e \in \mathbb{R}^{n_b}, \quad e = 1, \dots, n_e.$$

Matrices $R_e \in \mathbb{R}^{n_b \times n_n}, e = 1, \dots, n_e$ are restriction matrices from global to local indices. Note that elementwise evaluations inside the loop (lines 2 and 3) operate with local matrices and local vectors only. A fully vectorized MATLAB version of Algorithm 1 follows:

Algorithm 1 residual computation - looped version

1: **for** $e = 1, \ldots, n_e$ **do**

2:     $x_e = R_e x,$ (restriction)

3:     $r_e = b_e - A_e x_e,$ (local residual)

4: **end for**

5: $r = \sum_{e=1}^{n_e} C_e^T r_e.$ (assembly)

```
1   function r=residual_e(A_e,bt_e,x,ind_e,indt)
2   x_e=x(ind_e);                        %restriction - all
3   rt_e=bt_e-avtam(x_e,A_e);            %residual   - all
4   r=accumarray(indt(:),rt_e(:));       %assembly   - all
5   end
```

Clearly, matrices R_e and C_e of Algorithm 1 are not stored, but their operations are replaced by a convenient indexing using two index arrays:

$$\texttt{ind\_e} \in \mathbb{I}^{n_b \times 1 \times n_e}, \quad \texttt{indt} \in \mathbb{I}^{n_b \times n_e}.$$

Both arrays contain the same global nodes numbers corresponding to each element, but they are ordered differently with respect to their operations.

All objects indexed by elements are stored as full higher dimensional matrices and their names end with a symbol _e.

2.1   Richardson Iteration

We recall few examples of iterative methods based on a residual computation More details about them can be found eg. in [2,4]. One of the simplest iterative methods to solve (1) is the Richardson iteration for iterations $k = 0, 1, 2, \ldots$ in the form

$$r^k = b - Ax^k,$$
$$x^{k+1} = x^k + \omega\, r^k \tag{5}$$

with the initial column vector $x^0 \in \mathbb{R}^n$ and a given positive parameter $\omega > 0$. The optimal coefficient is equal to $\omega_{opt} = \frac{1}{\lambda_1 + \lambda_2}$ for $A = A^T > 0$, where λ_1 is the smallest and λ_2 the largest eigenvalue of A. For this ω_{opt} the convergence estimate is the fastest, i.e.

$$\|x^k - u\|_2 \leq \frac{\lambda_2 - \lambda_1}{\lambda_2 + \lambda_1} \|x^{k-1} - u\|_2.$$

Here, $u \in \mathbb{R}^n$ is the solution of (1). A MATLAB version follows:

```
1   function x=Richardson_e(A_e,bt_e,x0,ind_e,indt,iters,lam2,lam1,
        nd)
2   omega=2/(lam2+lam1);                    %optimal parameter
3   x=x0;                                   %iteration initial
4   for k=0:iters-1
5       r=residual_e(A_e,bt_e,x,ind_e,indt);  %residual comput.
6       r(nd)=0;                            %dirichlet condit.
7       x=x+omega*r;                        %iteration update
8   end
9   end
```

2.2 Chebyshev Iteration

The Chebyshev polynomial (of the first kind) of degree $N \in \mathbb{N}_0$ is defined by

$$T_N(x) := \cos(N \arccos(x)), \qquad x \in [-1, 1]$$

and it is known to have roots in the form

$$\alpha_k = \cos(\pi(k + 1/2)/N), \qquad k = 0, \dots, N - 1.$$

Consequently, a shifted and scaled polynomial

$$P_N(t) = T_N \left(\left(\frac{-2}{\lambda_2 - \lambda_1} \right) \left(t - \frac{\lambda_1 + \lambda_2}{2} \right) \right) / C_N, \qquad t \in [\lambda_1, \lambda_2],$$

with the scaling factor $C_N = T_N \left(\frac{\lambda_1 + \lambda_2}{\lambda_2 - \lambda_1} \right)$ satisfies the condition $P_N(0) = 1$. It also has N distinct roots

$$\alpha_k = \frac{\lambda_1 + \lambda_2}{2} - \frac{\lambda_2 - \lambda_1}{2} \cos \left(\frac{\pi(k + 1/2)}{N} \right), \qquad k = 0, \dots, N - 1$$

lying in (λ_1, λ_2). This polynomial has the smallest maximum norm on $[\lambda_1, \lambda_2]$ over all polynomials of degree less or equal N which are equal to one at zero.

Two-Level Chebyshev Iteration. The cyclic two-level Chebyshev iterative methods to solve (1) is in the form

$$r^k = b - Ax^k,$$
$$x^{k+1} = x^k + \alpha_{k \pmod N}^{-1} r^k. \tag{6}$$

The method is convergent if all eigenvalues of A are contained in $[\lambda_1, \lambda_2] \subset (0, \infty)$. The optimal convergence is accessed where λ_1 is the minimal eigenvalue and λ_2 the maximal eigenvalue of A. Note that after N iterations we get

$$x^N - u = \Pi_{k=0}^{N-1}(I - \alpha_k^{-1}A)(x^0 - u) = P_N(A)(x^0 - u). \tag{7}$$

and then after ℓN iterations we get $x^{\ell N} - u = (P_N(A))^{\ell}(x^0 - u)$. Note that the Richardson iteration (5) is the special case of this method with $N = 1$. This error formula gives us,

$$\|x^N - u\|_2 \leq \sum_{t \in [\lambda_1, \lambda_2]} |P_N(t)| \|x^0 - u\|_2 \leq 2\left(\frac{\sqrt{\lambda_2} - \sqrt{\lambda_1}}{\sqrt{\lambda_2} + \sqrt{\lambda_1}}\right)^N \|x^0 - u\|_2.$$

A MATLAB version follows:

```
1   function x=Chebyshev2Level_e(A_e,bt_e,x0,ind_e,indt,iters,lam2,
        lam1,N,nd)
2   d=(lam2+lam1)/2;  c=(lam2−lam1)/2;
3   k=0:N−1;  alphas=d+c*cos(pi*(1/2+k)/N);
4   x=x0;                                   %iteration  initial
5   for  k=0:iters −1
6       r=residual_e(A_e,bt_e,x,ind_e,indt);   %residual  comput.
7       r(nd)=0;                              %dirichlet  condit.
8       alpha=alphas(mod(k,N)+1);
9       x=x+(1/alpha)*r;                      %iteration  update
10  end
11  end
```

Three-Level Chebyshev Iteration. We now present the three-level Chebyshev iteration, cf. e.g. [2,4], The method is defined by the error equation, cf. also (7),

$$x^k - u = P_k(A)(x^0 - u), \qquad k = 0, 1, 2, \ldots \tag{8}$$

and its implementation is based on the following recurrence relation

$$T_k(t) = 2t\, T_{k-1}(t) - T_{k-2}(t), \qquad k > 1, \qquad T_1(t) = t,\ T_0(t) = 1.$$

This relation for t_k yields the recurrence formula for $k > 1$,

$$P_{k+1}(x) = 2\frac{\lambda_1 + \lambda_2 - 2x}{\lambda_2 - \lambda_1}\frac{C_k}{C_{k+1}}P_k(x) - \frac{C_{k-1}}{C_{k+1}}P_{k-1}(x),$$

$$C_{k+1} = 2\frac{\lambda_1 + \lambda_2}{\lambda_2 - \lambda_1}C_k - C_{k-1}, \tag{9}$$

where

$$P_1(x) = C_1^{-1}\frac{\lambda_1 + \lambda_2 - 2x}{\lambda_2 - \lambda_1}, \qquad P_0 = 1, \qquad C_1 = \frac{\lambda_1 + \lambda_2}{\lambda_2 - \lambda_1}, \qquad C_0 = 1.$$

For $k = 1$ we get $x^1 - u = P_1(A)(x^0 - u)$ and

$$x^1 = u + \frac{\lambda_2 - \lambda_1}{\lambda_1 + \lambda_2}\frac{\lambda_1 + \lambda_2 - 2A}{\lambda_2 - \lambda_1}(x^0 - u) = x^0 + \frac{2}{\lambda_2 - \lambda_1}r_0,$$

where $r_0 = b - Ax^0$. Note that x^1 is computed as one iteration of the Richardson method applied to x^0 with the optimal coefficient, cf. (5). Our method is defined by (8), thus using the above recurrence relation we get for $k > 1$,

$$x^{k+1} - u = \frac{2C_k}{C_{k+1}} \left(\frac{\lambda_1 + \lambda_2}{\lambda_2 - \lambda_1} I - \frac{2}{\lambda_2 - \lambda_1} A \right) (x^k - u) - \frac{C_{k-1}}{C_{k+1}} (x^{k-1} - u).$$

Since

$$1 = 2 \frac{\lambda_1 + \lambda_2}{\lambda_2 - \lambda_1} \frac{C_k}{C_{k+1}} - \frac{C_{k-1}}{C_{k+1}}$$

we see that

$$x^{k+1} = \frac{2C_k}{C_{k+1}} \frac{\lambda_1 + \lambda_2}{\lambda_2 - \lambda_1} x^k + \frac{4}{\lambda_2 - \lambda_1} \frac{C_k}{C_{k+1}} (b - Ax^k) - \frac{C_{k-1}}{C_{k+1}} x^{k-1}$$

and utilizing this identity once more we have the three level Chebyshev iterations

$$x^{k+1} = x^k + \frac{C_{k-1}}{C_{k+1}} (x^k - x^{k-1}) + \frac{4}{\lambda_2 - \lambda_1} \frac{C_k}{C_{k+1}} r_k, \qquad k > 1, \qquad (10)$$

$$x^1 = x^0 + \frac{2}{\lambda_2 - \lambda_1} r_0$$

with $r_k = b - Ax^k$ $k = 0, 1, 2, \ldots$. We remind that the scaling factors C_k are defined by (9). Note that x^N in the both 2-level and 3-level iterations, cf. (6) and (10), are equal to each other what follows from (7) and (8). A MATLAB version reads:

```
1   function x=Chebyshev3Level_e(A_e,bt_e,x0,ind_e,indt,iters,lam2,
        lam1,nd)
2   d=(lam2+lam1)/2;  c=(lam2-lam1)/2;
3   x=x0;
4   r=residual_e(A_e,bt_e,x,ind_e,indt);        %residuum comput.
5   r(nd)=0;                                     %dirichlet condit.
6   for k = 0:iters-1
7       z=r;
8       if (k==0)
9           p=z;  alpha=1/d;
10      else
11          beta=(c*alpha/2)^2;
12          p=z+beta*p;  alpha=1/(d - beta/alpha);
13
14      end
15      x=x+alpha*p;
16      r=residual_e(A_e,bt_e,x,ind_e,indt);    %residuum comput.
17      r(nd)=0;                                 %dirichlet condit.
18  end
19  end
```

3   Numerical Experiments

We consider for simplicity the case of the square domain $\Omega = (0,1) \times (0,1)$, no mass matrix ($\nu = 0$) and nonhomogenous Dirichlet boundary conditions $u = 1$ for $x \in \partial\Omega$. For a uniformly refined triangular mesh (see Fig. 1) with n^2 nodes (also counting boundary nodes), there are $(n-2)^2$ eigenvalues of $A = K$ in the form

$$\lambda = 4\left(\sin^2\frac{i\pi}{2(n-1)} + \sin^2\frac{j\pi}{2(n-1)}\right), \quad i,j = 1,\dots,n-2$$

and the minimal eigenvalue λ_1 is obtained for $i = j = 1$ and the maximal eigenvalue λ_2 for $i = j = n - 2$. We utilize these eigenvalue bounds for all mentioned iterations methods. Furthermore, we assume a constant function $f = 1$ for $x \in \Omega$.

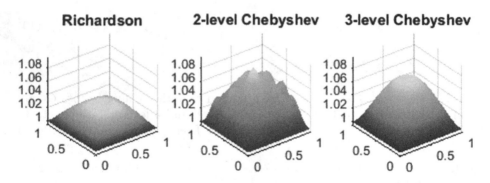

Fig. 3. Final iterates.

For a given number of iterations (we choose 124 iterations) and a (level 5) mesh with $1089 = 33^2$ nodes, final iterates are displayed in Fig. 3. Only the 3-level Chebyshev method converged optically to the exact solution. Richardson requires more steps to improve its convergence and the 2-level Chebyshev (with $N = 32$) demonstrates a known instability. The remedy to fix this instability would be to reorder values of precomputed parameters α_k to enhance the stability. Time performance is also reasonable for finer meshes. On a (level 10) mesh with $1050625 = 1025^2$ nodes, the assemblies of 3-dimensional arrays K_e, M_e take around 5 s each and 124 iterations take around 50 s for all iteration methods. The direct solver of MATLAB takes 5 s. Since number of iterations to obtain a convergence with respect to a given tolerance is known to grow as a function of condition number of finer meshes, we need to combine studied solvers with preconditioners or use several iterations of them as smoothers for instance in multigrid procedures.

Outlooks

We are interested in developing preconditioners for discussed solvers on multi-dimensional structures and extension to edge elements based on [1].

References

1. Anjam, I., Valdman, J.: Fast MATLAB assembly of FEM matrices in 2D and 3D: edge elements. Appl. Math. Computat. **267**, 252–263 (2015)
2. Hackbusch, W.: Iterative Solution of Large Sparse Systems of Equations. Applied Mathematical Sciences, vol. 95. Springer-Verlag, New York (1994). https://doi.org/10.1007/978-1-4612-4288-8. Translated and revised from the 1991 German original
3. Rahman, T., Valdman, J.: Fast MATLAB assembly of FEM matrices in 2D and 3D: nodal elements. Appl. Math. Computat. **219**, 7151–7158 (2013)
4. Samarskii, A.A., Nikolaev, E.S.: Numerical Methods for Grid Equations. Vol. II. Iterative Methods. Birkhäuser Verlag, Basel (1989). https://doi.org/10.1007/978-3-0348-9272-8. Translated from the Russian and with a note by Stephen G. Nash

The Approach to the Construction of Difference Schemes with a Consistent Approximation of the Stress-Strain State and the Energy Balance of the Medium in Cylindrical Geometry

Yury Poveshchenko[1], Vladimir Gasilov[1], Viktoriia Podryga[1,2(✉)], and Yulia Sharova[1]

[1] Keldysh Institute of Applied Mathematics, 4 Miusskaya Sq., Moscow 125047, Russia
hecon@mail.ru, vgasilov@yandex.ru, pvictoria@list.ru, yulia-shar@mail.ru
[2] Moscow Automobile and Road Construction State Technical University (MADI), 64 Leningradsky Prospect, 125319 Moscow, Russia

Abstract. In the paper, on unstructured metric grids of the theory of the support operator method, on the topological and geometric structure of which minimal reasonable restrictions are imposed, applicable to the symmetricized displacement tensor $t_{\mathbf{u}}$, discrete analogs of self-adjoint and sign-definite operations $\mathrm{div}(t_{\mathbf{u}})$ and $\mathrm{div}(\mathrm{tr}(t_{\mathbf{u}})\delta)$ which are invariants to solid rotations, were obtained for modeling of force fields of elastic processes, as well as approximation of integrals of the form $\int_{\Omega} \mathrm{tr}\left(t_{\mathbf{u}}^2\right) dV$ and $\int_{\Omega} \mathrm{tr}^2\left(t_{\mathbf{u}}\right) dV$, sufficient to simulate elastic-dependent energy balances of the medium taking into account the curvature of space of the cylindrical geometry of the system.

Keywords: Difference schemes · Support operator method · Theory of elasticity · Cylindrical geometry

1 Introduction

The present work concerns with the construction and investigation of difference schemes obtained by the support operators method on unstructured grids [1–6]. Difference approximations are constructed for the nonstationary system of equations of the elasticity theory, which takes into account the description of the balance between the elastic and internal energies of the medium [7]. For the construction of integrally consistent approximations of the equations of balance of the momentum and energy of the elastic medium, the support operator method is applied [8]. We consider the case of axial symmetric deformations, the description of the corresponding processes is performed in the cylindrical (r, z) geometry.

© Springer Nature Switzerland AG 2020
I. Lirkov and S. Margenov (Eds.): LSSC 2019, LNCS 11958, pp. 610–617, 2020.
https://doi.org/10.1007/978-3-030-41032-2_70

The discrete problem with axial symmetry was considered as three-dimensional with tensor objects, where in a certain way the grid functions were dependent only on variables (r, z) and did not depend on azimuthal rotation. This approach provided the divergence, self-adjointness and sign-definiteness of approximations of the operations $\text{div}(t_{\mathbf{u}})$ and $\text{div}(\text{tr}(t_{\mathbf{u}})\delta)$ both in 3d constructions and at the limiting transition $\theta \to 0$ and allowed us to use these properties in their two-dimensional (r, z) analogues. We note that the disclosure of uncertainties when using the limiting transition $\theta \to 0$ in the differential rotation (taking into account the azimuthal symmetry of tensor-dyadic objects) led to the appearance of a "curvature" of space in discrete analysis operations of the 2d problem associated with terms of the form u_r/r^2 and u_r/r in the corresponding representations of grid operations.

On the basis of the energy balance of the medium, families of integrally consistent approximations of vector analysis operations are constructed that are sufficient for discrete modeling of these processes taking into account the curvature of the space caused by the cylindrical geometry of the system.

On (r, z) unstructured grids by differential rotation in the azimuthal coordinate θ, the difference schemes of the method of support operators for the equations of the theory of elasticity in displacements are constructed and investigated. The approximations considered preserve the properties of divergence, self-adjointness and sign-definiteness of differential operators, and also are applicable to the solution of non-stationary problems of hydrodynamics with allowance for elastic processes [9, 10].

2   Formulation of the Problem

We consider the equations of the theory of elasticity in displacements [7] in the spatial domain $\hat{I}$ with the boundary $\partial \hat{I}$:

$$\text{div } X_{\mathbf{u}} = \mathbf{f}(\mathbf{r}), \quad X_{\mathbf{u}} = 2\mu\, t_{\mathbf{u}} + \nu\, \text{tr}(t_{\mathbf{u}})\, \delta, \quad t_{\mathbf{u}} = \frac{1}{2}\left(\frac{d\mathbf{u}}{d\mathbf{r}} + \nabla \mathbf{u}\right)$$

(with some boundary conditions) and with the corresponding integral relation

$$\int_O \text{tr}\left(\nabla \mathbf{u} X^T\right) dV + \int_O \mathbf{u}\, \text{div} X dV = \int_{\partial O} (X\mathbf{u}, d\mathbf{s}),$$

$$\text{tr}\left(\nabla \mathbf{u} X^T\right) = \text{tr}\left(\frac{d\mathbf{u}}{d\mathbf{r}} X\right) = \text{tr}\left(t_{\mathbf{u}} X\right)|_{X=X^T}.$$

Here $\mathbf{u}$ is the displacement vector, X is arbitrary tensor, $X_{\mathbf{u}}$ is stress tensor, $\mathbf{f}(\mathbf{r})$ is volume density of external forces at a spatial point $\mathbf{r}$, $\mu > 0$ and $\nu \geq 0$ are Lamé parameters, δ is metric tensor. The tr ( ) symbol means the trace of the tensor, and the index T means the transposition.

The contribution to the balance of the internal energy of the modeled medium associated with deformation processes (or their part, for example, only the shear deformation) is $E = E\left(\text{tr}\left(t_{\mathbf{u}}^2\right), \text{tr}^2\left(t_{\mathbf{u}}\right)\right)$. In addition, the change in this energy

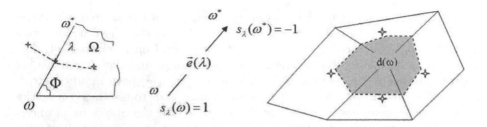

Fig. 1. Construction of 2d bases in (r, z) planes.

component E is associated with the dissipative function $d = \mathrm{tr}\,(X_{\mathbf{u}}\,t_{\mathbf{v}})$, where $X_{\mathbf{u}}$ is stress tensor (or its shear part) determined by displacements $\mathbf{u}$ in the medium, and $t_{\mathbf{v}}$ is symmetrized tensor of strain velocities, determined by the velocity field $\mathbf{v}$ of the moving medium.

Thus, to model the described elastic processes in a continuous medium (as well as more complex ones, for example, taking into account its plasticity), it suffices to build divergent, self-adjoint and sign-definite difference analogues of tensor operations of vector analysis $\mathrm{div}\,t_{\mathbf{u}}$ and $\mathrm{div}\,(\mathrm{tr}\,(t_{\mathbf{u}})\,\delta)$, for modeling the force fields of elastic processes.

To model the strain energies E and the dissipative functions d, which change the strain energies, the approximation of the integrals $\left(\int_{\Omega} \mathrm{tr}\,(t_{\mathbf{u}}t_{\mathbf{v}})\,dV\right)_{\underline{\Delta}}$ and $\left(\int_{\Omega} \mathrm{tr}\,(t_{\mathbf{u}})\,\mathrm{tr}\,(t_{\mathbf{v}})\,dV\right)_{\underline{\Delta}}$ on grid cells Ω is necessary. The further presentation of the work is devoted to this goal.

3   Metric Meshes of the Support Operators Method in Cylindrical Geometry

We consider problems with axial symmetry as three-dimensional, where the grid functions depend only on variables (r, z) and do not depend on the azimuthal coordinate θ. In the undeformed state, an elastic body takes a three-dimensional region O with a boundary ∂O. The region O is the result of rotation around the symmetry axis z of the two-dimensional (r, z) region. In a two-dimensional region, an unstructured grid is constructed on the (r, z) plane (see Figs. 1 and 2). This grid consists of two-dimensional cells (Ω), nodes (ω), as well as two-dimensional bases (Φ) and edges (λ) forming them. The corresponding node balanced domain $d(\omega)$ (see Fig. 1) is formed by a broken line connecting the center of the edges in the area of the node ω, the centers of gravity of triangular cells or the arithmetic mean of the radius vectors of the vertices of quadrilateral cells. We construct the grid in the three-dimensional region O by successive rotations of the two-dimensional grid around the axis of symmetry z at a "small" angle θ. The "thin" in the azimuthal direction bodies, which are "swept" by such a rotation with flat cells, we also call cells, but already three-dimensional and mark as (Ω). In this case, three-dimensional bases (φ) are formed from two-dimensional bases (Φ) (consisting of edges (λ)) by adding the "azimuthal" edge

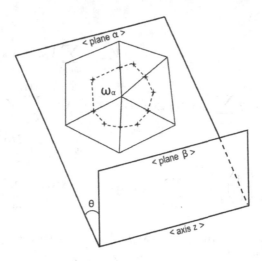

Fig. 2. Cylindrical geometry.

λ_θ of a three-dimensional cell Ω. In Fig. 2 the unit vectors $\mathbf{e}\,(\lambda_\theta)$ connect nodes ω_α and ω_β of neighboring (r, z) planes α and β in the direction of azimuthal rotation. The two-dimensional domains $d(\omega)$ around the nodes ω (see Fig. 1) form a three-dimensional balanced domain $d(\omega_\alpha, \omega_\beta)$ (see Fig. 2). Thus, the three-dimensional grid fills the entire three-dimensional area. Its cells (Ω) have the size of θ (in radians) on the azimuthal variable. Nodes (ω) are not on the z axis. It follows from the above that for a grid function $\mathbf{u} = \{u_r, u_z, u_\theta = 0\,\}$ defined in nodes (ω), we can write $u = u_r \mathbf{e}_r + u_z \mathbf{e}_z + 0 \cdot \mathbf{e}_\theta$. Here $\mathbf{e}_r$, $\mathbf{e}_z$ and $\mathbf{e}_\theta$ are the radial, axial and azimuthal unit vectors for the (r, z) plane.

4 Summary of the Formulas of the Support Operator Method for the Equation of the Theory of Elasticity in Cylindrical Geometry

We present a summary of the basic formulas of the support operator method [11, 12] obtained for approximation of the force fields of elastic processes using operations div $(t_\mathbf{u})$ and div $(\mathrm{tr}\,(t_\mathbf{u})\,\delta)$, as well as the corresponding deformation energies and dissipative functions changing these energies in the form of the integrals $\int_\Omega \mathrm{tr}(t_\mathbf{u} t_\mathbf{v}) dV$ and $\int_\Omega \mathrm{tr}(t_\mathbf{u})\,\mathrm{tr}(t_\mathbf{v}) dV$ on grid cells in cylindrical geometry.

$$\left(\int_{d(\omega_\alpha, \omega_\beta)} \mathrm{div}\,(t_\mathbf{u})\,dV \right)\Bigg|_{\triangle|_{\theta \to 0}} = \mathrm{DIN}\,\{t_{\triangle \mathbf{u}\varphi}\}\Bigg|_{\theta \to 0} =$$
$$= \theta \cdot \left[\mathrm{DIN}_2\,\{t_{\triangle \mathbf{u}\Phi}\} - \frac{u_r}{r^2} \mathbf{e}_r V_{2\omega} \right],$$

$$V_{2\omega} = \sum_{\Phi(\omega)} V_\Phi, \quad V_\Phi = S_\Phi \cdot r_{\Omega \supset \Phi};$$

$$\mathrm{DIN}_2 X = \sum_{\lambda(\omega)} s_\lambda(\omega)\, \tau_{2X}(\lambda), \quad \tau_{2X}(\lambda) = \sum_{\Phi(\lambda)}^{\{2|4\}} V_\Phi\,(e'_\Phi(\lambda), X_\Phi),$$

$$t_{\varDelta u \Phi} = \frac{1}{2}\left(\left(\frac{D\mathbf{u}}{D\mathbf{r}}\right)_\Phi + \nabla u_\Phi \right),$$

$$\left(\frac{D\mathbf{u}}{D\mathbf{r}}\right)_\Phi = \sum_{\lambda(\Phi)} \varDelta_\lambda \mathbf{u} \cdot e'_\Phi(\lambda), \quad \nabla u_\Phi = \sum_{\lambda(\Phi)} e'_\Phi(\lambda) \cdot \varDelta_\lambda \mathbf{u};$$

$$\left(\int_{d(\omega_\alpha, \omega_\beta)} \mathrm{div}\,(\mathrm{tr}\,(t_\mathbf{u})\,\delta)\,dV \right)\Bigg|_{\varDelta}\Bigg|_{\theta \to 0} = \mathrm{DIN}\,\{\mathrm{tr}\,(t_{\varDelta u \varphi})\,\delta\}\Bigg|_{\theta \to 0}$$

$$= \theta \left\{ \mathrm{DIN}_2 \left\{ \left[\mathrm{tr}\,(t_{\varDelta u \Phi}) + \frac{u_r}{r}\right]\delta \right\} - \mathbf{e}_r \left\{ \frac{1}{r}\sum_{\Phi(\omega)} V_\Phi\,\mathrm{tr}\,(t_{\varDelta u \Phi}) + \frac{u_r}{r^2}V_{2\omega} \right\}\right\};$$

$$\left(\int_\Omega \mathrm{tr}\,(t_\mathbf{u} t_\mathbf{v})\,dV \right)\Bigg|_{\varDelta}\Bigg|_{\theta \to 0} = \theta r_\Omega \sum_{\Phi(\Omega)} \left[\mathrm{tr}\,(t_{\varDelta u \Phi} t_{\varDelta v \Phi}) + \frac{u_r v_r}{r^2}\right] S_\Phi,$$

$$\left(\int_\Omega \mathrm{tr}\,(t_\mathbf{u})\,\mathrm{tr}\,(t_\mathbf{v})\,dV \right)\Bigg|_{\varDelta}\Bigg|_{\theta \to 0} = \theta r_\Omega \sum_{\Phi(\Omega)} \left[\mathrm{DIV}_2 \mathbf{u} + \frac{u_r}{r}\right]\left[\mathrm{DIV}_2 \mathbf{v} + \frac{v_r}{r}\right] S_\Phi,$$

$$\mathrm{DIV}_2 \mathbf{u} = \mathrm{tr}\,(t_{\varDelta u \Phi}) = \sum_{\lambda(\Phi)} (\varDelta_\lambda \mathbf{u}, e'_\Phi(\lambda)).$$

Here, the edges λ have a positive direction (see Fig. 1) and the grid function $\varDelta_\lambda \mathbf{u} = -\sum_{\omega(\lambda)} s_\lambda(\omega)\,\mathbf{u}_\omega = \mathbf{u}_{\omega'} - \mathbf{u}_\omega$ applies to them. Two-dimensional (r, z) grid tensor fields X are defined by their representations in bases X_Φ. $e'_\Phi(\lambda)$ are unit vectors of basis mutual to the original two-dimensional basis Φ, consisting of edges λ (see Fig. 1). In the designation $\{2|4\}$, the digit 2 corresponds to the number of summable bases $\Phi(\lambda)$ for the boundary edge λ in the (r, z) plane, and the digit 4 corresponds to the internal edge λ. S_Φ is two-dimensional basis volume (area), $S_\Phi = \frac{1}{6}|\mathbf{e}(\lambda_1) \times \mathbf{e}(\lambda_2)|$ is for a triangular cell Ω containing a basis Φ, and $S_\Phi = \frac{1}{4}|\mathbf{e}(\lambda_1) \times \mathbf{e}(\lambda_2)|$ is for quadrangular cell, if $\lambda_1(\Phi)$ and $\lambda_2(\Phi)$ are the edges forming a basis Φ. $r_{\Omega \supset \Phi}$ is the distance from the Z axis to the center of gravity of the cell Ω.

5   Calculation Results

To study the homogeneous finite-difference approximation of elastic forces in the framework of solving the coupled problems of hydrodynamics and elasticity [9] in the case when the substance remains in the solid state, the sound wave propagation in cylindrical and flat aluminum plates was modeled. Sound waves occur upon impact, followed by plate oscillations due to shear deformations.

The formulation of this problem is described in detail in [9]. On the right boundary in the plane case and on the axis in (r, z) geometry, the condition of reflection was set, while on the other boundaries the absence of external forces was specified.

Figure 3 shows the spatial density distributions in cylindrical and flat aluminum plates for times 2, 4, 6, 8, 10 µs. The obtained results are in qualitative agreement for various geometries.

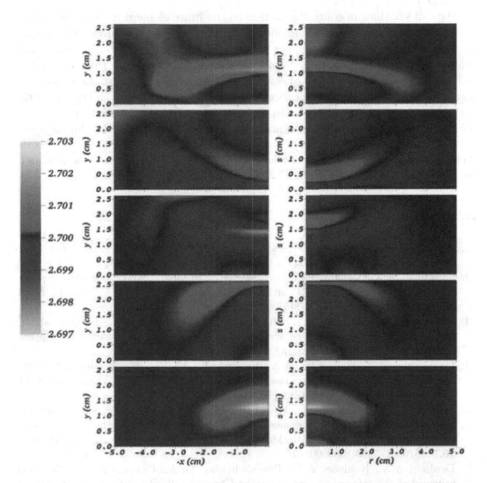

Fig. 3. Density distribution at moments 2, 4, 6, 8, 10 µs (bottom to top): (x, y) geometry is shown on the left; (r, z) geometry is shown on the right.

6   Conclusion

In this paper, discrete analogs of self-adjoint and sign-definite operations and differential operators div (t_u), div $(\text{tr}\,(t_u)\,\delta)$ [8, 10–12] were built for modeling the force fields of elastic processes and the approximations of integrals $\int_\Omega \text{tr}\,\left(t_u^2\right) dV$, $\int_\Omega \text{tr}^2\,(t_u)\ dV$, sufficient to model the elastic–dependent energy balance of the medium, taking into account the curvature of the space of the cylindrical geometry of the system were built. These constructions are applicable for coupled calculations of hydrodynamic and elastic-wave processes, including when the phase state of a material changes under the action of an energy flow of sufficient power [9, 12].

We can say that, in contradistinction to the finite element method, described difference constructions do not explicitly use continuous basis functions, and the integrals computed in each element are replaced by finite difference expressions that significantly reduces the computation time. We also note that, as applied to the equations of the theory of elasticity, the schemes of the support operator method have the property of rotational neutrality [10]. It lies in the fact that the elastic force and energy characteristics of such systems are invariant not only to parallel transfer, but also to instantaneous solid-state rotations of the medium.

Acknowledgments. The work was funded by Russian Foundation for Basic Research, projects no. 16-29-15081-ofi_m, 18-37-20062-mol_a_ved, 18-07-00841-a.

References

1. Samarskii, A.A., Tishkin, V.F., Favorsky, A.P., Shashkov, M.Yu.: Operator difference schemes. Differ. Equ. **17**(7), 1317–1327 (1981). (in Russian)
2. Samarskii, A.A., Tishkin, V.F., Favorsky, A.P., Shashkov, M.Yu.: On the representation of difference schemes of mathematical physics in operator form. Dokl. Akad. Nauk SSSR (DAN SSSR) **258**(5), 1092–1096 (1981). (in Russian)
3. Korshiya, T.K., Tishkin, V.F., Samarskii, A.A., Favorsky, A.P., Shashkov, M.Yu.: Variational-operator difference schemes for equations of mathematical physics, Tbilisi, TGU (1983). (in Russian)
4. Goloviznin, V.M., Samarskii, A.A., Favorsky, A.P.: Variational approach to the construction of finite-difference models in hydrodynamics. Dokl. Akad. Nauk SSSR (DAN SSSR) **235**(6), 1285–1288 (1977). (in Russian)
5. Denisov, A.A., Koldoba, A.V., Poveshchenko, Yu.A.: The convergence to generalized solutions of difference schemes of the reference-operator method for Poisson's equation. USSR Comput. Math. Math. Phys. **29**(2), 32–38 (1989). https://doi.org/10.1016/0041-5553(89)90005-0
6. Denisov, A.A., Koldoba, A.V., Poveshchenko, Yu.A.: Convergence of difference schemes of the reference-operator method to generalized solutions of the axisymmetric Poisson equation. USSR Comput. Math. Math. Phys. **30**(5), 140–147 (1990). https://doi.org/10.1016/0041-5553(90)90172-0
7. Landau, L.D., Lifshitz, E.M.: Course of Theoretical Physics, vol. 7, 3rd edn. Butterworth-Heinemann, Oxford (1987)

8. Samarskii, A.A., Koldoba, A.V., Poveshchenko, Yu.A., Tishkin, V.F., Favorsky, A.P.: Difference Schemes on Unstructured Grids. Kriterii, Minsk (1996). (in Russian)

9. Gasilov, V.A., Krukovsky, A.Yu., Poveshchenko, Yu.A., Tsygvintsev, I.P.: Homogeneous difference schemes for solving coupled problems of hydrodynamics and elasticity. Preprinty IPM im. Keldysha, M.V. [KIAM Preprints], vol. 13 (2018). https://doi.org/10.20948/prepr-2018-13. (in Russian)

10. Koldoba, A.V., Poveshchenko, Yu.A., Gasilova, I.V., Dorofeeva, E.Yu.: Numerical schemes of the support operators method for elasticity theory equations. Matematicheskoe Modelirovanie **24**(12), 86–96 (2012). (in Russian)

11. Poveshchenko, Yu.A., Gasilov, V.A., Ladonkina, M.E., Podryga, V.O., Nasekin I.S.: Difference schemes of support operator method for equations of the theory of elasticity in cylindrical geometry. Preprinty IPM im. Keldysha, M.V. [KIAM Preprints], vol. 142 (2018). https://doi.org/10.20948/prepr-2018-142. (in Russian)

12. Poveshchenko, Yu.A., Krukovsky, A.Yu., Podryga, V.O., Golovchenko, E.N.: Difference schemes of support operator method for equations of elasticity with azimuthal rotation. Preprinty IPM im. Keldysha, M.V. [KIAM Preprints], vol. 10 (2019). https://doi.org/10.20948/prepr-2019-10. (in Russian)

Two-Layer Completely Conservative Difference Scheme of Gas Dynamics in Eulerian Variables with Adaptive Regularization of Solution

Orkhan Rahimly[1], Viktoriia Podryga[1,2(✉)], Yury Poveshchenko[1], Parvin Rahimly[1], and Yulia Sharova[1]

[1] Keldysh Institute of Applied Mathematics of RAS, 4 Miusskya sq., 125047 Moscow, Russia
{orxan,pervin}@rehimli.info, pvictoria@list.ru, hecon@mail.ru, yulia-shar@mail.ru
[2] Moscow Automobile and Road Construction State Technical University, 64 Leningradsky Prospect, 125319 Moscow, Russia

Abstract. For the equations of gas dynamics in Euler variables, a family of two-layer in time completely conservative difference schemes profiled on the space with time weights is constructed. The effective conservation of internal energy in this type of divergent difference schemes is ensured by the absence of constantly operating sources of difference origin in the internal energy equation, producing "computational" entropy (including singularities of the solution). Considerable attention in this work is paid to the methods of constructing regularizing mass, momentum and internal energy flows that do not violate the properties of complete conservatism of difference schemes of this class, to the analysis of their amplitude and admissibility of adaptive use on variable structure grids in space and on implicit layers in time. The developed type of difference schemes can be used to calculate multi-temperature processes (electron and ion temperatures), where for the available number of variables, a single balance equation for the total energy of the medium is not enough.

Keywords: Completely conservative difference scheme · Support operator method · Gas dynamics

1 Introduction

The construction of a gas-dynamic difference scheme usually begins with the representation of a system of original equations in the form of mass, momentum, and total energy balances. Analysis of the corresponding systems of difference equations shows that in this case non-physical effects occur, leading to disruption of the balance of internal and kinetic energy. As a result of these studies, the principle of complete conservatism was formulated, according to which the difference scheme of gas dynamics should be built taking into account balances for

© Springer Nature Switzerland AG 2020
I. Lirkov and S. Margenov (Eds.): LSSC 2019, LNCS 11958, pp. 618–625, 2020.
https://doi.org/10.1007/978-3-030-41032-2_71

all types of energy - full, kinetic and internal [1,2]. The problem of constructing two-layer in time difference schemes satisfying the principle of complete conservatism was solved in [1] for the Lagrangian description of the motion of the medium. Certain difficulties arise when trying to construct such schemes for the equations of gas dynamics in Eulerian variables. In [3], a very wide family of two-layer difference schemes was considered and it was shown that it does not contain a completely conservative difference scheme (CCDS). New approaches were required. This work is a natural extension of [4–7], in which integral-matched (balanced) schemes were constructed using the support operator method. The system of equations of gas dynamics in a one-dimensional approximation is considered. The approximation of mass, momentum, and internal energy fluxes, satisfying the principle of complete conservatism, is also performed by means of a universal operator approach. A feature of the proposed two-layer scheme is the interpolation in time of the velocity of a substance, which is performed with weighted multipliers that depend on the mass of the knotted grid volumes. A regularization of the mass, momentum, and internal energy fluxes of the system is proposed, which gives the quasi-monotonicity property of difference schemes of this class, and at the same time does not violate the property of complete conservatism by adaptive artificial viscosity, following the results and recommendations of paper [8]. The amplitudes of regularized fluxes on the explicit and implicit layers in time are investigated.

2   Formulation of the Problem

The flow of a compressible medium is considered in Eulerian variables, in the Cartesian coordinate system. We denote the flow velocity by $\boldsymbol{u}$. The mass flux density is denoted by $\boldsymbol{\mu} = \rho \cdot \boldsymbol{u}$ (ρ is the density of the medium). For the basis of our constructions we take the system of "balance" equations, which follow from the Euler equations [2]:

$$\frac{D}{Dt}\left(dM\right) = -dV\,div\boldsymbol{\mu},$$

$$\frac{D}{Dt}\left(\boldsymbol{u}dM\right) = -dV\,gradP - dV\,div\left(\boldsymbol{\mu}\cdot\boldsymbol{u}\right),$$

$$\frac{D}{Dt}\left(\varepsilon dM\right) = -PdV\,div\boldsymbol{u} - dV\,div\left(\boldsymbol{\mu}\varepsilon\right) + dQ,$$

$$\frac{D}{Dt}\left(\frac{\boldsymbol{u}^2}{2}dM\right) = -\boldsymbol{u}dV\,gradP - dV\,div\left(\boldsymbol{\mu}\frac{\boldsymbol{u}^2}{2}\right),$$

$$\frac{D}{Dt}\left(\left(\varepsilon + \frac{\boldsymbol{u}^2}{2}\right)dM\right) = -dV\,div(P\boldsymbol{u}) - dV\,div\left(\boldsymbol{\mu}\left(\varepsilon + \frac{\boldsymbol{u}^2}{2}\right)\right) + dQ$$

Here thermodynamic variables are used: ρ is the gas density, P is the pressure, ε is the specific internal energy. The traditional model of the medium and the corresponding designations [4] are adopted: a particle with mass dM is enclosed in a volume dV through the boundaries of which the mass flux $\boldsymbol{\mu}$, carrying momentum $\boldsymbol{\mu}\cdot\boldsymbol{u}$ and internal energy $\boldsymbol{\mu}\varepsilon$ is flowing. Here the term dQ characterizes

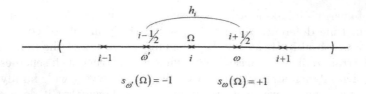

Fig. 1. Difference grid

internal energy released by an external source in a volume element per unit of time. For practical calculations, the system must be supplemented with some kind of gas state equation, for example, connecting pressure with density and internal energy.

3   Two-Layer Time Difference Scheme in Euler Variables

Fig. 1 shows the difference grid, where ω are the nodes of the difference grid, Ω are its cells. Thermodynamic quantities ρ, P, ε, as well as the volume of the cell V and its mass $M = \rho V$ will be related to the cells Ω. Velocity $\boldsymbol{u}$, mass m and volume v will be referred to nodes ω.

If for the cell Ω its direction of the outer normal in the node ω is positive, then the sign function $s_\omega(\Omega) = +1$, respectively, with a negative direction of the outer normal to the same cell Ω in the node ω', we have $s_{\omega'}(\Omega) = -1$.

It is clear that:

$$m_\omega = \frac{1}{2} \sum_{\Omega(\omega)} M_\Omega, \quad v_\omega = \frac{1}{2} \sum_{\Omega(\omega)} V_\Omega, \quad \mu_D = \frac{1}{2} \sum_{\omega(\Omega)} \mu_\omega.$$

Here μ_ω and μ_D are matched nodal and cellular mass fluxes. Let's introduce vector analysis operations $DIV : (\omega) \to (\Omega)$, that $DIV\boldsymbol{u} = \frac{1}{V}\sum_{\omega(\Omega)} s_\omega(\Omega)$ $u(\omega)$ and $GRAD : (\Omega) \to (\omega)$, that $GRAD\, P = \frac{\Delta P}{v}$, where

$$\Delta P = -\sum_{\Omega(\omega)} s_\omega(\Omega)P_\Omega + S_{\partial\omega}P_{\partial\omega}, \tag{1}$$

and also vector operations for approximating transfer processes $DIV_D : (\Omega) \to (\omega)$

$$DIV_D\, \boldsymbol{\mu}_D = -\frac{1}{v} \sum_{\Omega(\omega)} s_\omega(\Omega)\, \mu_D(\Omega) \tag{2}$$

for the balanced domain (connecting the centers of the cells around the node ω).

Also under dyad divergence $DIT_D : (\Omega) \to (\omega)$ we will understand:

$$DIT_D\, (\boldsymbol{\mu}_D \cdot \boldsymbol{u}_D) = -\frac{1}{v} \sum_{\Omega(\omega)} s_\omega(\Omega)\, \mu_D(\Omega)\, \boldsymbol{u}_D(\Omega). \tag{3}$$

In (1), if the node $\omega = \partial\omega$ is a boundary node, it is added the term of the magnitude $P_{\partial\omega}$ on the border and of the sign function $S_{\partial\omega} = \pm 1$ depending on the direction of the boundary normal.

On time layers t and $\hat{t} = t + \tau$ ($\tau > 0$ is time step), we introduce difference time derivatives and spatial-point (i.e., at grid nodes ω) time interpolations:

$$a_t = (\hat{a} - a)/\tau, \quad a^{(\delta)} = \delta\, \hat{a} + (1 - \delta)\, a.$$

Here the interpolation weight δ may depend on the node of the spatial grid ω, for example, according to the law:

$$\delta = \sqrt{\hat{m}}/(\sqrt{\hat{m}} + \sqrt{m}).$$

Also, by arbitrary time interpolation of the grid functions a, $\hat{a}$ between the layers t and $\hat{t}$ we will understand some grid value $a^\sim$.

Similarly to [4,5], we write out a two-layer completely conservative difference scheme (CCDS) in Euler variables:

$$m_t = -v\, DIV_D\, \boldsymbol{\mu}_D^\sim, \tag{4}$$

$$(m\,u)_t = -v\, GRAD\, P^\sim - v\, DIT_D\, (\boldsymbol{\mu}_D^\sim \cdot u_D^\sim), \tag{5}$$

$$(M\,\varepsilon)_t = -P^\sim\, V\, DIV\, u^\sim - V\, DIV\, [(\rho\varepsilon u)_\omega^\sim\,], \tag{6}$$

$$\left(m\, \frac{u^2}{2}\right)_t = -v\, (u^\sim\,,\, GRAD\, P^\sim\,) - v\, DIV_D\left(\boldsymbol{\mu}_D^\sim\, \frac{u_D^{2\,\sim}}{2}\right). \tag{7}$$

Here in the cell formed by the nodes ω and ω', the values are entered:

$$\boldsymbol{u}_D^\sim = \frac{1}{2}(\boldsymbol{u}_\omega^{(\delta_\omega)} + \boldsymbol{u}_{\omega'}^{(\delta_{\omega'})}), \quad \boldsymbol{u}_D^{2\,\sim} = (\boldsymbol{u}_\omega^{(\delta_\omega)},\, \boldsymbol{u}_{\omega'}^{(\delta_{\omega'})}).$$

Further, by $\boldsymbol{u}^\sim$ we will understand $\boldsymbol{u}^\sim = \boldsymbol{u}^{(\delta)}$. By $(\rho\varepsilon u)_\omega$ some approximation of the flux of internal energy in a node is understood.

4   Artificial Viscosity for Completely Conservative Difference Schemes in Euler Variables

4.1   Regularization of the Continuity Equation

We write the equation of continuity in the cell:

$$\frac{\hat{\rho}_i - \rho_i}{\tau} + \frac{\mu_{i+1/2}^\sim - \mu_{i-1/2}^\sim}{h_i} = 0, \tag{8}$$

from which (4) follows, where:

$$\boldsymbol{\mu}_D^\sim = \frac{1}{2}\sum_{\omega(\Omega)} \boldsymbol{\mu}^\sim(\omega), \quad \boldsymbol{\mu}^\sim(\omega) = \frac{1}{2}(\hat{\boldsymbol{\mu}}(\omega) + \boldsymbol{\mu}(\omega)).$$

Further, the mass flux density will be understood as

$$\mu(\omega) = u_\omega \rho_\omega - (\eta\, GRAD\, \rho)_\omega = \mu_{i+1/2}, \tag{9}$$

where $-\eta\, GRAD\, \rho$ is adaptive artificial viscosity, $\rho_\omega = \frac{1}{2}\sum_{\Omega(\omega)} \rho_\Omega$. For the spatial steps of the grid, we introduce the notation:

$$V_\Omega = h_\Omega = h_i, \quad v_\omega = h_\omega = \frac{1}{2}\sum_{\Omega(\omega)} h_\Omega = \frac{h_i + h_{i+1}}{2} = h_{i+1/2}.$$

Then $\mu_{i+1/2} = 0.5u_{i+1/2}(\rho_i + \rho_{i+1}) - (\frac{\eta}{h})_{i+1/2}(\rho_{i+1} - \rho_i)$

When choosing a viscosity $\hat{\eta}$, we apply the method of "freezing" the variables used in [8], namely, in (8) we make the assumption that the components of the grid velocity vector are constant $\hat{u}_{i-1/2} = \hat{u}_{i+1/2} = \hat{u} = const$. Also on a explicit time layer when choosing the viscosity η we "freeze" $u_{i-1/2} = u_{i+1/2} = u = const$. We will assume that the following estimates are performed:

$$|\hat{u}| < \left(\frac{\hat{\eta}}{h}\right)_{i\pm1/2}, \quad |u| < \left(\frac{\eta}{h}\right)_{i\pm1/2}, \quad \frac{1}{2}\left[(\eta/h)_{i-1/2} + (\eta/h)_{i+1/2}\right] < \frac{h_i}{\tau}. \tag{10}$$

The following theorems are proved in [9].

Theorem 4.1-1. *For two-layer in time CCDS* (4) - (7) *in Eulerian variables, the regularization of mass fluxes with adaptive viscosity in the form of* (9) *for the continuity equation does not violate the properties of complete conservatism of this family of difference schemes.*

Theorem 4.1-2. *When choosing adaptive viscosity* $(\eta/h)_{i\pm1/2}$ *for the continuity equation in the form* (8) *with zero homogeneous boundary conditions on the density* ρ *in the boundary cells* Ω *and with the "frozen" velocity* $u_{i-1/2} = u_{i+1/2} = u = const$ *at the cell boundaries of the spatial grid* Ω_i *on the explicit and implicit layers in time, as well as fulfilment of the conditions* (10) *on the uniform spatial grid the following estimation is performed:* $\|\hat{\rho}\|_c \leq \|\rho\|_c$.

4.2   Regularization of the Momentum Flux

Let's transform the momentum Eq. (5) in the node ω. Previously denote

$$m_\omega = \frac{1}{2}\sum_{\Omega(\omega)} \rho_\Omega V_\Omega = \frac{\rho_i\, h_i + \rho_{i+1}\, h_{i+1}}{2} = m_{i+1/2}.$$

From (1) it follows $\Delta P^\sim = P^\sim_{i+1} - P^\sim_i$, and from (3) it follows:

$$v\, DIT_D\,(\boldsymbol{\mu}_D \cdot u_D) = \mu_{Di+1}\, u_{Di+1} - \mu_{Di}\, u_{Di}.$$

Introducing momentum $I = mu$ in the node ω of the difference grid for (5) we have

$$I_t = -\Delta P^\sim - v\, DIT_D\,(\boldsymbol{\mu}_{\tilde{D}} \cdot u_{\tilde{D}}). \tag{11}$$

As an additive to the pressure P_Ω, given in the cells Ω, we will use the linear von Neumann-Richtmyer artificial viscosity $-(\eta_u\,DIV\,\boldsymbol{u})_\Omega$ in adaptive form [8] so that by the value $P^\sim$ in (11) we will understand

$$P_\Omega^{\widetilde{}} = P_i^{\widetilde{}} = [P_i - (\eta_u\,DIV\,\boldsymbol{u})_i]^{(0.5)} = [P_i - (\eta_u/h)_i\,(u_{i+1/2} - u_{i-1/2})]^{(0.5)}. \tag{12}$$

On explicit and implicit layers of time, when choosing the viscosity η_u, the mass flux density in the cells is "frozen" $\mu_{\widetilde{D}\,i} = \mu_{\widetilde{D}\,i+1} = \mu_D = const$. Also, the node masses that are not included in the node momentum $I = mu$ are "frozen" $m_{i-1/2} = m_{i+1/2} = m_{i+3/2} = m = const$. Then from (11) we obtain

$$(I_{i+1/2})_t = \frac{1}{m}\,\left[(\eta_u/h)_{i+1}\,(I_{i+3/2} - I_{i+1/2}) - (\eta_u/h)_i\,(I_{i+1/2} - I_{i-1/2})\right]^{(0.5)}$$
$$-\frac{\mu_D}{2m}\,\left[(I_{i+3/2} - I_{i-1/2})\right]^{(0.5)} = 0. \tag{13}$$

The value $-(\Delta P)_{i+1/2}^{(0.5)}$ on the right side of the Eq. (11) is not used when calculating viscosity η_u. Also, when $m = const$ the following relations are used:

$$\delta = \frac{\sqrt{\hat{m}}}{\sqrt{\hat{m}} + \sqrt{m}} = 0.5, \quad u^\sim = u^{(0.5)}, \quad u_{\widetilde{D}\,i} = 0.5\,(u_{i+1/2} + u_{i-1/2})^{(0.5)}.$$

We will assume that the following estimates are performed:

$$\frac{|\mu_D|}{2} < \left(\frac{\hat{\eta}_u}{h}\right)_{i,i+1}, \quad \frac{|\mu_D|}{2} < \left(\frac{\eta_u}{h}\right)_{i,i+1}, \quad \frac{1}{2}\left[\left(\frac{\eta_u}{h}\right)_i + \left(\frac{\eta_u}{h}\right)_{i+1}\right] < \frac{m}{\tau}. \tag{14}$$

The following theorems are proved in [9].

Theorem 4.2-1. *For the family of two-layer in time CCDS (4) - (7), the regularization of momentum fluxes with adaptive viscosity in the form of (12) does not violate the property of complete conservatism of this family of difference schemes.*

Theorem 4.2-2. *When choosing the adaptive viscosity $(\eta_u/h)_{i,i+1}$ for the regularizer of the momentum equation in the form of (13) with zero homogeneous boundary conditions for velocity at the boundary nodes ω and with "frozen" mass fluxes $\mu_{\widetilde{D}\,i} = \mu_{\widetilde{D}\,i+1} = \mu_D = const$ in the cells adjacent to the node "$i+1/2$", as well as with "frozen" on the explicit and implicit layers in time the node masses $m_{i-1/2} = m_{i+1/2} = m_{i+3/2} = m = const$ and also the fulfillment of conditions (14), the following estimation for the node moments takes place: $\|\hat{I}\|_C \leq \|I\|_C$.*

4.3 Regularization of the Internal Energy Flow

The equation for the internal energy balance (6) in the cell Ω is written as

$$E_t = -p^\sim DIV\,\mathbf{u}^\sim - DIV\mu_{\widetilde{E}}, \tag{15}$$

where $E_\Omega = \rho_\Omega \varepsilon_\Omega$ is internal energy per unit volume in the cell Ω, $\mu_{\widetilde{E}} = \mu_E^{(0,5)}$.

Under the density of the flux of internal energy similar to 4.1 we will understand the value:

$$\mu_E(\omega) = u_\omega E_\omega - (\eta_E \, GRAD \, E)_\omega = \mu_{E\,i+1/2} \qquad (16)$$

where $-\eta_E \, GRAD \, E$ is adaptive artificial viscosity, $E_\omega = 0.5 \sum_{\Omega(\omega)} E_\Omega$.

The value $-p^\sim DIV \, \mathbf{u}^\sim$ on the right side of the internal energy balance Eq. (15) is not used when calculating viscosity η_E. Hence, to calculate the viscosity, we obtain the equation

$$\frac{\hat{E}_i - E_i}{\tau} + \frac{\mu_{E\,i+1/2}^{(0,5)} - \mu_{E\,i-1/2}^{(0,5)}}{h_i} = 0, \qquad (17)$$

$$\mu_{E\,i+1/2} = 0.5u_{i+1/2}(E_i + E_{i+1}) - \left(\frac{\eta_E}{h}\right)_{i+1/2}(E_{i+1} - E_i).$$

When choosing the viscosity $\hat{\eta}_E$ we "freeze" in (17) velocities $\hat{u}_{i-1/2} = \hat{u}_{i+1/2} = \hat{u} = const$. Also on the explicit time layer when choosing viscosity η_E we "freeze" $u_{i-1/2} = u_{i+1/2} = u = const$.

We will assume that the following estimates are performed:

$$|\hat{u}| < \left(\frac{\hat{\eta}_E}{h}\right)_{i\pm1/2}, \quad |u| < \left(\frac{\eta_E}{h}\right)_{i\pm1/2}, \quad \frac{1}{2}\left[\left(\frac{\eta_E}{h}\right)_{i-1/2} + \left(\frac{\eta_E}{h}\right)_{i+1/2}\right] < \frac{h_i}{\tau}. \qquad (18)$$

The following theorems are proved in [9].

Theorem 4.3-1. *For two-layer in time CCDS (4) - (7) in Eulerian variables, the regularization of internal energy fluxes with adaptive viscosity in the form (16) for the internal energy equation does not violate the properties of complete conservatism of this family of difference schemes.*

Theorem 4.3-2. *When choosing an adaptive viscosity $(\eta_E/h)_{i\pm1/2}$ for the regularizer of the internal energy equation in the form (17) with zero homogeneous boundary conditions for the internal energy E in the boundary cells Ω and with "frozen" velocity $u_{i-1/2} = u_{i+1/2} = u = const$ at the cell boundaries of the spatial grid Ω_i on the explicit and implicit layers in time, and also the fulfillment of the conditions (18) on a uniform spatial grid, the following estimation is performed: $\|\hat{E}\|_C \leq \|E\|_C$.*

5   Conclusion

For the equations of gas dynamics in Euler variables, using the operator approach, a family of two-layer in time completely conservative difference schemes with space-weighted multipliers, used for the approximation of the momentum and energy fluxes, was constructed. A regularization of the flux terms of the equations of gas dynamics using adaptive artificial viscosity is proposed. It is shown that regularized fluxes make the scheme quasi-monotonic, and ensure the coordination of momentum, kinetic and internal energy balances, retaining the property of complete conservatism. In other words, in the constructed class of divergent difference schemes, in accordance with the laws of thermodynamics, there are no "approximation" sources (or sinks) of internal energy. Schemes have a second order of accuracy. They are implemented through simple iterative processes. After some natural generalizations, the developed schemes can be used for gas-dynamic calculations with more complex models, for example, in the case of fast processes in plasma with the electron and ion component temperatures taken off, when a single balance equation for the total energy of the medium is not enough, for example, in plasma dynamics models [2].

Acknowledgments. The work was supported by the Russian Science Foundation (project No 16-11-00100).

References

1. Popov, Yu.P., Samarskii, A.A.: Completely conservative difference schemes. USSR Comput. Math. Math. Phys. **4**, 296–305 (1969). https://doi.org/10.1016/0041-5553(69)90049-4
2. Samarskii, A.A., Popov, Yu.P.: Difference Methods for Solving Gas Dynamics Problems. Nauka, Moscow (1992). (in Russian)
3. Kuzmin, A.V., Makarov, V.L.: An algorithm for constructing completely conservative difference schemes. USSR Comput. Math. Math. Phys. **1**, 128–138 (1982). https://doi.org/10.1016/0041-5553(82)90170-7
4. Koldoba, A.V., Poveshchenko, Yu.A., Popov, Yu.P.: Two-layer completely conservative difference schemes for the equations of gas dynamics in Euler variables. USSR Comput. Math. Math. Phys. **3**, 91–95 (1987). https://doi.org/10.1016/0041-5553(87)90086-3
5. Koldoba, A.V., Kuznetsov, O.A., Poveshchenko, Yu.A., Popov, Yu.P.: On one approach to the calculation of gas dynamics problems with a variable mass of quasi-particles. Preprinty IPM im. M.V. Keldysha [KIAM Preprints], Moscow, **57** (1985). (in Russian)
6. Koldoba, A.V., Poveshchenko, Yu.A.: Completely conservative difference schemes for the equations of gas dynamics in the presence of mass sources. Preprinty IPM im. M.V. Keldysha [KIAM Preprints], Moscow, **160** (1982). (in Russian)
7. Poveshchenko, Yu.A., Podryga, V.O., Sharova, Yu.S.: Integral-consistent methods for calculating self-gravitating and magnetohydrodynamic phenomena. Preprint IPM im. M.V. Keldysha [KIAM Preprints], Moscow, **160** (2018). (in Russian). https://doi.org/10.20948/prepr-2018-160
8. Popov, I.V., Fryazinov, I.V.: Method of Adaptive Artificial Viscosity for Numerical Solution of Gas Dynamics Equations. Krasand, Moscow (2015). (in Russian)
9. Poveshchenko, Yu.A., Ladonkina, M.E., Podryga, V.O., Rahimly O.R., Sharova Yu.S.: On a two-layer completely conservative difference scheme of gas dynamics in Eulerian variables with adaptive regularization of solution. Preprinty IPM im. M.V. Keldysha [KIAM Preprints], Moscow, **14** (2019). (in Russian). https://doi.org/10.20948/prepr-2019-14

Some Problems of Modeling the Impact on Gas Hydrates on the Basis of Splitting by Physical Processes

Parvin Rahimly[1], Viktoriia Podryga[1,2](✉), Yury Poveshchenko[1],
Orkhan Rahimly[1], and Yulia Sharova[1]

[1] Keldysh Institute of Applied Mathematics of RAS,
4 Miusskya sq., 125047 Moscow, Russia
{pervin,orxan}@rehimli.info,
pvictoria@list.ru, hecon@mail.ru, yulia-shar@mail.ru
[2] Moscow Automobile and Road Construction State Technical University,
64 Leningradsky Prospect, 125319 Moscow, Russia

Abstract. In this work we consider an equilibrium joint model of a two-component three-phase (water, gas, hydrate) filtration fluid dynamics and two-phase processes in the thawed zone with no gas hydrates, for which splitting by physical processes is performed. Algorithms for the joint calculation of hydrate-containing and thawed states of a fluid-dynamic medium are described. Examples of calculations of technogenic depressive effects near the wells on the dynamics of spatial distributions of gas hydrates' thawing and the formation of thawed two-phase zones are given.

Keywords: Gas hydrates · Filtration · Thawed zone · Splitting by physical processes

1 Introduction

The method of modeling based on the splitting of gas-hydrodynamic processes occurring during the dissociation of gas hydrates in a porous medium by physical processes is presented. As a basis for mathematical modeling of underground fluid dynamics taking into account the dissociation of gas hydrates the mass, momentum and energy balance equations are taken. It is assumed that the thermodynamic equilibrium nature of the process corresponds to the time scale typical for the development of deposits. The filtration area is naturally divided into two zones: three-phase, where gas, water and hydrate are present, and thawed - with the absence of gas hydrates. Systems of differential equations in partial derivatives describing the motion of fluids in each zone have their own, and for the unified description of the entire filtration area it is necessary to perform the matching of solutions of systems of equations of gas hydrate fluid dynamics for all areas of the P, T plane within the unified computational scheme

© Springer Nature Switzerland AG 2020
I. Lirkov and S. Margenov (Eds.): LSSC 2019, LNCS 11958, pp. 626–633, 2020.
https://doi.org/10.1007/978-3-030-41032-2_72

[1,2]. Note that, according to the rule of the Gibbs phase, the thermodynamically equilibrium two-component (H_2O, CH_4) three-phase (hydrate, free water and gas) system has only one thermodynamic degree of freedom. Those there is a thermobaric connection $T_{dis} = f(P)$ between the temperature of dissociation of gas hydrate and the pressure [3]. However, in calculations in the thawed zone without hydrate in the medium there are two independent thermodynamic parameters (P, T). In practice, the dynamics of joint behavior of spontaneously arising spatially separated thawed and hydrate-containing zones is interesting. The initial problem, formulated as conservation laws (masses of H_2O, CH_4 and total energy of the medium), with a common system matrix for functions S_ν, S_w, pressure P, and temperature T, has mixed hyperbolic and parabolic properties. Direct use of such a system for the purpose of determining the dynamics of variables of thaw, water saturation, pressure and temperature (S_ν, S_w, P, T) and constructing an implicit difference scheme required for calculating parabolic equations with large time steps is difficult.

2 Formulation of the Problem

2.1 Three-Phase Medium with Hydrate Inclusions

In a spatial domain O with a boundary ∂O, we consider thermodynamically equilibrium two-component (water, methane) three-phase equations of filtration fluid dynamics with gas hydrate inclusions [4]:

$$\frac{\partial}{\partial t} \{m [S_\nu S_w \rho_w + (1 - S_\nu)\rho_\nu \beta_w]\} + div[\rho_w \mathbf{V}_w] + q_w = 0, \tag{1}$$

$$\frac{\partial}{\partial t} \{m [S_\nu (1 - S_w)\rho_g + (1 - S_\nu)\rho_\nu (1 - \beta_w)]\} + div[\rho_g \mathbf{V}_g] + q_g = 0, \tag{2}$$

$$\mathbf{V}_w = -\frac{k \cdot k_{rw}}{\mu_w}(\nabla P - g\rho_w \mathbf{k}), \tag{3}$$

$$\mathbf{V}_g = -\frac{k \cdot k_{rg}}{\mu_g}(\nabla P - g\rho_g \mathbf{k}), \tag{4}$$

$$\frac{\partial}{\partial t} \{m [S_\nu (S_w \rho_w \varepsilon_w + (1 - S_w)\rho_g \varepsilon_g) + (1 - S_\nu)\rho_\nu \varepsilon_\nu] + (1 - m)\rho_s \varepsilon_s\}$$
$$+ div \{\rho_w \varepsilon_w \mathbf{V}_w + \rho_g \varepsilon_g \mathbf{V}_g + [P(\mathbf{V}_w + \mathbf{V}_g)]\} + div\mathbf{W} + q_\varepsilon = 0, \tag{5}$$

$$\mathbf{W} = - \{m [S_\nu (S_w \lambda_w + (1 - S_w)\lambda_g) + (1 - S_\nu)\lambda_\nu] + (1 - m)\lambda_s\} \nabla T, \tag{6}$$

$$T_{dis} = f(P) = A \ln P + B. \tag{7}$$

The indices g, w, ν, s refer to gas, water, hydrate, skeleton of porous medium; l is the index indicating the phase; P is the pressure, T is the temperature, S_w is the water saturation, ν is the hydrate saturation, $S_\nu = 1 - \nu$ is the thaw, $\rho_l(P, T)$ and $\varepsilon_l(P, T)$ are the densities and internal energies of the unit mass of the phases, $\mathbf{V}_l$ is the filtration velocity of the corresponding phase; β_w is the mass fraction of water in the hydrate, t is the time, q_w, q_g and q_ε are the respective sources densities depending on the parameters $(t, \mathbf{r}, S_w, S_\nu, P)$, $\mathbf{r}$ is the radius vector. $\mathbf{W}$ is the heat flux, $\lambda_l(P, T)$ are the coefficients of thermal conductivity. $g\mathbf{k}$ is the vector of acceleration of gravity, directed vertically downwards, $k(r, S_\nu, P)$ is the absolute permeability, $k_{rl}(S_w)$ are the related phase permeabilities, μ_l are the viscosities. According to the Gibbs phase rule, the three-phase two-component hydrate system is multivariant, i.e. has one degree of freedom (temperature or pressure) [3]. Consequently, for a gas hydrate that is in equilibrium with liquid water or ice, the dependence $T_{dis} = f(P)$ is unambiguous. The enthalpies $i_l = \varepsilon_l + P/\rho_l$ of hydrate, free water and gas are thermodynamically consistent in the sense of the following relation

$$\beta_w i_w + (1 - \beta_w) i_g = i_\nu + h, \tag{8}$$

where h is the latent heat of the phase transition of a unit of hydrate mass. For a gas phase the equation of state is

$$\rho_g = \frac{PM}{z_g RT}. \tag{9}$$

with a coefficient of supercompressibility z_g, M is the molar mass of gas.

From Eqs. (1), (2), (5), an equation for piezoconductivity for the fluid dynamics with hydrate inclusions can be obtained in the following form [1]:

$$m\delta_\varepsilon \left\{ S_\nu \left[\frac{S_w}{\rho_w} \frac{\partial \rho_w}{\partial t} + \frac{(1 - S_w)}{\rho_g} \frac{\partial \rho_g}{\partial t} \right] + \frac{1 - S_\nu}{\rho_\nu} \frac{\partial \rho_\nu}{\partial t} + \frac{1}{m} \frac{\partial m}{\partial t} \right\}$$
$$+ \frac{\psi}{m\rho_\nu} \left\{ m \left\{ S_\nu \left[S_w \rho_w \frac{\partial \varepsilon_w}{\partial t} + (1 - S_w) \rho_g \frac{\partial \varepsilon_g}{\partial t} \right] + (1 - S_\nu) \rho_\nu \frac{\partial \varepsilon_\nu}{\partial t} \right\} \tag{10}$$
$$+ \frac{\partial[(1 - m)\rho_s \varepsilon_s]}{\partial t} \right\} + \delta_\varepsilon DIG + \frac{\psi}{m\rho_\nu} DIG_\varepsilon = 0,$$

$$DIG = \frac{1}{\rho_w} div(\rho_w \mathbf{V}_w) + \frac{1}{\rho_g} div(\rho_g \mathbf{V}_g) + \frac{q_w}{\rho_w} + \frac{q_g}{\rho_g}, \tag{11}$$

$$DIG_\varepsilon = [div(\rho_w \varepsilon_w \mathbf{V}_w) - \varepsilon_w div(\rho_w \mathbf{V}_w)] + [div(\rho_g \varepsilon_g \mathbf{V}_g) - \varepsilon_g div(\rho_g \mathbf{V}_g)]$$
$$+ div[P(\mathbf{V}_w + \mathbf{V}_g)] + div\mathbf{W} + (q_\varepsilon - \varepsilon_w q_w - \varepsilon_g q_g) = \rho_w \mathbf{V}_w \nabla \varepsilon_w + \rho_g \mathbf{V}_g \nabla \varepsilon_g \tag{12}$$
$$+ div[P(\mathbf{V}_w + \mathbf{V}_g)] + div\mathbf{W} + (q_\varepsilon - \varepsilon_w q_w - \varepsilon_g q_g).$$

Here

$$\frac{\psi}{m\rho_\nu} = \left(\phi - \frac{1}{\rho_\nu} \right) \geq 0, \qquad \phi = \frac{\beta_w}{\rho_w} + \frac{(1 - \beta_w)}{\rho_g}, \tag{13}$$

$$\delta_\varepsilon = \beta_w \varepsilon_w + (1 - \beta_w) \varepsilon_g - \varepsilon_\nu \geq 0 \tag{14}$$

are respectively specific jumps (per unit mass) for the phase transition of the volume and internal energy.

Equation (10) is the main piezoconductive-dissipative thermodynamically equilibrium equation of three-phase two-component fluid dynamics with hydrate inclusions physically splitted with the saturation block (1)–(4) possessing mainly hyperbolic properties on the background of the fixed thermodynamic parameters of the medium [1].

Assuming thaw $S_\nu = 1$, we obtain a two-phase equation in the thawed zone analogously. Further, excluding the function S_w from under the sign of the time derivative, we obtain the equations that determine the nonisothermal process of piezoconductivity in the thawed zone:

$$\frac{S_w}{\rho_w}\frac{\partial(m\rho_w)}{\partial t} + \frac{1 - S_w}{\rho_g}\frac{\partial(m\rho_g)}{\partial t} + DIG = 0, \tag{15}$$

$$m\{S_w\rho_w\frac{\partial\varepsilon_w}{\partial t} + (1 - S_w)\rho_g\frac{\partial\varepsilon_g}{\partial t}\} + \frac{\partial[(1 - m)\rho_s\varepsilon_s]}{\partial t} + DIG_\varepsilon = 0. \tag{16}$$

Here the combination of mass (DIG) and energy (DIG_ε) divergences together with the action of the corresponding sources $(q_w, q_g, q_\varepsilon)$ are defined similarly to (10). Difference algorithms for the described problems are presented in [2].

2.2 Algorithms for the Joint Calculation of Hydrate-Containing and Thawed States of a Fluid-Dynamic Medium

Let assign to the node balance domain of the grid a fixed unit volume and the whole mass of water molecules M_w, the mass of methane molecules M_g, and the total internal energy of the system E, including the skeleton located in this volume. Then, according to these parameters $\{1, M_w, M_g, E\}$, the local thermodynamically equilibrium state of the medium is uniquely determined. We will also assume that the range of variation of the balance parameters $\{M_w, M_g, E\}$ is such that either a melt zone or a three-phase hydrate containing medium occurs. Thus, there is a mandatory alternative: either a solution $\{S_\nu, S_w, P, T\}$ in a three-phase hydrate-containing thermodynamically equilibrium state, or a solution $\{S_w, P, T\}$ corresponding to the thermodynamically equilibrium two-phase thawed zone. These two problems are considered separately in [2].

Outlined in the previous sections, we can propose some methods for regularization of evolutionary transphase calculations of joint filtration problems in a piezoconductive medium with gas-hydrate inclusions and in the thawed zone without hydrate preserving the complete conservatism of the corresponding difference algorithms.

Double Skeleton. We choose a value $\Delta_\nu < 1$ close to unity. In this node, we fix as a parameter the thaw $S_\nu \to 1$ close to unity, such as $\Delta_\nu < S_\nu < 1$. In the physical sense, in the balance domain of the grid we produce hydrated encapsulation, i.e. we believe that the new solid skeleton of the system (marked with an index k) consists of two parts: the old skeleton with a density ρ_s, the volume fraction of which is in space $(1-m)$ and the encapsulated hydrate with density ρ_ν and volume fraction $(m-m_\nu)$. Here $m_\nu = m\,S_\nu$ is interpreted as the encapsulated porosity of the two-phase system, i.e. that fraction of the volume in which the flow of free fluids (water and gas) occurs. The transition from a three-phase medium with gas-hydrate inclusions to a two-phase thawed hydrate-free zone by the double skeleton method at this time step is used as one of the possible types of regularization of transphase calculations. Further, in the subsequent time steps, the double skeleton is transferred into a simple skeleton, if the system has enough energy in the node balance domain to remain two-phase. Thus, the condition $T \geq T_{dis}$ is fulfilled. Or the system finds its thermodynamic equilibrium as a three-phase hydrate-containing medium if its temperature is below the dissociation temperature T_{dis} (see (7)).

Overheated Thaw Method. Overheated thaw with a balanced transition to a two-phase thawed zone with a simple skeleton is as follows. If a three-phase medium with gas-hydrate inclusions was calculated in the node balance domain and the thaw S_ν exceeded a single value ($S_\nu \geq 1$), this means that the three-phase thermodynamic equilibrium determined by the parameters M_w, M_g, E does not exist. Since the thermodynamically equilibrium state of the medium is determined uniquely, then the solution $\{S_w, \ P, \ T\}$ of the corresponding thermodynamically equilibrium two-phase thawed zone is determined by the same parameters $(M_w, \ M_g$ and $E)$. Further calculation in this node on subsequent time steps takes place already in the two-phase thawed zone with a simple skeleton.

Supercooled Thawed Zone Method. Let the two-phase thawed zone (with a simple skeleton or a double skeleton) was calculated in the node balance domain and at this time step in the node the temperature was below the dissociation temperature (i.e. $T < T_{dis} = f(P)$, see (7)). Then, using the known values of $\{M_w, M_g$ and $E\}$ in the thawed zone, $\{S_\nu, \ S_w, \ P$ and $T\}$ are calculated for the three-phase hydrate-containing state. Further calculations in this node on subsequent time steps occur in the three-phase hydrate-containing zone. It is possible to modify this approach, when the condition $T < T_{dis}$ is fulfilled in this node, no recalculation is performed, $S_\nu = 1$ and the values S_w, P and T known from the thawed zone and are also considered to be a three-phase hydrate-containing state on an explicit time layer. In this case, the thermobaric condition (7) for the three-phase calculation is performed only on an implicit time step.

3   Calculation Results

Consider the following spatial one-dimensional process on an interval $x \in [0, l]$, l is the length of the computational domain. In it, at the initial moment of time, a three-phase equilibrium is observed, including a body-distributed solid hydrate phase. In this state of the system, pressure $P(x,0) = 6 \cdot 10^6 \, Pa$, water saturation $S_w(x,0) = S_w^*$ and thaw $S_\nu(x,0) = S_\nu^*$ are uniform in space, and $0 < S_w^* < 1$ and $0 < S_\nu^* < 1$ are constant values. The acceleration of gravity is not counted ($g = 0$). The left boundary of the computational domain is assumed to be an impermeable solid "wall", i.e. the mass flux through it is zero: $V_w|_{x=0} = 0$, $V_g|_{x=0} = 0$, $t > 0$. While the depression pressure $P(x,l) = 10^5$ Pa is set on the right boundary. Heat fluxes at the boundaries of the region are absent. Volumetric sources of mass and energy in the medium are also considered absent: $q_w = 0$, $q_g = 0$, $q_\varepsilon = 0$. Methane gas in the calculations was taken as the ideal ($z_g = 1$). The pressure dimension in (9) was measured in Pascal: $[P] = Pa$.

For the calculation, the following values of the parameters, characteristic for the Messoyakha gas hydrate deposit were also chosen:

$$\rho_w = 10^3 \frac{kg}{m^3}, \ \rho_\nu = 910 \frac{kg}{m^3}, \ \rho_s = 2800 \frac{kg}{m^3}, \ \beta_w = 0.9, \ m = 0.35, \ A = 7.28K,$$

$$B = 169.7K, \ \mu_w = 10^{-3} Pa \cdot s, \ \mu_g = 0.014 \cdot 10^{-3} Pa \cdot s,$$

$$c_{pw} = 4200 \frac{J}{kg \cdot K}, \ c_{pg} = 2500 \frac{J}{kg \cdot K}, \ c_{ps} = 873 \frac{J}{kg \cdot K}, \ M = 0.016 \frac{kg}{mol},$$

$$h = 514810 \frac{J}{kg}, \ R = 8.31 \frac{J}{mol \cdot K}, \ S_w^* = 0.6, \ S_\nu^* = 0.7, \ k(S_\nu) = k_0 \cdot (S_\nu)^3,$$

$$k_0 = 10mD = 10^{-14} m^2, \ k_{rw}(S_w) = 1.477 S_w^5 - 1.587 S_w^6 + 1.11 S_w^7 - 0.0473,$$

$$k_{rg}(S_w) = 1.044 - 1.7 S_w + 0.6 S_w^2$$

The minimum value of water saturation is $S_{w\,min} = 0.55$.

$$k_{rw}(S_w) = 0, \quad k_{rg}(S_w) = k_{rg}(S_{w\,min}) \ \ at \ \ S_w \le S_{w\,min}.$$

The maximum value of water saturation is $S_{w\,max} = 0.9$.

$$k_{rw}(S_w) = k_{rw}(S_{w\,max}), \quad k_{rg}(S_w) = 0 \ \ at \ \ S_w \ge S_{w\,max}.$$

The thermal conductivity of the medium was taken into account according to formula (6) and was equal to $\lambda_w = 0.561$, $\lambda_g = 0.0342$, $\lambda_\nu = 2.11$, $\lambda_s = 0.2 \, W/(m \cdot K)$. The model tube length is assumed to be equal to $l = 1$ m, the step along the spatial coordinate is $h = 0.01$ m. The calculations are given for times $t = 500, 1000, 2000, 6000, 9000, 12000$ s.

In Figs. 1, 2, 3, 4, 5 and 6, it can be seen that in the calculations a joint transphase spatially expanding process from right to left inside the depressed zone of bulk phase transitions of the medium in the emerging thawed zone and in the rest of the medium of the collector with gas hydrate inclusions takes place. Such transphase calculations, in particular, make it possible to study local processes of anthropogenic depressive effects directly in the vicinity of wells on the dynamics of the spatial distributions of gas hydrates thaw and the formation of thawed two-phase zones. The pressure graphs (see Fig. 3) show that the presence

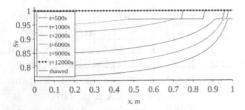

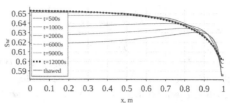

Fig. 1. Distribution of the hydrate thaw. On right two-phase thawed zone is highlighted in red. (Color figure online)

Fig. 2. Distribution of the water saturation. On right two-phase thawed zone is highlighted in red. (Color figure online)

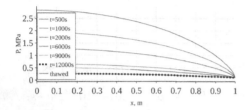

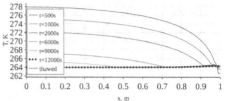

Fig. 3. Distribution of the pressure. On right two-phase thawed zone is highlighted in red. (Color figure online)

Fig. 4. Distribution of the temperature. On right two-phase thawed zone is highlighted in red. (Color figure online)

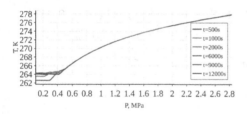

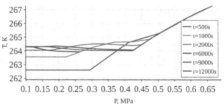

Fig. 5. Temperature versus pressure in the entire plane P, T.

Fig. 6. Temperature versus pressure in the zone of three-phase thermobaric equilibrium imbalance with the transition to the thawed zone.

of water saturation and thaw fronts has little effect on the nature of the pressure distribution. The pressure changes almost as in the single-phase case, the graphs for which (in the heat conduction problem similar to the one-phase elastic filtration problem) are given in [7]. At a developed stage of the process, the pressure tends to be constant, and, accordingly, the filtration velocities of gas and water, proportional to the pressure gradient, and the divergent terms of the equations in the thawed zone depending on them also tend to zero. Thus, the solution stabilizes. Those, the values of water saturation and temperature determined in this case are found from the stabilization of solutions of the non-stationary problem. From a comparison of the graphs $S_\nu(x)$, $T(x)$ (see Figs. 1 and 4) for identical times t, one can see the transition from the three-phase zone to the two-phase zone, where the process is almost isothermal, which corresponds to the assumptions that two-phase filtration is isothermal in most cases. This is confirmed by the $T(P)$ plots (see Figs. 5 and 6), where two characteristic regions are visible, corresponding to the three-phase and two-phase zones.

4 Conclusion

The paper describes the method of joint solving systems of equations for processes in various fields, each of which is characterized by its own set of coexisting phases, and the adjustment of computational schemes for them is not an automatic process. The results of the calculations numerically allowed to investigate the area of three-phase volume phase transitions by a single calculation with a variable number of phases in the entire plane of the P and T parameters. Using the example of the Messoyakha gas hydrate deposit, local processes of anthropogenic depressive impact directly in the vicinity of the wells on the dynamics of the spatial distributions of gas hydrates and formation of thawed two-phase zones were studied.

Acknowledgments. The work was supported by the Russian Science Foundation (project No 17-71-20118).

References

1. Poveshchenko, Y.A., Kazakevich, G.I.: Mathematical modeling of gas hydrate processes. Math. Mach. Syst. **3**, 105–110 (2011). [In Russian]
2. Rahimly, P.I., Poveshchenko, Yu.A., Podryga, V.O., Rahimly, O.R., Popov, S.B.: Modeling the processes of joint filtration in melted zone and piezoconductive medium with gas hydrate inclusions. Preprinty IPM im. M.V. Keldysha [KIAM Preprints], 40 Moscow (2018). https://doi.org/10.20948/prepr-2018-40. (In Russian)
3. Landau, L.D., Lifshitz, E.M.: Course of Theoretical Physics. Theory of Elasticity, vol. 7. Pergamon Press Ltd., Oxford (1970)
4. Rahimly, P., Poveshchenko, Y., Podryga, V., Rahimly, O.: Completely conservative difference schemes for simultaneous calculations of thawed hydrated zone and piezoconductive medium with gas hydrate inclusions. In: Dimov, I., Faragó, I., Vulkov, L. (eds.) FDM 2018. LNCS, vol. 11386, pp. 427–434. Springer, Cham (2019). https://doi.org/10.1007/978-3-030-11539-5_49
5. Poveshchenko, Y.A., Podryga, V.O., Rahimly, P.I.: About one approach to free volumetric approximation of a piezoconductive medium with gas hydrate inclusions. Math. Montisnigri **40**, 68–89 (2017). [In Russian]
6. Bogatyrenko, R.S.: Features of the development and operation of gas hydrate deposits (on the example of the Messoyakhsky deposit). Dissertatsiia, Moscow (1979). (In Russian)
7. Karslow, G., Eger, D.: Thermal Conductivity of Solid. Nauka, Moscow (1964). (In Russian)

Correction to: Impact of Data Assimilation on Short-Term Precipitation Forecasts Using WRF-ARW Model

Evgeni Vladimirov⑩, Reneta Dimitrova⑩,
and Ventsislav Danchovski⑩

Correction to:
Chapter "Impact of Data Assimilation on Short-Term
Precipitation Forecasts Using WRF-ARW Model"
in: I. Lirkov and S. Margenov (Eds.): *Large-Scale*
Scientific Computing, **LNCS 11958,**
https://doi.org/10.1007/978-3-030-41032-2_30

In the originally published version of chapter 30 an acknowledgement was missing. This has been corrected.

The updated version of this chapter can be found at
https://doi.org/10.1007/978-3-030-41032-2_30

© Springer Nature Switzerland AG 2020
I. Lirkov and S. Margenov (Eds.): LSSC 2019, LNCS 11958, p. C1, 2020.
https://doi.org/10.1007/978-3-030-41032-2_73

Author Index

Printed in the United States
By Bookmasters